10/23/01

The Death
of Comedy

The Death of Comedy

ERICH SEGAL

HARVARD UNIVERSITY PRESS
Cambridge, Massachusetts
London, England
2001

Library of Congress Cataloging-in-Publication Data
Segal, Erich, 1937–
The death of comedy / Erich Segal.
p. cm.
Includes bibliographical references and index.
ISBN 0-674-00643-7 (alk. paper)
1. Comedy—History and criticism.   I. Title.

PN1922 .S44 2001
809.2′523—dc21   2001024437

To Karen, Francesca, and Miranda,
with love

And in memoriam Harry Levin (1912–1994),
teacher, scholar, friend

Contents

Preface

The "Death" of Comedy is a metaphor, not a history. It traces the evolution of the classical form from its early origins in the misogynistic quip by the quasi-legendary sixth-century B.C. Susarion of Megara, through countless weddings and happy endings, to the exasperated monosyllables of Samuel Beckett—the Buster Keaton of modern dramatists—whose characters cannot even *say* "I do," much less "do" anything.

This makes no claim to be an exhaustive study, but rather is an exploration—some might say exploitation—of various landmarks in the history of a genre which flourished almost unchanged in the more than two millennia that followed Terence's death. It would be impossible to deal with every play of every author studied within the confines of a single volume. The aim has been to illustrate comedy's glorious life cycle and ultimate destruction by the "intellectuals" of the so-called Theater of the Absurd.

The chapters that follow are the product of more than thirty years of teaching comedy at Harvard, Yale, Princeton, and then Yale again. During this time the young men and women I was privileged to have as my students contributed immeasurably to my own perspective. This was a golden age of my academic life in which, like that described by Don Quixote, there was no *tuyo* or *mío*. At nearly forty years' remove I forget who taught whom.

Many ideas were formulated in conversations with Kenneth Cavander, who shared the podium with me for several terms at Yale, and Carroll Moulton, who did likewise at Princeton. At Harvard *I* was the assistant, first to the late Stephen Gilman, a fount of erudition and enthusiasm, and then to the late Harry Levin, to whose memory this book is affectionately dedicated. I will always be grateful to him for dissuading me from writing a doctoral dissertation on Renaissance translations of Vergil and encouraging me to concentrate on the subject which has occupied the rest of my academic life.

For the preparation of this book itself I am indebted to many friends and colleagues—the terms are not mutually exclusive—who ferreted out numerous inaccuracies and infelicities. I of course am responsible for any that remain. Kenneth Reckford read an early version and kept me from going totally overboard. Sander Goldberg read a slightly less anarchic draft and offered many sobering suggestions. Geoffrey Arnott undertook the Herculean task of reading the entire manuscript of what I had naively regarded as the "final" draft, and generously gave me a dozen handwritten pages of detailed corrections—and eight months' further work. Hugh Lloyd-Jones, a great scholar whom I am proud to call my friend, read a still later draft and offered wise comments and astute corrections.

Many scholars tolerantly indulged me in the diverse domains in which I was brash enough to poach. Harold Bloom, genial in all senses of the word, read the Shakespeare chapters and gave me the benefit of his great learning. Lauro Martines was kind enough to appraise what I had done to his countryman Machiavelli. Michel Fabre of the Sorbonne gave a welcome approval of my approach to Molière, as did Marie-Odile Fortier-Masek. Michael Screech, my colleague at Wolfson College, Oxford, was most generous with his advice, although he disagreed with some of my arguments. Andrew Calder of University College London, and his study of Molière, were most helpful. Ian Donaldson of Kings College, Cambridge, kindly offered a wealth of advice on both Jonson and Wycherley.

Though I began this book more than a quarter-century ago, I could never have finished it without the help of John Franklin, whose intelligence and creativity—and above all his friendship—made an incalculable contribution. Leofranc Holford-Strevens, a modern Aulus Gellius, shared his wisdom on authors both ancient and modern. Matthew Robinson and Jeannie Cohen were keen-eyed readers of the final draft. Any errors that remain are my own.

I also owe a great debt to the knowledgeable librarians of the Institute of Classical Studies and the London Library, as well as to Mr. Peter Saxel of Blackwell's, the legendary Oxford bookshop, who for more than thirty years satisfied my insatiable craving for ever-newer books on the classics.

Finally, to my beloved wife Karen and daughters Francesca and Miranda, the joy of whose company I denied myself while *serenas noctes vigilans:* I will now be back at the dinner table, where we can have a little *kōmos* of our own.

Earlier versions of some of the discussions in this book were published in journals and volumes of essays. They include "The Etymologies of Comedy," *Greek, Roman and Byzantine Studies* 14, no. 1 (1973); "The *physis* of Comedy," *Harvard Studies in Classical Philology* 77 (1973); "Aristophanes and Beckett," in *Orchestra: Studies in Honour of Helmut Flashar,* ed. Anton Bierl and Peter von Möllendorff (Stuttgart and Leipzig, 1994); "'The Comic Catastrophe'": An Essay on Euripidean Comedy," in *Stage Directions: Studies in Honour of Eric Handley,* ed. Alan Griffiths, *Bulletin of the Institute of Classical Studies* 66 (1995).

A word about the translations, which, except for instances duly signaled in the notes, were prepared by the author for this volume: Rather than render the foreign languages literally, which is traditional scholarly practice, it seemed better to try to recreate something of the *vis comica* of the original. My argument is, of course, based on the original texts, but I confess that my translations were, to some extent, based on my argument.

Wolfson College, Oxford
March 2001

The Death
of Comedy

I

Etymologies: Getting to the Root of It

Comedy was born at night. At least this is the fanciful conclusion of some long-ago scholars who derived "comedy" from *kōma* ("sleep") and *ōidē* ("song"). The ancients believed that essential truths were evident in their very speech, that words could both denote and describe. *Nomen omen,* as the Romans rhymed it.[1] Hence certain Byzantine word-wizards distilled *kōma* from comedy and pronounced the genre a creature of night.[2]

No one disputes the second verbal element. We are indeed dealing with a kind of song which figuratively and often literally ends harmoniously on the tonic chord. But although *kōma* is linguistically impossible, there are still some whimsical minds that allow a filigree of fancy to outweigh a philology of fact and give some credence to this derivation.[3] Since comic spirit traditionally disregards reality, we too can be grateful for this etymology of *kōma*. As the proverb says, it may not be true, but it's a great idea.

What then would a Nightsong be? Perchance a dream. On several occasions Freud equated the psychodynamics of the comic and the oneiric, once alluding to his essays on jokes and dreams as "twin brothers."[4] These mental actions have many important features in common, among which are punning word-play, the relaxation of inhibition, and the liberation of "primary process thinking."[5] Nightsong thus represents a temporary return to childhood, which Wordsworth called "the glory and the freshness of a dream." Freud presents the same picture with "the mood of our childhood, when we were ignorant of the comic, when we were incapable of jokes and when we had no need of humour to make us feel happy in our life."[6]

In both dream and comedy, the impossible wish comes true. In each case the aim is pleasure, and the joy comes with no loss of energy or pang of conscience—the normal expense of spirit borne free. Plato describes the dream process as one in which, as reason slumbers, "unlawful pleasures are awakened." In dreams, says Plato, the animalistic *(to theriōdes)* and "uncivilized" *(agrion)* aspect of man "breaks loose, kicks up its heels" *(skirtai).*[7] This is the dance of comedy—the precise activities of the antic world envisaged by Wrong Logic in the Great Debate of Aristophanes' *Clouds:*

> Indulge your lusting *(physei),* kick up your heels *(skirta),* laugh up.
> Remember—nothing's shameful![8]

Plato censures what Aristophanes celebrates, but both recognize the characteristic action of both comedy and dream.[9]

Moreover, *kōma* is a rare word with rare connotations, whenever it appears instead of the more common *hypnos.* It can have an erotic sense of letting go, not merely nodding off. In the *Iliad,* for example, Hypnos, the god of sleep, declares that he has covered Zeus with an especially soft slumber *(malakon kōma)*—just after Zeus and Hera have made love.[10] The sense of indulgence and release adds a metalinguistic validity to the alleged etymology of comedy.

Indeed, what they lacked in philological acumen, the Byzantine scholars seem to have made up in psychological intuition. Several of them argued that *kōma* begot comedy because of the uninhibiting nature of the nocturnal mentality, and that this special time is extremely conducive to the actions of a comic play.[11] Other critics of late antiquity preferred the derivation from *kōma* on the grounds that "sleep [plays] a considerable role, because only at bedtime did the country people dare to bring their mocking songs into the cities."[12]

Furthermore, dreams are often likened to comedy by the characters in the plays themselves. In Plautus' single comedy of mistaken identity, the long-lost twin who has just arrived in Epidamnus is astounded by the fact that people greet him familiarly in the street. "All this business seems to me like nothing other than a dream," he exclaims.[13] And similarly in *A Midsummer Night's Dream,* the dim-witted Bottom, on his return from the fairy kingdom, reports:

> I have had a dream . . . The eye of man hath not heard, the ear
> of man hath not seen, man's hand is not able to taste, his
> tongue to conceive, nor his heart to report what my dream
> was. I will get Peter Quince to write a ballad of this dream.
> It shall be call'd "Bottom's Dream," because it hath no
> bottom.[14]

Last but not least there is *erōs.* Like comedy, night is instinctively sensual. In Shelley's *Ode* it can actually seduce the daylight: "kiss her until she be wearied out." Moreover, only at night would Cupid visit Psyche, and according to the nocturnal vision recounted by Apuleius, the child of their union was the pleasure principle: *Voluptas.*[15] So much for the truth in the false etymology.

The first genealogy proposes a time, the second a place. Aristotle is among the many ancients who gave some credence to a Doric tradition which derived "comedy" from *kōmē,* "country village."[16] The validity of this etymology has been argued in the Middle Ages, the Renaissance, and, to a lesser extent, even in our own day.[17] Why "country song"? The conjecture reported by Aristotle is provocative: the "comedians" *(kōmōidoi)* were originally a group of roisterers who had to take to the hamlets with their singing after being kicked out of the city proper.[18] Either their subject matter or their behavior—or both—offended the urbanites.[19]

Aristotle does not indicate whether this was thought to have happened but once or on every festive occasion. But we need not hunt after historical truth here. *Kōmē* is related to comedy because the country has always stood vividly in the human imagination as a place of greater freedom.[20] In Plato's fretful description cited earlier, dreams bring out "uncivilized" *(agrion)* fantasies, a term which may be rendered more literally as "rustic." The *agroikos* or "country bumpkin" is an archetypal comic figure, the hero of the first extant comedy (Aristophanes' *Acharnians*) and attested still earlier for Epicharmus, the traditional founder of the genre.[21]

Elsewhere, Plato contrasts the *kōmē* and the city, and a passage in Thucydides suggests that the significant distinction was that the *polis* was walled, the *kōmē* wide open.[22] The myth survives in latter-day fables of farmers' daughters, and is certainly ingrained in the mind of one noted Danish prince:

> HAMLET: Lady, shall I lie in your lap?
>
> OPHELIA: No, my lord.
>
> HAMLET: I mean, my head on your lap?
>
> OPHELIA: Ay, my lord.
>
> HAMLET: Do you think I meant country matters?[23]

The persistent association between license and "country matters" does in fact have some historical validity.[24] In the ancient world, freer behavior could be sanctioned when it was geographically beyond the jurisdiction of the city fathers. Logically, the country is where fertility rites would take place. Sir James Frazer, whose *Golden Bough* was one of the seminal works of twentieth-century thought, amply demonstrated that these occasions have always involved uninhibited speech and sexuality.[25] Many cultures have had reinvigoration festivals characterized by such "stepping out of bounds." There was orgiastic indulgence beyond the city limits not only during *Akītu,* the Babylonian New Year, but also following the expiatory solemnity of the Jewish Yom Kippur.[26] That many comedies take place in the country is no accident either. One thinks of the country inn for Goldsmith's *She Stoops to Conquer,* Shakespeare's Forest of Arden *(As You Like It),* or better still, the enchanted wood outside Athens in *A Midsummer Night's Dream.*

It may have been so dark on the night Comedy was conceived in the country that—as in so many Menandrian plays—the mother could not recognize the father. But the linguistic doctors illumined all with their postpartum perceptivity. To the modern philologist, the true father of "comedy" can only be *kōmos,* the wild, wine-soaked, no-holds-barred revel which characterized most Aristophanic finales—and which, not incidentally, typically took place at night.[27]

And yet this is not a call for a serious ethnographic investigation. It is fatuous to think that one specific ritual may have engendered a precise theatrical form. This was attempted in the early twentieth century by acolytes of Frazer, the so-called Cambridge anthropologists. Jane Ellen Harrison argued that a "tragic rhythm"—the vestiges of seasonal rites—was still discernible in Greek drama.[28] Gilbert Murray saw the outline of a "ritual pattern" in these same works, consisting principally of an archetypal contest—the Old Year against the New, Light against Darkness, Summer against Winter.[29] F. M. Cornford detailed what he perceived as relics of the seasonal ritual in the comedies of Aristophanes. According to his view, the *agōn* or "conflict" of Old Comedy—most usually a debate of principles—reflected an ancient ritual struggle between the Old and New Kings, and ultimately led to the hero's sacred marriage *(hieros gamos)*.[30]

These were stimulating notions, but a later editor put things into perspective, noting that "Cornford's enthusiasm led him not infrequently to overshoot the mark."[31] Other critics were not so tolerant. A. W. Pickard-Cambridge, perhaps their leading foe, demonstrated that the ritualists had merely singled out in Greek drama elements that were common to humanity everywhere.[32]

Nevertheless, while deficient in detail, these contributions maintain some broad validity and should not be dismissed out of hand. Indeed, Pickard-Cambridge did not put the issue to rest forever. In 1966 Walter Burkert rehabilitated the ritualist approach by tracing the origins of Greek sacrificial rites, not to some Frazerian vegetative or seasonal worship, but to a real prehistoric event—the communal killing of an animal. The original participants of tragedy *(tragōidoi)* were not dressed in goatish satyr costume, as the etymology of *tragos* ("goat") had suggested to earlier scholars, but were instead the actual witnesses of a victim's sacrifice at the Dionysian festivals. The primal horror of the onlooker at the original sacrifice confirms mankind's innate and basic respect for life. The essence of drama was thus to be found in psychology and biology rather than the natural world: "the main problem for man is not winter, but man."[33] Though the thesis is not accepted in its entirety by many, Burkert's approach, subsequently elaborated in several important books, revitalized the study of ancient myth, ritual, and religion in the light of modern anthropological and biological theory.[34]

More recent criticism has steered away from the "anterior, even uto-pian moment in the development of theater,"[35] focusing instead on the social and political contexts in which these universal patterns are pre-sented. According to one view, for example, participation in the tragic chorus was a rite of passage in the presence of the polis for the young men of Athens (the *ephebos*), the term "goat-singers" referring to the goatesque physical changes of their adolescence.[36] Others have demon-strated beyond doubt that the Athenian comic festival had not only re-ligious importance, but a social and political dimension as well which had been neglected by earlier scholars:

> The city and its citizens were the festivals' theme and focus.
> Comic festivals were not "carnival" but civic business—and
> big business.[37]

This valuable approach has deepened our insight into the genre. Clearly, neither comedy nor tragedy nor any other work of art can be appreciated outside of its cultural context.

But even this does not tell the whole story, for there are always "comic forces" at work which are as much psychological processes as social, and lend themselves to a broader perspective.[38] The phenome-non of "holiday humour" is not confined to fifth-century Attica. It ex-ists in every society, whether it be called Saturnalia, Feast of Fools, or Homecoming Week. Inasmuch as drama arose from such festivals, "the holiday occasion and the comedy are merely parallel manifestations of the same pattern of culture."[39]

Thus, though comedy changes form from one culture and period to the next, there remains a truly universal aspect to the comic process it-self. Take Ovid's classic description of the *festum geniale* of Anna Perenna, the Roman holiday by the banks of the Tiber which celebrated the eternal rebirth of the year:

Common folks come and drink their fill while scattered everywhere in the
    Green grass, and each fellow lies next to his girl.[40]

The festivities conclude with the girls singing lewd songs *(obscaena)* and dirty ditties *(probra)*—a phenomenon we will return to in the next chap-ter. On these occasions, as Frazer commented, "many a girl may have

gone in a maid who came out a maid no more."[41] This crucial event inspired many a New Comedy plot. Terence describes the key forces at
work here:

> He was overcome by night, love, wine and youth—
> it's only human.[42]

This is *kōmos* pure and simple, a revel without a cause. There was no
need to enjoin the Romans to observe these rites, for the very essence of
kōmos is its irresistibility. Ovid does not dwell on the political aspects of
this festival; he chronicles the fun. As Horace describes it, "after the
rites have been performed, the spectator feels both drunk and beyond
the law" *(potus et exlex)*.[43] The entire description bespeaks an atmosphere of surrender to the senses, best exemplified in the words of
Shakespeare's Rosalind:

> Come, come woo me, for now I am in a holiday humour and
> like enough to consent.[44]

Kōmos then is less a state ceremony than it is a state of mind—what
Mikhail Bakhtin called carnivalesque.[45] One psychologist has defined
comedy as a "holiday from the superego,"[46] a view anticipated by Freud
when he wrote:

> A festival is a permitted, or rather an obligatory, excess, a sol-
> emn breach of a prohibition. It is not that men commit the
> excesses because they are feeling happy as a result of some in-
> junction they have received. It is rather that excess is of the
> essence of a festival; the festive feeling is produced by the lib-
> erty to do what is as a rule prohibited.[47]

From a Freudian perspective, the progress of comedy goes hand in
hand with an intensifying pall of repression which harnesses the natural anarchic instincts of man to ensure a civilized society. The linguistic
association between "civilized" and the Latin *civitas* ("town") once again
suggests a contrast between the couth behavior of the city dweller and
the boorish antics of the country bumpkin. Thus we again find reinforcement for the "erroneous" derivation of comedy from *kōmē*, a coun-

try village. We will inevitably find ourselves returning to this "rural" derivation and the truth it conveys.

Thus, despite the advance of civilization—perhaps because of it—we have never lost our zeal for *kōmos*. As Plato understood, the unconscious desire to break society's rules is one of the prime appeals of comedy.[48] Johan Huizinga might explain that ritual had not died, but merely metamorphosed into its twin—"play."[49] As the church father Tertullian railed, "a theater is also a temple—of Venus and Bacchus."[50]

What then is the truest etymology of comedy? We have already argued that there is a valid psychic dimension to all three of the words proposed. And though *kōmos* is the "authentic" parent of Comedy, the enormous poetic validity of the other hypotheses gives pause. Indeed, there is tantalizing if tenuous evidence that *kōmos* and *kōmē* may have a single remote source in the lexical Shangri-La of Indo-European. Both carry the notion of "shared activity."[51] In fact, traces of this ancestral connection may still be seen in the Greek adjective *enkōmios,* which can mean either "of a revel" or "in the village."[52]

One philologist links *kōmē* with various words in the other Indo-European languages which connote communal activity—including English "home"—arguing persuasively that all derive from an ancient Indo-European social institution, the communal settlement.[53] Thus "home" was originally less a place or building than a social concept, the focus of community spirit. The development of this word reflects the gradual narrowing of "the common" from community to family, accompanied by progressive alienation—one of civilization's Discontents—which comedy seeks to overcome.

Given these etymological interconnections, we might suppose a fairly close historical relationship between *kōmos* and *kōmē,* the first perhaps developing from the second as the village population marshaled for festival. Indeed, each hamlet seems to have made its own contributions to the larger Greek festivals, sponsoring choruses, dramatic skits, and so on.[54] A striking parallel is still to be found in the Italian Palio at Siena. Each neighborhood, spearheaded by its men, leads the chosen horse to the piazza, competing with other groups in song, invective, and finally the race itself. The event has the unmistakable flavor of sacrificial ritual.

If such a connection between *kōmos* and *kōmē* is supportable, then the conflict between the ancient etymologies of comedy becomes more intelligible, and each could rightly claim a degree of historical validity. The old Doric derivation of comedy as "song of the village," recorded by Aristotle, may have been as correct in its way as the philologically-approved "song of the *kōmos*."

More mist surrounds the origins of *kōma*.[55] But the earliest uses of the word tend to have erotic overtones, and the idea of "sharing" would be very appropriate for a post-coital slumberous trance. This free-floating notion would imply that sleep, village, and *kōmos* all offer opportunities for untrammeled freedom. Which they do, in life if not in lexicons.

Thus, psychically, all three etymologies are related and legitimate. Dreams, "country matters," and revels are all licensed indulgences of fantasy, releases from Civilization and its Discontents, with all's well that ends well. This alleged triple linkage offers its own valid dimension to the *idea* of Comedy. For it matters less who Comedy's true father was than what its true nature is. *Kōmos* is a rule-breaking revel in the flesh, Comedy an orgy in the mind. Perhaps with "holiday humour" we can entertain all three proposals and argue that Comedy, the mask that launched a thousand quips, is named with as provocative an etymology as Helen of Troy: a dreamsong of a revel in the country.

2

The Song of the *Kōmos*

To begin with, the Happy End. Aristotle calls it the *oikeia hēdonē*, the essential joy—literally "home pleasure"—of Comedy.[1] He cites a hypothetical example in which Orestes and Aegisthus, mortal enemies of tragic legend, confront each other and, instead of dueling to the death, make friends and stroll happily offstage. "Nobody kills anybody," the philosopher adds almost ruefully.[2] In the typical comic dénouement, High Noon turns magically into lunchtime.

The Homeric epics can serve as archetypes for both serious and light drama. Consider the action of the first tragic hero. When Patroclus is killed, Achilles, already estranged from his fellow Greeks, is now cut off from all that is human. He does not eat or drink, and he broods on the fated brevity of his life, his only consolation the promise of a glory that will survive him. He has become the loneliest man on earth, not merely by force of events, but by character as well. Not once does he mention his wife or the son who will fall heir to his "glory." Even Sophocles' Ajax does this much before his death, as does Hector, the social hero whom Homer has presented as a contrast to Achilles. Hector struggles for the solidarity and preservation of family and society. Achilles has no such concerns, and he moves further and further from mankind, ultimately to become merely "inhuman fire" *(thespiades pur)*.[3]

The *Odyssey,* by contrast, begins with its hero at the farthest point from humanity, and the theme of the entire poem is his struggle to return to it. When we first see Odysseus, he is symbolically unborn, hidden in the middle of nowhere at the geographical "womb of the world" (*omphalos thalassēs,* literally "the navel of the sea").[4] He has spent the past seven years with the immortal nymph Calypso, their nights a perpetual *kōmos,* yet Odysseus grieves by day and longs to regain his homeland and home. For the fleeting and fragile domestic existence with his wife and son, he is willing to sacrifice the unending eternity of transcendental bliss which the "immortal and immutable"[5] goddess offers him. He longs for the "fruitful day of his homecoming" *(nostimon ēmar).*[6] This adjective, which also connotes "fertile, productive," reinforces the rebirth symbolism of the poem. Indeed the symbolism of rebirth pervades the poem, whether it be Odysseus' liberation from the "hollow cave"[7] at the "navel of the sea" where Calypso (whose name means "to hide") lies with him—or his actual descent and return from the Underworld. Not to mention his awakening after a "death-like" sleep when he is carried home on the ship of the Phaeacians to Ithaka at last (Book 13):

> A sweet sleep passed over his eyelids,
> An unwaking sleep, the sweetest slumber, almost like death.[8]

While the *Iliad* concludes with a blazing pyre which anticipates the conflagration of Troy, the *Odyssey* ends with Odysseus becoming a father again, embracing Telemachus in the flickering light of the swineherd's cottage. He becomes a husband once more, reunited with Penelope at his own fireplace. After being rejuvenated by Athena, the storm-tossed hero enjoys a symbolic remarriage with Penelope. At last, Odysseus fully re-enters the family structure when he identifies himself as his father's son. What Horace Walpole referred to as "the great eating poem" reaches its climax with all three generations sitting down to a huge festive banquet. The entire poem emphasizes the reintegration of society. It is the fire of heart and hearth and the cooking of supper.

Emphasizing the joys of this world, the *Odyssey* is a complete rejection of Iliadic otherworldly glory. Homer makes this explicit when Odysseus hails Achilles in the Underworld as mightiest among the dead, and the noble shade bitterly retorts that he would rather be "a live peasant working a field that he did not own than to be a king of all the dead."[9] And then he asks about his son and his aged father. Achilles expresses the philosophy of the entire poem—"Give me life."

With these same words Falstaff justifies his hasty retreat from the dangers of Shrewsbury Field. Shakespeare contrasts the faint-hearted fatman with the heroic Hotspur, who cares only for intangible ideals such as his good name:

> I better brook the loss of brittle life
> Than those proud titles thou hast won of me.[10]

By comic standards, Falstaff is a genius and Hotspur, so Achillean in his thirst for glory, is a fool. As Fat Jack reasons sophistically:

> What is honour? A word. What is that word honour? What is
> that honour? Air—a trim reckoning. Who hath it? He that
> died a-Wednesday. Doth he feel it? No . . . Therefore I'll none
> of it.[11]

The tragic hero dies for what is nobler in the mind, the comic hero *lives* for what is humbler in the flesh. Unlike Hotspur's obsession with his "proud titles," the comic hero will surrender his good name to save his life. Thus Odysseus—Lord of Ithaka, Trojan War hero, sacker of many cities and renowned adventurer—forfeits these titles and tells the hungry anthropophagous Cyclops that he is no heroic morsel. In fact, he insists, "my name is Nobody." Better shamefully *hors de combat* than famously someone else's *hors d'oeuvre*. And so Falstaff retreats shouting "give me life," while Hotspur stands fast and becomes "food for worms."[12]

> All tragedies are finished by a death,
> All comedies are ended by a marriage
> The future states of both are left to faith
> For authors fear descriptions might disparage
> The worlds to come of both.[13]

Byron's whimsical over-simplification hides a paradoxical fact. From earliest times, even the darkest of the great tragedies contained a penumbra of consolation: a flickering vision of a release from agony and, ultimately, eternal life after death. Gilbert Murray commented on the relatively "happy" endings of the *Oresteia* and the *Prometheia,* both concluding with triumphant torchlight parades:[14]

> Greek tragedy does not fear the "unhappy ending." Nonetheless it is haunted by the thought of some life after death, and the nearer it keeps to its proper Dionysiac form, the stronger is the note of rebirth.[15]

The *Oresteia* supplies the fullest example. The trilogy begins with a search for light: a watchman on the tower, searching the blackened horizon for a trace of the signal fires that will announce the victory at Troy. This imagery is reinforced at crucial moments. When the torch at last becomes visible, Clytemnestra hails it as an "auspicious herald," adding her wish that dawn will emerge from night.[16] Later, as Cassandra walks bravely to her death, she evokes "the ultimate shining of the light" that will avenge her unjust murder. Most memorable is the chorus' anguished cry for revenge as they lean over Agamemnon's butchered corpse: "Does Orestes live in the sunlight still?"[17] It is not until the end of the *Eumenides,* the concluding play, that the grand torchlight procession finally dispels the darkness of the House of Atreus.[18]

Conversely, at the core of even the most frivolous comedies lies a heart of darkness. Somewhere in the vast, shadowy recesses of man's memory lurks a distant vestige of primordial fear: at the darkness of sunset, at the onslaught of winter, at the dying of the year—and most fundamental, at the prospect of his own death. Perhaps this is most clearly expressed in the plays of Shakespeare. The early *Comedy of Errors* is framed by the death sentence pronounced on the elderly Egeon, hapless father of the twin protagonists, who is to be executed at the setting of the sun. And the late romance *A Winter's Tale* presents, with the passage of time, purification, forgiveness, and symbolic rebirth.

Indeed, in a fundamental sense every comedy is a thinly disguised reenactment of the rebirth of the world. In the common imagination the universe was created as the result of a cosmic coupling: a primal hierogamy in which a masculine Heaven mates with a feminine Earth.[19] Indeed, the fanciful Elizabethan euphemism for sexual intercourse, "to dance the beginning of the world," must surely have emerged from some nocturnal corner of the collective unconscious, from a time when *kōmos* was not merely a metaphor, but an act of magic.[20]

Often one couple alone did not suffice. And so the stimulative magic was intensified by mass-mating, the untrammeled sexual activity currently and disapprovingly associated with the term "orgy." The catalogue of such festivals is time-honored and timeless. Frazer remarked upon the great number of fertility rites involving sexual intercourse, and Theodor Gaster and Mircea Eliade widened the panorama still further. We have already mentioned the Roman celebration of Anna Perenna, the equinoctial New Year's festival celebrated on the Ides of March which involved picnicking by the Tiber, inebriation, the singing of bawdy songs, and sexual promiscuity.[21] Analogous practices, also designed to stimulate crops, have been observed in South America, Java, Africa, China, and India.[22]

In ancient society, the orgiastic *kōmos* represented no dissolution of morals. Quite the contrary: it was serious and honorable, a combining of forces to intensify the magic of prayer.[23] Frazer did not fail to ascribe a religious urgency to "the profligacy which notoriously attended these ceremonies." As Eliade explains,

> Whatever is done in common will have the most favorable results . . . unbounded sexual frenzy on earth corresponds to the union of the divine couple . . . the orgy sets flowing the sacred energy of life.[24]

The wild mayhem of the drunken *kōmos* also had psychological significance. However unconsciously, the celebrants were experiencing yet another feature of the original genesis: primordial chaos, the condition immediately preceding the beginning of the world. In the Old Testament it is called *tohu v'vohu,* onomatopoetically evoking a helter-skelter violent void of cosmic anarchy.[25]

The unleashing of instinct helped maintain the stability of society by a periodic if circumscribed orgiastic release. As Burkert observes, at the end of the wild, phallic explosion, "aggression dissolves into laughter."[26] We are back to the nocturnal etymology of comedy: the man in a *kōma* dreaming the fundamental dreams described by Freud as archetypes of the human imagination. The *kōmos* is thus a brief regression which sanctions ancient behavior no longer licensed by the encroaching advance of civilization. It celebrates the triumph of instinct over intellect, *la forza di natura,* nature's bias.

Is it any wonder then that Old Comedy teems with the myth of the Golden Age, a wishful return to a time when everything was easier, food grew spontaneously, and there were no laws?[27] This happy time was succeeded by an Iron Age—our own—in which *Labor omnia vicit* ("Work conquered all").[28] During the Roman Saturnalia, the normal code of conduct was overturned: slaves were kings for a day, while their masters served them a feast.[29] It was the symbolic return of Saturnus, the deposed father of Jupiter and king of golden-age Italy,[30] who ruled a pastoral paradise like that of Vergil's *Eclogues,* where love—erotic love—was the only law: "*Love* conquers all, and we should surrender to it" *(omnia vincit amor et nos cedamus amori).*[31] When *amor* has given way to *labor,* it is no surprise that mankind now needs a "holiday for the Superego."[32]

Accordingly, the Greek *kōmos* fell within the domain of Bacchus—whom the Romans labeled *Liber* ("Free"). In Greek art we find numerous *kōmos* scenes in which men dress as women—released temporarily from the everyday bonds of gender.[33] As the art historian Philostratus reports in the second century A.D.:

> *Kōmos* allows a woman to be a man and a man to put on a woman's clothes and a woman's walk.[34]

This "comic" transvestitism is found in dramatic form in, for instance, Aristophanes' *Lysistrata, Women at the Thesmophoria,* and *Assemblywomen;* in *Frogs,* Dionysus himself appears in drag.[35] Pentheus' cross-dressing in Euripides' *Bacchae* provides a tragic version of this Dionysiac theme (although this too may have a comic overtone typical of Euripides).[36] As we shall see, Shakespeare takes this motif to extremes in the "transvestite comedies" such as *Twelfth Night.*

But of course this is just one aspect of the liberty granted by the *kōmos.*[37] More fundamentally it is a license to lose one's social and sexual identity—aided by costumes, masks, and intoxication. Indeed, this is the basic principle of dramatic character. In the earliest theory of laughter, Plato held that the ridiculous is essentially a reversal of the precept "know thyself"—it is the lack of self-knowledge.[38] Henri

Bergson echoes this idea in his theory that a character is comic in pro-portion to his ignorance of himself.[39] This "loss of face" is reflected in a number of familiar motifs. The setting is often beyond the limits of normal society: Roman comedy is set in Greece, Shakespeare prefers a forest beyond the laws of the city, and we often find a utopian mirror world.[40] Comedy abounds in madness, enchantment, separated twins representing a bifurcated psyche, and other temporary losses of iden-tity. These are often the result of shipwrecks—the anger of nature disor-dered—which ostensibly destroy, or at least scatter, entire families.

And yet somehow in the end people and pieces come joyfully to-gether. For the license to kōmos is limited. As Prince Hal puts it, "If all the year were playing holidays, to sport would be as tedious as to work."[41] Thus at the very center of the kōmos is the "home pleasure" of the Happy Ending, the comic katastrophē. Like Odysseus after his ten-year orgy of outrageous behavior, however freely the celebrants may be-have during the festival, when it is over they return to the order of the everyday world. For laughter is an affirmation of shared values. Society, renewed and reintegrated by a huge comastic release, is made happy and inhabitable again, just as nature must return from the wild chaos of winter to perform the expected duties of spring and summer.

Ultimately the orgiastic sex became institutionalized as festive gamos, the familiar wedding finale of comedy. The Greek word itself denotes both the legal and the carnal act. The incitement is erōs, and in the words of Shakespeare's Don Armado, "the catastrophe is a nuptial."[42] But a distant memory of the less inhibited group gamos is reflected in the many plays which close with double, triple, and even quadruple weddings—As You Like It, for instance. (With the advent of literary com-edy, as we shall see, some rewards of the comic triumph are no longer what psychologists refer to as "primary" pleasures, but "sublimated" ones like the acquisition of money.)

We can thus recognize in comedy psychic vestiges of two original ele-ments of the ancient kōmos: Chaos and Eros—by no coincidence the progenitors of the Birds in Aristophanes' boldest comedy. These vi-brant feelings are stored up not in the tables of man's memory, but rather in the locker room of his libido, ready to play at a moment's no-tice. We can still sense this vital presence in the most sophisticated comic authors: Shakespeare, Molière, Gilbert and Sullivan, and even parodistically in absurdist authors like Ionesco.

But all this is prologue. Now let us enter the theater itself. Aristotle saw tragic drama as evolving after many changes *(pollas metabolas metabalousa)*[43] from the dithyramb, a choral hymn sung in honor of Dionysus, the best-known practitioners of which were Pindar and Bacchylides, with Arion himself as its inventor. As legend has it, Tragedy was born c. 535 B.C. when the semi-mythical Thespis stepped away from the Chorus and announced to all: "I am Dionysus."[44]

Comedy was only granted official status in Athens half a century later at the Great Dionysia of 486 B.C., when Chionides is recorded as having won the first victory.[45] The festival itself was a very special time in the Greek calendar, when by law all government and legal business was suspended.[46] (The same was true of Roman holidays.)[47] Curiously, when drama was added to the more modest Lenaean festival in the Winter season of 440, the emphasis was on the lighter genre. In fact, comedies exclusively were produced at this festival for the first decade of its existence. Even when tragedy was finally added to the program, it remained essentially a comedian's holiday.[48]

Aristotle's apparent unwillingness to discuss in full the development of comedy has given rise to a widely held theory that he devoted an entire additional book of the *Poetics* to this subject, now lost. This hypothetical document has given rise to much speculation. There is an important manuscript (probably from the third century A.D., but discovered only in 1839) known as the *Tractatus Coislinianus,* which some have regarded as the epitome of this semi-mythical treatise.[49] Umberto Eco's tongue-in-cheek murder mystery, *The Name of the Rose,* almost allegorizes the medieval attack on laughter, positing the existence of the "lost" Aristotelian essay on comedy in the library of an isolated monastery. The mad killer is so incensed by the existence of a document so potentially dangerous to Christian gravity that he murders any fellow cleric who comes across it. The novel concludes, tantalizingly enough, with the burning of this subversive manuscript by the humorless maniac.

The flames leave us to speculate upon Comedy's various evolutionary stages. All that extant Aristotle vouchsafes is that the dramatic form evolved from "the leaders of the phallic procession" *(apo tōn exarchontōn ta phallika)*.[50] These were clearly participants in a special kind of *kōmos*. We can begin by trying to appreciate the importance of this type of worship in ancient Greece. Of course, institutionalized celebration of the male member is hardly restricted to the Aegean world or the distant past. Indeed, the Hindu Lingam is still in active worship. In the West, the familiar Maypole is itself probably a vestige of such a ceremony.[51]

There is an elemental rationale for this kind of worship which, from earliest times, was an integral part of fertility rites. The Greeks imagined gods in their own image—or at least with similar reproductive parts. But the phallus was not merely a symbol of male sexuality: the female celebrants at *ta phallika* were worshiping not masculinity, but a metasexual embodiment of the most human of feelings.[52] The potent phallus was a symbol and instrument not only for the continuity of the species, but for the flowering of the fields as well. In a study of these rites in various cultures, Eliade observes the frequent parallels between sexual and agricultural terminology.[53] (In the following chapters, we will see how Old Comedy uses similar imagery of flora and fauna for its obscenity.) Even a reticent Frazer had to acknowledge the omnipresence of the phallus:

> In the thought of the ancients no sharp line of distinction divided the fertility of animals from the fertility of plants; rather the two ideas met and blended in a nebulous haze. We need not wonder, therefore, why the same coarse but expressive emblem figured conspicuously [in the ritual of both Dionysus and his Italian counterpart].[54]

Herodotus suggests that the phallus had so long been a feature of Athenian religious life that its beginning was now forgotten, and accordingly offers his usual theory of Egyptian origins. The historian also reports an important use of the priapic symbol in religious magic—to protect one's home by placing before it a figure of Hermes-erectus. This custom too was clearly very ancient; this time Herodotus explains it as a Pelasgian importation.[55] The protective function is paralleled by the boundary stones of the ancient Near East and the Roman crossroad markers which scandalized St. Augustine.[56]

Yet despite its forgotten beginnings, Aristotle reports that phallic rites were still widespread and vital in his day.[57] The sanctity which the Greeks ascribed to these icons may be seen in Thucydides' account of the fear and trembling which gripped Athens in 415 B.C., when unknown vandals mutilated the Hermes statues.[58] Is it merely coincidence that Aristophanes' *Birds,* which appeared shortly thereafter, is the most detailed celebration of the phallus in extant Greek comedy?

Whatever the ultimate source of phallic worship, by the Classical period it was closely associated with the cult of Dionysus—Herodotus tells us that it was a central feature of his festival. This was the focal point of the Greek religious calendar, and it was on this occasion that drama was first presented. Greek comedy was thus born with the phallic god as presiding deity. As Aristophanes tells us, "Phales" was Bacchus' "partner in the *kōmos*" (*synkōme*).[59] It is this connection which accounts for the omnipresence of the icon in Attic Old Comedy, as we shall see.

We have no idea exactly what went on at the Attic phallic ceremonies mentioned by Aristotle. We do, however, have texts from fraternities like the so-called "straightrods" (*ithyphalloi*), who would enter the theater bearing the emblem of their membership to sing:

> Get it up, get it up
> Make a great wide space
> For hale and hardy Holy Him
> Whose rod may overflow the brim
> Would like to march right through the place.

Another confrérie, the "phallus-bearers" (*phallophoroi*), after parading in, would sing a hymn to Bacchus while their icon-bearer, straight and tall, rushed forward to hurl insults at various people in the audience.[60]

Here we find a second important feature of ancient Greek fertility rites, which would persist into iambic poetry and literary comedy: invective.[61] In the very beginning, prayer and curse were all but synonymous. The Greek *araomai* bears these dual, apparently antithetical connotations: the priest Chryses in the *Iliad* is referred to as an *arētēr,* but we know the destructive nature of his prayer.[62] It may strike the modern sensibility as somewhat odd—if not sacrilegious—that insult and scurrilous abuse *(aischrologia)* could be a form of worship. Yet Frazer and many others have documented the universal use of invective and "obscenity" as magic to promote fertility and avert evil spirits.[63]

But virtually nowhere is the hurling of invective more conspicuous than in Greek ritual. The Anthesteria, the Lenaea, and even the solemn rites of the Eleusinian Mysteries included the shouting of obscenities. So did the Thesmophoria and Haloa, festivals celebrated exclusively by women in honor of Demeter.[64] Accounts of verbal excess on the part of Greek matrons have caused at least one scholar to raise an eyebrow at "cet oubli de la pudeur féminine."[65] Yet it is precisely the sanction to unremember *pudeur* which gives *kōmos* such instinctive appeal. We are reminded of the Roman maidens—or maidens no more—described by Ovid, who stripped off their prim chastity to sing *obscaena* and *probra*.

While few moderns would allege that a curse is a prayer, few would deny it remains a pleasure. And a childish pleasure at that. As Sándor Ferenczi believed,

> In the fourth or fifth year of life . . . a period is interpolated between the relinquishing of the infantile modes of gratification and the beginning of the true latency period, one characterised by the impulse to utter, write up, and listen to obscene words.[66]

In word and symbol, ithyphallic invective, the curse that blesses, has a long and hardy history. There is the Roman tradition of fescennine verses, hostile scurrilities bandied on at least two significant fertility occasions: weddings and harvest-time. Not surprisingly, there is a Greek parallel. Sappho is known to have written bawdy mocking songs for marriages,[67] and Herodotus recounts how the Epidaurians tried to counteract the sterility of their fields by organizing choruses of cursers.[68] But the "rough and ready"[69] Roman *fescennina* are better known and better documented. At Roman weddings the phallus would be displayed to provide apotropaic magic, a power which we have seen in the Hermes-erectus. Catullus' epithalamium (Poem 61) is spiced with *iocatio Fescennina,* the same volleys of insult that characterized the Roman fertility festivals.

It is all for the sake of fertility. The same is true of the Roman *opprobria rustica,* "country cursing" which had accompanied the gathering of the harvest from time immemorial. We recall the "false" derivation of Comedy as "village song," an etymology that persists in radiating a fictional truth. Horace admiringly describes one such simple festival. With all agricultural duties completed, the farmers convene with their families to "renew body and soul," sacrifice to local agrarian gods, and then relax for the traditional volleys of insult:

> From this practice arose the tradition of licentious "fescenning," torrents of rustic abuse in bantering verse. This sort of freedom was welcomed and played merrily along year after year.[70]

At both wedding and harvest the obvious aim was invigoration by invective. And it is of more than incidental interest that the word "fescennine" was thought by some ancient scholars to derive from the Latin *fascinum,* meaning *"phallus."*[71]

The career of Ausonius of Bordeaux, often regarded as the last "classical" Latin poet, attests that these practices were still flourishing in the fourth century A.D. In fact, he composed a particularly bawdy wedding song for the Emperor Gratian's son, prefacing it with a professorial apology that, after all, this was a time-honored practice. He then recites the *Cento Nuptialis* ("Marital Patchwork Quilt"), a poem on a bride's deflowering, distinguished as much for its Virgilian parody as its priapic hyperbole. With his encyclopedic command of Latin poetry, Ausonius stitches together lines and half-lines from the *Aeneid* and the *Georgics,* to evoke a ribald description. His double-entendres are anything but subtle ("he whipped out his blade . . .").

Just as the origins of fescennine-style mockery stretch back beyond the horizon of centuries to an unknown distant origin, so too the practice continued unabated in subsequent ages. It is present in the invective aspect of all comedy, and in a sublimated form in the hurling of rice or flowers at weddings, which was once a hurling of derision—and ultimately of stones.[72] Interestingly, the Greek *ta katachusmata*—handfuls of nuts or figs with which bride and groom were showered—also describes the Old Comedy practice of throwing offerings to—or at—an audience in order to win its favor (a practice perpetuated in some modern productions).

Fescennine practices came into conflict with the sexual austerity of the early Church, already firmly established by the fourth century A.D. For the Christians of this period, sexuality replaced mortality as the magnetic pole to which all reflection on the extent of mankind's frailty must turn.[73] An outraged St. Augustine, in his discussion "about the turpitude of the rites held for Bacchus," recounts the pervasiveness of phallic adoration in Roman society, drawing (as so often) on Varro, that most diligent of Roman scholars.[74] Incredibly, there were statues at crossroads for public worship. Still worse, on holidays, this "filthy organ" (turpe membrum) was paraded on a wagon around the city, while the faithful were enjoined to employ the foulest possible language (verbis flagitiossimis). More shocking still, a matron from the noblest family would publicly place a wreath on "this most ignoble of organs." All this, cried Augustine, bringing ire and irony to a boil, to appease the gods, enrich the crops, and "to frighten evil spirits from the country with a mighty rod" (ab agris fascinatio repellenda).

Yet all the stormy fulminations from the pulpit were in vain, for instinct will master intellect. So universal and so ingrained in the country folk (pagani) was phallus-worship that, despite its early efforts, the Church could not dispel it. Augustine's tirade fully demonstrates how the icon he decried never lost its fascination, and that kōmos could outdraw communion. Thus, whatever the Church might preach about otherworldly glory, they were nonetheless obliged to temper piety with expediency. And so they arranged for their holidays to coincide with pagan kōmos-days, whose names were simply euphemized. Old instincts were aroused in the faithful.

Such obvious "paganisms" as New Year's Day were simply incorporated into the ecclesiastical calendar. The birthday of Jesus was wisely ascribed to the same day in December on which the return of the unconquerable sun (sol invictus) was formerly celebrated in the Western empire. (The older Eastern date—January sixth—is still kept by the Russian and Armenian Orthodox churches as Christmas day.) Saturnalia, the festival of lights for the shortest days of the year, was celebrated from the seventeenth of December to the twenty-third, a kind of run-up to Christmas.[75] The early spring holiday Carnevale, celebrating the return of life, was incorporated into the Lenten and Easter festivals.[76] And in 1545 the Council of Trent officially sanctioned the Maypole and May Day celebrations.

Extraordinary license had to be countenanced even in the highest echelons. In the medieval Feast of Fools the lowly clerics assumed high office, and hierarchy dissolved into Saturnalian high jinks. Certain frivolities had to be admitted along with the solemnity, as may be seen in this account of Christmas Day in Rome, 1503. A group of revelers, satirizing the College of Cardinals, held a rowdy banquet after which, the report states:

> They went out into the street, thirty of them. Wearing masks, which had long, thick noses of priapic shape—which is to say, like the male organ . . . and they exhibited themselves to the Pope who was in the window.[77]

These medieval practices resemble *kōmos* more than theatrical performance. Comedy had once again dissolved into ritual. We must bear in mind the important distinction that the one is a revel in the flesh, the other an orgy in the mind. Like the stern Church fathers, the mind allows an occasional holiday and permits pagan thoughts to frolic. And yet all is not mental. For, in the nightsong-country-revel that is Comedy, we still enjoy one physical reaction of the primitive orgy: laughter.[78]

All Comedy aspires to laughter—although not all laughter is related to Comedy. To begin with, as Aristotle long ago remarked, laughter "is the unique characteristic of human beings,"[79] an observation echoed by Rabelais among others.[80] The younger Pliny justified his occasional reading of comedies, saying, "besides, I laugh now and then, after all I'm human."[81] In fact, laughter is now understood to be a unique product of human evolution.[82]

Laughter is thus a vital sign of humanity. Quintilian observed that humor is a means of "dissipating melancholy and pressure, unbending the mind . . . renewing its powers and recruiting its strength."[83] Psychologically, it signals the triumph of instinct over intellect.[84] Kant saw it as "the furtherance of the vital bodily processes."[85] It is a way in which the Life Force is made manifest. In Susanne Langer's words, it is "the crest of a wave of felt vitality."[86] Indeed, recent research shows that laughter is restorative and health-inducing.[87]

Nor does it heal the individual alone. Laughter is universally recognized as a social gesture which binds the community and integrates society.[88] It expresses to other members of the same species a feeling of euphoria.[89] Darwin observed that for a great many animals a sound more or less like laughter is employed—either as a call for sex, or as "a joyful meeting between the parents and their offspring, and between the attached members of the same social community."[90]

Legends of many cultures link laughter and fertility. In one Greco-Egyptian myth, the beginning was not the Word, but the Laugh—and the Laugh was God.[91] According to Apache legend, when the first man awakened to discover the first woman beside him, he spoke. Then she spoke. He laughed. Then she laughed. And as they went off together, the world burst into springtime and song.[92] Theirs was a laughter of *erōs* which set the world in bloom, just as in Hesiod's account of Aphrodite's birth grass sprang up "beneath her lovely feet" as the goddess stepped newborn from the ocean.[93]

Conversely, when Demeter loses Persephone, she is drained of youth and wanders the earth as an old woman. She not only refuses food and drink, she is *agelastos,* "unlaughing." Then the earth starves, the flowers wilt, the fields are barren. (Only the aptly-named Iambe, with her obscene language, can make Demeter smile and laugh.)[94] The joyful reunion of mother and daughter is accompanied by the return of a spring so intense that "the entire earth and the salty sea all laughed for joy."[95]

Here on a cosmic level we can see the same association between motherhood and laughter evident in the biblical tale of Sarah, who laughed when told she would conceive at the age of ninety.[96] Hence it is understandable that various apotropaic or mimetic fertility rites feature laughter. This phenomenon is found in a diversity of cultures, and observers are quick to note that ritual laughter expresses not merely the life force, but rebirth as well.[97] This may be seen in the famous Easter laughter *(risus paschalis)* of the Greek Orthodox Church, which greets the Resurrection of Christ.[98]

Of course, laughter always has its foes. Employing a Rabelaisian coinage, George Meredith gave this dour personality type a name which will be useful in our discussion:

> We have in this world men whom Rabelais would call "agelasts," that is to say, non-laughers, men who are in that respect as dead bodies, which, if you prick them, do not bleed . . . In relation to the stage, they have taken in our land the form and title of Puritan.[99]

The agelast (Greek *a-gelastos,* "not laughing"), like the barren Demeter (who was also *agelastos*) or Eco's crazed monk, is thus the antithesis of the comic hero. Since laughter is an affirmation of shared values, such mean spirits can be dealt with in one of two ways: they are either persuaded—usually after a bit of rough-housing—to join the dance (which better suits a festive mood), or else they are expelled from the holiday society.[100] This figure is typified by Knemon, the title character of Menander's *Dyskolos* ("The Grouch"), whose ill-temper threatens to prevent the other characters from achieving the happy ending before he himself is finally softened and browbeaten to "let the world slip." He is anticipated by Demus in Aristophanes' *Knights,* the grumpy little old man (*dyskolon gerontion*)[101]—representing Athenian society as a whole—who is successfully rejuvenated at the play's end. The impenitent agelast who is not included in the final reintegration of society appears in Shakespeare's *Twelfth Night* as the ill-wishing Malvolio, and as Molière's obsessive miser Harpagon.

Rebirth. Reunion. The Happy End. In fact, what we have distinguished as the essential feature of Comedy is closely related to what has been called "Elemental Laughter"—that of a newborn child. As early as Darwin, scientists have observed that a baby's first laugh is likely to occur when, after a brief separation from his mother, he sees her return once more.[102] Thus the elemental laugh is related to the elemental happy end: the reunion of the family. There is a curious human need for this kind of simple resolution. Aristotle saw the Happy End not merely as pleasure for the audience, but one which they collectively longed for.[103] Perhaps it is appropriate to recall Freud's observation that the essential comic pleasure lies in the temporary recreation of the psychic state of childhood.[104]

A little poem of Catullus beautifully expresses the basic but complex delight of elemental laughter. Journeying in far-off places, he finally returns to his native Sirmio. After the anxieties of separation, he can now rest on the bed he has dreamed of:

> O what is more glorious than when the mind sets down
> its baggage, and worry-free, worn out from the efforts
> of travel, we come to our home and rest softly on our
> longed-for bed.[105]

This vision, at once infantile and erotic, is perhaps the dual essence of comedy's Happy End, a satisfying conclusion which in music is not co-incidentally known as the "home-tone."[106] The poem ends with Catullus asking to be welcomed by his beloved home: "Laugh out all the joyous laughter in the house."

The essential human comedy is an odyssey from estrangement abroad to reunion at home. And the happiest of Happy Endings is . . . laughter in the house.

3

The Lyre and the Phallus

A broad-shouldered man clubs a scrawny cripple. The victim staggers in pain, bleeds, begins to weep. Far from being a police report of felonious assault, this is an objective account of the first recorded stimulus to human laughter in the history of Western literature. Though the modern sensibility may recoil at the thought of such brutality as "comedy," Homer is unequivocal in reporting the delight of the Greek leaders when Odysseus beats Thersites: "Though sad and homesick, they laughed with pleasure at him."[1]

We can only speculate on what sort of effect the Thersites episode had upon the bard's audience. And yet it is not unreasonable to think that Homer's listeners would laugh much the way the Greek leaders did. They too might even regard the manhandling of Thersites as "the very best thing Odysseus had done since he got to Troy."[2] Homer's audience knew that he would go on to better things, but it is worth noting how much attention and comment his actions attract among his fellow warriors. The episode is especially important as presaging the character we will come to know, the comic hero who will "live up to his name."

For the essence of Odysseus is in his name.[3] The newborn son of Laertes was named by his grandfather, Autolycus ("Lone Wolf"), who said: "I have odysseused many in my time, up and down the wide world, men and women both; therefore let his name be Odysseus."[4] As one scholar states: "In the *Odyssey odyssasthai* means essentially 'to cause pain *(odynē)* and to be willing to do so.'"[5] (Contrast the joyous laughter explicit in the name of Isaac.) Thus from birth, by name, and by nature, the first comic hero in Western literature is an inflictor of pain. We should not seek psychological explanations for his behavior. Rather, we should acknowledge its psychological appeal.

It is almost universally accepted that comedy provides an inward release for various antisocial instincts. Freud believed that one of the prime effects of wit was the release of aggressive feelings that normally must be suppressed:

> Since our individual childhood and, similarly, since the childhood of human civilization, hostile impulses against our fellow men have been subject to the same restrictions, the same progressive repression, as our sexual urges.[6]

Freud also observes that the closer we are to the original aggression, the greater the comic delight. Of course none of this is new. The modern view of laughter-as-aggression subtends the Hobbesian "sudden glory" theory.[7] By the nineteenth century, this idea "became crucified through various physiological, psychological and primitivistic analogies."[8] W. K. Wimsatt, for one, questioned the worth of such inquiries:

> Why do I laugh . . . when an old peddler stumbles and spills his pencils all over the street? I don't know. Maybe I don't laugh. But a Fiji Islander would! He will laugh when a prisoner is being roasted alive in an oven! Confident proclamations about the nature of anthropoid laughter are invested with importance by equally confident assumptions that reduction to the lowest common factor is the right way of proceeding . . . Are such theories of hidden elements and forgotten origins supposed to increase my appreciation of jokes or comic situations?[9]

The argument of the present book dissents somewhat from this view, believing that there can be value in recalling "forgotten origins" of ancient stimuli to laughter. For the answer to "why they laughed" may provide many insights into literature of the past—particularly that of Greece, the birthplace of Western comedy.

Consider what purports to be the earliest extant bit of comic dialogue from the Greek theater.[10] As tradition has it, these lines were spoken by Susarion of Megara, who, according to a scholiast, was "the originator of metrical comedy."[11] When his wife left home, he stormed to the theater during the Dionysian festival, took the stage, and shouted these iambic lines:

> O fellow citizens, all women are the bane of life.
> But how could we have a home without a baneful wife?[12]

This is not exactly a great piece of wit, but it does tell us a lot about the comic process. The battle of the sexes is as old as the beginning of time: Susarion's quip is merely a sixth-century version of the anti-wife joke that has been a staple of comedy from the day after the first wedding.[13] The bonds—sometimes painful—of holy matrimony are an obvious target, since they put a legal restraint on emotions and require man to suppress his natural urge toward polygamy.

Misogynistic humor entered comedy via the long tradition of iambic poetry, which used the eponymous meter described by Horace as "proper to rage."[14] The best-known composers of this genre were Archilochus and Hipponax (seventh and sixth century respectively); the latter of whom left us with a famous epigram:

> a wife will give you two good days:
> the day you marry her—and the day you bury her.[15]

But the most scathing piece of misogyny is the bravura set-piece by the seventh-century poet Semonides, which likens the traits of women to various members of the animal kingdom—sow, ass, cat, mare, ape, and bee. His canine description is a memorable example:

> And one is a meddlesome bitch—just like her own mother.
> She wants to hear everything, and know everything,
> And, going around poking into everything,
> She barks even if there is nothing to see.

A man could not control her with threats,
Not even if he angrily smashes her teeth with a
Stone; nor if he speaks sweetly;
And even if she's sitting among house-guests
She keeps up her useless yapping.[16]

The anti-wife humor which underlies such classics as *Taming of the
Shrew* and Plautus' *The Brothers Menaechmus (Menaechmi)* and *Casina* is
evident even in so-called avant-garde plays like Jarry's *King Ubu* and
Ionesco's *Bald Soprano*. It is alive and well today, as in the rather unso-
phisticated remark of a husband to his better half: "Darling, whoever of
us dies first . . . I'm moving to Florida."[17] (The technical name for this
kind of joke is *para prosdokian*, "against expectation," where the dupe is
led down the path toward a logical conclusion which is unexpectedly
switched.) Of course, it works in both directions. As John Gay (1685–
1732) wrote in *Beggar's Opera*, "the comfortable state of widowhood is
the only hope that keeps up a wife's spirits." Freud's trenchant analysis
of the comic process reveals another dimension to Susarion's "First
Joke":

> The object of the joke's attack *(Angriffsobjekte)* may equally
> well be institutions, people in their capacity as vehicles of in-
> stitutions, dogmas or morality or religion, views of life which
> enjoy so much respect that objections to them can only be
> made under the mask of a joke and indeed of a joke con-
> cealed by its façade.[18]

There is no little hostility in Susarion's "witticism." In fact,
Strachey's translation as "the object of a joke's attack," while faithful to
Freud, still lacks the sheer hostility of *die Angriffsobjekte*, which could be
rendered more literally as "the targets of assault." What Julius Caesar
may have intended by "comic violence" *(vis comica)*, the absence of
which in Terence led the great general to prefer Menander,[19] is sometimes taken to almost unbearable extremes, as we shall see in Marlowe's
Jew of Malta. This comedy of cruelty is found in all cultures, but has
been most aptly named by the Germans—*Schadenfreude*.[20]

In the millennia since Susarion, none of the stimuli that arouse laughter have changed. At the beginning of Aristophanes' *Frogs,* Dionysus and his bondsman Xanthias take the stage and the slave immediately offers to warm up the audience by telling them "some of the old jokes—the ones that never fail to raise a laugh."[21] His master, the patron saint of the dramatic arts, replies that the idea is excellent, except that Xanthias must avoid certain lightweight subjects—and authors like Ameipsias and Phrynichus (two rivals of Aristophanes), because their jokes are *too* old.[22]

Yet paradoxically, there is really no such thing as a "new" joke. Laughter depends upon familiarity, and all of them have been told before. The emphasis may have varied in particular societies, and as time goes by the jokes may get better. But the essence remains. Comedy attacks restraints—it dares to say the unsayable. Laughter is liberating.

After all, in everyday conversation the Greeks did not go around making scatological remarks, joking about phalluses, or discussing explicit sexual matters as extravagantly as we find at the comic festivals. We notice that Susarion addresses the *dēmotai,* his fellow citizens. He is providing them with a comic escape for their own urges to break the very laws which make them a society. Thus, though we may never know what the leaders of the Athenian phallic procession sang, we can see from the sparse surviving remains of the Old Comedy poets that their repertory of abuses contained attacks on the most respected of institutions.

The fragments of Attic comedy are full of misogynistic quips like Susarion's. Women are stereotyped—as drunkards, blabbermouths, and nymphomaniacs.[23] One flaming example is Rhodia, wife of the politician Lycon, who is blasted twice by Eupolis, once in *Cities:* "Every man [who gets to town] goes straight to—Lycon's wife."[24] Apart from any personal habits she may have had, her name, "Rosy," also had sexual overtones—in this case it is almost a job description.[25] Eupolis again lampooned Lycon and his pliant spouse in the lost *Friends.*[26] (It serves Lycon right, since he was later one of the accusers of Socrates.)

Plato Comicus contributes a bit of anti-wife advice to husbands: "never stop beating your wife—although it is hard to keep it up. Other-

wise she will go elsewhere and that would be disastrous."[27] His *Phaon*
has a scene in which Aphrodite refers to typical female drunkenness
and describes women's hyperactive libido with a dozen lines of (virtually untranslatable) sly synonyms for male and female sexual parts.[28] In
another fragment, Aristophanes has a woman concede:

> It's not unreasonable, O women
> that the men should beat us regularly
> for all the trouble we cause.
> For they catch us doing
> the most dreadful things.[29]

Among the fragments we also detect numerous topical references to
politicians and other dignitaries. But this is not satire, strictly speaking,
as many scholars have alleged. (One thinks of the Algonquin wit
George S. Kaufman's wry definition: "satire is what closes Saturday
night.")[30] In fifth-century Greece it was invective for invective's sake, exploiting the "characters" of Athenian society by exposing their personal
foibles.

Avant-garde intellectuals, especially of the pseudo variety, are also a
popular target for assault, in keeping with comedy as the triumph of
instinct over intellect. We know that in the *Flatterers* Eupolis ridiculed
Callias, one of the most influential men in Athens, for consorting with
the newfangled Sophists.[31] In the same play he makes what seems to be
the first reference to the philosopher Protagoras, whom he presents as a
mere boaster *(alazōn)*.[32]

By comic license, Socrates was numbered among the Sophists,
even though the more familiar impression which has come down to us
is not one of an intellectual snake-oil salesman. Ameipsias twitted Socrates,[33] and in 423 B.C. brought on a chorus of pedantic nerds
(phrontistai) in his *Connus* to defeat Aristophanes' presentation of Socrates and the Thinketorium *(phrontistērion)* in the *Clouds.* Eupolis calls
Socrates the babbling beggar *(ptōchon adoleschēn),* and in another fragment someone says, "Take him, O Philosopher, and teach him how to
babble *(adoleschein)*."[34] This could fit well into Aristophanes' *Clouds,*
produced in 423. It is very likely the remark of a father bringing his son
to be educated by the great philosopher. Plato Comicus had a play ex-

pressly called the *Sophists,* while Cratinus mentions "a swarm of sophists."[35] And in Middle Comedy, Plato the Philosopher's name appears repeatedly.

Even motherhood is not sacred. Take for example the conclusion of the *Clouds,* where the young man Pheidippides, with his "new learning," justifies the beating of his father, which he is doing with gusto:

STREPSIADES: Ow! Ow! Why do you show me no respect?

PHEIDIPPIDES: Okay, I'll be fair—I'll go whip mother too![36]

This gambit became a staple in Comedy, at least as early as Aristophanes, and it had lost none of its vigour by the time of Plautus, one of whose comedies begins with a slave warning his master:

PSEUDOLUS: If I can't swindle someone else, I'll fleece your father . . .

SON: Oh please, by all that's sacred—fleece my mother too![37]

Indeed, in keeping with its origins in iambic invective, Old Comedy's primary characteristic was the unfettered use of language. Freedom of speech, referred to by Eupolis as *isēgoria,* was Athens' most prized possession.[38] It is better known from Aristophanes as *parrhēsia* (from *pas,* "everything," and *rhēsis,* "utterance"), the permission to say anything. As we have seen, obscene language was a traditional part of the festive rituals from which comedy grew. We know that at the women's festival, the *thesmophoria,* the participants shouted "disgusting, unholy things" *(aischra kai asemna).*[39]

In a famous passage, Horace describes the use of invective by the fifth-century Attic comedians:

> Whenever Eupolis or Cratinus or Aristophanes—the truly great poets—and their Old Comedy contemporaries encountered anyone worthy of being pilloried as a villain, or a crook, or a pervert, or a cut-throat, or something else notorious, they would brand him *(notabant)* with the greatest of freedom.[40]

Horace does not mention any poet from the first generation of Attic comic playwrights. In fact, there are only a few textual bits and pieces from this period. Certainly it would have been metrically possible to include the patriarch Magnes, but Horace begins rather from the second generation with Cratinus. But then it was a common practice of Alexandrian scholarship to pick three great authors as representatives of a given genre. Or perhaps the comedy of the first generation was too crude—for in the beginning, Old Comedy totally lacked what we would recognize as a plot. It still showed signs of its origin in improvisation by being relatively unstructured. The best that can be said is that it contained various themes, which some scholars prefer to call "Happy Ideas." Its structure was unique, and Old Comedy is classified as a genre unto itself.

But even to speak of "structure" is a bit of an exaggeration. We know that the ancient critics continually emphasized the *dis*organization *(ataxia)* of these early comedies. The great Cratinus himself, though he is credited with bringing some order to the chaos, was noted for his sloppy structuring. Only Aristophanes displayed "more proficiency and technical skills."[41] One may excuse or explain this as the necessary result of Attic comedy's attempts to absorb the disparate elements of various popular traditions (Dorian, Megarian, traditional choral structures). But the fact needs no apology. For Aristophanes and his colleagues were great artists whose theatrical forte happened to be a kind of episodic vaudeville.

Nevertheless, Old Comedy—at least as exemplified by Aristophanes—does show some broad consistency of form. The genre seems to have developed from, or integrated, an earlier but standardized performance type—the so-called epirrhematic *agōn*, comprising two choral set-pieces, the disappearance of which would mark the end of the genre.[42]

The *agōn* ("contest, struggle") itself was a kind of debate usually on a topic relating to the theme of the play, a battle of words rather than swords, and perhaps descends from the slanging matches of the invective tradition.[43] The Chorus split into two "teams" that would exchange insults (and sometimes blows) in their furious efforts to emerge victorious and persuade the protagonist. At other times there were two individual opponents—as in Aristophanes' *Clouds,* where Right Logic and Wrong Logic debate the relative merits of the old and new moralities. In *Wasps,* the argument is about the role played by the jurymen in politics.

Conversely, the plays as a whole, each exploring a certain issue, might themselves be viewed as extended *agōnes*. The victorious protagonist, like the Olympic champion, is cheered with *tēnella kallinikos,* "Hail the Victor."[44] He also "gets the girl"—a kind of "Miss Olympia" *avant la lettre*. She is often a piper, the party-girl who enlivened Greek symposia with a full range of entertainments (played onstage, of course, by a man in appropriately exaggerated padding). Often nameless but always naked, she lends her unbridled enthusiasm to the dramatic recreation of a loud, crapulous *kōmos,* with decorum and restraint thrown completely to the winds. And if modern incarnations are anything to go by, the actor who played the "lovely girl" was probably a hulking brute. We find this continued, for example, in the 300-year-old tradition of Harvard's annual Hasty Pudding shows. They nearly always feature a chorus line of the most muscular—and hairy-legged—specimens from the Varsity Football Team.

In the *parabasis* ("stepping forward"), the Chorus steps up to the very rim of the stage, breaking the dramatic illusion to deliver a message directly from poet to audience. It is frequently a polemic, advocating some civic action (the appointment of a general, for example) or defending the originality of the author. Often it was simply shameless flattery to convince the judges to give the author first prize.

As would be natural in a genre which was evolving from a group performance, the role of the Chorus is far more prominent in the early fragments than in Aristophanes himself, whose early plays nevertheless still give it an ample role. The Chorus was often presented as a pack of animals, harking back to the theriomorphic participants of early fertility celebrations and displaying the notion of impersonation which is fundamental to drama. Like Aristophanes, several other comic authors composed *Frogs* and *Birds,* and there were productions featuring choruses of bees, horses, fish, storks, vultures, nightingales, goats, ants, flounders, and simply "animals."[45]

It is important to remember that in Old Comedy the phallus was onstage at all times. Every actor wore an outsize replica which dangled between his legs.[46] Even the gods, and Zeus himself,[47] were so equipped. This indispensable feature of their get-up could be manipulated by a string to indicate sexual excitement. One thinks of the classic example in *Lysistrata* where the Spartan herald reports his country's reaction to the women's Sex Strike:

> All Sparta's totally aroused, and our allies will remain
>   absolutely firm.[48]

But the outsize organ is more than just a piece of stage business. It harks back to time immemorial when it was a religious icon, and maintains a potent effect on the themes of all Old Comedy.

The language of the genre was very special. From the beginning it consisted of a variety of meters—ranging from the hexameter of Homer to the invective verses of the Iambic poets to the lyric strains as used by Sappho, Alcaeus, Pindar, and the Tragedians. The anapestic septenarius—more familiar to modern playgoers as the "Gilbertian" meter (Sullivan, perhaps unfairly, does not get mentioned)—was known in earlier times as the "Aristophanic."

All the playwrights show remarkably rich inventiveness in the coining of words, puns, and other verbal acrobatics and gymnastics. Take for example Aristophanes' almost surreal creation of *englōttogasterōn genos,* "the tongues-in-stomach tribe."[49] In particular, he was fond of giant compound words, such as *orthrophoitosukophantodikotalaipōrōn,* "early-morning-going-out-and-judging-trumped-up-lawsuit-toil-and-troublous-habits."[50]

And, of course, at the other end of the scale there is *aischrologia*—the gross humor involving such primitive bodily functions as defecating and vomiting, both favorite Greek topics. Indeed, the chamber pot is so omnipresent that it is almost a stock character in the comedies.[51] There are an endless number of synonyms for private parts, both masculine and feminine.

The poetry of Old Comedy is heterogeneous, to say the least. It is a unique confection of the lyre and the phallus, a counterpoint of melodic delicacy and discordant grossness. A fragment of Pherecrates demonstrates well this unique aspect of the ancient playwrights. At first glance, it seems like a lovely—if slightly odd—floral arrangement, in a style reminiscent of "Lucy in the Sky with Diamonds":

Sweet mallow belching and hyacinth breathing
Green clover wordlets and Rose-smiles divine
Peppermint kisses and celery thrusting
Wild olive laughter and lovely blue lusting
Whip out your pitcher, sing paeans for more wine![52]

But there is more. Each of the "blossoms" mentioned—from roses to hyacinths to celery—would give an added frisson to the audience, because they are all familiar slang words for male or female private parts.[53] The song is a tour de force of lyricism and obscenity.

None of Aristophanes' contemporaries or predecessors has left us more than fragments and notices. We know of twenty-seven titles for Cratinus, of which eight won first prize at the comic festivals (the first in 453, though his career must have begun earlier), and some five hundred fragments, the longest of them being bits and pieces of 89 lines.[54] His peculiar titles deal in plurals, often of literary or intellectual interest—the *Odysseuses* and the *Archilochuses*, for example, where the choruses must have been rather odd. His extant work is predominantly in iambic trimeters with an admixture of hexameter and Archilochean meters—the latter an obvious inheritance from the seventh-century iambic poet whose subject matter was equally caustic and hostile. Much of his subject matter too is like Aristophanes'. Among the targets of Cratinus' abuse were Euripides and Pericles himself.[55]

Interestingly enough, Cratinus also blasts the latter not for his policies but his person, calling him "bulb-headed" *(schinokephalos)*.[56] The public ridicule of minor physical flaws is typical of the comic process. One thinks of Aristotle's definition of "the comic" as arising from a defect (but not a harmful one) in the person targeted.[57] This might well justify the amusement at Thersites' expense, since he was "the ugliest man who came to Ilium."[58] Thus the noble Socrates was often mocked as a satyr for his particular sexual appetites and disheveled wardrobe—and simply because it was true.

Comic performers throughout the ages have even exploited their own physical defects to arouse laughter. Aristophanes alludes to his own baldness.[59] Cratinus satirized his own alcoholism. Everyone who has seen a Marx Brothers film will recall the funny walk of Groucho, but it is not widely known that he had a genuine physical handicap which made him walk like a ruptured duck.

Cratinus also attacks women, dabbles in bathroom humor, and makes fun of dramatic conventions. For example, he pillories the stereotypical comic portrayal of Heracles as a glutton and buffoon,[60] an example of which we will see in Aristophanes' *Birds*.[61] But, of course, he himself tells all the old gags. In *Knights*, Aristophanes praises the old playwright in his prime:

> Then Cratinus came to mind, who before his star declined
> swam in streams of wild acclaim, a torrent sweeping down a
>   wooded plain
> Like Ajax in heroical tradition uprooting his entire competition
> And the songs that they sang at every dinner were all *his*—and
>   each one of them a winner![62]

In the *Frogs*, Aristophanes praises the "bull-eating Cratinus" as being loyal to Dionysus both as dramatist and drunkard.[63] A bull was the prize in the Comic Festival, and Aristophanes is insinuating that Cratinus was both a frequent victor and, like Heracles, a glutton.[64]

But the good life eventually took its toll on Cratinus. He ended up a drunken has-been:

> But the old man wanders
> Like Connas "wearing a wilted crown and dying for a drink,"
> When for his past victories he ought to be in the Prytaneum—
>   quaffing.[65]

Of course, it is hard to know how accurate this picture is, since Aristophanes loved to lampoon his rivals.[66] Indeed, Cratinus managed to defeat Aristophanes with his *Bottle,* a comedy about his own dipsomania, at the age of ninety-seven.

Crates was a contemporary of Aeschylus.[67] He began as an actor in Cratinus' company, and gained a reputation for being "jolly and ridiculous." He has the dubious distinction of being the first to bring drunken characters onto the stage.[68] One of the longest fragments in our possession includes an apostrophe to kitchen equipment.[69]

Aristotle cites Crates as the inventor of dialogue and plots, *logous kai mythous,* and praises him for abandoning sheer iambic raillery.[70] His largest fragments come from *The Animals*—a play whose charming plot is a unique concept in extant Greek comedy.[71] It tells of the yearning of edible creatures for a vegetarian utopia in which consumption of meat—themselves, that is—would be forbidden:

> CHORUS: From now on, just stick to eating cabbage
> Or fish—fried or with pickled brine on
> But *us* you cannot eat—
> ACTOR: Why? You're such delicious meat
> Now we'll never get the treat
> Of coming from the agora with sausages to dine on.[72]

Pherecrates is praised for abandoning the use of *ad hominem* attacks, for introducing novelty *(kaina),* and for being skillful with plots *(heurētikos muthōn).*[73] Another critic calls him "super-Athenian" *(Attikōtatos)*—for reasons not readily comprehensible.[74] Picking up where Crates left off, Pherecrates made food and cooking his stock in trade—many of his fragments read like recipes or menus. One of his plays is even entitled *The Kitchen.* The prominence of cuisine in Attic comedy may be partially explained by the fact that so many fragments are preserved in Athenaeus' *Deipnosophistae (The Learned Banqueters)* as appropriate material for dinner conversation. But there is more to it than this.[75] As one scholar observes of comic comestibles, "food is at the heart of the polis, in many of its dealings and negotiations and in the center of its social organisation."[76] As such, the various delicacies as well as the contexts in which they are consumed at times carry the weight of comic and social commentary.

Comic eating is often given a sexual overtone, in keeping with the *kōmos* as "wining, dining and concubining."[77] Crates has a delightful description of a pretty woman: "Her breasts are like apples and strawberries, fine and ripe."[78] In Aristophanes' *Peace,* the hero's name, Trygaeus, alludes to the grape harvest *(trygē),* while Opora, the lovely *kōmos*-girl who is his reward, means "Autumn Fruits." And of course there is the illicit affair as *paropsis,* a side-dish or snack. Pherecrates uses this old gag to satirize women's infidelity: "Your side-dishes *(paropsides)* are almost as delicious as the main course."[79] He uses the same joke again elsewhere:

> The enjoyment of someone else's wife is just like an hors d'oeuvre:
> it's tasty—but a single swallow is enough.[80]

Pherecrates also wrote *The Wives of Athens and Their Wifely Lies,* in which someone remarks, "The older women get hot to trot again."[81] The fragments of Pherecrates also contain the first example of a character type that will appear throughout all comedy: the *senex amator,* the lecherous oldster. Indeed, in his *Korianno* the old man seems to have been in rivalry with his son for the same courtesan, a motif later found in Plautus' *Casina* and Molière's *Miser.*

There is also a tantalizingly Oedipal fragment from Pherecrates' *Jocasta* in which the heroine observes, with remarkable understatement, "How extraordinary to be both a wife and mother too." Notwithstanding the claims of the Byzantine scholars, we have evidence that, like the other Old Comedy poets, Pherecrates attacked well-known Athenians and wrote the following about a controversial leader's sexual habits:

> For Alcibiades it seems is not a man and yet he "plays a man" to
> all the wives he can.[82]

Eupolis also took a swipe at the bisexual shenanigans of the controversial politician, and in a fragment from the *Cities* an unnamed character, who may very well be Alcibiades, boasts about his vigorous pansexual activities: "I did it with women, boys, and even old men."[83] Eupolis was regarded in later antiquity as second only to Aristophanes.[84] We have nineteen titles and nearly five hundred fragments. He indulged in the traditional jokes against old age, wives, and the Sophists, as well as the usual *ad hominem* attacks. He enjoys making fun of Euripides. In another fragment he has Miltiades, the victorious general at Marathon, parody two verses from Euripides' *Medea.*[85] Eupolis also seems to have satirized the pusillanimous Cleonymus, an infamous coward and a favorite Aristophanic target.[86] Aristophanes himself he insulted as "old baldy," and even claims he had a hand in writing his colleague's *Knights.*[87] Aristophanes retaliated in the *parabasis* of the *Clouds,* accusing his rival of resorting to cheap gags to win his victory.[88]

We may also find in Eupolis an early example of the *medicus gloriosus,* the boastful quack, usually with a foreign accent, who would be such a frequent character on the comic stage thereafter.[89] Naturally, even at this early point in history, the physician had mastered the mysteries of his profession. The playwright presents a mock trial, with Aristides the Just presiding. The doctor is being indicted for overcharging:

> QUACK: I don't care what happens after I get paid my fee . . .
> FRIEND(?): Good lord, Asclepius himself
> Would never charge as much
> For treating galumping diabetes or systolic emphysema—
> Not to mention psycho-social appendectomy!
> ARISTIDES: I say to you in closing, that you're guilty guilty guilty!
> QUACK: *(disdainfully)* I don't deny I've charged my patients
> through the nose.
> Of course, they're dead—and death's the most expensive
> malady of all.[90]

Eupolis' character Plutus anticipates Aristophanes' play of that name by boasting that "Wealth" brings man his greatest blessings.[91] He also ridicules Nicias, the skillful Athenian who succeeded in making the peace with Sparta of 421 which bears his name.[92] Once again the town of Megara is mentioned as a source of low comedy. He quotes one man's comment on another's *phallos,* "Look at that—you're as flaccid as a bad Megarian joke."[93] But Eupolis himself was not above the usual gross sexual innuendos, as when he wrote: "No, I made Hestia a sacrifice of a musical and very lovely piglet," where "piglet" was common slang for "vagina."[94]

In terms of his later reputation, Plato Comicus had the misfortune of being born with the wrong name. Indeed, throughout the ages some of his lines were sometimes ascribed to the philosopher. He was roughly a contemporary of Aristophanes and has left some three hundred fragments from thirty plays. His subject matter is the same as that of his Old Comedy colleagues. Plato wrote a comedy called *The Ants* and, interestingly enough, a *Nux Macra* which dramatized the "Long Night" created by Zeus so that, disguised as Amphitryon, he could enjoy cuckolding the luckless man's wife. Some scholars have argued for the influence of this on Plautus' *Amphitruo,* which we shall examine in a later chapter.

If we had to judge Aristophanes exclusively by his fragments, we would have regarded him as just another one of the boys. The plays that remain as shards do not reveal his distinctive quality. In one sense they constitute merely an anthology of the same old jokes we've seen his colleagues use. In fact, one of the old jokes that Xanthias is forbidden to pronounce in the *Frogs* is, despite his protestations, used by Aristophanes himself in fragments.[95] His fragments display traces of chamber pots, vomiting, and the illicit-affair-as-"side-dish" (again!).[96] Once again he justifies the beating of wives, having a chorus of women say:

> It is right that we are pummelled now and then
> Especially when we're caught with other men.[97]

He praises the freshness of his own style, attacks Euripides, and at one point combines the two elements by stating that he "learned everything he knew" from reading Euripides—although he has improved on the tragic author.[98] There are many examples of Aristophanes mocking senior citizens—his chief subject, as we shall see—one of which is from the viewpoint of a youthful bride: "To a young wife an old man is disgusting,"[99] a remark which at the same time parodies Euripides.

Though most of his Old Comedy colleagues dabbled in mythological pastiche, this is not the basis of any complete extant Aristophanic comedy. The fragments, however, do show that he wrote at least one outrageous parody of a well-known myth. The *Dress Rehearsal (Proagōn)* deals with the theme of Atreus' appalling act of infanticide and tecnophagic cookery which causes his brother's unwitting cannibalism. When he discusses the nature of the menu, Thyestes splutters:

> Oh wretch that I am, I've dined on my own children's giblets-
> how can I ever eat roasted pig again?[100]

Not much later, he exclaims:

Oh woe is me! What stirs within my stomach now?
Go to hell—tell me where I find a chamber pot![101]

The fragments of Aristophanic comedy are squarely in the tradition of his predecessors. In fact, there is nothing to distinguish them. And yet, in the plays themselves he introduces an innovative theme which would change forever the course of comic drama. Having groped through the fragments, let us turn to the single Old Comedy author whose plays are extant.

4

Aristophanes: The One and Only?

To many readers, Aristophanes is still synonymous with "obscenity." To these over-simplifiers, the epithet "Aristophanic," usually interchangeable with "Rabelaisian," merely denotes coarse humor, addenda to pudenda, and the comic cacophony of belches and slaps with a stick. True, his characters speak in *le langage vert,* as the French refer to the four-letter words which titillate an audience (colorfully transmuted as "blue" words in English). But if this were all there was to it, it would be no reason to rank him as a classic.

Then there is the joyless view of the playwright as high-minded denouncer of despotism and militarism, the passionate pacifist. Yet Aristophanes is not what the modern intellectual would have him be, essentially because he is neither modern nor intellectual. He wrote more than two thousand years ago, before half the concepts he is said to espouse were even invented. Pacifism, for example: it is sad but true that not every civilization has despised war. No less a philosopher than Plato viewed belligerency as man's natural state.[1] And Aristophanes' comedy not only presupposes the typical and traditional values on the part of his audience, it also does nothing to alter them.

And what about his politics? The poet has been called both radical and conservative, both apolitical (Jaeger) and *überpolitisch* (Reinhardt).[2]

But in truth, he is on the side that will get him the most laughs. All comic authors know there is much mileage in attacking the establishment. Even where the target is something innocuous like a mother-in-law, marriage is still an institution. With his objection to the foolish internecine war, Aristophanes many times covered the distance from Athens to Sparta to seek his comic subjects. But does he not assail the bad? Yes, but he also assails the good. He vilifies demagogues—scurrilously—but, to Cicero's concern, he has no kind words for the likes of Pericles either.[3] Or any politician.

The power of Aristophanic satire to influence political events is also grossly overestimated. Some have compared the Greek poet to the crusading Thomas Nast, the nineteenth-century satirical cartoonist. By this analogy, Cleon, the tyrannical demagogue, would be Boss Tweed. But this is not really a fair comparison. After all, Tweed ultimately succumbed and fell from grace whereas, right after the *Knights* was produced, Cleon was elected to a generalship by the very people who had witnessed Aristophanes' attack on him. In Plato's *Apology,* Socrates mentions the comic playwright's portrait alongside the widespread envy and slander he has suffered among the Athenians. But it may well be without rancor: no firm evidence can connect the philosopher's condemnation and the comic poet's caricature. Nor was Aristophanes the only playwright to lampoon Socrates and other intellectuals—they were fair comic game. Indeed, consider Plato's affectionate sketch of the pair enjoying each other's company in the *Symposium.* It would hardly have been to Aristophanes' credit if he could not keep a rogue out of office but could hemlock a man of principle.[4]

In most discussions of Aristophanes, it is common to lament the lost plays of his so-called "mentor" Cratinus and the other worthies of the Old Comedy stage. But there is another way of looking at it: it would be nice to believe that Aristophanes' eleven plays survive because he was in some way superior to his rivals.[5] There is no way of verifying this. And yet, as the playwright boasts, even the Persian King knew his comedies[6]—a joke, of course, but not impossible.

Unlike what we are able to judge from the fragments of those playwrights whom Horace referred to as "the others," Aristophanes had an organizing principle even in his most ramshackle "plots" (or Happy Ideas). His typical hero is a dyspeptic old man who gets fired up by an idea and in pursuing it turns the world topsy-turvy. With one significant exception, the hero succeeds in his revolution and fulfills his quest. But in addition to the satisfaction of victory, he gets a special physiological reward—sexual rejuvenation.[7]

In later comedy, of course, the son always beats the father figure. For it is a common *donnée* in all other comedy that youth always wins the battle of the generations. We see this already in the *Korianno* of Pherecrates. We have scraps from what may well be an *agōn*—a young man berates his father for claiming that he is still young enough for amorous adventures: "No dad, it's cool for *me* to move and groove, but not someone of your age—you're absolutely bonkers."[8]

The comedies of Aristophanes, however, are unique in presenting the reinvigorated father defeating his own inept son. Take *Wasps,* for example, where in the grand finale the old Philocleon literally beats up his young son. Cornford saw the pattern as an echo of Frazer's Old King/New King ritual, which in turn symbolized the rejuvenation of the Old Year, Harrison's *eniautos daimōn.* From a psychological perspective, Ludwig Jekels, as a corollary to Freud's reading of Oedipal conflicts in classical tragedy, saw the comic conflict as a kind of *reversed* Oedipus situation.[9] It is the lie of lies, the Oedipus complex overthrown.

Naturally, the aches and pains of the senior citizenry had been a favorite topic of other Old Comic poets.[10] As Pherecrates wrote:

> O Senescence, how burdensome you are to mankind.
> Miserable not in one way but in every.
> Only when we've lost our brains and brawn
> Do you teach us wisdom.[11]

Cratinus also satirized the Viagra generation, as can be inferred from his "Old codgers are babies for the second time."[12] The exact sentiment is found in Aristophanes' *Clouds,*[13] and was probably proverbial. This observation is important for understanding the psychology of Aristophanic comedy, as we watch the hero retrace the steps of libidinal development on his way to complete sexual rejuvenation.[14]

By transforming the old proverb into a stage character, Aristophanes found his formula for success. None of his predecessors has left us a large enough segment to judge the structure of the play from which it came. And yet, though many further fragments have been discovered since Cornford wrote, we still find no trace in the others of the Aristophanic hero, who appears in six out of the nine extant Old Comedies (his *Assemblywomen* [*Ecclesiazusae*] and *Wealth* [*Plutus*] are a different type of dramaturgy altogether, verging on the so-called Middle Comedy). There is no evidence that either Eupolis or Cratinus depicted a character like Dicaeopolis *(Acharnians)*, Trygaeus *(Peace)*, Demus *(Knights)*, Philocleon *(Wasps)*, Peisetaerus *(Birds)*, or, in an incomplete way, Strepsiades *(Clouds)*.

This rejuvenation-of-the-old-man theme is anything but subtle. It is so explicit that it shouts at the reader, usually with four-letter words. And yet few are aware of the extent to which this theme permeates the plays. This is because it has not been accessible to Greekless readers or students using bowdlerized English texts—or even Greek texts with bowdlerized notes. But in a new millennium, where a liberal education has become a liberated one, let us examine what Aristophanes really does with this character.

The playwright burst upon the scene with the *Banqueters (Daitales)* in 427, which—because of his youth (he was in his early twenties)—was produced by one Callistratus.[15] The play is lost to us, but its fragments suggest that it was a variation on the battle of generations, not unlike the *Clouds*. We have not only the derision of an old man who can't learn new tricks, but a comic morality play involving the conflict of two brothers, one a responsible good-boy *(sōphrōn)*, the other a sybaritic reprobate and buggeree *(katapygon)* who not only behaves badly but even taunts his father with insults like "you coffin-head." Evidently anticipating the *Clouds,* the old man has taken his sons to some institution to be educated by a certain learned man.[16] Soon afterwards, the brothers compare notes:

KATAPYGŌN: Did you learn any tricks *(sophismata)*?
SŌPHRŌN: Of course . . . I studied hard, but you cut class from the first day we went.[17]

In 425 Aristophanes won first prize with the *Acharnians,* still an example of his "apprenticeship" but differing from his earlier plays in three important respects. Though produced by Callistratus, it bore

Aristophanes' own name. It also marks the introduction of the rejuvenated old man presented above. And best of all, it is extant.

Its action begins in Athens, where all but one of Aristophanes' plays are set. Our hero is Dicaeopolis, a typically Aristophanic "charactonym" meaning "John Q. Righteous City," which hints at the renewal of society at the end of the play. He is a poor old farmer, forced by the Peloponnesian War to flee his home in the country and take refuge in the crowded city. Indeed, the play presents a clear contrast between the free life of the country village *(kōmē)* and the pressures of the city. There is no end in sight for the conflict with Sparta, and no one in Athens seems to care about making peace. He sits alone on the stage, bemoaning the political situation: "O Polis Polis: what has happened to the state of the state?"[18]

Dicaeopolis has come to all the meetings of the Assembly and lobbied for peace, but to no avail. He sits disconsolate, terribly bored by the lack of action, "plucking himself"[19] and sighing: "I sigh, I yawn, I stretch, I fart."[20] His superannuated phallus is clearly inoperative. For, if he had been actively masturbating, Aristophanes, with his rich vocabulary for onanistic activities, would not have hesitated to say so.

As he watches the unsuccessful Greek embassy trudge wearily back home, Dicaeopolis gripes that the only men left in the city are "assfucked" *(katapygones)* and "cock-suckers" *(laikastai)*.[21] (It should be noted that in Old Comedy the references to passive homosexual partners are almost entirely pejorative.)[22] Dicaeopolis is so preoccupied by this that he continues his tirade against "unnatural" sexual practices, tarring the unintelligible Persian ambassador and the delegate from Thrace with the same brush.[23] And while he is on the topic, he takes the opportunity to assail his lewd countryman Cleisthenes—a favorite target because of his cowardice and effeminacy.

At last Dicaeopolis' frustration comes to a boil, and, instead of his phallus, he takes matters into his own hands. At least his ideas are still potent. He proposes to perform a "great and fearful cocky deed" *(ti deinon ergon kai mega)*.[24] He gives eight drachmas to Amphitheus, the self-styled peace emissary of the gods, and urges him to hasten to Sparta to negotiate a personal peace for him alone. Amphitheus traverses the nearly 300 kilometers from Athens to Sparta and back in a mere 43 lines of text. Breathless from having outrun the Chorus (still offstage) who want to wreck his mission, he announces that he has obtained not one but three flavors of peace for Dicaeopolis to taste, each in the form of wine—the Greek *spondai* means both "treaty" and the "wine libation" with which it was ratified. Naturally, after careful sipping, our sexagenarian hero picks a truce of 30-year-old vintage as the most delectable because it smells of the injunction to "go and screw wherever you want."[25]

After Dicaeopolis has made a personal peace, he then decides to present his personal version of the Rural Dionysia. This scene is a bold metatheatrical stroke—the comic dramatization of a festival during a festival. It is even more significant for the argument here because it is a holiday in the freedom of the country, normally celebrated in the evening of the year, which inevitably makes us think of the *libertà di Decembre* and elements characteristic of the Saturnalia.[26] We seem to keep returning to the possible derivation of comedy from *kōmē*, "country village."

At this moment the chorus of charcoal-sellers enters. They are decrepit old codgers from Acharnae, a town ten miles to the north of Athens. Like Dicaeopolis, they are impotent ("our music is gone—our instruments are worn out").[27] They have suffered terribly from the Spartans' yearly brutal attacks. Like Dicaeopolis, they have been forced to retreat into the city, unable to defend their land from destruction. As a result, they are pro-war, arch-conservative militants.[28] In a way they are replicas of the protagonist—ancient, slow-moving, frustrated, and discontent.

They have tried in vain to catch Amphitheus. They lament that their creaky senectitude has made them "stiff and heavy-legged" so they can no longer run as fast as they did in the old days when (they boast) they could keep up with the legendary Olympic sprint champion—conveniently named Phallus of Croton.[29] When he sees Dicaeopolis approaching, the chorus leader silences his colleagues and they watch him leading other Dionysian celebrants from his household in a traditional phallic procession much like the ones described by Athenaeus in connection with the *ithyphalloi* and *phallophoroi*. One of them bears the sacred icon.

As this play within a play is prepared, the ribald jokes come fast and furious. Dicaeopolis admonishes his slave: "Xanthias, make sure the phallus remains good and erect" *(orthos)*.[30] While his wife has been unceremoniously relegated to watch from an upstairs window, his young daughter now comes out of the house with a basket. (Dicaeopolis is already showing a predilection for youth.)[31] He praises her: "He'll be a lucky man who marries you and makes pussycats as good as you at farting during the early morning."[32]

He then intones a hymn to Phales, at once reverential and laden with sexual allusions, one of which tells us something important about the play's hero:

> O Phales Phales, companion of Bacchus
>> Fellow reveler *(synkōme),* wanderer by night,
>> Adulterer, pederast,
> I call you after five years
>> Coming gladly into the country,
>> After making a treaty for myself,
>> Shrugging off business and battles
>> And arrogant leaders.
> For it is much sweeter, O Phales Phales,
>> To catch a ripe young girl carrying off stolen wood . . .
>> Grab her by the waist, lift her up,
>> Throw her down, and pit her cherry.[33]

Dicaeopolis has not celebrated the phallic rites for a full five years, suggesting that he has been totally abstinent during this time. The war—and old age—have made him lose his sexuality. But now at long last his mind seems to be turning again to ripe young girls. Though his joy is understandable, his sexual plans seem a bit of a nonsequitur. He has not mentioned a wife, a girlfriend, or any sexual urges until now. He seemed content to toy with his member, not even indulging in what Woody Allen refers to in *Annie Hall* as "sex with someone I love."

The chorus breaks its silence, clamoring for revenge on Dicaeopolis for making his private peace.[34] After a protracted exchange of verbal abuse, during which our hero offers to put his head on a chopping block, the Acharnians at last agree to hear his case. But suddenly, before speaking, the old man has a novel idea: he insists on dressing himself as shabbily as possible to arouse his audience's pity. Naturally, the best man to see in Athens would be Euripides, who, in the *agōn* of the *Frogs*,[35] is mocked by Aeschylus for his presentation of "shredded heroes." He hurries to the stage structure which serves as Euripides' home (it would later be Socrates' "university"). Dicaeopolis inquires of the slave who opens the door, "Is Euripides home?" The bondsman replies with the kind of chopping logic for which the tragedian was famous (and notorious):

> SLAVE: He's in and *not* in, if you get my meaning sir.
>
> DICAEOPOLIS: *(puzzled)* What—"in and *not* in"?
>
> SLAVE: Erect—I mean correct, old man. His mind is off wandering in the clouds, but he himself is inside with his feet in the air, consorting with his Tragic Muse.[36]

But Dicaeopolis is insistent. He must see the great playwright. At this point the ingenious stage machine used for depicting interiors reveals the controversial tragedian in the throes of "creative intercourse" with his muse.[37] After much literary banter (which overflows with snippets from Euripides), Dicaeopolis is at last suitably costumed as Telephus, the titular hero of one of Euripides' lost plays.

This is not a random choice—for the *Telephus* was no ordinary tragedy. Produced in 438 B.C., it was an early attempt at the melodrama which Euripides would bring to perfection in his *Helen* and *Iphigenia Among the Taurians*. Telephus, king of the Mysians, was wounded by Achilles before he came to Troy. Told by the Delphic oracle that his cure could only come at the hands of the man who had injured him, Telephus then disguised himself as a beggar and stole into the Greek camp. When he was discovered, he snatched the infant Orestes and held him hostage on an altar (which granted him immunity). This action was reminiscent of the "rather comic" finale in the *Orestes*—as the scholiast described it—where a grown-up Orestes threatens to kill Menelaus' daughter Hermione. Dicaeopolis' choice of Euripidean hero will color the rest of Aristophanes' comedy.

According to legends preserved by later fabulists, another aspect of the Telephus myth involved a quintessentially comic plot. Abandoned at birth like Oedipus, he went to Mysia in quest of his parents on the

advice of the Delphic oracle. When Telephus arrived there, King
Teuthras offered his foster-daughter Auge to him in marriage if he
would help him put down a rebellion. Just as the newlyweds are about
to consummate their union—shades of Figaro—Telephus recognizes
the bride as his own mother.[38] Oedipus interruptus! This situates
Telephus as a prime character for comic treatment. This facet of the
myth was treated in Euripides' lost *Augē,* alluded to by Aristophanes in
the *Frogs,* and quoted by Menander in the *Epitrepontes (The Arbitrants).*[39]
Along with the *Ion,* it may have provided a model for the rapes of New
Comedy.

Now suitably attired, Dicaeopolis returns to direct his comments to
the audience, echoing Euripides' words:

> Do not be offended, though beggar that I be,
> For I may speak in Athens, where the speech is always free,
> And talk about the city, even in a comic play—
> For comic authors also have important truths to say.[40]

This shattering of the dramatic illusion is typical of comedy—and
Aristophanes—with the actor calling attention to his own theatricality.
This "metatheater" also encompasses his many allusions to tragedy,
calculated to amuse an audience who would recognize the original
texts being parodied.

After these introductory remarks, Dicaeopolis then delivers an even-
handed plea to the Athenians to recognize that although the Spartans
are to blame for some wrongs, they themselves are not blameless. Just
as Shakespeare's Ulysses reduces the Trojan War to "the argument of a
cuckold and a whore,"[41] Dicaeopolis diminishes a story of epic proportions to the "kidnapping of local whores by both sides." As is to be expected, his long oration is peppered with parodies of the *Telephus.* He
concludes by saying that in these circumstances even Telephus would
make peace.

Half of the chorus is convinced by Dicaeopolis and begins to fight
with the other half in a kind of proto-*agōn* between the advocates of war
and peace.[42] It all ends in a slapstick mêlée which is only interrupted by
the entrance of General Lamachus, the earliest caricature of the *miles
gloriosus* or "braggart soldier."[43] (Of course, the historical Lamachus was

an energetic and respectable leader.) He carries a gigantic shield embla-zoned with a gorgon and bellows: "Who has aroused my trusty sleeping monster from its slumber?"[44] (The audience is free to construe "mon-ster" as it wishes.) Lamachus embodies and advocates everything to which Dicaeopolis is opposed. He will be the perfect foil for agonal pur-poses.

Dicaeopolis immediately engages Lamachus in a slanging match. In one of the tried and true Old Comic jokes, Lamachus gives him a feather from his helmet—into which Dicaeopolis proceeds to regurgi-tate.[45] When Lamachus tries to hit him, the old man protests:

DICAEOPOLIS: No, no, Lamachus—if you want to get physical, your
weapon's big enough—why don't you skin my cock?[46]
LAMACHUS: (offended) What—a general like me with a beggar like
you?[47]

At this moment, the dramatic progression is completely halted as the chorus steps out of character, walks downstage, and delivers the *parabasis* in the author's name. The chorus is here in its fullest form as it evolved from the phallic procession. Like its ceremonial predecessor, it lambastes political dignitaries while advocating rectitude as well as praising the playwright's talents and pleading with the judges to give him the prize. (It obviously worked.) Aristophanes here alludes to praiseworthy advice he has previously given to the Athenians to reject the leadership of foreigners—in other words, Cleon (whom he mocks in the *Knights* as a Paphlagonian), "a faint-hearted and open-assed bugger."[48]

The chorus continues the *parabasis* with a traditional element—a par-ody of a religious hymn to their "fiery Muse," Miss Charcoal, as it were. Afterwards they return once again to their eternal preoccupation: the woes of old age. Aristophanes is clearly laying the groundwork for the dramatic turnaround to come.

Then Dicaeopolis returns and lays out a market *(agora)* for himself, announcing that he intends to sell his products to every state in Greece. We will later learn that the produce he is selling has grown spontane-ously *(automata)*, a hint that his peace has brought him a new golden age, a familiar theme in all of Old Comedy.[49]

Word that Dicaeopolis has opened for business has obviously traveled around Greece, for he receives an immediate train of visitors—a common Aristophanic convention.[50] A starving old Megarian enters intending to sell his two daughters, whom he has disguised as "piglets." As we have seen, his city of origin would be an immediate clue to the audience that the scene would be crude and tasteless. The action is bizarre, something that the surrealist Magritte might paint. The father makes innumerable porcine puns, all of which refer to the girls' private parts.[51] "Dicaeopolis, do you want to buy some of my cunt-ry piglets?"[52] When Dicaeopolis takes one of the girls out of the sack, he is surprised. "What is this?" he asks. The other replies, "it's a little Megarian pig-pussy." By this time, Dicaeopolis is showing an increasing interest in sex. Eyeing the girls' nether parts, he quips, "I can see the family resemblance."[53] Growing ever more interested, he embarks upon an interrogation laced with double-entendres:

DICAEOPOLIS: What do they like to eat best?
MEGARIAN: Anything you give them—ask them yourself.
DICAEOPOLIS: Piggy piggy, how about a cock-tail (literally "chickpeas")?
"PIGLETS": Oink! Oink!
DICAEOPOLIS: How about some *organic* figs?
"PIGLETS": Oink! Oink! Oink![54]

After concluding the deal, the Megarian bids (an obscene) farewell and *bon appétit* to his daughters, and their new owner takes them into his house. How would his wife react? Dicaeopolis has conveniently forgotten that he is married and is living in the here and now of the *kōmos*. After he has chased off a series of intruders, he is confronted by one of Lamachus' slaves, who is to purchase eels and thrushes (both sexual symbols). Clearly the general wants to get a piece of the peace. Dicaeopolis refuses. "Let him shake his crested helmet and eat his army salt-fish"—an innocuous answer which conceals several gross puns.[55] Something is obviously astir in his groin, since he disappears inside with "wings on his shoulders" *(epterōtai)*.[56] The Greeks would not be confused by this metaphor: "to fly" clearly conveyed the action of an erection rising, a motif which would be developed extensively in the *Birds*. Indeed, the chorus reveals that there are "*feathers* before the *door,*"[57] another very clear double-entendre for male and female sexual parts.[58]

Just as Dicaeopolis is about to go in to prepare his dinner, a gorgeous female appears. The chorus recognizes and hails her as "Reconciliation" *(Diallagē),* the companion to Aphrodite and the Graces. Their appreciative description continues with many phallic puns. Reconciliation curvaceously embodies all the aspects of the chorus's (and by extension Dicaeopolis') lost sexuality—which has suddenly returned to them. They ogle the new arrival and address her:

> Would that Eros would grant *me* an audience with you.
> For you may think I'm old and past it,
> When I screw you for the third time black and blue
> You'll see that I can last it.[59]

They continue in this vein with graphic agricultural images. (Recall the common overlap of sexual and farming terminology found in many cultures.) The reinvigoration of the Chorus prefigures the return of the hero's own sexual prowess. In fact, something in his intensifying libido already seems to radiate new sexuality. This can be seen in the subsequent episodes. As Dicaeopolis proceeds to grill *thrushes* on a *spit* (yes, another innuendo), some new intruders plague him with requests for some of his peace, including the emissary of a new husband who begs him to pour "a little spoonful of peace" into his waiting bottle. Dicaeopolis turns them all down, until the maidservant of the bride whispers a plea into his ear: she wishes for something to enable "her husband's cock to remain at home" (instead of going out to war). To this request Dicaeopolis agrees. He then gives the woman a few drops of his oinomorphic Treaty-wine with precise instructions: when the soldiers are called up, she is to "anoint her husband's dick" with a bit of the potion and all will be well.[60] Quite an aphrodisiac!

In the finale of the play, the priest of Dionysus has invited Dicaeopolis for dinner, which is clearly going to be a wild and woolly wedding, a complete *kōmos* and *gamos.* Dicaeopolis, still blithely ignoring the fact that he has a wife at home, is the triumphant victor-bridegroom (perhaps he can even outrun Phaÿllus). His trophy-bride Reconciliation enters suitably undressed for the wedding, accompanied by two other nameless (but not shapeless) lovelies—played of course by men with the appropriate padding.[61] The menu contains all the traditional matrimonial delicacies, as well as "whores and dancing girls."

As the feast begins, General Lamachus reappears only to be called off—now unwillingly—to war again. He departs, singing a duet with Dicaeopolis which aptly summarizes their preoccupations of the moment. It is almost unnecessary to state that the song is full of obscene references. For example:

> DICAEOPOLIS: The pigeon meat's deliciously cooked.
> LAMACHUS: O you man, stop laughing at my personal weaponry.
> DICAEOPOLIS: *No,* you man, stop looking at my little birds . . .
> LAMACHUS: *(to his shield-bearer)* Look sharp boy, and concentrate your
> mind on fighting . . .
> DICAEOPOLIS: *(to his servant)* Get ready boy, and let's concentrate on
> drink-all-nighting![62]

Lamachus then goes off to war, and Dicaeopolis to dinner. At which point the chorus leader sings:

> Godspeed and enjoy on each of your encounters
> How dissimilar the roads you two now tread.
> For one there is drinking with a wreath around his head
> The other freezing on cold ground for a bed.
> For the first there is sleeping with a gorgeous young girl
> And plenty of rubbing-of-cock.[63]

A mere 30 lines later, the boastful general returns from battle badly wounded and moaning:

> LAMACHUS: Carry me my friends O carry me, grab round my legs and
> quick.
> DICAEOPOLIS: *(mocking)* And you my friends grab *me* around the middle
> of my cock.
> LAMACHUS: My head hurts, I'm fainting—someone put the light out.
> DICAEOPOLIS: And me, I'm hard as anything—I want to screw the night
> out.[64]

Thus at the end of the play Dicaeopolis has regained his sexuality, and with a vengeance. The vigorous attractions of "Reconciliation" and her two handmaidens will certainly keep him up straight till the dawn.

Aristophanes' hero has come a long way since first we found him old and weary, in despair, playing distractedly with his lifeless member. In addition to his complaints about the political situation, he was obviously sexually dysfunctional. Not only was the state in disarray, but the state of his own libido was misdirected and debilitated. His talk was obscene, but it was only about the prevalence of buggery and male prostitutes in Athens. Along his road to a triumphant *gamos,* he shows growing signs of sexual renewal. His thoughts turn to young women (some very young). As he rises in the polity, his phallus rises with him, culminating in the resurrection of his genital prowess and the rebirth of his "awesome tool"[65] to play the role for which it was originally created. Indeed, from every indication it would seem that his new vigor surpasses anything in his previous experience. He is going to enjoy the favors of Reconciliation—and perhaps her two handmaids as well—which is a rather staggering feat for any senior citizen.

Lest we doubt that our hero is a complete winner, as Dicaeopolis struts off priapically with his ladies, the final chorus hails him as *kallinikos*—the victory cry for Olympic champions.[66] The dramatic hero, like the athletic one, reinvigorates the world.[67] Thus Aristophanes concludes the play with an affirmation of a centuries-old practice which obviously still continued to fulfill a public need.

We must not make too much of this, however. Aristophanes is not necessarily allegorizing a symbolic regeneration of the fields or alluding to Dionysiac mysteries. He is talking about the male member plain and simple, which, in the course of the play, goes from flaccid to rigid. Naturally, we realize that this does not happen in real life. It is merely a fantasy, and in all later comic genres the vigorous phallus at the end belongs to the younger generation. But here in Aristophanes it belongs to the newly young *re*-generation. We will see how this—obviously successful—pattern would be repeated in the next five plays of Aristophanes (*Knights, Peace, Clouds, Wasps,* and reaching a sublime peak in the *Birds*).

But Aristophanes' use of the rejuvenation motif in his next offering, the *Knights,* seems rather perfunctory. One could speculate that he grafted it on rather awkwardly merely because of its promise of success. Indeed, the *Knights* is not Aristophanes' best play. The general tone is rancid; the characters are unlikable and seem to engage in nothing but endless volleys of insults. No one in the play arouses sympathy in the audience.

And yet the *Knights* has many of the elements of the better ones: the miserable quality of life for the citizens of Athens, a *parabasis* lobbying on behalf of the playwright, and, of course, the transformation of an old man quite literally into a sexual athlete. For, as in *Acharnians* and *Birds,* the codger is ultimately hailed as *kallinikos*—the cheer for the Olympic champions.

The outward "plot," such as it is, is more like a political pageant written by a malcontent. The play begins with a dialogue between two slaves in the house of Demus ("the Athenian people"), a veteran of Marathon, a battle fought nearly seventy years earlier, now an agelastic and "bad-tempered little old man."[68] The two servants are worried about the destructive influence of Cleon, a demagogue with whom Aristophanes had earlier locked horns and who took the poet to court over his invective in a play now lost. It is clear that the playwright's resentment has not abated. Aristophanes here presents Cleon as a Paphlagonian foreigner and a fellow slave. They must get rid of him, and to this end they plan to fight fire with fire by enlisting the aid of a Sausage-seller, the greatest rogue in Athens, whom they promise to promote to make the "biggest dick" *(ho megas)* in the city, when he will perform oral sex at state expense in the *prytaneum.*[69] Only a villain like this could beat Cleon at his own game. The Sausage-seller agrees to take on the challenge—thereby taking center stage in the drama—as he and Cleon vie for the favors of Demus. This rivalry is so prominent that the ancient "hero" is all but reduced to a supporting player. (He doesn't even enter until the play is halfway through.)

At first Demus is totally infatuated with Cleon. They are lovers in the literal sense. The passion is conveyed by Aristophanes explicitly and without euphemism or sniggering innuendo. The metaphor of Athens as the beloved boyfriend goes back at least to Thucydides, and is also echoed in *Acharnians.*[70] This practice in itself would not shock the Greek audience, for pederasty was an institutionalized part of their culture.

But they would react to the precise *nature* of the relationship depicted. Perhaps a fuller explanation is in order.

The basis of the classical Greek system of education was an erotic association between a role model *(erastēs)* and his protégé *(erōmenos)*. There was a "consistent Greek tendency to regard homosexual erōs as a compound of an educational with a genital relationship."[71] It was the duty of the younger man to inspire the older man by his good looks. The senior partner would strive to show himself worthy of his beloved by precept, in the stadium and on the battlefield. This relationship took precedence over all others, even that of father and son.

Yet the portrayal of Demus here is out of joint, for the playwright makes the old man the passive partner. To play this role at his age was not only unseemly but actually regarded as a perversion. Correspondingly, the Paphlagonian is referred to as the *erastēs*,[72] and is therefore screwing Demus the way Cleon did the Athenian people. The Sausage-seller proclaims himself a "rival lover" *(anterastēs)*,[73] and vies with Cleon for the favor of Demus, much as two *erastai* would contend for the same handsome boy.

But Demus is not entirely naive, and later confesses to the audience that he has been playing the ingenue in order to profit from his suitors' efforts.[74] As he tells the chorus who criticize his behavior:

> You have no brain within your long hair
> When you think that
> I'm so stupid: my silly behavior
> is all an act.[75]

Although his new slave succeeds in his revolution, it is Demus who gets the real Aristophanic hero's reward. For the Sausage-seller, after Cleon is deposed, sends the old man to a rejuvenatory health spa, where he is boiled up with the proper herbs and spices. This is more than simply a metaphor for literary effect. It seems to be important that this is a ritualized action properly performed. This motif of "symbolic baptism" is found throughout the later history of comedy, as we shall see.

When the doors of the baths open again, Demus reappears, restored to youthful vigor and smelling of peace libations and myrrh. The chorus then hails him as the "monarch" *(monarchos)* of all Greece and "king" *(basileus)* of all Greeks.[76] He is now as fit as when he was in the bloom of his youth—the good old days when he was a mere foot soldier along with Aristides and Miltiades, the future generals at Marathon.[77]

The first indication of Demus' renewal is his promotion from the passive *erōmenos* to active, homosexual *erastēs*. He is given a "well-hung boy" who will carry his camp-stool . . . "or be one."[78] This is already a more acceptable role for a man his age. "I'm made blessed again like in the good old days!" he declares.[79]

But the process is not yet complete. The Sausage-seller now offers two lovely treaty-pies *(spondai)*.[80] At this point two curvaceous lovelies appear, clearly from the same stable as the brace of bimbos who accompany Reconciliation to Dicaeopolis' bridal chamber in the *Acharnians.* Demus, astounded, remarks with the dirtiest language in a very dirty play:

> DEMUS: Oh much-honored Zeus, how gorgeous they are! By the gods, I'll ram my pole in each of them three times![81]

With the deposed Cleon banished to argue drunkenly with cheap whores and drink waste-water from the public baths, Demus invites the Sausage-seller to a festive dinner in the Prytaneum (the Athenian banquet hall) and to sit in Cleon's former seat. The palace revolution is over, and the city is upright once again. As is the old man Demus. All this obviously fits the pattern established in the *Acharnians.* Indeed, this jolly ending, loosely tacked on, is perhaps what won Aristophanes an otherwise puzzling first prize. Clearly, this motif had a great appeal for his audience, and they would endure a lot of bitter antipathetic antics just to experience it again.

Some detractors regard *Peace,* Aristophanes' offering in 421 B.C., to be a pale rewrite of *Acharnians,* his big success four years earlier. Indeed, the similarities are many. Both center around a displaced farmer (here Trygaeus—the wine-grower whose very name suggests the Greek *trygē,* the harvested grape) who longs for peace and a return to his rural home. But here the treaty he seeks, unlike the private agreement of Dicaeopolis in the *Acharnians,* is a full-fledged public treaty. Once again we find the country village *(kōmē)* associated with the hero's comic dream. (Opora, one of the play's *kōmos* lovelies, personifies the harvest fruits.)[82]

The play offers a kind of sympathetic allegory in which a citizen rescues the embodiment of Peace. In both plays the hero explicitly associ-
ates the country with sexual freedom. Both heroes have wives and children who are "forgotten" in the *kōmos-gamos* finale—as they go off with
new and luscious partners. (In the *Peace,* Trygaeus actually marries
again, whereas Dicaeopolis merely lives in sin.) And of course, both are
sexually rejuvenated.

But merely to catalogue the thematic dittographies in the *Peace* is to
overlook the play's own merits, which include an air of fantasy, a bucolic tone, a cheerful outlook, a "Happy Idea" that is better organized
and might even be called a "plot," and some lively lyrical language—
along with some shamelessly vulgar scatological humor.

The comedy begins with the hero—in the words of one of his slaves—
"struck by a novel madness."[83] (The word *kainos,* "fresh, brand new,"
used twice here, is an adjective which we will see again in connection
with the *Birds* and Euripides' *Helen.*) Trygaeus' brainstorm bears an undeniable relationship to the *Acharnians,* for it presents a bold little man
who takes matters of great pith and moment into his own hands. But
whereas Dicaeopolis' actions are to secure his peace, Trygaeus aims for
the heavens—an act specifically forbidden by Greek morality (consider
the myths of Bellerophon and Icarus)[84]—where he intends to wrest
Peace from the hands of Zeus.

As a precedent for this quest he invokes Bellerophon, the mythical
hero who rode to heaven astride the wingèd horse Pegasus, but was
punished for this sacrilegious act and became—in Homer's words—
"hated by all the gods."[85] Euripides wrote a tragedy on this subject,
from which the protagonist quotes liberally throughout the action.
And of course, since it is a comedy, he succeeds where the tragic hero
failed.

Being a humble creature, Trygaeus is naturally not fit enough to ride
as noble a steed as Pegasus, and so for his astronautical engine must resort to traveling on a *kantharos,* a "dung-beetle." This insect actually exists, but Aristophanes blows up his stage replica to fantastic size *pour le
spectacle.* The non-existent curtain goes up on two slaves preparing
dung-cakes to satisfy the beetle's unusual diet and engaging in outrageous scatological dialogue. It is excremental in the extreme, even to
the degradation of Zeus from, as it were, "God the Father" to "God the

Farter."[86] The unrejuvenated hero is completely regressed to infantility, judging from the preoccupation with these anal matters.

Now that the beetle has grown to a suitable size, Trygaeus embarks on his journey—"one of those great leaps into outer darkness which mark the career of the great comic hero."[87] He mounts his courser and begins to ride to heaven, breaking the dramatic illusion by calling to the crane operator in the wings to hoist him up. This metatheatrical reference to the machinery of the theater of Dionysus is another typical feature of Old Comedy, and one of the "old gags" that never fails to work. In its way, it puts greater emphasis on the "play" aspect of the play.[88]

Seconds later Trygaeus arrives in Olympus where Hermes, the outraged doorkeeper, scolds him for his impiety. In the course of this angry dialogue, the divine messenger informs him that all the gods have abandoned Olympus—only War remains on the premises, raging completely unchained. We also learn that this hypertrophied *miles gloriosus* has captured the goddess Peace and hurled her into a pit, where she now languishes. When War himself appears on stage, a gargantuan fugitive from the Macy's parade, he notices the new arrivals and bellows:

> O Mortals Mortals, Long Suffering Mortals—
> How creamed you're going to be in just a minute![89]

Much like another behemoth, the Cyclops in the *Odyssey*, this creature is preparing to make a meal of the chorus (who represent the various Greek states), intending to crush them first with a huge mortar and pestle. When the monster disappears into his house, Trygaeus tries to engage the chorus to help him pull Peace out from her prison. Cables, shovels, and crowbars suddenly appear and they set to their task, huffing and puffing until they rescue her from her tomb. Although the beautiful goddess appears as a statue, she magically smells of fruit-harvest and thrushes, not to mention Sophocles' music and Euripides' lightweight verses. More important from Trygaeus'—and our—point of view, she is accompanied by her two fetching handmaidens—Opora ("Ms. Bountiful") and Theoria ("Ms. Showbiz").

When Trygaeus is given Ms. Bountiful as "his lady grape-giver,"[90] he immediately recognizes the significance of Opora: she brings with her not only carnal entertainment but also represents the restoration of his vineyards, and fertility for the land in general. The moment they free her, Hermes can announce that peace reigns all over Greece. Therefore, the farmers can realize their fondest dream: they can return to their rural homes, "taking their agricultural tools into the field."[91] The chorus sings:

> O day longed for by upright men and farmers
> I am overjoyed to see you, I want to greet my vines,
> My deep desire has been swollen up so long
> To embrace the figs which I planted when I was a lad.[92]

With the first exploit accomplished, the troop readies itself for the homeward journey. Hermes offers Bountiful to Trygaeus as his bride, and, in a parody of the marriage formula, says, "Take this beauty here to be your wedded wife, be with her and beget your own . . . grapes."[93]

But our hero is taken aback, having some qualms about consorting with a damsel so young and luscious:

> TRYGAEUS: Do you think, Lord Hermes, that it might . . . hurt me if
> I piled into Ms. Bountiful after being . . . inactive for so
> long?[94]

As with Dicaeopolis, this festive occasion has been preceded by a period of enforced abstinence. While the hero of the *Acharnians* had been *hors de combat* for six years, Trygaeus has not had a woman for more than twice that time.

They now look for the beetle to waft them home, and discover that he has disappeared. Hermes then calmly informs them that the creature has gone up and away, having been promoted to be a bearer of lightning on the car of Zeus. (The beetle is now a stablemate of Bellerophon's legendary steed Pegasus—quite a promotion!) But although they are marooned high in the sky, they do not seem as distressed as an astronaut abandoned on the moon would be. Quite the contrary—they are not perturbed in the least. This is a fantasy, after all, and on Hermes' instruction they walk simply and safely down a stairway to the stage floor. While Zeus caused Bellerophon to fall tragically to earth, Trygaeus has not only visited the domains forbidden to mortals—very significantly, he is in Olympus when Zeus is not, which makes him akin to another Aristophanic hero who displaces the father of the gods—but he can also return to the earth unharmed, with the greatest of ease.

As the veterans of the Olympic expedition head offstage, Trygaeus addresses a final few words to the ladies, setting the tone for the second half of the play:

> Come quickly follow me dear ladies
> For many men await you with hungering lips and hard-ons.[95]

At this juncture betwixt heaven and earth, the actors retire, leaving the chorus to deliver the *parabasis*.[96] This time Aristophanes' message is totally conventional—criticism of other playwrights and celebration of his own talents, including the usual disclaimer that he will not stoop to using old jokes. He protests that he would not present heroes in rags (except that he did in the *Acharnians*), nor Heracles the glutton ruled by his gigantic appetite (as he would do in the *Birds*). This self-evidently ironic boasting was part and parcel of the traditional form.

After this interruption, the players reappear to continue the comedy with what can quite legitimately be called the second act. The play seems to fall naturally into two halves, the first containing the fantasy flight to heaven and the rescue, the second a long and outrageous preparation and celebration of a *kōmos* during which Trygaeus enjoys a cornucopia of the new fruits—and other dainties—of his victory. Once he is back from Olympian heights there is no further allusion to his heroic journey, and the play dissolves into a long and happy orgy. And, after nearly eight hundred lines of relatively non-sexual dialogue, the play gets raunchy.

Appropriately enough, the graphic language begins when the old man must be rejuvenated. Although the chorus made one or two allusions to the process in the first part,[97] this notion still comes up somewhat unexpectedly. For Trygaeus does not bemoan his old age in the beginning of the play. But now, as he appears on stage with Ms. Bountiful on his arm and gives her to a slave to bathe, the chorus predicts that he will be physically fit for the wedding night:

CHORUS: You will be envied, ancient old man
            When your youth is restored again
            Anointed with scents and sensuality.
TRYGAEUS: You're right. And what about when we're coupling, and
            I'm squeezing her little boobies?
CHORUS: You'll be as snug as a bug in a rug.
TRYGAEUS: And don't I deserve it? I'm the one who
            astride my trusty beetle-horse
            rescued the Greeks so that
            they can all go live in the fields,
            then safely screw and sleep it off.[98]

The victory then is for everyone, and the couplings will be multiple. Moreover, they are taking place in the ideal venue for this activity, the countryside. It is an old-fashioned fertility festival like those we have already examined.

And now the rejuvenation begins in earnest. A slave appears to inform Trygaeus that:

SLAVE: The bride has been cleansed and the pretty parts of her
          ass are all freshened.
      Her wedding cake is baked, and sesame balls[99] are being
          fingered now.
      Everything else is ready. There's only one thing missing
          . . . a tasty penis.[100]

For all his fluent and creative obscenity, Aristophanes still manages to startle his audience by using the bluntest possible non-metaphorical word for the male member (to peos).

Moreover, Ms. Showbiz is to entertain the members of the Council. In addition to her other charms, she is apparently quite adept at fellatio—a talent likely to have been perfected by a pipe-girl—which she has performed on the gods. And lest we fail to appreciate that she is a multi-talented champion, Trygaeus delivers a multi-faceted pun on her sporting prowess at the "Isthmian" ("crotch") games.

She is adept at all events—wrestling, horse-riding, and chariot-racing. These metaphors are traditional and are used by many poets in other ages, for example, the Roman elegists, who took their cue from Hellenistic epigrams.[101] Even Aristophanes' reference to the phallus is in the form of a pun on a particular hold in the *pancration,* a brutal free-for-all contest more like a street fight than an Olympic event:

> Wrestle her to the ground, stand her on all fours,
> Grease up like young men and fight her with
> no-holds-barred, puncture her with fist and dick.
> After that, the next day, you can hold a horse race,
> Where one jockey will outride the other
> And chariots tangled-up
> Will thrust a-gasping and a-panting,
> And other drivers will be lying with their cocks all skinned.[102]

While this would be a logical moment for a concluding *kōmos,* the playwright carries on with several manifestly anti-climactic scenes. Finally, after beating off various intruders, Trygaeus disappears into the house and the chorus begins the feast. After a moment he re-emerges dressed as a bridegroom and sings a solemn wedding song:

> Come with me into the field my dear wife
> And Beauty, beautifully you'll lie with me.[103]

As the chorus begins an antiphonal wedding hymn, they raise up Trygaeus on their shoulders and carry him—just like an Olympic winner—to the victory *kōmos,*[104] continuing their song with an obscene pun on the verb *trygan,* "to pick fruit":

> CHORUS: What shall we do with her?
>   Well, shall we all screw with her?
>   Let's go and pluck her!
>   Let's go and fuck her![105]

The chorus leader predicts that they will live happily ever after, cultivating their figs:

> SEMI-CHORUS A: His fig is big and thick
> SEMI-CHORUS B: And hers is sweet and slick.[106]

Young Trygaeus takes his bride off stage to enjoy the fruits of a sensual *gamos* to the fullest, while the audience is left to cheer the triumph of fantasy over fact. Strangely enough, Aristophanes only won second prize, defeated by Eupolis' *Flatterers*.[107] The fragments of his contemporary's winning comedy do not give us any hint of why this play would have been judged superior to Aristophanes'. But then this was the City Dionysia, at which Aristophanes never won. Whatever the reason, Aristophanes did not seem to take his defeat to heart. This was not the case, however, with his beloved *Clouds,* which we shall turn to in the next chapter.

5

Failure and Success

In Athens, the playwright had only one chance. The evidence of many theaters throughout Attica suggests that plays might have been repeated or even premiered "off-Broadway."[1] But in the city itself the playwright's work, whether comic or tragic, would be performed but a single time for the entire population at the festival. That was all. If he failed, he had no chance to fix it for another occasion. The only example we have on record of a play being repeated was Aristophanes' *Frogs*—and that was because it was such a big hit. That is why the *Clouds,* as we have it, is the best comedy Aristophanes never presented.

Playwrights always have a soft spot for their failures. In 423 B.C., after two successive first-place victories (*Acharnians* and *Knights*), Aristophanes offered the *Clouds,* a play he regarded as "his finest and best."[2] In many ways the play was ahead of its time—a change of pace for Aristophanes, who was bored with churning out the same old jokes year after year.

Yet, to paraphrase a theatrical dictum, innovation, like satire, is what closes on Saturday night. Aristophanes' high hopes were dashed when the play failed, finishing third and last at the great Dionysian festival.[3] To the best of our knowledge, in fact, Aristophanes never won at the

Great Dionysia. Perhaps his comedy was not suited to the larger theater with its vast stage machine, although it may have been used to good effect for Socrates' descent to earth.[4]

It is not insignificant that the winning comedy was called *Pytinē (The Bottle)*—by none other than Cratinus, the very gray eminence of the previous generation, still active at (according to legend) age 97.[5] He proves that the old dog's old tricks were still better than the young puppy's new tricks (Aristophanes was still under 30). The veteran playwright employed the time-honored standbys—wine and women. Aristophanes was galled, not only because he had been defeated by such a superannuated rival, but because he felt his own play was so fresh and new while Cratinus' entry was safely in the well-worn groove of traditional—that is, hackneyed—farce.

The difference is evident in a simple comparison of the "plots"—and for the *Clouds* we dare use that term.[6] From what we know of the *Bottle*, it was almost a domestic comedy, sounding an unusually personal note for an ancient play, since it was drawn from the most painful aspects of the poet's real life. For the older playwright's predilection for alcohol had ruined his creativity, as Aristophanes testified in the *Knights*, a passage which Cratinus seems to have answered.[7] Cratinus' choice of subject was brave, just as Molière, who, cuckolded in real life, could make humorous plays out of his sad predicament.

The author made the titular hero in his image—typecasting?—as the husband of "Lady Comedy," whom he abandons to go off on a spree with "Ms. Hooch," a femme fatale who was obviously congenial to his own reputation for dipsomania.[8] As Cratinus' wife complains:

> Before this, if he ever spoke me ill,
> With his mind on some other woman—I would laugh it off.
> But now it seems to me that
> Old age and Ms. Hooch combine to never
> Let him be his own master.[9]

At some point the playwright seems to have repented, saying ruefully, "I realize now too late the wretchedness my folly has brought me."[10] But the true "moral" of the comedy is surely that "you can't compose anything clever by just drinking water."[11]

Husband and wife are reunited at the end but, in an obviously wild *kōmos (anti-kōmos?)*, Lady Comedy breaks all the bottles of wine in the house to keep her husband from straying again.[12] We are unable to judge if Cratinus' comedy was of particularly high quality—we only know it won first prize. As a French editor notes logically, "having proved the best at provoking laughter, it was judged the best of all."[13]

Aristophanes was relegated to third place by the other competitor, Ameipsias, whose *Connus* was a comedy that, curiously enough, also featured Socrates and a chorus of thinkers *(phrontistai)*. It would appear from one fragment that he was fairer to the philosopher than was Aristophanes,[14] and it may be that this is why the play was preferred.

Stung and embarrassed, Aristophanes sat down and revised the *Clouds* in the vain hope of earning another performance.[15] Perhaps he was relying on the remote possibility that the authorities would accept the rewritten manuscript as a new play with an old name (it was common practice for Old Comedy poets to re-use their titles).[16] The text that has come down to us is the incomplete second draft, with the *parabasis, agōn,* and finale largely rewritten, and with minor changes throughout.[17] Details remaining from the first version also create certain inconsistencies. Both versions were known at least as late as the second century A.D.[18] But the revision was never performed.[19]

The primary defect which made the play a non-starter is that it lacks the essence of the festival spirit. The audience may well have used the old proverb: "What has this to do with Dionysus?" *(ouden pros ton Dionuson)*.[20] In this play Aristophanes lets slip every possibility for traditional comedy. Indeed, by the playwright's own admission, this was his "most intellectual comedy."[21] There are none of the other features which had heretofore served Aristophanes so well—no celebration of fertility, no ode to the erection, no rejuvenation. Perhaps most glaring is the absence of any women at all—not even one silent pipe-girl—besides the aloof, anemic Cloud chorus who only bestow the intellectual gifts of "knowledge and dialectic and brainpower."[22] There can be no comedy without a *kōmos,* and no *kōmos* without ready, willing, earthy females.

At the beginning, it seems as if we are in for a typical Aristophanic romp. Strepsiades certainly is cast in the same mold as Dicaeopolis—a displaced rustic, old and querulous. As he himself concedes, he is "ancient, forgetful and slow."[23] Unlike Dicaeopolis, however, who undertakes the grand heroic enterprise of trying to obtain a peace with Sparta, Strepsiades has decidedly more mundane aspirations: he longs to avoid paying his debts. The emphasis on money is a new element in Aristophanic comedy. Heretofore we have seen little or no mention of financial matters. But as we will see, this bourgeois element will play an ever more significant role as comedy evolves, from Aristophanes' *Assemblywomen* and *Wealth*, to Plautus' *Aulularia (The Pot of Gold)*, and culminating in Molière's *L'Avare (The Miser)*.

Strepsiades' financial predicament is a result of his son's passion for horses—an expensive habit. The play begins with a night watch: the old man is unable to sleep because he is upset about "the interest mounting" from the lavish spending of his son, who is given the amusing charactonym Pheidippides ("Horsethrift"). Almost as compulsive as Harpagon, Molière's miser, Strepsiades calls for his red-inked accounts to be brought out so he can read them once again and weep by candlelight.

Meanwhile, he watches his son blithely sleeping—and passing wind—without a care in the world, mumbling various remarks about horseracing in his sleep. ("How many more laps to drive?" To which his father replies, "You are driving me—into deep debt.")[24] As an early indication of the play's intergenerational rivalry, Strepsiades lies down next to him and snores in agonistic counterpart to his son's aggressive flatulence. As we saw in the fragments of Old Comedy, such activity was a favorite item on the Greeks' comic agenda. It may seem infantile to modern sensibilities, but bathroom jokes have inspired centuries of low comedy, as for example Subtle in the beginning of Ben Jonson's *Alchemist*, who insults Face with "I fart at thee."[25] Indeed, the bathroom joke is still alive and well in twenty-first-century England.

But the old man cannot sleep and soon turns to another complaint: his unequal marriage. He was a simple farmer from deep in the country and his wife a gluttonous city girl of snobbish family—the contrast is strongly made[26]—and a very demanding woman both financially and sexually.[27] He has spent himself supplying both needs. We have here a precursor of the *uxor dotata*, the rich dowried wife who was a favorite character in Roman comedy, and is mercilessly developed by Molière in *George Dandin*.

But in the midst of his problems, like many other Aristophanic protagonists, Strepsiades is suddenly struck with a Happy Idea: "Eureka, I
have found it—a brilliant, god-sent plan to solve my problem!"[28] He
quickly rouses his son, who must be the instrument of his inspiration.
He orders the boy to change his life-style completely and points to a
building across the stage (once Euripides' house in the *Acharnians*). He
wants the boy to learn Wrong Logic at the newly established
Thinketorium *(phrontistērion)*, where the "Intellecto-pensive noble gentlemen"—they are described as *alazones*—are led by a boasting impostor
called Socrates who teaches "how to make the worse seem the better
cause."[29] Armed with this knowledge, he will then be able to talk his father's creditors out of their demands. But the son refuses, since, if he
enrolled, he would lose his tan.

The old man has no alternative but to send himself to school. Even
this familiar motif had great comic possibilities. (Recall the spate of
films in the 1950s with titles like *Grandma was a Freshman*.) It is the eternal problem of teaching an old dog new tricks. This being the case, it
was still not too late to embark on a rejuvenation plot. But Aristophanes does not move in this direction.

Strepsiades enters the Thinketorium and encounters students performing childish experiments like investigating how far fleas can leap
and how gnats pass air "through their rumps."[30] (Of course, equally absurd experiments take place today.)[31] We now see that the flatulence in
the first scene was merely an overture to a cacophony of scatology
which fills the play. It is everywhere, even informing Socrates' theology
and meteorology.[32] From a psychological point of view, the humor remains firmly at the anal stage, never acquiring the phallic dimension
essential to the *kōmos* state of mind. The best Strepsiades will manage is
to cling timorously to his member in his first "on the couch" interview
with Socrates.[33] This is a far cry from other Aristophanic heroes, who
overcome the state of second infancy represented by old age, and this
may be one key to the failure of the play.

Even at this late stage, Aristophanes still could have snatched victory
from the jaws of defeat by adding women to his comedy—perhaps by
making Socrates' college coed, thereby opening a whole new horizon of
comic possibilities. The only thing close to a female figure in the play is

the chorus of Clouds, who are apparently not that attractive, for the very sight of them frightens Strepsiades to the extent that he feels a need to loose his sphincter—scatology yet again.[34] They do nothing to help the anti-*kōmos* atmosphere when they praise the hero for "pursuing the intellectual."[35]

As it is, the only *erōs* in the play is anal and pathic: the word "bugger" seems to be on everybody's lips.[36] In fact the only erotic feeling on the part of Strepsiades is his "lust" to avoid paying his debts.[37] This too may have its scatological dimension. As Freud wrote in the fundamental article, "The connections between the complexes of interest in money and defecation, which seem so dissimilar, appear to be the most extensive of all."[38] In mythology and literature, Freud alludes to the devil's gold which turns into excrement, the *Dukatenscheisser* ("Shitter of ducats"), and the Babylonian view of gold as the feces of Hell—Mammon was another name for the god of the underworld.

Though Aristophanes, as he himself claimed, may well have broken new ground,[39] he was traveling down the wrong road. The vast majority of his audience was not interested in the "new learning" of the sophists who were just appearing on the scene—unless, of course, they were treated with ribald humor like the intellectuals who formed the chorus of thinkers in Ameipsias' bawdy *Connus*.

We have already seen Aristophanic heroes who "attack and replace" Zeus, for example in the *Peace*. This familiar motif is present in the *Clouds*, but in a very rarified way. Alluding not only to Anaxagorian theory, but punning on the Greek word *dinos* (which can mean either "mixing bowl" or "vortex") and some forms of Zeus' name (for example, *Dios, Zenos*), the dean of the college explains the latest theology:

SOCRATES: Zeus doesn't even exist.

STREPSIADES: What are you saying?
            Who makes the rain then? I always thought it was
            Zeus pissing through a sieve.

SOCRATES: Not in the least: now a celestial Vortex *(Dinos)*
            Rules the universe instead of Zeus.[40]

God is reduced to a piece of pottery. Meteorological phenomena are reduced to excretory functions (Socrates likens thunder to Strepsiades' noisy farts).[41] How much of this bathroom humor could even the Greek audience tolerate?

Aristophanes uses the *parabasis*—which belongs entirely to the revised edition[42]—for a vigorous defense of his dramaturgy. He castigates the audience for rejecting his first version of the *Clouds,* "my most intellectual of comedies, for which I was defeated undeservedly by vulgar men."[43] He flatters the higher tastes of the spectators and defends the quality and chastity of his art in this play:

> And consider how pure she is by nature, this Comedy
> Who comes not having stitched on a leather appendage,
> Red at the tip, thick, so the kids could have a laugh.
> And she does not make fun of baldies, nor dance the *kordax.*
> Nor does an old man beat a bystander with a stick
> When speaking his lines, so as to hide the lame jokes.
> And she has not come in with torches yelling "Help! Help!"[44]

He asserts:

> No: she has come relying on herself and the script.
> And I, though I am a poet of such a calibre, do not grow my hair
> Nor seek to trick you by bringing on the same thing two or three
>   times.
> No: I am clever, always bringing on fresh new ideas *(kainas
>   ideas),*
> None like the other and all smart.[45]

If the *Clouds* had been the usual Aristophanic comedy, the antiquated hero would have discovered a gymnasium and baths in the college and be cooked to youthfulness. But Strepsiades remains frustratingly old, and when he is kicked out by Socrates for ineducability, he begins a kind of regression. With payment day impending, he finally succeeds in convincing his son to enroll in the college—although, as the chorus ominously warns, this may have dire consequences for him.[46]

Socrates begins the boy's curriculum by letting him hear an *agōn* between the Right and Wrong Logics. Both debaters are of the homosexual persuasion. Right Logic, obsessed with boys revealing their genitals, begins the argument by invoking the good old days when lads were dutiful and crossed their legs chastely.[47] In fact, they were so scrupulous that "they even smoothed the gymnasium sand so when they stood up they would not leave traces of their manhood."[48] His speech concludes with a plea to the young Pheidippides to choose him as a role model, "and you'll avoid the *agora* and shun the bathhouses . . . respect your elders . . . and go down to the Academy and run track with your agemates."[49] And all this will mold him into a proper man:

> But if you follow my advice
> And keep it ever in your mind
> Your chest will bulge, your skin will shine
> With muscley shoulders, tiny tongue
> A big fat ass and little dick.[50]

The Right Logic curriculum clearly would qualify its students to be models for the best classical vases. The overlarge buttocks appear commonly on pottery (along with bulging thighs) to indicate athletic prowess. The small penis represents the ideal of sexual behavior, which is moderation, hence a demure instrument. Even a swashbuckling hero like Hercules is not portrayed with priapic exaggeration, whereas satyrs, barbarians, and other lowlifes are characterized by oversize genitals. This is also made clear in Right Logic's deprecation of his opponent's doctrine:

> But if you follow *that* man's teachings
> You'll be pale, your chest concave
> Your ass minute, your tongue grown huge
> And worst of all, a big bad attitude.[51]

The Chorus sings out in admiration of this speech and doubts that Wrong Logic can answer it.

But the villain rises to the occasion. If Pheidippides follows the advice of his rival, he will miss all the real pleasures of youth: "Boys, women, fun and games, good food, drink and laughter. What is life without these things?" In short, he urges,

> Indulge your instincts, leap and dance.
> Consider nothing shameful.
> Your mastery of rhetoric will even allow you to commit adultery,

convincing the young lady's husband that you haven't done a
thing the gods don't do.[52]

We have already seen how this passage demonstrates all that is typical
of comic behavior. Like free thoughts in the Platonic dream process, we
will leap and dance beyond the shadows of morality, and even get away
with adultery by arguing that if it's good enough for Zeus, it's good
enough for man.

In the twinkling of a theatrical eye, it is suddenly a month later;
Strepsiades picks up his son just in time, for the creditors appear. Surprisingly, it is Strepsiades, and not his newly graduated son, who chases
them off with Socratic theology, philology, and pseudo-science. What
was the point of sending the boy to school if the old man has to do the
chasing himself?

The answer comes immediately. Strepsiades returns home, but he
has no time to savor his triumph. An instant later he bolts hysterically
out again, chased by his son, who begins to choke him and beat him.
Strepsiades appeals to him, asking for mercy, reminding his son that he
treated him well as a child, always providing food and drink:

> No sooner did you say "kaka" than I would pick you up, carry you
> out of doors and hold you over the ground. But just now you
>   were strangling me
> and I cried out that
> I needed to drop a load . . .
> But you kept choking me
> so I had to do it on the floor![53]

Strepsiades has now regressed to a state of pre-toilet-trained infancy.
"Do you dare to strike your father?" he repeats twice incredulously.[54]
"Yes," the boy replies with learned assurance, "and I'll demonstrate to
you logically that I'm in the right."[55] Pheidippides justifies his actions
by adducing the proverb that "old men are in their second childhood."[56] Therefore, just as his father beat him "for his own good" when
he was young, now that his father is senile and regressed, he is obliged
to whip him for the same reason. Moreover, the hostile son intends to
widen his aggression and attack his mother as well (1446).[57] Whereas

the play began with the genial enough idea that the old man would take his young son's place in college, it ends bitterly with the son reversing the reversal. It is the comic equivalent of double jeopardy.

We do not know how Aristophanes ended the original *Clouds*, but the error in his "more moral" second ending is glaringly obvious. Unlike the more traditional Old Comedy endings, *Clouds* seems to lack an ending worthy of a *kōmos*—not to mention a *gamos*. The old man is not rejuvenated from his second babyhood, and the comic behavior espoused by Wrong Logic is crushed. For the play concludes with Strepsiades entering with a lighted torch to set the college of Thinkers on fire: "Chase them, slave, beat them, for many reasons, but most of all because they have blasphemed the gods."[58] For Socrates had compelled Strepsiades to forswear the gods and recognize only Chaos, the Clouds, and Tongue.[59] Many scholars see in the Cloud chorus the forces of nature, more closely aligned to the traditional values of Right Logic. Thus, although Wrong Logic triumphs in the *agōn*, Right ultimately wins the victory as the sophistic perversions of the Thinketorium are swept away.[60]

The *Clouds* nevertheless leaves a distinctly bitter taste. When the comic hero, instead of overthrowing Zeus as he would in the *Birds*, places him firmly back on the throne, something is radically amiss. Even the burning of Socrates' college (definitely written for the revised draft), which in another context could have been a college prank, presents a kind of rough justice which is alien to Old Comedy, whose essence is the *avoidance* of judgment; the revolution establishes a new order. In Eric Bentley's formulation, "In farce as in dreams one is permitted the outrage and spared the consequences."[61] By not perpetuating the outrage, Aristophanes had to pay the penalty: failure. The lesson we—and he—could learn from this unusual exercise is that comedy is asphyxiated by morality.

But Aristophanes came back with a vengeance. At the Lenaean festival of the following year (422) he presented the *Wasps*, nothing less than a direct riposte to the detractors of the *Clouds*, and proof that he was still master of the very material that he had innovated. Every one of the typical elements is here without the burden of an intellectual "message." As one scholar observes, the play "is free of the moralizing and dispassionate analysis that made the *Clouds* so unsatisfying and ambivalent."[62]

Philocleon, the oldster-hero, is in the grand tradition of Aristophanic protagonists, one whose particular focus is on self-gratification. He does not have a "higher purpose" like the hero of the *Acharnians* or the *Peace,* but rather pursues "the comedy of wish fulfilment, where pleasures are either erotic or aggressive but always physical."[63]

The rejuvenation pattern follows the traditional motif of Old King/New King, as Cornford conceived it, but with an Aristophanic touch. His usual practice is to present an oldster who becomes a youngster. We see a variation of this in both the *Clouds* and the *Wasps,* where the *agōn* is between father and son.[64] But the conflict is decided in a radically different way in each play. In the *Clouds,* the father is not rejuvenated at all, and the son wreaks terrible vengeance on him, punishing him physically. In the much more elaborate conflict in the *Wasps,* while Bdelycleon first beats up his father, the reinvigorated Philocleon later punches him to unconsciousness. Thus the characteristic Aristophanic theme is re-emphasized.

The play begins at night (like the *Clouds*) with a dialogic duet between two slaves with familiar names, Xanthias and Sosias. After an exchange of banter—perhaps to warm up the audience the way another Xanthias offers to at the beginning of the *Frogs*—Aristophanes finally calls an end to the jocularity so that he can "explain the plot to the audience."[65] He then warns the spectators not to expect anything too big *(mega),* or any "gags from *Megara,*" and, he protests, they don't have a brace of slaves scattering nuts among the spectators.[66] He also claims that they will not see Heracles trying his usual tricks to get his dinner (the audience would have to wait for the *Birds* to get around to that again), nor any of those common attacks against Euripides (only lots of parodies and paraphrases).[67] Once again this is Aristophanes protesting too much—for he himself presented the very crude "Megarian" scene in *Acharnians* and a slave scattering barley grains in *Peace.* This is yet another example of the playwright's boasts of novelty when his dramaturgy obviously undercuts his claims, and these obviously false claims would themselves be funny.

Xanthias then explains that they are guarding their master, Philocleon ("Cleon-lover"), who is suffering from an odd malady:

> He is more of a judge-a-holic *(philēliastēs)* than any other man on earth.
> He's madly in love with passing verdicts, and he groans if he can't cast his vote.[68]

Philocleon is our earliest example of a "humorous" character, one whose function is to "repeat his obsession" on the principle that "unincremental repetition . . . is funny."[69] One of Bergson's most important general laws is that we laugh at "something mechanical stuck onto the living . . . when a person gives us the impression of being a thing."[70] This kind of character was very popular in Renaissance drama, and derives from the ancient theory of the four humors—blood, bile, black bile, and phlegm—which are equally balanced in a healthy body. A person becomes obsessive in some way when one of the humors dominates over the others.[71]

One thinks of Harpagon in *The Miser (L'Avare),* who cannot stop counting his money, and only wishes to marry for the sake of the dowry—his normal sexual appetites are replaced by an unfleshly preoccupation. Philocleon's preoccupation also comes straight from his libido. As a regular member of one or another of the famous Athenian juries, he is passionately in love with judging: it is a "pure" appetite for power, expressed in the unambiguously erotic verb *eran.*[72] He has even been known to scrawl graffiti in praise of jury-duty on the same walls on which lovers carve their beloveds' names.[73] So intense is his passion that he will even attempt suicide when forced to give up his love.[74]

The hero's son, Bdelycleon ("Cleon-hater"), has shut up every orifice of the house to keep his father from going to the courtroom, setting out nets all over the place since Philocleon in the past has proved slippery enough even to slip out of drain-pipes.[75] Indeed, our first sighting of Philocleon finds him with his head sticking out of the chimney after another escape attempt.[76] Aristophanes here anticipates the imagination of cartoon comedy in what was doubtless surreal *avant la lettre* even to the Greek audience. (Recall the absurdity of Aristophanic compounds like *englōttogasterōn genos,* "the tongues-in-stomach-tribe.")

In this play the conflict of the generations has a political aspect as well. The names of father and son indicate their relationship to the demagogue Cleon. Philocleon is reactionary, still adhering to the values of radical democracy, whereas Bdelycleon, the smart young man, moves in circles where the rule of the best—oneself and one's friends—is in fashion. The battle between public and private is thus played out in their home.[77]

When the guards eventually drift into sleep, the chorus enters. Once again they are old-age pensioners whose aches and pains will add counterpoint to the hero's melodious rejuvenation. These twenty-four angry men are churlish Wasps who share Philocleon's passion for judging. They may have lost their "sting," but they still have the vestiges of the implement between their legs. In fact, it goes without saying that these stings are phalluses.[78] The restoration of their powers will thus have a graphic impact.

They come to pick up their jury-mate Philocleon and find him imprisoned, calling out for help. They remind him of how fit he once was when he was the best commando in the army. "I was young then," he laments, "and I had my own strength and I could have escaped scot-free."[79] As an alternative, they urge him to dream up some trick or scheme *(mēchanē),*[80] and he proceeds to gnaw like a beaver on the nets. A moment later he slides down on a rope he has suddenly discovered.

But before he can abscond with his friends, Bdelycleon appears, fuming at his father and the Wasps. He orders Xanthias and Sosias to *chain* his father, and the two leap to the fray as the Chorus wails, "Isn't old age terrible? Those two are manhandling their former master."[81]

The formal *agōn* epitomizes the essential conflict in the play: loving or hating Cleon. Father and son square off against each other to debate Cleon's treatment of the jurors. Bdelycleon argues that Cleon is exploiting the predicament of the old men who serve as jurors. Because they are dependent on the three-obol fee, he can control them politically. But Philocleon does not deviate from his reactionary position and counters that pronouncing verdicts gives him kingly power *(basileia).*[82]

He enjoys the attention of the people who plead with him to vote for their cause, flattering him and supplicating: "'take pity on my son,' or, if I prefer 'pork cuntlets' I can take heed of his daughter."[83] Indeed, his own daughter rewards him with tongue-kisses when he brings home his jury pay.[84] As one critic puts it, "what the old men really want . . . is the experience of sexual potency that makes them feel really alive."[85]

But Philocleon's appetite does not yet tend to "porcine delicacies." On the contrary, he prefers the opportunity the job affords him to look at boys' genitals when they are being examined for registration.[86] This situation is subject to change. For the moment, however, Philocleon rejoices in his position as a juror, which he likens to that of the king of Olympus:

> PHILOCLEON: Is not the power I wield no less than Zeus'?
> After all, the same things that are said of Zeus are said of
>   me . . .
> If I make lightning
> the rich and very grand men gulp and
> soil their pants because of me.[87]

But Bdelycleon at last coerces his father to go freelance with his judging—that is, to set up a court in the house and to hear cases in the comfort of his home. Philocleon attacks his new job with zeal, and immediately embarks on a prosecution of the house dog, who has eaten all the cheese—a thinly disguised allusion to Cleon and his detrimental effects on the city.

In the *parabasis* which follows, Aristophanes reviews his professional life.[88] Understandably, he is still smarting from the wounds of last year's rejection of the *Clouds*. Castigating the audience for neglecting his masterpiece, he praises his own behavior throughout his theatrical career. He never exploited his celebrity status by base actions, scouring the wrestling schools to make a pick-up. Nor did he pimpify his Muse. And he tried to present new ideas. This complaining, however, is to no avail. His newfangled *Clouds* had anything but a silver lining and would forever rain on the parade of his ego (he continued to sideswipe Socrates in *Frogs*).[89]

As the play races toward its conclusion, the theme of rejuvenation comes to the fore. The chorus, who have already shown signs of reinvigoration when they cast away their staffs in the *parabasis*,[90] express their personal geriatric nostalgia:

> O, were we heroic in the good old days in the choruses,
> And on the battlefield—
> And we were most heroic of all in this domain *(indicating their*
> *phalluses)*
> Those were the days—the good old days.[91]

They exhort themselves to summon up their youthful strength—especially since today's bunch of youngsters are nothing but a "generation of buggerees."[92] They then turn to their stings, once potent weapons in any number of battles: "There was nothing more macho (*andrikōteron*) than a good old Attic wasp."[93]

In the final allegro of the play, Bdelycleon rehabilitates his father (or so he thinks), training him in social graces to prepare him for a fancy dinner at a friend's home. He condescendingly reminds him to be on his best behavior. And "don't forget to sing your part in the drinking songs."[94]

As they leave for the festivities, a self-satisfied Bdelycleon proposes that they both get drunk. Unrejuvenated, Philocleon resists the call of the *kōmos*. Like a *senex iratus,* he says sternly:

> PHILOCLEON: Heavens no!
> Drinking is bad for you. Wine leads to
> the door breaking and beating and stoning—
> lots of expenses, on top of a headache.
> BDELYCLEON: Not with these elegant guests. If someone goes wild, just
>   calm him down with a tale of Aesop or one from good
>   old Sybaris, and they'll dissolve in laughter.[95]

Philocleon promises that he will learn a lot of those jokes. But Bdelycleon's best-laid plans go awry with his father's explosion, which is recounted by a breathless slave, shouting the old joke: "I'm finished, I'm beaten black and blue."[96] He explains that the old man has gone

wild at dinner and was the most outrageous *(hybristatos)* of the guests:[97]
"The old man was the bane of the party. He was the drunkest guest of
all, even though there were some heavy drinkers there."[98] As soon as
Philocleon had stuffed his face with food, he jumped up and began to
frolic:

> He leaped, he danced, he farted and he laughed . . .
> He beat me with the vigor of a young man, shouting "boy!
>   boy!" . . .
> He insulted every single person there with
> Rustic jokes and anecdotes. Then drunk to his gills he headed
> Home while punching everyone who came his way.[99]

The verb "to dance" *(skirtan)* is the same one used by Wrong Logic in
the *Clouds,* and also in Plato's account of dream-psychology. The reinvigorated hero is the life-force personified. Philocleon has re-channeled
his energies, from seeking the thrill of potency from jury life, to ordinary—or, in his case, extraordinary—heterosexual indulgence.

For Philocleon enters in triumph with Dardanis, a naked pipe-girl,
on his arm, his other hand holding a torch. (Yet one more comic device
Aristophanes never uses!) The hero pokes the passers-by with his
brand. His behavior with his girlfriend is anything but subtle. He has
stolen her away from the party as she was about to perform fellatio on
the guests, and he now requests this attention for himself alone:

PHILOCLEON: Come here, my lovely,
>>> grab this rope with your hand:
>>> Hold on to it. Easy, because it's a bit frayed—
>>> Still, a little rub won't hurt it.
>>> Do you see how cleverly I rescued you
>>> From the others when you were about to blow them?
>>> Now pay me back by servicing *my* dongle! . . .
>>> Are you going to cheat me and just stand there open-
>>>   mouthed?
>>> I mean, you *have* done it for lots of other people before!
>>> And if you're not a bad girl now,

Then when my son dies

I'll free you and keep you, my little piggy, as my official
　　mistress.

But at the moment I'm too young to handle my own
　　money.[100]

This is more like it! This genuine twenty-four-carat rejuvenation reverses the generations and stays there—nor does Philocleon remain
mired in an infantile state, unlike Strepsiades.[101] Hostility is vented in
abundance. The son will predecease the father. The father will outdo
him in every physical domain.

Bdelycleon storms onstage and derides his father, using various images of senility ("you've got a hard-on for a coffin") and vowing that "he
won't get away with this."[102] But Philocleon gets away with everything.
And when Bdelycleon tries to take the pipe-girl back, his father threatens to punch him and knock him to the ground.[103]

The chorus then sings of their admiration for our newly-minted
"young" hero:

> I envy the old man his good fortune, changing his
> Dry behavior and his arid way of life
> To learn other things,
> He'll experience a mighty transformation
> Towards the cushy comfy and the ultra-hedonistic.[104]

Philocleon has fought the good fight for sense and sensuality.
Whereas the hero of the *Clouds* ends up old, lonely, and passing judgment atop Socrates' roof, Philocleon's judge-a-holic life has become a
mighty *kōmos*. Our hero breaks out in a dance—with ithyphallic
overtones[105]—yet another element that Aristophanes never presents. He
is joined by the chorus, who claim all the while that no one has ever
ended a play with a dancing chorus.[106] Aristophanes had once again
demonstrated that in his heart he really knew what they wanted and
could present a comedy as they liked it.[107]

6

The *Birds:* The Uncensored Fantasy

The *Birds* takes comedy as far as it can go. It dramatizes, with a unique combination of the lyre and phallus, the fullest expression of the comic dream. In a word, it is Aristophanes' masterpiece. While producing a work of transcendent brilliance, he also captured the historical moment at which it was composed. Aristophanes can thus share Ben Jonson's praise of Shakespeare: he is at once the "soul of an age" as well as "not for an age but for all time."

In the summer before the *Birds* was presented at the Great Dionysia (414 B.C.), Athens undertook, at the urging of Alcibiades, the most audacious venture in the long Peloponnesian War, launching a vast armada—according to Thucydides, the most magnificent force ever assembled by a Greek city[1]—to conquer Sicily and sever Sparta from her western allies. It was ultimately to prove a disaster, but at the time of the play, the Athenians were still drunk with hope and dreams of power. Sicily was El Dorado to them, a land of infinite wishes. Like Hamlet, they "ate the air, promise crammed."

Euripides' description of Orestes' voyage in the Black Sea does equally well to describe the Sicilian expedition:

Or did they sail . . .
upon a distant quest
to increase their halls' treasures?
For hope is fond, and, to people's misfortune,
insatiable for the persons
who bring back the rich cargoes,
wanderers over the sea to the cities of the outlanders.
All with one single
purpose; sometimes their judgement of profit
fails; sometimes it attains.[2]

But, of course, this was written a few years later, *after* the destruction of the fleet. In the *Birds,* Aristophanes is not necessarily mocking his countrymen's imperialistic urges directly.[3] Nevertheless, he perfectly captures the feeling that was in the air.[4] In Thucydides' account of the Athenians' mood at this time, the note of their being "drunk with hope" *(euelpides)* is sounded several times.[5] Small wonder that Aristophanes has named one of his wandering heroes Euelpides, and the other Peisetaerus ("Friend-Persuader").

Moreover, there was a special phallic dimension to the events of 415. As mentioned earlier, the Athenians had been placing priapic icons of Hermes outside their front doors for centuries to ward off the evil eye. The night before the fleet sailed, these statues were mutilated by unknown vandals. Thucydides recalls the shock of the Athenians, who regarded it as "a very grave incident."[6] *Birds* is an artistic reaction to what Aristophanes elsewhere refers to as the "Hermes-choppers."[7] For although the *Birds* is in one sense a traditional comedy—the hero's goal is not unlike that of Dicaeopolis or even Strepsiades—on a more fundamental level the play is about, in no uncertain terms, the re-invigoration of the phallus. And on a more universal level, its psychological significance goes back to the dawn of man—a fantasy which even predates its expression in ritual (which is why the poet is "for all time").

The general theme is the acquisition of wings by men—itself a great sexual metaphor. Freud explains the erotic dream symbolism of "flying fantasies" and the remarkable characteristic of the male organ which enables it to rise up in defiance of the laws of gravity, one of the phenomena of erection . . . But dreams can symbolize erection in yet another, far more expressive manner. They can treat the sexual organ as the essence of the dreamer's whole person and make him himself fly.[8]

It should come as no surprise then that the Greek word for "wing" also served as a euphemism for phallus. After all, "bird" is still used to refer to the male member in the slang of many modern languages. Besides the English "cock" and "flip the bird," the Greek idiom is matched in French by *le petit oiseau*, in Italian by *l'uccello*, in Spanish by *pajarito*, as well as by the German verb *vögeln* ("to bird," that is, to have intercourse).[9] In both Greece and Rome, birds were lovers' gifts. One thinks of the vivid connotation of the sparrow with which Catullus delighted Lesbia—until it "died."[10]

Intimately related to this imagery is the Greek symbol of the winged phallus, familiar from various artifacts since the earliest times.[11] This is doubtless what Plato refers to in *Phaedrus,* where the philosopher, discussing *erōs,* quotes two verses from one of the Homeric apocrypha, which, he warns, are "very obscene" *(panu hybristikon):*

> All men refer to him as love-on-the-wing.
> But the gods simply call him *Pterōs* ["Wingèd *Erōs*"] since he needs
> his wings to grow before he flies.[12]

Clearly the obscene word must be *Pterōs*—a fusion of *pteron* ("wing") and *Erōs*. By this principle Aristophanes' entire play, elaborating the familiar literary and artistic trope, becomes one magnificent erection. It is evident from the first that the two tramps are driven by an erotic impulse to seek out the birds: "no other play of Aristophanes, not even *Lysistrata,* is so pervaded, so saturated by the language of desire."[13]

Comedy, as we have seen, was born of the *kōmos,* engendered by the same two forces that the Birds will claim as their parents in the Birdogony of the *parabasis:* Eros and Chaos. Alongside it marched the bawdy banter of the phallic procession, which ultimately made its way to the stage. These primal elements are nowhere more clearly preserved

than in this comedy. Indeed, the play concludes with a triumphant procession—a phallic play within a play—this time on a much grander scale
than the one we saw in the *Acharnians*. The *Birds* is thus the ultimate
destination toward which *ta phallika* had been leading for centuries, and
it perfectly reflects the orgiastic mood of the Athenians before the defeat of the Sicilian Expedition.

The scene is spare: a rock and a tree. The phallic theme is firmly established by the very first word of the play, *orthēn* ("erect").[14] Two aged
hoboes shuffle onstage, each holding a bird. The first is asking his avian
pet for directions:

EUELPIDES: Hard on *(orthēn)* down the road, is that the way you are
            suggesting?[15]

In similarly phallic terms, his companion inquires of *his* bird:

PEISETAERUS: Why are you making us exhausted humping up and
              down *(anō katō)*? This trip is going to wear us out com-
              pletely![16]

Thus the note of tumescence and detumescence is struck at the very
outset. It is a theme whose variations will be played throughout the entire comedy.

This pair of drop-outs from the city are on a quest. As Peisetaerus explains to the audience, they are anxious to flee Athens and its discontents:

PEISETAERUS: It's not that we hate the city as such, or that we don't
              want it to be "huge" *(megalēn)* and happy—and welcome
              everybody who wants to come and pay fines. But in
              Birdland the cicadas only chirp on branches for a
              month or two, while Athenians chirp away at lawsuits
              all the time.[17]

Sick of the rat-race, they are looking for a "hassle-free place" *(topon
apragmona)* to live out the rest of their lives.[18] This phrase would have
had an ironic ring to the Athenian ear because it is the precise opposite
of what they regarded as their quintessential virtue. The Athenians
viewed themselves as exemplars of *polypragmosynē* ("hyper-busybody-

ness"). Pericles emphasizes this trait in his famous funeral oration.[19] But the tramps want a holiday from being Athenian, far from the urban hurly-burly they have left. Knowing Aristophanes, they may also be seeking some sort of health-spa for rejuvenation, since they are both burnt-out cases.

The tramps are trying to find Tereus—formerly a star of the tragic stage (most recently appearing in the play of that name by Sophocles). The familiar Tereus of myth married Procne and raped her sister Philomela, cruelly cutting out her tongue so she could not report his deed. But Philomela informed her sister by weaving a tapestry. For revenge, the two women killed the couple's young son Itys and served the dish to the unwitting Tereus, who, when he discovered the true nature of his feast, attacked the sisters. But before he could do them harm, Zeus changed all three of them into birds.

The two men believe that Tereus can help them find a place, since he has seen the world with the eyes of both men and birds.[20] They arrive at Tereus' home (the erstwhile Thinketorium and Euripides' house) and knock. A huge-beaked servant opens the door, and both men are terrified: frightened to death—or rather, to "deathecate," unheroically befouling themselves with fear. The puzzled serving-bird demands:

SERVANT: What are *you* then?
PEISETAERUS: I'm a bird from Libya, a Frightengale.
SERVANT: Come on now!
PEISETAERUS: Well, my pants are like Turd-le Doves.[21]

Precisely what it is about the servant that scares them is not apparently clear, but we have good reason to believe that they were astounded by the enormity of the servant's phallus. There is an Attic red-figure vase painting (the so-called "Getty Birds") which shows two cocks, endowed with massive phalluses and representing a chorus (as shown by the piper). Some have argued that this represents an actual performance of Aristophanes' play, though the view remains controversial.[22] Whatever its true identification, the vase painting at least provides a convincing precedent for the dramatization of a chorus of phallus-birds. How much more likely then that bird *actors* would be similarly endowed.

They beg the servant to call his master, and Tereus appears straight from the Sophoclean stage.[23] The playwright has rehabilitated the wretched man into a socially acceptable hoopoe with an awe-inspiring crest.[24] And—curiouser and curiouser—he is reconciled with his tawny-throated wife, the former nightingale—though she still sings her lament and mourns Itys.[25] This gorgeous creature has retained enough of her anthropomorphic charms to stir up a mighty passion ("I'd be more than pleased to help her spread her legs").[26]

The travelers inform the Hoopoe that they are anxious to avoid paying their debts and have somehow heard that he did the same by becoming a bird.[27] More specifically, they ask Tereus if he knows of some cushy city, "as soft as a fleecy bed to lie down in."[28] This is hardly a noble quest. In fact, their aspirations seem childish. But that is precisely the point—both men are infantile, regressed characters without grown-up sexual feelings. In fact, when the birdman asks them what sort of place they are looking to live in, Euelpides says:

> EUELPIDES: I'm looking for a place where the father of a good-look-
> ing boy would chide me for having wronged him: "you
> didn't give my boy much of a kiss when he was all
> washed and leaving the gym, you didn't talk to him or
> embrace him, and you didn't even finger his balls. And I
> thought you were my friend."[29]

Aristophanes leaves us in no doubt as to the protagonists' sexual orientation. At this point they are still old and very weary—a necessary precondition for ultimate rejuvenation.

The travelers are eager to know what bird life is like. The Hoopoe replies with innuendo, implying abundant sexuality:

> TEREUS: Folks really give you a hand here.
> Most of all, you don't need any money . . .
> And we feast on cunt-ry flowers like white sesame, myrtle,
> poppies and mint.
> EUELPIDES: Sounds like one long wedding night![30]

The plants mentioned are not only aphrodisiacs, they are also—as we have seen elsewhere in Old Comedy—double-entendres for female sexual parts.[31] The Hoopoe's suggestive speech inspires the Happy Idea. Peisetaerus suddenly exclaims: "Oh boy, I see a great big cocky *(mega)* plan for all you birds, and power too, if you'd just listen to me."[32] Peisetaerus will lead the birds on a Sicilian expedition of their own. Their aims have expanded greatly from a longing for personal comfort to universal domination: our heroes' *erōs* has metamorphosed into a lust for power. For, in the words of Henry Kissinger, "Power is the great aphrodisiac."

The first step in world conquest is to found a city for the birds. As with all real estate, the three most important factors are—location, location, location. The site Peisetaerus chooses is midway between sky and earth. It is the same territory as Socrates in the basket, writ large. Here they can block the sacrifices which mortals make to the gods, and prevent the gods from flying down with their Olympian erections to "screw the Alcmenas and Alopes and Semeles."[33] And if they *do* insist on coming, the Birds will infibulate their divine genitals.[34] In short order, they reckon, the gods will cede their dominion.

Tereus is thrilled and calls the other birds to gather for a meeting. Birds of all feathers—in other words the chorus—now flock together to hear what the Hoopoe describes as "some great huge windfall"—the thought of phallic arousal is never far from view.[35] Like a fashion commentator at a catwalk, Tereus identifies each species as it enters. Aristophanes' catalogue of ancient Greek birds has been the delight of ornithologists for centuries.

The chorus gather around Tereus as he explains that a brace of old men have arrived bearing the "shaft of a prodigious thing."[36] The birds are hostile at first and threaten to attack the mortals, whom they regard as enemies to "our feathers and forefeathers."[37] The potential conflict between the chorus and the heroes takes the form of a cockfight, the model bird for aggressive virility. Peisetaerus' and Euelpides' weapon is the phallically-shaped ritual skewer *(obeliskon)*.[38]

As soon as the rough-house subsides, Tereus introduces the two men, explaining that they have approached the birds out of "lust to have 'intercourse'" with them.[39] (The verb *syneinai*, "to be together," also has a coital overtone.) The chorus is excited by Peisetaerus' companion-persuading plan and feel their "wings grow straight" (anepterōmai).[40]

The agōn ensues. This time it is not a debate between two opposing forces, but rather an exhortation by the hero to convince the Birds to join him in his revolution. His recruitment speech is interrupted by some slapstick skirmishing between speakers and audience, but at last they listen carefully. According to legend, says Peisetaerus, the Birds antedated not only Cronus and the Titans, but even Earth itself.[41] The chorus leader is amazed, never having heard this "ornithogony" before. "That's because you're not polypragmōn," Peisetaerus quips—in other words, "you don't have the intellectual assets of an Athenian." We recall the hoboes' earlier desire to avoid the polypragmosynē of Athens. Yet now Peisetaerus praises the very quality he sought to escape!

After he punningly cites three or four examples of the Birds' previous phallic potency, all of which sexually exploit traditional and fabular attributes of birds,[42] his once hostile audience is won over into joining him to recover their lost power. Peisetaerus emphasizes that the kingdom (basileia) of the world will be theirs "inphallibly" (orthōs).[43]

They begin to build their city and proclaim a "holy war" against Zeus.[44] The celestial roadblock will continue until Zeus capitulates. Their eyes are now on much higher goals. Why settle for avoiding debt when you can avoid death itself?

At this point all the actors leave the stage and the chorus delivers the parabasis—the only instance in all of Aristophanes where it is integrated dramatically with the rest of the play. The chorus does not drop its persona for delivering "a word from our sponsor": they speak for themselves, once again extolling the life of the birds. It is one of Aristophanes' finest pieces of music.[45]

They address frail, ephemeral, earthbound mankind and, parodying Hesiod, present a new cosmogony in which Eros mated with winged Chaos and hatched the birds. Eros was the ancestor of all the gods, which is why the birds have primacy of rule. "It is clear in many ways that we are creatures of Eros: we fly and we have intercourse (syneinai again) with lovers."[46]

The Birds represent primal sexual origins for both aggression and transgression. Witness their claim that in Birdland "everything which is shameful (aischron) in the world of men is perfectly lovely

(kala) here. For example, striking one's father . . ." This bears a startling resemblance to Wrong Logic's argument in *Clouds* that followers
of his philosophy can enjoy a life in which nothing is shameful
(aischron).[47]

Indeed, some of the greatest advantages of birdhood are "comic"
joys—to begin with, the gross element of circumventing toilet-training,
and the subtle advantage of being able to vent hostility in the most
primitive of fashions:

> If anyone sitting in the theater had to heed the call of nature,
> he wouldn't have to soil his clothes.
> He could just fly up and dump his load.[48]

Aristophanes presents an even more drastic image in the *Ecclesiazusae*
(Assemblywomen), where one character's greatest fear is that, if the
young people were to gain control over their parents, they would strangle and then excrete on them.[49] But the birds offer joys of a loftier and
more phallic nature as well. For example, if a man happened to see his
mistress's husband in the VIP section of the theater, he could take advantage of the man's cultural involvement, fly down to her bedroom,
and fly back again.

With this the action resumes. Peisetaerus and Euelpides re-enter—
now wearing wings. They have achieved the first important stage of
their goal: they are sexually potent creatures and could conceivably fly
up as high as heaven. They direct the building of Birdland—
Nephelococcygia, more literally "Cloudcuckooville"—which is what they
have decided to call the city.

At this point Euelpides, having outlived his usefulness—and because
the actor is needed to play another part—walks offstage to supervise the
building. Even this is dramatically motivated by the two of them bick-
ering over Peisetaerus' imperious manner. Yet in truth Euelpides would
be out of place in the fine dignity of the finale.

There now ensues a series of annoying visitors whom Peisetaerus has
to chase away. As we have seen as early as the *Acharnians,* this is a typical
Aristophanic (and possibly Old Comic in general) motif. And gradually
it begins to dawn on Peisetaerus that in seeking to flee the city of Athens, they have ironically recreated it in their Utopia. The intruders include a priest who wants to establish the metropolitan religion, a

versifier who wants to be the poet-laureate, and an oracle-monger who wants to legislate morality on the citizens.

When the city-planner Metōn arrives, he immediately begins to take the specification of spaces in the city with "measuring rods of the air." With geometrical innuendos and double-entrendres, Metōn tries to bugger Peisetaerus—and it is hardly subtle.[50] The next intruder is an inspector who wants to delve into people's private lives, as does the decree-seller, who punctuates his annoying appearance by also breaking wind.[51] The episode concludes with another choral lyric in praise of the birds and yet another plea to the judges to grant the poet victory. If they should fail to do it, the birds will punish them with their unique form of aerial bombardment.

The action now accelerates as a messenger announces the completion of the city wall, built entirely by the birds and now patrolled by them. War is declared on the Olympians. His rejuvenation dramatically advanced, Peisetaerus now begins his ascent toward sexual supremacy. He begins at the top with a goddess. When the divine Iris trespasses into the territory of Birdland, Peisetaerus accosts her and asks whether she has official permission to pass through this area. She haughtily denies the need for one. Peisetaerus then declares that for this infringement of their laws she must die:

> IRIS: But I'm immortal!
> PEISETAERUS: It makes no difference, you'll have to die anyway . . .
> IRIS: My father has sent me to tell mankind to sacrifice to the
> Olympian gods . . .
> PEISETAERUS: Gods? What gods?
> IRIS: Why us of course, the gods in heaven . . .
> What other god is there?
> PEISETAERUS: Birds, my dear. And men must sacrifice to *them* and not,
> by Zeus, to Zeus.[52]

When Iris protests with overblown tragic rhetoric, Peisetaerus tells her to shut up—he has half a mind to "lift up her legs and screw her."[53] Moreover, he declares, "you'll be amazed that a guy my age can get it up for three full sessions in a row."[54] We have encountered a similar exclamation on the part of the old Acharnians.[55] The rejuvenation process is well under way.

He now motions off stage and a huge crane lifts Iris and carries her away (this was the Great Dionysia, after all, with its elaborate machinery). The next second the messenger he has sent to mankind arrives to report that men have all become passionate lovers *(erastai)* of Cloudcuckooville and people are going birdmad *(ornithomanousi)*.[56]

Peisetaerus' plan now reaches a speedy conclusion. One of the divinities sneaks down from Olympus—Prometheus, the friend of man. The fire-giver brings intelligence of what the situation is above. In a word, Zeus is *history*. The birds' strike is working so well that the gods are shrieking with hunger. With victory imminent, Prometheus gives Peisetaerus an important bit of advice:

> PROMETHEUS: Don't pour any peace libations unless Zeus gives the
> sceptre back to the birds and gives you . . . Basileia as
> your wife.
> PEISETAERUS: *(intrigued)* Who's this Basileia?
> PROMETHEUS: She's a gorgeous maiden
> Who guards the thunderbolt of Zeus
> And absolutely everything else . . .
> If you've got her, you've got everything.[57]

Having divulged the secret of the universe, Prometheus slinks back to heaven just in time to avoid Heracles, Poseidon, and Triballus, a barbarian god invented by Aristophanes—there is no doubt a pun here, Triphallus—arriving in a peace embassy to negotiate terms with Peisetaerus. Heracles is his usual swaggering self: a hooligan *gloriosus,* blustering threats of bodily harm to Peisetaerus. But the latter is in the process of supervising the preparation of a meal—the wedding feast— and Heracles' gluttonous mind is predictably turned off assault and battery to salt and buttery.

One by one they agree to his conditions—until Peisetaerus makes his final demand:

> PEISETAERUS: As far as Hera goes, Zeus can keep her—
> But young Basileia must be given to me as wife.
> POSEIDON: *(outraged)* No deal![58]

As Poseidon turns to storm off, Heracles chastises him with an epic allusion, "Why fight a war over one woman?"[59] His Olympian uncle is adamant, but the tie-breaking decision is left to Triballus, whom Heracles bullies into grunting agreement by misinterpreting his unintelligible Greek. He happily informs Peisetaerus of the result and bids him: "Come with us to heaven so you can get your hands on Basileia . . . and everything else!"[60] Peisetaerus has surpassed even Athenian ambitions—he has succeeded in conquering the world. He then calls off to the stage manager to prepare his bridegroom's costume.

The play concludes with a grand phallic wedding procession, with the hero dressed splendidly as the new king. Constant reference is made throughout the festivities that this is exactly like the wedding of Zeus and Hera:

> Once upon a time the Fates brought together
> The well-endowed (megan) ruler of the gods
> With Olympian Hera with such a wedding-song as this . . .
> And young Eros, golden wings,
> Double-blooming (amphithalēs), directed the
> Back-stretched reins, the best man at the
> Wedding of Zeus and blessed Hera.[61]

Eros, the driver of the matrimonial chariot, is described by the adjective amphithalēs ("all-powerful" or "all-flourishing"). This should surely be construed in the context of its root thallein ("to grow or rise"), since the usual meaning of the word ("flourishing on both sides of one's family") is otherwise ill-suited to describe this god.[62] "Rising on both sides" would aptly describe male arousal, the growing of wings. Peisetaerus' sexual journey from mutilated herm to priapic godhead is thus completed.

As the play nears its conclusion, the chorus-leader calls the chorus to celebrate Zeus' "awesome thunderbolt" (deinon keraunon) in the most elegant lyric strains.[63] The bolt of Zeus now seems to have replaced Peisetaerus as the central character. The bolt has been described as both "winged" and the "firebearing spear" (enchos pyrphoron).[64] Like any good wedding hymn, the song that ends the play is emphatically ithyphallic. The image of the phallus overshadows the individual people, as it did the celebrants in the ancient phallic procession. It is an emblem of how Peisetaerus feels as he approaches the wedding-bed of Basileia.

But to repeat our hero's question: who is this bride really? Critics have tended to avoid the most obvious conclusion. For despite Peisetaerus' facile disclaimer that Zeus can keep Hera, the resemblance of Basileia to Hera is too Olympian to be ignored. The chorus describes her as *paredros Dios,* "Zeus' constant companion," or more literally "she who sits beside Zeus."[65] Some scholars have used the superficial meaning to identify the goddess as a minor deity like Themis (Justice), who is sometimes referred to by this same epithet.[66] But there are no details in the text to justify this view.

Throughout the finale, Peisetaerus is specifically spoken of as a new Zeus: in the choral song just examined, his wedding is compared to that of Zeus and Hera.[67] Moreover, in some of the most ancient cities of Greece there was a long-established cult of Hera *Basilis.* This title relates to Hera's role in the Sacred Marriage with Zeus, father of gods and men—an ancient cosmic belief with deep implications for the history of comedy, as we have seen.[68] These facts cannot be ignored. The figure of Basileia would not be obscure to Aristophanes' audience: Basileia *is* the mother of gods and men. It is as close an identification as, in our own day, "virgin mother" would be for Mary.

Some critics have gone to great lengths to dispute this outrageous view.[69] But did not Freud write that the objects of wit are the *most* respected institutions, which cannot be approached in any other way? What more sacred institution than the mother of the gods and men, who is normally beyond the pale of comic treatment? Man was born with animal libido, propelling him toward aggression and unfettered sexual behavior. Opinions differ as to the origin of the incestuous instinct, and few now hold strictly to Freud's belief that totem and taboo originated in a historical "dethroning" of father by son.[70] Later thinkers, blurring this stark vision, saw them as "an infantile fantasy created out of nothing by the infantile ego in order to sequester by repression its own unmanageable vitality (id)."[71] But all agree that the urge to restrain this impulse forms the basis of religion, morality, and the family, and that vestiges of the original impulse survive in myth.[72] As Otto Rank explains:

> From the development of the ancient religions, it seems that
> many things that mankind had renounced as "criminal"

were attributed to a god and still permitted in the name of the god. Recourse to the deity was the way man freed himself from evil, socially harmful drives. It is therefore no coincidence that all human characteristics and the misdeeds associated with them were attributed to the old gods without restriction.[73]

This mythic pattern has been an integral part of human thought since the beginning of time and cannot be ignored. Aristophanes presents it boldly in the *Birds*. Peisetaerus not only rises in the city but above it, ultimately achieving godhead. According to Rank's formulation, he is now permitted to enjoy the incestuous experience because he has become "the very highest of the gods" *(daimonōn upertatos)*.[74] The only difference between these fantasies and Aristophanes' play is the aura of comedy which he has constructed in order to bypass the censors in the spectators' psyche. Psychologists would explain Basileia as "an ostensible other" who represents a displacement by which feelings of incest can be defused.

Thus, it is less important that Peisetaerus acquire Hera explicitly as that he win the female prize that comes with dethroning the "Old King." For Zeus himself did not take his mother Rhea to wife after deposing Cronos, nor did Cronos do likewise after castrating Uranus. After all, in the spirit of Aristophanic rejuvenation and *kōmos,* the New King would surely prefer a beautiful young New Queen, just as in the *Poenulus* of Plautus the lovestruck young hero exclaims: "If I were Jupiter himself / I would marry that girl and kick Juno straight out!"[75] We recall Peisetaerus' contemptuous outburst:

> As far as Hera goes, Zeus can keep her—
> But young Basileia must be given to me as wife.[76]

In a widely influential essay, Northrop Frye described the "argument of comedy" as unfolding from "what may be described as a comic Oedipus situation."[77] More specifically, it is the realization that the heroine "is not under an insuperable taboo after all, but is an accessible object of desire." Frye also adds that the Oedipal dilemma is often "thinly concealed by surrogates or doubles."

This is precisely what is at work in the *Birds*—with a magnificent difference. Whereas in "classic" comedies, like the *Marriage of Figaro,* the hero is about to marry his mother and a last-minute *cognitio* prevents the catastrophe, here the ultimate triumph is *not* denied the hero. He not only unseats the ruler and assumes control of his kingdom, but also marries his wife as well. It is the Oedipal situation *consummated.* It is Oedipus unchained.

The conflict of the *Birds* is the quest of a hobo with no fixed address, an old codger who ultimately becomes the rejuvenated king of the universe. It reverses the ancient succession myth and brings back the Golden Age, as the Old King becomes young again and defeats the Young King, who has since grown old.[78] It was a theme of ancient potency, deriving from that prehistoric time before the taboo of incest existed.

As he heads for the nuptial bed, Peisetaerus bids his bride to grab hold of his "wings" and dance.[79] He is hailed as an Olympic victor *(kallinikos).*[80] He has gained what Prometheus suggestively describes as "everything."

Long ago Gilbert Murray inquired rhetorically,

> Greek doctrine is full of the punishment of those who make themselves equal to even the lowest order of the Gods—yet Peisetaerus dances off in triumph. *What* did the audience feel?[81]

The answer is that, on the *kōmos* level, they would have felt enormous satisfaction. The *Birds* is the product of an uncensored imagination whose boldness would not have been lost on the Greek audience. It represents the culmination of comedy's evolution from *ta phallika,* and the *ne plus ultra* of Aristophanes' rejuvenation theme—writ large in the universe and writ small in the human body. The erotic element is uninhibited. It is an orgy of the mind as unfettered as its physical antecedents. The audience would have lived the ultimate fantasy, committing the primal crime without consequences. It is Frazer's Old Year against the New, with man challenging deathless gods and triumphing. Its audacity and magnitude make it a unique work.

Indeed, the fantasy may have been *too* bold, and the judges were hesitant to give the play first prize. For Aristophanes was once again bested by Ameipsias (with *The Comasts*), and had to settle for second place.[82] Yet even the *Oedipus Rex* earned only a second.[83] One scholiast offered the explanation that the judges were either stupid or bribed. Aristophanes would write at least a dozen more comedies, but none would equal the matchless bravery, beauty, and vision of the *Birds*.

7

Requiem for a Genre?

The *Birds* sounded the death knell of Old Comedy, although it took another decade until rigor mortis set in. After that it was no more possible to revive this unique art form than it was to resurrect Aeschylus, the subject of Aristophanes' last fifth-century play presented in 405—the year before the city of Athens and its theater collapsed.

The *Frogs* is *sui generis.* We still find the formal ingredients of the integrated chorus (two, in fact) with *parabasis* and *agōn,* albeit in an atypical structure. It has its amusing, indeed memorable, comic moments: the switching of identities between master and man, mock-heroic burlesque, and even an amusing literary *agōn.*

The comic dream of restoring the good old days was not new. In *The Demoi* nearly a decade earlier, Eupolis had resuscitated four of the most popular leaders of Athens (Miltiades, Aristides, Solon, and Pericles) to dissuade his countrymen from their headlong rush to ruin. (An early imperial critic remarked, "even as a dead man Pericles triumphed over Cleon.")[1] And as we have seen, the myth of the Golden Age and the return to simpler, better times resonates strongly with *kōmos,* and was accordingly a frequent theme in Old Comedy.

And yet something is missing from the *Frogs.* For lack of a better word, we might call it the hormonal element. In contrast to the other comedies we have examined, the theme of the *Frogs* is not fertility but rather its polar opposite. There is a peculiar kind of *Liebestod,* a sexual language surrounded by an imagery of death, which pervades everything. We no longer see a decrepit old man rejuvenated to the delight of all, and the attempt to restore the beleaguered city to the glory of the past is futile. Aeschylus is revived but not rejuvenated, and enjoys neither *kōmos* nor *gamos.*

In a way, then, *Frogs* is about the art of playwriting—and the impossibility of producing any more comedies in the traditional manner. It can thus be seen as "a definition of Old Comedy itself, which could flourish only in the atmosphere of confidence, in the unity of the *polis* which Aristophanes is attempting to promote."[2] Other scholars have also stressed the play's somber tone, and go as far as to call it "a tragedy in comic form."[3] Whether this designation is helpful or not, it is undeniable that *Frogs* is no longer Aristophanes as we have come to know him.

The long, farcical opening scene is a *katabasis* or downward journey to the underworld. We find the comic routine of master and man switching identities, later exploited in the *Captivi* (*The Captives*) of Plautus and Goldsmith's *She Stoops to Conquer* (1773). Here as elsewhere—*The Admirable Crichton,* for example—the slave proves to be the "better man." While the bondsman is the familiar Xanthias (perhaps a little savvier than his namesake in the *Wasps*), the master is none other than Dionysus, god of the theater, travestied—not for the first time in Old Comedy[4]—as a kind of dim-witted Bertie Wooster in contrast to his ever-resourceful man-servant Jeeves.

Dionysus makes his appearance in the bisexual garb that is characteristic of him: a saffron dress and lion skin, carrying a club, with tragic buskins on his feet. His slave follows on a donkey, weighed down by an enormous load of luggage (evidently a favorite bit of Old Comedy business). In a familiar gambit to "warm up the audience," he asks his master if he should tell the spectators any of the old jokes that never fail to make them laugh—those stock scatological gags which offend his master's sensibilities, but which are found so often in the fragments of Old Comedy and in Aristophanes himself. The theater god is too fastidious for this sort of humor, which, he says, "makes me grow older by a full year"—of course it has been just that long since the previous theatrical festival.[5] Are we to infer that his own jokes will rejuvenate? Alas not.

As in the *Birds,* the duo is on a quest. Yet Dionysus is not seeking advice from a hoopoe on avoiding debts, but rather trying to obtain suggestions for a "heroic" journey to Hell from an even more familiar figure of the comic stage, his half-brother Heracles. The blustering muscle-man laughs uproariously at Dionysus' outfit[6]—although he himself was frequently associated with transvestitism.[7]

When Heracles asks his sibling why he wants to undertake such a daunting mission, Dionysus explains that, while reading Euripides' *Andromeda,* he was suddenly seized with an erotic desire *(pothos).*[8] The activity of reading in itself would have caused a stir in the audience, for in addition to their physical distress, the Athenians were in the throes of a serious cultural crisis: the transition between orality and literacy— an experience with considerable psychological repercussions, as evidenced by the moral anarchy visible in the dramas of Euripides and the teachings of the sophists.[9] The *Frogs* abounds with references to the revolutionary new art.[10] Not only does Dionysus' entire inspiration for his journey come from his *reading* of a published version of the *Andromeda,* but the prominence of books is emphasized again in the word-weighing scene when Aeschylus challenges his younger rival to step bodily onto the scale "along with all his books."[11] Further emphasis is found in the remark that everyone in the audience has a book and is an old hand at reading.[12]

But the stolid Heracles, a man of flesh, leaps to the wrong conclusion:

HERACLES: Desire for a woman?

DIONYSUS: No.

HERACLES: For a boy?

DIONYSUS: Wrong again.

HERACLES: For a man?

DIONYSUS: Heavens no.

HERACLES: Then that faggot Cleisthenes?

DIONYSUS: Don't make fun of me, brother. I'm burning up with
            passion for the late Euripides.

HERACLES: (flabbergasted) You've got the hots for a *dead* man?[13]

This rather coarse exchange typifies the entire first half of the play. Dionysus later refers to the current (living) playwrights as "pissing on

the goddess of Tragedy,"[14] conveying the impotence of the new dramatists.[15] By contrast, the theater god wants to visit the underworld and
take back to earth a truly "fertile" poet, one who is *gonimos*—a term
which appears only twice in Aristophanes, both times in this passage,
unmistakably implying that the playwrights on earth lack creative
power.

In a certain sense we have here the makings for the usual rejuvenation plot. Indeed, the chorus of Mystics will hint at this motif later
when they sing the praises of Iacchus, another cult god who embodies
the festive *kōmos* aspect of Dionysus:

> Aged men all dance with boldness
> Shaking off their grief and
> Oldness.[16]

There are other suggestions. The chorus of eponymous Frogs—whose
immortal onomatopoetic refrain of *brekekekex koax koax* has been perpetuated in our own day in the Yale football cheer—joyfully refer to
their delight at having caught a glimpse of a young maiden's "titty"
(titthion).[17] In some ways this earthly chorus is in a different play. For
Frogs consists of two distinct sequences: the initial slapstick of the
katabasis ("journey down"), and the amusing—and astute—literary debate which Dionysus witnesses in Hades. Although the humor is both
broad and conventional, this opening gambit is, according to our ancient sources, the reason for the play's enormous success and immediate reprise.[18]

And yet these tantalizing hints of *kōmos* are never realized. Dionysus
himself—though famously, in Xanthias' words, the god of "quaffing
and boffing" *(pinein kai binein)*[19]—barely has a single sensual thought.
The only female figure in the play is the silent if naked pipe-girl, referred to as Euripides' rather threadbare "muse."[20] And besides being
tired and tatty—she is also dead!

Instead of revitalization, this opening farcical interlude teems with a
medley of idiotic jokes. When Dionysus asks Heracles for the easiest
way to Hell, the impudent lout quips: "get a rope and hang yourself!"[21]
(Would Aristophanes' audience have known, as the tramps in Beckett's
Waiting for Godot certainly do, that hanging causes an erectile response?)

Aristophanes obviously enjoyed this joke immensely, for he immediately repeats it when Heracles suggests an alternative route:

HERACLES: Well, go to the starting line of the tragic races.

DIONYSUS: *(nodding eagerly)* And then . . .?

HERACLES: Climb up to the tip-top of the tower.

DIONYSUS: *(more eagerly)* Yes, yes . . .?

HERACLES: From there, watch the torch-race starting up. And when the spectators say "They're off," off you go too.

DIONYSUS: *(breathless)* Go where?

HERACLES: *(pointing to the ground)* Straight down there . . . to Hades.[22]

The humor is so elemental in this part of the play that, frightened at the sight of the monster Empusa, Dionysus—like Strepsiades before him—actually befouls his pants.[23] "My master was so scared he shat all over me," Xanthias complains. The god again loses control of his sphincter soon after.[24]

At the gates of hell, Dionysus is "recognized" as Heracles by Aeacus, normally judge of the underworld but here demoted to mere doorman. He sends for the police to arrest Heracles—the deadbeat who left so many unpaid bills on his last visit. In terror, Dionysus changes his twice-soiled costume with his bondsman. Here we have another traditional comic gambit, reappearing in later plays like Plautus' *Menaechmi (The Brothers Menaechmus),* Shakespeare's *Comedy of Errors,* and Gogol's *Government Inspector,* all instances where a new arrival to town is mistaken for someone else more important and therefore given a lavish welcome.

Strangely, when the hardy travelers reach the underworld, the tone changes radically, as does ultimately the goal of Dionysus' quest. This occurs after the longest and most famous *agōn* in Aristophanes: the oft-quoted debate between "Aeschylus" and "Euripides," a *tour de force* of parody and pastiche. It is the source of many observations that become critical commonplaces in later ages, like Euripides' boast of his innovation in presenting household affairs *(oikeia pragmata),*[25] and his colloquial style as opposed to Aeschylus' hypertrophied language (what Marlowe called "high astounding terms").[26] The elder playwright attacks Euripides for presenting "monarchs in rags."[27] He also blames his audacity in writing improper tragedies, decadent melodramas full of "shameful tales of incestuous vice"[28] and other inappropriate themes:

> His bawds and his panders, his women who give
> > birth in the sacredest shrine.
> Whilst others with brothers are wedded and bedded . . .[29]

As the debate heats up, Aeschylus proposes to deflate all of Euripides' prologues by inserting the phrase *lēkythion apōlesen,* "lost his little bottle of oil":

EURIPIDES: When Egypt with great strain and toil
> > Brought fifty sons to Argos and then—
AESCHYLUS: —Lost his little bottle of oil![30]

For many years scholarly argument has raged about whether the bottle is or is not an allusion to the male sexual organ. We need only hark back to the beginning of the *katabasis,* where Dionysus complained of the "impotence" of contemporary dramatists, to see that this is a logical conclusion.[31] The humor is especially ironic since the mighty loins of Aegyptus fathered fifty sons. Obviously, having sired, he is now too tired. His bottle of oil must be exhausted.

The *Frogs* concludes with what seems like a happy ending. Dionysus' passion is diverted from a pang for Euripides to a zest for Aeschylus, and he takes the older playwright with him to the upper world in the hope that he can restore the glory of Athens. For Aeschylus does not merely represent the greater artistry. He is an emblem of the golden days of Athens, the battle of Marathon (in which he fought), and the mighty flowering of the arts.

The *Frogs* was an enormous success, the only play on record to have won a repeat performance.[32] For yet another fleeting instant the Athenians could ignore their imminent catastrophe. But less than a year after the *Frogs* was performed, Athens was starved into submission at the brutal hands of Lysander's Spartans and their Peloponnesian allies. Eupolis had prophesied the course of events, chastising the city (as Dicaeopolis had) in a painfully elegiac fragment:

> O polis, polis [polis]!
> Up to now you've been so lucky—but not so wise.[33]

The world—at least temporarily—had lost its sense of humor. Euripides' famous paradox, "Who knows if death be life or life death?"[34]— which Aristophanes delighted in mocking—was now no laughing matter.

It is often said that Old Comedy died intestate, that Eupolis, Cratinus, and Aristophanes had no influence on the subsequent comic tradition.[35] To a certain extent that is true. Despite efforts to prove Aristophanic influence in every age,[36] the spirited style of the early Athenian plays went the way of the dinosaur and pterodactyl (the latter for the *Birds*, of course). Alexandrian scholars found Aristotle's distinction to be helpful: the drama of "the old playwrights" *(tōn palaiōn)* was characterized by obscenity—*aischrologia*—and that of "the new" *(tōn kainōn)* by innuendo—*hyponoia*.[37]

But was it in fact a genre unto itself? A separate artistic entity? Or were Aristophanes and the other playwrights merely a stage, several stages perhaps, of a work in progress—the development of the single artistic form we now call "comedy"? There have been many frustrating attempts to define and describe Old Comedy as an independent genre.[38] A. W. Schlegel was among the traditional scholars who were outraged at the notion of Aristophanes being considered a mere way-station to Menander. To him the Attic playwright was "a genre original and pure."[39]

On the other hand, subsequent scholars have offered arguments in support of a "comic continuum," and view New Comedy as a natural outgrowth of its Attic predecessors.[40] Indeed, when Crates is praised by Aristotle for abandoning sheer invective,[41] we see a hint of actual dramatic structure. Another ancient commentator records that Pherecrates stopped indulging in raillery and became especially inventive at plot-making.[42] Moreover, we may infer that his *Corianno* presented some sort of romantic rivalry between a *senex amator* and his son—in other words, a typical New Comedy scenario as in Menander's *Aspis (The Shield)*, Plautus' *Mercator (The Merchant)*, and eventually Molière's *L'Avare (The Miser)*. As one critic has observed, "the fragments of Krates and Pherecrates are hardly distinguishable from the manner of the New Comedy."[43]

Perhaps there would be no dispute if the entire *Poetics* were extant. As it is, we have merely enough to justify our hypothesis. In chapter five of *Poetics* Aristotle gives but fleeting reference to the development of comedy and tragedy, with tantalizing and ambiguous explanations of their origins.[44] He then considers whether tragedy is a fully developed form and decides affirmatively.

Having begun as improvised episodes, tragedy "underwent many changes" and finally "came to rest" having reached its fullest natural form, its *physis*.[45] Aristotle's essential view is that tragedy had been fully developed since the early days of Sophocles' career. This would, of course, admit the *Oresteia* as mature tragedy as well.

Then, in the next chapter, Aristotle turns to comedy. He discusses how certain of its elements originated, but he does not consider whether comedy has reached its *physis*. He does note that comedy got a much later start, receiving an official chorus long after the public presentation of tragedies was an old and accepted tradition.[46] But even from the scant remains of fifth-century comedy we can see what drastic changes it underwent in a very short time. And it is of no small significance that Aristotle never once uses the term *kōmōidia* in reference to Eupolis, Cratinus—or Aristophanes.

Ironically, comedy was reaching its *physis* at precisely the moment Aristotle was composing the *Poetics*. For in Menander we find the first stage of "classic" comedy, what has been called *Normalklassik*.[47] In Menander the form is canonized; there are no more changes *(metabolai)* until Terence. Menander and Marivaux are cut from the same comic cloth; the *Birds* and the *Assemblywomen* are certainly not. Meter, as Aristotle notes, does not a genre make.[48] Indeed, most Plautine comedies have more lyrics than the *Assemblywomen,* three-quarters of which is in iambic trimeter. Moreover, every definition of comedy, from antiquity to our own day, refers exclusively to the Menandrian form.

At the same time, however, the notion of a "Middle Comedy"—a term coined by the third century B.C. scholar Aristophanes of Byzantium to refer to the sixty-year period between the end of Aristophanes' career and the beginning of Menander's—has recently been redeemed.[49] This middle ground is strewn with confetti of small quotations, and it is impossible to characterize it in detail except for a few generalities. We find a pronounced emphasis on food and drink, mythological burlesque, and the elaboration of the stock character types of New Comedy (cook, parasite, pimp doctor, and later the slave and soldier). All of these elements set it apart from the antipodes of the two more familiar genres.

But even here Old Comedy offers precedents for most of these features. We have seen the braggart warrior in *Acharnians,* the quack doctor in Eupolis.[50] The cook is prefigured in the Sausage-seller of *Knights,* while Xanthias in *Frogs* is an early impudent slave. Nor are mythological subjects totally absent from the early fragments, which feature such characters of legend as Prometheus, Agamemnon, Achilles, Odysseus, Amphitryon, Oedipus—and even Priapus. Middle Comedy provides its own distinctive view of these tales, and this establishes, however subtly, an unmistakably continuous evolution.

Menander, however, was so far ahead of his time, so mature, that he bears little resemblance to his fragmentary predecessors and contemporaries. In fact, this may well have been responsible for the later tripartition into Old, Middle, and New that we find articulated in Apuleius' description of Philemon as a "writer of Middle Comedy."[51] All in all, then, a clear picture of a continuous evolution emerges, albeit articulated by key figures—Aristophanes, Alexis, Menander—and the changing aesthetics of each generation.[52]

We may briefly note some of the aspects of Attic comedy which succumbed to the evolutionary process. The genesis of comedy resembles the Creation as told by Hesiod (and parodied by Aristophanes): in the beginning there was Chaos. The earliest comic writers were criticized for formlessness and chaotic construction. The cry is as old as comedy itself, for even Susarion, its semi-legendary inventor, is accused of managing things sloppily *(ataktōs).*[53] This is a charge hurled often at Aristophanes, and Cratinus was likewise criticized for *ataxia.*[54] One may excuse or explain this as the necessary result of Attic comedy's attempts to absorb all its variegated dramatic influences, for example, subliterary farce, the skits of Epicharmus, and so forth.[55]

Yet comedy ultimately rejected loosely-jointed vaudeville, growing more and more into tightly structured *mythos* or plot. The chaos in

Aristophanic Cloudcuckooville became the cosmos of Menandrian Athens. (We shall see a parallel phenomenon in the development of Roman comedy.)

When Athens fell to the Spartans in 404 B.C., not only were its famous Long Walls destroyed but a greater victim was the city's fabled freedom of speech, lauded by Herodotus as the source of the Athenians' valor.[56] The dramatic poets no longer dared to attack specific citizens by name—or to express themselves in *le langage vert*. And although the Spartan occupiers were gone within two years, perhaps their ascetic values lingered. For even in Menander's day the polis was still in a state of political turmoil: "during the thirty years of [his] career, everyday life in Athens rolled in a welter of war, siege, bloody rebellion and cruel vendettas."[57]

Still, although the overall metamorphosis was drastic, it was not wholly due—as some would have it—to the radical changes in political climate, however sweeping they may have been. The Athenians had lost their freedom, but not their marbles. Not even the savage war, the famine, the economic crisis, and the bankruptcy of everything, including hope, can explain all the changes that occurred in subsequent comedy.

The chorus, for instance—the original nucleus of the genre—was gradually but ineluctably marginalized. Complex lyrics, the *agōn*, and the *parabasis*, with all its overt political commentary, were eventually eliminated. By the time of Menander the chorus only performed *embolima*, "interludes" or *entr'actes* (literally "throw-ins"), completely divorced from the plot of the play. This was only partially a result of Athens' military difficulties, for they could have economized on such expenses as costumes and still had twenty-four singers in the chorus.

But somehow the chorus had gradually lost its impact on the audience. Greek theater was growing ever more detached from its ritual beginnings. An integrated chorus tended to break the coherent dramatic illusion that became so important in New Comedy. Moreover, elaborate lyric songs were a liability in plays that were increasingly exported to other parts of the cosmopolitan Greek world, for it was obviously impractical to train a new citizen group in each locale.[58] We shall see in the next chapter that the chorus was already waning in Euripides, and there is some evidence to suggest that this was true even of Cratinus.[59] But here too we must see the change as an evolution.[60]

There have been numerous attempts to explain why fifth-century comedy discarded its political and allegorical elements in favor of more personal and domestic matters. But the abandonment of attacks on public figures was not necessarily a result of the curtailment of political freedom. The topical allusions in Aristophanes proved to be impediments to the plays' afterlife, so time-bound that they became unintelligible within a few years. (Samuel Johnson admired Shakespeare for his observations on human nature, deploring his particular allusions that could mean nothing to later readers and audiences.)

In any event, there began a long period of transition in which the humor modulated from insult to innuendo. There is always the possibility of a change in taste, as there was in England in the late 1690s when the public seemed to tire of Restoration bawdiness and enjoy—if that is the right word—the sentimental drama of *comédie larmoyante,* brought by the likes of Colley Cibber to the London stage. Some scholars have suspected that the *theōrika,* a state subsidy which in the good old days had enabled poor, unpropertied citizens to attend the theater, had been suspended because of economic difficulties, and thus the theater became the exclusive property of the well-born and well-to-do.[61]

The New Comic playwrights' sudden concern with the private lives of mundane, if well-heeled, individuals was thus less the result of external agents than an ever-evolving awareness of what the average spectator really wanted to see. The comic theater had progressed and would ultimately present universal truths that would apply to all nations and all time—to the cosmopolis, a new concept, relating, if not to the brotherhood of men, at least to the improved cultural communication between the world's cities.

New Comedy—that is, the plays of Philemon, Diphilus, Menander, and many others—flourished between the late fourth and early third centuries. It was the hallmark of the Hellenistic age. In fact, the first play of Menander in 321 was presented only two years after the death of Alexander (and seventy years after the death of Aristophanes). We will examine in detail the defining features of New Comedy in Chapter 9; here we will simply observe that the metamorphosis of the older form was marked by a move from the fantastic to the realistic, from the crises of political celebrities to the mundane everyday problems of mundane everyday people. The haphazard *ataxia* of Old Comedy was abandoned for a logical, fixed structure which more and more satisfied the Aristotelian (later Horatian) desideratum of artistic unity,[62] culminating in the seamless dramas of Terence. This included the replacement of the *deus ex machina* with the long-lost-relative *ex machina* who unravels so many Menandrian and Terentian plots.[63] But perhaps its most striking feature was the "automatic" happy ending, much more mechanical and formulaic than the festive *kōmos* of the older playwrights.

The first author in whom we can discern these changing tastes is none other than Aristophanes himself. Like every great artist, he remained abreast of dramatic innovation—and probably even had an influence on it. Indeed, even his earlier plays show traces of what would become New Comedy. Under the reciprocal influence of Euripides, who was pioneering a comic *embourgeoisement* of myth and presenting the "domestic affairs" *(oikeia pragmata)* of great heroes, Aristophanes tended more and more to abandon the field of fantasy and focus on the home base of New Comedy: the humble—or even fashionable—home.

In fact, this locale had been impinging upon the Greek comic imagination from the earliest comedies on record. We need only recall the "first joke" of Susarion: it is an attack not on some sixth-century demagogue, but on the playwright's wife—the most domestic of *oikeia pragmata*. Cratinus's *Bottle,* although it contained a few allegorical characters, expanded the husband-wife dispute to a full-length domestic comedy in which the hero leaves his wedded wife for a mistress. One fragment shows Cratinus pondering what sort of plot *(paraskeuē)* the members of his household are concocting.[64] This intrigue-making suggests Plautus' *Casina,* not to mention Feydeau. And the universal comic concern with drink, sex, food, and invective is nothing if not *oikeia pragmata,* what Aristotle would have accepted as *ta phaulotera* ("the trivial"), which he regarded as the essential subject of comedy.[65]

Even in Aristophanes' earliest plays we can distinguish a tendency to domesticate as well as politicize. His dramatic style characteristically tends to the reduction of statecraft to housekeeping. Take the *Acharnians.* Is the hero really concerned with the state at large? Or is Dicaeopolis rather a private person who makes a private peace for private gain and celebrates a private Dionysia in his private home? His treaty is nothing more than a trade agreement enabling him to run his

own common market open to all cities.[66] The chorus observes that the
hero is out to make a fast profit and has amassed a good supply of
household items and luscious foodstuffs.[67] His motives are so egocen-
tric and personal that they are downright selfish. He flatly refuses to allow anyone else to enjoy his peace.[68] The chorus emphatically comments for a second time: "and he didn't want to share with anybody."[69]
In the finale, Lamachus leaves to fight a national war while Dicaeopolis
stays to continue his personal *kōmos*. The *Acharnians* does indeed celebrate the joy of peace and condemn the folly of war, but the tone is as
much domestic as polemic.

We find this same tendency in the *Knights,* when the slave
Demosthenes explains to the Sausage-seller that ruling the city is no
different from cooking up meat patties:

> It's a piece of cake: just do what you do now.
> Shake everything and chop it into mincemeat.
> Always try to catch the people's appetite
> With sprinklings of spicy rhetoric—sweetened to taste.[70]

This recipe anticipates Lysistrata's description of how women will
run the state as they do their households, untangling political problems the same way they sort out wool:

> As when we have a snarled thread, taking it like this,
> And working it gently this way and that within our spindles:
> We'll unravel the war in just the same way, if we may,
> Sending out emissaries hither and yon.[71]

The *Knights* and *Lysistrata* bring the government into the kitchen. In
an ironic bourgeois reversal of the *Oresteia,* which establishes Athenian
justice atop the Areopagus, the *Wasps* relocates the courtroom into the
living room. Here even the judgment urn is less important than certain
household crockery. Philocleon can prosecute the family animals while
close to the comforts of his chamberpot.[72] As he remarks when his son
has convinced him to remain at home:

PHILOCLEON: Look at this situation—how the oracles are coming true!
　　　　　　　For I had heard that the Athenians would some day

> Try cases in their homes, and before their doors
> Every man would set up a law-court in miniature.[73]

Finally, there is Praxagora in the *Assemblywomen,* who advocates the women's rule of "home economics"[74] and will refurbish the municipal buildings to turn the Athenians into one big happy family.[75] She explains to her husband Blepyrus her plans for the new administration:

> BLEP.: What way of life will you bring?
> PRAX.: Common for all. For I say that I'll turn the town into a
>   single house,
>   Breaking all together into one, so that everyone can visit
>   one another easily.
> BLEP.: But where will you serve dinner?
> PRAX.: I'll turn the lawcourt and the colonnades into dining
>   rooms.[76]

Moreover, the *Assemblywomen* presents more references to money than any previous Aristophanic comedy.[77]

This growing tendency toward domestication and financialization culminates in the *Plutus* (388 B.C.). Indeed, translating the English title as *Money* rather than the usual *Wealth* would give us a better idea of what has changed onstage, where private concerns dominate the atmosphere. This change of focus is also reflected in the name of the hero, Chremylus, a charactonym which might be translated as "Mr. McMoney" (from *chrēma,* material wealth). In Figaro's words, *l'or c'est le nerf de l'intrigue.*

Traditionally we think of the comic hero in terms of Balzac's definition in *La Comédie Humaine* as a young man seeking *une femme et une fortune.* Love and lucre are fundamental aspects of the genre. But where in his previous plays has Aristophanes presented the pursuit of money for its own sake? Does Dicaeopolis mention the prices of his market in the *Acharnians?* Does Peisetaerus in the *Birds* or Strepsiades in the *Clouds* specify anything except the desire to avoid their debts? Numerals never cross their lips. Logically, we know that the pipe-girls who graced the Athenian symposia must have been paid a fee.[78] But in the *kōmos* of Old Comedy we never see or hear about this—the comic hero gets his gratification gratis. The earlier Aristophanic heroes did not have any financial resources as such. They had no need for mundane matters like bank accounts—or even pots of gold.

This is because comedy in its most basic form presents an unmediated fulfillment of libidinal instincts. Money, by contrast, requires a certain intellectualization and abstraction of appetites. Freud considered the advent of currency one of the "sublimating" forces that began to inhibit the instincts. Quite simply, "money is not an infantile wish."[79] Banknotes are an abstract and dehumanizing concept. As Norman O. Brown explained:

> The desire for money takes the place of all genuinely human needs . . . thus the apparent accumulation of wealth is really . . . the impoverishment of human nature and desires, asceticism. The effect is to substitute an abstraction, *Homo economicus* . . . and thus to dehumanize nature.[80]

In other words, money is one of the earliest Discontents of Civilization. Comedy is growing up alongside civilization, progressing from the *kōmē* to the city. Indeed, if we accept Freud's analysis of obsession with money as the sublimation of anal eroticism, we might see the gradual rise of comic finance as a mature substitute for the scatological humor which was the stock-in-trade of Aristophanes and his colleagues. We shall see what this entails in New Comedy.

By the end of the fifth century and throughout the fourth, Plutus began to replace Phales as the central divinity of comedy as financial matters came more and more to the fore. The speeches of Lysias (c. 450–380) show a new preoccupation with money.[81] The orator constantly harps upon the poverty of the state—at the very time the *Plutus* was presented. Athens was not so rich as she had been. The invalid's pension, for example, was a meager *obol* per day—half of what Philocleon received for jury duty. Naturally this state of affairs would be paralleled by a changing comic aesthetic, since Old Comedy never ignored the interests of society at large.

Even in the *Acharnians* we have an indication of troubles to come when Dicaeopolis complains that before the war no one in the country ever used the verb "to buy," and "Mr. Purchase" was nowhere to be seen:

DICAEOPOLIS: Longing for my village
Where nobody ever said, "buy charcoal"
Nor "buy vinegar" nor "buy olive oil." They didn't even
know the verb "to buy"!
No: it produced everything itself and Mr. Purchase was
nowhere on the scene.[82]

The fabled Golden Age, alluded to here and treated so frequently by other Old Comedy poets, was a time when the food was said to grow, cook, and even serve itself. As Ovid tells it (note the agricultural language):

The first age sown was Golden, which cultivated
Of its own will faith and right, without a law or law-enforcer.[83]

But the decline from the Golden Age was marked by lustful materialism, "the love of possessions" *(amor habendi)*.[84] Among the many evils introduced by Zeus/Jupiter in the Iron Age was the introduction of money:

They went into the bowels of the earth,
And the wealth which [the creator] had hidden in the Stygian
gloom
They dug out, an incitement to evils.[85]

Here and elsewhere, Ovid condemns—or at least affects to—the "ferocious lust for riches" which brought the republic low.[86] Yet even in the days of Plautus, Roman comedy was already saturated with the language and humor of finance.[87] And one of Menander's characters even blasphemes, "For my part I consider the most useful gods to us / are silver and gold."[88] (We find in the same author the sentiment "you can't take it with you.")[89]

But in *Plutus* the interest in money is an innovation. We are now dealing exclusively with hard currency, a literally gilded age that will be stamped on coins of legal tender—Mammon as we know it today. Aristophanes is no longer dealing with the abuses of political power, theories of education, dramatic literature, or even sex strikes. In fact, the phallus seems tangential to the fabric of the play.[90] Likewise, all the plot elements that it symbolizes—unfettered, uninhibited, and unpurchased sex—are gone as well. Some have seen this as "the ultimate emas-culation of the genre."[91] And yet the organ was still hovering in the wings and remained so throughout later comedy, for human nature stays the same even when the codpiece is covered by robes and trousers. Thus, Aristophanic *aischrologia* yielded the stage to Menandrian *philanthrōpia*—an example of the change observed by Aristotle, from ob-scenity to innuendo.

Like the *Birds, Plutus* begins with two men—Chremylus and his slave Cario—following a trail that will change their destinies. But significantly, in contrast to the stark tree and rock of the earlier play, the decor of the *Plutus* is a street in Athens. This is but a few paces from New Comedy, which, as Donatus describes it, always deals with "private people living in town."[92] Indeed, the characters in the *Plutus* seem more human than in Aristophanes' previous plays, bespeaking a new realism.[93]

To the audience's initial puzzlement, the two are following a blind beggar. The first person to speak is the slave, who is likewise puzzled. He is not like the other bondsmen we have encountered in Aristophanes' earlier work. In fact, Cario has the largest part in the play. And he is far cheekier than, for example, Xanthias and Sosias, Philocleon's slaves who gossip irreverently in the prologue to the *Wasps*. The bondsman of *Plutus* is anticipated only by Xanthias of the *Frogs,* who outfaces his master Dionysus and proves himself the better man. But Cario is constantly insubordinate, insulting, and crafty. He rules Chremylus with a stunning lack of respect (does he not realize that a Greek master could put his disobedient slave to death?).[94] To begin with, he questions his master's sanity, complaining to the audience that he is "following a blind man—just the opposite of what he ought to be doing."[95]

When his master threatens him with a beating, Cario trumpets his immunity. It is true that he still wears the garland from the shrine at Delphi, which ostensibly protects him. But literary considerations are more important. Cario is the first in a long line of clever, scheming slaves whose prime talent was outwitting punishment, a character painted with particular ingenuity by Plautus. The barrier between slave and free in the ancient world was a "dividing-line stricter and more difficult to cross than any social barrier has been since."[96] Slavery was a subject of both awe and fear, and the subversive behavior of the *servus callidus* was always a prime source of laughter.

Chremylus is an old man—Aristophanes' last portrait of this character. But he is neither a buffoon nor a hero of any sort. And although he will enjoy a new lease on life thanks to his association with the title character, he will not be rejuvenated in the manner we have come to enjoy in Aristophanes. He is more anal-acquisitive than phallic.

The pair have been to the Oracle of Apollo. (We are in Ion-land: we shall see a number of Euripidean parallels when we consider the *Ion* in the next chapter.) Chremylus has asked the god how he should raise his son—to be righteous or a rogue. The slave interprets the reply as advising the more shamelessly the better, and tells his dull-witted master *(skaiotatos)*, "It's obvious, even to a blind man in this day and age."[97] With a parody of Euripides,[98] the slave is showing himself to be cultured. Not many of his low-born colleagues—or even high-born masters—could quote the classics. A similar character appears often in comedies of the Spanish Golden Age. The *lacayo latinizante* (latinizing lackey) is a familiar figure in the plays of Lope de Vega. Like so many slaves in Plautus, the lackey is far more clever than his master, and can quote—more often misquote—some learned tags from Latin literature. Holofernes, the stolid, pedantic schoolmaster in Shakespeare's *Love's Labour's Lost*, is a similar fount of old saws.

The old man reveals that the Oracle instructed him to follow the first man he encountered when he left the shrine. (This is obviously a conscious return to Ion-land: Aristophanes uses the same word—*ex-iōn*, "going out"—as Euripides.) The first person that Chremylus met was the disheveled vagabond. Cario now accosts the stranger and they run a familiar comic gamut of "misunderstanding":

> CARIO: Tell me your name immediately.
> MONEY: Go-to-hell!
> CARIO: O master, did you hear him say his name is "Go-to-hell"?
> CHREMYLUS: You asked him rudely. Now watch me. Kind sir, would
> you be kind enough to vouchsafe your name to me?
> MONEY: Go-jump-in-a-lake![99]

At last this odd creature relents, though not without qualms, for his name had always gotten him in deep trouble.[100] To the Athenian duo's consternation, he reveals that he is the god called Money and explains that he has had so many bad experiences that he does not wish to communicate with mankind. For he has always wanted to serve the good and shun the bad. Chremylus volunteers, "You won't find a better man than I," whereupon quickly Cario tops him by interjecting "Except for me."[101]

This quip is typical of the full-blown comic slave character, who is always flaunting his superiority to his master. As Beaumarchais' archetypal servant Figaro remarks:

> Considering the talents demanded in a servant, does Your Excellency know many masters who would be good enough to be valets?[102]

Beaumarchais' character is usually traced back as far as Plautus. But its true antecedent is not Plautus but *Plutus*.

The god goes on to say that, in a fit of jealousy, Zeus has blinded him because of his intention to do good, and now he cannot tell the honest citizens from the dishonest. If only he could, he would go only to the righteous—whom he has not seen for a long time. At this Cario again jokes to the audience, "Nothing surprising in that. I haven't seen any either—and I've got perfect vision."[103] Recalling the Oracle, Chremylus promises to cure Money and then uses logic to prove that the sightless deity is more powerful than Zeus (a replay of Peisetaerus' pitch to the Birds). He explains that mortals sacrifice to Zeus because they want to acquire wealth, yet they cannot perform the rites without money to pay for an ox or cake. But now that they have Wealth, "if Zeus proves troublesome, single-handed you can crush his power."[104]

Chremylus goes on to enumerate the many good things one can acquire with Wealth. Cario chimes in with his own earthy desiderata, which are exclusively for food (one thinks of Euelpides' enumeration of the eatables he would long to eat in Birdland). His attitude is typical of the comic slave in antiquity:[105]

CHREMYLUS: No one ever has enough of you.
Man can have too much of every other thing,
Of love—
CARIO: Of bread—

CHREMYLUS:	Of the arts—
CARIO:	Of sweets—
CHREMYLUS:	Of honor—
CARIO:	Of cakes—
CHREMYLUS:	Of courage—
CARIO:	Of figs—
CHREMYLUS:	Of seeking glory—
CARIO:	Of barley-loaves—
CHREMYLUS:	Of soldiery—
CARIO:	Of juicy stew![106]

Understandably, as the unique heir to *parrhēsia,* the slave is the only character who can speak boldly: the slave's bill of fare is a sexual menu with all the usual double-entendres.[107]

Cario now anticipates the Roman comedy figure of the *servus currens* or sprinting slave, as his master bids him race to the country to fetch his fellow farmers so he can share the wealth with them. The servant is extremely swift, for he returns only one line later, leading a group we have often seen—the familiar chorus of rustic antiques. Cario addresses them as "labor-loving"[108]—a rare use of libidinous language in this play. Like earlier Aristophanic characters, they are driven by their lusts, and, also consistent with the theme, the farmers' initial instinct is diverted into work—the precise antithesis of *erōs.* Cario (who does all the talking) offers them surcease from their "frigid and bad-tempered life"[109]— in other words, the joys of money.

The delighted oldsters break into a lively dance (instant reinvigoration?). And yet they have the smallest role of any chorus in Aristophanes. They sing but one number about the Cyclops, perhaps a parody of a recent and popular dithyramb on that subject by Philoxenus, one of the avant-garde New Musicians.[110] (It is also the most prominent of the rare moments of scatology in the play.) This *embolimon* bears at best a tenuous link to the rest of the play, unless it be the reference to the Cyclops' meager wallet.[111] The Old Comedy chorus has now been marginalized, to say the least.

And yet there is a dying vestige of the earlier plays in their anticipation of the reinvigorated protagonist. But, as we have seen, Money revives only Chremylus' purse, not his person. It is a secondary rebirth, not from youth to age, but merely from poverty to plenty. All the old-sters can now afford to hire pipe-girls the likes of Ms. Bountiful in the *Peace*. But remember—Trygaeus got her for free. This is not, like the *Birds*, a primal fantasy realized. It is pleasure compromised by business.

Like Aristophanes' typical geriatric protagonists, Chremylus has a plan, although it was really Apollo's—to take the blind god to the shrine of Asclepius.[112] This was an increasingly popular cult in late-fifth and early-fourth-century Athens.[113] After the unwelcome visit of the semi-allegorical Poverty, who argues stridently and agonistically that *she* is the Mother of Invention and is swiftly kicked out, Chremylus and Cario take Money for a vigil in the healing-god's temple.

The next morning, in a bravura set-piece for the leading actor, Cario narrates the dramatic occurrences of the previous night. The snakes of Asclepius restored the sight of Money, who is now completely healed. The long narrative is punctuated only by brief interrogations from Chremylus' nameless wife. (At least in this play she has a speaking part. Her younger sisters would have to wait until Menander to get a name.)

As Cario returns to his master's house, the chorus now re-enters skipping joyfully behind him. They persuade old Chremylus' wife to join them: "Kick your heels up, skip and dance away."[114] Here is another suggestion that they are reinvigorated, for in their terpsichorean activity we hear a faint echo of Wrong Logic's invitation to indulge the senses, Philocleon's uninhibited behavior, and Plato's description of the dream state.[115]

The reconditioned god of finance himself now enters with great pomp, greeting the mortals in grandiloquent tones reminiscent of Aga-memnon's arrival in the *Oresteia*.[116] As if to prove *plus ça change plus c'est la même chose*, even in this late play, Aristophanes gets in a last bit of self-praise. This time, since the chorus is not available, he uses the god as his mouthpiece.[117] Plutus declares that he will not celebrate outside, since the action would involve lowbrow behavior like tossing figs and candies to the audience to get a laugh—so unworthy of a great comic poet like Aristophanes. Of course we have seen the playwright use this very device in the *Peace*—among others. Even in his dotage the old man is up to his old tricks.

After Cario has chased away some of the familiar intruders who, as usual, want a piece of the action, Chremylus greets the most distinguished visitor of them all—none other than Hermes, messenger of the gods. Here is a vivid reflection of the finale of the *Birds*. Since Money acquired his sight, mankind has not put anything at all on the altars of the gods. In fact, the gods are starving and must sue for peace. A priest of Zeus will later testify that the temples are now empty and just used as toilets.[118] The mention of divine starvation would surely evoke memories of Lysander's siege of Athens even among the festive spectators.

Hermes has defected to the new ruler of the universe—Chremylus—and now seeks employment. He offers to serve in his most "comic" incarnation—a priapic herm. But this job is no longer open. The *hermai* had proved that they had lost their magic in the defeat of the Sicilian expedition. Besides, with all the money in circulation, the population would no longer need a garden statue to protect their homes—they could all afford live security guards. And so the god must settle for a job as an athletic coach.

In this pale echo of Peisetaerus' achievement in the *Birds*, Chremylus succeeds in getting the ruler of Olympus to submit to his authority: "Zeus the savior is within our house, coming of his own free will."[119] And now the cast, singing, parades off to reinstall Money in his former abode in Athena's temple.

All's right with the world. And yet is it not odd that we never see Chremylus spending any of his newly acquired lucre? Perhaps, like Ben Jonson's Volpone, he glories more in the acquisition than the disposition of his money. (Has the change from the moneyless society now gone too far in the opposite direction?) Perhaps the new emphasis on getting rather than spending was due to the impoverishment of Athens compared with the great days. In the *Plutus* this was channeled into a moral fable that prefigures the tone of New Comedy. Financial concerns will become the focal point in Menandrian drama, centering around the dowry. Thus we have seen the preoccupations of the comic stage move 180 degrees in the opposite direction, from the irrelevance of money to preoccupation with it.

That is all there is to the *Plutus*. It is a slight play, and not very carefully crafted. Its greatest interest lies in its chimerical form—half old, half new; half good, half bad (much like the bizarre half man/half horse used by Horace at the beginning of the *Ars Poetica* to describe an ill-formed work). There is certainly a discernible *kōmos* at the end of this play, but no one's thoughts are on a *gamos*. And, *pace* Mrs. Chremylus McMoney, there are no women to join the wedding dance.

The *Birds,* though Aristophanes' greatest play, was not his greatest hit. The most successful comedy in the poet's lifetime was the *Frogs,* produced triumphantly in 405 B.C., winning popular acclaim and first prize, with a reprise in the following season. Toward the end of the twentieth century, the "bawdy" *Lysistrata* with its themes ostensibly congenial to the agendas of both the women's liberation and anti-war movements (both concepts would have been alien to the author himself) became the play most often produced.

But during the more than two millennia between the poet's death and his recent "relevance," the *Plutus* was the best known of his plays. We need no better proof than to look at the number of surviving manuscripts for this anemic play: there are at least 148 editions of the *Plutus* extant as compared with the *Birds'* 18 and *Lysistrata's* 8—a rout by anyone's calculation. *Plutus* was the most acceptable Aristophanic comedy for teaching the young, since it contains none of the obscure deviant demagogues or rude language—or difficult meters—that characterize his other plays.

And yet Aristophanes' career did not end with the *Plutus.* According to ancient sources, he also composed what could almost have been a full-fledged New Comedy. We are told that his *Cocalus* contained "rapes and recognitions and all the other things that Euripides loved."[120] Some scholars, loath to accept the association of Euripides with the lighter genre, have insisted on emending "Euripides" to "Menander,"[121] who of course used these devices in almost every play he wrote. But in a way, both readings are correct—as we shall see in the next chapter.

8

The Comic Catastrophe

At every Aristophanic comedy there is always more than one Euripides: the poet onstage and the poet in the audience enjoying the flattery of being parodied as well as picking up a few dramaturgical tips for himself. For despite Aristophanes' constant derision of Euripides, he was a great admirer of the controversial playwright's works and, as we have seen, borrowed freely from his style, from burlesque to parody.[1] Aristophanes even boasted that he had improved on Euripides.[2]

But this was a two-way process. We find an equal and opposite reaction on the part of Euripides, who appropriated Aristophanic elements for his "tragic" style.[3] As but one example, the first stationary choral song *(stasimon)* in Euripides' *Helen* and the song of the hoopoe in the *Birds*—both odes to the nightingale—contain unmistakable verbal echoes, like the striking participles *elelizomenes* and *elelizomena,* which appear nowhere else in extant Greek literature in the sense "to trill."[4] The symbiotic relationship of the two playwrights was such that Cratinus, Aristophanes' ancient Old Comedy rival, coined the verb "to Euripidaristophanize."[5] This was not merely a joke. It was sound literary observation.

The relationship was recognized in antiquity. The lexicographer Pollux (second century A.D.) declared that Euripides was unique among tragic playwrights in borrowing techniques of the Old Comedy stage. The tragedian's (now lost) *Danae,* for example, had a comic *parabasis.*[6] Furthermore, Pollux adds, he did this not occasionally but "in many dramas."[7]

Euripides' earliest extant play, *Alcestis* (438), already reveals his bifurcated psyche. Here the sorrowful mourning for Alcestis is contrasted with the shameless roistering of their unwelcome guest Heracles in another part of the palace. With his bluster and excessive gorging and swilling, he is a character straight from the Old Comic stage. Not surprisingly, since it was produced in place of the usual satyr-play, the *Alcestis* ends happily when this bullying incarnation of *élan vital* conquers death and brings the heroine back to life.

But the *Alcestis* is not comic simply because of its happy ending: its setting and dialogue are frequently mundane and unheroic. The lavatory, for example, is never mentioned in "serious" Greek tragedy (or the nineteenth-century novel, for that matter). But Euripides broke down the barriers of intimacy and, for the first time, showed "rooms never before seen on the tragic stage."[8] As we have seen, Aristophanes makes the Euripidean caricature in the *Frogs* boast that he introduced *oikeia pragmata* ("domestic affairs," literally "household objects") to the tragic stage.[9] In the *Alcestis,* we hear about such mundane details as the unmade bed, the unwashed floor, and crying children.[10] As A. W. Schlegel complained, Euripides democratized myth, letting us "eavesdrop on gods and heroes in their pyjamas."[11]

Perhaps the most extreme example is the eerie *fin de siècle* black humor of the *Orestes.* At the climactic moment, Apollo appears *ex machina* just as Pylades, Electra, and Orestes—already a condemned murderer—are about to slaughter their hostage Hermione. Not only does the god stop the massacre, he orders Orestes to marry the girl at whose throat he is holding the knife. In addition, Pylades is to wed Electra. Most surprisingly, none other than Menelaus, the archetypal monogamist (whose wife this time has not been abducted but translated to heaven), is to take another wife. In this cadenza of whitewashing matrimony, Orestes is forgiven his matricide and all the antagonists go off on honeymoons. This black-humored example is in the spirit of the hypothetical comic ending posited by Aristotle, in which Orestes would confront his arch-nemesis and invite him for a drink (and nobody kills any-body).[12] Small wonder then that the scholiast remarked that "the play has a somewhat comic *katastrophē*" (an early critical term for the dénouement of a comedy).[13]

Even in the late fifth century, genre distinction was already a matter of scholarly debate, beginning with Socrates—as portrayed by Plato—who insisted on the outrageous (to the Greeks) paradox that tragedy and comedy could be written by one and the same playwright.[14] This conversation occurred at the party which celebrated the victory of a tragedy by Agathon, who, as a "new musician" like Euripides, may have provoked Socrates' observation through an unorthodox combination of comic and tragic elements.

The age-old question was given new impetus by the Menander finds in the 1950s, then by new Euripides fragments discovered among the Oxyrhynchus papyri, and finally by an influential article in which the *Ion* is identified as the "first modern comedy" because it contains, among other things, a lost baby play, a trickery play, and a wish-fulfillment play.[15] It also presents a humorous treatment of sex, as well as a traditionally comic character, the cuckolded husband. A simple reading from this perspective will demonstrate how *Ion* represents a significant step toward New Comedy.

The *Ion* begins with an "omniscient prologue" by the god Hermes, who provides the background to the drama and other information the audience will need to know in advance. In outline it sounds like a typi-cal Menandrian or Terentian plot. Years earlier the Princess Creusa was violated by the god Apollo in a nearby cave. Nine months thereafter she gave birth to a son whom, for fear of scandal, she exposed in his cradle in the place of her violation. In New Comedy, as we shall see, a rape has typically taken place before Act One, and the woman has either given birth or is about to. Naturally, what Aristotle called an *anagnōrisis*[16]—a recognition—is a common device in tragedy. The mother will be exoner-ated, and the baby will prove to be of distinguished parentage. The only difference here is that Creusa is a princess and her seducer is a god. The plot is more exalted—although the god's behavior is not.

While Creusa knew nothing of the boy's fate, Hermes has also told us that the Prophetess of Delphi found the child and raised it as her own. The boy, now grown, has entered the service of Apollo and has been entrusted with the responsibility of monitoring the temple's gold.[17] Meanwhile, Creusa has been given in marriage to Xuthus, a foreign ruler who had come to help her father in battle. The fact that he is a foreigner is much harped upon. As Creusa will tell Ion, "My husband is not a citizen of Athens, but an immigrant from another land."[18] Xuthus is neverthless a grandson of Zeus and, in the absence of any direct successor, the throne of Athens has passed to him. But his marriage to Creusa has been childless, and this problem has brought them to Delphi to consult the Oracle. Before he leaves, Hermes predicts that the young boy's parentage will be discovered and his name will be "renowned through all of Greece."[19]

We meet Ion as an innocent-looking young man, hard at work scrubbing the temple floor and serenading his broom. The absurdity of a piece of household equipment addressed in highly ornate language is furthered by the sight of Ion carrying a bow and arrow to prevent local birds from "befouling" the statues, a rare moment of tragic scatology. He emphasizes his fitness for divine service, being "holy and chaste."[20] All in all, it is a remarkably unselfconscious picture of a carefree youth leading a pure and dutiful life.[21]

The chorus enters, fifteen little maids from Athens on a day trip, all wide-eyed at the mythological carvings on Apollo's temple. As we will see, they scarcely have a role in the drama. Ion greets them cordially, remarking that "they look noble."[22] At that moment, Creusa enters in tears. When Ion asks why her "noble" face is wet, she answers that Delphi has stirred up unhappy memories. Identifying herself as the wife of the "foreign" King of Athens, she explains that they have come to the Oracle because they have no children. Ion reacts with surprise:

ION: No children? You've never given birth?
CREUSA: Apollo knows my childlessness.[23]

But Creusa is struck by something in the boy's presence, and now she questions him: "What is your name? Your mother must be very proud of you—I wish I were she." A sudden fog of ignorance descends upon the protagonists. For when Ion states that he was a foundling brought up by the prophetess ("I think of her as mother"),[24] Creusa inexplicably fails even to suspect that he might be the very child she is seeking. With mounting irony she proceeds to tell him in confidence about "a friend of hers":

CREUSA: This woman claims the god Apollo bedded her.
ION: *(disingenuously)* Not Apollo and a mortal woman—don't even say it!
CREUSA: But she insists it's true—and even bore a child by him and never told her father . . .
(with difficulty) She exposed the baby.
ION: What happened . . . is it still alive? . . .
CREUSA: She went back and couldn't find him . . .
ION: How long ago was this?
CREUSA: He would have been about your age by now.[25]

Even this statement falls on deaf—or stupid—ears. What will it take for this pair of innocents to put two and two together? Not only does Creusa pay no attention to her statement that Ion is the same age as her lost son, but Ion, who has been obsessing about his own parentage, likewise fails to see a spark, and merely offers his sympathies.

Suddenly, catching sight of her husband approaching, Creusa breaks off the conversation and with a frisson of incest begs Ion not to reveal what they have been chatting about, for "even the affairs of good women are always irritating to their husbands."[26] Ion watches silently as Xuthus tells Creusa the good news that the priest has prophesied that they will both leave Delphi with a child.[27] Anxious to consult the Oracle for further details, he hurries into the temple as Creusa leaves the stage.

At the end of a choral song—a prayer for fertility, a celebration of the joys of children, and a recapitulation of Creusa's dilemma—the maidens announce that Xuthus is about to appear. They know this because their leader has heard a melody that will re-echo throughout the centuries of all subsequent comedy—the sound of the door creaking. (Menander uses the same device in *The Samian Woman*.)[28] "But hark the sound of hinges—the master is approaching."[29]

The next scene is the touchstone for the argument.[30] Xuthus appears, beaming with joy. He spies Ion and rushes to embrace him, creating a misunderstanding of his intentions owing to the ambiguity of the Greek word *teknon* (literally "child," but also used by the *erastēs* as a term of endearment for his young beloved—like English "baby").[31] The boy's reaction indicates which of the two ways he has interpreted the salutation. Of course, his conclusion is colored by the fact that Xuthus is rushing towards him with open arms. Even the meter of the scene, trochaic tetrameter catalectic, is most often used for comedy:[32]

> XUTHUS: My child *(teknon)*, greetings. For this is the proper way to start.
>
> ION: *(resisting)* Er . . . thank you sir—but let's not get carried away.
>
> XUTHUS: *(lunging)* Let me kiss your hand and put my arms around your body.
>
> ION: *(shrinking back)* Stranger, are you crazy? Has some deity made you berserk?
>
> XUTHUS: Me, mad? When I have found my beloved boy and want to kiss him?
> *(He lunges again wildly)*
>
> ION: Stop—if you touch me you'll break Apollo's holy wreath!
>
> XUTHUS: I *will* embrace you. I'm not going to rape you.[33]

At this point, Ion draws his bow. Xuthus protests that if the boy looses the arrow, he will "kill his father," adding that Apollo has just told him that the first man he encounters upon leaving *(ex-ion-ti)* the temple would be his son—punning on the boy's (future) name, and recalling the same word-play in Aristophanes' *Plutus*. A moment later, the logical Ion asks the very logical question, "Who is my mother?" But the hapless Xuthus replies, discomfited, "Uh . . . I was so overjoyed for myself that I forgot to ask Apollo."[34] Ion is still looking for a human explanation:

> ION: Did you ever take a slut into your bed?
>
> XUTHUS: Er, yes. When I was young and foolish . . .
>
> ION: Have you ever been to Delphi?
>
> XUTHUS: Yes, some years ago—at the festival of Dionysus.
>
> ION: And you stayed with one of the organizers?

XUTHUS: Er, yes—and there were also some local girls there . . .

ION: *(finishing his thoughts)* And the steward introduced you?

XUTHUS: Yes, they were Bacchantes in the midst of their rites.

ION: Did you drink a lot?

XUTHUS: *(nodding sheepishly)* Well, after all, it *was* the festival.[35]

The lines anticipate Terence's neat description of a young man's loss of self-control at a similar festival:

> He was overcome by night, love, wine and youth—
> it's only human.[36]

New Comedy abounds in incidents of rape (or, as one scholar more charitably describes it, "forceful seduction").[37] This had a real basis in Greek life. For the fertility festivals were the only occasion at which young men could meet *proper* young ladies, who were otherwise closeted away in the *gynaikēiē*. These occasions had through the centuries maintained their uninhibited nature, and the participants indulged in much drinking and sexual freedom that would not have been tolerated under normal circumstances. As we have seen, the *kōmos* long preceded its theatricalization by Susarion, Epicharmus, et al., and persisted as an indispensable feature of the Old Comedy finale. The *kōmos* is just as important in New Comedy—but with a significant difference: it takes place offstage *before the comedy begins*. In New Comedy, the ultimate discovery of the pregnancy resulting from the peccadillo precipitates a recognition of identities and status which leads to a better life for all. Nonetheless, it is the act of fertility that sets the entire plot in motion. Thus the Old and New genres simply present different, complementary phases of the comic cycle.

This first *anagnōrisis*, though erroneous, elevates Ion's status from an orphan of unknown parentage to Athenian heir apparent (he will of course ultimately be revealed as Apollo's son). Here, Xuthus adds in an uncharacteristically mercenary tone: "you'll inherit not only your father's scepter, you'll get a lot of money. You won't be a bastard anymore but noble and rich."[38] This bourgeois attitude is part of the fabric of New Comedy, and we have seen that even Aristophanes' later plays display an increased amount of financial language, culminating in *Wealth*.

By the time of Menander, money is practically a protagonist in the drama.[39]

Xuthus announces a public birthday banquet, at which he will officially dub his newfound and symbolically reborn son Ion (he seems to have had no name before). There are many hints of rebirth all through this scene, especially in what follows.[40] Despite the public nature of the planned celebration, Xuthus nonetheless swears the chorus to silence, for he does not want Creusa to be hurt by learning of his newfound son. Since they have been standing awkwardly by, merely watching—incongruous in a plot involving secret stratagems— Xuthus' exhortation seems to comment metatheatrically on changing theatrical convention.[41] And yet, when Creusa enters with an elderly family servant in the next scene, the chorus immediately breaks the oath and tells her everything—a bid to assert its traditional dramatic rights.

Creusa is now at the depth of despair and, like so many other Euripidean heroines, longs for wings to fly away from her present pain.[42] She confesses her predicament to the old servant, who convinces her to kill Xuthus' newfound son. She agrees, quickly fetches a deadly poison made of Gorgon's blood, and gives it to the ancient culprit to slip into Ion's cup.

The geriatric retainer hastens to fulfill his mistress's commission, exhorting himself in an anticipation of early Hollywood black stereotypes like Mantan Moreland and Stepin Fetchit ("Feet don't fail me now!" / "Feet do your stuff").[43] Fortunately, Creusa's unwitting attempt at infanticide fails. As a messenger describes it, a flock of Apollo's birds swoops down on the party *just in the nick of time,* and one of them unfortunately drinks the poison intended for Ion and dies horribly. The old man is immediately discovered and confesses all. The crowd is incensed and demands that Creusa be punished. But, *just in the nick of time,* Creusa takes refuge at the altar on stage—a familiar motif in later Greek and even Roman comedy (Plautus' *Rudens,* for example, based on a play by Diphilus).

Ion now enters brandishing a sword, violently angry. Just as the young man is about to kill Creusa, the priestess appears—his "mother in deed if not in blood"[44]—carrying a small wooden object. With maternal severity, she orders the warring parties to cease and desist. Remarkably, she has chosen this, of all moments, to reveal to Ion the cradle in which she had first discovered him. Euripides has withheld the major *anagnōrisis* until the last possible moment. "These were the clothes that you were wrapped in," she says, and promptly leaves Ion in tears, suggesting that he embark on a search for his parents. He stares at the neonatal basket. He sobs that he was never held to his mother's breast and was abandoned "without a name" (*anōnumos*).[45] At last he summons the courage to look at his mother's trinkets. Tension mounts.

Creusa reacts first. "What image beyond hope and dreams do I now see?" she shouts,[46] rushing to throw her arms around the boy, who shrinks away from her forwardness. (Both Ion's "father" and mother are clearly demonstrative Mediterraneans.) Creusa tries to convince him by identifying the tapestry inside the basket. It features a Gorgon—what was nearly the source of his death is now the source of his rebirth. Yet Ion is still dubious, even when she states correctly that the cradle will also contain a golden necklace wrapped in an evergreen wreath of olive.

Finally, the young man, overcome with emotion, embraces his mother and starts to kiss her, and both express their ecstasy at actually holding one another in their arms. Ion sums up the feelings of both: "This is the thing I least expected in the world."[47] Creusa exults, "I am childless no more."

But she says more to make this a comic moment. Invoking her distinguished ancestors, she declares that Erectheus, founder of Athens, "has been reborn." The King whom she calls upon to return to the living has long been ruling as a deity of the Underworld. Her language is strengthened by the familiar—but here very appropriate—metaphor of the situation going from darkness into the clear light of day.[48]

But all the loose ends are not yet tied up. There is still the matter of his father. When he questions her, she is still evasive, causing Ion to jump to the mistaken conclusion that he is of ignoble parentage. After spinning out the tension a bit longer, she reveals at last that Apollo had made love to her long ago.

Now her son is overjoyed. Contrast this elation with his harsh judgment in the earlier conversation, incredulous that Apollo could go to bed with her "friend." Yet now it is acceptable because *he* is the child concerned. "What wondrous things you speak—if they are true."[49] When he finally assimilates the good news, Ion sings an ode to Tychē, ever-changeable Fortune—the arch-deity of New Comedy—who has made things right at last.[50]

And yet doubts linger. Ion whispers to his mother, "Are you sure you're telling the truth and not just fobbing it off on Apollo?"[51] Suddenly, a god appears *ex machina* to untie the final knots. Surprisingly, it is not whom we expect. Instead, Athena has come since Apollo himself is "too embarrassed" to show his face.[52] The goddess immediately explains who's who, foretelling that Ion's descendants will be the Ionians, and that Creusa and Xuthus will give birth to the other eponyms Doros (whence the Dorians) and Achaeus (whence the Achaeans). And she reminds Creusa to maintain Xuthus' "happy deception" to ensure that Ion's accession goes smoothly.[53]

All's well that end's well, and they go off singing.

But has it really ended well for Xuthus? Henceforth he will live in ignorance—knowing less, in fact, than the lowly members of the chorus. As the butt of other people's trickery, he is the most "comic" character in the play. The reason is archetypal. As Euripides emphasized earlier, Xuthus is "not of this city" (*ouk astos*), but an "outsider" (*xenos*) in a closed society, an alien among citizens.[54] As with all traditional comedies, just as with the predramatic *kōmos*, the conclusion involves the reintegration of society, with the alien spoilsports ostracized. Euripides employs this theme prominently in his other comedies, and it returns to play a vital role in Menander and New Comedy.

Xuthus is also the ancestor of another comic type, the *mari philosophe*—the husband who knowingly, or semi-unknowingly, opens his wife's door to visitors. Dr. Nicia, the fatuous old pantaloon in Machiavelli's *Mandragola,* is another example of this type. More brutal is Jupiter's cuckolding of Amphitryon in Plautus' play of that name. And in our own day the willingly-cuckolded husband appears in Sidney Howard's Pulitzer Prize-winning *They Knew What They Wanted* (1924).

The pattern of the *Ion* conforms to what Freud and Rank would describe as a *Familienroman* ("family romance"). In this fantasy an adolescent dreams that he will discover he is really from a noble family, or at least has a "better" parent than his current one; or, if he is an orphan, he will be discovered to be of noble birth:

> The entire endeavour to replace the real father by a more dis-
> tinguished one is merely the expression of the child's long-
> ing for the vanished happy time, when his father still ap-
> peared to be the strongest and greatest man, and the mother
> seemed the dearest and most beautiful woman.[55]

Ready examples from the English novel include *Tom Jones* and *Oliver Twist*. Ion is thus but one early example of a long tradition. Certainly, Apollo and Creusa are better parents than a basket and a cave.

Why the audience takes so much joy from such discoveries can be ex-plained by Aristotle's assertion that the happy ending is demanded by the "weakness of the audience" *(astheneia tōn theatrōn)*.[56] As John Gay ex-pressed it at the end of *The Beggar's Opera*, when the rogue MacHeath is saved from the gallows: "All this we must do to comply with the taste of the town." The *anagnōrisis* in *Ion* prefigures the hundreds of recognition scenes in New Comedy where a child thought to be foreign turns out to be Athenian after all.

The watershed year in Euripides' development was 412 B.C. A number of scholars argue that the *Ion* was performed that very year, though there are other opinions.[57] It is more than the evidence of the perfor-mance records *(didaskalia)* that strengthens the argument: there is a psychological reason why at this time the Athenian audience would have particularly hungered for tragedies with more happy, "comic" endings. The much-vaunted Sicilian Expedition, whose high hopes we saw parodied in the *Birds*, had been utterly destroyed the year be-fore. In addition, according to Thucydides, Athens was beset by over-crowding, a financial crisis, lack of food, and a "great fear and trem-bling" in general.[58] The sophists—those radical new educators who were lampooned in the *Clouds*—had called traditional values into question. The Ionian cities were in revolt (which makes the Ion myth topical). Worst of all, the polis was on the brink of oligarchic revolu-tion.

The date of the *Ion* may be in doubt, but we have certain knowledge of two of the plays presented by Euripides in 412: the *Helen* and the lost *Andromeda*.[59] Some scholars regard the *Ion* as the third play of the trio. The *Helen* was anticipated two years earlier in another Euripidean proto-comedy, commonly referred to as *Iphigenia in Tauris*.[60] (It literally means *Iphigenia among the Taurians,* because a place called Tauris never existed. In fact, there is a strong argument that Euripides invented the entire plot.) The *Iphigenia* has so many traits in common with the *Helen* that some have referred to them as two versions of the same play.[61]

One scholar has offered a detailed comparison as a springboard for discussing the influence of "operatic Euripidean drama" on later operas like Mozart's *Abduction from the Seraglio* and Rossini's *Italian Girl in Algiers*. The recognition scenes of both the *Iphigenia* and the *Helen,* for example, are highly melodramatic lyric dialogues:

> The *pathos* is underscored by the grand duet in lyric meters,
> exquisitely melodramatic, between Orestes and Iphigenia . . .
> a key moment brought out especially by . . . the unusually
> lofty and excited music and rhythm.[62]

It was for such metrical and melodic complexity that Euripides and other contemporary musicians were frequently parodied by the comic poets. And yet Aristophanes indulges in the same broad range of musical innovations in his own lyric, which cannot all be attributed to parody.[63]

Both the *Helen* and the *Iphigenia* present a damsel in distress rescued from a barbarian land by a hero whom at first she does not recognize. In addition, in each play the escape of the noble Greeks is blocked by a cruel barbarian ruler. Both dramas make ample use of the essentially comic meter employed in the *Ion* recognition scene. And the heroine of each dreams up a trick to dupe a gullible monarch into letting her go off and escape—the sort of action Plautus would call a *frustratio*.[64]

The *Iphigenia* begins with yet another expository prologue. As with all comedies of mistaken identity, the audience has to be carefully instructed as to who is related to whom. Iphigenia establishes her mythological credentials by identifying herself as the great-granddaughter of

Pelops, and dispels the myth of her death at Aulis. Betrayed by her father into believing that she was to marry Achilles, she arrives in bridal white only to be seized by the Greeks and sacrificed to Artemis.[65]

In this version, however, she has been saved by the goddess at the last minute and wafted to a far-off land, where she is forced to serve as priestess and sacrifice any strangers that might trespass. Iphigenia longs for rescue from this barbaric place. In fact, she had dreamed the night before that she was at home again and saw the palace in ruins: "one pillar alone was left in my father's house."[66] This was clearly her brother Orestes. She then saw herself sprinkling water on the column and takes this to mean that Orestes is now dead.

No sooner does she re-enter the temple than her brother appears (very much alive) with Pylades, his loyal friend. They are aware of the dangers they are risking. For the trespass of strangers is punishable by death, and the place is already dripping with blood.[67] Still persecuted by Furies—albeit "freelance" ones who continue to hound him for killing his mother[68]—Orestes has been told by Apollo that he will get surcease from his punishment if he can bring back the statue of Artemis from the temple. Seeing the high security, he is disheartened at the prospect, and suggests that they escape. Pylades gives him courage, and they start back to the ship.

A moment later they are captured (offstage) by the Taurians and dragged before Iphigenia in chains to be sacrificed as alien trespassers. The swiftness of the scenes and the speedy exits of the characters lack only the slamming of imaginary doors to be farce. She gazes at the two strangers and wonders who their mother and father were, and whether they have a sister who will miss them when they are killed. And Orestes wonders who *she* is. She asks him for his name, to which he replies, somewhat perversely:

> ORESTES: Call me Unlucky *(dystychēs)*.
> IPHIGENIA: That's the name that fortune gave you. What's your real one?
> ORESTES: "The nameless die unmocked."
> IPHIGENIA: Are you so great that I can't know your identity . . . ?
> ORESTES: You'll only execute my body, not my name.

IPHIGENIA: Can't I even know what city you are from?

ORESTES: Why should I help you, since I'm going to die?[69]

At last he vouchsafes that he is from Mycenae. Iphigenia is excited at the mention of her native city. She then asks about Troy and, in stichomythic question-and-answer, gets all the good and bad news. This includes her father's death at the hands of Clytemnestra and Aegisthus, and Orestes' revenge by killing the killers. Iphigenia does not mourn her mother: she is more anxious to know if the avenger is still alive. Orestes replies enigmatically, "He lives both everywhere and nowhere."[70]

Hearing this, Iphigenia proposes to send a letter back home. Orestes nobly insists that Pylades be the messenger while he stays and is sacrificed. "Would that my sister's hand could lay out my corpse," he laments.[71] Iphigenia reassures him with unconscious irony that she will perform these offices.[72] While she goes to get her letter, Orestes and Pylades discuss this unusual priestess, and speculate that she must have "some connections" in Argos—a logical conclusion since she is going to great pains to send a letter there. Iphigenia reappears with her message, and, as a dramaturgical trick, Euripides portrays her as so worried about Pylades' losing the letter that she has him memorize the message. Thus Orestes gets to hear it:

IPHIGENIA: "Dear son of Agamemnon, your sister was not slain at
          Aulis, she is alive."

ORESTES: *(stunned)* Iphigenia alive? Has she come back from the
          dead?

IPHIGENIA: You're looking at her right now. But don't interrupt my
          letter.[73]

Orestes' head is spinning as Iphigenia continues to dictate, concluding with a plea for her brother to rescue her. She then explains to Pylades how Artemis rescued her at Aulis, and hands him the letter for Orestes. Pylades turns to his friend and delivers it to him. "It's from your sister," he quips.[74]

But Orestes has already got the message and rushes to his sister to throw his arms around her. At this point the chorus—who has been watching the episode in silence—senses rape and chastises him: "Stranger, to touch a priestess of the goddess is sacrilege. Do not embrace her robes."[75] We are reminded of the recognition scene between Xuthus and Ion, where the older man's powerful emotions were comically misinterpreted as a sexual pass. It is once again time for the characters to demonstrate their inability to put two and two together, for again the *anagnōrisis* must be spelled out in excruciating detail.

Iphigenia adamantly refuses to accept his claims:

> IPHIGENIA: You cannot be Orestes; he's in Argos.
> ORESTES: *(frustrated)* Your brother is *not* there, you wretched girl.
> IPHIGENIA: *(still incredulous)* Was Tyndareus' daughter your mother?
> ORESTES: My father was the grandson of Pelops.[76]

Even at this, she still is incredulous and interrogates him further about domestic details. He speaks of incidents that occurred with their sister Electra—and, most important, gives the details of a tapestry that Iphigenia once wove.[77] Finally won over, she throws her arms around her brother. (There is much emphasis on the tactile: "I am actually holding you, Orestes.")[78]

This scene marks what could well be designated Act One. Just as the first part was a mini–recognition drama, the second will be a trickery play, which might be subtitled "The Bamboozled Barbarian." Iphigenia at first offers to arrange Orestes' escape, though she would have to remain among the Taurians and face certain death.[79] But then she has a brainstorm, a stratagem that will trick King Thoas.[80] Since the Greek visitors are matricides, their approach has sullied the precinct and they will need to be purified along with the statue (before putting the trespassers to death). This obscure ceremony involves taking the statue into deep water far from shore. At that point they will make off for Greece.

Orestes approves of the plan and comments: "Women are good at finding tricks *(technas)*."[81] (As one critic remarked light-heartedly, "Euripides was a misogynist, or else he was the first feminist, or else the charges cancel out.")[82] Then, in the kind of scene we have encountered in the *Ion,* Iphigenia makes the chorus—all of whom are now privy to the secret plans—swear to be silent.

At last King Thoas enters, hoping he is in time to witness the aliens sacrificed. He is dumbfounded to see Iphigenia emerge from the temple carrying the statue of Artemis. But she has an act prepared, the same tactic employed by the clever slave Tranio in Plautus' *Mostellaria* (which Ben Jonson in turn copied in the *Alchemist*). To mask the mischief, someone blocks the way to the evidence (usually the front door to a party) and scares off intruders by pretending that the house is haunted. Here Iphigenia terrifies the king by asserting that Artemis' statue is cursed and he must keep his distance lest he himself be defiled:

> THOAS: How do you know the victims are contaminated?
>
> IPHIGENIA: I saw the statue move when they approached.
>
> THOAS: Couldn't it have been a little earthquake?
>
> IPHIGENIA: No, I even saw her close her eyes.[83]

The gullible king is shocked. When he asks if they could now slaughter the two Greek visitors as a sacrifice, Iphigenia objects, quoting an unfamiliar temple "law":

> IPHIGENIA: We must first purify them—in the sea . . .
>
> THOAS: Well, at least that would please Artemis.
>
> IPHIGENIA: *(with a wry smile)* It would please me much more.[84]

She suggests meekly that the royal dupe have the strangers tied up so they won't escape. The king is puzzled. "This is the end of the earth. Where could they possibly run?" At which point Iphigenia melodramatically says, "You can never trust a Greek in anything." This joke would raise a laugh of Aristophanic magnitude. Finally, she warns the king not to look:

> IPHIGENIA: Cover up your eyes with your sleeve—
>
> THOAS: Lest I be contaminated?
>
> IPHIGENIA: *(nodding)* And if I do seem to take a lot of time—don't be upset.
>
> THOAS: Take as long as you like—just do it properly.
>
> IPHIGENIA: *(meaningfully)* I hope it succeeds the way I want it to.
>
> THOAS: *(naively)* I hope so too.[85]

The procession to the beach begins with Iphigenia confiding (to the audience? to the chorus?) that she has used "the blood of lambs" instead of her friends.[86] The action is the mirror image of Iphigenia's original rescue from the beach at Aulis. There Artemis saves her by substituting an animal; here she rescues *Artemis* by doing exactly the same thing.

One hymn to Apollo later, a wounded soldier appears bellowing frantically for King Thoas, to whom he immediately spills out that they have been tricked. The prisoners and Iphigenia have all escaped, and, from the departing ship, one of the Greeks shouted that he was Orestes:

> THOAS: Which Orestes do you mean? Not the son of Agamemnon?
> ... *(amazed)* That's like some sort of miracle.
> SOLDIER: Stop standing there in wonder, King—think about how you can catch them!
> THOAS: They won't get away. Our spears will bring them back.[87]

But the ship is already at sea "like wings above the deep."[88] This "flight" from danger is the fulfillment of three impossible wishes for winged escape voiced throughout the play.[89] At this crucial moment, Athena suddenly appears *ex machina* and bids the king desist from trying to capture the escapees. She cleans up some unfinished business, obtaining the return of the chorus of Greek maidens, whom Orestes and Iphigenia have carelessly left behind. Thoas' anger is completely dissipated, and he meekly wishes Orestes and Iphigenia a *bon voyage* back to Greece.[90] Once again, all's well that ends well.

Then, in 412, came the *Helen.* It is not a coincidence that the notorious protean creature Alcibiades, leader of the Sicilian expedition as well as one of the fomenters of the Ionian revolt, was reviled by his contemporaries as a Helen. So, in its way, Euripides' play of that name had its own topical dimension. Scarcely a year after *Helen* was performed, Aristophanes parodied it—and other escape plays—in his *Thesmophoriazusae (Women at the Thesmophoria)*.[91] This comedy presented the fanciful idea of the women of Athens attacking Euripides for slandering them. Needing someone to speak on his behalf, Euripides has convinced his "In-law" to disguise himself as a woman and sneak into the women's festivities. (Indeed, with the minor exception of the Scythian archer, all the male characters dress up as, or resemble, females.)[92] When the "In-law" is discovered and captured by the women, he tries to free himself by enacting some of Euripides' most famous escape dramas. He recites from the prologue to the *Helen,* among other passages, giving us the best evidence of what struck the audience most about Euripides' innovations.

And innovations they were. In the *Thesmophoriazusae,* Aristophanes refers to Euripides' play as *hē kainē Helenē,*[93] most frequently translated as "his recent Helen." But the adjective *kainos* means more than that. In the *Birds,* for example, the Hoopoe convokes the avian assembly with the news that a senior citizen from Athens has brought them a "novel" idea for a "novel" enterprise:

> Here comes a shrewd old codger,
> New in notions, new in planning,
> Innovative.[94]

Kainon is something invented fresh—and it is the most significant characteristic of the comic poet's task.[95] In a famous fragment, the fourth-century comic playwright Antiphanes compares the tasks of writing tragedy and comedy, arguing that whereas the tragedian retells stories already known, his opposite number does not have this advantage:

> But we comedians aren't so lucky. We must
> make it all brand new (*kaina*)—brand new names,
> brand new plots, brand new dialogue.
> The past, the action, the dénouement,
> even the opening—all must be brand new.[96]

Euripides actually announced the *Helen* as a coming attraction the year before in the epilogue to his *Electra.*[97] In a sort of "trailer" at the end of the play, Castor and Pollux *ex machina* announce to the matricides Orestes and Electra that they will be exiled and that Menelaus will come to bury Clytemnestra when he arrives with Helen from Egypt, adding "she did *not* go to Troy. Rather, Zeus sent a phantom to try to cause passion and strife."[98]

In Euripides' *Helen* the "novelty" is in evidence from the outset. The first scene of the play is a visual paradox. The heroine—like Iphigenia for her "wedding"—is dressed in bridal white, seated on a tomb (of "deathless" Proteus!) in the center of the stage. Helen sings that to preserve her chastity she has taken refuge here by the "beautiful virginal waters."[99]

This ascription of "purity" to the notorious femme fatale would certainly come as a shock—and doubtless a laugh—to the audience. Helen, of course, was usually perceived as a nymphomaniac. Witness Hecuba's accusation in the *Andromache* of her "insatiable bed-hunger."[100] Or Martial's epigram about the chaste Roman matron who went off to the seaside at Baiae:

> She fell into the flames: and leaving her husband ran off with her
> lover.
> Penelope she came, but she went home a Helen.[101]

Quite the opposite of the woman in Martial's epigram, Euripides' Helen has been Penelopized. The erstwhile femme fatale has never thought of going to bed with any other man, and is clinging to the grave of Proteus "to keep her bed unsullied."[102] Despite years of waiting, she has kept her honor intact: "though I bear the name of infamy in Greece, yet I have kept my body *(sōma)* free of shame."[103] Moreover, the epic poets were wrong to tell us that she caused the Trojan War. On the contrary, when Paris stole off with her she was saved from disgrace much the way Iphigenia was rescued at Aulis. Hermes snatched her up and wafted her to Egypt, where all those years she could "keep my bed *(lechos)* safe for Menelaus."[104] Euripides chose this unlikely variation of the myth for a supreme comedy.[105]

This play thus asks the question, "Was this the face that launched a thousand ships?" and answers "No." Surely our reaction is that of Theseus in *A Midsummer Night's Dream,* who comments that this is "hot ice and wondrous strange snow" when told that the rude mechanicals will present a play of "very tragical mirth."[106]

The drama is set on the island of Pharos "near the mouth of the Nile." The exoticism of distant countries becomes a traditional comic motif, setting a tone of unreality to create an inversion of the normal, mundane world in which there is not always a happy end. Here Euripides' dramatic setting seems to have been directly inspired by Herodotus.[107] In fact Menelaus' travels have an intertextual aspect. Before coming to Egypt he has been buffeted about the sea, even as far as the lookout-tower of Perseus (on the west side of the Nile delta):

> MENELAUS: You ask me much in one word and of one road.
> Why should I tell you of the losses in Egypt, and the Euboean watch-fires of Nauplius, and Crete and of the cities of Libya, which I wandered, and the Heights of Perseus?[108]

Euripides not only draws on Herodotus' description of the boundaries of Egypt,[109] which also extend to the self-same Heights of Perseus, but simultaneously gives a dramatic preview of the *Andromeda*, which would be presented later that same afternoon.

The action takes place on a single day. The play begins with Helen's plaint that her chastity is imperiled. The benevolent old king Proteus, who had protected her all these years, has now died, and his son Theoclymenus, a barbarian in every sense of the word, "hunts me to have me."[110] Helen has taken refuge on the altar of the deceased but "deathless" king Proteus. She is preoccupied with the threat of rape and the violation of her bed—a word she repeats seven times in her opening speech alone. In fact, this play has more references to the marital couch than *Medea*, where the heroine is likewise obsessed by the bedroom.[111]

First Teucer arrives, a refugee from Troy. He is shocked to see Helen in this godforsaken place, which reminds him of Hades.[112] When he recovers enough to speak, he gives her news of what has happened since Ilium fell. Menelaus, he reports, has vanished in a shipwreck. The literary motif of the shipwreck, which became common in later comedy, develops the theme of chaos and loss of identity that is an essential part of the *kōmos*. One thinks of comedies like *Twelfth Night* and *The Tempest* (not to mention Plautus' *Menaechmi* and Molière's *Miser*), in which the drama is launched by a storm splitting the characters' ship and separating them. In Shakespeare's words, it "does make divorce" of the characters, who will unite only in the finale.

Thus Teucer can only say that Menelaus has been reported dead. Helen also learns that her twin brothers, Castor and Pollux, are "dead and not dead": rumor has it that they have been made stars.[113] Teucer then leaves on his winged ship to go to Cyprus to start life afresh and live happily ever after in a New Salamis.

Helen warns him to be careful because, as in the *Iphigenia,* any Greek found trespassing must be put to death. Teucer thanks her and pays her the utmost compliment—she may have the body *(sōma)* of Helen, but she does not have her evil nature.[114] The chorus, exactly as in the *Iphigenia,* is composed of captive Greek women as pure as the new Helen herself—and dramatically just as superfluous. They enter and ask Helen if she has succumbed to "barbarian beds."[115] Helen then sings of how, when Paris tried to make off with her, Hermes swooped her up as she was picking fresh flowers. We had a similar example of innocence violated in Apollo's rape of Creusa.[116] This image also evokes the myth of the blameless Persephone kidnapped by the infernal god Hades as told, for example, in the Homeric *Hymn to Demeter.* Here, in the Euripidean simile, Helen's rehabilitation attains a cosmic level, for she becomes a kind of seasonal goddess like Persephone, who, we recall, would spend half the year in the underworld and then return with the spring to bless the crops.

A few moments later, Menelaus, who has just been mourned as dead, arrives alive and dripping. He is a typical Euripidean hero in rags, and his unfashionable garb prevents Helen from recognizing him. He indicates his own self-consciousness at his torn clothing and expresses his discomfort ("when a great man has bad luck it makes him feel worse than an ordinary beggar").[117] In fact, his wardrobe proves a source of discomfort to Helen throughout the play. He identifies himself to the audience with the same genealogical boast which Iphigenia used, claiming descent from Pelops.[118] He has been wandering ever since the Greeks' victory, trying to win his homecoming (as he repeats several times). But now he has been shipwrecked and has drifted alone up onto the shore. He thinks he has left Helen in a cave guarded by sailors.

He is wretched and penniless.[119] Catching sight of the imposing palace of the King, he decides to knock and get his due as a famous guest. There ensues a broadly comic scene with a cranky old lady who guards the royal door. It is a battle in which the stakes are his own identity. Immediately upon seeing him, she castigates Menelaus: "You are a Greek and Greeks are not allowed here." She then unceremoniously pushes him. He protests, "I am a shipwrecked foreigner of inviolate race."[120] But she cuts him down to size: "You may have been a great man at home but you are not one here."[121]

At this Menelaus bursts into tears (not usually considered a heroic reaction). He incredulously asks the woman to repeat herself. The irate woman replies, "It is because Zeus' daughter, Helen, is in this house." Menelaus' shocked reaction must be of epic proportions:

MENELAUS: What? What is this you are telling me? Say it again.
OLD HAG: I mean Tyndareus' daughter who lived in Sparta once.
MENELAUS: Where did she come from? What is the explanation of this?
OLD HAG: She came from Lacedaemon and made her way here.
MENELAUS: When? Has the wife I left back in the cave been carried off?
OLD HAG: No, no, she came before the Achaeans sailed for Troy. So get away from here quietly. The state of things inside is such that all the great house is upside down.[122]

Some commentators have tried to explain away Menelaus' obtuseness.[123] But the Greek hero's conclusion shows that he is merely a comic fool:

All the while some other woman with the same name
As my wife has been living in this house. She said
That this one was by birth the child of Zeus. Can there be
Some man who bears the name of Zeus and lives
Beside the banks of the Nile? There is one Zeus—in heaven . . .
I suppose it must be that in the great world a great many
have the same name, men named like other men, cities
like cities, women like women. Nothing to wonder at.[124]

So much for the uniqueness of the tragic hero. By contrast, Menelaus' attitude is exactly like that of the slave Sosia in Plautus' *Amphitruo*. When outfaced by Mercury, who claims he is the real Sosia, the bondsman can only conclude, "we've all been twinned"—and slink off in surrender, muttering: "I've got to find myself another name."[125]

At last the long-awaited *anagnōrisis*. Having just learned that Menelaus is alive, Helen suddenly emerges from the temple (compare Xuthus in the *Ion* having just heard that he had a living son). She cries passionately to her absent (she thinks) husband: "Would that you were here, dear one."[126] This is another of the self-fulfilling wishes that would pervade Greek New Comedy, for Menelaus stands right before her eyes. (Compare Iphigenia's longing for Orestes, who enters immediately after she despairs of seeing him.)[127]

Yet when Helen first sees Menelaus, she thinks he is just another of Theoclymenus' thugs "hunting her" with rape in his eye.[128] She also adds the gratuitously bourgeois comment that this stranger is dressed like a "hick" (*agrios*)—the inhabitant of the country village *kōmē*, and the archetypal comic figure.[129] Helen rushes back to the tomb for asylum. They talk it over:

> MENELAUS: You are more like Helen, woman, than any I know.
> HELEN: You are like Menelaus, too. I don't know what to say.
> MENELAUS: But that is my name. Look—I am Menelaus.
> You recognize me as a most unhappy man.
> *(Her eyes suddenly widen)*
> HELEN: Oh, at last returned to the arms of your wife![130]

As she reaches out to embrace him, Menelaus suddenly shrinks back:

> MENELAUS: Wife? What do you mean? *(As she tries to touch him again)*
> Take your hands off my clothes![131]

This is similar to Orestes' misunderstood "rape attempt" of Iphigenia as well as Xuthus' lunge to embrace Ion.

At long last Menelaus and Helen convince each other that they are who they claim to be. Dreading the thought of cuckoldry, Menelaus inquires whether Helen has "held off" the barbarian king. She replies that she has kept her bed (again!) unsullied for him,[132] to which Menelaus exclaims, "How sweet if true!" The plot then proceeds from the husband's stupidity to the wife's ingenuity. Just as Iphigenia concocts "a brand new escape plan,"[133] Helen hits upon "an ingenious plan for escape" *(mēchanē sōtērias)*.[134] She will tell the king that Menelaus is a humble messenger—his disheveled wardrobe now serves a useful dramatic purpose—who brings news of her husband Menelaus' death, and she will play upon the aged monarch's barbarian superstition for permission to perform a symbolic burial on a ship. Menelaus agrees to being pronounced dead (though he's careful to remind Helen that he is not!). Like a similar point in the *Iphigenia,* this juncture could well be described as the end of Act One. As in the earlier play, the first half was a recognition drama and the second half a trickery comedy.

King Theoclymenus is a barbarian bully cut of the same cloth as King Thoas of the *Iphigenia.* He has heard that a Greek man has been spotted and urges his men to find him, for he fears that his bride-to-be may be stolen. And then the lady herself appears, her costume radically changed. The king reacts:

> THEO.: Helen, why have you changed your white clothes
> for black ones—and why have you cut your hair?[135]

She then tells him that Menelaus is dead, and indicates the bearer of these sad tidings—Menelaus. The king's immediate reaction is that the hero is dressed terribly ("what rags he is wearing").[136] Helen indicates coquettishly:

> HELEN: You may make the wedding arrangements now.
> THEO.: I've been waiting a long time but I am glad.
> HELEN: Yes, let's forget the past.[137]

This softens Theoclymenus, and he gives her permission to bury "the shadow" of Menelaus according to the Greek custom. The king then remarks that Greeks are very knowledgeable about such things. Helen explains that the custom is to bury their dead at sea and indicates that Menelaus will know what equipment is needed. The monarch then asks Menelaus how the Greeks bury their heroes and he answers, in typical bourgeois fashion, "as lavishly as a man's wealth allows." Theoclymenus responds, "Then, for Helen's sake, the sky's the limit."[138]

In parting—though Theoclymenus does not know for how long—Helen promises him ironically that "I shall be the wife you deserve . . . today will show the quality of my love for you."[139] After the chorus sings an ode expressing their longing for escape on wings, as in the *Iphigenia* ("O, that we might fly in the air / wingèd high over Libya"),[140] a servant rushes in with the "brand new news" of Helen and Menelaus' great deception.[141] Theoclymenus' immediate reaction is as much shame as rage ("I've been duped and tricked with *women's* artful cunning").[142]

As the king's fury mounts, Helen's brothers Castor and Pollux appear *ex machina:* twins, sea gods, stars—and well known predators on women.[143] (Rape seems to be everywhere in Helen's family—not to mention the threat of it in Egypt.) They calm the outraged king, explaining that the gods willed Helen to leave Egypt, and predict her future deification. She too will become a heavenly body and a light for sailors.[144] Meanwhile, Menelaus will be granted a home on the island of the blessed.[145] Theoclymenus instantly forgets his anger and relinquishes any claim on Helen, remarking (perhaps with irony), "there are not many women like her."[146]

Recalling Ion's ode to Tychē, the play ends with a choral song (repeated verbatim in four other Euripidean plays)[147] celebrating the unexpected:

> Many are the shapes of the divine,
> Much that is unforeseen the gods bring to pass;
> The expected is not accomplished,
> And the God finds a way for the unexpected.
> Thus did this affair fall out.[148]

Both *Helen* and the *Iphigenia* emphasize rebirth from the sea (Hades lies beyond). So does the securely dated offering of 412, *Andromeda* (also parodied by Aristophanes in the *Thesmophoriazusae* and declared Dionysus' favorite play in the *Frogs*).[149] Although the play exists only in fragments, we know that it also dealt with a damsel in distress on an exotic shore. As in *Helen,* the heroine is dressed in bridal white, chained to a boulder in the sea as an expiatory sacrifice to a sea monster sent by the angry Poseidon, who has been angered by her mother's vanity—a scene which has been the subject of much iconography.[150] The Greek novelist Achilles Tatius gives us a detailed description of a painting of Euanthes in the temple of Pelusium, in which a maiden, dressed in bridal white, bound to a hollow rock, resembled "one who was assigned to be the bride of Death."[151] Even in Euripides' version, Perseus seems at first to have thought Andromeda a statue.[152]

We can reconstruct the early part of the play, namely the rescue. Our best source is a calyx krater of the late fifth century in the Berlin Museum.[153] It depicts Andromeda bound to a cliff in the sea just off Joppa in "Ethiopia" (modern Jaffa)—whence St. George was to rescue a damsel of his own. King Cepheus and Queen Cassiopeia had exposed her with much precious jewelry to appease the god. In fact, her royal parents are standing by on the shore, waiting to see what will happen. Perseus is hovering over the scene in his famous winged track shoes. There is, in fact, a bourgeois feeling to it all, as in one fragment which says: "I am fortunate with money, but otherwise not fortunate."[154] Is her father offering Perseus a bribe? If so, to do what? In any case, the subject of money is a prime element of the *res privata* of Menander's world (as opposed to the *res sacra* of Tragedy and the *res publica* of Old Comedy).[155]

Two other fragments suggest that, after the rescue, King Cepheus reneged on his promise to give Andromeda to Perseus in marriage, on the grounds that he was a pauper and a bastard.[156] If, as Oscar Wilde would later assert, "a handbag is not a proper mother," surely a shower, even a golden one, is not a proper father (his mother Danae could not have been telling Perseus the truth about his lineage). For that matter, a cave and a basket were not much better for Ion.

But all will be well—all *must* be well, since this is a comedy. The krater suggests that the crisis was resolved by the eleventh-hour appearance of Aphrodite *ex machina,* who doubtless revealed that Perseus was not a thing of shreds and patches but the son of Zeus, the celestial Mikado himself. Now all the problems are suddenly solved. As the god Castor remarks in the epilogue to the *Electra, toisde melēsei gamos*[157]—"the rest is marriage," to paraphrase Hamlet.

And *gamos* it is, in the literal sense of the word. For in the *Helen* we have a symbolic remarriage in the departure of Menelaus and his faithful love from Egypt (for a honeymoon). As one scholar comments, "Something like comedy is at work, both in the sense of life renewed and in the reduction in size of the heroic and terrible."[158] Some scholars would even discern a fescennine jocularity in Menelaus' leering exit-line: "from now on my troubles are over. I'll be walking on hard-on highway" *(orthoi de bēnai podi)*.[159] This would hardly be in keeping with the tone of tragedy (and is perhaps going too far).

So much for Euripides' offerings of *kaina pragmata* on the so-called tragic stage of 412 B.C. Significantly, this was also a watershed year for the comic festivals. It was the season of Eupolis' *Demoi,* in which four dead Athenian leaders—Miltiades, Solon, Aristides, and Pericles (the last, we are told, to great cheering)—were resurrected from the underworld and asked to advise the city.[160] Whatever the issue of this comedy, its avowed aim, like that of the *Frogs* in 405, was "to make our city gush and bloom again,"[161] in other words to be fertile *(gonimos)*.[162] It was a dream of spring, rejuvenation, and healing—all impossible in real life.

Can we explain this universal hunger—for purification, for rebirth, for a Happy Ending—via wish-fulfillment? The Athenian climate around 412 B.C. was one of intellectual regression. Symptomatic of this atmosphere was not only the waning of all creative activity (except comedy), but a greatly increased interest in new healing cults which "within a generation or two transformed Asclepius from a minor hero into a major god—and made his temple at Epidaurus a place of pilgrimage as famous as Lourdes."[163] Recall the temple scene in Aristophanes' *Plutus.* There was also a heightened participation in foreign, orgiastic, mystical religion—"magic for the many," quick cures, easy answers for those desperately searching for solutions. As one critic so eloquently puts it, "they felt the need for some space larger than the confines of despair."[164]

In *Beyond the Pleasure Principle,* Freud describes the perpetually warring forces within the human psyche—the life drive and the death instinct—as man's unconscious search for an earlier state of things, a quest for the recapture of time.[165] Another way of denying time among primitive peoples is the mimetic cosmogonic ceremony—rites which give the spectator-participants the feeling that their world will enjoy a fresh new beginning. These are often in the form of a *hieros gamos*. We are back to the ritual ancestors of comedy. In other words, we are back to the beginning.

Could these theories possibly explain the near-ridiculous emphasis on marriage (sacred or otherwise) in the later plays of Euripides? We recall the dénouement of the *Orestes*, where Apollo *ex machina* turns imminent manslaughter into mass mating. The three pairings at the end of Molière's *Miser* (brother, sister, father-in-law) pale by comparison. Comedy in the late fifth century B.C. had a social function, providing a troubled city with needed psychic balm or a draught of hope. Even in the securest of times, as Aristotle rightly noted, audiences always crave the *hēdonē oikeia* ("home joy") of comedy. Like every comic author, Euripides was merely "complying with the taste of the town."

There remained but two significant variations which would transform the Euripidean formula into Menandrian New Comedy—the "classical" genre. The first is the "blocking character," who in Euripides is a non-*Greek* (the barbarians Thoas in the *Iphigenia* and Theoclymenus in *Helen*), but who characteristically becomes in Menander a non-Athenian.[166] The relationship can be schematized as follows:

E = Non-Greek (Blocking Character)	M = Non-Athenian Citizen (Blocking Element)
vs.	vs.
Greek	Athenian Citizen

In Menander, the loved one (usually the woman) is initially thought to be foreign (or sometimes a slave) and is ultimately discovered to be Athenian and therefore . . . marriageable. In the *Sicyonians* both hero *and* heroine turn out to be citizens.[167] The law against marrying foreigners was not comic fabrication. According to legislation instituted in 451/450 B.C., marriage with a non-Athenian carried grave penalties—because, among other things, the children would not be legitimate.[168] In fact, the whole Menandrian corpus could be subtitled "The Importance of Being Athenian."

The more general xenophobia found in Euripides had a comic dimension of its own. In the *kōmos*, society is made whole and outsiders, like Xuthus, Thoas, and Theoclymenus, are expelled or "ducked." Likewise, the hero frequently finds himself in a hostile kingdom facing a death penalty—as in *Iphigenia Among the Taurians,* the *Menaechmi,* and the *Comedy of Errors*—as he seeks to reunite his family. By contrast, in Roman comedy with its Saturnalian reversal, characters suffer comic punishment for behavior that is *too* Roman.

New Comedy wrought a second variation on the Euripidean formula. The tragic playwright's later dramaturgy forms a diptych of *anagnōrisis* followed by *mēchanēma,* recognition followed by intrigue, a sequence so often repeated that "it threatened to become a pattern."[169] But that is precisely the point about New Comedy: the essential *sameness* of its plots, as we shall see in the next chapter. The similarities between the *Iphigenia* and the *Helen* are a harbinger of the later genre.[170]

The structural change made by the New Comedy authors was to reverse the order of Euripidean *anagnōrisis* and *mēchanēma.* Whereas in Euripidean comedy, the plays we have just studied, the *anagnōrisis* comes first and the trickery follows, in fully developed comedy the *frustratio* comes before the *cognitio* (to use the Latin translations of the Greek terms which modern scholars since Northrop Frye have employed when discussing comedy—a mere matter of fashion). So it is that we laugh at the rogueries of the Plautine slave—or of Molière's Scapin—and *then* discover all those long-lost, legitimate, marriageable daughters.

These, I would argue, constitute the significant differences between Euripidean and modern comedy. Our ambidextrous playwright had already sensed the crowd-pleasing potential of the comic *cognitio.* For in that watershed year of 412 B.C., one of his characters remarks: "How utterly divine it is to recognize your loved ones again!" This is the impassioned exclamation of none other than "the brand new Helen."[171] It was written by the man who perfected the recipe for what Henry James would later refer to as "the time-honored bread-sauce of the Happy Ending"—if not the father, certainly the grandfather of modern comedy: Euripides.

9

O Menander! O Life!

At first the problem with Menander was that his plays were lost. Then the problem was that they were found.

After an indifferent career—with only a few victories[1]—the Hellenistic playwright received a great deal of posthumous praise which elevated him over rivals like Philemon and Diphilus as a literary paragon.[2] He was praised for his simple eloquence and psychological insights, for managing to "suit the action to the word, the word to the action."[3] (Hamlet would have been pleased.) Aristophanes of Byzantium, an early Alexandrian editor, ranked him second to Homer himself,[4] and praised his realism with these famous lines:

> O Menander and Life!
> Which of you is imitating which?[5]

And Plutarch, while dismissing the playwright Aristophanes as boorish, vulgar, and obscene ("like an aging whore"), praised the matchless style of Menander: "what other reason would a cultivated man have to go to the theater?"[6]

Then, after a happy existence in many manuscripts, Menander's plays were lost in the wake of Arab imperialism and Byzantine indifference.[7] Thereafter he was extant only in Atticist pedantry and the scholar's commonplace book—anthologies of quotable quotes like "whom the gods love dies young."[8] Thus, when later scholars praised him—Goethe, for example, celebrated his "unattainable charm," and George Meredith spoke of Menander and Molière as the two great comic playwrights—they were talking of an author who no longer really existed.

Then magically, like a sudden discovery at the end of one of his own plays, a major manuscript of Menander (containing parts of five works) suddenly reappeared in 1905, resurrected, appropriately enough for the romantic playwright, in "love-town"—the Egyptian city of Aphroditopolis. It was one of the major scholarly breakthroughs of the twentieth century, greatly augmenting the meager fragments previously known. Then after 1959 when a complete copy of the *Dyskolos (The Grouch)* was published, unearthed under mysterious circumstances,[9] Menander was at last on his way to becoming an Oxford Text—and a critical cottage industry.[10]

But this rebirth occasioned a bit of postpartum depression. The initial reaction of most Hellenists seemed to echo Horace's dismissal of a poetaster's work: "the great mountains labor and give birth—to a silly little mouse."[11] G. S. Kirk once remarked, "tell me why Menander is anything but a wet fish."[12] The initial disappointment stemmed from the fact that he seemed to be a "Johnny-one-note": his plays kept saying the same thing, or so it seemed. Yet mature reflection has established that, from the point of view of influence, Menander is arguably the single most important figure in the history of Western comedy.

Unlike Aristophanes, Menander and his New Comedy colleagues are not overtly political.[13] In an oft-quoted phrase, Gilbert Murray distinguished between the matter of Old Comedy as *res publica* and that of New Comedy as *res privata*.[14] In fact, the transition from Old to New may be epitomized as a journey from the topical to the typical. There is a delimited cast of familiar characters: cranky old fathers, hyperventilating young lovers, blustering soldiers, and scurrying slaves. The women belong to one of two distinct groups: virgins or prostitutes. Hardly a nuanced view of the opposite sex, it is nonetheless a social dichotomy of fundamental importance. One group is suitable for partying, the other for parturition.

In either case, Menander's quintessential plot is motivated by love—almost always at first sight. Though we have evidence that not every one of Menander's plays ended in marriage,[15] we have Ovid's testimony that this was Menander's favorite subject: "Never did charming Menander write a play without romance in it."[16] Ovid, who was still exposed to a living tradition, was certainly in a position to know. For Plutarch attests that Menander, of all Greek authors, was the one most read and discussed at banquets, in the classroom, and at competitions.[17]

A sample plot might go as follows: during one of the Athenian fertility festivals, under cover of night, a well-bred young man, intoxicated by wine and the spirit of the *kōmos*, "forcefully seduces" a well-bred young girl. In his haste to decamp, he neglects to notice that he has somehow lost his ring. Sometime later, in the daylight, he falls in love "at first sight"—with the same girl, unaware that she had been his victim. But then, learning that she is pregnant, he refuses to wed her. Finally, after much ado, all is resolved in Act Four (Act Five is reserved for the party: Menander canonized the five-act format, which Horace insisted upon for all dramas in his day)[18] when he spies her souvenir, recognizes his property and fault, and says "Hey, that's my ring—I love you, let's get married!" And thus the line of Athenian upper-class twits is perpetuated.

Menander tells this same rape and recognition plot again and again with what seem to be merely cosmetic changes. Yet close scrutiny reveals that although he appears to repeat himself, he does so in subtly different ways. Indeed, for his subtle depictions of formerly stock character types and plot formulas he may have sacrificed a certain amount of popularity in his own lifetime.[19]

One source of variety comes from a mixture of comic and tragic modes.[20] For example, the playwright's small number of plots reveal many diverse *situations* as well as surprise modifications of stock figures and motifs. In the language of Lévi-Strauss, Menandrian drama presents a "common armature, union of youth and girl in spite of obstacles ... clothed in sixty different ways to produce sixty different plays."[21]

A famous anecdote bears this out. When a friend chastised Menander about not having completed his comedy for the upcoming festival, the poet replied: "The play is finished. Now all I have to do is write the dialogue."[22] This certainly conforms with Aristotle's dictum that in drama "plot is the soul."[23] This is as good a summary as any of Menander's subtle dramatic technique. And herein lies the playwright's charm—and the secret of his appeal.

In some ways, New Comedy is little more than suburban Euripides. Philemon, a contemporary of Menander, might well be speaking for himself when he has one of his characters say that he would hang himself if he thought he would meet Euripides in the next world.[24] As we have seen, the *Ion,* with its offstage rape, lost child, distressed heroine, parental recognition through tokens, and happy ending, provided the paradigm for all Menandrian drama. This relationship is in fact attested by a near-contemporary source—in his third century B.C. biography, Satyrus maintains that most of the New Comedy elements can already be found in Euripides:

> Raped maidens, swapped babies, recognitions through rings
> and necklaces: these are the devices which hold the new com-
> edy together, and which Euripides brought to a peak.[25]

Some four centuries later, Quintilian still held the same strong opinion that Menander, "as he often demonstrates, admired [Euripides] fanatically, and copied him—albeit in a different kind of work."[26] The schoolmaster's eulogy goes on to say that "a study of Menander would develop all the qualities necessary [for an orator]":

> So brilliant is the picture of life he presents to us, there is
> such an abundance of invention and turn of phrase, he is so
> adept in every situation, characterization, and emotion.[27]

Nevertheless, for all the similarities between the two playwrights, Euripides still presented his plays of uncertain genre at the *tragic* festivals. His characters, though often verging on the bourgeois, are nonetheless kings, queens, and princesses. It was left for the poets of New Comedy to bring the dramatic focus from Homer to home sweet home.

The new genre can be best described by observing what it is *not.* While Greek tragedies ended with an Aristotelian *anagnōrisis*[28]—the hero's discovery of the bitter truth about his identity—the analogous moment in comedy, the *cognitio* (simply a Latin translation of Aristotle's term), entails the opposite kind of outcome.[29] Even the *Oedipus Rex* was amenable to comic treatment—as was reportedly done in antiquity.[30] At the comic conclusion Oedipus would discover that he is in fact the real son (not the stepson) of the King and Queen of Corinth. Thus parricide and incest instantly vanish and the hero can marry the lovely widow Jocasta, with everything concluding in a joyful *gamos*. It all can be explained by *Schadenfreude:* whereas tragedy evokes the *Schade* ("there but for the grace of the playwright go I"), comedy inspires *Freude*. This is a substantial reason for the appeal of Menander's stereotyped drama.

Often with the *cognitio* there is what we might call a *cognatio* ("kinship"). Ion and Creusa are mother and son. Iphigenia and Orestes are brother and sister. In Menander, long-lost daughters abound. The *Georgos (The Farmer)* even has long-lost parents *and* children. In New Comedy it is usually the identity of the girl that enables the happy ending. Occasionally it is a long-lost son as in the *Sicyonians,* where in the end the lad turns out to be Athenian.

The barrier is elementally tribal: it prevents exogamy. It is essentially a dramatization of the daydream of the family romance fantasy, as described by Freud and Rank—a growing boy's dream of more noble (and usually richer) parents. This basic plot, already prefigured in Euripides, has provided the raw material for innumerable versions throughout the ages in many genres in and out of the theater. It is also the basic stuff of the typical nineteenth-century novel where, for instance, Oliver Twist, after his ordeal amidst the underclass of London, is discovered to be a good bourgeois lad with an inheritance awaiting him.

Although Menander was praised for his realism, this *cognitio-cognatio* plot may seem rather far-fetched.[31] Yet as Frye remarked, "happy endings do not impress us as true, but as desirable."[32] This is why New Comedy made Tychē—Chance, Lady Luck, ever-changeable Fortune— its presiding deity.[33] The goddess was always ready to operate without motivation to unite people and pieces, no matter how complicated the situation, in an "automatic" happy ending. Menander frequently invokes "the usual machinery" *(to automaton)* to explain away the inexplicable and free both himself and his characters from any responsibility.[34]

According to a well-known proverb made famous by Theophrastus, "All human affairs are Chance, not well-laid plans."[35] As Menander himself says:

> Everything we think or say or do,
> Is Luck (*Tychē*)—we just sign our names to it.[36]

But it was for his characters, not the realism of his plots, that Menander was justifiably celebrated. Henry James's famous dictum, "What is character but the determination of incident? What is incident but the illustration of character?" was in fact anticipated by Aristotle's discussion in the *Nicomachean Ethics*.[37] The philosopher divided characters into four broad types: the *alazōn* or boasting impostor (recall Lamachus, Socrates, and the *medicus gloriosus* in Eupolis), the knowing but disingenuous *eirōn*, the buffoonish *bōmolochos,* and the *agroikos,* the boorish bumpkin (Dicaeopolis, Trygaeus, and Strepsiades).[38]

If Aristotle did not directly influence Menander, Theophrastus (371–288)—Aristotle's successor as head of the Lyceum and Menander's own teacher—certainly did.[39] This polymath's voluminous writings included the *Characters,* a Hellenistic forerunner of Wilhelm Reich's similarly-titled twentieth-century classic, *Character Analysis.* Again we find the boor (*agroikos),* and his boaster (*alazōn*) is a strutting peacock who drops such casual remarks as "the Regent Antipater has just offered me a license to export timber tax-free . . . but I turned it down so that no one would accuse him of favoritism."[40] Theophrastus took Aristotle's categories much further, developing them into thirty amusing—and remarkably accurate—portraits.

Many of Theophrastus' vignettes seem like sketches for Menander's plays. The *Dyskolos (The Grouch),* for example, has many of the traits of Theophrastus' examples of *authadeia* (stubbornness) and *mempsimoiria* (resentment).[41] For this reason scholars have tended to link the philosopher and the playwright in a kind of spiritual collaboration. At least, both were simultaneously engaged in a growing area of inquiry in the Hellenistic age—the *dramatis personae* of the human comedy.[42] In any case, Menander was a good student. One of his famous utterances—"how human is a human when he acts humanely"—encapsulates his celebrated *philanthrōpia.*[43] How different from the cartoonist Al Capp's famous dictum that all comedy is based on "man's delight in man's in-humanity to man"!

Because the characters are reduced to types, it is nearly impossible to recall the names of Menander's young heroes. They are unmemorable because they are interchangeable. Nearly all his characters are given *redende Namen* ("speaking names") which do not designate a person but reveal his personality. This was standard practice in New Comedy. As Donatus prescribes: "Strictly speaking, the names of characters in com-edy should have both meaning and etymology."[44]

Actually, this practice goes back to the beginnings of Greek comedy. We find a character named Colaphos or "Mr. Striker" in the *Agrostinos (The Rustic)* of Epicharmus. And as we have seen, Aristophanes abounds in such charactonyms as Dicaeopolis ("Just City") and Pheidippides ("Horsethrift"), the prodigal son of Strepsiades ("The Twister"). This is still more evident in the *Plutus,* where the old man is called Chremylus, "Mr. McMoney," while his friend Blepsidemus is "John Q. Clearsight"—in obvious contrast to the title character, the blind god of wealth.

But this convention really came to the fore in New Comedy. Menander and his colleagues go beyond the colorful Aristophanic coinages which usually indicate a specific character's agenda within the play. Rather, they use appellations which, although in some cases real names, tend to bespeak general character or personality types. Cleostratus and Straton, for example—"General Martial" and "Sergeant Slaughter"—are pompous soldiers descended from Lamachus in the *Acharnians* and the very model of Theophrastean *alazoneia.* Smicrines, who appears in several plays, is "Mr. Stingy," a perfect caricature of the miserly old man, recalling the Theophrastean *aneleutheros* ("tight-wad") and *micrologos* ("penny-pincher").[45]

Whereas the people of Aristophanes are fantastical, consorting with Clouds and flying to Olympus on dung-beetles, Menander's everyman lives next door. These characters are almost always Athenian and bour-geois—or want to be—and so are their values.[46] He depicts no Hades as in the *Frogs,* no heaven as in the *Peace,* and nothing in between as in the *Birds.* It is all very much down to earth—on the same city street.[47] The setting is metropolitan, even cosmopolitan—a word which comes into current use at this time. The dialogue is chaste; unchaste words are rare, and explicit sexuality rarer still.[48] It is particularly noteworthy that, although it was still a familiar part of Athenian life, there are almost no examples in Menander of homosexuality (an exception is made for the cook, of course).[49] Menander has few songs and only simple meters—mostly iambs, which, as Aristotle noted,[50] are closest to human speech.[51] Compared to Aristophanes he has precious few jokes, puns, or coinages, avoiding verbal acrobatics and eschewing what Vladimir Nabokov referred to in *Ada* as "performing words." This is not to say that Menander has no sense of humor: as Plutarch wrote, "his comedies abound in the witty and amusing."[52] Laughter comes rather from his mastery of diction, irony, visual effects, and comic structuring.[53]

Though at first glance the urbanity of Menandrian characters suggests that he is presenting merely a bland comedy of manners, in his hands the Hellenistic drama is closer to its formative roots than is often recognized. New Comedy crystallizes—one might say canonizes—some of the key elements that we have distinguished as far back as the pre-dramatic rituals. For example, unlike the transitional *Plutus,* Menandrian drama does have *gamos* as well as *kōmos.* Just as the Aristophanic endings often repeat in dramatized form the ritual sacred marriage, so too Menander's *gamoi*—in the sense of legal marriage without the same onstage license—end nearly all his plays. It is the one constant in Menander.

But *gamos* in the physical sense is still present. The significant difference is that it takes place *offstage,* before the beginning of the play, at one of the fertility festivals. Thus *kōmos* is still the driving force, but rather than being the hero's reward at the end of the play, as in Old Comedy, it is the heroine's problem at the beginning. And many newlyweds receive what we might in a holiday humor refer to as a baby prize.

The comastic revel is clearly described in the prologues, although of course not graphically and without double-entendre. Although the young hero has lost control during the festival, when he—and society—discovers what he has done, he ultimately fulfills his duty as a citizen and formally weds the girl. Most of Menander's extant plays end with the tintinnabulation of wedding bells and iterations of the marriage formula: "I pledge my daughter to you as your wife for the plowing of legitimate children."[54] The reader is correct to infer a sexual overtone in

the plowing metaphor. At the same time, it is without any hint of cru-
dity: recall the ancient hieratic association between the language of ag-
riculture and sexual fertility documented by Eliade. Thus the phallus—
so prominent in Old Comedy and discreetly worn in Middle—is still
present by inference in New Comedy.

The good burghers of Athens always opted for matrimony and pater-
nity. This "urge to merge" for the propagation of humanity is a conspicuous theme in Shakespeare as well. One thinks of his opening
sonnet:

> Of fairest creatures we desire increase,
> That thereby beauty's rose may never die.[55]

This is no mere flattery for the addressee of the poem. With Shakespeare, it was an article of faith. And when the confirmed bachelor
Benedick in *Much Ado About Nothing* finally succumbs to marriage, he
justifies his change of heart by protesting that "the world must be
peopled."[56]

Thus, like Aristophanes and the pre-dramatic rituals, New Comedy
remained focused on the continuity of the species. Whether it be a sacred marriage to the shouts of phallic abuse, or the prim and proper
atmosphere of "nice" bourgeois Athens, comedy remains at its epicen-
ter a fertility rite. This was as true of early Greece as it was for Elizabethan England, and (to take a modern example) for Dustin Hoffman
and Katherine Ross in *The Graduate*. (If we were to press this argument
to its ultimate conclusion, we might interpret Hoffman's affair first
with Mrs. Robinson and then with her daughter as equivalent to the replacement of the Old Queen by the Young Princess—in other words, a
legitimate modern variation on an old theme.)

Moreover, all through Menander there is an almost subliminal leitmotif of resurrection, continuing the Aristophanic theme of rebirth.
People thought to be dying are miraculously cured; those presumed
dead are revived or reappear. With the frequent birth of babies there is
an ever-present emphasis on a new beginning. This may explain the ongoing appeal of Menander's formulaic plot, which was presented with
scarcely an alteration each year. For the audience it was still essentially
a subliminal dramatized fertility rite, a maypole dance of the imagination. Menander's appeal is similar to the joy felt by a husband whose

wife gives him a tie each year which varies by one stripe or polka dot. Although it is practically a copy of last year's gift, he appreciates the festive gesture. By analogy, this is Menander's dramatic practice.

Some have criticized Menander as fairly anemic, lacking the red blood of comic gusto. But closer examination reveals that in his sophisticated manner he still deals with all the fundamental elements of traditional comedy. Aristophanes and "the others" were a unique phenomenon. They waxed and they waned. Menander was an unquenchable fount of comic possibilities. And, in contrast to his Attic predecessor, no *Who's Who* of Athens was required to understand his plays.

Here we see themes previously treated by Aristophanes now recast for a different sensibility. Comedy still deals with the basic elements of life—birth, death, and resurrection. While Menander's dramaturgy is never as outrageous as Aristophanes' *Birds*, which presents onstage the ultimate fulfillment of the Oedipal fantasy, it does at times conform to the paradigmatic definition of comedy offered by Ludwig Jekels, and since rearticulated by Frye: an Oedipal crisis narrowly averted.

Of course, this too had its precedent in plays like Euripides' *Augē*, with the near-incest between mother and son, or even Sophocles' fragmentary *Thyestes in Sicyon,* in which the title hero rapes his own daughter to beget an avenger who will punish his brother Atreus.[57] But Menander translates the motif to the day-to-day world of Athenian society. While never quite crossing the boundary into tragedy, Menander sometimes flirts with outrage, softening the shock of incest with what we might call "displacement" (just as in the *Birds* the Oedipal shock is absorbed through the faceless Basileia):

> We do not find in New Comedy a man marrying his mother, but a man who is suspected by his adoptive father of being seduced by his father's mistress; a wife does not murder her husband upon his return from war, but a soldier's mistress does desert her lover in his absence and seek refuge in a temple. The patterns of sexual attraction and antagonism are the same, but they have been given a more mundane, realistic treatment.[58]

Consider, for example, *Perikeiromenē (The Shorn Bird)*. Here the young man Moschion falls in love at first sight with Glycera, the girl next door—unaware that she is really his long-lost sister. The presiding deity of the play, Agnoia (Miss Apprehension), speaks a delayed prologue in which she explains:

> At dusk [he] happened to spy
> Her sending her maid off somewhere,
> And when he saw that she was at the door, he ran straight up,
> And kissed and hugged her.
> And she didn't try to resist, knowing he was her brother.[59]

The goddess admits that she encouraged Moschion's passion "for the sake of the story," revealing her awareness of how daring the plot is and warning the audience not to be upset: "If anyone is shocked or outraged by this, let him think again, for a god can turn bad fortune into good."[60]

Then the plot thickens. The girl has been the sweetheart of a tenderhearted and (barely) braggart soldier (the aforementioned "General Martial," Polemon) whose slave chances to spy Moschion and Glycera kissing. Totally in Agnoia's sway, he wrongly concludes that the girl is being unfaithful to his master. Thus when the play begins the soldier has mistakenly punished his faithful sweetheart and shorn her locks as a sign of disgrace. In despair, Glycera has fled to the next-door neighbor where, of course, Moschion happens to be living with his foster family.

The incest fixation persists unabated throughout the first three acts and into the fourth. An overheated Moschion confides his passion to the audience (who, thanks to the prologue, are better informed than he), encouraged by the fact that:

> When I ran up to hug her, she didn't try to flee
> She put her arms around me and drew me near.
> *(self-satisfied)* I guess I'm not bad looking, by Athena—
> No, I'm quite the lady's man.[61]

Daus the slave then appears to stoke the fires in his enraptured master by describing how their newly arrived, close-cropped family guest has just stepped daintily from the bath—all fresh and lovely.[62] Mightily pleased, Moschion repeats his previous observation about his physical appeal.[63] The audience's tension is increased by further ironic references to the "love affair," and in the dialogue between two slaves, Glycera's slave Sosias refers twice to Moschion as the *moichos* (adulterer) of his mistress, and refers to him as Glycera's love-object *(melēma)*.[64]

With every scene Moschion's passion burns more intensely. Consumed by thoughts of Glycera, he is unable to sleep. He describes how, aching with passion, he tossed and turned in bed, too "aroused" to sleep.[65] He adds that he is waiting for "my mother to come as a messenger from my lover *(erōmenē)* with details for our tryst."[66] The young man is truly carried away. As one scholar notes, "in his ignorance he thinks that Glycera's moving from the house of Polemon to his mother's house is a proof of her secret desires for him, and is eager for an opportunity to realize his erotic fantasies about her."[67]

At last, well into the climactic fourth act, Moschion dramatically realizes Glycera's identity. The sad discovery occurs as he is eavesdropping on a conversation between his inamorata and the soldier's best friend, Pataicus, as the latter discovers that Glycera is his long-lost daughter. As he looks at the tokens and listens to the details, Moschion realizes that Pataicus must be *his* father too. And therefore, horrible to say—"if that's true, then she's my sister and my whole damn life is over."[68] He presents himself to his father—and his sister—and the bittersweet reunion is complete. This triple *cognitio* averts what could have been a tragic *anagnōrisis*. Now the jealous Polemon does not worry about Glycera's affection toward Moschion, because "you kissed a brother not a lover."[69] The newfound father immediately entrusts his daughter to the sentimental soldier, and they prepare for the wedding, where Pataicus pronounces the usual marriage formula and adds the substantial dowry of three talents.[70]

Not only does the play conclude with the wedding of Glycera but, Menander being Menander, he adds a second marriage, that of Glycera's long-lost brother Moschion (to the unnamed daughter of the unknown Philinus).[71]

Like the *Perikeiromenē, Misoumenus (The Hated Man)* presents a "dead" soldier and a fleeting smidgen of incest. For reasons not readily apparent, this comedy was extremely popular in the post-Menandrian era, and one scene from Act Five is even the subject of a third-century A.D. mosaic found on Lesbos.[72] Possibly the play was appealing for its innovative technique of having the actors narrate off-stage conversations in which they get to impersonate both interlocutors.[73]

The heroine, Kratea, believes that her master, the *miles* Thrasonides, has killed her brother, whence he is the eponymous *misoumenos*. This is of course a sure indication that he will reappear at the climactic moment. But about halfway through the play there is a *cognitio* between Kratea and her long-lost father, who has arrived from Cyprus in search of his long-lost daughter.

This recognition precipitates a misunderstanding similar to that in the *Perikeiromenē*. This time, the slave Getas sees Kratea and her father embracing and jumps to a naughty conclusion:

> GETAS: She's just come outside . . . Whoa! What's this?
> *(calling out)* What's she to you, mister?
> You—what are you doing? I told you so!
> That's the man I've been looking for, caught red-handed!
> He may look an old grey geezer, some sixty years old,
> but he'll still be moaning!
> Whom do you think you're kissing and embracing?[74]

But elsewhere Menander does not make a play of it. It is a simple sequence, creating a confusion that is very quickly clarified. The audience experiences only a brief frisson at the suggestion of incest as Menander harks back to a theme which he has dealt with at full length.

These are not the only such plots in the corpus.[75] But whereas in the *Perikeiromenē* the forbidden act is narrowly avoided, and in the *Misoumenus* it is suggested by a wrong suspicion, the *Samian Women* provides an extended example of a misapprehension that an Oedipal outrage has been committed. The play combines a stereotypical Menandrian dilemma—boy rapes girl-next-door at a festival, and does not realize who she is or that she is marriageable. To this standard formula is added the suspicion that he has seduced his father's "wife."

As in the *Perikeiromenē,* the young hero is again called Moschion. He begins the play on a note of *pudeur* and contrition. First he tells us of his adoptive father's falling in love—with a Samian courtesan named Chrysis.[76] Evidently the older man was ashamed of himself,[77] but finally took the woman to live with them. From the boy's account, she quickly became little less than a real wife, establishing friendly relations with the neighbors and even arranging to have the Adonis Festival celebrated in their house, where she entertained the local ladies' group.

At this untrammeled occasion, while the women celebrants were running around in the darkness, the boy committed his stereotypical sin. He had seen a girl, Plangon, and is too ashamed to confess what happened next. All that he can bring himself to say is that—typical of the New Comedy—she got pregnant.

The young man then went to her mother, who happened to live next door, and promised to marry the daughter as soon as he could get permission from his father Demeas, who was then abroad. But when the baby was born, Demeas was still away, and so to avoid embarrassing the girl Moschion took the baby into his own house. By a scarcely believable coincidence, Chrysis, his father's Samian partner, also happened to have a baby while the old man was away. So both women are breastfeeding at the same time. But when Chrysis loses her child, the young couple ask her to nurse theirs to protect the mother until she can be legitimized.

Suddenly the slave Parmeno announces that Moschion's father has just returned. He must now plead for the promised marriage. But the boy is hesitant. He is ashamed, of course. The Samian herself assures the lad that his father will be sympathetic, if only because Demeas was as much in love with her as Moschion is with Plangon. She then pronounces a typically quotable Menandrian proverb: "love kills the ire even of the most irate man."[78]

Two old men now enter (the substantial losses of text in Acts One and Two make this plot seem more streamlined than it probably was in its entirety): Demeas, the adoptive father, and his neighbor Niceratos, father of the young girl and unwitting grandfather of her baby. By coincidence—*to automaton* is frequently invoked in this play—they are in the midst of planning the marriage of their respective children, unaware that the youngsters are already involved. But when Demeas meets Moschion, he quips bitterly: "I didn't know that Chrysis had become my lawfully wedded mistress" *(hetaira gametē).*[79] For somehow he has learned that Chrysis has given birth, and he is ready to kick her and "the little bastard" out. Moschion tries to dissuade him with another gnomic utterance: "no one can be called illegitimate who is born a man."[80]

But then comes the twist. While strolling through his house, Demeas chances to overhear Moschion's old wet nurse helping Chrysis take care of the baby, which he still thinks is his own. The woman babbles: "Not long ago I was lovingly nursing Moschion himself and now I'm taking care of his own baby."[81] Demeas is rocked to his core. Is his son really the father of his "wife's" child? It is technically true that an affair with his father's mistress—who is not a blood relative—does not really constitute incest in the letter of the law, but the sense of outrage is still very much there. Like Theseus in Euripides' *Phaedra,* Demeas now believes that his son has defiled his bed. To compound the shock, as he bolts for air he sees his Samian nursing the baby. As he tells the audience paratragically, whom he has taken in confidence:

> Aha—so the baby's hers!
> But as to the father . . . whether the baby's mine, or . . .
> And to think that Moschion was always such an obedient and
>   respectful boy![82]

From this misunderstanding the errors multiply geometrically. There are several scenes of equivocation. First Demeas confronts his slave Parmeno, asserting: "I know everything about Moschion's baby."[83] Then Moschion misunderstands when his father tells him he knows everything. He erroneously assumes that the old man knows the truth—and that Chrysis is rearing the baby now for *his* sake. The consequences proliferate. Before the play began Demeas had learned of Chrysis' own baby and sent word that he wanted it exposed. He now thinks that she has not only disobeyed him but that it is not even his own baby. As Parmeno dashes off, Demeas goes into a towering rage and then restrains himself and once again confides to the audience that his son is not to blame. After all, he is young and he has expiated his sin by agreeing to marry Niceratos' daughter:

> He wants to escape here, away from my *Helen.*
> *She*'s what's behind all this.

She must have got a hold on him when he was drunk, that's clear,
When he wasn't in his right mind. Youth and unwatered wine
cause seamy thoughtlessness, especially when it finds
A ready and willing partner-in-crime.[84]

His male chauvinist tirade continues with an exhortation to himself to stop loving her ("drive the beautiful Samian straight out of my house").[85] We see that *he*, not Moschion, offers the standard excuse for immoderate youthful behavior—night, love, wine, and youth—and he rushes in to drive his confused *hetaira* out of his home "with all her servants and possessions."[86] He then storms off stage leaving the young woman confused and upset. As Chrysis stands there weeping, Niceratos arrives—in the midst of preparing his daughter's wedding. He notices his neighbor's "wife" in tears and asks:

NICERATOS: What on earth has happened?
CHRYSIS: What else? Your nice friend Demeas has thrown me out!
NICERATOS: But why?
CHRYSIS: Because of the baby.[87]

Act Four begins with Moschion impatiently waiting for sunset and the ceremony. He has already taken three baths.[88] Niceratos hurries up to him, thinking he is *au fait* with events, and reveals that he knew Chrysis had taken in someone else's child:

NICERATOS: Don't you know what's been going on here? . . .
Your father has just chucked Chrysis out of the house.
MOSCHION: What are you saying!?
NICERATOS: Just what has happened.
MOSCHION: But why?
NICERATOS: Because of the baby . . .
MOSCHION: (*in astonishment*) What a strange, horrible thing![89]

Niceratos thinks that Demeas has caught some sort of brain fever on his journey and invites Chrysis to come to his house.

Just then the lunatic himself rages onto the stage again, and the other two approach him timorously:

MOSCHION: Why are you treating Chrysis this way?

DEMEAS: (*confiding to the audience*) Look who's trying to suck up to
me. . . .

(*looking in his eyes*) Stop playing games, I know the child is
yours.

MOSCHION: But how has Chrysis wronged you, if the baby's mine?[90]

This begins another long equivocation in which each misunderstands the other. Demeas berates his son for his foul deed, but
Moschion thinks it is because of his precipitous affair with Plangon
and argues: "But father, it's not so bad, lots of people have done this
sort of thing."[91] Demeas is enraged and calls his neighbor to witness.
He orders his son to answer:

DEMEAS: Who is the mother of your child then? Tell Niceratos,
If you don't think it's terrible!

MOSCHION: Yes, but to *him* it *will* be dreadful. He'll be furious when
he finds out![92]

Niceratos suddenly catches on—or thinks he does—and wildly leaps
to the wrong conclusion. But now the "incest" is out in the open, and
the *senex* adduces the worst arch-perpetrators of incest in mythology:
Oedipus, the most infamous of all; Thyestes, the seducer of his own
daughter; and Tereus, the miscreant who raped his wife's sister (and
whom we saw as a rehabilitated hoopoe in the *Birds*). In a paratragic
outburst he castigates young Moschion:

NICERATOS: O deed most dreadful of them all! You have made the
outrages of Tereus, Oedipus, Thyestes, and all the rest
pale in comparison![93]

Until this moment no one in the play has dared mention outright
the potentially incestuous aspect of Moschion's alleged seduction of
his father's "wife." Though Chrysis is only his father's "woman," it follows naturally that she is the mother figure—or at least the Phaedra
figure—in his life. The Greek audience would regard Chrysis and
Demeas as Moschion's father and mother. Menander has conveniently
camouflaged the bald realities of incest, knowing that the spectators

would make the intended association. The psyche knows no step-relatives.

Whatever their own practice may have been,[94] the Greek spectators would have enjoyed a frisson-by-association, making the mental leap in the privacy of their imaginations. For this moment of false *cognitio* is hardly lighthearted and could—in a tragic drama—bode ill for all concerned. But, of course, Tychē has made this a comedy, and after this *folle journée* of mistaken identities and incestuous intimations, everyone will return to his rightful (and respectful) place in society.

But for the moment, Moschion's so-called "crime" has torn his family asunder, with grave implications. Menandrian characters are always likely to compare their crises to those of tragic heroes, and the old man's most literary allusion is particularly apt, especially since it is from Euripides. Niceratos invokes Amyntor in the *Phoinix* who, outraged by the rumor that his stepson has seduced his concubine, blinded the young man. He incites Demeas to explode with anger and punish Moschion for his abomination.

Niceratos then rushes into his house to bring out the "perpetrator of these horrors"[95]—whom he believes to be Chrysis. Left alone on stage with his father, Moschion finally confesses that *he* is the father of the child, but that the mother is none other than Niceratos' daughter. He further explains why Chrysis was suckling the baby. Suddenly seeing the light, Demeas is immediately overcome with shame. Regretting that he has wronged his son, and consistent with his character as described at the opening of the play, he expresses his deep contrition.

None of this has been heard by Niceratos, who stomps back on stage screaming hysterically. He has just seen his daughter suckling the baby.[96] He is beside himself. Demeas calms the old man down and turns the stylistic tables on him by dressing his own revelation in yet another mythological allusion. He bids his neighbor recall the tragic story of Danaë, locked in a tower by her father to keep her from being ravished by Zeus. But the god then paid him the dubious honor of entering the girl's fortress in the form of golden rain and impregnating her.[97]

Demeas glances knowingly at Niceratos and adds, "You had better check and see if there are any leaks in your roof," and then pats him on the back.[98] Niceratos is still baffled. Demeas glosses his allusion. "Congratulations, you're as lucky as Danaë's dad. For it seems that Zeus has visited your own daughter as well."[99] Ignoring the literary references, Niceratos is suddenly clearheaded and realizes that Moschion has seduced his daughter. He fumes while Demeas good-humoredly reassures the old man that his son very much wants to make his daughter an honest woman. There is no shame at all: "I can tell you there are thousands of people going around the city today who are 'children of the gods.' It's very common."[100] The humor is wry and would have provoked a laugh of recognition from the spectators. We think again of the *Ion*, where the protagonist mocks Creusa's "friend," who (he thinks) is clearly masking her promiscuity by claiming to have been seduced by Apollo.[101]

The intrigue is now over, and the play ends on a note of spiritual reunion. The appeal of the story is the portrayal of a close call with incest which temporarily seizes the mind of the household and hypnotizes them into thinking something Oedipal or Thyestian has taken place in their family.

The plays we have looked at thus far are not the only instances of Menander's audacious flirting with incest. There is also the fragmentary play *Georgos (The Farmer)* in which a young man has raped Hedeia, the girl next door, and of course made her pregnant. The young man bemoans the fact that his father, who has just arrived from Corinth, has decided that he should marry his own half-sister.[102] But this is not the incest in the play—for this kind of union was permissible. The young man is unhappy about the marriage as well as upset about the consequences for the girl he has wronged. If he obeys his father, Hedeia will now be alone and disgraced.

Clearly, the parents-to-be will end up married, since it could not be otherwise in Menander. What ensues is the shocking part. Hedeia's brother Gorgias is out working in the fields with a wealthy farmer, Cleainetus, who suddenly injures his leg. Gorgias gives him first aid so conscientiously that the older man decides to marry the boy's sister. Now two people want Hedeia, and we have a helpful hint as to the outcome of this complication when the slave reports that Gorgias tended to his employer's injury "as if he thought the man was his own father."[103] The audience will soon appreciate (retrospectively) the irony

here. Nothing is too far-fetched for the muse of Menander. And now
the original premise, the pseudo-incest of step-siblings, palls when it is
discovered that Cleainetus is the long-lost father of both Hedeia and
Gorgias, and was about to marry his own daughter! This could occur in
Greek mythology, but not Greek reality. Menander saves the day by
having the affable—and older—Cleainetus decide to marry the woman
he had raped so long ago, and thus families past, present, and future
are reunited at the play's end.[104] Again, *Oedipus interruptus*.

Incest is one staple in the Menandrian repertory which not only
presents the internal preoccupations of the Athenian bourgeoisie but
touches an all-too-human chord in people of every culture as well (for,
as it has often been noted, the Oedipus complex is universal to all societies). A modern example of the Menandrian treatment of incest may
be found in Gilbert and Sullivan's *Iolanthe*.

Menander's most famous (or at least most discussed) play is the
Dyskolos, the only one of his works that has survived in its entirety.
Ironically, it is somewhat different from the more typical but fragmentary works: it has a bucolic setting, rustic characters, and an out-of-
town ambience. Nevertheless, it does contain the conventional New
Comedy elements of boy sees girl, boy loves girl, boy must suffer set-
backs before ultimately marrying her.

There are also some bold strokes of dramaturgy which may not be
apparent to the modern reader at first glance. For example, the old
man's daughter herself appears on stage all flustered because their
bucket has dropped into the well.[105] She even has a few lines and a scin-
tilla of a personality. Like Juliet on the balcony, she is in fear of her father: "He will spank me if he finds me out here."[106] Her admirer
Sostratus engages her in conversation.[107] Though he wants to marry
her, the girl's father Knemon, the grouch of the title, stands in the way.

Indeed, the young romance is only secondary to the portrayal of the
title figure. As Northrop Frye notes, "In the comedy of manners the
main ethical interest falls as a rule on the blocking characters."[108] The
same will be true of the mothers-in-law of Terence's *Hecyra*, the miser
Harpagon in Molière's *The Miser*, and the ill-willed Malvolio in *Twelfth
Night*—a figure so memorable that his name in Stuart times was often
used as the title for the play.

A loner, a misanthrope, and a melancholic, Knemon would today be labeled a depressive. In fact, we find in comedies of all ages what one might almost designate an archetypal pattern: a character who suffers from, for lack of a better word, "The Dyskolos Syndrome."[109] In dramatic terms he represents the agelast, and is typical of a whole breed of anti-*kōmos* men who are antagonists to the comic spirit. Sometimes the character is so unredeemable that he must be scapegoated by society, as with Malvolio. But Knemon, like the "grumpy little old man" Demus in *The Knights*,[110] is typical of the agelast won over. The *cognitio* of this play leads Knemon to a brief *self*-recognition.[111] Paradoxically, he becomes less comic as his self-ignorance evaporates.

At the beginning, Knemon is introduced by the god Pan, who speaks the prologue, as "the most inhumane of all humans on earth"[112]—in other words, the ultimate Menandrian anti-hero, the mortal enemy of *philanthrōpia.* He hates people and avoids talking to them whenever possible. By contrast—and this is a frequent occurrence in comic drama— he has a lovely daughter whom he guards zealously against the outside world, none of whom can live up to his strict values of perpetual work.

As Pan predicts, into this drab life of isolation comes Sostratus, a young man from the city who is extremely rich. His father's fields are worth "a pile of talents."[113] He is lovestruck the moment he sees the grouch's daughter. When suing for her hand from Knemon's estranged son Gorgias, he learns that the old man will not allow his daughter to marry anyone except an industrious farmer. Sostratus gamely agrees to go into the fields and toil next to his would-be father-in-law. He does not make much progress until—the single dramatic event of the play— the old man falls down his own well (foreshadowed by the bucket falling in earlier). The slaves stand by idly, and the cook even sniggers: "I hope you drown."[114] Gorgias helps to rescue him, and when he emerges from this bath, Knemon appears to have undergone a sea change—or at least a well-change—and his entire outlook on life is altered. He soliloquizes about the error of his former ways:

> I did make one mistake, thinking that I, alone among all men,
> was self-sufficient, and that I wouldn't need anybody else.

But now, having seen that the end of life can be swift and unpre-
dictable,

I've discovered my belief was not well-founded.

People always need somebody near them who can lend a hand.[115]

This theme, which we might call a symbolic "baptism," is already discernible in Odysseus' rebirth from the sea and the *Helen* and *Iphigenia in
Tauris* of Euripides. It persists throughout the subsequent history of
comedy in what we might call "water comedies." In Plautus' *Menaechmi*
and *Rudens,* Shakespeare's *The Tempest, Twelfth Night,* and *Comedy of Errors* (from *Menaechmi*), and Molière's *The Miser,* the protagonists are separated by a shipwreck, a catastrophe which is magically reversed in the
finale. The theme harks back to the "loss of face," an inherent part of
the *kōmos,* and is surely related to the frequent use of water in ritual ab-
lution (the antecedent of baptism).[116] When the "baptism" involves an
agelast like Knemon, we might look to the accounts of holiday "ducking":

> A rough and ready form of punishment . . . against the rustic
> code of conduct. The churl who will not stop working, or
> will not wear green on the feast-day, must be "ducked."[117]

Knemon is thus most directly anticipated by Demus in the *Knights,*
who is boiled up in a rejuvenating cauldron. We will see the motif
again in Marlowe's *Jew of Malta,* when the villainous anti-hero is finally
hurled into a boiling pot—a more gruesome way to cleanse his sins.
Falstaff too is thrown into the water as one of his torments in *The Merry
Wives.*

A story in Boccaccio's *Decameron* (Second day, Fifth tale) provides a
more extended illustration of the "baptismal" suggestion in the
Dyskolos. Andreuccio da Perugia, a simple lout and a greenhorn, arrives
in Naples to buy horses. His bag of money attracts the local Mafiosi (so
to speak) who cozen him out of it with the help of a con-woman, at
whose house he trips and falls into the cesspool. He emerges soiled and
despoiled. Thereafter, penniless, he falls in with other thieves, who
cleanse him by dipping him into a well for a wash, and then press him
into stealing a ring from the tomb of the recently-buried archbishop,

where they abandon him "almost as dead as a corpse." But when two predatory priests open the tomb again, our hero "rises from the dead"—at dawn—and runs off with the ring.

The element of resurrection is more obvious in Boccaccio, but it is implicit in the case of Knemon. The old man emerges from the well a different person.[118] (The verb *ekbainein* means both "to exit" and "to become.")[119] In gratitude to Gorgias he divides his property in two, offering half for his son to support "your mother and me,"[120] and the rest as a dowry for his daughter—whose wedding arrangements he also entrusts to his son. Thus, in a subtle echo of the principal love plot, the harmonious Knemon is also reconciled with his estranged wife and enjoys the *oikeia hēdonē*—this time literally the joys of home.

Gorgias presents Sostratus as a candidate for groom. Knemon approves of the lad because of his farmer's tan,[121] and the fiancé prepares a further act to strengthen the ties between their families. He persuades his father to allow his sister to marry Knēmōn's son. The older man demurs, grumbling about acquiring two poor relatives in one day.[122] (Interestingly enough, Knemon is not particularly poor.)[123] Sostratus admonishes him gnomically: "Remember money is a sometime thing—it may not last forever. Tychē may take it away. But goodness is immutable."[124]

The plutocratic patriarch sighs in defeat and gives his daughter's hand to Knemon's stepson, pronouncing the formula and even proposing a massive dowry of three talents.[125] At the same time, he rejects Gorgias' counter-offer of a one-talent dowry for his sister, since it represents the young man's entire share of Knemon's farm. This is a dramatic symbol, and the grouch's family is now reconciled and reunited.[126]

A moment later Gorgias leaves to try to convince his churlish father to attend the double wedding ceremony. At which point a jubilant Sostratus proposes that his father arrange a festive *kōmos* to precede the *gamos*:

SOSTRATUS: Now we need some good drinking, Papa,
And an up-all-nighter for the ladies.

CALLIPIDES: *(wryly)* That's topsy-turvy, son. *They'll* do the boozing, and *we'll* be the ones who stay up all night![127]

The reader would be correct in sensing a rather tame (when compared with Aristophanes) sexual double-entendre, for the verb *pannychizein* ("hold a vigil") can also mean "make love through the night."[128] Thus we discern a faint glimmer of Old Comedy gusto.

If one counts as a "new beginning" the reconciliation of Knemon and his wife, at the end of the play the world would have three more married couples—this seems to be an article of faith with Menander. In this case, the players also celebrate with an onstage revel which includes drinking and dancing. And yet at first the grouch resolutely refuses to join the merrymaking and sits dourly outside the party, determined not to enjoy himself. But Callipides' slave Getas and the cook badger him till he relents and finally agrees to join the dance. This agelast has been converted—or perhaps merely bullied—to a sociable being. The play concludes with a shout of Olympic victory ("O kallinikoi!")[129] as a torchlight parade escorts the title character in for a celebration of the *kōmos* and *gamos* of Old Comedy. One thinks immediately of the grand finales of *Acharnians, Knights,* and *Birds.*

Aspis (The Shield) is an example of the playwright at his best, a delightful piece that combines many Menandrian features and seems to emphasize the very elements that will be picked up and accentuated by the Roman adapters. These include a genuinely clever slave, a plot of trickery, an artfully depicted miser, a strong tinge of poetic justice and—*mirabile dictu*—some moments of hearty laughter. Plus the standard rebirth and wedding motifs. There is even a brief but hilarious house call by a comic doctor. The play also graphically presents the now familiar triumph of youth over age (as opposed to the reverse in Aristophanes), anticipating the likes of Molière's *School for Wives.* Daus' description of Smicrines' prancing around the house with his keys and dreaming of wealth[130] even anticipates Subtle in Ben Jonson's *Alchemist,* who will also ultimately be duped.

Menander's play begins somberly, presenting an incident which was unfortunately all too familiar to the audience. Daus, the slave who had accompanied his young master to war, enters carrying a battered shield and bears the heartbreaking news that Cleostratus is among the fallen.

As many have noted, the tenor of his speech approaches tragedy, for he is totally convinced that Cleostratus—who has gone to war only to acquire a dowry for his sister—has perished. The victim's uncle, the old miser Smicrines, overhears Daus' lament and accosts the slave. Shedding crocodile tears, he begs for details.

Still in an elevated tone, the slave recounts that the death occurred after the battle, when many of the soldiers were gathering booty. He adds, almost parenthetically:

DAUS: Everybody came off with lots of stuff.

SMICRINES: *(eagerly)* Goody![131]

Then in mock-epic tones, Daus describes the manifold riches his master acquired in the ensuing conflict (from which he was absent, cataloguing the spoils). When he returned three days later, the corpses were bloated beyond recognition, but Cleostratus' shield was found and that was proof enough of his heroic demise. After the mass cremation, the slave returned to Athens.

Smicrines cannot suppress his awakened appetite for treasures and greedily interrogates the slave again, making him repeat the inventory of plunder. The amount of gold, silver, and other precious items is impressive, but instead of commenting on their lavishness, the miser remarks with unctuous hypocrisy, "I don't care about all you've brought home, any of that. I only wish *(sob)* the boy had lived."[132] Moments later, Daus departs into the house of Chairestratus and the miser confides to the audience, "Now I think I'll go inside to figure out the smoothest way of . . . dealing with the rest of them."[133]

There follows a delayed prologue, this time spoken by a female deity, who does not identify herself until her very last word. She quickly explains that Daus is unaware that Cleostratus has *not* died. In the panic of battle, when the soldiers were ambushed by the enemy, someone else picked up Cleostratus' shield, and it was *this* person's body that the slave mistook for his master's. Moreover, the young man himself will be home very soon (in Act Four). The prologue also confirms our strong suspicion that Smicrines is the nastiest man in the world, far more offensive than other crabby old men like Knemon in the *Dyskolos* or Euclio, the miser in Plautus' *Aulularia:*

This guy has given no thought to
Family and friend, nor to any of the shameful things in his life:
He wants to have everything—that's all he knows.
He lives all alone, with only an old slave woman.[134]

The goddess also explains that Chairestratus, younger brother of the miser and likewise uncle of the deceased, has been taking care of his niece, the dead man's sister. This uncle is the polar opposite of his brother. Menander uses two evocative words to make the contrast: *ponēros* ("wicked") to describe the evil uncle, and *chrēstos* ("noble") for the good one.[135]

Finally, the prologue reveals that the "good uncle" has betrothed his niece to his son by a previous marriage—along with a not inconsiderable dowry of two talents.[136] In fact, the wedding was to have taken place that day. But catastrophe has struck. The greedy Smicrines, realizing that by law all of his nephew's wealth, gold, slaves, mules, and girls would now go to the dead man's sister, exercises his legal right as her guardian to marry her himself (for lucre, not love). The prologue assures us that he will not succeed. In fact, he will be totally disgraced all over town.

Her duty discharged, the speaker at last identifies herself:

It's only left for me to tell my name.
Who am I, who's running this whole show?
I am Tychē.[137]

It is none other than Chance, who, with her exposition "the dead will rise, the good will be rewarded, and the villain punished," removes all doubt (and thus all suspense) from the rest of the play. All will end well. Smicrines informs Daus of his intention to follow the law *(nomos)* and marry the young girl. The slave treats him with ironic indulgence and also scoffs at remarks from the old man like "So no one will say I'm greedy, I didn't even count the treasure."[138]

At the beginning of Act Two the good uncle, Chairestratus, accompanied by his son Chaireas, who was intending to marry the girl, confronts the bad. Smicrines repeats his intent to wed her and, reminding his brother that he is the elder, commands him not to offer their niece to anyone else. Chairestratus is staggered. "Be civilized," he retorts angrily. "Let her marry the young man she grew up with. I'll even give you the money."[139] But Smicrines is too canny and sees possible legal ramifications in such an offer (ultimately the girl's son could sue him);[140] he declines, insisting upon the maiden herself:

> CHAIR.: Don't you care for decency, Smicrines?
> SMIC.: What? What?
> CHAIR.: Are you going to marry that child at your age?
> SMIC.: (*disingenuously*) What do you mean "my age"?
> CHAIR.: I think you're way too old.
> SMIC.: Am I the only older man who's ever gotten married?[141]

The miser is resolute and his younger brother retreats in a state of shock, threatening to die if this proposal is enacted. Young Chaireas once again laments that the law (*nomos*) is keeping him from his beloved.[142] His father appears again and tells Daus he is going mad from his brother's villainy (*ponēria*):

> CHAIR.: For he's going to get married.
> DAUS: Are you serious? Is he even . . . capable?[143]

Chairestratus reiterates that he will die before letting this wedding go through. This chance sparks a scheme in Daus, and he tells father and son that "we must enact a very tragic drama."[144] Chairestratus must follow his avowed depression to the limit and pretend to be on his deathbed . . . and then die:

> DAUS: Then we'll call a doctor, a real learned type.
> He'll say it's pleuritis or phrenitis or one of those other
> things that kill you quickly.
> CHAIR.: And then?
> DAUS: And then you're dead. Of course, we'll start to mourn
> you.[145]

Note how, in contrast to the mumbo-jumbo of the traditional foreign physician (*iatros xenikos*), Menander's quack doctors use the names of real diseases. Nevertheless, father and son exchange baffled looks. Daus explains further:

> DAUS: Don't you see? Your daughter thus becomes an heiress
>   too, just like your niece . . . except, your estate is worth
>   at least *sixty* talents, your niece's not more than four.
>   The old miser is the same relation to them both. He'll
>   gladly drop the poor girl for the rich one.
> CHAIR.:   Now I get it.
> DAUS: Of course, if you're not a numbskull.[146]

Now they catch on. They like the idea, and Chaireas is sent off to find a friend to play "the foreign doctor—sophisticated and a trifle fraudulent."[147] For this play within a play he will get all the necessary papers and costumes, including a toupee, cloak, and foreign accent. As the two masters rush to do the slave's bidding, Daus himself addresses the audience:

> DAUS: This little show will be entertaining, if once it gets going,
>   And our doctor plays it convincingly.[148]

This is an ideal note for the end of an act—which it indeed is. Although some scholars have asserted that Daus is more of a bungler than a clever slave, a look at the evidence proves otherwise.[149] Although when Cleostratus comes back "from the dead" Daus' brainstorm is made superfluous, this does not diminish the fact that his stratagem has fooled the miser. The mean-spirited uncle is suitably punished.

Daus is indeed a worthy forerunner of the Plautine *servus callidus*.[150] (Incidentally, the *servus currens* or "running slave" is also found in Menander.)[151] Ovid provides the best confirmation that Menandrian drama had already given birth to the clever slave, as shown by his justification for the Greek playwright's immortality,[152] which Ben Jonson—drawing heavily on Marlowe's translation—rendered with:

> While slaves be false, fathers hard, and bawds be whorish
> Whilst harlots flatter shall Menander flourish.[153]

A fragment attributed by some to Menander corroborates the existence of these clever slaves in Greek New Comedy, and the fact that it is told as a proverb suggests that they were a familiar type:

> [Master], take me as an advisor in your troubles:
> Don't despise the counsel of a slave:

Often the slave of good character
Is smarter than his masters.
And even if Tychē gave his body into slavery,
His character still has a free mind.[154]

After an irrelevant but pleasant choral interlude, Act Three begins
with Smicrines gloating over his new possessions when Daus runs in
with "bad news," which he prefaces with a series of quotations from the
tragic playwrights (Euripides, Aeschylus, and lesser-known authors like
Carcinus). It is perhaps the funniest extant moment in Menandrian
comedy. The miser tries to stop this "fit of citations" and get to the
point. His words interspersed with even more tags, Daus announces
that Chairestratus is dying and they have called the doctor, who is on
his way. No sooner has Daus spoken these words than the pseudo-
quack appears, announced by a pretentious quote from Euripides'
Orestes. Chaireas' friend turns out to be a master jokester and plays the
part to the hilt, spouting nonsensical jargon to Smicrines, who inquires
after his brother's health, and imitating the Doric accent that to the
Greeks conferred medical authority, as a Viennese tone might to us in
certain medical situations:[155]

DOCTOR: Zere ist no prayer to zavink him. Zuch konditions are
Fatale—I don't vant to komfort mit false hopinks.
SMICRINES: Don't make it easy: just tell me the truth.[156]

The consultant scurries off, having baited the hook which the miser
has eagerly bitten. Acts Four and Five are both in tatters, but we know
that the fourth act included the expected arrival and revival of the
"dead" brother. Young Cleostratus enters, and Smicrines is doubly
foiled. He can now marry neither of his nieces. His younger brother sets
a double wedding (not only will his son marry Cleostratus' sister, but
the young man himself will marry his uncle's daughter). This dual
gamos shuts out the miser, who must now endure the shame of his actions—and perhaps worse.[157]

There is also the comic gambit of an old man wanting to marry a
young girl. In Aristophanes there would be no problem—for in the
course of his comedies the protagonist evolves from senile sexagenarian into sexy sexbomb. But New Comedy presents the now more famil-

iar triumph of youth over the aged agelast who tries to block his way to natural fulfillment. By the time of the Renaissance, the girl, who has no name and no lines in Menander, would have both in the works of Molière. She would doubtless speak of her disgust at the prospect of marrying a prunish senior citizen. The playwright makes a wonderful comic moment of this theme in a scene in *The Miser,* as we shall see. This law of nature is defined in the final lines of Beaumarchais' *Barber of Seville:*

> FIGARO: Let's be candid, doctor: When youth and love combine to trick an Oldster, anything he does to try and stop it could rightfully be called a useless precaution.[158]

Menander represents both the mainstream and the canonization of the new comic code. The occasion for performances was still seasonal. Just as with Old Comedy, each presentation coincided with the celebration of a Greek fertility rite. In a real sense, comedy had not gone far from its roots.

Like Aristophanes—but far more subtly—Menander provides an anodyne for the painful realities of everyday life. He dares not say all's right with the state, because manifestly it was not. But he can offer that a happy ending is still possible in the private life of the spectator. This has been the balm of comedy ever since.

10

Plautus Makes an Entrance

Ever the comic poet, Philemon died of over-laughing.[1] The year was 263 B.C., and the date is conventionally regarded as the end of the era of New Comedy. Diphilus and Menander had left the scene much earlier—the latter in 292 at the age of fifty-two, when, according to tradition, he drowned while swimming in the harbor of Piraeus.[2] We are told by the ancient biographers that Menander created over a hundred and eight comedies.[3] His rival Philemon could only manage a mere ninety-seven in almost twice the life-span. Yet it is quite unlikely that either could have produced this quantity without Athens having many more festivals. But in fact theaters were burgeoning all over Attica. Although these venues might be regarded as what in modern times is commonly referred to as "the sticks," in this case they were high-paying sticks like Sicily and Magna Graecia. Those wandering minstrels made a tidy living.[4]

But none of these colonies could have been more enthusiastic than Tarentum (Greek Taras), inside the heel of Italy, which already had its own native comic tradition in the *phylax* farce which is depicted on so many vases.[5] This lively town gave birth to the first "Roman" playwright, the bilingual scholar Livius Andronicus, a former slave who—

after being relocated to Rome—rendered into Latin a Greek tragedy and comedy for the harvest festival *(ludi Romani)* of 240 B.C.[6] This set the pattern for centuries: Latin plays "with a plot,"[7] based on Greek models; such comedies were known as *palliata,* "in Greek dress." As the third century neared its close, many more performance dates were added at other festivals.[8] The Romans were stage-struck.

They were a puritan folk, at once fascinated by and suspicious of the theater; for centuries they soothed their ambivalent psyches by having their productions performed on a makeshift wooden stage which was dismantled after each festival.[9] Even when Pompey the Great built the first permanent venue in 55 B.C., he had to dedicate it as a temple to Venus Victrix, the stairs of which doubled as seats on theatrical occasions—and could hold forty thousand spectators. As an agelastic, theater-hating church father commented, "Thus he deceived discipline with superstition."[10]

Rome had also long enjoyed a native type of improvisatory comedy, known as the *fabulae Atellanae* or Atellane farces, named after the Campanian village where the genre probably originated.[11] This crude entertainment presented little skits with stock low-life characters like Bucco the babbling fool, Pappus the foolish old codger, Dossenus the hunchbacked buffoon, and Maccus, another type of simpleton.

It was from these lusty, popular entertainments that, scarcely a generation after Livius, the first true genius of Roman literature literally took the stage. Horace recalls the artist's roots in the native tradition:

> Look at how Plautus
> Portrays the characters of a lovestruck youth,
> A stingy father and cunning pimp,
> How much of Dossennus there is in his hungry parasites,
> How he runs about the stage with sloppy slippers![12]

Titus Maccius Plautus (c. 250–184 B.C.) is very likely a theatrical pseudonym, for what kind of parent would call a child "Dick O'Fool McSlapstick"?[13] What little we know of this poet's life does not help to explain how he rose from humble origins in the north Italian town of Sarsina to become what Aulus Gellius would later praise as the "Glory of the Latin Tongue."[14] The imperial scholar also preserves Plautus' "bi-

ography," which states enigmatically that the playwright made a fortune in some kind of "show business."[15] It is pleasant to imagine our
author in a band of strolling players. That would certainly help explain
his unique instinct for pleasing the Roman crowds.[16]

"Roman Comedy," however, is a misleading term. For, unlike
Aristophanes and Menander, none of the Roman *palliata* playwrights
produced entirely original compositions. Rather they were, to a greater
or lesser extent, based on Greek models. The very art of their
dramaturgy lay in the manner in which they rendered the Hellenic
originals. And yet what Plautus and his colleagues created in their
adaptations of Menander and the others was nothing short of revolutionary.

But, as in the case of Aristophanes, either merit or capricious fate
(Tychē perhaps?) has allowed only a single playwright to survive and
represent the entire Roman genre, while his contemporaries—who seem
to have written in much the same style—left only fragments. (Terence,
as we will see, wrote a completely different style of comedy.) Thus, we
should caution ourselves that Plautus may be only the tip of an iceberg
of laughter.[17] Since Livius Andronicus, Naevius, Caecilius, Accius, and
their colleagues have all melted away, we must, in Vergil's words, *crimine
ab uno / disce omnis* ("From the crime of one learn that of all").[18]

Like his contemporaries, Plautus appears to have used the Greek
models as a mere springboard, a process which he called *vortere* ("convert, adapt"), a term still recognized by Terence and, perhaps obliquely,
by Horace—and in the English "version."[19] As the playwright describes
Trinummus, "Philemon wrote it: Plautus made the 'barbarian' version."[20]

But Plautus is much too modest. His method transformed the Greek
works into something entirely "rich and strange." He seasoned the
bland fodder of the Greek models with the piquant sauce of native Italian farce, refurbishing the sedate originals into brash musical comedies
by using his innate operatic sense to recast simple Greek dialogue into
eminently singable, polymetric Latin songs *(cantica)*.[21]

That he knew Greek well is unquestioned. That he translated faithfully is out of the question. Indeed, like the Old Comedy poets of Athens, Plautus' language is so colorful and idiosyncratic that there can be

no doubt that he took great liberties. Plautine style became synonymous with verbal virtuosity and neologisms. Despite his criticisms of the playwright elsewhere, Horace invokes the master as a precedent for his own poetic coinages.[22] Centuries after the playwright's death we find the second-century A.D. critic and scholar Aulus Gellius coining a superlative adjective, *Plautinissimus,* to describe a really juicy piece of dialogue,[23] calling to mind such Plautine super-superlatives as *occisissumus sum omnium qui vivont* ("I'm the very dead-dead-deadest man alive").[24] As one of Plautus' slaves says, when questioned about the unusual word *parenticida*—a *hapax* or "one off" in Latin—"I don't deal with dated, dissipated diction."[25]

Plautus' *vortere* contained all this and more. Like Shakespeare and Molière, Plautus begs, borrows, and steals from every conceivable source—including himself. But once the play begins, everything becomes one hundred percent Plautus.[26]

Gellius has preserved some passages of Menander's *Plokion (The Necklace)* alongside the Latinized version of the same passage by Caecilius, a younger contemporary of Plautus in whom we can discover elements of the "Plautine" style.[27] Caecilius was much praised in antiquity, ranked by some above both Plautus and Terence.[28] This early exercise in comparative literature provides some insight into the methods of the popular Roman playwrights. Menander's original described an ill-favored heiress whose only attractive feature was her family's money. This creature now rules her husband, and has just fired the maid whom she thinks he lusts for (he does). Caecilius' Latin version is much coarser and more vivid. He spells everything out in broader detail, interlarded with not a few well-turned jokes like "I'm dying for her death. A very living corpse am I." It gives a much more vigorous picture of the woman's badgering:

> With pleading, demanding, insisting, and scolding
> She so bludgeoned me that now I'm selling her.

Gellius sums up disparagingly what—with few exceptions—has been the attitude toward Roman comedy throughout the ages: to the elegant Greek models "he stuffed in a lot of slapstick."[29]

A similar comparison was not possible with a Plautine text and its Greek original until the discovery in 1968 of a long fragment from Menander's *Dis Exapaton* ("Double-deceiver"), adapted by the Latin playwright as the *Bacchides.* In a memorable inaugural lecture to the chair of Greek at University College London, Eric Handley presented the results of this landmark exercise.[30] Plautus had combined what were two separate speeches in Menander, changed the rhythm (from the simple iambic to the jauntier trochaic), and added several snappy jokes and a distinctly Roman attack on the usually-revered moral notion of *pietas.* Handley also substantiated many of Eduard Fraenkel's brilliant conjectures about Plautine verbal techniques,[31] and concluded that by comparing the two playwrights we could see "on a very small scale but by direct observation how [Plautus] likes his colours strong, his staging more obvious, his comedy more comic."[32]

Of the many paradoxes in Latin comedy, the greatest is that these Roman entertainments are called *fabulae palliatae,* "plays in Greek dress," as opposed to *fabulae togatae.* The characters are pretending to behave "Greekly," playing on the commonly accepted notion that the decadent denizens of Athens were the precise moral and social opposites of the citizens of Rome. Plautus even uses the verb "to Greek it up" (*pergraecari* or *congraecare*) as a synonym for immoral, debauched behavior. This Greek license enabled the players to engage in activities that normally would be frowned upon by the censors—both Roman and psychological—and so is a vivid example of the "losing of identity" that is part of the *kōmos* mentality. Thus at the finale of *Stichus* when a lively slave arranges a booze-up for his fellow bondsmen, the author has him explain to the audience:

> Don't be surprised that lowly little slaves like us
> can drink, make love, invite our friends to supper.
> In Athens, we're allowed to do this sort of thing.[33]

With similar freedom, the characters onstage can eat foods normally forbidden to Romans, delicacies prohibited by the strict puritanical "blue laws."[34] In the *Menaechmi,* for example, when the would-be errant husband asks his mistress Erotium to prepare a meal for their assignation, the following passage would give the audience a vicarious thrill:

MENAECHMUS: Please arrange a feast at your house, have it cooked for
three of us.
Also have some very special party foods bought in the
forum—
glandiose, whole-hog, and a descendant of the lardly
ham.
Or perhaps some pork chopettes, or other treats along
these lines.[35]

This is gastronomic delinquency on the husband's part, as all these
foods were normally forbidden by the puritanical sumptuary laws.
Even if one cavils that these laws were passed after Plautus' death and
were already dead letters, such food would nevertheless be prohibitively
expensive to the average Roman.

But the real rule-breaker is Plautus' consummate creation: the clever
slave. Though this figure was anticipated in previous comedy, Plautus
presents the bondsman in his ultimate apotheosis. This is not mere
metaphor, for the *servus callidus* is as boastful as the Romans are never
supposed to be, and is even not loath to compare himself to a god. He is
the "architect of trickery" *(architectus doli)*[36] who acts out his young master's worst fantasies, for example by swindling the lad's own father for
the money needed to purchase the young man's girlfriend:

CALIDORUS: Will you get me twenty minae—cash—today?
PSEUDOLUS: Of course. Now don't annoy me any more.
But so you won't deny I told you, let me say:
If I can't swindle someone else—I'll fleece your father.
CALIDORUS: What, what? By all that's holy—fleece mother too![37]

This is, of course, an infringement of the most sacred prohibition: respect for parents was one of the cardinal Roman virtues. In this topsy-
turvy comic world the young man has invoked *pietas,* the cornerstone of
Roman morality, only to violate it.

In a sense the saucy Plautine slave and the bland Plautine lover are
really two facets of the same character. For the boldfaced bondsman
acts as an alter ego for the young man's love pangs, "disobediently"
flim-flamming father while the *adulescens* remains in the shelter of os-

tensible *pietas*. (It is not until Beaumarchais' *Figaro* that the slave and hero are fused into a single comic character without class distinctions.)

This bit of dialogue reveals an important difference between the treatment of "love" on the Greek and Roman stages. We have seen how Menander's plays regularly conclude with a lawful marriage.[38] Plautus avoids this ending like the plague. His heroes seek fun, not marriage—its polar opposite. They are almost exclusively interested in fast women (*hetairai*), and hence most of his plays center around the swindling of money to pay for the young men's pleasure. The playwright is not sentimental. To Plautus, "happily ever after" is a prepaid year with—or better still the outright purchase of—a concubine.

Only a handful of the twenty extant plays conclude with a girl being recognized as free and marriageable. And even in some of these instances, at least in *Casina* and *Cistellaria*, the wedding is scarcely mentioned in the text and is merely predicted at some point in the future. One assumes it will take place . . . sometime, but it is not a consummation devoutly to be wished. In the epilogue to the *Casina* the spectator, in exchange for his hearty applause, will be rewarded with the ability to have the mistress he wants and to always deceive his wife.[39] At the end of the *Trinummus*, marriage is even meted out as punishment to the remorseful *adulescens*, who stoically accepts it for misbehaving:

> SON: I will marry, father—
>   her and any others you want me to.
>   FATHER: No. Though I was cross with you,
>   One wife is suffering enough for any man.[40]

Plautine comedy can best be viewed as a "Saturnalian" inversion of normal values. Everyday life is turned on its head, everyday values are topsy-turvy. The slave, the lowest man on the totem pole of life, emerges triumphant—and grandiloquent—over his esteemed Roman master (occasionally even a distinguished senator). And yet, in reality, every master had in his everyday power the ability to put a slave to death for this kind of audacity. Only during the Saturnalia was this right waived. What Plautus presents is, in the truest sense, a Roman holiday.[41]

After the young man's quest for pleasure, the most frequently treated subject in Plautus is the institution of marriage, which he does not exactly celebrate. In Aristophanes we frequently find a husband ignoring the bonds of marriage and going freelance (at least for the duration of the play). As we have seen, Dicaeopolis in the *Acharnians* and Trygaeus in *Peace,* though married with children, both break loose and seek extracurricular activities. Cratinus too, in the somewhat surreal *Bottle,* left his wife for a spree with Ms. Hooch.

By contrast, while the husbands in Roman comedy go to great lengths to avoid their very vigilant spouses, they *never* succeed in consummating an extramarital *gamos* at the end of the play. This itself seems to be a kind of Saturnalian inversion, since Roman husbands normally had license to commit adultery—whereas their wives could be put to death for similar behavior. As we will see in the next chapter, Plautus stands this institutionalized double-standard upon its head in the *Amphitruo.*

The animus against women is so pervasive in Roman comedy that even slaves take any opportunity to rail at the opposite sex. In the *Casina,* for example, the respective slaves of both the husband and the wife comment acerbically on Cleostrata's character. "You're a real hunter," says Olympio to his master, "because you spend all your time with a dog."[42] And when the woman asks her slave Chalinus what he thinks her husband wants with her, the slave responds:

> CHALINUS: I think he wants to see you blazing on your pyre beyond
> the city gates.[43]

But the worst type of wife, and Plautus' best target for comic hostility, was the *uxor dotata,* the henpecking, big-dowried *matrona* who makes her husband's life a misery. She is foreshadowed in Aristophanes as Strepsiades' wife in the *Clouds.* We recall the first scene, in which the frantic oldster complains bitterly of his mismarriage: he was a country bumpkin, she a wealthy and conceited city girl with insatiable sexual appetites.[44] There is also the fragmentary sketch of the figure in what we have of Menander's *Plokion*[45]—an *epiklēros* or heiress is in a position to boss her husband, as described by Aristotle.[46] Plautus is so fond of the *uxor dotata* that, if the drama will not allow for her inclusion in the cast, he will have a character deliver a gratuitous tirade against her.[47]

The *Menaechmi (The Brothers Menaechmus)* provides a good illustration of Plautus' entire attitude toward wives and matrimony. Though the prologue protests that the setting is particularly Greek, in truth it is essentially Roman.[48] In fact, one scholar has even argued that it is based on no Greek model whatsoever.[49] We do have evidence of at least three comedies by Menander which dealt with twins, but none seems to have been a comedy of errors like *Brothers Menaechmus,* which Harry Levin aptly characterized by saying: "We are at the roulette wheel, not the chessboard."[50] It was at the very least a Plautine experiment, for he never wrote another play like it again.

The prologue, which in Plautus (with the exception of the *Amphitruo*) is never spoken by an Olympian god—he seems to secularize his Greek originals[51]—provides the audience with the knowledge necessary to understand the initial setting of the play. Twins have been separated in childhood—an enduring comic theme. (Pascal remarked that "two faces that are alike, although neither of them excites laughter by itself, make us laugh when together, on account of their likeness.")[52] The one called Menaechmus was kidnapped by pirates. To commemorate the loss of the stolen brother, the grieving father changed the name of the remaining twin, Sosicles, to Menaechmus. Menaechmus I is now settled down in Epidamnus with the necessary wife and mistress, and during the play Menaechmus II, who lives in Syracuse, will return to look for his long-lost brother.

On this day of days Menaechmus I plans a special outing. He confides in his parasite Peniculus that his aim in short is "to have a good time" *(pulchre habere)* with his mistress: "hidden from my wife we will live it up and burn this day to ashes."[53] With perfect symmetry, his wife's behavior has the opposite effect—"to always give him a hard time" *(semper male habere)*.[54] When the beleaguered husband first appears on stage, he is doing battle with the shrewish woman, complaining that she badgers him about his every movement: "she's not a wife, she's a snoopy customs officer!"[55] He threatens to divorce her and continues with a song of castigation:

> Watch out for trouble, if you're wise,
> A husband hates a wife who spies.
> But so you won't have watched in vain, for all your
> Diligence and care,
> Today I've asked a wench to dinner, and we're going out
> Somewhere.[56]

Plautus emphasizes the deliberate contrast between Menaechmus' wife and his lady-friend in a lapidary outburst when he first sees his mistress Erotium, whom he refers to as *Mea Voluptas* ("pure pleasure"), a grander form of the more common *Voluptas Mea:* "My wife—O my purest pleasure—when I see you, how I hate her!"[57] He also pays her the unusual compliment of being *morigera* ("dutiful")—a principal Roman wifely virtue, here ironically used not of the homemaker but of the housebreaker.[58] Plautus often toys with this serious attribute, as we will see.

After ordering his menu of forbidden foods, Menaechmus I wanders off to the forum—inexplicably putting business before pleasure. Invariably in Roman Comedy, the stage left exit was the way to the forum, stage right the road to the country. This provides a sort of comastic index: the closer to the forum a character is, the more tied up he will be.

His exit naturally signals the arrival of his twin, who has just reached Epidamnus and whose earnest (but not clever) slave Messenio warns him about the local inhabitants. They are, he explains, "huge drinkers and great pleasure-lovers."[59] Moreover, the ladies here are sexier and more "enticing" *(blandiores)*[60] than anywhere else:

> Now here's the race of men you'll find in Epidamnus:
> The greatest libertines, the greatest drinkers too,
> The most bamboozlers and charming flatterers
> Live in this city. And as for wanton women, well—
> Nowhere in the world, I'm told, are they more dazzling.
> Because of this, they call the city Epidamnus,
> For no one stops off unscathed, "undamaged," as it were.[61]

Although Plautus refers to a town that really existed in his own day, he is rather insouciant in his geography, for the itinerary his slave outlines is a jumble of ancient names.[62]

No sooner is Menaechmus II forewarned than the confusion of identities begins. This is facilitated by the outrageous coincidence that both brothers are wearing the same outfit. Indeed, until the final scene when the twins are reunited, both brothers could be played by the same actor (and if the characters were masked, the similarity would be all the more apparent).

When the newly arrived twin is recognized and hailed by name by both Erotium and her cook, he is puzzled that people already know who he is, but is too clueless to recognize the clue he has been given. Ignoring his slave's admonitions, he succumbs to the courtesan's blandishments and enters her house to enjoy the festivities that his unwitting brother has arranged. Several hours later he emerges from the ecstatic *kōmos,* drunk and garlanded and carrying a very elegant lady's gown on his arm:

> By all the gods, what man in just a single day
> Received more favors, though expecting none at all?
> I've wined, I've dined, I've concubined—and of this dress I've
>   robbed her blind.[63]

The garment was a gift to Erotium from his brother, who stole it from his wife. The meretrix has coaxed him (she thinks) to take it and have more gold embellishment added—and for a bracelet as well.

A moment after the lucky traveler skips offstage, the local brother reappears, furious and frustrated. While he was in the forum, a pesky client caught hold of him, demanding that he defend him in a case. He could not refuse (he is, after all, a Roman *patronus*). As he explains:

> I was just now delayed, forced to give legal aid, no evading this
>   client of mine who had found me.
> Though I wanted to do you know what—and with who—still he
>   bound me and tied ropes around me.[64]

The client's clinging behavior echoes his description of his busybody wife: "You detain me, delay me, demand all details."[65] Citizenship, like marriage, places certain restraints upon a man. Menaechmus has just now been "tied up" in the forum on business.[66] The special Romanness of this scene has often been commented on.[67] Both ties prevent Menaechmus from following his natural instincts.[68]

To compound the poor man's misery, his virago wife appears and berates him for his bad behavior—especially for stealing her dress, which she demands that he return—and storms off to seek her father—and perhaps a divorce. Nothing daunted, Menaechmus proceeds to Erotium to ask her for the garment back. His mistress is outraged, insisting that she has only just given it to him a moment ago, and accuses him of trying to cheat her. Though he denies it, she too slams her door in his face, leaving him alone on stage.

The entire fabric of Menaechmus' existence seems torn to shreds. Everyone is angry at him. All doors are closed. He is—to use his own, typically Plautine coinage—*exclusissumus*, "the most kicked-out man in the world."[69] He rushes off to seek advice from his friends. But there is worse to come.

Immediately thereafter (of course) Menaechmus II reappears (still carrying the dress). The wife—who has a big part but no name—emerges and subjects her husband's facsimile to a rabid tongue-lashing. His retort is reminiscent of Semonides:

> WIFE: O Shameless brazen wicked man!
>
> MEN. II: *(with quiet sarcasm)* Do you have any notion why
> The ancient Greeks called Hecuba a total . . . bitch?
>
> WIFE: No.
>
> MEN. II: Because she acted just the way you're acting now:
> She barked and cursed at everyone who came in sight.[70]

At this moment, the wife's father enters. When Menaechmus II denies knowing either of them and pretends to go berserk to scare them away, the old man, believing his son-in-law is completely insane, runs off to the city center to get a doctor. The traveler rushes off in the other direction toward the harbor and the safety of his ship.

No sooner does the *senex* reappear with the doctor than the angry Menaechmus I re-enters. The learned medical practitioner, obviously a classmate of the quack in Menander's *Aspis* and an ancestor of the physician in the St. George plays, questions Menaechmus. The patient must suffer for his twin brother's actions. The psychiatrist *gloriosus* has pronounced him in need of an expensive cure, and orders several burly porters *(lorarii)* to drag him off for "treatment."

Messenio, seeing what he thinks is his master struggling with a group of nasty-looking strangers, comes to his aid and beats the attackers off (Plautus is fond of presenting mayhem onstage). The rescued Menaechmus shrugs at Messenio's insistence that he is his slave—as far as he is concerned, Messenio can be as free as he wants. Thrilled by his "emancipation," the former slave skips off ecstatically.

All this mounting confusion is resolved when the two brothers finally confront one another onstage. The slave Messenio looks at the local twin and tells his master that he sees *speculum tuum*, "you in the mirror."[71] This is a portentous phrase. For in a very real sense, the visiting brother is the alter ego of the local twin. In short, what this play really represents to its audience is a married, responsible Roman citizen who desires temporarily to break all the rules of his normal life: to avoid litigation, eat forbidden food, and cheat on his harridan wife. Someone with the same name—his mirror image—*does* savor all these illicit joys. But this is another Menaechmus—who is unmarried and free to consort with Erotium without any repercussions. And, as a foreigner, he is not required to abstain from the forbidden delicacies. The only joy that the local, married brother can derive from all this is vicarious:

> MEN. I: Wonderful! By Pollux I'm delighted you had fun because
> of me.
> She asked you to dine because she thought that you were
> me.[72]

Earlier in the play, at the height of the confusion, the married brother cried out that all these wild goings-on seem to him like a dream: "haec nihilo esse mihi videntur setius quam somnia."[73] He does not realize how right he is. For this comedy represents the *kōma* of Menaechmus I, an upstanding, married Roman citizen whose fantasies have conjured up a surrogate self to indulge in forbidden pleasures while he himself preserves outward everyday respectability. In fact, as the recognition scene demonstrates, there is really only one Menaechmus: the married one. After this day of errors, this *folle journée*, everything will return to normal. Identities will be properly redistributed, and Menaechmus II (his "Greek" twin) must take back his original name—Sosicles. Menaechmus I retains his respectability. Both brothers will decide to return to Syracuse and the family business. *Voluptas* today, but *industria* tomorrow.

This is, in its way, a kind of rebirth, for in Syracuse they will begin life anew. In their hometown, with their family made whole, they will enjoy new life; the past will become a *tabula rasa* with no obligations for either of them. For that reason the play closes on a commercial note, with Messenio announcing an auction of all the local twin's property. Anxious to divest all the impedimenta of his master's former life, he adds, "we'll sell the wife as well—if anyone will come and take her."[74] This is Susarion's misogynistic humor taken to the ultimate degree. One thinks of the modern stand-up comic's *para prosdokian* quip, "Take my wife . . . *please.*"

However much the strife between married couples is the stuff of comedy, the fact remains that it is disproportionately prominent in Plautus. The battle is even more explicit in the *Casina,* where at one point it comes to actual blows. Probably one of the master's late creations, and definitely his bawdiest, this play is a no-holds-barred attack on the Menandrian ideal of marriage as the natural culmination of a love affair. It was one of Plautus' most successful plays, often revived after his death. Indeed, the manuscript we have shows traces of revision for a later performance.

The prologue explains that the play is a Latin adaptation of Diphilus' *Cleroumenoi* ("the Lot-Casters"). But Plautus stresses that he has given it a fresh coat of paint—"again and anew" *(rursum denuo),* he says pleonastically.[75] He goes on to explain the situation. In its outline it is fairly Euripidomenandrean.

Sixteen years earlier one of the household slaves discovered a baby girl who had been exposed and brought it to her mistress, begging permission to bring it up. Casina has now grown into quite a beauty, and has begun to serve as a lady's maid in the house, where the *senex* Lysidamus falls madly in love with her—as does his son. The single remark of the good uncle in Menander's *Aspis*—"aren't you a bit old to get married?"—is expanded into a leitmotif, representing not merely an abstract conflict of age versus youth but a familial battle of the generations.

Each desperate to have the girl to himself, father and son select their favorite slaves as their proxies to wed Casina formally so that they may exercise what is popularly known as *ius primae noctis* ("the road test of first night"), the patronal prerogative to "pre-marry" a servant's bride. One thinks also of Count Almaviva in the *Marriage of Figaro*. (In antiquity, of course, a master could assert this right whenever he chose!) Thus the conflict is redoubled by the addition of the son's own slave Chalinus fighting on his behalf, and the father's farm-manager Olympio as his contender.

When the play opens, Lysidamus has already advanced his cause by sending his son out of the country. Moreover, the prologue reveals that the lad will not return during the entire comedy since "Plautus didn't want him to" *(Plautus noluit)*[76]—a declaration of artistic autonomy, and an assertion of originality on the part of the Latin adapter. But, the exposition continues, Lysidamus has an even more formidable foe left at home. His wife Cleostrata, a consummate harpy, knows of Lysidamus' devious plans and will take up the cudgels on her son's behalf to foil her wayward husband's best-laid plans. At this moment, the prologue suddenly "notices" some murmuring in the audience. Imagining that they are muttering to themselves in consternation, he soothes their qualms. He "hears" them saying:

> "Hey, by Hercules, what's going on—since when do slaves have
>   weddings?
> Since when do they get married or request a young girl's hand?
> This is really new—and never happens anywhere on earth."
> But I tell all you doubters that it's done, in Greece and Carthage
> And even in our nearby Apulia.[77]

Once again, as in the case of the slaves at the finale of the *Stichus*, Greek license is invoked to indulge in un-Roman behavior. The prologue is not merely making these geographical references for the sake of sounding exotic, but to emphasize that everyone's imaginations should be as far from the forum as possible.

The real star of this play is one of the funniest creatures on the ancient comic stage—Lysidamus, the ultimate antique lover *(senex amator)*, a colorful self-inebriate.[78] From his first entrance, he is intoxicated with passion, feeling lusty and rejuvenated. He appears singing of love:

> LYS.: Now that I'm in love with Casina I'm shining brighter
> and I feel more graceful than the Graces.[79]

And yet part of him is aware of his anomalous situation—that he is too old to act this young. In fact, later in the play, in a moment of metatheatrical candor, he even refers to himself as a *senex amator*.[80]

But all is not rosy in the old man's life. His marital relationship is a constant state of war. As he explains, "my wife is torturing me—by staying alive."[81] When his guilty conscience drives him to embrace her to allay suspicion, she spurns his advances. She snaps "You're killing me." He mutters "I only wish it were true." She scolds her husband, calling him a "white-haired gnat and an antique wretch wandering around the streets oozing all kinds of perfume," and demanding of him where he's been drinking and what whorehouses he's visited.[82] Her hostile interrogation reminds us of Menaechmus' meddlesome wife. But whereas she was an *uxor dotata*, Cleostrata seems to have the knack of being unpleasant even without the benefit of a large dowry.

The husband and wife address the current *casus belli:* which slave is to get the lovely Casina. The old man protests:

> LYS.: But why, dammit, do you want to give her to some little
> shield- and baggage-handler?
> CLEO.: Because, my darling, we should help the boy.
> Remember, he's our only son.
> LYS.: But what of that? Remember, *I'm* his only father![83]

Neither succeeds in convincing the other, so they agree to draw lots. The slaves are called on stage. As they stand next to one another, Lysidamus urges Olympio to punch his rival. At which point Cleostrata urges *her* slave Chalinus to hit back. As the two servants pound away at each other, the audience enjoys the spectacle of a Punch and Judy combat being held by proxy. Olympio loses the fight, but wins the lottery.

The old man joyously orders his wife to prepare the wedding.[84] A little later, the sulking Chalinus overhears Lysidamus telling Olympio that he intends to exercise his *droit de seigneur,* and the slave scurries off to tell the *châtelaine.*

The old man sends Olympio to buy delicacies for the nuptial feast, "soft and sweet, just like the girl herself."[85] He specifies seafood, commonly thought to have aphrodisiac properties. Then he goes to see Alcesimus, the senior citizen next door. Lysidamus is not an entirely one-dimensional character. As noted earlier, he possesses a degree of self-awareness. In this conversation with Alcesimus he shows that he is sensitive to expressions like "old whitehead" and "at your age" and "think of your wife," and he begs his friend not to criticize him.[86] Although Alcesimus agrees to provide his house for the dual wedding night, the moment the geriatric groom is out of earshot, he voices his resentment about "the trouble he's gotten into for helping that toothless old goat."[87]

And now, with his wedding but hours away, Lysidamus—like Menaechmus—has inexplicably gone off to stroll in the forum.[88] Cleostrata enters, harping on Lysidamus' senility; she is determined to confound her "dilapidated old husband," whom she derides, along with his elderly neighbor, as "castrated rams."[89]

Moments later the old goat returns from the forum as irate and frustrated as Menaechmus I, and for the same reasons. As he was wandering in the business district, a relative seized him and demanded that he act as a lawyer for him.[90] Once again, a would-be married lover learns that the forum is no place for festival, especially with the treats he has in mind.

Now the foolery begins in earnest. At this point a new character appears: the mischievous slave girl, Pardalisca, who from this point takes the role of a sports commentator. She first appears after a clamor is heard from inside Lysidamus' house. She rushes onstage, hysterical, claiming that Lysidamus is as good as killed. "What!" he snaps. She pulls herself together and explains that Casina has gone berserk (behaving in a "totally un-Athenian manner").[91] Indeed, according to Pardalisca, Casina plans to kill her husband on her wedding night.[92] She's already running around with the sword, threatening Lysidamus as well. After more of his frantic behavior, the old man cannot suppress his fright and cries out, coining a typical Plautine superlative (and paradox), that he is "the deadest man alive" *(occisissumus omnium qui vivont).*[93]

As they go in to prepare for the wedding, there is again a natural break,[94] which would argue for another musical interlude to indicate that some time has passed. Pardalisca races onstage again to keep us posted on developments. There are obvious metatheatrical overtones, since she is talking about *ludi* ("tricks") at the Roman *ludi* ("games"):

> PARD.: Never even at Nemea or Olympia
>   Was there seen such festive games
>   As those we are playing now
>   On our old man and his henchman.[95]

She reveals that the women are dressing up Chalinus to play the bride Casina for the ceremony—a unique instance in Plautus of an on-stage wedding, albeit a complete travesty thereof. Lysidamus is brimming with breathless anticipation at his good fortune and that of his "co-bridegroom" *(commaritus).*[96] Olympio enters similarly excited, even singing along with the wedding musicians. The women bring out the bride, whom they refer to in whispers as "Casin*us*,"[97] and he/she is given away to Olympio.

We now arrive at the most famous scene in the play, and by far the raciest in Plautus—what the neighbor's wife Myrrhine, another co-conspirator, calls the *ludi nuptiales,* either the "marriage games" or "wedding trickery."[98] Plautus has thus far structured the play so brilliantly that the spectators are now on the edge of their seats to see what will happen to the men inside the matrimonial chamber. As Myrrhine remarks metatheatrically, "no playwright could ever invent a play wittier than this."[99]

Finally, as the plotters watch eagerly, Olympio staggers out from the wedding bower, red with embarrassment. Cleostrata disingenuously inquires whether the bride has behaved accommodatingly *(morigera),* that is, as a good wife should. This casual use of a significant Roman expression would not be lost on the ears of the spectators. The single word *morigera,* which may have been spoken in the Roman marriage ceremony itself, subsumes the cardinal virtues of the ideal Roman *matrona:*

"the ideal of faithfulness to one man . . . of wifely obedience to a husband . . . and the marriage bond conceived as eternal."[100] As we saw with Erotium in the *Menaechmi*, Plautus often plays with this highly charged word. Compare the ironic quip, "She at long last pleased her husband by dropping dead" *(ea diem suom obiit, facta morigera est viro).*[101]

When Cleostrata finally persuades the groom to reveal what has happened, he relates:

> OL.: Oh, it was absolutely huge!
> I was afraid she had the sword, so I began to go for it.
> While I was searching I thought I grabbed the hilt,
> But when I think about it, that handle couldn't be a sword—
> it was too warm!
> *(embarrassed pause)*
> CLEO.: Say more!
> OL.: I'm so ashamed . . .
> CLEO.: Could it have been a radish?
> OL.: No.
> CLEO.: A cucumber perhaps?
> OL.: By Hercules, it wasn't any vegetable at all—
> but if it was, it was in perfect shape.
> And no matter what it was, it was gigantic.[102]

Plautus does not usually resort to euphemism, but he is rarely as explicit as this. This is broad farce pure and simple (with a *frisson* of homosexuality). After this invasion of her privacy, the "bride" then gave her first "husband" a good pounding.

But Olympio's speech merely sets the scene for his master. The audience now knows what is in store for Lysidamus, and their eyes immediately dart to the doorway. The ancient bridegroom appears, clothing torn and composure shattered. He begins by groaning a lyric. For the first few words it could possibly have been a love song:

> LYS.: I'm in flames and burning—with disgrace
> I don't know what to do about this situation.

> How can I ever look at my wife's face again?
> I'm absolutely finished.
> The whole affair's been exposed,
> In every way I'm deader than a doornail![103]

At this point "Casinus" appears, trying to coax Lysidamus back into the chamber. His wife takes this golden opportunity to scold her husband with righteous indignation. Ignoring his passionate pleas for forgiveness and his promise not to make any more advances on Casina,[104] she capitulates on metatheatrical grounds, "so we won't make this long play any longer."[105]

The epilogue makes a direct appeal to the adulterous yearnings of the spectators:

> Now it is fitting that you applaud us with appropriate
> appreciation.
> Whoever does will always fool his wife and bed the slut
> he longs for.
> But whoever doesn't clap his hands enthusiastically,
> Will find his strumpet has been turned into a foul-smelling
> goat.[106]

This denigration is in fact an accurate description of all the *senes amatores* that appear in Plautus. They always love with ignominy, yielding to the forces of the younger generation. Thus, although it is merely alluded to, the young son of Lysidamus and Cleostrata will marry Casina and enjoy her favors—legally, since she is discovered to be freeborn.

But this is not stressed by Plautus. The Roman playwright prefers to portray the defeated husband. And since most of the Plautine oldsters are pillars of Roman society, there is a kind of saturnalian inversion here. Though the notion of topsy-turvydom of social values in Plautine comedy has been accepted, it has not yet been adequately noted that, sexually, the hero of the comedies is not the slave but his clueless master, who provides the love as his servant provides the trickery. In a sense they are two parts of a single character (and will be literally fused in the comic ages to come).

It is also notable that the triumphant young lads in Plautus almost never opt for marriage. Is it because they are aware that—as the playwright emphasizes with his geriatric characters—marriage is more a chore than a pleasure? This would certainly be more likely if an arrangement with a dowry was involved. As one *senex* tells another:

> SENEX I: By Pollux, big fat dowries are a lot of fun.
> SENEX II: If only there were not a wife attached.[107]

There may be another reason for the avoidance of wedlock. Perhaps in Plautus' day there was a similar attitude to what we find in Greece, where a man was officially a youth until he married. By choosing to remain a hot-blooded bachelor in the spirit of *kōmos*, the Plautine *adulescens* remains a kind of sexual Peter Pan.

Plautus is consistent in this matter. The old men who hunger after adultery are doomed to failure. Could it be a question of morality? For there are certainly extramarital antics in prior as well as subsequent playwrights. The Romans may not have preached monogamy, and they certainly did not practice it. No less distinguished a figure than Cato the Elder, stern censor—and as such the "warden of the life and character" of the entire nation—as well as a strong advocate of laws against female extravagance and other societal excesses, had affairs with his slave girls,[108] as did the great Scipio Africanus, conqueror of Carthage. The latter's wife was so tolerant of her husband's liaison with his *ancilla* that when her husband died she freed the girl.[109] Rome being Rome, the privilege of adultery was not universal: it was strictly for men only. In fact, this was not mere custom, it was the law of the land. It is reported by Gellius that Cato, citing a law that apparently went back to Romulus himself, maintained that a wife, if caught in adultery—or even drinking wine—could be put to death:

> If you catch your wife with someone else you can put her to death without trial with impunity. If she catches you, she cannot lay a finger on you and has no legal right to do so.[110]

Thus in principle at least, Plautus could have depicted the sexagenarian lover succeeding in his amorous quest. And yet, with a single exception which we will examine in the next chapter, this element is conspicuously missing in his plays. For, in direct contrast with Aristophanes, Plautus writes in the mainstream of comedy, depicting the triumph of youth over age. The old men fail because, while they may be senators in everyday society, for comic purposes they are simply senior citizens and, as Berowne moralizes in *Love's Labour's Lost*, "young blood doth not obey an old decree."[111]

II

A Plautine Problem Play

We have seen ample evidence in the previous chapter of Plautus' severe—not to say savage—treatment of husbands and wives. This may have been a universally popular theme in Roman comedy. Our chance possession of a few fragments from Caecilius' adaptation of Menander's *Plokion (The Necklace)* shows how another Roman playwright retouches a Greek characterization with the broad strokes of farce to emphasize the hideous, henpecking, richly-dowered wife. In Menander's play she is unattractive. In Caecilius she is positively nauseating.[1] Unfortunately, since his contemporaries exist only in fragments even smaller than these, we can merely state with certainty that in Plautus at least no adultery is consummated in any play—except the *Amphitruo.*[2]

In many ways the play is unique. For one thing, it is the only extant Latin comedy that deals with a mythological subject: namely the birth of Hercules, a demigod much venerated in Roman religion from the earliest times. This has elicited theories that Plautus' play is based on an original from Middle Comedy, whose authors specialized in such mythological plots. There is even the more radical view that the play was an original creation based on no model whatsoever.[3]

It was commonly known in antiquity that Jupiter had a sweet tooth for mortal women, and was so relentless in his pursuit that he would never hesitate to change into a bull or a swan or even a golden shower— whatever was necessary—to fulfill his cravings. There was, however, one unattainable human exception: Alcmena, wife of King Amphitryon of Thebes. She was emphatically *univira*, the highly respected Roman quality of being a one-man woman. Her chastity and inviolability were legendary, and there was no creature into which the great Olympian seducer could transform himself to win her over—until he hit upon the stratagem of assuming her husband's form.

Taking this material which had been treated before in both Greek tragedy and comedy, Plautus invents a second "twin": while Jupiter is impersonating Amphitryon, Mercury is transformed into a facsimile of his slave Sosia. In a curious moment of comic rebirth, the dizzied slave mumbles to his master: "you've begotten another you. I've begotten another me. Everyone's twinified."[4] Plautus will bring this theme to a climax with the birth of twins. Indeed, to this day *sosie* remains in French a synonym for a double or look-alike.

Amphitruo proved to be one of the poet's most successful—and enduring—plays. According to the imperial writers Arnobius and Prudentius, it was never out of favor.[5] It was still being produced during the third and fourth centuries A.D., and has continued to be readapted in our time, for example in Harold Pinter's *The Lover*, an ironic reworking of the myth which stands in a long line of theatrical variations by such diverse authors as Vital de Blois, Camoëns, Molière, Dryden, and Kleist. Indeed, when in 1929 Giraudoux called his version *Amphitryon 38*, he may have underestimated the number of adaptations that preceded his own.

The play has also been a favorite with scholars, who have spared no effort in trying to unearth Plautus' source for this "tragicomic" admixture of myth and mirth. It would seem that no ancient author has been denied credit for having inspired the Roman playwright. Because of its multi-layered ancestry, the *Amphitruo* is often segregated from the rest of the Plautine corpus, taking Mercury's tongue-in-cheek prologue at its face value. For when he finishes tickling the Romans' interest by promising them huge profits—after all, he was among other things the god of financial transactions—he proposes to set forth "the plot of this tragedy."[6] He then pretends to see the audience frown:

> MERCURY: What's wrong, why are you knitting up your brows?
> Because I said that this would be a tragedy?
> All right then, I'm a god. I'll change it all, and if
> You want I'll turn this from a tragedy to a
> Comedy and do so with without altering a single word.[7]

Mercury pretends that the audience balks at this as well, and so he suggests an artistic compromise. In so doing he coins a new term:

> MERCURY: I'll make a mixture then. We'll make it "tragicomedy."
> Of course I can't make it a totally laughing matter—
> After all, it would not be quite suitable for kings and
> gods like us.[8]

Literary critics have spent more time on this light-hearted remark than any single dramatic concept after Aristotle's *Poetics*. We have seen in both Euripides' and Aristophanes' later plays how the two genres gradually converged to produce the New Comedy of Menander and his colleagues. Even so there is really no genre problem with the "tragical mirth" of this play, whose tone and purpose are not that far removed from the farcical *Casina*. In fact, the *Amphitruo* is even more "Roman." And if one wished to compare it to another comic author, Feydeau would be more appropriate than Philemon. It is very much related to the theme we have been pursuing—namely, the rocky relationship between Roman husbands and wives.

After his brief excursus into Lit Crit, Mercury proceeds to set the scene. Amphitryon is off at war as a *praefectus legionibus*.[9] In the meantime, "you know what type of guy my father Jove is . . . and how free and easy with the ladies."[10] The great Olympian Lothario has made Alcmena yet another conquest:

> MERCURY: Now he began—without her husband knowing it—
> To take a "heavy interest" (*usura corporis*) in her body's charms,
> And sleeping with her made her swell with child.[11]

Interest in her body? The phrase would inevitably strike a mercantile chord to the Roman ear, not merely in the sense of "borrowing" but for its varied other financial connotations.[12] For Jupiter is perpetrating *furtum usus,* the theft that consists in using something without its owner's consent. Plautus' language is very deliberate, as evidenced by Jupiter's near-verbatim repetition towards the end of the play.[13] Furthermore, in the course of the comedy, Alcmena is mentioned twice as *uxor usuraria* ("loaned-out wife"), first by Mercury, then by Jove.[14] This is the language of a sexual embezzler.

Throughout the play, the focus is on the sexual aspect of the myth. In the prologue, Mercury emphasizes his father's "bedding-down" (*cubare*)[15] with Alcmena, but does not mention any feelings of tenderness or affection. (There are no fewer than thirteen variations of *cubare* and *cubitus* in the play.) Referring casually to the most famous aspect of the myth, he tells us that Jupiter has protracted the night for the sake of his *voluptas.*[16] For "he's lying with the lady loving lustily as long as he would like," reveling in the fact that Alcmena innocently believes she is with her husband when in reality "she is with her adulterer."[17]

The action at last begins with Sosia the slave stereotypically complaining about his slavish lot. He has been sent from the front to bring Alcmena the news of Amphitryon's victory, and cannot help noticing that the night seems endless. He quips:

> SOSIA: Where are you, wild and wanton wenchers who can't bear
>   to sleep alone?
>   Here's the night to make a pricey prostitute worth every
>   penny.[18]

The eavesdropping Mercury then comments to the audience:

> MERCURY: My father's being very wise—he's doing just precisely that:
>   Lying with and loving Alcmena, obedient to his heart
>   (*animo obsequens*).[19]

Making an ironic pun on the wifely virtue of *obsequentia* ("obedience"), one of the cardinal virtues of the Roman *matrona,* Mercury emphasizes the carnality of it all.[20] In his tart comparison he seems to regard Alcmena as a cheap courtesan—except that she is not being paid for

"the use of her body" *(usura corporis)*. She has been unwittingly split between *kōmos* and legalized *gamos,* whore and madonna.

Here—nearly halfway through the play—Mercury delivers a second
prologue, this one slightly more "Euripidean" than the first. Again he
dwells on what is happening in the bedroom: Jupiter is still embracing
Alcmena in complete sensual abandonment.[21] At this point we are informed of Alcmena's double pregnancy and the storms brewing in
Amphitryon's household. But Mercury assures us that all will end well,
with a single parturition.[22] And, he adds almost parenthetically, "no
one will consider Alcmena to have sinned."[23] Hardly the greatest gift a
god could grant a mortal. Most important, in contrast to Euripidean
practice, which would have mentioned it as early as the prologue, the
birth of Hercules is not mentioned by name or even hinted at. This ac-
centuates the act of conception rather than its outcome.

At this moment, Jupiter enters with his beauteous "borrowed wife"
and, playing Amphitryon to the hilt, laments that his duties as "com-
mander-in-chief" oblige him to return to the army.[24] The irony is hardly
veiled. "What a shrewd impersonator he is," as Mercury says in praise of
his father's performance.[25]

This "counterfeit Amphitryon"[26]—again the words of Mercury—is exactly the opposite of Regulus, one of the towering figures in the Roman
past. Horace celebrates the bravery of this ascetic hero, captured by the
Carthaginians and sent as a hostage to persuade the Romans to make
peace.[27] He disobeyed; not only did he urge the senate to persevere in
their fight but, brushing off his "noble wife's kisses," he went coura-
geously back to Carthage to the torture and death he knew awaited
him.

By contrast, the very un-Roman Jupiter uses the flimsiest excuses
to remain at home. In fact, he does not even want to leave the bed.
Moreover, Jove hints at a certain clandestinity when he gives Alcmena
the golden trophy which he—that is, Amphitryon—has won: "I sneaked
away to give this little trophy-gift to you."[28] This mention of the trophy
would have had a contemporary resonance for the audience, for in
this period of Roman expansionism in Carthage and the east the subject of distribution of the spoils of war to soldiers was very much a live
issue.[29]

Finally, left alone on the stage, Jupiter "liberates" the night.[30] By delaying the sunrise, he has realized the traditional lovers' fantasy. One thinks of Ovid's *Amores*, "run slowly, horses of the night,"[31] and the words of John Donne: "Busy old fool, unruly sun . . . must to thy motions lovers' seasons run?"

And now we pass from the dream of a lover to the nightmare of a husband—as Plautus will emphasize. The real Amphitryon enters, followed by Sosia, who is in the midst of an identity crisis, not to say schizophrenia: "I'm here—and yet I'm over there as well!"[32] Indeed, Plautus emphasizes the oneiric element throughout the play, although the characters keep protesting that they are not asleep.[33] When his master insists he was acting "in a dream,"[34] his slave maintains:

> Wide awake I was, as wide awake as I am now and talking wide-
>   awakely,
> Wide awake to feel his punches while he punched me wide
>   awake.[35]

This at least is a play which can justify the etymology of comedy from *kōma*—except that here the dream fantasy is a nightmare.

At this point, Alcmena enters singing the joys of love. *Voluptas* ("pleasure," a word she repeats three times in 10 lines)[36] is "granted for but a brief time."[37] But, as a kind of compensation for the lack of *vir*, Alcmena can at least share in his *virtus*, celebrated in a song which she concludes as follows:

> The greatest prize of all is virtue;
>   The best of things—must ne'er desert you.
> Freedom, health, one's life, one's business and the nation's,
> One's parents and one's children and one's loving close relations,
>   Adversities of life will never hurt you
>   If you have virtue.[38]

She is arguably the greatest incarnation of feminine *pietas* on the Roman stage,[39] an image which is reinforced when Amphitryon hails his wife in words that are as much a Roman *laudatio* as a Greek salutation: "the unique and finest and noblest woman in all Thebes."[40] This is an ideal portrait of a woman who is *univira*, faithful to one man alone. But having barely seen him off, she is confused to see him again so soon. She senses that something is wrong. The household hurricane has already been stirred up, leading her to suspect that she is being put to the test.[41]

Amphitryon himself considers her behavior to be pure hallucination (*deliramenta*) or the fantasy of a daydream: "is she asleep while wide awake?"[42] But Alcmena swears she is as awake as he is. She has seen her husband, and "both were wide awake," twice echoing Sosia's protestation that this is not a fiction of slumber.[43] And when Amphitryon maintains that he spent the preceding night on board his ship, she retorts: "no, indeed, you dined with me and then afterwards you . . . reclined with me."[44] Though her virtues include "sexual restraint,"[45] Alcmena is flesh and blood and can appreciate conjugal joys.

Needless to say, Amphitryon is shaken to his boots—and he has not heard everything. Alcmena continues, reminding her increasingly anguished husband of their conversations the previous night, and insisting that he gave her the golden trophy which he had captured from the enemy.[46] Amphitryon is still obstinate: "By Pollux I didn't give you or tell you anything."[47] This use of the verb *dare* ("to give") to connote performing the sexual act recalls the protests of Menaechmus I to his wife regarding the stolen *palla:*

> MEN. I: By Jove and all the gods, I swear—is that enough for you,
> dear wife?—I didn't *give* it to her.[48]

Even when Alcmena displays the golden trophy to prove that Amphitryon *was* there the evening before, Sosia insists that his master "gave it to her secretly," echoing the double-entendre.[49] On the surface *dedi* ("I gave") would appear to refer to the golden trophy which Amphitryon has allegedly given to Alcmena. But in the acting of a play with so many double-entendres, the sense of having "given her one" could easily be conveyed by the actor.[50]

At this point Amphitryon begins to interrogate his wife about the events of the preceding night. And Alcmena is anything but reticent about the excruciating (for him) details: "You washed . . . you reclined . . . we dined . . . we reclined again."[51] We recall the *Menaechmi,* where the same language is used to describe the joys of consorting with Erotium.[52] Flabbergasted, Amphitryon cannot keep from asking:

AMPHITRYON: In the same bed?

ALCMENA: The very same.[53]

And again, wanting not to believe it:

AMPHITRYON: Where did you lie down?

ALCMENA: In the same bedroom and in bed with you of course.[54]

Amphitryon is shattered. "Someone in my absence has besmirched the *pudicitia* of my wife," he cries.[55] *Pudicitia* is one of the primary Roman wifely virtues, connoting fidelity of every sort. Alcmena's heartfelt protest is useless; he is offended that she does not even attempt to lie.[56] Still she swears by Jove and Juno "whom I should most revere and dread," a subtle echo of Mercury's quip in the prologue; and once more she insists with unconscious irony, "no other mortal except you has touched my body."[57]

As both their tempers rise, Amphitryon rages at his once paragonal wife's fall from grace and tells her in no uncertain terms that she is talking overboldly. "As befits a woman who is *pudica*," Alcmena replies.[58] With great dignity she makes the classic declaration of innocence which encompasses the virtues the Romans prized most:

ALCMENA: For myself, I don't believe my dowry is what people think
  a dowry is,
  But rather chastity and modesty and shyness when in bed
  with you,
  Fear of the gods, love of my parents and harmony with all
  my relatives,
  To be accommodating to you *(morigera)*, and generous
  and helpful to all good and honest people.[59]

As well as being heartfelt, her words are direct and to the point. (To this catalogue of virtues Jupiter himself later adds *pietas*.)[60] She is not afraid to pit her own virtues against such an accusation. Her "dowry" of character reminds one of Horace:

Their dowry is the great virtue of their
 Parents, that is fearful of another's husband,
Chastity in a sure bond
 Where sin is unspeakable and its wage death.[61]

But nothing can convince the outraged Amphitryon, who marches off to fetch Alcmena's kinsman Naucrates to act as arbitrator. The possibility of divorce looms.[62]

When the confused and troubled mortals leave the stage, Jupiter once more returns. In what resembles yet another prologue, he presents himself: "Now I play Amphitryon . . . and when I'm in the mood, I'll turn back into Jupiter again."[63] He has come to reassure the audience that they are still watching a comedy.[64] But in the meantime he will continue the intrigue by masquerading *(adsimulare)* as Amphitryon to create "a superb trickery play" *(frustratio maxuma)* in the household.[65]

Jupiter promises to reveal everything to Alcmena and Amphitryon at the end and constantly reaffirms his victim's innocence.[66] He promises to reward her—with a painless double-birth.[67] It seems a small thing in comparison with the devastation he has brought to her marriage. The supreme Olympian is a god, all right—he lacks all human feelings.

At last, we see Alcmena confront her unrecognized seducer. She approaches him burning with resentment at being accused of "infidelity" *(stuprum)* and "immorality" *(dedecus).*[68] But "Amphitryon" twists the knife deeper into her delicate sensitivies, pretending that he was only joking and asking forgiveness. She is not placated. How dare he vilify her virtue? She spits at him the precise Roman words that indicate intention to divorce: "Goodbye—take all your property, and just give me my dowry back."[69]

Jupiter-Amphitryon speaks an ironic and cruel curse: "If I'm lying to you let Jupiter supreme be ever angry with Amphitryon."[70] At this Alcmena's innate *pietas* and love are awakened again and she calls heavenward, "No no dear Jupiter—be kind to him!"[71] "Husband" and wife are momentarily reconciled. She goes in dutifully to prepare for a sacrifice while Jupiter remains outside to give his flunky more instructions. While he remains "faithful" *(morigerus)*—to himself—with his "loaned-out wife,"[72] his son Mercury-Sosia must keep all visitors away.

The Olympian slave continues the mockery that he and his father have indulged in, abusing adjectives which are typically used in Roman funerary inscriptions to record the special virtues of noble wives. As he stands guard on the roof, he praises his father's activities, recalling Wrong Logic's credo in Aristophanes' *Clouds:* "He makes love. That's wise. The thing to do, seeing that he's wholly 'faithful'—to his instincts."[73] He continues in the same vein, "It's only proper that I be 'accommodating' *(morigerus)* to my father and serve his every whim completely."[74]

If the reader is not yet persuaded that Plautus' comedy emphasizes the physical aspect of the adultery, this episode should dispel all doubts. For the principal characteristic of the classical myth of Amphitryon is that Jove had only a *single* encounter with Alcmena and on this one occasion lengthened the night and never visited a mortal woman again.[75] But let us remember that this is not "Zeus" but the very Roman deity Jupiter Optimus Maximus, under whose aegis the comedy itself was performed. Thus, to the audience's mind, the play deals with one Roman taking great pleasure in cuckolding another.

Plautus continues to run the gamut of possible confrontations with the twin masters and slaves and a single mistress. There is a moment of farce that is lost to us in a long lacuna of approximately three hundred verses.[76] Mercury seems to have spilled some water from the roof, and there was a general mêlée during which there was some farcical fighting as Mercury tried to keep Amphitryon from the house while his father continued to pursue his pleasure. One tantalizing fragment even suggests that Amphitryon fights physically with the divine imposter in a battle royal:

> I've got him, citizens of Thebes! I've got the foul debaucher
> Who sullied my wife's honor. I've got the fount of evil![77]

It was established myth that in the Golden Age the gods came to earth to join humans on special occasions like the wedding of Peleus and Thetis (Achilles' parents) or Cadmus and Harmonia. But there is no record of Jupiter going among mortals for a bloody street-fight![78]

We have no way of knowing exactly how the scene played out, but when it is over Jupiter leaves Amphitryon outside and repairs to the house because—as he informs us—Alcmena is going into labor.[79] Distraught, Amphitryon shouts to all the gods that he will not rest until he wreaks a dreadful revenge on the callous usurper, "and not even Jupiter and all the gods" will stop him.[80]

But before he can act, there is a monstrous peal of thunder and he falls to the ground in a faint. At this point a household maid, the aptly-named Bromia ("Thunderella"), makes her first appearance, her sole purpose to be a kind of hysterical messenger who rushes onstage to recount the wonders that have just occurred. While Alcmena was in labor there was a blaze of miraculous fire and, after "a loud thunderclap stunned her,"[81] a great voice came from the heavens telling her not to be afraid. And suddenly she gave birth to not one but two boys "without labor."[82]

The maid then notices an "old man" *(senex)* lying near the house.[83] Ironically, Mercury foreshadows this picture of Amphitryon as an old man *(senecta aetate)*.[84] It is indeed her master, once a vigorous young general. He not only appears dead, but buried as well *(sepultust quasi sit mortuus)*.[85] Has he been struck by one of Jupiter's bolts? In a way he certainly has. He groans to her:

AMPHITRYON: I'm dead . . . I'm trembling all over. That noise was like a
　　　　　　　bolt from Jupiter.
　　　　　　　I feel as if I'm just now coming back to life—from Hell.[86]

This is a perverse comic rebirth for Amphitryon. He has not come to life as the same person. Jupiter's thunderbolts have transformed the title character—and we must recall that the play is named after the mortal husband, not Jupiter or Alcmena—into a senior citizen, nay a corpse. And as he rises from the ground he reenters the still painful here and now in which his wife has been severely compromised. It is not a brave new world to which he has been reborn, but rather a harsh and cruel one.

The moment her master regains some of his composure, Bromia announces that Alcmena has given birth to twins.[87] To which he can only respond, "god save us."[88] There is surely more than a little ambivalence on the part of a father who has just suffered so much twinification—although he does not yet realize the full extent of the identity crisis that has beset his home.

The play ends with Bromia's description, quite Euripidean, of a supernatural event which occurred to one of the newborn twins (whom the audience would know to be Hercules, although his name is never mentioned). Two snakes suddenly appeared and glided menacingly toward the newborn hero's cradle—from which he leapt miraculously and rushed to strangle both of them. A voice suddenly speaks. Amphitryon is confused. "What man was this?" he asks *(Quis homo?).*[89] It is beyond his imagination even to think that the adulterer could be anyone but a mortal. But his maid replies:

> BROMIA: Supreme commander of all men and gods, great Jove.
>   He says that he's secretly been having an affair with
>   Alcmena.[90]

What is Amphitryon's reaction to this good news? When he hears about the Olympian visit and the resultant augmentation of his family, he says:

> AMPHITRYON: By Pollux, I'm not troubled in the least
>   If I am blessed to share my goods with Jove.[91]

Is he telling the truth? Not likely. Is he unhappy? Very probably. But what could he do? For though Jupiter has commanded the couple to return to their *antiqua gratia,*[92] from everything we have seen, Amphitryon's marriage has received an incurable stress fracture.

What would have been the reaction of the Roman audience? Is Amphitryon not what later Romans would call a *cornuto,* a cuckold?[93] Whatever their morality was in fact, the Greeks of the fifth century B.C. at least could laugh at theatrical adultery with great freedom. We have already seen the *gamoi* of Aristophanes, but we should also recall that even the Greek playwright's women make jokes about having lovers.[94] And in his comedy *Daedalus* we find the playful repartee stating that a lover is as necessary to every woman as a dessert to every meal.[95]

But note the moral contrast between Aristophanes and Plautus. There is no Roman comedy that celebrates the consummation of an extraconjugal *gamos.* Compare two husbands—Menaechmus and Philocleon; and two finales—*Acharnians* and the *Asinaria.* The difference is clear and emphatic. Plautine husbands dream and scheme about adultery, but they never succeed in their desires. In fact, the only

adultery that is consummated in all of Roman comedy is in the
Amphitruo.

It is fruitless to argue that Jupiter is a "god" and "it was only my
great power that made her submit,"[96] for only a few moments earlier
Mercury was praising his father's flirtation, encouraging all men to follow his divine example and feel free to seek their pleasure wherever they
can find it.[97] However we look at it, Alcmena has been compromised
and Amphitryon cuckolded. There is no way around these facts.

Although it is sometimes stated that the Romans had no word for
"cuckold"—or even the concept[98]—the onomatopoetic tidbit "cucu" is
heard distinctly in several portions of the dialogue (for example,
complexus cum Alcumena cubat),[99] culminating in the "explanation" of Jupiter as related by the maidservant: *cum Alcumena clam consuetum
cubitibus.*[100] *Cucu* is indeed the note which resounds across the entire
comedy, and it finds its diapason in the English word "cuckoldry," generally thought to derive from the cuckoo, who lays its eggs in other
birds' nests.[101] Since the Latin for "cuckoo" is *cuculus*, and the patron
saint of cuckolds in Renaissance Italy was still San Cuccù, we come full
circle to Plautus' ubiquitous word-play. It is a provocative theory, but
"such a joke would not be unworthy of the writer . . . who would make
[a drunken young man] deny his condition with *mammamadere.*"[102]

One might well describe the Plautine Amphitryon with Rostand's
play on words—*ridicoculisé* ("ridi-cuckolded"). This may seem a bitter
theme for comedy—which may be the real reason for calling the play a
tragicomedy—but it is nonetheless a perennial one. As we shall see, the
dramatic heyday for this theme was Restoration England, when adultery seemed to be the theme of almost every comedy.

Shakespeare testifies to this universality in a delightful song:

> The cuckoo then, on every tree,
> Mocks married men; for thus sings he,
>> "Cuckoo;
> Cuckoo, cuckoo"; O word of fear,
> Unpleasing to a married ear![103]

The ancient Roman husband, of course, had the remedy of divorce,
which the inhabitant of medieval Europe did not—and this makes
cuckoldry a more excruciating and interesting plight. But Alcmena was

the model of the dutiful, *morigera* wife, whose highest ambition would be lifelong devotion to a single man. The Romans surpassed the Greeks in their reverence for female chastity, and a Roman matron was praised for being *univira* (the actual term is of a later era). This meant that "chaste" widows were not supposed to remarry. Consider the following epitaph from the time of Accius (170–86 B.C.):

> This woman who preceded me in death
> Was loving, chaste, and of my heart possessed,
> Repaying love with love and faith with faith
> No greed in her put duty to the test.[104]

Jupiter's caprice has violated this ideal and destroyed Amphitryon's marriage, for both he and Alcmena know that she can never really be *univira* again. He announces his intent to go for a consultation with the savant Tiresias. There are many unanswered questions.

Yet another thunderbolt announces the arrival of the *deus ex machina*—none other than Jupiter himself. Brute that he is, he informs the stupefied husband for the *n*th time, repeating Mercury's words of the prologue:

> JUPITER: Now first of all I have invested my attention in Alcmena's
> body
> I slept with her and made her pregnant with a son.[105]

Here Jupiter predicts the glorious future of his newborn son, though not even he identifies him as Hercules. His final words are:

> JUPITER: Remember now—I forced Alcmena. Now I'm going back
> to heaven.[106]

Throughout the entire scene Amphitryon does not speak a single word. It was patently clear to all that he was less than honored. Nevertheless, he is obliged to accept the situation, and closes the play with resignation:

> AMPHITRYON: I will do as you wish, and I beg that you keep your
> promises.
> Now I'm going inside to my wife.[107]

Plautus' *Amphitruo* is a bittersweet comedy—in fact more bitter than sweet. It is exactly the opposite mood to that of Aristophanes' *Birds*. In the supreme Greek comedy a human displaces the king of the gods—gaining his dominion and his "companion." In Plautus' play the *god* displaces the *man,* exacting intertextual comic vengeance on humanity by touching the otherwise untouchable woman.

For all their obsessive qualms about the fidelity of their wives, Roman husbands practiced the well-known "double standard." We recall the philosophical attitude of Scipio's wife to her husband's mischief with their slave-girl.[108] Although divorce (for men) was already common in the time of Plautus, it was not really approved of. The Romans went to great lengths to distort their pasts and thus dreamed up a nonexistent golden age in which divorce did not exist.[109]

Female adultery, on the other hand, was a serious matter. As we have seen, an upper-class Roman who caught his wife with a lover could kill the woman as well as punish the malefactor in any way he chose.[110] But Amphitryon would have no such rights. All of this evidence could argue that the comic hero of this play is actually Jupiter, who is the embodiment of being "permitted the outrage and spared the consequences." Yet where would the audience's sympathy lie? Perhaps for once Plautus crowns the risible elements with a touch of *Schadenfreude?* There but for the grace of Jupiter go I. One thing is certain: the audience would see the victim as a Roman and be glad that Jupiter's visits were mere mythology. This, rather than academic considerations of genre, may be the best justification for Plautus' striking neologism *tragicocomedia.*

12

Terence: The African Connection

Is it better to be Salieri or Mozart? *Mutatis mutandis,* that is the relation of Plautus to Terence—at least during the younger playwright's lifetime (c. 195–159 B.C.). Plautus, the first as well as the most successful *professional* dramatist in the ancient world, had no dark *Clouds* or angry *Mother-in-Law* in his career. His name was magic. The mere mention of it could call a drunken, rowdy Roman mob to silence: you could hear a pun drop. At the end of a Plautine comedy the audience would often stand up and cheer for more. By contrast, at the *beginning* of a Terentian performance they might stand up—and turn their backs.[1] At least, this is what occurred twice with his *Mother-in-Law.*

Like Menander whom he so admired, Terence became a classic only after his death. Plautus, though wildly popular in his own day and performed until the Dark Ages, began to languish thereafter in decaying manuscripts, unread and unproduced. Even as early as the late Republic, Plautus was regarded in much the same way as Ben Jonson dismissed Edmund Spenser's *Faerie Queene:* "he writ no Language." Cicero tended to favor Terence in his quotations, as did Horace, who was almost hostile to the talents of the older playwright.[2] (Incidentally, both Cicero and Horace preferred *The Eunuch* and ignored *The Mother-in-Law* completely.)[3]

Of course Terence's victory—if one may call it that—was not entirely owing to his comic merits. Julius Caesar, leader, Latin stylist *par excellence,* and influential opinion maker—the Churchill of his day—belittled Terence's dramaturgy, drawing attention to his lack of *vis comica* or *comica virtus* ("comic verve" or "comic skill")[4] and calling him a "mini-Menander" *(dimidiate Menander).*[5]

But the playwright was widely admired for other reasons. Caesar also praised Terence for being *puri sermonis amator* ("a lover of pure speech"). The imperial critic Quintilian referred to his style as *scripta elegantissima.*[6] Aulus Gellius, who coined the superlative *Plautinissimus* to describe a really novel passage,[7] never needed to label a verse *Terentianissimus.* This explains the huge number of quotable quotes we find in his plays.

It was this superb oratorical quality that made the playwright an ideal school text.[8] Student editions of Terence date back as early as the first century A.D. and continue unabated throughout the Middle Ages, when the scribes and artisans produced beautifully illuminated manuscripts.[9] During this time Terence even had some scholarly imitators, like Hrothswitha, "learned nun of Gandersheim," who in the tenth century created biblical plays in the Terentian style, and the late sixteenth-century Dutch schoolmaster Schonaeus of Gouda.[10]

Meanwhile, Plautus was all but ignored. Not that the Middle Ages were allergic to laughter, but Plautine Latin is so idiosyncratic and inventive—and the plots so much bawdier—that he was completely unsuitable for tender schoolboys beginning their studies. In fact, in the fifth-century A.D. treatise *Terentius et Delusor* ("Terence and the Heckler"), an imaginary dialogue between the playwright and a contemporary theatrical producer, the latter states in confusion about the plays of Plautus that "we have no idea whether they are metrical or in prose."

When the twentieth century began, Terence was still high on a pedestal. Terence's adaptation of New Comedy, far from being mere translation, was on the same literary level as Shakespeare's transmutations of Plutarch.[11] At mid-century the pendulum swung in the opposite direction, as illustrated by the equally outrageous pronouncement that Terence is merely a translator and that "in his versions whatever is good comes from Menander, and what is bad is the fault of Terence."[12] After an important study of Terence's literary qualities marked a moment of critical equipoise in 1953, it was generally accepted that Terence enhanced his "Latin Menander" by adding greater realism, more detailed character studies, and less sententiousness, and in general by being a patriotic and moralizing poet. Terence was recognized as "the poet who shook up ancient convention and prepared the way for modern theatrical practice."[13]

The 1960s marked the beginning of a truly unblinkered appraisal of the so-called comedy of the unpopular playwright.[14] The rhapsodic and critical view of Terence as flawless was dispelled. On the positive side, both old and new critics acknowledge that he makes some scenes more dramatic by transforming what was a static monologue in Greek to a lively dialogue in Latin—as Donatus had remarked.[15] Yet some Terentian innovations were actually felt to spoil the Greek original.[16] But Terence's medium was itself a message, and as such "a great achievement":

> It meant the creation of a new literary language in Latin with the purity, refinement and flexibility of diction that had not previously existed and was capable of expressing complicated psychological processes.[17]

All in all, then, Terence has fared quite well at the hands of the critics. Yet as with all posthumous fame (remember Achilles) Terence's Mozartian standing in the Latin canon would be cold comfort to him, since in his lifetime—with one notable exception—he met with only indifferent success.

His background is interesting. Born in Carthage, he was taken as a slave to Rome by a senator, Terentius Lucanus. Enthused about the young man's mind *(ingenium)*—as well as his outward beauty *(formam)*—the lawmaker had him educated and then freed. At his manumission the young man took the *nomen* Terentius from his benefactor, while his *cognomen* "Afer" suggests roots on the African continent.[18] It is true that this name is attested for other Roman families,[19] but Suetonius' description of him as "dark-skinned" *(fuscus colore)* makes it likely that Terence was the first black author in the classical world.[20]

As legend has it, the aspiring young playwright was invited to join the Scipionic Circle, the semi-mythical literary coterie which also included the historian Polybius, the philosopher Panaetius, and the satirist Lucilius, who were gathered around the philhellenic Scipio Aemilianus. The "Scipionic Circle" was in fact largely devised by Cicero as a literary setting for his philosophical dialogues.[21] But it is certain that Terence enjoyed aristocratic patronage, under which he wrote six plays—four based on Menandrian originals and two by Apollodorus of Carystus, one of the Greek master's acolytes. Not long after 160 B.C., when his sixth play, the *Adelphoi,* was produced, Terence went to Athens to gather new material, and, like Menander, died a watery death—perishing in a shipwreck on the return voyage, along with a cargo of one hundred and eight plays adapted from Menander. This sudden fecundity is clearly exaggerated and most likely the result of a scribal error.[22]

Terence's approach to adaptation *(vortere)* was diametrically opposed to that of Plautus, Naevius, Caecilius, and the others of their generation, who were never loath to shatter the Greek illusion for the sake of a Roman joke.[23] He aimed to bring the masterpieces of Greek New Comedy to a Roman audience in their pristine Greekness (or so his prologues protest), and he did so with some success. He has been justifiably praised for the subtlety with which he glossed obscure Greek allusions to make them intelligible for the Roman audience. And yet the scene remained essentially Greek—without any deliberate Roman asides or dialogic winks at the audience. For this he won Cicero's high praise for having "conveyed and replayed Menander in a Latin voice."[24]

But these indisputable merits may have been lost on the typically drunk and rowdy festival audiences memorably depicted by Horace.[25] Terence's plays were caviary to the general—as the actors in *Hamlet* rationalize their recent theatrical failure: they lacked the common touch, the *nescio quae mimica*—the farcical additions of Caecilius and Plautus which corrupted the Greek but delighted the audiences. Terence himself admits in the *Heauton Timoroumenos (Self-Tormentor)* that his plays are more *statariae* than *motoriae,*[26] terms which the fourth-century scholar Euanthius glossed as *quietiores* and *turbulentae.*[27] As the polemic prologue, spoken by his producer, explains:

So you won't see a running slave or angry father,
Voracious parasite or brazen blackmailer
Or greedy pimp which I at my age always have to play,
At the top of my voice with maximum effort.[28]

Explaining to a rowdy, rough-edged audience that they will not get to see their favorite characters is hardly a *captatio benevolentiae,* as the prologue invariably had been in Plautus.

Of course, Terence himself presents some of these same characters—and more than once. He has not merely one but *five* running slaves in his six comedies, not to mention a parasite and a braggart soldier in the *Eunuchus,* and a greedy pimp—Sannio—in *The Brothers,* which also has an overbearing father, as does the *Self-Tormentor.* Indeed, Terence was even accused of being "not a bookish writer but a crookish writer,"[29] that is, of stealing characters from other authors' plays. In his own defense, the playwright protests that this was already a common practice by the masters of a previous generation:

Why can't a playwright use familiar characters?
Can no one else present a running slave?
Or wives of virtue, whores to hurt you,
Soldier boys bluffing, parasites stuffing,
Little babies nicked by knaves, older people tricked by slaves
Loving, hating, tricks anticipating.[30]

In short, "nothing can be said today that's not been said before."[31]

Despite his protestations, however, Terence really does put a few new wrinkles on the hackneyed masks of traditional comic personifications. He often adds touches of originality and realism, creating such novelties as a *nice* mother-in-law and an *honest* prostitute. Compared with his predecessors, his presentation of the rebellion of the young man against his father is markedly subdued. As we have seen, the typical Plautine *adulescens* gives in to outrageous comic impiety. Take for example the outburst of young Philolaches in Plautus' *Mostellaria,* who sees his sweetheart and voices this horrendous thought:

PHILOLACHES: I wish someone would bring me news right now that
father's dead

> So I could disinherit myself and give all my worldly
>   goods to her![32]

How much milder is Terence's "drop dead" scene in the *Adelphoe (The Brothers)* when the young man is informed of his father's inopportune return to town:

> I wish—as long as he stayed healthy—he would tire out
> And lie in bed for three whole days, unable to get up.[33]

Clearly, this Terentian lover is much more respectful than his Plautine counterpart. Donatus, commenting on this passage, contrasts its mild sentiments with the harsh and "Plautine" outburst of a young lover from a play by Naevius: "I pray the gods to snatch away my father and my mother."[34] Such assaults on parental *pietas,* with their violation of a fundamental taboo, must have had a special appeal for the Roman audience in their holiday humor.[35] Perhaps this is why Julius Caesar found Terence so lacking in *vis comica,* which we might translate here as "comic violence."

But the scene also sounds very much like a parody of Plautus and Naevius. It may in fact be a reaction to the general irreverence which characterized all Roman popular comedy. This is not to deny that Terence could write scenes as funny as those of Plautus when he wanted to (and he actually did once, as we shall see). But for the most part he chose to write polite comedies, which he preferred to call *fabulae,*[36] like the coterie dramas of John Lyly, the Elizabethan playwright whose refined plays were suited for the princes of the Court rather than the plebs of the Globe.

It has been argued that Terence's next meal was not wholly dependent on his next success: his aristocratic patrons protected him from the slings and arrows of the marketplace, and he could afford to scorn public opinion and deride his audience as *populus stupidus.*[37] Be that as it may, his plays are infused throughout with Menandrian *philanthrōpia,* transmuted as Roman *humanitas.* Indeed, the character struggle between the human and the inhuman is a dominant theme in Terence.[38] It was for this "Christian" dimension that Terence was quoted by church fathers. Cicero had already noted that this theme of Terence was quoted out of context.[39] Nevertheless, it became the watchword of

Renaissance humanism: "I am human; nothing of humanity is alien to me."[40]

Unfortunately, his close and profitable association with high-ranking intellectuals gave rise to the rumor that they actually assisted Terence in composing his comedies. Despite the excellent tutors his master provided, the young freedman was regarded by some as incapable of producing "classics" because of his humble foreign origins. Though his prologues are always polemic, Terence does not directly refute this charge.[41] And yet, if the anecdotes which have survived are any indication of the contemporary attitude, the view was rather widely held,[42] and persisted as late as Montaigne.[43]

But genius defies all cultural descriptions, especially linguistic. In modern English literature we can adduce Conrad the Pole, Tom Stoppard the Czech,[44] and Nabokov the Russian as ready examples. As we shall see, many of the French absurdists were not native francophones. In the Roman theater itself we can cite Seneca, who was from Spain, and Caecilius, who is said to have been a slave from Gaul.[45] Thus, Terence's African birth cannot itself prevent him from being regarded as one of the great early stylists in Latin letters.

Whoever wrote these plays, the fact remains that Terentian drama represents a milestone—in fact the final milestone—in the development of classical comedy. It established the classic paradigm for all subsequent comic drama until the twentieth century. For Terence *was* an important innovator, but in a way that has been taken for granted for more than two millennia. His contribution was, quite simply, the invention of dramatic suspense.

This Terence accomplished in several bold strokes. First, he radically altered the expository prologue. Menander—and Euripides before him—had almost always had a speaker, usually divine, offering the details of the drama the audience was about to see—and, most important, reassuring them that the outcome would be happy. (In some cases this expository "prologue" was delayed, as often in Menander.)[46] Until this point of history, the audience's concern was not *what* would happen, but *how*. This may seem silly or even primitive to us, accustomed as we are to Terentian suspense. (And yet even today how many people begin a novel by reading the last page? The urge to know "how it turns out" is almost irresistible.)[47] Shakespeare lampoons the convention, making it one of the dramaturgical "inspirations" of the rude mechanicals who stage the "merry and tragical" tale of Pyramus and Thisbe:

> BOTTOM: First, Pyramus must draw a sword to kill himself, which the ladies cannot abide. How answer you that? . . .
>
> STARVELING: I believe we must leave the killing, when all is done.
>
> BOTTOM: Not a whit. I have a device to make all well. Write me a prologue, and let the prologue seem to say we will do no harm with our swords, and that Pyramus is not killed indeed; and for the more better assurance, tell them that I, Pyramus, am not Pyramus, but Bottom the weaver. This will put them out of fear.[48]

Perhaps Terence took for granted that, after more than a century of watching essentially the same theme, the Roman audience would come to a comic play with a preconditioned mindset: the subliminal assurance that, however unmarriageable the heroine may seem in Act One, by the end of the play she will be discovered to be Athenian and nubile. It was a bold innovation for which he may have sacrificed a certain amount of popularity.

In the prologue to *The Brothers*—rated by Varro as better than Menander's original—Terence officially informs the audience that dramatic technique has been permanently altered:

> Don't count on hearing all the plot from *me* right now.
> The oldsters who are entering will tell you part of it
> And in the acting of it *(in agendo)*, by and by, you'll learn the rest.[49]

The absence of a specific prediction in the prologue allows the spectator to enjoy a special tension in which he not only suspends his disbelief but also invokes a certain deliberate amnesia so that he can be "surprised" by the happy ending. He is drawn into the world of the characters, and participates more closely in their emotions.[50] The playwright is in a position of power, and he leads the spectators by the nose, trailing crumbs of exposition in his wake. This is suspense.

Terence worked hard at developing the technique of artful exposition, which in his skilled hands became for comedy what the beginning *in medias res* was for epic. For lack of a better term we may refer to this practice (in Plautus as well as Terence) as the *in agendo* ("in the acting of it") technique, from the passage quoted above. Indeed, these words signal a new era in dramaturgical technique. The warnings of Terence's prologue become an *ars poetica*.[51] The result produces a kind of domino effect on the spectator's sensibilities. At each twist of the plot he discovers something that he has not known before. And when the traditional *cognitio* comes at the end, he has the pleasure of having his instincts confirmed. Indeed, when there is wish fulfillment without prediction the audience feels more personally involved in the happy ending, as though they helped to bring it about.

Of course, Terence was not the first to write a play without an expository prologue. As we have seen, Plautus himself had tried his hand at it,[52] and the practice may go back ultimately to Menander's *Samia*. In fact, "the form of the prologue belongs to competing dramaturgical theories among the Latin poets of the second century," and in this sense, Terence "brought to fruition an evolution which began with Plautus."[53]

But those who downplay Terence's contribution to dramaturgical technique on these grounds miss the point.[54] Terence represents a fundamental change from *irony*, the mode of Menander and Plautus, to *suspense*. As Lessing explained, an expository prologue gives a feeling of superiority to the audience, who know for certain what is to come at every minute: this is dramatic irony.[55] But the mere excision of the prologue does not *ipso facto* create suspense. It merely eliminates the element of irony, since the audience is no longer put in a position of complete power over the actors. This must be coupled with a sophisticated restructuring which parsimoniously parcels out exposition like a leaky faucet—drop by drop.

Plautus was not disciplined enough—or perhaps did not care—to keep the players one step ahead of the spectators. He is prodigal with "telegraphed" hints of the actors' identities and the ultimate ending. Terence, however, systematically suppresses these clues. Though the plays written by Terence's predecessors may have experimented with the elimination of prologues—and there are at times unpredicted surprises—they did not make suspense their single guiding artistic principle.

Throughout the ages scholars—perhaps jaded by millennia of suspenseful plays—have maintained that Terence replaced the conventional prologue for less artistic reasons. They argued that, wanting to
rebut his critics as publicly as possible, he took advantage of the opportunity to address a large audience by putting his rejoinders into a new-
style prologue. But perhaps too much attention is given to these argu-
mentative prologues and they should be viewed as merely set-pieces,
possibly to warm up the spectators with their passionate bile. The "failures" of the *Hecyra,* for example, might be mere fabrication intended to
intimidate the audience into good behavior, rather than behaving like
the uncultured louts who (allegedly) interrupted the previous performances.[56]

Be that as it may, it is ridiculous to suppose that Terence would undertake a drastic revision of dramatic technique, with all the additional
labor this would entail, *solely* to buy himself time for non-dramatic polemics. With the new emphasis on suspense, the prologue was no longer needed to provide exposition. Yet the convention of having a prologue itself could hardly be eliminated. Therefore, Terence took
advantage of this vacancy for fighting his theatrical feuds.

It seems that he was attacked by a jealous rival playwright, one
Lucius Lanuvinus, a mean-spirited old poetaster[57] who accused Terence
of all manner of crimes, including the use of ghost-writers. But would a
theater full of high-spirited spectators on a Roman holiday really care if
Terence had committed *furtum,* the "robbery" of several scenes from a
work that had previously been Latinized? Or *contaminatio* ("spoiling"),
the fusing of two Greek models into one Roman one? For the record,
Terence did not consider this an artistic felony:

> And about those rumors which his enemies have spread around,
>   that he has spoiled a lot of Greek plays just to make
>   one or two Latin ones . . . he won't deny it.
>   Nor is he ashamed, and he will keep on doing it.
>   He has distinguished precedents.[58]

Elsewhere he cites such worthies as Naevius, Plautus, and Ennius
who had done the same.[59] Instead of silencing the wretched old poet for
good, his defense of *contaminatio*—which until then was never part of a
formal critical vocabulary—caused it to be elevated to the status of a

technical term, far beyond the intent of the original accuser or accused. And if this be a fault, then Shakespeare, Ben Jonson, Molière, and countless other playwrights are to be condemned.

For Terence's use of multiple models was in the service of another cardinal stylistic innovation, and what others derided as *neglegentia* was preferable to the *diligentia* of the poetasters.[60] As he explains, "the plot of the comedy has been transformed from a single one into a double" (*Heauton Timoroumenos* 6). The double-plot, which often involved the introduction of a second pair of lovers, was a cardinal stylistic innovation, and is found in all but one of Terence's plays. It gave the playwright a chance to create a more complex counterpoint of the basic Theophrastian character sketches—in a word, to approximate real life more closely.

More specifically, we find the complicated love-relationships that were a Hellenistic fashion[61] developed into a very well thought out structure which often can be charted as a kind of chiasmus. For example, often boy 1 is engaged to girl 1 when he really wants to wed girl 2, and boy 2 is waiting in the wings desperate to woo girl 1, who has been plighted to his rival. As a result of the last-minute *cognitio* when true identities are revealed, girl 2 is found to be a freeborn Athenian. Boy 1 is now permitted to marry her, thus freeing boy 2 to wed his beloved girl 1. This is in fact a precise description of Terence's first play, *The Girl from Andros.*

A similar situation obtains in the *Brothers,* although the second couple does not have the benefit of clergy—one brother ends with a slut, the other with a wife. The same counterpoint between *amor* and *pietas, kōmos* and legalized *gamos,* is found in *The Eunuch,* perhaps Terence's most evolved example of the *duplex argumentum.* An elder brother is involved with a courtesan, while the younger rapes a slave girl—who in the end turns out to be freeborn and marriageable. In these plays there is a further level to the chiasmus, a concord between home and away. One couple reaches the "home pleasure" *(oikeia hēdonē)* of respectable marriage, while the other enters the arrested development of perpetual *kōmos.*

In the *Heauton* the chiasmus is of a slightly different dimension. One line charts the transformation of the title character from a harsh *senex* into an easy-going one, while the bisecting line traces the transformation of the mellow father into a disciplinarian. In fact, he who had at the outset proclaimed his tolerant humanism,[62] has become a grouch, acting "with too little humanity."[63] It is otherwise a conventional plot in which two sons woo two different kinds of girls, with a non-chiastic resolution.

Even the *Mother-in-Law* exploits the chiastic technique, as we shall see. On the surface it is a *simplex argumentum,* dealing with the relationship crisis of a single couple. But, as the title suggests when taken generically, the play explores this traditional stage figure—in two manifestations.

The potential of the double-plot was not lost on Shakespeare, who exploited it to great effect. *Twelfth Night,* for example, presents a chiasmus of sexual attraction: the Duke loves Olivia, Viola/"Cesario" loves the Duke, and Olivia loves Cesario/Viola. The cross-purposes are sorted out in the *cognitio* when Viola's carbon-copy twin brother Sebastian arrives to provide Olivia with a masculine version of her beloved Cesario.

Terence's innovations are apparent even in his earliest comedies, and he has to defend his dramaturgical technique in the polemic prologue to the *Girl from Andros* (thought to be his earliest play). The prologue explains the method of his *duplex argumentum* and identifies for the audience the two Greek models for this single play, Menander's *Andria* (*The Girl from Andros*) as well as his *Perinthia* (*The Girl from Perinthus*):

> Whoever knows just one already knows the pair
> For both their plots are very similar—
> And yet the dialogue is different and the style as well.[64]

According to Donatus, Terence's fourth-century A.D. editor and commentator, Menander's version of the opening scene was merely a monologue which the Roman playwright has recast as a lively dialogue. For this improvement, Terence must employ a "protatic" character—one who appears merely for the purpose of exposition.[65] We have seen an example of this in the *Amphitruo* with Bromia. But the expository *dialogue* has the advantage of better maintaining dramatic illusion by saving the character from speaking to the audience, who are thus addressed only in the prologue and the valediction at the end of the play.[66]

The action begins with Simo, an old man, who is speaking with his freedman Sosia. Terence even gives a few metatextual signals that he is manipulating a traditional character for his own dramatic purposes. Simo tells Sosia that he does not have need of his "guile" but of his "trustworthiness and silence."[67] In other words, Sosia is not to be, as the audience might expect, a Plautine *servus callidus,* but a mere sounding board for Simo, who is something of a windbag, forever wheezing proverbs like "everything in moderation" and "truth begets resentment."[68]

With the help of Sosia, Simo is making preparations for his son's wedding this very day. But, the old man explains, the wedding is a sham. Simo recalls that three years ago a woman came to Athens from Andros, and her dire financial straits forced her into the world's oldest profession. He has kept an eye on this woman ever since, to see if his son Pamphilus would fall under her sway. Three of his pals, who are already her clients, have told Simo that his son "paid his penny and ate his meal,"[69] referring to a type of potluck meal popular among well-to-do Athenian youths.[70] In other words, Pamphilus was not romantically involved with the fallen woman. The old man was overjoyed by this news.[71]

His son's high-minded reputation was noted by the whole town and brought an offer of marriage—with massive dowry—from Chremes (Mr. Cash), their next-door neighbor. It is this wedding that they are preparing. After all this good news, Sosia manages to squeeze in a logical question: "So what exactly is the problem, sir?"[72]

Simo rambles on, gradually explaining that the woman from Andros died and her customers banded together to pay for her funeral. At the obsequies, he saw his exemplary son Pamphilus "crying with everyone else."[73] Simo was pleased by the boy's tears, reasoning naively and selfishly that if the boy is this upset by the death of a relative stranger, "how much more will he mourn for me, his own father?"[74]

With a hint of intergenerational sexual rivalry, Terence tells us that the old man could not keep his eyes from starting at the sight of an exquisite mourner:

SIMO: My glance by chance hit on a lovely little lass.
     Her figure was . . .

SOSIA: Fantastic, maybe?

SIMO: *(nodding)*   And her face as well, Sosia.
So modest, and yet so attractive. Absolutely tops.[75]

From fellow mourners Simo learned that young Glycerium was the "sister" of the deceased. Light suddenly dawns: his son is in love with this young beauty. *Hinc illae lacrimae,* he says, a memorable and quotable Terentian line used by many later authors like Cicero, Horace, and Juvenal.[76] The literal "hence these tears" only approximates the delicacy, which could serve as a motto for Terentian dramaturgy.

For in direct contrast with Plautus, Terence substitutes tears for what in the older playwright would have been laughter. In *Phormio,* for example, a sobbing girl arouses love in Antipho, a sensitive Terentian *adulescens* who has come across the girl weeping for her dead mother. As his slave recounts, "It was really heart-wrenching—and she was good looking too."[77] All of which sets off the love affair. Lest we have any doubt, this is sentimental comedy. Certainly nowhere in Plautus would you find characters even blushing—much less sobbing.[78] *Lacrima* ("tear") and its cognates appear no fewer than twenty-four times in Terence's six plays, which is more than it appears in all twenty and one-half extant plays of Plautus.

Denis Diderot (1713–1784), the French polymath—and admirer of Terence, on whom he published a monograph—wrote dramas which were neither comedy nor tragedy. They could not be tragedies because they were about the bourgeois. They could not be comedies for the same reason. They are commonly referred to as *comédies larmoyantes,* "tearful dramas." But the grandfather of this genre was really Terence, as we shall continue to see in the *Andria.*

Simo goes on to describe how his son betrayed his secret love: he watched as the lovely girl stood by her "sister's" pyre, continually in tears.[79] When suddenly she tried to hurl herself into the flames, Pamphilus grabbed her, and:

> In a way that proved they were already lovers,
> she sobbing hurled herself into his arms.[80]

The very next day, his fellow *senex* Chremes, the father of the prospective bride, came to Simo furious that Pamphilus was treating the lachrymose lady ("that foreign woman")[81] as his wife. Understandably, he is no longer willing to let the lad near his daughter Philumena.

Simo is enraged in turn by his son's affair. At the moment, though, he has insufficient evidence to confront the boy, and must bide his time until Pamphilus gives him more solid grounds for reproach. Toward this end—and now that the exposition is complete—he finally proposes to Sosia that they pretend to go along with plans for the arranged marriage. If, at the moment of judgment, Pamphilus refuses to leave Glycerium, this will justify Simo in venting his anger. This curious situation, a flimsy pretext upon which the whole plot hangs, reveals both Terence's concern for realism and the metatheatrical playfulness with which he manipulates and comments on the stock comic figures. It is as though his son's marriage is less important to him than the need to live up to his role as *pater iratus*.

At this point Sosia exits. Forever. He has fulfilled his usefulness.

Now the young man's slave Davus enters. He and the old man have a snappy stichomythic exchange—the playwright was admired for such bursts of dialogue:

> SIMO: Davus.
> DAVUS: What's up?
> SIMO: Come here.
> DAVUS: (*to himself*) What does he want?
> SIMO: Any news?
> DAVUS: About what?
> SIMO: You even have to ask?
> I've heard a rumor that my boy's in love.[82]

Pretending that he is unwilling to act the "harsh father," he begs Davus to get the boy to "step back in line."[83] Davus, this time a true clever slave, likewise plays dumb, protesting, "please, I'm just a servant, not Oedipus the King."[84] Simo suspects a trick—*fallacia*[85]—in the making, and threatens Davus with torture should he scheme to stop the parentally-arranged wedding. The old man exits.

Alone on stage, Davus reveals to the audience that "this Andrian woman is pregnant with Pamphilus' child," and adds: "That's the way crazy folk begin, not lovers."[86] Once again we have the element of madness in comedy. He must find some way to extricate his master from the undesirable match with Philumena.

At this point, since we have no information from the prologue, we have no inkling of whether Pamphilus will get the girl he loves, or whether he must go through with the forced wedding. It is true that Terence alludes to the final *cognitio* when Davus informs us that Pamphilus believes his beloved to be a long-lost orphan of Athenian birth. But we are immediately thrown a red herring when Davus derides this "pure make-believe" *(fabulae!)* which his master has concocted as a trick *(fallacia)*.[87] Suspense has been created!

Davus leaves the stage to search for some plausible plan to help his master. The pace now accelerates. Mysis, Glycerium's servant girl, rushes onstage to explain to the audience *in agendo* that her mistress is in labor and she must fetch Lesbia the midwife. A moment later Pamphilus storms out, enraged, for just now his father has casually told him that his marriage to Chremes' daughter would take place that very day. Mysis quickly informs him that his beloved Glycerium is enduring not only the pains of childbirth, but the greater agony that she may lose his love. Waxing sentimental, young Pamphilus tearfully recalls his deathbed conversation with the girl's protector, who with her last breath all but married him to her young ward. Since the girl has until now been *morigera*,[88] he must now honor the dying wish. He hastens to be with his beloved.

Terence now introduces the second plot. (We should avoid using the word "underplot," for the term *duplex argumentum* presumes that the story lines are of equal importance.)[89] Charinus, another *adulescens*, enters with his slave Byrria. He is devasted by the news that his so-called friend Pamphilus has betrayed him and is actually going to wed Philumena—*his* own beloved. He hopes to dissuade his friend, but his earthy slave quips reassuringly, "Look, even if you don't succeed, after they're married you can always be her lover *moechus*"[90]—a rather risqué notion for Terence.

Pamphilus protests that he has no interest in wedding Philumena, and is as anxious to escape Charinus' beloved as Charinus is to marry her. His frantic friend replies, "I beg of you, don't go through with it." Pamphilus sighs forlornly, "I only wish I could!"[91]

Enter Davus—Terence's plots are lean and mean. He informs his master that the marriage is only a charade on his father's part: Chremes has heard of Pamphilus' impending fatherhood and now refuses to wed his daughter to him. Hope reborn, Charinus hurries off to begin his own suit for Philumena's hand. We now know the double problem—which, suitably enough, will be resolved with a single solution.

The slave advises Pamphilus to call his father's bluff by making all the motions to go through with the marriage. There is no real danger, he promises, since it is only a sham, and it will forestall his father from having Glycerium turned out of the country.[92] Accordingly, when Simo enters they tell him they accept his candidate for marriage. Unfortunately, Charinus' slave Byrria overhears and thinks that Pamphilus is now double-crossing his master.[93]

At this point the midwife Lesbia appears with Mysis and speaks of Glycerium's imminent parturition. Not knowing that Pamphilus and Davus are on to his scheme, Simo confides to the audience that he senses a sly *fallacia* designed to scare Chremes off from the arranged wedding. This is immediately belied by the offstage groans of the girl herself, but the old man remains willfully blind to the truth. Even when Lesbia the midwife appears to announce that Glycerium has given birth to a terrific boy, and expresses her fervent hope that it will not be exposed to die, Simo remains unconvinced.

Davus, who has promised Pamphilus not to reveal to his father that Glycerium is pregnant, adroitly switches tactics and agrees with Simo that it *is* an invention, and even predicts that they will bring a baby on stage as the grand finale, which will definitely stop the wedding.[94] Left alone, Simo muses that all that remains is to talk Chremes into agreeing to the match after all, and Pamphilus will be caught out.

Chremes, the father of the bride, now conveniently appears, livid at the thought that some of his friends think the wedding is still on. ("Who's crazy, Simo? You or they?")[95] Simo attempts to get across to Chremes that Pamphilus and Glycerium have had a lovers' quarrel. His friend is dubious (*fabulae!*), but Simo persuades him to relent and give his daughter in marriage.[96] Pamphilus is trapped, and Davus—whose schemes have failed—is in trouble.[97]

The infuriated lad now appears and threatens to have his slave whipped to death for having "hurled me from utter peace into utter matrimony."[98] Things go from bad to worse. Charinus enters, enraged at what he thinks is his friend's double-dealing. Pamphilus pleads with him, explaining that it is all the slave's fault.[99] Davus begs to be given one more chance,[100] but the young man fears that this will end in double trouble:

> PAMPHILUS: I'm sure if you keep up this good work
> you'll get me married not just once but *twice!*[101]

To add to Pamphilus' troubles, Glycerium has also learned of his impending marriage and believes that she has been betrayed in her hour of need.[102] At this climactic moment—because of the lack of expository prologue—the audience is genuinely in the dark as to how this *turba* will subside.

To cut a long comedy short, the double dilemma is solved by the totally unexpected appearance of Crito, a traveler *ex machina,* from the isle of Andros (and left field). He is in search of the late Chrysis' "sister." He spies Mysis, the maidservant, and immediately asks whether young Glycerium has found her parents in Athens yet.[103] When told she has not, being a kindly Terentian character, he decides not to go to law to seek his rightful inheritance (an heiress could be claimed by her nearest male relative)[104] but instead gives it to the poor girl who is all alone. He goes into Glycerium's house and informs her of his decision.

A moment later a euphoric Davus appears, shouting to the world his joy at Crito's appearance: "I never saw a man arrive so in-the-nick-of-time."[105] Simo confronts him, exploding with anger when he learns his son is still inside *that* house. Davus professes that "some swaggering old con-man" (*nescioqui senex . . . confidens catus*)[106] has just turned up, claiming that he knows for certain Glycerium is Athenian-born. As Simo remains obstinately unconvinced, the traveler suddenly reappears and the skeptical Chremes—of all people—recognizes him!

This is a revelation for everyone, on both sides of the stage. It is a surprise to the audience, although their unspoken wishes for the lover to succeed have been realized. "Do I really see Crito of Andros?" Chremes gasps incredulously.[107] He is further astounded to learn that Glycerium is his very own long-lost daughter and sister of Philumena:[108] a fully eligible, marriageable, and wealthy Athenian maiden. This is the first mention of a long-lost daughter, at the very end of the play. This is not *Tychē,* this is Terence.

Chremes is now overjoyed to have Pamphilus marry his daughter—Glycerium. He bestows on the couple a dowry of ten talents, one of the largest in all of Roman comedy.[109] Simo is doubly pleased by his son's good fortune. The audience, totally satisfied with the surprises that have worked out so happily for the first couple, now turn their attention to the second. The jubilant Chremes now gladly gives Philumena in marriage to the lovesick Charinus; conveniently, she is already dressed for a wedding. A double dream *(kōma?)* has suddenly been realized—"is this a dream or have I just awakened from a magic spell?"[110]—and all go inside to celebrate.

The epilogue declares what Terence has decided not to show: the double *kōmos* that will now be celebrated. Davus, alone on stage, bids the audience farewell:

> DAVUS: Don't wait around for them to come back out
> If anything is left to do it will be done inside.
> Now everybody clap![111]

13

The Mother-in-Law of Modern Comedy

We know that *The Eunuch* was Terence's most successful play—but we are hard pressed to understand why. It has something to do with the evolution of taste because, despite its bawdiness, it has not attracted much attention in the modern day.[1] Early in the twentieth century, the play was condemned in the strongest possible terms: it was not only "vulgar and useless," it was even worse—it was "abjectly Plautine."[2] This is of course a highly prejudiced evaluation. What should concern us is not how the play appears to us, but what it was that thrilled the Romans so much that they demanded an encore the very day it was presented.

Let us think positively and enumerate its virtues. To begin with, it has a full-blown *duplex argumentum,* featuring complementary love affairs. The plot is somewhat tangled and involves two brothers, and two lovely ladies: one a hooker, the other a looker. The older brother, Phaedria, is in competition with a soldier (braggart of course) for the exclusive attention of the fancy lady (Thais). They ply her with gifts. The soldier is by far the richer and presents Thais with a lovely young slave girl. When he sees the maiden Pamphila ("all lovely") being delivered, the younger brother Chaerea is lovestruck at first sight. To gain access to her he disguises himself as the present his brother is planning to give Thais—a eunuch. The moment he introduces himself they think of the perfect position for someone in his condition: bodyguard for the lovely Pamphila. The results are predictable. Not long thereafter, he reappears on stage triumphant in his "amorous rape." Naturally he bounds off to boast of his conquest.

This sort of sexual masquerade will reappear frequently in later comedy, most famously in Wycherley's notorious *Country Wife*. Horner, the protagonist, pretends he is impotent and thereby gains access to any woman he wants. It is hardly the most tender of themes, even before the substitution of Restoration cynicism for Terentian sentiment. Castration seems to be the way to a woman's heart—and her bed.

The audience would no doubt guess the outcome of the young girl's violation. For there is no rape in all of ancient comedy that is not set straight at the end by a lawful marriage. Therefore, by the rules of the game, the "forced seduction" of Pamphila will be righted by the revelation that she is in reality freeborn and therefore marriageable. This is accomplished when her ancient nurse is sent for, recognizes "all the clues" *(signa omnia),* and reveals the heroine to be the long-lost sister of a rich and noble lad named Chremes.[3] So much for the younger brother; we may even call this a conventional ending. But the experience of his older brother is a bit more problematic.

Terence has grafted onto the play the farcical figure of a braggart soldier, Thraso, who is (of course) silly, vain, and rich. (His name survives in the English adjective "thrasonic.") His sidekick Gnatho ("Mr. Gobbler") is both a vainglorious and (of course) groveling and professional parasite. The toady fancies himself a philosopher, but this is merely a sideline to his professional appetite. Not only are these characters taken from another play, they are barely integrated into Terence's comedy. We might say they are presented, for lack of a better term, as comic relief. Indeed this may be the very point, if Terence wished to answer his detractors and enhance the *vis comica* of his dramaturgy.

The unique aspect of *The Eunuch* is the older brother's campaign to win the favors of the good-natured prostitute, Thais. The family praises her generous actions whereby, as Chremes exclaims, "our house is all united."[4] This is thanks in part to the negotiations by Gnatho on behalf of his military master. The parasite proposes an unusual deal to the young hero, Phaedria—that he *share* the favors of Thais with his military rival (who is relatively harmless), in exchange for which the soldier will pick up all the bills. Phaedria agrees, and all three of them live happily ever after.

This *ménage à trois* may not seem sophisticated in the twenty-first century. But it would have been scandalous in the Rome of Cato the Elder. Could this piquant arrangement alone have been the reason for the crowd's demands for an instant replay of Terence's comedy? Why else would the *populus stupidus* insist on an immediate encore? Is this not the ideal reward for a comic hero, the advantages of wife and whore—sex with neither strings nor price tag attached? As one scholar remarks,

> Terence has gone for the surprise conclusion, the arresting ending, the coup de théâtre, as a calculated move to win the audience's approval; in both cases he is willing to sacrifice consistency for dramatic effect.[5]

Terence received the unprecedented prize of 8,000 *sesterces,* the largest sum which had ever been won by a playwright.[6] This is especially mysterious as he never seemed to hit the jackpot again. But we should bear in mind that the *Eunuchus,* with all of its slapstick and rude sexual humor, was Terence at his most "abjectly Plautine."

It was for other reasons, however, that Terence became a classic and a paradigm for all comic authors forever after. Paradoxically, it was his most problematic play that evinced the essence of his achievement. Let us try to unravel the mystery.

Since the earliest days of the theater, the stage mother-in-law has been a perennial figure of fun, an agelast whose only joy in life is making the happily-ever-afters miserable. The *belle-mère* was a familiar figure on the nineteenth-century French stage, always frantically scheming to be a spoilsport to the young lovers. This emotionally charged topic has deep cultural resonances with a kind of taboo which extends back to the beginning of time, and which is operative in the farthest-flung societies studied by Frazer.[7] Along with ejaculations like "slob," "son of a gun," and "hully gee," which the famous American vaudeville impresario B. V. Keith banned from his theaters, a single mention of "mother-in-law" would warrant a performer's immediate dismissal.[8] Nearer our own day this tradition has been given a deft new twist in Mike Nichols' brilliant 1967 film *The Graduate* ("Here's to you, Mrs. Robinson . . .").

Yet Terence's *Hecyra* (*Mother-in-Law*) would seem to be an exception to this tradition. As we will see, Sostrata, the *matrona* of the title, embodies an apparently unprecedented theatrical oxymoron: the sympathetic mother-in-law. Sostrata is so sensitive a parent that, upon learning she is the cause of the newlyweds' unhappiness, she offers to retire to the country and give them peace. Terence plays upon the preconceptions of the audience—and Laches, her husband—to create suspense through a bit of surprise characterization.[9] Nevertheless, despite this novelty—or perhaps because of it—the play was a singular disaster.

But perhaps "double disaster" would be more accurate. For the *Mother-in-Law* is notorious: it was unable to hold the audience on the first two times it was presented. Its maiden performance in 165 B.C. was rudely interrupted (according to a later prologue). When it was restaged five years later in 160 B.C., a similar disturbance chased the actors from the stage. Its third production finally won a hearing, if not a prize, later that same year at the *ludi Romani*.

The apologetic and defensive prologues to the second and third attempts are extant. The first of these is brief but nevertheless contains a hint of what might have displeased the multitude. It chastises the crowd for their unfriendly reception of the initial performance which, says Terence, was interrupted by "the unwashed mob" (*populus stupidus*)[10] who had heard that a tightrope-walker was about to perform. The prologue's sneering denigration of the theatergoers could hardly be classified as *captatio benevolentiae*: nobody likes to be called stupid, least of all on a festive occasion. Terence then concludes with a plea that, since the spectators have enjoyed his previous plays, they should give this one a hearing as well.

The long prologue to the third production, constructed like a formal Roman speech,[11] is spoken by none other than Ambivius Turpio—the veteran actor-producer who was a luminous legend for discovering new talent. He recalls how he once rescued Caecilius' reputation, and begs the audience to give Terence's play a chance to be heard in full.[12] He goes on to discuss the complete theatrical history of the *Mother-in-Law*, which seems to have been "so dogged by disaster" that it never really had a chance.[13] Curiously, this time Terence's account of the first failure states that, in addition to the disruption of the tightrope-walker, there were also rumors that there would be a boxing match.[14]

Why does Terence now change the details of the initial failure, adding fisticuffs to the highwire artistry? Why did the earlier excuse neglect to mention what was an extremely popular Roman spectator sport? It might make the play's rejection a bit more understandable, and a little less humiliating for the playwright.[15] Moreover, why remind people of your failures in what should really be a "warming up" of the audience? (Aristophanes also dwells on his first failure in the revised *Clouds*, but this does not constitute a true precedent since the revised version was never performed.) Unfortunately, the audience's response is not recorded.

The prologue goes on to say that the first act of the *second* production was going well—until someone shouted that there was about to be a gladiatorial display. This caused such a commotion, as Turpio tells it, that "I couldn't keep my place on stage."[16] In his peroration, he begs for their good will on this, the third effort, arguing cryptically that the Roman theatergoers should not allow the "creative arts to be dominated by a select few."[17] This time, in any case, they made it to the end.

By general agreement, this string of disasters is taken to illustrate how Terence was too refined to hold the attention of the rough-hewn Roman audience, in contrast to the universal popular appeal of Plautus. But this view has recently been challenged in a vigorous and learned paper which has to a certain extant absolved Terence of being "caviary to the general."[18] Unfortunately, the effort to stand apart from common opinion has somewhat strained the evidence—particularly regarding the failures of the *Mother-in-Law*.

By using the term *populus stupidus,* the argument goes, Terence does not condemn an audience whose interest he could not hold. Rather, it refers to a second body of festival-goers, a "gaping crowd" that burst into the theater in hopes of seeing the boxers and highwire act. The fact that they struggled with the mob for seats (*convolat*) suggests that there was already a full house.[19] The intrusion broke Terence's spell over this audience, and the play could not be continued.

This is important: clearly Terence had his devotees. But we must not make too much of this. There is no parallel, prior to Ovid,[20] for *populus* as "a crowd" as opposed to "the crowd as a whole." Thus, although it is right to distinguish the attentive audience from intruders,[21] the "idiot mob" must refer to the festival crowd as a whole—*who were for the most part not attending the play.* And what is more, since there was only one stage at such festivals,[22] we must conclude that the general public chose to entertain *themselves* rather than go to Terence's play. Perhaps its reputation preceded it. At any rate, Vergil describes what people liked best on these comastic occasions:

> The farmer keeps the festival days, lounging on the grass,
> Where friends wreath winebowls with a fire in their midst.
> He summons you with a libation, Bacchus, and for the keepers of
>   the herd
> He sets up targets on the elm tree for a contest of swift javelins,
> And the country folk bare their hardened bodies in wrestling.[23]

Clearly, the people who preferred Terence were a minority compared to those who enjoyed brutal sports and thrilling physical feats, and the *populus stupidus* with their rowdy, drunken behavior were absent from the theater until there was a possibility of something more to their liking. This sort of crowd, as Horace tells us, would not hesitate to "demand bears or boxers in the middle of plays."[24] Polybius records a curious event that typifies these popular aesthetics.[25] In 167 B.C. Anicius, to celebrate a triumph, hired musicians, actors, and dancers to perform on a stage in the Circus. Bored by their display, he forced the artists to engage in a mock-gladiatorial combat, as the audience roared their approval.

We must then ask whether Plautus, or any other playwright, would have fared better than Terence.[26] And yet it is abundantly clear from Plautus' own prologues that he faced—and succeeded in entertaining— just the sort of unruly Romans that avoided the *Hecyra.*[27] Plautus could hold their attention because, as Horace insists on remembering, he spoke the language of the *vulgus* and adhered closely to the popular touchstone of Atellane farce.[28] His very name, "Dick O'Fool McSlapstick," proves this.

Consider how often Plautus breaks the dramatic illusion, shame-lessly flirting with the spectators' good will. His characters are forever addressing the audience: "take a look if you will, it will be worthwhile for those present."[29] And in the farcical *Casina* the slave, who has just been mauled by a servant disguised as his bride, tells the audience:

> Pay attention while I tell you my experience. It will be worthwhile
>   for your ears to hear.
> What I've stirred up inside will be a laugh to listen to—and tell.[30]

A recent study of this metatheatrical element in Plautus even posits a "competition" for audience sympathy among the various characters, with the clever slave winning by constantly implicating the audience in the deception.[31]

Because of Plautus' great popular success, the rankings of scholars like Varro, Cicero, and Horace are of questionable value in assessing his impact on the audiences of his own day. It is well known that critics love to go against popular opinion, and like to believe that they appreciate subtleties that others cannot grasp. Accordingly, we should expect Rome's most populist comic author to suffer at the hands of the later pundits, and this seems to have been the case. Cicero rarely quotes Plautus, preferring Caecilius and Terence. Horace condemns the disorganization of Plautine dramaturgy.[32] Both Horace and Velleius Paterculus praise Caecilius and Terence while omitting Plautus.[33]

Donatus, as reliable as one can hope for in an ancient critic, recalls that "*The Mother-in-Law*, several times rejected, was only with difficulty performed right through."[34] Donatus was in a better position than we are to know if the third staging was as successful as any of Terence's other plays. But even if *vix acta est* ("was barely acted") refers to the play's history as a whole rather than the final performance specifically, some stain seems to have adhered to the play's *Nachleben*. That Donatus is not merely inferring from the prologues themselves is supported by the fact that Volcacius Sedigitus, only two generations after the performance (c. 100 B.C.), rated *Hecyra* sixth out of Terence's six plays.[35] It is true that Suetonius (early second century A.D.), who preserves this opinion, asserts that all six plays were equally popular.[36] But the historian himself may have merely inferred this from the fact that the third staging was uninterrupted.[37] Thus, in the absence of any further evidence, the early testimony of Volcacius is greatly to be preferred,[38] as is that of Aelius Stilo (c. 150–70 B.C.) still earlier, whose praise of Plautus was quoted by Varro, the diligent scholar and expert linguist:

> The Muses would have spoken with the words of Plautus, if they wished to speak in Latin.[39]

And Volcacius was surely aware of current opinion when he ranked Terence sixth out of ten playwrights of the *flos poetarum* ("flowering of poets"), with Plautus second only to Caecilius.[40] Obviously Terence's time had not yet come. Moreover, the neglect of the *Hecyra* continued throughout the play's later life. John of Salisbury (twelfth century), who quotes the playwright frequently, does not mention the *Hecyra* once.[41] And since most of his quotations come from classical anthologies, this reveals that the play was persistently stigmatized throughout antiquity.

What was it about the *Hecyra* that caused the otherwise successful playwright so much trouble? For there is no escaping the conclusion that, while the (Plautine) *Eunuchus* was a huge hit, the *Hecyra* was not. It was simply not comedy the way the majority of Romans liked it—broad, farcical, and obvious. Scholars admit that it is difficult to call the *Mother-in-Law* a comedy in the conventional sense. And yet, at first glance, the play seems to have all the stereotyped trappings of the genre, especially the violation of the heroine by an anonymous assailant ten months earlier, culminating in a *cognitio* which makes both mother and child perfectly legal. All ends well, and they live happily ever after.

There is, however, a significant exception here. Although everything in the *Hecyra* seems to be happening according to formula, there is no advance prediction by the prologue, nor any dramatic clue that a single important convention is being flouted. Perhaps the experienced instinct of the cleverer members of the audience could sense the intention, but it is nowhere clearly indicated in the text. It may well be that *Hecyra*, like *Clouds* before it, was too far ahead of its time: Terence's innovations may have been so subtle, the suspense he created so natural, that the fans simply could not follow the play.[42] For though not a laugh riot, and the only Terentian play with a *simplex argumentum,* the *Hecyra* is devilishly clever. Despite its traditional elements of the *nox-amor-vinum-adulescentia* ("night, love, wine, youth") variety, surprise follows surprise.

The first scene finds the slave Parmeno in conversation with two protatic prostitutes. We learn that the young hero Pamphilus, who has enjoyed a long liaison with the courtesan Bacchis, has been coerced by his father into respectability through marrying their neighbor's young daughter, a girl so proper that she is never even allowed to appear onstage. We will later learn from the "zany" slave, who echoes his master's words,[43] that Pamphilus had hesitated to obey his father, not knowing "whether he should succumb to duty or beauty."[44] But in the end *pietas* prevailed over *amor.* The play has thus begun at the very point where a conventional comedy would end—with a legal *gamos.*

Parmeno then vouchsafes a crucial bit of information. He reveals to the incredulous "professional ladies" that his master did not at first consummate his marriage: his wife Philumena was still (so he thought) an "untouched maiden."[45] He also claims that his master kept seeing Bacchis daily.[46] In point of Roman law, of course, this represents no problem and Philumena has no grounds for being upset. As we have seen, a double standard prevailed: a man was not bound to be monogamous—since this did not represent a threat to the integrity of the family—whereas women had to remain faithful under penalty of death. Still, we can assume that this was not to the liking of the Roman matron—recall Mrs. Menaechmus—and Philumena, especially as a young newlywed, would have been less than pleased with her husband's dalliance.

Nevertheless, as Parmeno continues to relate, the young husband came in time to appreciate Philumena's quiet qualities and grew genuinely fond of her.[47] Touched by *misericordia,* he now transferred his tender feelings to his wife and, two months after the marriage, finally made love to her.[48]

At this delicate moment, Pamphilus was obliged to go on an overseas business errand for his father, leaving Philumena in the care of her mother-in-law. In the young man's absence, his mother and wife seem to have had a falling-out, and Philumena has gone back home to her family (who conveniently live across the stage). Naturally, at this point, the audience assumes that Philumena has left because her mother-in-law is acting like a mother-in-law—a preconception reinforced in the next scene, when she is upbraided by her husband Laches in a lengthy tirade:

> LACHES: So every mother-in-law hates her daughter-in-law—and
>   while we are at it, hates her husband just as fiercely.
>   They seem to have all studied at a school for mischief
>   and, if there were such an academy, my wife would be
>   the headmistress.[49]

The encounter concludes with Laches making a facile generalization:

> LACHES: The minute you pressure them into marriage, you start
>   to pressure them to get divorced.[50]

When her husband storms off, Sostrata is left to lament that, though innocent, she will have a difficult time exonerating herself:

> SOSTRATA: So everyone believes
>   that mothers-in-law are sneaky. By Pollux, I'm not one of
>   them!
>   I treated my son's wife just like a daughter and never
>   dreamed of all this trouble.[51]

At last the hero appears for the first time.[52] He has clearly been briefed by Parmeno, and reiterates to his bondsman how he has grown to love his wife and is now happy with the marriage his father arranged for him. Furthermore, he has abandoned his extracurricular liaison. But he is very upset to learn that his wife and mother have had a falling-out, and assumes the older woman is to blame. Nonetheless, he realizes that *pietas* bids him take his mother's side.[53] Parmeno consoles his master, adding: "women—they're all scatterbrained, like children."[54]

This philosophical discussion is suddenly interrupted by a cry from within the neighbor's house. Pamphilus is stunned. Parmeno ingenuously mentions that Philumena has been feeling ill lately. The sensitive Terentian youth rushes in to comfort his wife, but a few minutes later emerges in tears, only to be greeted by his mother who is curious—as are we—about what has transpired inside. Philumena has a fever, Pamphilus tells her—it's nothing serious and she should go home. "But why then," his mother asks, "are you crying?"[55] He evades the question and she exits.

Left alone onstage at last, Pamphilus delivers a long monologue in which he recounts the horrors which have put him in utter shock. The moment is indeed lachrymose:

> After I saw her I cried "What a scandal!" and rushed out in tears.
> What I saw made me shout, staggered by this incredible sight.
> Meanwhile her tearful mother hurried after me
> and, at the very doorway to her house, fell to her knees
> pitifully wailing: I felt such pity for her.[56]

In typical Terentian style, both characters are crying copiously.

The groom's mother-in-law, Myrrina, now dominates the latter portion of the play, almost justifying a change in title to a plural—*Mothers-in-Law*. The singular *Hecyra* can be taken in a generic sense, that is, "the mother-in-law figure," and this is supported by the many generalizations made in the course of the play. This doubling allows Terence to explore the limits of the stereotype and, in a sense, compensates for the lack of a second plot. Indeed, it very nearly constitutes a *duplex argumentum* in its own right.

At last Myrrina tells her son-in-law the truth. One dark night, two months before they were married, her daughter was violated. The time has now come for her to deliver the child she conceived that night. Myrrina pleads with Pamphilus not to betray Philumena's shame, and to let the outside world think that he is the baby's father. After all, since no one but they know of both the rape and the newlyweds' initial abstinence, the timing would make it seem possible. Who said that Terence did not employ irony as well as suspense?

Pamphilus is angry and upset, but will honor his promise to keep his unfortunate wife's secret. He indulges in some self-pity:

I burst into tears when I ponder my future life and its
Solitude. O fortune, how briefly you smile upon us.[57]

He then spies Parmeno coming onstage, who alone outside of himself, Philumena, and Myrrina knows of his sexual abstinence during the first two months of the marriage. Since this would spoil Philumena's "alibi," Pamphilus gets rid of his chatty bondsman by sending him on a wild-goose chase. He then confronts his father and his father-in-law Phidippus and, true to his word, maintains the pretense that his wife's indisposition is owing to the spat (*discidium*) she has had with his mother.[58]

Pamphilus is torn. Clearly he must break with one of the women in his life. He echoes his earlier declaration of loyalty to his mother and explains to both fathers:

Either I must leave my mother or my Philumena.
But I now act out of loyalty not love.[59]

Naturally the two older men misinterpret the younger, who is faithfully camouflaging his wife's disgrace. Although he concedes that he still adores Philumena—"I love her, admire her, and deeply desire her"[60]—he remains steadfast in his loyalty to his mother. With stiff upper lip he marches offstage, prepared to suffer a divorce.

At this point Myrrina, the mother of the bride, who has thus far only appeared in Pamphilus' narrative, enters in person. She is frantic, fearing that her husband has heard the baby's cries. Indeed he has, and Phidippus storms back out in a fury to confront his wife ("Am I your husband? Do you take me for your husband or just some utter stranger?").[61] Phidippus knows that their daughter has given birth and is suspicious at what he believes to be the baby's prematurity (at seven months!). He demands, "who's the father?"[62] Caught off guard, Myrrina fabricates an answer: "Do you actually have the gall to ask? My God! Who else but her lawfully wedded husband!?"[63] The time-frame suggests that it could have been a honeymoon baby.[64] Her spouse is chastened, but still cannot understand why they would want to conceal the birth of a legitimate baby.[65] Myrrina throws out a red herring, convincing him to have a serious talk with "the young father" Pamphilus about abandoning his mistress. Meanwhile he goes in to see the new member of their family.

Alone on stage, Myrrina is afraid that when her bad-tempered husband discovers that the child is really fatherless, he will never believe the truth of what actually happened to their daughter. And she now conveys a startling bit of information:

> You see, when my daughter was attacked, it was too dark to tell
>   who ravished her,
> nor could she snatch from him a souvenir by which we could
>   identify the man.
> But he, the wretch, pulled off a ring from my poor daughter's
>   finger.[66]

The fact that it was too dark to see the culprit is a standard condition for New Comedy rapes. However, there is something unusual in this *modus rapiendi*—the attacker has taken *her* ring and not, as typically, vice versa. We have learned a lot of surprising information in a very few lines.

As one mother-in-law exits, the other re-enters. Sostrata is overflowing with gratitude that her dutiful son has sided with her rather than his wife. But she magnanimously offers to go to the country so as not to be in the young couple's way. High-mindedly, she wants to change the general negative reputation of all mothers-in-law.[67] Hearing this, the young man exclaims: "I wish my wife were like my own dear mother!"[68]

This is not the first such expression of maternal affection in dramatic literature, and certainly not the last. We see matrophilia in such diverse "mama's boys" as Telephus (who nearly does) and Oedipus (who does), Coriolanus, and Henry Higgins. (The reference is of course to Shaw's protagonist, not Broadway's, for "the ending of Pygmalion is the classic Shavian situation: someone is clamorously refusing to enter the bedroom.")[69] And of course there is the ever-popular song, "I want a girl just like the girl that married dear old dad."

Moments later Phidippus appears and a delighted Laches tells him that all is well; and since his wife Sostrata, the source of this trouble, has gone to the country, Philumena can now return to their house. But Phidippus insists that it is his own wife—the *other* mother-in-law—who has stirred up this whole mess and is the source of all the anxiety. Thus, in this moment of anger both mothers-in-law stand unjustly maligned.

Pamphilus is now stunned by the sudden change of events—especially when his duped father-in-law asks him to recognize the baby. In a brief but amusing stichomythia, all three men blurt out their thoughts:

> PHIDIPPUS: Do take the babe—
> PAMPHILUS: *(aside)*   O damn, he knows!
> LACHES: *(stunned)*   Babe? What babe?
> PHIDIPPUS: *(with naive pride)*   We both are now a grandpa.[70]

The codgers understandably rejoice, but young Pamphilus remains obdurate, refusing to accept either child or mother. They try to reason with him:

> LACHES: Do you imagine any man can find a wife
>   who's perfect? Don't you think that husbands have their
>   faults as well?[71]

But the angry young man storms offstage, leaving the oldsters to find a new plan of action. Phidippus then suggests that they go confront "this Bacchis woman,"[72] who they assume is the source of the trouble.

Right on cue, the courtesan in question emerges from the third house on stage. The audience is *still* in a fog as to what is really going on. Though she has often been alluded to, Bacchis' actual appearance comes very late in the play. She is therefore much like Crito, the relative in the *Andria,* who arrives as a convenient New Comedy version of the *deus ex machina* to untie all the knots and legitimize the heroine for marriage—only here in the *Hecyra* the new arrival reassures the characters of the legitimacy of the heroine's *baby.* Pedants still in search of a prologue to the play could best look here for this extremely delayed exposition, deftly transferred from what would have been a run-of-the-mill introductory speech in an ironic comedy, to grace the appealing finale of a suspense-packed drama.

The lady's sudden appearance on stage anticipates the grand tradition of such eleventh-hour entrances in later drama. In Molière's *School for Wives*, for example, a long-lost uncle ("Enrique from Amerique") suddenly materializes in the nick of time to save the heroine from a ghastly mismarriage. We shall see this convention invoked only to be destroyed in Beckett's *Waiting for Godot*, where the last-minute arrival never comes.

In Terence's *Hecrya*, Bacchis is the "Godot" who does appear. Almost at once she expresses her fears that the sleazy reputation of her sisters in the trade might prejudice the other characters against her. Unlike them, she herself is entirely decent.[73] Bacchis quickly swears to Laches that she has kept away from his son from the moment he married. This seems not be true: we have heard earlier from the slave Parmeno that his master kept up his illicit union, with daily visits even after the wedding.[74] Yet she is now prepared to go inside and deny it, showing her sterling character:

> BACCHIS: I must persuade Pamphilus' wife to go back home to
> him. I won't regret a gesture that my fellow floozies all
> would flee with fear.[75]

She praises the young man's virtue and diplomatically makes peace among the various wives and husbands. We see here Terence's manipulation of character type to create the almost oxymoronic persona of a good prostitute, foiling expectations in order to create suspense, realism, and surprise twists. The later critic Euanthius assures us that the Romans themselves viewed Bacchis this way:

> When he fashioned his plots, [Terence] alone dared, in the
> pursuit of verisimilitude, to go against comic conventions
> and even occasionally bring out prostitutes who were *not*
> bad.[76]

Can there be any doubt that Bacchis is a *bona meretrix*?[77]

But Terence has one final twist—the biggest surprise of all. Bacchis suddenly emerges from the bride's home, spies Parmeno, and urges him to fetch his master as soon as possible. She then announces to the spectators that inside the ladies have recognized a ring on her finger as once having belonged to none other than *Philumena*. And, what is more, she was given it by none other than *Pamphilus*—precisely ten months ago, after snatching it from someone he had raped! Of course, he had no idea until this moment that his victim was now his own wife. But suddenly he knows whom he wronged, and that the newborn child is in fact his own son!

This is not merely a last-minute turnabout, it is a significant landmark in the history of drama. With a verbal wink Pamphilus even remarks that they are avoiding the traditional hackneyed ending:

> PAMPHILUS: I don't want this play to end like other comedies,
> where all the characters learn everything about each
> other.
> This time the folks who have to know now know
> and those who *don't, won't* need to know.[78]

Yet in a way the *Hecyra* does in fact have a traditional comic finale—a symbolic rebirth. Indeed, Terence makes it quite explicit. Earlier when the young husband saw that all had been set right, he effusively thanked his slave:

> PAMPHILUS: You've brought me up from Hell into the light—
> How could I let you go without a token of my grati-
> tude?[79]

It is archetypal. The hero has, as it were, returned from the dead, a point that the zany Parmeno emphasizes by echoing his master's words: "I brought him from the dead in Hell just now."[80]

Whatever drew the audiences away from the first two aborted stagings of the *Mother-in-Law,* the third group of spectators who saw it all would have had the unique pleasure of tasting some new wine in old bottles, spiced by suspense (as well as irony.) The play at once sports with old conventions and canonizes a new form, one that would dominate the stage for the millennia to come. As Mikhail Bakhtin put it, the Romans taught the world how to laugh.[81]

14

Machiavelli: The Comedy of Evil

The death of Terence sounded the knell for the Roman *palliata* that Plautus and his brethren had developed for nearly a century. Not that the African playwright himself wrought a fatal innovation, but for some reason, today inexplicable, the genre lost its creativity and simply faded out. The *flos poetarum* had withered.

But Plautus and Terence did not wholly disappear. During the subsequent centuries, each was variously in and out of favor.[1] The elder playwright was revived again and again throughout the Republic; the last recorded revival of a Plautine play is a performance of *Pseudolus* in which Cicero's friend Roscius played the part of Ballio, "the vilest and crookedest pimp."[2] Terence, by contrast, remained in vogue throughout the early Empire. There are frequent references to acting and actors in Quintilian's manual of oratory, and Menander enjoyed a vigorous life in recital and dinner-party performances, as well as on-stage. With renewed interest in archaic poetry in the age of the Antonines, Plautus regained some scholarly attention as being a store-house of unusual words and expressions.[3] The fourth century saw the publication of important Terentian commentaries by Donatus and Euanthius.

But the posthumous productions were mere ghostly visits, mere revenants rather than true revivals. Indeed, according to Aulus Gellius, only fifteen years after his death the debate on Plautine authenticity had already become a cottage industry.[4] This is ample testimony to Plautus' unprecedented success, for unscrupulous promoters, anxious to cash in on the late master's cachet, would ascribe second-rate comedies to his authorship to enhance their appeal and price. The playwright and scholar Lucius Accius (170–c. 186 B.C.) divided the comedies into three categories: authentic, possible, or doubtful. Varro also speaks of a triadic division of comedies in existence in his own day. His careful research—Cicero praised him for being *diligentissimus*—must have done much to consolidate the corpus in the first century B.C. But questions remained for Gellius (second century A.D.) and even Macrobius on the threshold of the Dark Ages.[5]

All this time, of course, popular entertainment stayed as popular as ever. The indigenous mime and farce continued to flourish, as they did in Greece both during and after the heyday of Aristophanes and his colleagues. Even in the fifth and sixth centuries A.D., Greek mimes were still wearing the traditional leather phallus, known by then as a *phaletarion*.[6] There has never been a shortage of low comedy in any age. But in neither country was there anything quite so rich as the commedia dell'arte which was still to come.

Yet it is not our intention to chronicle an annalistic history of dramatic performances per se, but rather to follow through the ages the evolution and transmutations of the classical literary form as pioneered by Aristophanes, crystallized by Menander, and canonized by Terence. The distinction between the medieval play and the scripted dramas we have been examining can be seen, *mutatis mutandis,* in the difference between Woody Allen's monologues and his films. Both inspire laughter, but only the movies tell a story.

Moreover, this period was not fertile ground for any literary comedy. The European populace was faced with steely churchmen preaching against the diabolical dangers of all stage plays. The anti-theatrical polemics of the churchman Tertullian's second century *De spectaculis (On Theater),* though certainly acerbic, had enjoyed only relative success un-

til Emperor Constantine's conversion to Christianity.[7] This unrepen-
tant agelast warned:

> Yet [for Christians] are reserved other *spectacula* on judgment
> day . . . Then will be the time to listen to the tragedians,
> whose lamentations will be more poignant for their proper
> pain! Then will the comedians turn and twist, rendered nim-
> bler than ever by the sting of unquenchable fire![8]

Constantine's death early in the fourth century arguably marks
the end of the classical era. It coincided, on the religious scene, with
the entrance of the anti-*kōmos* saints Jerome, Ambrose—and especially
Augustine. After a wayward childhood during which he was passionate
about the theater, Augustine became wildly incensed by it—and his
attitude permeated the religious and secular life of Christianity
for centuries to come. The church preached *contemptus mundi*—
the rejection of everything terrestrial, to concentrate on the next
world. The theater was a principal *bête noire,* and comedy in particular
since the *kōmos* focuses on the joys of life in this world—with no
regard for the next. Heaven and the theater were irreconcilable opposites.

And yet, as we have seen, the church could not eradicate the pagan
kōmos days. Indeed, the patristic anti-*kōmos* sermons are, if anything, evidence that many people continued to prefer the old festivals to otherworldly glory. There are ample histories of medieval drama—which
could be both festive and funny. As Bakhtin insisted, "to ignore or underestimate the laughing people of the Middle Ages also distorts the
picture of European culture's historic development."[9] But the "theater"
was usually a marketplace or inn-yard set up for the day's performance;
the players were merely diverse performers like jugglers, sword-dancers,
singers, and assorted minstrels.[10]

Nevertheless, even at this level of disorganization and *ataxia,* theatrical performances faced continual opposition from the Church. So sinful was their occupation regarded that actors were often denied a
Christian burial, and their most glorious roles were as heroes of the
martyrologies. St. Genisius, now the patron saint of actors, who was

commanded to perform a comic mime in front of the Emperor Diocletian (died in 312, the very year Constantine beheld his vision), instead hailed the glories of Christ, but was slain for his disobedient expression of faith. The only happy end for a Christian would be a transport to heaven. The theater district was in hell.[11]

An architectural analogy demonstrates how things had changed. Drama in the ancient world flourished in the open air, in the sunshine of the here and now. Indeed, in the Greek and Roman religions there was no true sense of life after death. We recall Achilles' remorseful rejection of the existence in the underworld, when he laments, "Better to be a hired-hand with no property on earth than king of all the dead."[12] Whereas the early churches in the East had been almost as wide open as the theaters, the medieval cathedral became the quintessential expression of the severe Christian world-view.[13] Its tall, narrow spires pointed straight at heaven, all but shutting out the sun from mortal man's tenebrous existence. Attention was completely focused on the world to come.

Then at long last a light dawned in the shadows and men began to look once again at one another, and the world, with unblinkered eyes. The term "Renaissance" of course is a "movable feast." Traditionally it refers to the period beginning in the mid-fourteenth century. But the Middle Ages were not without moments of great illumination. The name commonly given to the period between 800 and 1300 A.D., the Dark Ages, is belied by enormous intellectual activity—particularly in Latin classics. There was the Carolingian revival in the late eighth and early ninth centuries, with the English scholar Alcuin the leading figure at Charlemagne's court. Terence was represented in the library, whereas Plautus was not.[14] Then there was the very active period brilliantly chronicled by Charles Homer Haskins in *The Renaissance of the Twelfth Century*.[15]

Nevertheless, the period most commonly referred to as the Renaissance saw a deep and permanent transformation in Europe, with the rebirth of classical literature and ideas—not just in scriptoria and courts, but throughout society. The human body was transformed from a constrictive garment imprisoning the soul to a new temple in which the priests did physical exercises and even danced.

Perhaps the supreme "Renaissance man" was Leon Battisa Alberti (c. 1404–1472)—priest, artist, architect, superb athlete, writer, musician, jurist, mathematician, physicist, and naturalist, as well as a prolific author both in Latin and Italian. As he himself expressed it, "Men can do anything if they want to."[16]

Among the comic innovators of this new infatuation with the world was Giovanni Boccaccio (1313–1375), one of the first writers to sing the body electric. His Latin works are long forgotten, but his famous *Decameron,* "written in very choice Italian," has never been unavailable since it was first published in the late fourteenth century. It was at once a *coup de grâce* to the Middle Ages and a hearty harbinger of the reborn secular civilization. Thus the work is often referred to as the *commedia humana,* in contrast to Dante's divine medieval epic. In fact, among Boccaccio's works is a commentary on Dante's massive poem. He was a veritable Janus, looking both to the past and to the future.

When he published the first three *giornate* (days of tales), Boccaccio received much criticism from the straitlaced members of society for daring to describe such audacious—not to say slanderous—fictions as women's sexuality and the concupiscence of the clergy. His treatment of these outrageous subjects earned him much opprobrium—not least with women and the clergy. To counter these many attacks, the author published a riposte in the preface to the subsequent seven *giornate.* He felt obliged to tell a story in his own persona and in his own defense.

It concerns one Filippo Balducci, an upstanding citizen of Florence whose wife has died. Grief-stricken, he retires from the world with his young son to a small monastic cell atop Mount Asinaio. Here, for many years, the two lived an ascetic existence, the father teaching the boy "nothing of the world except prayers and the glories of the next." As Filippo grew older, the occasional trips to Florence to get what meager supplies they needed became more and more fatiguing. Since he assumed that his son, now sixteen, was inured to "the things of this world," he took the young lad along to help him carry their provisions back.

The boy was enchanted at the sight of the cathedrals and the other buildings of the city, and never ceased to ask his father questions about the various wonders he was seeing. The old man readily explained. And then . . . they passed a group of young girls dressed for a wedding. The boy's mouth fell open. "And what may those be, father?" he asked. "Those are a bad thing," Filippo growled, not wanting to stir up any feelings in his son that were "not really useful." The boy replied ingenuously, "but father, those bad things are so beautifully built!"

Boccaccio's tale may be read as a metaphor. On the stony heights of the mountain, Filippo keeps his son's libido suppressed by prayer and thoughts of angels. Yet, in a moment of weakness, Filippo allows his son to visit the earthy metropolis where he learns, to his dismay, the basic human truth—the comic truth—that the power of intellect is nothing compared to the power of nature.

The *Decameron* reflects the change in European sensibilities that came with the Renaissance. Broadly speaking, this period saw humankind descend from the lofty heights of self-denial, with all eyes on heaven, to the world of here and now, the glories of Florence, and the temporal life. Love and lust. Women. Boccaccio's *apologia* hails this transformation. It is with this metamorphosis in mind that we approach the rebirth of classical culture that characterized the florescence of Florence and the other Italian city-states.[17]

Yet despite the discovery and editing of many Latin texts, the plays of Plautus and Terence were at first all but ignored. Even by the beginning of the fifteenth century, only eight plays of Plautus were known. Then in 1429 Nicolas of Cusa came to Rome with an incredible find—a manuscript with no fewer than sixteen comedies of Plautus, twelve of them newly brought to light.[18] In 1433 he returned, this time with Donatus' commentary on Terence.[19]

Several of the newly discovered Plautus comedies were produced in 1502 at the wedding of Lucrezia Borgia (no poison was served!).[20] One of the guests recorded that the bride was rather bored by the Latin comedies, but enjoyed the musical *intermezzi*. In England, St. Paul's School produced the *Phormio* before Cardinal Wolsey in 1528, and Westminster played Terence before Queen Elizabeth in 1569 (and at the end of the twentieth century it was still a regular event). Sometime around 1553 Nicholas Udall, the "whipping master" at Westminster, produced the curious *Ralph Royster Doyster,* a *contaminatio* of Plautus' *Braggart Soldier* and Terence's *Eunuch.* It was a hit—of a theatrical sort.

In Italy, classical comedies were often performed by child players. Castiglione, author of *The Courtier*, remarked how pathetic it was to see little children trying to take the parts of Menander's old men.[21] It was probably not the first time—and certainly not the last—that the scenery outshone the dialogue.[22] There is an old saying in the modern musical theater that "the audience never goes out humming the scenery," but this was belied by those early productions in the Renaissance courts. Plautus and Terence were staged with spectacular effects which did overshadow everything else, and the audience did go out singing their praise. Angels flew in and out; Apollo would come down from heaven. Some theater companies had the great good fortune of using stage machinery invented by none other than Leonardo da Vinci.

Not surprisingly, the first attempts to mimic ancient works were feeble efforts. But in time the Italian playwrights began to master the classical material. Among the earliest important authors was Ludovico Ariosto (1474-1533), better known for his splendid epic *Orlando Furioso*. At the Court of Ferrara he wrote, among other things, *I Suppositi* in 1509 (*The Substitutes*), an identity-comedy based on Plautus' *Captivi* and Terence's *Eunuch*.

But the first author of stature to write stage comedies in the classical tradition was Niccolo Machiavelli (1469-1527). The author of *The Prince*, the famous manual of political machinations, was himself a high official in the republic of Florence, by turns a republican or a supporter of autocracy, depending upon which way the wind blew. A passionate idealist with a highly cynical world-view, he was ahead of his time—a fervent nationalist in an age of dynasts, hoping that one day Italy would be united as a single country.

Machiavelli used the outward form of Roman comedy to compose a biting satire on the Florence of the Medici, a corrupt society he knew well from the inside. It would be like Henry Kissinger lampooning the Nixon administration. The period in which he lived has been called "the Italian carnival," and he was very much a man of this age, with all its verve and contradictions. Machiavelli wished to sweep away the medieval detritus: his targets were no less than the Papacy, the ruling classes, feudalism, and hypocrisy in general.

Taking his cue from Boccaccio's tale, he countered the *vita contemplativa* of the Middle Ages with a *vita activa* based on a triadic aspiration of country, action, and the pursuit of glory. Dante, the quintessence of the Middle Ages, had preached "we must *love*." By contrast, Machiavelli urged that "we must *know*." At the center of the poet's world was the *soul;* at the politician's, the *brain*. The supreme good was knowledge of oneself and the world as it really is. It was *Realpolitik avant la lettre*.

In *The Prince*, Machiavelli argues that a ruler should govern, not by violence, but by knowing his subjects and controlling them with *l'inganno*, deception. His world-view was like that of Marlowe's later stage caricature, Machevill, who would say "I count religion but a childish toy." But what the real Machiavelli might have believed was closer to "I count religion but a clever *tool*." How, one wonders, could the author of such a treatise as *The Prince* write anything as frivolous as the works of Plautus or Terence? In fact Machiavelli could not. He was the polar opposite of Terence. For whereas the Roman playwright's humanistic outlook might be epitomized as "every man has his worth," the calculating Machiavelli would say "every man has his price."

Nevertheless, Machiavelli began his theatrical career with an adaptation of Terence's *Andria*, and concluded with an extremely vulgar adaptation of Plautus' *Casina*. These were ostensibly in the classical tradition. But the Florentine playwright added his own peculiar touch of bitter pragmatism to the Roman models.

The prologue to *La Clizia*, Machiavelli's adaptation of Plautus' *Casina*, turns earthy Latin comedy into Florentine amorality. Indeed, the setting has been quite literally changed. He first announces that the play will take place in Athens, "a noble and most ancient city in Greece." But then he quickly corrects himself and changes his mind, saying of Athens:

> its streets, its piazzas, its noble structures can scarce be recognized, and since the people there speak Greek, a language which you people don't understand—imagine that all of this took place in Florence.

It is a significant moment in theatrical history. Whereas Plautus and Terence had set their comedies in foreign lands as a way of creating a parallel—but antithetical—comic universe, Machiavelli brings it closer to home. He is conscious of his place in the history of the classical form. For Athens was in ruins more than architecturally. Both Menander and Aristophanes were gone. The Greek theaters were little more than marble quarries. The form and style of the ancient models were viable, but the content of the plays was too tame for the new age. The theater needed a new infusion (or perhaps transfusion). Machiavelli's hard-nosed *Realpolitik,* added to the classical models, provided the ingredient that made his plays relevant to the new age.

Unlike the comedies we have studied so far, Machiavelli's were in prose. *La Clizia,* despite its coarse Plautine humor, has a more sophisticated Terentian structure. For the prologue withholds information about the real identity of the girl so there can be a genuinely suspenseful *cognitio* and *cognatio.* Only at the end is it discovered by the girl's noble and *ricchissimo* father, who arrives at the eleventh hour, that she is well-born and marriageable.

But Machiavelli's masterpiece transcended both his Roman predecessors. This was the *Mandragola* (*The Mandrake*),[23] for which Voltaire said he would sacrifice all the plays of Aristophanes. (The Greek playwright was unfit for eighteenth-century sensibilities, with his inventive word-play and jokes against individuals long since forgotten. Of course, few people yet knew the ancient language.) Carlo Goldoni, the master comic playwright of the eighteenth century, recalled his youthful encounter with the play:

> I devoured it on the first reading, and reread it ten times . . . it was not the libertine tone nor the shocking machinations . . . on the contrary, its filthiness revolted me . . . but it was the first character-play that had come to my eyes, and I was enchanted by it.[24]

Mandragola is wholly "Machiavellian." Toward this end the author has modified the classical form to suit his needs. Its moral—or immoral—sympathies mirror the author's own political philosophy, which has been articulated in such simplistic epitomes as "the end justifies the means," "might makes right," and "the only sin is ignorance." Nothing happens by chance. There is no Tychē, no felicitous *cognitio,* and no *deus ex machina.* It is all scheming, knowledge, and manipulation.

First, the title. What did the playwright intend by it? Since antiquity, the mandrake root was thought to be an aphrodisiac, no doubt because of its phallic shape. It clearly appeared as a remedy or drug in Alexis' lost *Mandragorizomenē (The Mandraked Woman)*.[25] In the extant fragments we hear how people are taken in by foreign doctors—the *medici gloriosi* we have seen before, and who constitute a central theme in the *Mandragola:*

> If a local
> Doctor tells you "give this man a bit of
> Broth at dawn," you despise him at once.
> But if he says "given sie ein bowl mit broth," you're awe-struck by
> his learning.[26]

The mandrake is also celebrated in John Donne's famous poem, "Catch a Falling Star," which is worth quoting at length because its cynicism matches the tone of Machiavelli's play:

> Go and catch a falling star,
> Get with child a mandrake root,
> Tell me where all past years are,
> Or who cleft the Devil's foot . . .
> And find
> What wind
> Serves to advance an honest mind . . .
> And swear
> No where
> Lives a woman true and fair.
> If thou find'st one, let me know,
> Such a pilgrimage were sweet.
> Yet do not; I would not go.
> Though at next door we might meet,
> Though she were true when you met her,
> And last when you write your letter
> Yet she
> Will be
> False, ere I come, to two or three.

Clearly, at this moment in his life, the future Dean of St. Paul's shares with his Italian predecessor a bitter, misogynistic outlook. Neither the medicinal powers of the mandrake nor female fidelity can be trusted. For every woman is corruptible. If Jonson's *Volpone* reduces man to bestiality, Macchiavelli's *Mandragola* further reduces him to a vegetable—albeit a phallic one. And should this not be demeaning enough, the heroine makes her first appearance as a urine sample!

The *Mandragola* also presents one of the first Renaissance articulations of a classical theme, which has since reappeared many times in modern literature: the *mari philosophe* or complaisant husband who receives "procreative intervention" on his behalf by someone younger and fitter. We saw this motif adumbrated as early as Euripides' *Ion*, where Xuthus goes home blindly from Delphi thinking that the young priest he is taking home is his own son—when in fact he is a scion of Apollo whom the god had abandoned even before Creusa had given birth. We saw it developed more painfully in Plautus' tragicomic *Amphitruo*, where Jupiter cuckolds the title character to impregnate Alcmena with the baby Hercules.

Closer to our day it was the theme of Marcel Pagnol's French trilogy *Marius/Fanny/César* (1931-1936), and was seen on the American musical stage in Frank Loesser's *Most Happy Fellow*, a musical adaptation of Sidney Howard's Pulitzer Prize–winning 1924 stage play *They Knew What They Wanted*. The protagonist is pleased because he is going to have a child: he is a cuckold, but a most happy one. Just like Messer Nicia, the doddering would-be daddy in the *Mandragola.*

And yet "horning," the theme of the *Mandragola*, is peculiarly Italian. To this day, one of the worst terms of abuse in modern argot remains *cornuto*, "you horned bastard." And as modern Italian cinema demonstrates, the cruel pleasure of making someone else a *cornuto* is as popular as ever, as illustrated in the classic film *Divorce Italian Style*, which has as its climax the cuckolding of Marcello Mastroianni, the amorous husband. It was also a favorite theme of the commedia dell'arte, of which some of the characters in this play are forerunners.[27]

Except for the addition of a priest, the cast of characters in the *Mandragola* is essentially Plautine: a *senex amator*, a parasite who takes over from the clever slave, and a young lover who doubles as a pompous doctor or *medicus gloriosus*. And of course the pure-hearted ingenue. The age of Machiavelli saw the appearance for the first time of real women with real names playing real female roles—in certain productions.

Also in the mode of Plautus is the explosiveness of the language and the extensive use of trickery. Yet the prime mover is not Siro, a bit too dim to be a "clever" servant—though Renaissance Florence did in fact have some non-Christian white slaves, nearly all of them were women— but the parasite Ligurio (did this classical stage figure really exist in six-teenth-century Italy?) One critic has described Ligurio as someone "entirely destitute of moral sense, who would have betrayed Christ for a good tip."[28]

But the parasite is not the sleaziest character in the play. That dubious honor goes to Fra Timoteo, the canny friar. Machiavelli does not mince words in his characterization. Like the church he ostensibly serves, Timoteo is corruptible, corrupt, and corrupting. As he explains to the audience, his constant confidant, "I hang around the church because it's the best place to do business." It was this portrait of immoral clergy that was so shocking to the dour Germans in the throes of Martin Luther's Reformation. By contrast, Pope Leo X had the *Mandragola* performed for him and was reported to have laughed heartily (of course, this was a Medici Pope).[29] Times had clearly changed since Boccaccio's day.

But the focus of all attention in the *Mandragola* is Lucrezia, the lovely young girl married to Dottore Nicia, a rich but foolish lawyer who knows little more than a few scraps of legal Latin. His exquisite and innocent wife bears the name of the legendary Roman heroine who was the paragon of purity. Cruelly raped by the Roman General Sextus Tarquinius, she waited to tell her husband and father of her disgrace— and then stabbed herself to death. So pure and modest was Lucretia that, according to Ovid's wry account, even as she collapsed to the floor she was careful to hold her robe about her lest she reveal anything immodest.[30]

But whereas Sextus Tarquinius raped his victim, Machiavelli's hero will not use force. He will win his prize by *l'inganno,* trickery. And this time the woman "dies" only in the erotic Elizabethan sense of the word.[31] This is the Florentine appetite for the flesh, which exploits Machiavellian means to bring it success.

The opening scene of the play is a parody of the Roman legend.[32] It begins with the hero Callimaco in Paris—a code word to the Italian audience that he was up to no good with women. (Of course, the French regarded the Italians and Spanish as lewd. This perjorative stereotyping persists in the Euro clichés of our own day.)[33] A group of young lads in a Paris saloon are discussing who the best-looking woman in the world might be, and it is quickly established that Madonna Lucrezia of Florence, the wife of a certain Dottore Nicia, clearly owns this title. Consumed with a mad desire to have her, Callimaco hastens to Florence.

There are initial problems. As the would-be seducer explains to his servant, he has no hope of possessing her. Although she is *onestissima*, above reproach, her *marito ricchissimo* keeps her locked up in the house and allows no worker or delivery boy to come near. The comic motif of the older husband trying to isolate his young wife from the advances of a young, masculine world is familiar, and would be seen later in Jonson's *Volpone*, Wycherley's *Country Wife*, and Molière's *School for Wives*.

Naturally, her inaccessibility merely whets Callimaco's appetite. He quickly exchanges his servant for Ligurio, the slimy parasite, to whom he expresses his utter desperation:

> CALLIMACO: I've got to try something—be it huge, dangerous, harmful, shameful, or unspeakable. It is better to die than live like this.[34]

Note that, like his Roman forebear, the lustful Callimaco desires to spend only *one* night with her. There is no tenderness here: all that matters is the conquest. For this he is ready to go to hell, the burning inferno—but anyway there are so many fascinating people there.

He has come to the right man. Ligurio knows the old man's weakness: Messer Nicia is desperate for a child. Therefore the con-man proposes to introduce Callimaco as a *xenikos iatros*—a fertility expert from Paris who has helped many grand ladies to have children. Now in disguise, our anti-hero speaks to the *senex* and is instantly recognized as a great medical mind—because his Latin is so much better than Nicia's.

"Dottore" Callimaco first questions the old man to determine whether the fault might lie with him: are his own sexual functions healthy? In a burst of *alazoneia,* the old man retorts:

> NICIA: Me impotent? Don't make me laugh, I don't think there
> is any man more rock hard or masculine in all of Flor-
> ence.[35]

Despite Nicia's protests of virility, the fertility expert proposes that they put a "visiting possessor" in his wife's bed. The old man hesitates. "I don't want to make a whore of my wife and a cuckold of myself," he says.[36]

At last he relents. But only half the battle is won. For Nicia believes that his virtuous wife would never agree to a stranger in her bed. Ligurio proposes that the only logical way to reach a woman of such virtue is through her spiritual father. And yet:

> CALLIMACO: Who will convince the priest—you?
> LIGURIO: Me, money, our own sleaze—and theirs.[37]

Fortunately Fra Timoteo is less incorruptible than Lucrezia. In fact he quite willingly collaborates. Throughout the play the churchman dances to the tune of money. They also enlist the collaboration of Lucrezia's mother, a semi-retired slut who is also inspired by money to try to convince her daughter to visit the church. And yet the old woman too is skeptical that this seduction plan will succeed. The priest reassures her with the sardonic and Plautine remark: "brains—no woman has them."

The mother and the friar reason with the girl, using sophistry worthy of the Spanish bawd Celestina:

> It's the will that sins, not the body . . . it's something that a
> few drops of holy water will wash away.[38]

Lucrezia's very goodness will undo her. They convince the girl that the potion the doctor has given her will kill the next man who sleeps with her, and it is better that the husband not run the risk. Timoteo cites the biblical example of the daughters of Lot, who, thinking they were the last people on earth, slept with their father without sin to re-populate the world. Even the devil can quote scriptures. Reluctantly Lucrezia assents, expressing her wish that the young man who will sacrifice himself need not die.[39] She returns to her bedroom to prepare herself.

Callimaco quickly doffs his medical disguise and becomes the hand-some lute-playing minstrel who, by previous arrangement with the parasite, will be strolling past in time to be "kidnapped" as the sacrificial victim. As Nicia and Fra Timoteo go out into the night "in search" of this "candidate," the Captain (Ligurio, as *miles gloriosus*) informs them:

> LIGURIO: The password will be Saint Cuccù.
> NICIA: Who is he?
> LIGURIO: The most highly honored saint in all of France.[40]

Our old friend is back. It is San Cuccù, the patron saint of cuckolds.

In disguise, with the servant bringing up the rear to make sure the "troops don't droop," the kidnapping is successful. They hustle the prisoner back to Lucrezia's bedroom—Nicia himself helping to drag the disguised Callimaco into his own bed. He is astounded by the readiness and speed with which the man takes off his clothes. And the view there-after—well, he very much likes the musician's physique:

> You never saw such a gorgeous body—so white, so soft, so tender. And about the other things, don't even ask![41]

Nicia cannot keep from probing the victim's sexual parts to see how things are going, an operation which seems to excite him ("I wanted to touch him and feel that he had all the right equipment").[42]

When all retire to await the good news, Fra Timoteo addresses the audience with a wink and a grin:

> TIMOTEO: Tonight no one will sleep, so that the Acts are not broken up by the time. Callimaco and Signora Lucrezia won't get any rest, and I know if you or I were in that bed we wouldn't get any either.[43]

The aesthetic requirement for the unity of time within a play is thus cleverly exploited to ribald effect.

The final act is replete with mordant ironies—a cruel travesty of the usual *gamos* ending typical of classical comedy. Unable to sleep this past night, Fra Timoteo describes how he has spent the nocturnal hours doing various tasks in the church—all of which could be construed as sexual double-entendres.

Dottore Nicia and Ligurio appear and recount to the eavesdropping friar the successful "issue" of the previous evening. Nicia tells of the difficulty they had pulling the unfortunate visitor from Lucrezia's bed, and expresses pity at the young lad's imminent demise. And yet he is such a supreme dupe that at the height of his fantasies he imagines that "his" child is already born:

> NICIA: I'm going home and have my wife get up and wash up
> and I'll make her come to church to say the childbirth
> blessings.[44]

Nicia is indeed getting ahead of himself, and Fra Timoteo remarks once again on the *sciocchezza* (stupidity) of the other players (a theme emphasized by Machiavelli throughout the play).

At last the "bridegroom" appears. Intoxicated from the delights of the evening, he describes (to the audience) how he approached the pious lady and how she reacted:

> CALLIMACO: She has tasted the difference between my style and
> Dottore Nicia's, having compared the kisses of a new
> young lover to those of an antiquated husband . . .[45]

Callimaco revealed his true identity to her. Upon learning of the shameful trick that had been played upon her, Lucrezia reacted in a surprising manner. Accepting that the "heavens" have willed Callimaco into her life, she adds a twist of her own to outwit the would-be one-night-stander and his fellow conspirators. It is hard to say whether she is being candid or sophistic when (as Callimaco reports) Lucrezia sighs philosophically and declares:

> Because of your cleverness, my husband's foolishness, my
> mother's simplicity, and my confessor's duplicity, I have

been forced to do what I myself would never have done, I accept it is the will of heaven . . ."[46]

She has had a genuine awakening, and we note the new powers of rhetoric—Wrong Logic—as she comes to the sophistic conclusion:

> LUCREZIA: I therefore take you as husband, lord and master, father and protector—you will be everything to me. And what my husband wanted you to do for one night, I want you to do for him always.[47]

If this sounds suspiciously like a wedding vow, that is Machiavelli's ironic intent. It matters little that Lucrezia is already "married." For, with the curious exception of the Aristophanic oldster, in comedy youth must always triumph over age.

This fundamental law is indeed at work here. When in the next scene Lucrezia appears before her husband, Nicia remarks on her radiance: "It seems indeed as if you've been reborn this morning."[48] This sentiment is anticipated by Lucrezia's worried remark at the end of Act Three: "I am satisfied—but I don't think I'll be alive tomorrow morning."[49] And as if the implications were not clear enough, the old man adds to his mother-in-law: "why, only last night she seemed half-dead."[50]

Thus there is not only a symbolic rebirth, but a symbolic marriage as well. This is evident not only from the aforementioned "vows" of Lucrezia to Callimaco, but in the grateful naiveté of Nicia toward the great "doctor":

> NICIA: Professor, I want you to take my wife by the hand.
> CALLIMACO: With pleasure.
> NICIA: Lucrezia, thanks to this lad's efforts we will have a rod and staff for our old age.[51]

The subtle inferences are anything but subtle. And in the unlikely event that the spectator has missed the sexual overtones in this dialogue, Nicia then offers Callimaco the "key" (la chiave) so he can visit his house privately at his leisure. His ingenuous gift would raise laughter, since the verb chiavare ("to key") is slang for sexual intercourse—even today. Callimaco graciously accepts the key, indicating that he will use it "at his convenience."[52] Thus the final statement in the play is not that he will always be a faithful lover, but harks back to his initial heart-less—Machiavellian—desire to have Lucrezia *once*.

Despite its cynical eccentricities, the *Mandragola* conforms in its sala-cious way to the mainstream of comedy, concluding with a lusty *gamos*—with a difference. Machiavelli represents a moment in history where classical tradition meets Florentine cunning—and the result is a theatrical masterpiece. Machiavelli became synonymous with evil. We will meet him again as Old Nick, delivering the prologue to the next comedy of evil.

15

Marlowe: *Schade* and *Freude*

Many theorists of the comic have explained *Schadenfreude* delight at someone else's misfortune—from a psychological standpoint. But it is important to recognize that not a few would decry it from a moral point of view. We think immediately of Plato, an enemy of laughter in general and Homeric laughter in particular. How wrong of the gods to enjoy "unquenchable laughter" at the sight of the crippled Hephaistos.[1]

Cruelty should never be a laughing matter, argues Socrates in the *Philebus* and Aristotle in the *Nichomachean Ethics*.[2] In the *Poetics*, Aristotle draws the line at what is properly ludicrous: we may laugh at a kind of ugliness which is "neither painful nor harmful."[3] And yet Aristotle's own prescription might well justify the amusement at Odysseus' brutal clubbing of Thersites, since he was "the ugliest man who came to Ilium."[4] Besides, even Socrates allows that we may rejoice at the misfortunes of those we hate[5]—a standard aspect of the ancient heroic code. And barely hidden beneath the moralizing in both Plato and Aristotle is the implicit concession that, however ethically reprehensible it may be, people do rejoice at their friends' misfortunes.[6]

As we have seen, comedy provides a release for antisocial instincts; even Plato often grants this. But one finds less willingness to acknowledge that among the instincts satisfied is an inherent thirst for cruelty.

That man is innately hostile has always been a more difficult notion to accept than the idea that he is innately erotic. And yet the sex and aggression drives are very closely connected.[7] Alfred Adler first posited the "aggression drive" in 1908 ("every individual really exists in a state of aggression"),[8] but Freud fought the concept for twenty years until, in *Civilization and Its Discontents,* he finally conceded its validity:

> The element of truth behind all this—which people are so ready to disavow—is that men are not gentle creatures who want to be loved, and who at the most can defend themselves if they are attacked; they are, on the contrary, creatures among whose instinctual endowments is to be reckoned a powerful share of aggressiveness . . . *Homo homini lupus.*"[9]

Later in the essay, Freud restates this even more emphatically: "the inclination to aggression is an original, self-subsisting instinctual disposition in man . . . it constitutes the greatest impediment to civilization."[10]

Considering how difficult this was for modern psychologists to accept, one readily understands the moral indignation of the ancient philosophers at the raising of brutal laughter.[11] Moreover, Aristotle's position was distorted by subsequent misinterpretations. Sir Philip Sidney saw the philosopher as forbidding "laughter in sinful things,"[12] and Ben Jonson even argued that Aristotle was against laughter of any kind: "[it is] a kind of turpitude, that depraves some part of man's nature without a disease,"[13] We are but one small step from the ultimate agelastic attitude, which Chesterfield urges upon his son—that he never laugh at all in his entire life.[14]

Naturally, times change. Our "greater civilization" may come to reject certain brutalities as too painful to be risible. And yet every age produces new cruelties and new possibilities for comic *Schadenfreude.* In the preface to *Joseph Andrews,* Fielding discusses the limits—the *ne plus ultra,* in fact—of the Ridiculous:

> What could exceed the Absurdity of an Author who should write *The Comedy of Nero,* with the merry Incident of ripping up his Mother's Belly; or what would give a greater shock to humanity?

The absurdity of *The Comedy of Nero* would be exceeded in 1959 by *Oh Dad, Poor Dad, Mamma's Hung You in the Closet and I'm Feelin' So Sad.* The spirit of von Masoch has become increasingly congenial to modern comedy.[15] And who could have imagined a comedy that would invite us to relish the annihilation of the human race? But then who could have imagined that the absurd optimism of Dr. Pangloss would be surpassed by the insouciant glee of Dr. Strangelove?

But our concern is cruelty in comedy past. There is a famous incident in Spanish literature, when Lazarillo de Tormes tricks his blind master into jumping into a post, causing very painful injury:

> He hit his head against the post and it sounded loud as huge pumpkin. And then he fell down backwards, half dead, his head all gashed.[16]

However it may affect us today, this episode was enormously popular in sixteenth-century Spain and was imitated by other writers in prose and song. It may even have been a part of the folklore well before it found its way into the Lazarillo novel.[17] Suffice it to say that this cruel trick earned as much admiration for Lazarillo as the beating of Thersites did for that proto-pícaro, Odysseus.

It is also useful to consider a story which is told in a "framed" context, because it includes the reaction of a fictive audience. The Eighth Day of Boccaccio's *Decameron* contains many tales of brutality, much of it perpetrated by two rogues, Bruno and Buffalmacco: "Fun-loving men who were also perceptive and shrewd."[18] In the third story, they dupe Calandrino, hit him with stones till he whines in pain, and then abandon him. The victim then vents his frustration by brutally beating his wife. Boccaccio's fictive listeners welcome this story with great delight. Their reaction is even more enthusiastic for the ninth tale, in which Bruno and Buffalmacco victimize one Master Simone, a dim-witted doctor, finally hurling him down a latrine. Unlike other "baptisms" we have seen, this ducking does not occasion a symbolic rebirth. But the malodorous mayhem does evoke enormous laughter:

> No need to ask how much the story . . . made the women laugh. Every single one of them laughed so hugely that tears came to their eyes at least twelve times.[19]

And yet there are limits. The seventh tale of this same Day, the cruel revenge wrought by the scholar Rinieri on a woman who scorned him, evokes icy silence. Unlike Panurge's revenge upon the haughty Parisienne, this tale engages our pity. As Bergson explains, "to succeed, the comic demands something like a momentary anesthesia of the heart. Its target is purely the intelligence, and the intelligence only."[20] Emotion is ever and always the foe of laughter. As Nietzsche remarked, "Wit is the epitaph on the death of a feeling."[21]

The *Canterbury Tales* afford another opportunity to study the success or failure of comic *Schadenfreude* on an audience. Oswald the Reeve tells a lusty tale which involves aggressive sexuality: two scholars "swyve" the wife and daughter of a miller as revenge for his having shortchanged them. At the end there is much physical violence:

> And on the nose he smoot hym with his
> Doun ran the blody streem upon his brest.[22]

As a final coup, the miller's wife accidentally smashes him with a staff "on the pyled skulle":

> That doun he gooth and cride, "Harrow I dye!"
> Thise clerks beete hym weel and lete hym lye.[23]

And yet, although the Reeve can tell such a story, he is the only pilgrim who did not laugh at the Miller's tale, which immediately preceded his own. On the contrary, Chaucer describes him as angry and upset. Surely this is not due to the grossness of the Miller's tale (which involves some hostile flatulence), or even its explicit brutality:

> The hoote kultour brende so his toute
> And for the smert he wende for to dye.[24]

Actually, the scatology and cruelty help to explain the near-universal laughter with which the pilgrims greet the tale.[25] Oswald the Reeve is discomfited not because the young student was branded, but because the old carpenter was cuckolded. As he himself explains his ill-humor:

> But ik am oold, me list not pley for age
> Bras tyme is doon, my fodder is now forage . . .
> We olde men, I drede, so fare we . . .[26]

For Oswald the Reeve, the cuckold in the Miller's tale was too close to himself. He sympathized; he feared ("We olde men, I drede . . ."). This is *Schade* without *Freude*. Successful comedy must subliminally reassure us that the victims could not possibly be ourselves. How curious, though, that Chaucer's Reeve could tell of cuckoldry and yet not listen to it. One thinks of Molière, who could transmute the pain of his personal life into the joys of his plays.

The argument thus far has been but a prologue to a discussion of Marlowe's *Jew of Malta*. T. S. Eliot pointed out the essential truth about this play: it is not tragedy but farce. Marlowe, like Ben Jonson, writes what Eliot calls "savage comic humour."[27] But Jonson's brutality has been discussed far more often than Marlowe's cruelty. And yet it is ever-present in his plays, as in Tamburlaine's torture of Bajezeth and sack of Babylon, and in Faustus' willingness to "offer luke warme blood of new borne babes."[28] And in Barabas' entire *raison d'être*.

Barabas is related to the Vice of morality plays, "a single intriguer, a voluble and cunning schemer, an artist in duplicity, a deft manipulator of human emotions."[29] But Barabas existed long before medieval drama, before Christianity, and even before morality as Socrates "invented" it. Before he was called Vice, he was called Odysseus: like Marlowe's Jew, "a hand and a mind against every man, by nature, or as a matter of policy."[30] As Harry Levin has pointed out, "policy" is a key word for Barabas.[31] Curiously enough, "policy" enters the English language in 1406—associated with Ulysses.[32]

By now the Romanticized views of Marlowe's hero have lost currency, although at least one late twentieth century critic has referred to Barabas as "a sensitive and helpless victim" for whom the Elizabethan audience might have felt "genuine sympathy."[33] But rationalism dies even harder than Romanticism. There are still critics who try to argue cause and effect for Barabas' behavior. No doubt the earnest attempts to "understand" the Jew of Malta were influenced by the dimensions Shakespeare later added to his Jew of Venice. But Barabas is not Shylock; if you prick him, he will not bleed. One does not have to explain Philocleon's jurymania, Harpagon's greed, or Volpone's acquisitiveness; that's the "humour of it." And Barabas is also a humorous character.

All of Marlowe's heroes are what Levin calls "monomaniac expo-
nents of the first person."[34] This is certainly true for Barabas: he contains multitudes, a cast of thousands in a malevolence of one. He is not
only every thing that orthodox Elizabethans were against, he is every
one. A Jew was a gargoyle much the same as a Turk. In fact, an Elizabethan writing in 1590 remarks: "Turkishness is quite closely related to
Jewishness."[35] Both figures were associated with the Devil.[36] The Devil/
Jew/Vice was a familiar stage persona, but surely there never was an
abundance of villainy to match that of Marlowe's "hero."

The prologue sets the tone. It is our old friend Machiavelli's first appearance on the English stage:[37]

> Albeit all the world thinke *Macheuill* is dead
> Yet was his soule but flowne beyond the *Alpes*
> And now the *Guize* is dead, is come from France . . .

Here is yet another Elizabethan bugbear: atheism and villainy incarnate. Machiavelli himself was frequently considered an incarnation of
the Devil. Moreover, his soul (unlike Faustus') seems to have enjoyed a
Pythagorean metempsychosis, for after having visited that infamous
Protestant-killer the Duke of Guise, he has now flown across the Channel to present this "Tragedy of a Jew."[38] To Machevill, of course,
Barabas' ultimate fall is a tragedy, "because he fauours me."[39] To add to
his other innate sins, the Jew is also a Machiavellian, and it should be
noted that when he boasts of his successful co-religionists throughout
the Mediterranean world, he specifically points out that there are
"many in *France.*"[40] Is this perhaps an oblique reference to the murderous Duke of Guise, and the massacre he perpetrated in 1572?

But of course the Maltese are more or less Italians—and there is no
need to emphasize what that nation evoked in the Elizabethan imagination. In *Pierce Penniless* Thomas Nashe calls Italy "the Academie of
manslaughter, the sporting place of murther, the Apothecary-shop of
poyson." And worst of all, these men are Catholics. Here again we confront the diabolical, for the Pope is in league with the Devil, as Satan
himself admits in the morality play *The Conflict of Conscience* (1581):
". . . the Pope, who is my darling dear, / My eldest Boy, in whom I do delight."[41] Indeed, Malta is a kind of Devil's Island.

The name Marlowe chooses for his protagonist makes it perfectly clear that he is the antithesis of Christ. Quite simply then, Barabas plays "hate thy neighbor." And his primary humor is not miserliness. He does not even share Volpone's enthusiasm for lucre. Even for silver the fox of Venice would not say, "Fye, what a trouble 'tis to count this trash."[42] To Barabas, fantastic wealth is only useful "to ransome great Kings from captiuity";[43] money is equated only with policy.

Since the real essence of Barabas is motion, the instant he has told us the sole value of "infinite riches in a little roome,"[44] he asks the first question of the play: "But now how stands the wind?"[45] Barabas will always be moving and shifting with the wind. The importance in what follows is not so much that his ships immediately arrive laden with goods, but rather the interesting revelation that he is always taking risks. When he asks about his argosy at Alexandria, a merchant replies:

> We heard some of our sea-men say,
> They wondred how you durst with so much wealth
> Trust such a crazed Vessell, and so farre.[46]

But Barabas knew that his ship was damaged: "Tush . . . I know her and her strength."[47] Yet four lines later the "crazed Vessell" arrives safely in Malta port. Barabas will risk sinking more than once in this play.

When his co-religionists tell him that the Turk has arrived in Malta, Barabas implies his concern for them all. But he immediately tells the audience in an aside:

> Nay, let 'em combat, conquer, and kill all,
> So they spare me, my daughter, and my wealth.[48]

Yet we cannot take too much stock even in his feelings for his daughter, since he has already told us he loves her "As *Agamemnon* did his *Iphigen*."[49] Hardly a deep affection, since Homer's hero sacrificed his daughter so the fleet could sail. And by the same token that he is richer than Job,[50] Barabas surely owns more than a thousand ships. His first love is not even Volpone's for gold, "far transcending . . . children, parents, friends."[51] Rather, Barabas salutes his co-religionists, "Assure your selues I'le looke vnto [*aside*] my selfe."[52]

Barabas' true policy is selfmanship—which he indulges immediately after the departure of "these silly men."[53] He is not concerned with the Jews' problem, or even Malta's:

> How ere the world goe, I'le make sure for one,
> And seeke in time to intercept the worst,
> Warily garding that which I ha got
> Ego mihimet sum semper proximus.
> Why let 'em enter, let 'em take the Towne.[54]

He is always against the universe itself, even in moments of prosperity. This is not the only time Barabas wishes the rest of humanity dead. In Act Five he exclaims, "For so I liue, perish may all the world."[55] Marlowe's Faustus is tempted with a Deadly Sin who says much the same.[56] This unchained aggression is also evident in Alfred Jarry's bizarre King Ubu, as we shall see in a later chapter.

Those who would have us feel for the plight of Barabas inevitably point to his "persecution" in the scene of the confiscation of his wealth. But there is no reason why Barabas should refuse to pay something in order to keep much more than half his property (remember what he has hidden away). He could, in fact, keep all his wealth merely by the application of a little holy water. After all, to a Machiavellian, religion is "but a childish Toy"[57]—or a childish tool; and he will immediately persuade his own daughter to feign conversion, arguing that

> A counterfet profession is better
> Then vnseene hypocrisie.[58]

When Abigail tells him his house (with hidden horde) has already been occupied, it becomes a challenge to outfox the little foxes, or as Barabas himself says in more Odyssean language:

> No, I will liue; nor loath I this my life:
> And since you Ieaue me in the Ocean thus
> To sinke or swim, and put me to my shifts,
> I'le rouse my senses and awake my selfe.[59]

With the reawakening of his militant self, his splendid creative malice will now be fully displayed. He will epitomize his last advice to his daughter, "be cunning *Abigail*."[60] Marlowe's "balcony scene" ends with Barabas and his gold reunited and his ecstatic effusion: "hermoso placer de los dineros."[61] Why in Spanish? It could be a tag in any one of the many languages he knows, but Marlowe is ironically anticipating the arrival (in the next line) of one more Elizabethan devil, the Spaniard del Bosco, "Vizadmirall vnto the Catholike King."[62] In granting del Bosco permission to sell his slaves, the Maltese governor is breaking faith with his ex-allies, whom he now calls "these barbarous mis-beleeuing Turkes."[63] This note of international treachery sets the stage for the most memorable confrontation in the play: between the Jew Barabas and the Turk Ithamore.

Barabas enters, brimming over with sweet hostility, for he is not really bitter or vengeful. He is already as rich as he ever was,[64] and now can devote himself entirely to mischief. To Lodowick, his hostility is but thinly veiled:

> 'tis a custome held with vs,
> That when we speake with Gentiles like to you,
> We tume into the Ayre to purge our selues.[65]

He speaks of the "burning zeal" with which he regards the nuns who live in his former home, adding in an aside, "Hoping ere long to set the house a fire";[66] but then he must excuse himself to buy a slave. We need seek no emotional reason for Barabas' wanting a new servant. It is not, as some critics would have it, that he feels lonely, for Barabas does not feel anything. He has always been alone; there has never been a Leah to whom he gave a ring. He lives in a continuum of active aggression. And Ithamore will merely be a weapon.

At their first meeting, Barabas and the lean Turk each sing an aria of evil, an amoebean song of cruelty. This is a set-piece with much precedent in comic literature—for example, in Aristophanes' *Knights,* where there is a perpetual rivalry between the Sausage-seller and the Paphlagonian, "a super-panurgist and super-diabolist."[67] The two constantly exchange threats of violence and scatological attack. The Chorus enjoys the prospects of the Paphlagonian being bested—or worsted:

> We are delighted to say that a man has
> come on the scene, far more corrupt than you, and it's

clear he'll harass you and surpass you in villainy,
boldness, and dirty tricks.[68]

The *agōn* here is nothing less than a bragging contest of crimes past and
better crimes to come. At the end, the Paphlagonian must concede defeat, with a uniquely Aristophanic play on words: "Aieeh, bad luck—I'm
absolutely ab-rogue-ated!"[69]

But the "aria of evil" which can best be compared with that of
Barabas occurs in Boccaccio's *Decameron*. Although, strictly speaking, it
is prose narrative, we everywhere sense the speaker's rhapsodic delight
in presenting the achievements of Ser Ciapelletto:

> He gave false witness with supreme delight—and whether
> asked to or not . . . He took inordinate pleasure in stirring up
> enmities, scandals, and other misfortunes among friends,
> relatives, and anyone else. And the greater the misfortune,
> the greater his amusement. If invited to a homicide—or some
> other dastardly event, he not only always accepted and went
> with great enthusiasm, but very often his enthusiasm found
> him striking the blows and killing men with his own hands
> . . . But why am I going on at such length? He was perhaps
> the very worst man who was ever born.[70]

Ciapelletto is like Molière's Dom Juan, who was, according to
Sganarelle, "le plus grand scélérat que la terre ait jamais porté."[71]

But Barabas is more than a match for the grandest rogues of comedy, and his outrageous *curriculum vitae* is worth quoting at length:

> As for my selfe, I walke abroad a nights
> And kill sicke people groaning under walls:
> Sometimes I goe about and poyson wells . . .
> Being young, I studied Physicke, and began
> To practise first vpon the Italian;
> There I enric[h]'d the Priests with burials,
> And alwayes kept the Sexton's armes in vre
> With digging graues and ringing dead mens knels:
> And after that was I an Engineere,
> And in the warres 'twixt France and Germanie,

Vnder pretence of helping Charles the fifth,
Slew friend and enemy with my stratagems.
Then after that was I an Vsurer,
And with exorting, cozening, forfeiting,
And tricks belonging vnto Brokery,
I fill'd the Iailes with Bankrouts in a yeare,
And with young Orphans planted Hospitals,
And euery Moone made some or other mad,
And now and then one hang himselfe for griefe.[72]

There are, of course, aspects of Barabas' "career" which derive from medieval stereotypes of the Jew. In any case, we are not meant to take his words at face value or believe that he has actually traveled to all the places he mentions. Marlowe's style is always one of exaggeration, especially in this play.[73] We note in Barabas' brag, which begins significantly, "As for my selfe,"[74] that his interest is always in malice, not money. As a doctor, his specialty was enriching the priests with burials. As a usurer, his joy was in the pain he caused (suicides, insanity, and so on). Most interesting is his behavior while "helping" Charles the fifth, for here he slew friend as well as enemy.[75] Some have sought a historical model for Barabas among the Jews who were skilled at designing war machines. But in fact the best model is Dr. Faustus, who also "helps" Charles V.

This delight in totally indiscriminate cruelty is exactly like Ser Ciapelletto's in stirring up pain and trouble among relatives and friends. Both Boccaccio's and Marlowe's descriptions are intended to arouse the laugh of *Schadenfreude* through a comic hero who unabashedly relishes the inflicting of pain, "o qualunque rea cosa."

Whereas Barabas' exploits may be imaginary, before the play is out he will have committed almost all the atrocities of which he boasts. And Ithamore, who begins as one of Barabas' dupes, will end as one of his victims. For the Jew merely baits his slave with the Volpone-trick. While he may flatter him as "my second self,"[76] and chant litanies of "I here adopt thee for mine onely heire,"[77] Barabas wastes no time in telling the audience that he is but gulling Ithamore:

Thus euery villaine ambles after wealth
Although he ne're be richer then in hope . . .[78]

How little veiled is the hostility in Barabas' expression of gratitude to his collaborator in the poisoning of the nuns: "Ile pay thee with a vengeance, Ithamore."[79] In fact, Barabas buys Ithamore to enlarge his own scope of hate.

Barabas' purchase is followed by a crescendo of comic cruelty. First, the Jew schemes to set Lodowick against Mathias in a heartless perversion of what Sir Toby stirs up between Viola and Sir Andrew Aguecheek. But in Shakespeare the trick adds to the midsummer madness; here it adds to Maltese murder. And there is so much gusto on the part of the murderer that we feel no sympathy at the death of the two young men.

It is even difficult to grieve for Abigail. We cannot but be amused by the notion of an offstage chorus of her fellow nuns all dying at the same time. The many other murderous pranks of Barabas which have analogues on the comic stage are too numerous to list here. Sometimes Ithamore will lend a helping hand—to strangle a friar, for example (Boccaccio's Ser Ciapelletto was likewise generous when it came to killing people). But he is a mere Zany to his master, who has no real need of him. In fact, after Ithamore's defection, the speed and scope of villainy actually increase. Here, as throughout the play, Barabas' single aim is to outdo himself in evil:

> Now I haue such a plot for both their liues,
> As neuer Iew nor Christian knew the like . . .[80]

That is why he persists in scheming even after he becomes governor, which could be ambition's *ne plus ultra*. He must continue in malice; it is his humor. This reflects the Odyssean quality in Barabas—and we cannot ignore how he led the Turk through the city walls in Ulysses-like fashion. Similarly, Mosca believes that he and Volpone have achieved "our master-peece: We cannot thinke, to goe beyond this"—and Volpone immediately comes up with yet another scheme to "torture 'em rarely."[81] So too Barabas' instinct urges him to undo others till he himself is undone.

Thus, immediately following the brutal sack of Malta, Barabas switches sides. We need seek no explanations in reason or *Realpolitik*. The motive is far more basic: are there not Turks to kill? Barabas is a man who could laugh at the annihilation of the world. He cares no more for Turk than for Christian;[82] he cares for himself. And at the end he is quite the same person he was at the outset, ever risking, shifting, testing the wind, and delighting in his villainy:

> Why, is not this
> A kingly kinde of trade to purchase Townes
> By treachery, and sell 'em by deceit?
> Now tell me, worldings, vnderneath the sunne,
> If greater falshood euer has ben done.[83]

This clearly recalls his views from the opening monologue on "the policy" of riches.

Barabas' last trick is both his best in quantity of victims and his worst—since he is one of them. Shakespeare's Jew ends at the baptismal font, but Marlowe's ends in hotter water. As we have seen, Barabas' cauldron is also an ancient comic prop, rejuvenating among others Demus in *Knights*. Surely the last glimpse of Barabas, boiling mentally and physically, and cursing the "damn'd Christians, dogges, and Turkish Infidels" was intended to raise a "heartless laugh."[84] It must have, for audiences packed Henslowe's playhouses to see Marlowe's wildly successful play. Today we may find such laughter as foreign as that of the Fiji Islander delightedly watching a prisoner roast.[85] That was in another country. Yet so was Barabas, and as Baudelaire wrote in his essay on laughter: "To find savage comedy—indeed *very* savage comedy—you have to cross the channel and visit the misty realms of melancholy [*spleen*]."[86]

Schadenfreude is a childish pleasure, say the psychologists, and Marlowe often displays a rather adolescent delight in cruelty. It is perhaps difficult to accept this as a laughing matter, but the beast in man does not always evoke pity and terror—as in the case of Lear's pelican daughters or that Spartan dog Iago. There is also Jonson's fox of Venice, and Marlowe's snake of Malta, both of whom make laughter of what Freud had to concede was a basic human trait: *homo homini lupus*. Did Freud know he was quoting Plautus?[87]

16

Shakespeare: Errors and *Erōs*

Even great poets begin by mimicking their masters. Yet already in his journeyman days, Shakespeare was incapable of merely aping his distinguished predecessors. For *The Comedy of Errors,* possibly his earliest play and certainly the shortest, is a great deal more than an adaptation of Plautus' *Brothers Menaechmus (Menaechmi).* Shakespeare's *vortere* represents a "departure as a dramatist [and] his borrowings from classical comedy show the direction in which his mind was moving."[1] Coleridge called the play the "only poetical farce in our language." Documentary evidence dates the play around 1594 (or even earlier), but its thematic richness has inspired Harold Bloom to argue—contrary to the majority of critics—that it "does not read or play like apprentice work."[2] Northrop Frye affirms that "here as in so many other places this early experimental comedy anticipates the techniques of the romances."[3] Shakespeare was a natural, and he infused his very first offering for the stage with a sophistication bordering on genius.

In the Plautine play, we recall, a young man leaves Syracuse to search the entire world—or at least *Graecia exotica*—for his long-lost twin, in whose memory he has been redubbed Menaechmus. He likens the task to finding "a needle—as they say—in a haystack."[4] (The original Latin, *in scirpo nodum quaeris,* translates literally as "you're looking for a knot in a bulrush.") At long last he reaches the town of Epidamnus, where he is mistaken for someone who bears both his name and his likeness (a rather obvious clue). After a series of comic episodes or errors, the fraternal mirror images are reunited and both sail for Syracuse—leaving the Epidamnian twin's wife behind.

But this was not enough for the young Shakespeare even in his maiden effort. He recast the material, not merely to conform to the Elizabethan convention of the triple plot, but to add a depth and dimension that greatly enhance the Latin original. For a start, he increased the number of players. To the Roman twins he adds a pair of identical servants, both named Dromio—an apt name for these *servi currentes* (Greek *drom-*, "to run")—who by incredible coincidence were born the same day as their masters. And whereas the Menaechmus boys' parents disappear after the prologue, Shakespeare has built a rich finale in which not only are both braces of brothers reunited, but the Antipholus twins' father and mother as well.

Yet these additions transcend the mere multiplication of *dramatis personae.* The piece is suffused with a Christian coloration which makes the theme one not merely of discovery but of redemption.[5] As we will see, the change of locale from the Plautine Epidamnus to Ephesus has a number of Christian implications. Nevertheless, Shakespeare retains the Plautine setting of "Epidamium" [*sic*] as a place in the twins' past. Thus the playwright both asserts his command of the ancient material, and underscores the important change of dramatic setting.

The overplot is somber. The music at the beginning of *Twelfth Night* may have a "dying fall," but *Errors* commences with a note more suited to tragedy than comedy: the threat of actual death. The elderly Egeon has been condemned because of the strife between the neighboring towns of Syracuse and Ephesus—the setting of the play: "If any Syracusian born / come to the bay of Ephesus he dies."[6] The exclusion of foreigners on pain of death is a motif familiar from Euripidean melodrama (*Iphigenia in Tauris,* for example). The only way Egeon can "redeem his life" is by paying one thousand marks; lacking the necessary ransom, the old man is resigned to his doom. This is the first of many instances in the play which mix religious and monetary imagery. For the currency of redemption—"marks"—finds a contrapuntal echo in two themes which pervade the play. First there is a running joke of the blows inflicted on the two slaves. More seriously, there is an ongoing allusion to the stigmata of Christ, with all its implications for the theme of resurrection.

In an expository dialogue with the Duke of Ephesus, Egeon recounts how many years ago his pregnant wife followed him to Epidamnus, where he was doing business. Not long thereafter she produced "two goodly sons," twins:

> And which were strange, the one so like the other
> As could not be distinguish'd but by name.[7]

By happy coincidence, on the same day another woman in the town, who was "exceeding poor," also gave birth to "twins both alike." Pitying her, Egeon purchased her newborn lads to be servants to his own identical neonates.

But on the voyage home all were caught in a storm and scattered from one another in the ensuing shipwreck—a motif whose comic significance we have already seen in Euripides. It represents the chaotic loss of identity and upheaval of natural order that is part of the *kōmos*. Shakespeare is certainly using the imagery consciously, as his carefully chosen words demonstrate:

> Our helpful ship was splitted in the midst;
> So that, in this unjust *divorce* of us,
> Fortune had left to both of us alike,
> What to delight in, what to sorrow for.[8]

As we will later learn, the mother with one son and his servant boy were picked up by one passing ship, while the father and the other two babes were rescued by a second vessel. By this time Egeon is in tears (thus the actor can give his voice a rest, and the audience a breather). Fascinated, the Duke bids him continue his sad tale: "For we may pity, though not pardon thee."[9]

Eighteen years later, the son who had survived with Egeon—renamed, as in the *Menaechmi*, in memory of his lost brother

Antipholus—left Syracuse with his similarly renamed servant to search for their other halves. When after five years they did not return, Egeon set off in pursuit, now in search of four people. His quest has brought him to Ephesus where he has been arrested and condemned to death. Touched by this tale, the sympathetic Duke postpones the old man's execution until sunset, in the hope that he may somehow obtain the money he needs to save his life.

As they leave the stage, the traveling Antipholus II and his slave appear, concluding a business deal with Balthazar, a local merchant. By artful coincidence, the tradesman pays the visiting twin a thousand marks—precisely the sum of money needed for his father's salvation—which Antipholus II entrusts to Dromio II to take to their inn. The merchant warns the visitor of the harsh law that imperils the lad's countrymen—one of whom (he adds with parenthetical irony) is scheduled to be executed that very day for violating the law.

Left alone on stage, Antipholus II decides to take a walk in the city and "lose myself."[10] He explains his predicament to the audience:

> I to the world am like a drop of water
> That in the ocean seeks another drop,
> Who, falling there to find his fellow forth,
> (Unseen, inquisitive) confounds himself.[11]

The image of water drops seems to have been inspired by the exclamation of Messenio in the *Menaechmi* when he sees both twins together for the first time:

> Never have I seen two men more similar than you two
> Water isn't more like water, milk's not more alike to milk
> Than he to you and you to him.[12]

But whereas in Plautus this same speech comes toward the climax, Shakespeare has introduced the theme at an early stage, and he carefully develops the imagery throughout the play—harking back to the storm which divorced the Antipholus family. Thus intertextual allusion once again demonstrates Shakespeare's self-conscious awareness of the Latin play and the transformations he has wrought. For Antipholus effectively betrays his awareness of Messenio's words toward his own Latin incarnation, as though he himself had read Plautus.

Yet the contrast is intensified by the joy in Messenio's ejaculation versus the more Terentian melancholy in Antipholus' speech:

> So I, to find a mother and a brother,
> In quest of them, unhappy, lose myself.[13]

Here we encounter another somber moment continuing the mood of the opening scene, something that is quite anomalous for the beginning of a rollicking farce. Why is Antipholus not happy? Plautus' twin has been searching just as long and shows no such despondency. Even in this early play, we can see Shakespeare's greater depth of character and seriousness as compared with Plautus' Roman farce.

As Antipholus II strolls off stage, there follows the first of the many errors. The local Dromio mistakes the traveling twin for his master, and urges him to come home to dinner at his house, the Phoenix—an apt name in a play of rebirth. Antipholus II of course has no idea what "his" servant is talking about and demands, "as I am a Christian . . . where is the thousand marks thou hadst of me?"[14] The servant is confused. Dromio I only knows "his mistress's marks" upon his shoulders:

> The clock hath strucken twelve upon the bell;
> My mistress made it one upon my cheek.[15]

The angry traveler immediately gives him some more marks for his face and chases him off, confiding to the audience:

> They say this town is full of cozenage
> As nimble jugglers that deceive the eye,
> Dark-working sorcerers that change the mind,
> Soul-killing witches that deform the body,
> Disguised cheaters, prating mountebanks,
> And many such-like liberties of sin.[16]

This is perhaps Shakespeare's closest echo of Plautus. There, punning on "Epidamnus," Messenio warns his master of the usual perils of an urban red-light district: "no one leaves here un-epi-damaged."[17] By changing the dramatic setting from Epidamnus to Ephesus, Shakespeare has added not only the theme of transformation and deception, but also a Christian dimension, echoing St. Paul's description of Ephesus as a place where

> exorcists took upon them to call over them which had evil spirits . . . Many of them also which used curious arts brought their books together, and burned them before all men.[18]

Shakespeare develops the theme of sorcery and witchcraft throughout the play. Moreover, his portrayal of the characters' perplexity goes far deeper than Plautus' silly dupes. For "damaged" is not "transformed," nor in any way psychotropic. As the play proceeds, Shakespeare will strengthen this Christian dimension, which reaches its fullest expression in the finale.

The second act begins with a scene that Plautus could never have written. Two freeborn young women are having an intimate conversation: Adriana, the wife of the local Antipholus, and her gracious sister Luciana (both of course paradoxically played by young boys). Adriana is complaining about her husband's infidelity. In Plautus the fille de joie is called Erotium, while the wife is left nameless. Shakespeare reverses this, giving the married woman "a local habitation and a name," leaving the courtesan merely as "wench."

It is clear where the playwright's interests lie. In a bygone age the local Antipholus might have invoked the Roman husband's privilege of extramarital promiscuity. But fidelity was a subject close to Shakespeare's heart. Though he himself was separated by distance from Anne Hathaway, he was nonetheless a fervent advocate of marriage and procreation. This theme is everywhere in his plays and in the sonnets:

> From fairest creatures we desire increase,
> That thereby beauty's rose might never die . . .[19]

The two women present a contrast. Adriana, the bad-tempered wife, bitterly complains of her husband's indifference to her. Her unmarried sister reminds her that "a man is master of his liberty."[20] To this the wife retorts with a strikingly modern sentiment, "why should their liberty than ours be more?"[21] Luciana's subsequent discourse on her view of the proper role of a woman in a marriage contains St. Paul's advice ("Wives, submit your selves unto your husbands, as unto the Lord"),[22] paraphrased by Luciana in her remark, "Ere I learn love, I'll practice to obey."[23] She is clearly good wife material. But Adriana remains adamant. For this display of proto-feminism she has been called a shrew. Yet hers is a voice of a genuine, plausible lament, and in a real sense these two women provide the emotional core of the play.

Dromio I comes in to report that "his master" is mad, since he kept asking him for a thousand marks. And when told that Adriana wanted him home for dinner, his outraged master had replied, "'I know,' quoth he, 'no house, no wife, no mistress.'" Thus, to the women's perception, Antipholus I has abrogated his marriage vows. Divorce looms.

After the slave is given more marks for his efforts, the scene concludes with Adriana's mournful plaint that her marriage is disintegrating. She pines away "and starves for a merry look":

> What ruins are in me that can be found
> By him not ruin'd? Then is he the ground
> Of my defeatures; My decayèd fair
> A sunny look of his would soon repair.[24]

In a kind of reversal of the Petrarchan conceit that love bestows loveliness on the beloved, Beauty thinks that she has become the Beast as a result of her husband's neglect. Yet another scene concludes with a plangent note:

> Since that my beauty cannot please his eye,
> I'll weep what's left away, and weeping die.[25]

Adriana and Luciana soon confront Antipholus—the wrong one—who has been transformed into another person. They continually and unwittingly pun on the two connotations of "strangeness," the one in its modern meaning, the other in the sense of "foreign." It is as if Adriana subconsciously recognizes that he is an outlander:

> Ay, ay, Antipholus, look *strange* and frown . . .
> How comes it now, my husband, O, how comes it,

That thou art then *estrangèd* from thyself?—
Thyself I call it, being *strange* to me,
That undividable, incorporate,
Am better than thy dear self's better part.[26]

Her remark that Antipholus' personality is somehow divided into good and bad is our first hint that in Shakespeare's mind, as in Plautus', the twins might be two parts of a schizophrenic whole. The local twin is terribly bourgeois, complacent, and oddly detached from his wife and family.

He is also unfaithful and in debt—which may be construed as feelings of guilt. As Ferenczi observed, "debt" and "guilt" are, in many languages, expressed by the same word. Indeed, "debt" is repeated most often in this of all the comedies, and three times in this scene alone—hammering home a cardinal element in the play, the sentence lying over old Egeon's head. For in Elizabethan times "debt" was pronounced the same as "death"—and in Egeon's case both meanings are clearly operative. We find a similar pun in *1 Henry 4*, where Prince Hal reminds Falstaff on Shrewsbury field:

HAL: Why, thou owes't God a death.
FALSTAFF: ... I would be loath to pay him before his day.[27]

The pedant Holofernes explains in *Love's Labour's Lost*:

HOL.: I abhor such fanatical phantasimes, such insociable and
point devise companions, such rackers of orthography, as
to speak "dout," fine, when he should say "doubt"; "det,"
when he should pronounce "debt"—*d, e, b, t*, not *d, e, t* ...[28]

By contrast, his alter ego the traveling Antipholus, innocent of the world despite his years of voyaging, arrives in Ephesus unattached and "unhappy, to lose myself." But is not his entire purpose to *find* his other self? This theme of alienation of the self is often associated with the word "strange," repeated in this context again and again. The passage quoted above develops a motif begun in Egeon's remark that even at birth the twins' complete similarity was "strange."[29] The traveling twin reports that he "is as strange unto your town as to your talk,"[30] while the merchant Balthasar finds it "strange" that the local Antipholus is being kept out of his own house.[31] When at the end the Duke confronts the various twins, he will remark "Why this is strange."[32] Likewise Egeon, staring at the "wrong" son, and pained that he does not recognize his own father, wonders: "Why look you so strange on me?"[33] In other words, each brother needs to unite with the other to restore chaos to order and become an entire person.

Despondent at her (putative) husband's strangeness, Adriana begs him not to break their marriage tie with "deep-divorcing vow." We recall the "unjust divorce" of the storm that separated the Antipholus brothers. She too invokes the simile of water drops, once again to suggest a single person with two personalities:

> For know, my love, as easy mayst thou fall
> A drop of water in the breaking gulf,
> And take unmingled thence that drop again
> Without addition or diminishing,
> As take from me thyself, and not me too.[34]

Shakespeare employs similar imagery to express the insolubility of love in other plays, as in the balcony scene of *Romeo and Juliet,* when the heroine says:

> My bounty is as boundless as the sea,
> My love as deep: the more I give to thee
> The more I have, for both are infinite.[35]

Taken aback, the traveling Antipholus protests that they could not possibly know each other because "In Ephesus I am but two hours old . . ."[36] In other words, he has just been born again. Luciana, of course, does not understand, and reproves him for denying that he is married to her sister. She too employs the imagery of transformation: "Fie brother! How the world is *changed* with you!"[37]

Still protesting that he does not know these women, Antipholus reminds us of the archetypal association of comedy with dreams. False etymologies can sometimes be truer than real ones:[38]

> What, was I married to her in my *dream*?
> Or *sleep* I now, and think I hear all this?
> What error drives our eyes and ears amiss?[39]

The kinship between comedy and dream is never far from Shake-speare's mind, whether it be Sly's drunken hallucinations in the Induction to *The Taming of the Shrew*, or an episode as zany as "Bottom's Dream," a nocturnal fantasy on a midsummer's night. And of course Puck's epilogue:

> PUCK: If we shadows have offended,
>
>   Think but this and all is mended,
>
>   That you have but slumber'd here
>
>   While these visions did appear.[40]

Dreaming or not, the traveling Antipholus accepts "his wife's" invitation to dinner, and sets Dromio to keep any intruders out. (There will only be another Antipholus and another Dromio trying to disturb their own house.)

Yet it is more than the possibility of *kōma* here. Before entering, Antipholus II expresses his stupefaction:

> Am I in earth, in heaven, or in hell?
>
> Sleeping or waking, mad or well advised?
>
> Known unto these, and to myself disguised![41]

Shakespeare here raises the notion of insanity for the first time, as Antipholus questions his own lucidity and identity. Can he really be true "to myself disguised"? In a play which presents the "other self," he imagines that new feelings of love have awakened a better identity within him. In fact, he has been "reborn" as a lover "two hours old." Sane or mad, he is bewitched into accepting the hospitality of these lovely women who profess to know him. He will certainly get a good meal—and who knows what else for dessert?

And here is another significant variation on the Plautine theme. In the Roman play, the visiting twin gets to enjoy a free dinner and free love from Erotium, his brother's *mistress*. There is a wholly different dimension to Shakespeare's version. For here the traveling brother receives an affectionate offer to wine and dine—and perhaps recline—with his brother's *wife*. In Plautus the twin's greatest risk would be being accused of robbery, while in the *Comedy of Errors* there is the hazard of incest with his brother's wife. According to scripture—*au pied de la lettre*—the act would be both a sin and a moral outrage.[42]

The errors compound. As Harry Levin observed, "there is an inherent lack of dignity—I am almost tempted to call it a loss of face—in being indistinguishable from, in always being mistaken for, someone else."[43] The visiting Dromio, left to guard the home gate, turns away the rightful owner and his slave, insisting "*my* name is Dromio." We need not wonder that Antipholus I does not notice the striking similarity between the two bondsmen. It requires of us what Coleridge would call a "willing suspension of disbelief... which constitutes poetic faith." This causes his local twin to echo the lament of the slave Sosia in the *Amphitruo* when *he* is turned away from his own household by Mercury. After the god punches him into believing that he is *not* Sosia any more, the bondsman exclaims: "Where did I get lost? Where was I transformed? Where did I lose my self?"[44]

In Shakespeare the local servant complains to his newly discovered mirror image: "O villain, thou hast stol'n both my office and my name!"[45]—another echo of the *Amphitruo* where Sosia retreats in anguish from Mercury, exclaiming: "I've got to find myself another name."[46] It is only *now*, when locked out of his own house, that Antipholus thinks of his courtesan.

No sooner does the husband depart for his "licensed" adultery than Shakespeare presents his twin making amorous advances to Luciana, his "wife's" sister. Luciana is shocked, but Antipholus II persists, twice referring to the "wonder" of her already knowing his name. He once again presents himself as a newborn baby: "Smother'd in errors, feeble, shallow, weak."[47] His astonishment re-emphasizes the theme of rebirth and metamorphosis through the power of love:

> Are you a god? Would you create me new?
> Transform me then, and to your power I'll yield.[48]

This anticipates Romeo's burst of affection when Juliet asks him "to doff thy name." He answers, "call me but love and I'll be new baptized."[49] In Shakespeare love is renewal, regeneration, and rebirth.

But in the *Comedy of Errors,* a quite similar expression of affection has the opposite effect on the affrighted Luciana. "Why call you *me* love?" she protests. The visiting twin insists, "It is thyself, mine own self's better part." Once again we have the intimation that the twin is but half of another person. But here it is more conventional—one thinks of the Latin proverb *amicus est alter ego*. In truth, this twin must find his own self's other part before gaining license to marry the woman with whom he has fallen in love at first sight. But in the meantime Luciana is horrified and runs off from the confused visitor.

Dromio too has an identity crisis as well as a possible metamorphosis. He rushes in and asks his master in a panic:

> DROMIO: Do you know me, sir? Am I Dromio? Am I your man? Am I myself?
>
> ANTIPHOLUS: Thou art Dromio, thou art my man, thou art thyself.
>
> DROMIO: I am an ass, I am a woman's man, and besides myself.[50]

In a parody of the main plot, the servant also experiences the transforming power of "love." He will prate on about being changed into various animals (ass, dog, and so on) as he suffers from the amorous advances of the kitchen wench, a "mad mountain of flesh" who has mistaken him for his twin brother, to whom she is married. In a vaudevillian turn, the slave likens various parts of her anatomy to different countries:

> ANTIPHOLUS: Where America, the Indies?
>
> DROMIO: O, sir, upon her nose, all o'er embellished with rubies, carbuncles, sapphires, declining their rich aspect to the hot breath of Spain . . .
>
> ANTIPHOLUS: Where stood Belgia, The Netherlands?
>
> DROMIO: O, sir, I did not look so low . . .[51]

He concludes: "I, amazed, ran from her as a witch."[52] His master concurs, and they plan to leave Ephesus immediately.

But before they can sail, Angelo the Goldsmith enters to give the visitor a chain commissioned by his indigenous brother. Antipholus II is confused—but naturally accepts the gift:

> But this I think, there is no man so vain,
> That would refuse so fair an offered chain.[53]

Five o'clock nears. In the end, the many gifts bestowed on the traveling twin must be paid for. And they will be—by the local twin, who, in a reversal of Bentley's formulation of comedy, "is *denied* the outrage but *pays* the consequences." Thus the traveling twin could represent the libido, the local the superego. Antipholus of Ephesus, confused by Angelo's dunning him for the money he owes for the chain, denies that he has received it. But this is no time for levity. The Goldsmith needs to pay a merchant at five o'clock. The specific sum provides irony for the cleverer spectators, and serves to remind all others that this is the scheduled time of old Egeon's execution. As a debt collector arrests Antipholus for non-payment, he sends Dromio—the wrong one, of course—to run home and get bail money from his wife.

As these confusions come hard and fast, we have a scene between the two sisters. Luciana is troubled by the sudden change both in her "brother-in-law's" interior and his exterior. Adriana is more upset by her "husband's" attempted seduction of her sister. Neither can fathom what has happened, and the only charitable conclusion they can reach is that he is mad. Note the rhetorical emphasis on psychic symptoms made physical:

> He is deformèd, crooked, old and sere,
> Ill face'd, worse bodied, shapeless everywhere;
> Vicious, ungentle, foolish, blunt, unkind,
> Stigmatical in making, worse in mind.[54]

To a play that emphasizes the similarity of exteriors (the Plautine model), Shakespeare has added the dimension of interior changes.

Meanwhile the traveling Dromio arrives to ask for bail money. Adriana is astonished that her husband is "in debt," but gives the gold to Dromio, who rushes off.

The following scene is an elaboration of a moment in the Plautine original, when Menaechmus of Sicily enters dazed and amazed by the fact that people recognize him in this strange city:

> What unworldly wonders have occurred today in wondrous ways:
> People claim I'm not the man I am and close their doors to me.
> Then this fellow said he was my slave and that I set him free!
> Then he says he'll go and bring a wallet full of money to me . . .
> All this business seems to me like nothing other than a dream.[55]

Again we encounter the oneiric aspect of comedy. For, etymology aside, comedy is in a very real sense a wish-fulfillment. Just like his naive Plautine forebear, Antipholus II has not yet understood why everybody in Ephesus seems to recognize him:

> There's not a man I meet but doth salute me
> As if I were their well-acquainted friend;
> And every one doth call me by my name:
> Some tender money to me; some invite me . . .
> Sure, these are but imaginary wiles,
> And Lapland sorcerers inhabit here.[56]

Once again Shakespeare has added the dimension of sorcery to the Syracusan twin's hypnotic experience. But the local Antipholus is not having the same good luck. For one man's pleasant dream is another man's nightmare. When the (nameless) courtesan, who has provided entertainment, confronts the local Antipholus for the chain he promised, as well as the ring he took at dinner, the astounded twin denies having received either. The lady immediately concludes, "Now out of doubt Antipholus is mad"[57]—a diagnosis she repeats three times in eight lines. And in a comic reversal of the "other woman" who normally keeps a low profile—if that is the word—she rushes off to tell his wife he is "lunatic." It is clear to the audience which twin will *pay* for the swindle.

Adriana reappears with a psychiatric consultant-cum-conjurer, the ridiculous Dr. Pinch. Much like the *medicus gloriosus* in Plautus' play, he pronounces the patient insane ("both master and man is possessed")[58] and orders his strong-armed helpers to grab hold of Antipholus and Dromio. His prescription, that "they be bound and laid in some dark room,"[59] was a normal therapy for insanity in Elizabethan times; Malvolio is subjected to the same treatment in *Twelfth Night*. Here in the dark, one cannot help perceiving an additional intra-uterine adumbration of the symbolic rebirth that is to come. Now both father and son can only be redeemed by payment of a debt.

The final act takes place not in the familiar city street, but before a Christian Priory (formerly the famous temple of Diana, one of the listed wonders of the ancient world) in whose cloisters the visiting Antipholus and Dromio have taken refuge to avoid the local brother's creditors. The lady Abbess is both a kind of *dea ex machina* and an early marriage counselor. Adriana explains to her with unconscious irony, "this week he hath been . . . much different from the man he was."[60] The holy woman immediately seeks to reconcile the estranged couple. She begins by admonishing Adriana for her bad temper (taking Luciana's position), and concluding that she was partially to blame for her husband's going mad:

> The consequence is, then, thy jealous fits
> Hath scar'd thy husband from the use of wits.[61]

Moreover, although Adriana wants custody of her afflicted husband, the Mother Superior insists upon keeping Antipholus under her supervision.

But Adriana takes her plea to a higher court. For at that moment the merchant announces that "the dial points at five," and the noble Solinus himself enters, leading Egeon to his imminent execution. Adriana appeals to him with a cry—"Justice, most sacred Duke, against the Abbess!"—and begins to describe her husband's madness—just as he himself appears with a perfect antiphonal shout ("justice, most gracious Duke").

Both husband and wife put their case before the noble ruler, who then overrules the Roman double standard with Christian fidelity. Other voices are raised. The merchants, and even the courtesan, vent their ire. At this cacophony of indictments, the Duke exclaims:

> Why, what an intricate impeach is this!
> I think you all have drunk of Circe's cup.[62]

Shakespeare yet again calls our attention to the witchcraft and transformations that permeate Ephesus. The comparison to the enchantress in the *Odyssey* is particularly apt. A pernicious *femme fatale*, Circe used her seductive appeal to bewitch men and turn them into pigs—itself a kind of metaphor for male sensuality. Nor is this the only reference in the play to Homer's "reunion poem." Like Odysseus, Antipholus has spent years wandering throughout farthest Greece. His love for Luciana is like the siren's song that distracts and lures him from his quest:

> ANTIPHOLUS: O, train me not, sweet mermaid, with thy note,
> To drown me in thy [sister's] flood of tears.[63]

The twin's long travels have been a voyage of rebirth and discovery. Is this not the very theme of the *Odyssey?*

And yet, although comedy focuses on the swinish parts of man, this reductive view of the relationship between the sexes is about to be refuted with the purity of love displayed by the protagonist. Suddenly Egeon catches sight of a possible savior, and quickly questions the much-beleaguered local twin:

> EGEON: Is not your name, sir, called Antipholus?
> And is not that your bondman, Dromio?[64]

Just as it seems that this gambit of identities can go no further, Shakespeare, by having Egeon appeal to the wrong set of twins, wrings one final twist from the conventional material. Neither his son, nor his son's slave, recognizes him. Egeon is staggered, but still persists:

> EGEON: O time's extremity,
> Hast thou so crack'd and splitted my poor tongue
> In seven short years, that here my only son
> Knows not my feeble key of untun'd cares?[65]

To Plautus' simple reunion, Shakespeare has added a deft *non-cognitio* as the local Antipholus answers bluntly but truthfully, "I never saw you in my life till now." And when Egeon claims again to be Antipholus' father, the local twin protests—with a touch of sadness—"I never saw my father in my life."

And now tragedy looms. In a moment it will be too late to save Egeon's life. And so the playwright expediently sends the Abbess onstage, leading the Syracusan man and slave—who of course immediately recognize their father. At this climactic moment, Adriana's eyes widen as she exclaims, "I see two husbands, or my eyes deceive me."[66] And with equal astonishment, the Duke adds:

One of these men is *genius* to the other;
And so of these, which is the natural man
And which the spirit? Who deciphers them?[67]

As the traveling twins affectionately embrace their elderly father, the Dromios introduce themselves. The family reunion is made astonishingly complete by the wholly unexpected cry of the Abbess, who suddenly realizes that she is Mrs. Deus Ex Machina: the doomed prisoner is none other than her long-lost husband. For his part, the wide-eyed old man exclaims, "If I dream not, thou art Emilia." And yet he is not dreaming: this *is* indeed his long-lost wife—back from the divorce of death. His son thinks it is a sleeping fantasy, and echoes his astonishment: "If this be not a dream I see and hear." We are continually brought back to the strong link between *kōma* and comedy—if not etymologically, at least psychologically.

The Duke himself has a sudden *cognitio*—of the veracity of Egeon's plaint in the prologue. Not only two pairs of sons but a father and mother have unexpectedly reappeared from the depths of the ocean. The mysteries, mistakes, and merchandising of this mad day are straightened out—and, most important, the money that will redeem Egeon. Antipholus offers to ransom his father from death, but the Duke pardons the old man so his son can keep the money. It is an archetypal ending, a world of dreams and wish-fulfillment. All anger is dispelled, and love can triumph.

Best of all, the traveling twin can now marry Luciana. Unlike the identical heroes in the Plautine model, who return home to Syracuse insouciantly leaving the Epidamnian wife behind, Shakespeare celebrates the symbolic remarriage of all four couples in a mighty quadruple *gamos*. We can safely assume that the local Antipholus will never visit the courtesan again. And, thanks to the intercession of the Duke, Adriana will be a shrew no more. His twin will marry his beloved Luciana and remain deeply in love. Even Dromio and his frumpy kitchen wife are reunited. This is perhaps too much like a fairy tale. But Shakespeare believed in the sacrament of marriage in a way that transcends words.

The play ends on a very Christian note as the Abbess exclaims:

Thirty-three years have I but gone in travail [pains of childbirth]
Of you, my sons; and till this present hour
My heavy burdens ne'er delivered.[68]

It is a curious speech. We have already been told that the shipwreck occurred *twenty-five* years ago when the twins were neonates. This is surely not, as some pedestrian critics have argued, a mere *lapsus calami:* it is neither slip of pen nor memory. In this play full of christological allusions, we immediately recognize the age of Christ at the crucifixion—another direct reference to resurrection.[69] In Frye's view, "the imagery of the final recognition scene suggests a passing through death into a new world."[70] In other words, as Antipholus of Syracuse demonstrates, you must lose yourself to find yourself. Everyone in the play has experienced a rebirth, and the Mother Superior invites them to come to church to celebrate "a gossips' feast"—a highly significant choice, for this was the celebration of a newborn child's baptism. The bemused Duke puns, "with all my heart I'll gossip at this feast." The local Dromio invites his brother to join "their gossiping," and they joyfully leave the stage hand in hand.

Yet, strangely, the reunion of their masters is muted, to say the least. Nowhere in the final scene does either of them exchange a single word of affection or enthusiasm. Could this be a dramaturgical error?[71] After all, the traveling twin earlier expressed his longing to meet his brother. Could it be that, having lost himself, he will only find himself again when reunited with his other self? The two can be viewed as two parts of a single whole—one married with responsibilities, the other a carefree traveler.[72] They only share the same name because of the loss which has now been recovered. Perhaps they need heavenly benediction for the restoration of their wholeness, their humanity—and their speech. Then at last the wandering twin will find himself.

This first comedy by Shakespeare set the tone for all those that followed. For in one way or another, every one of them is about lost selves, absence, recognition, and reunion—whether it be the parodic transformation of Bottom into an Ass which mocks the lovers' imbroglios wrought by Puck, or time recaptured in *The Winter's Tale* with the discovery of the lost Perdita and the magical rebirth of her wronged mother, Hermione. Or Pericles reunited with his wife Thiasa, long thought dead, now magically rescued from her watery tomb and—like Emilia in *Errors*—serving as a nun at the temple of Diana in Ephesus. Pericles, embracing his beloved wife, lovingly invites her, "come be buried / a second time within these arms."[73] Ultimately, all these themes were refined into the most delicate gold in *The Tempest,* with which Shakespeare ended his career.

17

Twelfth Night: Dark Clouds over Illyria

*T**welfth Night* is the last of Shakespeare's so-called happy comedies. It is more refined and characteristic of the author than his *Comedy of Errors* (for which Plautus deserves some credit). The primary inspiration for the plot was Barnabe Riche's novella "Of Apolonius and Silla" (1581).[1] Its theme was again mistaken identity—with the added complication of confused genders.

However, for this motif there was ample Italian precedent in comedies like *Gl'Ingannati (The Deceived)*. But the pioneer on the English stage of what we might also call transvestite comedy was arguably the Oxford wit and court poet John Lyly (1554–1606), who blazed the trail—or perhaps "maze" is more appropriate—with *Gallathea* (c. 1582).

Once upon a time, this story goes, the folk of Lincolnshire sought each year to find "the fairest and chastest virgin in the country" to sacrifice to the God Neptune. To save them from this harsh fate, two fathers independently disguise their beautiful daughters Phillida and Gallathea as men. These two "draft dodgers" fall in love, each thinking the other is a man. They escape the knife, but when Venus reveals their true genders they are left with a rather serious problem:

> PHILLIDA: It were a shame if a maiden should be a suitor (a thing)
> hated in that sex, that thou shouldst deny to be her ser-
> vant.
>
> GALLATHEA: If it be a shame in me, it can be no commendation in you,
> for your self is of that mind.
>
> PHILLIDA: Suppose I were a virgin (I blush in supposing my self one)
> and that under the habit of a boy were the person of a
> maiden, if I should utter my affection with sighs, mani-
> fest my sweet love by my salt tears, and prove my loyalty
> unspotted, and my grief intolerable, would not then that
> fair face pity thy true hart?
>
> GALLATHEA: Admit that I were as you would have me suppose that
> you are, and that I should with entreaties, prayers, oaths,
> bribes, and what ever can be invented in love, desire your
> favour, would you not yield?[2]

Gallathea reciprocates the feeling and is likewise perplexed. Unfortunately, Lyly does not find an artful way to solve the gender quandary,
and the play ends rather lamely with Venus vaguely promising to "work
things out."

Shakespeare was captivated by this theme, and added the improve-
ments needed to bring it to a state of perfection. In *Twelfth Night* he
transcends both Lyly and Plautus to create a work uniquely his own. At
least one contemporary spectator appreciated its genealogy. One John
Manningham, a law student at the Middle Temple, reports in his diary
on 1 February 1602:

> At our feast we had a play called ["mid" crossed out] *Twelve*
> [*sic*] *Night or What You Will,* much like the *Comedy of Errors* or
> *Menaechmi* in Plautus, but most like and near to that in Ital-
> ian called *Inganni* [*sic*]. A good practice in it to make the stew-
> ard believe his Lady widow was in love with him by counter-
> feiting a letter . . . making him believe they took him to be
> mad.

Twelfth Night is arguably Shakespeare's finest comedy, the culmination of his "first comic phase." Here we find the lovely heroine Viola

separated from her carbon-copy twin brother in a shipwreck (the oblig-atory catastrophe). Thinking that Sebastian is dead, she dresses in mas-culine garb and gains employment with Duke Orsino, with whom she immediately falls in love.

The sexual ambiguity had an added frisson in Elizabethan romantic plots for, unlike Machiavelli's Florence, the female parts were played by boys. Hence when a heroine assumes masculine garb we have a boy playing a girl, disguised as a boy. This protean sexuality is of course to-tally alien to modern sensibilities, where both genders share the stage. It was not until the Restoration that women began to appear on stage. This may account for the absence of mother figures in Shakespeare, since a boy could plausibly play a girl, but not an older woman.

In one way Shakespeare's heroines all share a "masculine" trait. With the early exception of *The Comedy of Errors,* where the visiting Antipholus briefly woos Luciana, *they* take the initiative. Being dis-guised as men—the otherness granted by the *kōmos*—enables them to act more aggressively. One thinks not only of Viola, but of Rosalind in *As You Like It,* Julia (who calls herself Sebastian) in *Two Gentlemen of Verona,* Helena in *All's Well That Ends Well,* and even Portia in *The Merchant of Venice.*

The sexual confusion of *Twelfth Night* is reflected in its subtitle, *What You Will.* Besides being a pun on the author's name, "will" is also a syn-onym for sexual desire.[3] But all will be right in the end, and the errors ultimately serve to distinguish the sexes. And as we shall see, this cru-cial difference is only "a little thing"—which is how Viola refers to her non-existent phallus. Without it the world would be unpopulated.

In the famous opening words of the play,[4] Duke Orsino sounds the note of melancholy which pervades Illyria:

> If music be the food of love, play on,
> Give me excess of it, that, surfeiting,
> The appetite may sicken, and so die.
> That strain again. It had a dying fall.[5]

These lines contain no fewer than five words with sexual connotations: "play", "excess," "surfeit," "appetite," and "die."[6] Clearly all of Illyria is "sicklied o'er with the pale cast" of sadness. Affection and desire are waning, and the whole tone is one of longing and lack of consummation.[7]

In the rather conventional mythological images which he uses throughout the play, the Duke—and we must remember this is not a soliloquy—addresses his gathered courtiers, protesting (too much) his love for Olivia:

> Methought she purg'd the air of pestilence;
> That instant I was turn'd into a hart,
> And my desires, like fell and cruel hounds,
> E're since pursue me.[8]

This is not a random simile. Using a conventional Petrarchan language of love, Orsino idolizes his beloved as being too pure for him. He likens himself to Actaeon who, when he gazed upon Diana, the chaste goddess of the hunt, was torn to pieces by his own hounds. This is the first of several important classical similes which appear at crucial moments.

And yet, despite his poetic aspirations, it is clear that the Duke is more in love with love than with Olivia—as St. Augustine famously expressed it, *amare amabam*.[9] The more she spurns him, the more ardent he gets. For his courtier Valentine—an apt choice of name for this protatic character, and surely not a chance reference[10]—reports that the object of his affection has vowed to mourn her dead brother for seven years during which:

> . . . like a cloistress she will veilèd walk
> And water once a day her chamber round
> With eye-offending brine; all this to season
> A brother's dead love . . .[11]

Somehow one cannot keep from doubting Olivia's protestations of grief, and her determination to endure a seven-year period of mourning displays as much invention as intention. Perhaps it is merely a posture to stoke the Count's ardor. It has certainly succeeded. Orsino is ablaze at the thought that if she shows that much passion for a dead brother, how much more will she feel for a live husband?[12]

But in Shakespeare, no such oath of self-denial ever lasts very long. A vow made by intellect is always defeated by instinct. We see this again with the noble male "undergraduates" in *Love's Labour's Lost*. Although they have sworn to study for a year, exiled from the fair sex, the arrival of the Princess of France and her lovely ladies-in-waiting once again demonstrates that instinct will inevitably triumph over intellect.

As the Duke exits, the heroine enters. Viola is suffering from a traditional "comic" loss of identity, having just survived a shipwreck, an upheaval of nature in which she fears that her twin Sebastian has perished:

> VIOLA: My brother he is in Elysium.
>   Perchance he is not drowned. What think you, sailors?
> CAPTAIN: It is perchance that you yourself were saved.
> VIOLA: My poor brother! And so perchance he may be.[13]

The very heavy emphasis on chance (it is echoed for the fourth time in the next line) is in the best tradition of Menander.

The captain, trying "to comfort [her] with chance," reports that "after our ship did split" he had seen Sebastian clinging to a mast:

> Where, like Arion on the dolphin's back,
> I saw him hold acquaintance with the waves.[14]

Arion, the semi-legendary bard of antiquity, when thrown overboard, enchanted the sea creatures with the power of his music and was carried to safety.[15] This is the first note of a musical figure which will play on throughout the play, celebrating the saving grace of song. And yet, as we hear from the Duke's opening speech, this comedy has begun in a distinctly minor key.

When Viola learns from the captain that a certain Duke Orsino rules Illyria, she recalls her father once mentioning him—and as a female reflex asks if he is still a bachelor. Despite her grief, Viola's natural instincts are immediately aroused. The captain tells her with Euripidean paradox that he is, and he isn't. For he loves a noble lady called Olivia, but the lady's seven-year vow of abstinence makes her untouchable.

When Viola hears of Olivia's pledge to mourn her dead brother, her own sorrow arises afresh, and she is drawn to her as a fellow sister in mourning ("O, that I serv'd that lady").[16] But this is a comedy,

and the force of nature prevails as her mind returns to the bachelor
Duke. Viola takes the initiative to woo—and win—him. She bids the
captain:

> Conceal me what I am, and be my aid
> For such disguise as haply shall become
> The form of my intent. I'll serve this Duke;
> Thou shalt present me as an eunuch to him.[17]

That she chooses to disguise herself is understandable. But why
does she ask the captain to "present me as an eunuch"? Critics
have gone to great lengths to explain this enigmatic decision on
her part, some arguing that the first Viola was played by a high-voiced
boy who sang all the songs, which, in later productions, were re-
assigned to Feste.[18] Shakespeare failed to adjust the text and, so the
argument goes, the requirement for "an eunuch" was left in—much
as Aristophanes' *Clouds* has inconsistencies deriving from partial
revision.

But this cannot be right. In the original production Feste was played
by Robert Armin, renowned for his glorious voice, who later that year
would immortalize Shakespeare's greatest clown—the fool in *King
Lear*.[19] Thus it is most unlikely that Feste would not have been given the
songs in the first place—not to mention that the Fool was a natural entertainer. Which leaves us with the question: why does Viola choose to
be "an eunuch"? And yet this persona could not be more appropriate,
since the confusion of sexual identities is the play's central organizing
principle. Neither man nor woman, the eunuch is unable to love and be
loved.

As Viola goes off with the captain so he can "conceal her what she is,"
Shakespeare begins his subplot, which is all misrule, *kōmos*, and carnival. It involves Olivia's uncle, Sir Toby Belch, the maid Maria, and
their guest, the feckless Sir Andrew Aguecheek. Sir Toby is a latter-day
alazōn, and an unfettered *kōmos*-man. When scolded by Maria: "you
must confine yourself within the modest limits of order," he retorts,
"Confine? I'll confine myself no finer than I am." He lives only for
"cakes and ale" and dancing through life:

My very walk should be a jig; I would not so much as make
water but in a sink-a-pace.[20]

The life force incarnate and a minor-league Falstaff, Toby complains
to the wench Maria of his niece's persistent mourning: "I am sure care's
an enemy to life."[21] Toby regards his fellow knight as a possible match
for his niece: after all, "he speaks three or four languages word for word
without book."[22] Yet later when Andrew proposes to go home, since his
suit has not made any progress, Toby asks "*Pourquoi,* my dear Knight,"
and the gallant replies:

> What is "*pourquoi*"? Do, or not do? I would I had bestowed
> that time in the tongues that I have in fencing, dancing, and
> bear-baiting.[23]

Later we will see that Sir Andrew's time in fencing has also been spent
to no avail. (It may be of interest that King James I was notorious for
devaluing knighthoods.)

The revelers trip offstage and Viola reappears, disguised as Cesario in
company with the Duke. He asks "him" to plead with Olivia on his behalf. He is already on intimate terms with his page, who has replaced
Valentine as his confidante. As the Duke himself remarks:

> I have unclasped
> to thee the book even of my secret soul.[24]

Of course this subliminal heterosexual attraction will ultimately be explained by an influence of "nature to her bias." Viola is the least
successful of all Shakespeare's she-males, for the Duke's hormones
already seem to sense something distinctively female in "him":

> Diana's lip
> Is not more smooth and rubious; thy small pipe
> Is as the maiden's organ, shrill and sound,
> And all is semblative of a woman's part.[25]

We find the same bifocal sexuality in Shakespeare's Sonnets when he
describes his boy-love:

> A woman's face with Nature's own hand painted
> Hast thou, the master mistress of my passion . . .[26]

Has Viola's epicene beauty caused Orsino to fall in love with her?[27] For her part Viola, left alone on stage and smitten, confides to the audience:

> I'll do my best
> To woo your lady: *(aside)* yet a barful strife!
> Whoe'er I woo, myself would be his wife.[28]

Sex is never far from the surface in this play, especially among the *kōmos* revelers in the subplot. When Feste the clown appears, Maria chides him for his absence:

> MARIA: My lady will hang thee for thy absence.
> CLOWN: Let her hang me; he that is well hanged in this world
> needs to fear no colours.[29]

His very first joke is a familiar phallic double-entendre. The clown once again employs this suggestive metaphor in his proverb "Many a good hanging prevents a bad marriage."[30] The Fool himself is the very spokesman of the phallus:

> Historically, the Fool and indecency cannot be parted. To make up for his mental shortcomings, Nature was commonly believed to have endowed the Fool with an excess of virility, symbolized by his bauble. Priapus used to be described as "that foolish god."[31]

The Fool also represents the survival of an independent medieval comic tradition, thrust into the midst of the classical tradition of comedy. His hallmark is the anarchy of carnival, "ready to subvert at any moment the playwright's prescription for action."[32] This counterpoint runs throughout Twelfth Night in the form of a Saturnalian commentary by the Fool on the progress of the action.

Olivia now makes her appearance in the company of her steward, the humorless Malvolio, whose name—from the Italian *mala voglia,* "ill will"—reflects his alliance with the forces of anti-*kōmos*.[33] Both mistress and man wear black, and Malvolio, "sad and civil," has the keys to the house around his neck—revealing his compulsion to shut away the "cakes and ale," and a visual indication that his emotions are also "locked up." His dark costume and even darker temperament symbolize the melancholy pandemic in all Illyria. For a comedy, the mood is unusually dark.

The scene ends with the entrance of Cesario/Viola. Even Malvolio, with all his misanthropic self-involvement, somehow senses the new arrival's sexual neutrality and makes what for him is a bold statement, describing the visitor as:

> Not yet old enough for a man nor young enough for a boy; as
> a squash is before 'tis a peascod, or a codling when 'tis almost
> an apple. 'Tis with him in standing water, between man and
> boy.[34]

The Elizabethan audience would construe "codling" as a reference to "his" prepubescent masculinity. Curiously, of all the characters only Malvolio actually pierces Viola's concealed sexual identity. He is not a fool—nor even a villain. Yet he cannot act on his perception because, as Olivia says,

> O, you are sick of self-love, Malvolio, and taste with a distem-
> pered appetite.[35]

(Many critics have viewed Malvolio's "humorless" behavior as being a caricature of Ben Jonson.) With some ambivalence Cesario/Viola woos the mourning lady, asking her to remove the veil which covers her face. When Olivia does so, and betrays her innate vanity, Viola's reaction betrays her innate jealousy:

> OLIVIA: Look you, Sir . . . Is't not well done?
> VIOLA: Excellently done, if God did all.
> OLIVIA: 'Tis in grain, sir; 'twill endure wind and weather.[36]

Olivia is wrong. One of the lessons this play teaches us is that we must not believe that beauty will last forever. Indeed, only briefly for the time of this comedy are we free from the wind and the rain, for in real life "the rain it raineth every day." Viola tries to persuade Olivia to forsake

her self-imposed celibacy and marry so she will "leave the world a copy."
Again we hear an echo of the playwright's first sonnet:

> From fairest creatures we desire increase,
> That thereby beauty's rose might never die,
> But as the riper should by time decrease,
> His tender heir might bear his memory.[37]

Shakespeare employs the imagery of the brief blossoming of a rose
throughout the play, as when Viola tells the Duke:

> For women are as roses, whose fair flow'r,
> Being once displayed, doth fall that very hour.[38]

The simile is as old as Aristophanes, who puts the same poignant lament in Lysistrata's mouth:

> But the season of a young girl is brief and if she fails to find a love
> No one will want to marry her and she is left all alone at home.[39]

By the Renaissance this was a well-worn—yet ever fresh—conceit. Thus
Ronsard's lines, oft-repeated (even by himself):

> Believe me love, live now—this moment—don't delay
> Pluck from the rose of life the blossoms of today.

This conceit was employed by all European poets. Another prime example is the Spaniard Garcilaso de la Vega (1503–1536), who urges his beloved to enjoy the prime of life:

> For as long as the rose and lily
> Show themselves on your lovely face . . .[40]

and concludes with the admonition:

> Pluck from your joyous springtime
> Its honeyed fruit—before the angry cold of winter
> Covers your lovely hair with all its snowfall.

Misguided about the length of her springtime, Olivia remains unassail-
able and bids Cesario report that she is not interested in any more messages from the Duke—unless they be brought by the same messenger.

Clearly she has taken a fancy to the young emissary—one that could ultimately cause her to come to grief.

The problem of mistaken gender is immediately followed by its potential solution—this play could have been constructed by a Swiss watchmaker. Viola's male twin Sebastian, the ultimate solution to her phallic problem, arrives on stage. He is mourning a sister, just as Olivia is a brother. He describes Viola to Antonio, the sea captain who saved him: "it was said, she much resembled me, was yet of many accounted beautiful." He then adds, "she is drowned already sir, with salt water, though I seem to drown her remembrance again with more."[41] His tears reflect those that Olivia sheds for her brother as he joins the universal lachrymosity that pervades Illyria.

No sooner does Sebastian leave the stage but his "undrowned sister" Viola enters, accosted by Malvolio who returns her ring. She sees the problem all too well, and the moment she is alone confides in the audience:

> I left no ring with her: what means this lady?
> Fortune forbid my outside hath not charm'd her . . .
> Poor lady, she were better love a dream.[42]

Here we have another Shakespearean "error," but one that is far more sophisticated and serious than the wandering Dromios of Ephesus. For Viola distinguishes between the inner and outer person and between superficial infatuation and genuine love. The error is deeper than mere appearance; we are not dealing with reflections in mirrors but rather the fundamental feelings of real men and women. This "midsummer madness"[43] evokes the same hallucinatory atmosphere of Shakespeare's comedy about a midsummer night's *kōma.* The doings in Illyria have the same unreality as those in the Forest of Arden. There too, identities are masked and lovers are confused. It is the time-honored chaos before the *kōmos.*

Viola tries to make sense of the current confusion:

> VIOLA: My master loves her dearly,
> And I, poor monster, fond as much on him;
> And she, mistaken, seems to dote on me:
> What will become of this? As I am man,

My state is desperate for my master's love:
As I am woman (now alas the day!),
What thriftless sighs shall poor Olivia breathe?[44]

One thing is certain: Shakespeare's solution will be more artful than Lyly's.

As Viola exits, the clown sings a ditty which encapsulates the attitude of the party people in the play:

> FESTE: What is love? 'Tis not hereafter;
> Present mirth hath present laughter;
> What's to come is still unsure:
> In delay there lies no plenty;
> Then come kiss me, sweet and twenty,
> Youth's a stuff will not endure.[45]

This is the philosophy of *Twelfth Night,* the quintessence of Carnival, in which the celebrants are freed from their everyday identities to melt into the festive throng. The emphasis is solely on the "now," on *present* mirth and *present* laughter. It recalls the rhapsodic lines of Lorenzo di Medici:

> Youth is lovely—but it's fleeting
> It will disappear anon!
> Give each day a joyous greeting
> Tomorrow it may all be gone.

The revelers do not live by any clock: their life is one continuous party. Falstaff, in his very first appearance on the Shakespearean stage, is chided for his insouciance about "the time of day" by Prince Hal:

> FALSTAFF: Now, Hal, what time of day is it, lad?
> HAL: . . . What devil hast thou to do with the time of the day?
> Unless hours were cups of sack, and minutes capons, and
> clocks the tongues of bawds, and dials the signs of leap-
> ing-houses, and the blessed sun himself a fair hot wench
> in flame-coloured taffeta, I see no reason why thou
> shouldst be so superfluous to demand the time of the
> day.[46]

But Malvolio does not share this view. The agelast interrupts the merry-makers with stern castigation—revealing a bit of social snobbery when he likens them to lower-class tradesmen (who is he to talk?):

> MALVOLIO: My masters, are you mad? Or what are you? Have you no
>   wit, manners, nor honesty, but to gabble like tinkers at
>   this time of night? Do ye make an alehouse of my lady's
>   house, that ye squeak out your coziers' catches without
>   any mitigation or remorse of voice? Is there no respect of
>   place, persons, nor time in you?[47]

Can this punctilious fool be implying that they should conform with Aristotelian dramatic unity?

After his tirade, Toby dismisses the humorless steward with the famous retort:

> Dost thou think, because thou art virtuous, there shall be no
> more cakes and ale?[48]

Here we find the essence of the special melancholy of the play. The other denizens beyond Toby's circle are not merely sad, but each in his own way *depressed*. This is the central conflict of the play, which, as we will see, does not reach a wholly satisfactory conclusion.

After his fulmination against Sir Toby's "uncivil rule," Malvolio storms offstage. The party-people now speak of a "revenge" by playing a practical joke on the straitlaced major domo. Maria's proposal is that they forge a letter to him in Olivia's name, pretending that the mistress of the house is enamored. If he reciprocates, he should wear his yellow stockings to please her. Sir Toby is keen: "Excellent, I smell a device."[49]

In the next scene the Duke reappears, still playing the stereotyped lover. He asks Cesario/Viola whether he has ever known the love of a woman. When Viola nods her head, Orsino immediately pursues the subject: "What kind of woman is't?"[50] The sexual reversal becomes increasingly intensified as she tries to speak of the "woman" she loves who was:

> VIOLA: Of your complexion.
> DUKE: She is not worth then. What years, i' faith?

VIOLA: About your years, my lord.
DUKE: Too old, by heaven . . .[51]

The Duke then bids the clown sing. And Feste obliges with the famous
song:

> Come away, come away, death,
> And in sad cypress let me be laid
> Fly away, fly away, breath,
> I am slain by a fair cruel maid.[52]

The theme of dying for love was already established in the very first
speech of the play with the Duke's "It had a dying fall." Here, as often in
Shakespeare, the word "die" has sexual overtones. As Benedick pledges
to Beatrice at the climax of *Much Ado About Nothing*:

> I will live in thy heart, die in thy lap,
> And be buried in thine eyes.[53]

The song is followed by another intimate exchange between the
Duke and Viola. Orsino is chauvinist enough to tell his disguised female page that no woman can love a man the way he loves Olivia. Viola
replies that she knows this too well:

VIOLA: My father had a daughter lov'd a man
As it might be perhaps, were I a woman,
I should your lordship.[54]

There has always been debate about how soon the Duke knows that Viola is Viola and not Cesario. In any case he asks the history of "his"
fictive sister and Viola replies, further developing the image of a rose
(here of the damask variety):

VIOLA: A blank my lord: she never told her love,
But let concealment, like a worm i' th' bud,
Feed on her damask cheek: She pined in thought,
And with a green and yellow melancholy
She sat like Patience on a monument,
Smiling at grief . . .[55]

The conversation concludes with a sympathetic question which she answers ambiguously:

> DUKE: But died thy sister of her love, my boy?
> VIOLA: I am all the daughters of my father's house . . .[56]

Once again we find the mixture of *erōs* and *thanatos,* and always lurking in the background are the sexual connotations of "dying." In *As You Like It,* Shakespeare's Rosalind debunked this poetic hyperbole:

> Men have died from time to time, and worms
> have eaten them, but not for love.[57]

Yet here in Shakespeare's last "happy comedy" we have something closer to a real death. In a sense, the old Viola has died in the shipwreck—and this play presents her rebirth and renewal (from the sea) by the power of love. The conversation ends with the Duke sending her/him to continue the suit on his behalf with Olivia.

The subsequent scene shows us why in King Charles's day, the play was presented under the title of *Malvolio.* It was in fact already renamed for a production at the court of James I in 1623.[58] For it is the unforgettable figure of the steward—the most original character in *Twelfth Night*—that struck people's fancy in the ages to come. Though a grim martinet, he is not wholly antipathetic, and ultimately he does elicit sympathy from some. The romanticized argument that Malvolio is a tragic figure is dismissed by the level-headed Levin: he is "a sycophant, a social climber, and an officious snob."[59]

As the steward dreams out loud of marrying Olivia and becoming "Count Malvolio,"[60] the lowlife characters Sir Toby and Maria spy on him. One of the eavesdroppers sneers: "Look how imagination blows him."[61] Malvolio even fantasizes about scolding his future cousin, Sir Toby: "You must amend your drunkenness."[62] And then he spies the forged letter that the roisterers have left in his path. He thinks he recognizes the writing:

> MALVOLIO: By my life, this is my lady's hand: these be her very C's, her U's, and her T's; and thus makes she her great P's. It is in contempt of question, her hand.[63]

Malvolio certainly does have a "distempered appetite," for to the Elizabethan audience the C, the U, and the T are none too subtle and together suggest—except to the dolt Sir Andrew—the female genital organ.[64] The joke of her great "P's" is as gross as it is obvious.[65] Malvolio is
infatuated by the injunction to be "unafraid of greatness":

> Some are born great, some achieve greatness and some have
> greatness thrust upon 'em.[66]

The letter concludes with an appeal for him to wear his yellow stockings "cross-gartered" in order to please Olivia. He rushes off to prepare
himself by reading politic authors.

The act concludes with Olivia revealing her love to "Cesario." The
conversation is fraught with conscious and unconscious ambiguities:

> OLIVIA: I prithee tell me what thou think'st of me.
> VIOLA: That you think you are not what you are.
> OLIVIA: If I think so, I think the same of you.
> VIOLA: Then think you right. I am not what I am.[67]

Olivia takes the initiative and declares her love openly—with the usual
Petrarchan conceits. She swears by the "roses of the spring,"[68] and so
forth. To which Viola replies cryptically that:

> VIOLA: I have one heart, one bosom, and one truth,
>   And that no woman has; nor never none
>   Shall mistress be of it, save I alone.[69]

But Olivia is so enraptured that she does not notice the subtlety of
Viola's reply.

Illyria is a never-never land for people who never seem to do anything
but fantasize—and drink. We now move from dreams to drams. The
mischievous Toby urges his dim-witted guest, Sir Andrew, to demonstrate his prowess to Olivia by challenging the Duke's young emissary
to a duel and "hurt him in eleven places."[70]

Lest the audience be concerned about Viola's lack of "swordsman-
ship," Shakespeare immediately reassures us by bringing her twin
brother back on stage—the man who (we sense) will ultimately do the
dueling. He enters in the company of his rescuer Antonio, and in many

ways their conversation echoes both the *Comedy of Errors* and the *Menaechmi,* and ultimately Euripides. For when, like the traveling Antipholus, Sebastian proposes that they "go see the relics of the town,"[71] Antonio must decline, since he is a wanted man in this country. He then gives Sebastian his purse for safekeeping in case his "eye shall light upon some toy / you have desire to purchase." They plan to meet in an hour.

This is pure Plautus. But Shakespeare's defter touch does not leave the audience a moment to breathe or be bored. Malvolio appears, intoxicated with *alazoneia* and preening before a puzzled Olivia, who does not understand his allusions to a letter she did not write. She is further astounded by his odd attire—especially when Malvolio reminds her:

> MALVOLIO: "Remember who commended thy yellow stockings"—
> OLIVIA: Thy yellow stockings?
> MALVOLIO: "And wished to see thee cross-gartered."
> OLIVIA: Cross-gartered?
> MALVOLIO: "Go to, thou are made, if thou desir'st to be so:"
> OLIVIA: Am I made?[72]

Malvolio's comic delusion brings a symbolic change of seasons. For the play that began in winter (on the Twelfth Night of Christmas) has moved into a warmer climate. Olivia's exclamation, "this is all midsummer madness,"[73] is reinforced by Fabian's subsequent comment: "More matter for a May morning."[74] References to May Day need not be taken literally, for "Maying" can be thought of as happening on a midsummer night—even on midsummer eve itself. To this day, "May Week" at Cambridge University still takes place in June.[75] This may be confusing to us as well as the characters, but one thing is sure: we have seen a progression from wintry cold to summer warmth.

Malvolio's interview with his mistress is cause for universal embarrassment. It so defies credibility that it could only be concocted by a dramatist, as Olivia's servant Fabian comments with Plautine metatheatricality:

> If this were played upon a stage now, I could condemn it as
> an improbable fiction.[76]

Toby then proposes that, since Malvolio is clearly mad, he be bound and shut in a dark room. We have already seen this Elizabethan treatment for lunacy in the *Comedy of Errors*.

Then at last we see Sir Toby delivering a challenge, coaxed out of Sir Andrew, to the timorous Cesario/Viola. Note how Shakespeare has prepared his audience so perfectly for the "confrontational" scenes that the plots seem to run simultaneously:

> SIR TOBY: Dismount thy tuck [sword], be yare [swift] in thy prepa-
> ration, for thy assailant is quick, skilful, and deadly . . . or
> strip your sword stark naked; for meddle you must, that's
> certain . . .[77]

These hardly subtle phallic suggestions remind us of Viola's disguised gender. When Toby melodramatically exaggerates Andrew's prowess with a blade, Viola's womanish fright is intensified and she remarks:

> A little thing would make me tell them how much I lack of a
> man.[78]

Viola's lament for "a little thing"[79] (another phallic reference) inspired the unabashed title for a successful twentieth-century musical version of this play, *Your Own Thing* (1968).[80] This single line alone sums up the crux of transvestite comedy:

> The most fundamental distinction the play brings home to
> us is the difference between men and women . . . Just as a sat-
> urnalian reversal of social roles need not threaten the social
> structure, but can serve instead to consolidate it, so a tempo-
> rary, playful reversal of sexual roles can renew the meaning
> of the normal relationship.[81]

But whenever real swords are needed, real men arrive in the nick of time to provide them. As Sir Andrew draws, the sailor Antonio, thinking Viola/Cesario is Sebastian, comes to her/his defense—and chases the silly knight off. But the sailor's bravery costs him dear. He is immediately recognized as a wanted criminal and arrested by the Duke's officers. Much like the twin in the *Comedy of Errors*, he asks Viola/Cesario, whom he still takes to be Sebastian, for the money he entrusted to "him" so he can pay his bail. She responds, with perfect honesty, that she does not know what he is talking about.

As he is being dragged off, Antonio vilifies his friend:

> Thou hast, Sebastian, done good feature shame.
> In nature there's no blemish but the mind;
> None can be called deform'd but the unkind.
> Virtue is beauty.[82]

Once more we find the notion that moral ugliness can deface beauty, here applied to describe the outward similarity of one person to another who lacks the inner virtues of the first. It is the only way the victims of mistaken identity can explain a "familiar" character acting *out of character*. (Recall the case of the visiting Antipholus making "illicit" advances to his sister-in-law.)

Unlike Menaechmus and Antipholus, Viola instantly realizes what is happening:

> Prove true, imagination, O, prove true,
> That I, dear brother, be now ta'en for you! . . .
> He nam'd Sebastian. I my brother know
> Yet living in my glass.[83]

In the mirror of her imagination Viola immediately sees the reflection of her beloved brother. In contrast to previous plays of lost identity, Shakespeare here tries to offer dramatic motivation for some of the coincidences—why she happens to be wearing garb exactly like Sebastian's, for example:

> Still in this fashion, colour, ornament,
> For him I imitate. O if it prove,
> Tempests are kind, and salt waves fresh in love![84]

As the next act begins, her twin brother is suddenly confronted by the two farcical worthies. Sir Andrew hits Sebastian—who responds by beating his inept attacker black and blue, exclaiming: "Are all the people mad?"[85] Defeated, Sir Andrew limps off, threatening to sue for assault and battery.

Now it is Sir Toby's turn. He draws a sword to engage Sebastian.

We have reached the acme of lunacy. Which is why at this very moment Shakespeare brings on Olivia who, seeing "her beloved Cesario" assailed by her ruffian uncle, sternly orders Toby to retreat. She then turns affectionately to Sebastian and says softly, "I prithee gentle friend . . . Go with me to my house."[86]

She is more than ever enamored with a dream, but enamored she is. Paradoxically, in Elizabethan English the word "lover" meant friend, and "friend" meant lover. Olivia is saying—in so many words—"darling, let's go to my place." Sebastian is not loath to accompany this gorgeous creature, and yet is bewildered:

> What relish is this? How runs the stream?
> Or I am mad, or else this is a dream.
> Let fancy still my sense in Lethe steep;
> If it be thus to dream, still let me sleep![87]

The masculine twin has no qualms about following so lovely a lady without asking what he is getting into. When he reappears on stage, he is still so vertiginous that he must reassure himself that "'tis not madness"[88] and repeats "this may be some error but no madness," but then concludes, "I am mad, / or else the lady is mad." Olivia then emerges in the company of a priest and invites Sebastian to be her husband. Although Shakespeare argues in *As You Like It* that "who ever love'd that lov'd not at first sight?"[89] this is the first instance of a hero experiencing *marriage* at first sight.

Sebastian immediately pledges fealty and "goes with the flow," for his instinct has completely mastered his intellect. Surely this *must* be a *kōma*—and it is certainly leading to a *kōmos*. In a holiday humor (like Rosalind) he lets "the world slip," surrendering to this fantasy:

> I'll follow this good man and with you
> And having sworn truth, ever will be true.

Needless to say, there is no intent of reality here. This is true *midsummer madness*—Cesario has been transformed into a real man, and the law of comedy will be served.

In the final act of the play—which is all one scene—Orsino makes his first excursion from the ducal palace in the company of Cesario/Viola to visit Olivia. What has inspired him to make the journey at this precise moment? (The playwright, obviously.) With perfect timing, the Duke's officers bring out the captive Antonio, and Viola bids her master pardon him. Antonio protests to the Duke:

> A witchcraft drew me hither:
> That most ingrateful boy there by your side,
> From the rude sea's enrag'd and foamy mouth
> Did I redeem. A wrack past hope he was.[90]

These words hark back to the metaphor of redemption in *Comedy of Errors*. The playwright does not choose his words at random. Not only does he mention witchcraft, but he also presents in a far more sophisticated form the shipwreck of life which in Shakespeare can bring a rebaptism and Christian redemption.

And now the errors compound geometrically before they are ultimately resolved. Unlike the classical tradition, in this play the wedding occurs before the *cognitio*. Olivia dressed in her bridal whites appears, thinking to join her husband, Cesario. Despite Viola's frightened protestations that she has not been married to anyone, the priest confirms that he has performed the ceremony. The Duke is outraged and, snarling at his erstwhile confidante "O, thou dissembling cub," banishes Viola from his presence forever. The attractive young woman has now been metamorphosed into a beast.

An operatic finale and spectacular *cognitio* ensue, prefaced by the arrival of the clown and the much-battered Sirs Toby and Andrew. Their antagonist Sebastian enters, and is busily apologizing to Olivia ("I am sorry, madam I hurt your kinsman")[91] when the Duke utters perhaps the most famous lines in the play:

> One face, one voice, one habit, and two persons—
> A natural perspective that is, and is not.[92]

Shakespeare continues in his use of optical metaphors, here alluding to a scientific device that could produce multiple copies of the same image. He repeats the notion again when he refers to the mirror image ("the glass seems true").[93] But here we are not dealing with artifice and science. We are dealing with natural perspective and human nature.

An amazed Antonio then gasps: "Which is Sebastian?" Whereupon Viola experiences both *cognitio* and *cognatio:*

> Sebastian was my father;
> Such a Sebastian was my brother too.[94]

Brother and sister embrace and then Sebastian turns to his bride, exclaiming that her "error" was nothing less than *la forza di natura* at work:

> So comes it, lady, you have been mistook
> But nature to her bias drew in that.[95]

As in all of Shakespeare's transvestite comedies, the natural attraction in the world between man and woman prevails, for "Jack will have Jill and nought will be ill."[96] The Duke suddenly realizes the truth behind Viola's earlier enigmatic utterances:

> Boy, thou hast said to me a thousand times
> Thou never should'st love woman like to me . . .
> Give me thy hand,
> And let me see thee in thy woman's weeds.[97]

Paradoxically, although he sensed the female in her when she was disguised as a man, the Duke suddenly needs sartorial reassurance of Viola's femininity and will not embrace her until he sees her as a woman. He awaits the full resolution of the happy end, the complete return from comic otherness.

La commedia è finita. But not quite. There is still "the madly-used Malvolio" (as he signs a written plea to Olivia), who is instantly freed. He enters to complain of his cruel treatment and, when he is told that Olivia never wrote any letter to him, the roisterers admit their skulduggery. As always, the agelast is offered a chance to renounce his anticomic values and join the party. But Malvolio is unmoved and storms off to his self-appointed exile, heedless of the Duke's efforts at conciliation. As Northrop Frye explains:

> Comedy often includes a scapegoat ritual of expulsion which
> gets rid of some irreconcilable character, but exposure and
> disgrace makes for pathos, even tragedy.[98]

All this would have ended according to tradition were it not for Malvolio's ominous parting words:

I'll be reveng'd on the whole pack of you![99]

In the end he did wreak a terrible vengeance on his abusers—and the light-hearted "cakes and ale" pastimes of the Elizabethan audience. For scarcely a generation later (1642), the Puritans closed the English theaters.

But not yet. Merriment is still unbounded in Illyria as the play, like the *Comedy of Errors,* ends with a mass *gamos.* All the baubles will ornament the triple wedding night. For in addition to the correctly-gendered twins, Sir Toby suddenly decides to wed Maria. The equilibrium of man and woman has been satisfied. Nature has had her, or his, way. *Vive la différence!* What exactly does all this signify? The answer is as old as Aristophanes. As Benedick says in surrendering to the life force in *Much Ado About Nothing:* "the world must be peopled."[100] For comedy at its heart is a fertility ritual and a celebration of the phallus.

This is made eminently clear by Feste's final song:

> When that I was a little tiny boy,
> With hey, ho, the wind and the rain,
> A foolish thing was but a toy,
> For the rain it raineth every day.[101]

In Shakespeare, a "toy," like "bauble" (as for example in *Romeo and Juliet*),[102] can refer to the male member. The rest of the song is likewise phallic in word and spirit:

> A great while ago the world begun,
> With hey, ho, the wind and the rain,
> But that's all one, our play is done,
> And we'll strive to please you every day.[103]

Even the simple word "rain" can have sexual overtones in Shakespeare.[104] But more important is the allusion "a great while ago the world begun," for to "dance the beginning of the world" was an Elizabethan euphemism for the sexual act. We recall the sacred marriage of the ancient cosmogonies. This adds a new dimension to Feste's philosophy. Indeed, what is Feste if not the phallus incarnate? His song is a kind of life cycle of the organ, beginning with the tiny boy's "foolish thing" and concluding with the winter rain which sees man old and cold in bed.[105] Moreover, Feste's song recalls a famous passage in Corinthians:

> When I was a child, I spake as a child, I understood as a child,
> I thought as a child: but when I became a man, I put away
> childish things. For now we see through a glass, darkly; but
> then face to face.[106]

Comic rejuvenation thus involves the stripping-off of disguises to reveal the natural perspective, the return to what Freud described as "the mood of our childhood . . . when we had no need of humour to make us feel happy in our life."[107]

And so the play ends with both connotations of *gamos*. First wedding, then consummation. Not just marriage, but fertility. The dead have been reborn and rebaptized by the tempests which wrecked their previous lives. Olivia and the others have learned that although it raineth every day, today exceptionally it did not rain in Illyria at all. It was a *kōmos* day of errors, an odyssey of sexual confusion which went from comic chaos to cosmic order: marriage, which sets God in heaven and man and wife in each other's arms.

18

Molière: The Class of '68

Sometimes the border between comedy and tragedy is barely visible, with the greatest laughter born from the greatest pain.

There is a tale—perhaps apocryphal—of Grock, a legendary clown of the early twentieth century, whose success encompassed all of Europe, and most notably England. He made nations laugh, yet in private life he was so nightmarishly depressed that, while playing Zurich in his native Switzerland, he booked an appointment with Dr. Carl Jung under his real name—Charles Adrien Wettach. The famous psychiatrist counseled his deeply troubled patient to go see Grock perform, "and all your troubles will vanish with laughter."

The agonized man replied, "I *am* Grock!"

Such pain was also the case with Molière, who was a genius in an age of geniuses—Corneille, Pascal, Descartes, La Fontaine, and Racine. When asked by King Louis XIV whom he regarded as the greatest writer of their age, the critic Boileau answered without hesitation—Molière. The Sun King was surprised, but time has proven the validity of Boileau's assessment.[1]

Despite his success, the playwright led a tortured life. The immortal Victor Hugo remarked:

Those men that make us laugh so much become in the end profoundly sad. Beaumarchais was morose, Molière gloomy, Shakespeare melancholic.[2]

In volume three of the vast study entitled *La Personalité,* the authors state once again that the term *mélancolie* precisely denotes what today is known as clinical depression.[3] Molière's psyche has been the subject of serious medical analysis in a recent two-volume, 1600-page study.[4]

And yet, despite his agony, the playwright had the superhuman gift of being able to laugh at himself—and make the world laugh with him. Up until the end he was putting his heart and soul and finally even his blood onto the stage. He died in 1673, following a performance of his last play, ironically called *Le Malade imaginaire (The Imaginary Invalid).* Whereas Shakespeare was endowed with what Keats rather infelicitously called "negative capability"—the skill of being able to portray both a Falstaff and a Lear, a Juliet and a Lady Macbeth—Molière painted only one character who appears in various guises in all of his plays—himself. No author we have studied thus far has put so much of his own inner life into his plays. Indeed, he all but dramatized his own death—but here we anticipate ourselves.

Jean-Baptiste Poquelin, born in 1622, was the son of the royal carpet-maker. He received a thorough classical education, and even went on to qualify for the bar. But he preferred not to follow the family business and, rebaptizing himself "Molière," risked the uncertain life of the theater. But unlike Shakespeare, he was not sprung full-grown from the head of Dionysus. He benefited greatly from an "out of town" apprenticeship, touring the provinces for thirteen years with a group called *L'illustre théâtre,* whose prima donna was Madeleine Béjart. It goes without saying that during these long *Lehrjahre* the two were lovers.

Upon their return to Paris, the king granted Molière partial use of the Petit-Bourbon theater, which the playwright had to share with a troupe of commedia dell'arte players led by the legendary Scaramouche. Thus he was able to reinforce the lessons he learned from Tabarin, the improvisational clown from the Pont-Neuf. Critics have found many points of genuine biography in his very early skit *Elomire Hypocondre* (1670), which deals with a struggling young actor who wants to master his technique:

To hone his art of producing laughter to perfection
Guess what this clever chap does?
He goes morning and night to the great Scaramouche,
And there, holding a mirror in his hand,
Standing opposite the chief of clowns
Learns his every single expression, stance
And repeats them over and over a hundred times.

Molière's art is a brilliant synthesis of the Latin comic tradition and the more popular commedia dell'arte. But stern critics like Boileau disapproved of those of his works which, in his view, contained too much low comedy—thus echoing Aulus Gellius' opinion of the Roman comic playwrights who inserted farcical slapstick *(nescio quae mimica)* into the Greek originals.[5] The *Mischief of Scapin* was an egregious example. In the words of Boileau:

> Would he had not pandered straight to the crowd,
> And all those artistic misjudgments allowed,
> And for some cheap humour abandoned good taste
> Spoiling Terence with Tabarin—Oh what a waste!
> When Scapin hides himself in that ludicrous sack
> The *Misanthrope*'s author becomes just a hack.[6]

Perhaps it is for this quality that Molière was never accepted by the Académie Française. And yet it is wrong to assume that he only aimed at pleasing the groundlings:

> One must never forget for whom Molière principally wrote: without the court and the nobles his renown would have been rather meagre. Indeed the bourgeois spectators themselves adapted *their* tastes in emulation of the beautiful people.[7]

In 1662, at the age of forty (equivalent to at least sixty today) and in the grand tradition of the Aristophanic old man who is rejuvenated and goes off with a young pipe-girl, Molière married Armande Béjart, the daughter of his long-time mistress Madeleine. If not completely illicit, this was certainly scandalous and most definitely ill-advised. From the beginning there were malicious whisperings that Armande was actually Molière's own daughter. After all, his two-decade liaison with Madeleine makes it chronologically possible. In his *Life of Monsieur de Molière,* Mikhail Bulgakov finds some credibility to the rumor,[8] but the majority of twentieth-century scholars dismiss this unsettling and unfounded hypothesis.[9]

Yet from earliest antiquity actors have been regarded as immoral. Aulus Gellius entitled one chapter "That the passion and love of theatrical artists is shameful and reprehensible."[10] We recall from both *Acharnians* and *Wasps* that Aristophanes was not afraid to portray *erōs* between father and daughter. (A similar charge had been leveled at Alcibiades.)[11] In a curious coincidence, Woody Allen, a modern master of comedy—and depressive—has been assailed for the same outrageous behavior as that of Molière.

The early years of his marriage to Armande saw the birth and death of his first two sons and Molière's initial battle with a serious illness. Still, when they were barely newlyweds, his young wife could not suppress her sprightly inclinations and—to put it politely—put horns on her despairing husband.[12] The quantity and quality of her lovers were prodigious, and Molière's conjugal difficulties became the bane of his life—and the stuff of his comedies.

While we are not suggesting that Molière wrote psycho-dramas, it is clear that the later plays are to some extent reflections of his wretched life. By his unique genius, the playwright could transmute personal anguish into public laughter. This is most clearly evident in the three full-length theatrical works he produced in the year 1668 when, after composing more serious masterpieces like *Tartuffe* and *The Misanthrope,* his dramatic powers were at their height: *Amphitryon* (13 January, a very personalized version of the Plautine original), *George Dandin* (18 July) and *The Miser* (9 September, also based on a Plautine model). Not coincidentally, all three deal to a greater or lesser extent with the pains of cuckoldry.

To Plautus, *Amphitruo* may have been merely a mythical *tragico-comoedia,* but to Molière it was nothing less than a thinly disguised *cri du coeur.* This was not the first French adaptation of the Latin play. Earlier in the seventeenth century, Jean de Rotrou had rendered the *Amphitruo*—which he entitled *Les Sosies* (c. 1636)—from which Molière drew liberally. As with Rotrou, his text is mainly Plautine. But we shall see how Molière's subtle touches vivify the play, making it an "original" adaptation.

It was widely held that the *Amphitryon* celebrated Louis XIV's taking of Madame de Montespan as his new mistress.[13] To provide his royal audience with the masque-like splendors to which they were accustomed, the production was on a grand scale, with elaborate theatrical machines flying divinities in and out.[14]

The play begins with a Prologue scene in which Mercury, aloft on a cloud, tries to persuade Madam Night, aloft in a chariot, to hold back the dawn for Jupiter's *douce aventure* (the adjective is repeated three times—at the beginning, middle, and end of the prologue). Despite their altitude, they are having a less than celestial conversation. Night expresses her disapproval of the various animal forms—bull, serpent, swan, *ou quelque autre chose*—that Jupiter has previously employed to win the objects of his terrestrial desires. Mercury defends this practice since:

> He completely leaves his own identity
> And the man who appears is no longer Jupiter.[15]

As the familiar myth recounts, with Amphitryon's exemplary bride, Alcmène, the supreme god had to take desperate measures. The lady was so famously faithful that he could only hope to succeed if he seduced her in the guise of her own husband. This he does at the height of the couple's passion. For, in contrast to the Roman model, here Amphitryon and Alcmène are newlyweds, still basking in the glow of first love.[16]

The action of the play begins with the timorous Sosie carrying a lamp and frightened of his own shadow. He has been sent to Alcmène to report Amphitryon's glorious victory. The next scene is a considerably elaborated replica of the Plautine original. Sosie confronts his divine mirror image, and there follows a series of vaudevillian exchanges—and blows:

> SOSIE: I'm his manservant.
> MERCURY: You?
> SOSIE: Me.
> MERCURY: His manservant?

SOSIE:	Absolutely.
MERCURY:	Manservant to Amphitryon?
SOSIE:	To Amphitryon, yes him.
MERCURY:	And your name?
SOSIE:	Sosie.
MERCURY:	What's that?
SOSIE:	Sosie.[17]

As in Plautus, however, the terrestrial servant must ultimately surrender his identity: "I've got to find myself another name."[18] But Molière expands Plautus' succinct cry of anguish into Sosie's long-winded, existential *crise* (note yet another association of dream and comedy):

> I can't just annihilate myself for your sake,
> And endure a conversation so incredibly implausible.
> Have you got the power to be what *I am?*
> Can I just stop being *me?* . . .
> Am I dreaming? Am I sleeping?
> Have I been driven mad by powerful emotions?[19]

As in Shakespeare's *Comedy of Errors,* Molière has given the manservant an unappealing and cloyingly faithful wife, Cléanthis, who despite her amorous behavior is unable to get either her divine or human husband into bed. When she contrasts their situation with the passionate newlyweds, Mercury/Sosie reminds her:

> Hey, for heaven's sake, Cléanthis, they're still lovers,
> There comes a certain age when all this is done with; and
> what in the beginning suits them well enough, would
> look quite out of place in old married folks like us.[20]

This unromantic, farcical subplot stands in ironic counterpoint to the sensualities of the principal one. Cléanthis reacts to Mercury/Sosie's rejection of her amorous advances with the plea—much like that of Shakespeare's Nell, the scullery maid in *The Comedy of Errors*—"How can you find fault with me for being too virtuous?"

In the next protracted scene, Sosie tells his incredulous master that "another me" has preceded him to the house and beaten him away. Amphitryon dismisses this as another oneiric illusion:

AMPHITRYON: Is this a dream? Is it drunkenness?

Have you gone mad?

Or is this some unfunny joke?[21]

But the bondsman protests that the blows on his back are all too real. There follows a seventeenth-century version of the classic Abbott and Costello "who's on first" routine—lifted straight from Plautus:

AMPHITRYON: You've been beaten?

SOSIE: Yes I have.

AMPHITRYON: By whom?

SOSIE: By myself.

AMPHITRYON: You beat yourself?

SOSIE: Yes, *me*; not the *me* that's here, but the *me* from the house —who hits like four.[22]

Molière amplifies this comic conceit into a virtual operatic crescendo, wringing out its last drop. The superfluous repetition of a word or phrase is another instance chosen by Bergson to illustrate his theory of laughter.[23]

In the following scene, Alcmène, still aglow from last night's love-making with the disguised Jupiter, is astounded to see her husband back so soon. Amphitryon protests, and echoes a theme already introduced by ascribing his wife's impression to a nocturnal fantasy:

AMPHITRYON: In your dream last night, Alcmène, your heart
sensed what has now come true.[24]

The notion of a sleeping fantasy is mentioned no fewer than four times in the dialogue between husband and wife until Alcmène calls an end to it. Once more we have *kōma:* the comic plot as dream—in this case nightmare. The cry of madness is not far behind.[25] The Plautine scene is elaborated here, as the innocent wife describes "their" previous night together:

ALCMÈNE: We whispered a thousand loving questions to each other.
The meal was served, we dined tête-à-tête;
Then after supper we went to bed.

AMPHITRYON: Together?

ALCMÈNE: Of course, why do you ask?

AMPHITRYON: (aside) Ah, this is the most unkind cut of all,
And what my burning jealousy had feared
has turned out to be true.[26]

Events quickly turn grave. Her husband's outrage leads Alcmène to assume he wants a divorce, and she is now angry enough to be willing to give him one.

Amphitryon, certain that he has been cuckolded, is determined to prove he is in the right and goes off to find his wife's brother Naucratès to vouch that he spent the previous night in the army camp. These serious events are interrupted by an interlude between Sosie and his wife, Cléanthis. The scene is again reminiscent of Shakespeare—the confrontation between (the wrong) Dromio and Nell, his brother's unappetizing wife. At first husband and wife discuss the problems of their master. The manservant offers his earthy opinions—if he had the problem, he would prefer *not to know*. This is clearly the unheroic alternative. But it sets the difference between lord and lackey into bas-relief.[27]

Cléanthis now complains of her husband's neglect in bed the previous night—ignoring her overtures of *chaste ardeur*, and not doing "his husbandly duty." Unlike his master, Sosie is pleased with his abstinence, and offers lame excuses to continue it. Molière's subplot forms a deliberate counterpoint to the main story. Whereas the master complains of one seduction too many, the servant's wife complains of no seduction at all.

A moment later, Jupiter reappears to mollify his "wife's" anger and tries to dissuade her from breaking up their marriage. He harps on the distinction between lover and husband, arguing with a sophistry reminiscent of Aristophanic Wrong Logic that he is innocent:

JUPITER: It is the husband in me, darling, who is in the wrong;
So it's just the husband you must look on as the guilty
one.
The lover in me has no part in this harsh treatment—
My heart is totally incapable of hurting you.[28]

The great god's pettifoggery has a nasty edge. He posits two aspects of a husband—one the lover, one the spouse—and argues ironically that the two are literally divided. While Jupiter is her ardent lover, the real

Amphitryon is relegated to being merely a husband. He concludes with the ultimate irony that he (an immortal) can no longer live since her anger overwhelms him.[29] The god's eloquent pleas finally wear down the wounded Alcmène. They retire to dinner—and what would logically follow.

There follows a brief interlude of low comedy between Cléanthis and Sosie (the real one this time) in which she—in contrast to the divine characters—complains of the disadvantages of being virtuous. Alcmène "sins" unconsciously, and Cléanthis displays a simple loyalty. It is really only the gods who deliberately plan adultery. Could this be a veiled allusion to the *dolce vita* of King Louis' court?

The final act begins with a long brooding monologue by Amphitryon, who oscillates between self-pity and anger, while still desperately trying to rationalize the abomination he has seen. With deep sadness he concludes that he cannot believe his wife's excuse:

AMPHITRYON: Now and then nature creates a likeness
             Which imposters have exploited.
             But it is unimaginable that
             A man could disguise himself as someone else's husband.
             Because despite all the similarities there are a thousand
               differences
             That any wife could easily detect.[30]

His one possible hope is that this may all turn out to be illusion and witchcraft—again a parallel with Shakespeare's *Comedy of Errors*.

After these solemn ruminations, the hero has an agonizing encounter with Mercury/Sosie (they are becoming increasingly painful). The god treats him rather sadistically, claiming that the real Amphitryon is inside enjoying himself:

AMPHITRYON: What! Amphitryon is there inside?
MERCURY: Absolutely—
             Crowned with wreaths and sharing his
                Great triumph with the fair Alcmène, enjoying her and
                whispering sweet nothings. After a little lovers' quarrel
                they are enjoying all the pleasures of a reconciliation.[31]

We next find Amphitryon alone—as he has been throughout the play, both literally and metaphorically—and so disconcerted and angry that he fears he is going mad:

> AMPHITRYON: What strange blow has struck within my soul?
> What a painful deed has rocked my mind![32]

He then storms off and returns immediately with Naucratès and several other generals. They knock on the palace door. At this moment Jupiter appears at the bedroom window to complain of the noise. At the sight of this *Doppelgänger*, a dumbfounded Naucratès gasps:

> NAUCRATÈS: Ye gods, what's this uncanny sight?
> I now see two identical Amphitryons![33]

This is a moment both tragic and comic. It certainly lacks the levity of, for example, the reunion of the Menaechmus twins. Here too, Molière has literally divided Amphitryon's psyche into superego and libido, embodied respectively by Amphitryon and Jupiter. One is the dutiful husband, and the other the immoral, lascivious lover. This interpretation is substantiated by what follows. As Amphitryon lunges to kill his likeness, Naucratès restrains him—perhaps Molière's way of confronting the lacuna in the Plautine text:

> NAUCRATÈS: We can't tolerate this strange battle—
> Amphitryon against his own self.[34]

Molière here displays an astute awareness of the polarities of the masculine subconscious. Their alter egos rage as each asserts his authenticity. This combat concludes with the most famous lines of the play, Sosie's earthy epitome:

> SOSIE: The genuine Amphitryon's
> the one who pays for dinner.[35]

From this point onward, the play is entirely Molière's invention. And it hardly ends happily. As Amphitryon's slave concludes, both of them have been robbed of their own personality:

> SOSIE: O master, I am dis-a-Sosie-ated,
> Just as you've been un-Amphitryoned.[36]

This is far more serious than the traditional comic loss of face. We have here a grave identity crisis (albeit graced by some wonderful verbal inventiveness).

As the mortals stagger in confusion, Jupiter appears on a cloud, heralded by a peal of thunder. He brings Amphitryon some dubious consolation:

> JUPITER: To share a love with Jupiter
> is surely no disgrace.[37]

Rotrou's earlier treatment of the myth, following Plautus, has the hero himself stress the "honor" accorded him by the father of the gods:

> AMPHITRYON: I should complain about this glorious disgrace to my
> own honor
> To have had as my rival the ruler of the skies.
> My bed is "shared," Alcmène is unfaithful.
> Yet the insult's sweet and the shame is lovely.
> The outrage is a kindness—the rank of the seducer
> Balances disgrace with this great honor.[38]

In Molière's conclusion this sentiment is expressed not only by Jupiter but by Alcmène's brother Naucratès as well, who is flattered with the luster that Jupiter has bestowed on their family. Yet the servant's final comment is a significant departure from the Plautine original, a sort of intertextual "correction," and is spoken with unabashed candor by the pragmatic Sosie:

> SOSIE: With things like this it's always best
> to shut up and say nothing whatsoever.[39]

The bitterness of this "comedy" is emphasized by the fact that his master Amphitryon has done precisely that. During the entire final scene he has not uttered a single word. For even if having one's wife visited by the father of the gods were a credible honor for the credulous Romans, the cuckolds among Molière's audience would hardly share this reverent opinion. Some of the gentlemen may have been awarded their horns (and knighthoods) by the contemporary "Jupiter," Louis XIV.[40]

Perhaps most sad is that, while both Plautus' and Rotrou's comedies end with the birth of two boys, one fathered by Jupiter and the other by Amphitryon,[41] in Molière's play Alcmène is pregnant with only a son by Jupiter. This Amphitryon, like the playwright himself, is deprived of a son of his own. It would perhaps be too facile to read the play as merely Molière's own marital disasters clothed in mythical garb. But then again, it would be equally naive to totally ignore the unquestionable similarities. After all, were not the nobles with whom Molière's wife dallied the "gods of society," whose rank brought him as little consolation as Jupiter's does Amphitryon? Clearly, in this play, only Jupiter lives happily ever after.

⁂

George Dandin, produced in the summer of 1668, tests the limits of comedy. Indeed, it is virtually a case report on Molière's anguished state of mind.

The plot itself is conventional, surely antedating even the *Clouds,* in which the rustic Strepsiades has married above his station and lives to regret it. Molière may have based the outline of the play on a tale in Boccaccio's *Decameron,* wherein a rich businessman has married a woman of an allegedly higher rank by whom he is deceived and who, despite all his efforts to catch her *in flagrante,* succeeds in turning the tables on him.[42] Indeed, Molière had already assayed this theme himself in what is very likely his earliest extant play, *La Jalousie du Barbouillé (Mr. Barbouillé's Jealousy,* c. 1646). In fact, that farce is very much a rough sketch for the theme's full-fledged treatment in *George Dandin.* But what was formulaic in the earlier play has now acquired a certain bitter edge.

From one standpoint, *Dandin*[43] is little more than a crescendo of humiliations for the title character—played of course by Molière. (We are not certain whether Armande played Angélique, but it is a fairly safe inference.) It is a play in which the same thing happens—three times. If not Johnny-One-Note, it is certainly a single theme with two painful variations. On the surface, it looks like a sketch for the better-known *Would-Be Aristocrat (Bourgeois Gentilhomme),* produced two years later and showing much more restraint—or was it perhaps resignation?—in its characterization.

Like Monsieur Jourdain, the shameless social climber (also played by the author, with his flirtatious young wife as the flirtatious young wife), George Dandin is another socially ambitious buffoon, whose rise from the peasantry to bourgeois affluence enables him to marry the daughter of second-rate, seedy provincial gentry—to his eternal regret. Though Angélique's parents have welcomed the match, the young girl herself has other intentions—fun—and chooses to follow her fancy, leaving her stolid husband to moan. Indeed, a large part of the play consists of George's lament and self-reproach for his terrible error.

At the beginning we find "the hero" conversing with himself—he is his own friendliest interlocutor—regretting the social aspirations which brought him, who had nothing to offer but money, to this painful pass. For he has married:

> GEORGE: A wife who acts as if she's far above me, who wouldn't stoop to take my name—and thinks that all my money's not enough to purchase the great privilege of being called her husband.[44]

His concluding remarks of self-castigation set the tone for the entire play:

> GEORGE: George Dandin, George Dandin, you've committed the greatest stupidity in the world!

But his troubles are only about to begin.

He suddenly notices a man loitering outside his house. It is the simple peasant Lubin, who ingenuously confides to Dandin (whom he does not recognize) that he is delivering a *billet doux* from a "young nobleman," Clitandre, to a vivacious demoiselle:

> LUBIN: The husband, from what I hear, is jealous as hell and won't allow anyone to flirt with his wife. He would certainly go beserk if he knew about this. Now do you get me?
>
> GEORGE: *(trying to control himself)* Very well.[45]

The simple fellow further reveals that Angélique was extremely receptive to his master's approaches and is anxious to devise *quelque chose* so that they can get together. The scene ends with the discomfited protagonist once again alone on the stage, chastising himself:

GEORGE: George Dandin, look at the disdain with which your wife treats you![46]

He hurries to complain to her parents, the de Sotenvilles ("Imbeciles-in-Town"), pompous—yet shrewd and sly—aristocrats. They pretend to be sympathetic, but in fact cannot conceal their disdain for George's lowly social status. They constantly criticize his manners and will not permit him to address them as "father-in-law" and "mother-in-law," but insist on "Madame" and "Monsieur." They even go so far as to forbid him to refer to their daughter as his "wife." This is the last straw, and Dandin explodes:

GEORGE: What? My own wife is not my wife?

MME DE S.: *(condescendingly)* Of course, son-in-law, she is your wife. But you have no right to call her that. For after all is said and done, you haven't married one of your own social class.[47]

They constantly remind him of the *grands avantages* he has received from marrying into their exalted family. To which the hero can only retort with his peasant bluntness:

GEORGE: And what advantages, Madam—since "Madam" is the way I must address you? This hasn't exactly been a bad bargain for you folks. For, with due respect, until I came along your own finances were in pretty shoddy shape and my cash helped to patch up quite a few hefty holes . . .[48]

He is no longer even pacified by the thought that his children with Angélique will be aristocrats. He treats this "advantage" with new cynicism:

GEORGE: *(sarcastically)* Oh! that's really wonderful, my kids will be noblemen. But I'll be a cuckold if I don't set things straight.[49]

With the proper nomenclature at last established, Dandin lodges his complaint against their daughter (we dare not refer to her as his wife). He reports that Angélique is "flirting" with a blade called Clitandre—and, if immediate action is not taken, he will be cuckolded. The parents protest that their daughter would never do such a thing. She is too full of "honor," a word repeated almost as often—and with the same irony—as in the *Country Wife*.

In the following scene, Monsieur de Sotenville and his son-in-law accost the nobleman in question. Clitandre of course protests his innocence—his high rank does not admit of such low behavior.

In the plenary session which follows, we meet the lovely Angélique for the first time, as she enters with her saucy maid. In the presence of her parents and her would-be lover, she protests her innocence, scolding the young man (with a wink), and forbidding him—even for the fun of it *(par plaisir)*—to send her messages or write little love letters. If he dares to do so, she says ironically, he will see how she responds:

> ANGÉLIQUE: All you have to do is come here, and I assure you, good
> sir, you will be received in the manner you deserve.[50]

In but a few moments she will storm off, indignant at her husband's accusations.

Not for the last time, the tables turn on George Dandin. Madame de Sotenville upbraids him:

> MME DE S.: Come now, you are not worthy of the virtuous wife that
> we've granted you.[51]

At this Clitandre protests that his "honor" has also been impugned. Monsieur de Sotenville explains to the spluttering husband that a nobleman's word is sacrosanct. To which Dandin retorts:

> GEORGE: You mean if I discovered him in bed with my wife he
> could get away with it by simply denying it?[52]

That remark is not even worthy of a response. Tired of this punctilious attitude, his father-in-law demands that George apologize to Clitandre, reminding him that "this man is a gentleman and you're not."[53] To which Dandin mutters, not for the last time, "j'enrage." As in *Amphitryon*, we see the in-laws refusing to acknowledge the disgrace of a husband's cuckoldry. Crestfallen and defeated, George reluctantly repeats the words of apology his stepfather dictates, begging Clitandre's pardon for even suspecting him.

The act concludes with George once again alone on stage, sputtering and castigating himself:

> GEORGE: You brought it on yourself, you brought it on yourself, George Dandin, you really brought it on yourself. And it serves you right. They've really put you in your place. You've got exactly what you asked for.[54]

He vows to have his revenge—but the audience has little doubt that he will never get it.

Act Two brings further frustration and humiliation to the hapless hero. We find George scolding Angélique for acting so flirtatiously. He demands that she show him some respect and behave like a wife. Her retort, skillfully manipulating a "feminist" argument, is not wholly without merit—criticizing the *mores* of the time, when marriage was arranged without considering the feelings of the bride herself. Here, as elsewhere, she protests that she "has no intention of renouncing the world—and lie down in a coffin while I am still alive."

> ANGÉLIQUE: What! Just because a man deigns to marry us, does that mean everything else in the world is all over for us? And that we break all contact with the human race? The tyranny of husbands is incredible—it's very considerate of them to wish us dead to all joys, and live only for them. I say to hell with that. Get ready for your punishment![55]

Angélique's argument has a curiously modern ring to it, and reflects the dilemma of seventeenth-century young women:

> ANGÉLIQUE: Did you ask about my feelings before we got married? Or find out if I loved you at all? No, you only asked my mother and father. The fact is *they* really married *you!*[56]

It would not be surprising to find Molière unsympathetic to this feminist cause *avant la lettre*, yet he cannot restrain his urge to speak truthfully. Angélique evokes a certain sympathy—especially among the female spectators.

On the verge of exploding again, George rushes out. Later—in a direct adaptation of *The Jealousy of Barbouillé*—he discovers the young lovers together when peeking through the keyhole of his own front door, and exults:

> GEORGE: Ye gods! There's absolutely no doubt now. I've just spied
> them through the keyhole. Fate has given me a chance to
> foil my enemy completely![57]

Once again Monsieur and Madame de Sotenville are fetched to see their daughter caught *in flagrante*. They arrive to find Clitandre taking leave of Angélique. But the young couple put on a farce in which Angélique pretends to be outraged at Clitandre's advances and in a "rage" beats the young man with a stick. By some curious stroke of fate her blows land on her husband instead, who is hiding in the bushes.

Dandin's "proof" has once again turned against him, and his wife's parents depart in a huff. Could he possibly be any more humiliated than this? The answer is yes. The final act culminates in a farcical night scene which anticipates the nocturnal antics in Beaumarchais' (or Mozart's) *The Marriage of Figaro*. In the darkness the characters mistake the obscured figures for the wrong people. Somehow George manages to trap Angélique and Clitandre together in the garden, and once more sends for his in-laws. At first the "victorious" Dandin gloats at his foiled wife and refuses all pleas to admit her to the house:

> GEORGE: No, no, no. I want your parents to see what a bitch you
> really are, and expose your deceit to the world.[58]

But when his frantic wife threatens to kill herself *à la* Lucretia, the worried Dandin rushes out with a candle to see what has happened—during which time Angélique and her maid rush into the house and immediately lock *him* out. Thus, when her parents arrive once more (this time in their nightshirts), it is their daughter who complains about the roistering behavior of her husband.

Can things possibly get any worse for George Dandin? They can. The de Sotenvilles insist that he apologize to his wife on his knees. This he does, painfully begging her forgiveness and promising to "behave himself from now on."

The play concludes with George Dandin now totally defeated and once again alone with the audience, whom he warns to learn from his devasting experience:

> GEORGE: I give up, there is nothing more I can do about it. *(to the spectators)* You see, when you've married such a heartless woman like mine, the best thing you can do is throw yourself into the water—head first.[59]

This is hardly the traditional comic conclusion. On the contrary, we are certain that George will live *un*happily ever after. For while the divorce which he dearly longs for existed at the time,[60] her parents will not hear of it: it would stain their escutcheon—and sever them from Dandin's money.

The plot of *George Dandin*—such as it is—is hardly original. Indeed, cuckoldry was already a staple of the Roman mime and continued to flourish at least through Feydeau with his widely popular farces. Ironically, comedies tend to deal with either the joys of love or the pains of marriage. Yet Molière's play was not a mere exercise in a familiar genre. The parallels to his own marriage are too glaring—and the pain of the hero too palpable. There were many "Clitandres" in Madame Molière's life, and the playwright must have endured even more than George Dandin.

❧

But it was Molière's third production of 1668 that was destined to become one of the most popular plays in theatrical history. Harpagon ("Mr. Grasper"), the title character of *The Miser (L'Avare),* is the oldest father in all of Molière's comedies: sixty was an extremely advanced age for that time, the equivalent nowadays of eighty. Like the playwright, he had "heard the chimes at midnight." As usual in Molière, there is a double plot, united by the miser's compulsion to hold onto his money by interfering with both his son's and daughter's love affairs to control their futures. It is both a comedy of intrigue and a fantasy of recognition.[61]

The first act is almost completely exposition. We find Élise, the miser's daughter, and her paramour Valère expressing their love for each other in language that parodies contemporary sentimental novels. Only she knows that he has concealed his true rank as a gentlemen and "reduced himself" to become a lowly valet in her father's house just to be near her. The young man, who has recently risked his life to rescue Élise in a storm at sea, hopes that he can gain some proof of his real social rank by locating his parents—although he fears they may have drowned in a shipwreck years ago.

We next have a dialogue between Élise and her brother Cléante. He sums up his problem in a single word: *J'aime*. He is in love with young Mariane, who "shines with a thousand graces in everything she does," but whom he cannot woo properly because of his dire financial straits:

> CLÉANTE: Because of father's stinginess there's absolutely no way I can do it. I am thwarted from tasting the joy of trumpeting to my beloved any evidence of my love.[62]

Furthermore, he has already revealed that his beloved is without resource or social position—just a nice girl who lives with her widowed mother. And yet she has "a tenderness which would touch your soul." Much will be made in the play of the double meaning of the verb *toucher* ("to touch"), which can also be construed as getting money from someone. Just then, they hear the sound of their father's voice—and brother and sister quickly retreat from the stage.

With our appetite whetted by the extravagant complaints of his children, Harpagon finally appears. As always, he is carrying his monomania with him—the obsessive fear of being robbed. The intensity of his obsession all but animates his pot of gold. True to comic convention, his paranoia is pathological: for in Frye's construct, the typical beginning of comedy finds society in the bondage of humorless characters.[63] His anxiety justifies the later comment of one of his servants:

> LA FLÈCHE: Our Master Harpagon is of all humans the least humane human—the most hard-hearted and the most tight-fisted.[64]

Harpagon is even inhuman in the treatment of his horses. His stinginess will not allow him to feed them, and they are too weak to stand. To laugh at this requires more Bergsonian anesthesia of the heart than most modern audiences can muster.[65] Their sentiments are more those of Maître Jacques, who criticizes the "fast days" his master imposes on the beasts:

MAÎTRE JACQUES: A man would be pretty cold-hearted, sir, to have no pity for his fellow creatures.[66]

As we will see, this same attitude is displayed by Jarry's King Ubu, whose horses cannot bear his weight because they have not been fed for five days.

Harpagon is suffering from a typical Menandrian personality disorder. Like Knemon in the *Dyskolos,* he too is an "absolutely inhuman human."[67] Harpagon feels but one emotion: greed. Like a Bergsonian machine, he can compute interest to the minutest decimal point without the benefit of a pocket calculator. Yet he is so drastically twisted that:

LA FLÈCHE: "To give" is a word that so sickens him he never says "I give you" but "I *lend* you a good morning."[68]

He is constantly interrupting conversations to rush offstage to make sure his money is still there—a classic example of Bergson's "Jack-in-the-box" theory of laughter.[69] It is comic self-ignorance, for he cannot control his own thoughts nor his actions. When La Flèche curses "miserliness and all misers," Harpagon asks quite ingenuously, "about whom are you talking, pray tell?" And in his mad obsession he reveals the very fact he is trying to hide. For the more he tries to convince La Flèche that he has not concealed any valuables anywhere, the more the lackey begins to think that he has. Worse still, Harpagon's manic searching of his servant's clothing awakens the desire for revenge for this treatment:

LA FLÈCHE: A man like this deserves to get exactly what he's scared of and I'd have a lot of satisfaction out of robbing him![70]

At the beginning of Scene Four, Harpagon reveals the magnitude of the fortune he has buried in the garden. The monomaniacal miser suspects everything—even inanimate objects:

> HARPAGON: I don't trust strongboxes—they're always the first thing
> burglars go for. It is a real enticement to them. Still, I
> don't know if I was right to bury in the garden the ten
> thousand golden écus someone sent me yesterday.[71]

When his son and daughter arrive to discuss their plans for marriage, Harpagon is so paranoid that he thinks they have overheard him talking about his buried treasure—and reflectively fears the worst:

> HARPAGON: Isn't this unnatural—my own children are betraying me
> and have become my enemies?[72]

He even goes so far as to think that they are going to murder him. Of course there is a psychological truth to this—at least as far as the son is concerned.

What Ovid said of Menander is no less true of Molière: he writes no play without romance. And so to the Plautine character of the miser he adds the equally Plautine *senex amator*. Thus to the children's surprise, before either can broach the subject of matrimony, Harpagon stuns them by making a wholly unexpected announcement.

Their dialogue conforms to Immanuel Kant's theory of laughter as arising from "a strained expectation leading to nothing."[73] The old man casually asks his children:

> HARPAGON: Have you, pray tell, come across a young lady named
> Mariane who lives not far from here?
> CLÉANTE: (*eagerly*) Yes father.
> HARPAGON: (*to Élise*) And you?
> ÉLISE: (*warily*) I think I've heard of her.[74]

The miser leads his son along with ambiguous questions about the young girl's looks and demeanor. Cléante, thinking he is discussing the qualities of his own future bride, testifies enthusiastically to Mariane's virtues. When the gambit reaches its climax, Harpagon drops the bombshell:

> HARPAGON: I'm keen on marrying her—as long as I find something of
> real value among her other values.
> CLÉANTE: (*astounded*) What?
> HARPAGON: What what?

CLÉANTE: Did you say *you're* keen?

HARPAGON: *(nodding)*—to marry Mariane.

CLÉANTE: What, you, *you!?*

HARPAGON: Yes, me, me, *me!*[75]

The audience would realize the double meaning in Harpagon's resolution to wed the impoverished Mariane: to seek something *bien* refers to the young girl's net worth as well as spiritual values.

Cléante is indeed beset with problems: he and his father are now rivals for the same girl.[76] We have already seen this theme in classical antiquity (recall Plautus' *Casina*), but in Molière this normally conventional Oedipal rivalry strikes a special chord. Did the playwright see himself in the elderly Harpagon—the role *he played*—foolishly marrying a girl young enough to be his own daughter? The notion should not be dismissed out of hand.

Yet the miser has further shocks for his children. He reveals that he has arranged a match for Cléante "with a certain widow." And as for Élise:

HARPAGON: Yes, a mature man, careful and wise, scarcely more than fifty years old—and said to have a massive fortune.[77]

Both son and daughter are outraged at these unnatural proposals. But Harpagon ignores their protestations, and the scene ends with the miser's firm belief that "it's all settled."[78]

Valère, the newly hired "manservant" and Élise's secret lover, then tries to reason with the old man, who retorts that his daughter's future husband is especially attractive because he is willing to take her *sans dot,* "without a dowry." This is one of Molière's more famous *mots de caractère*—words or phrases repeated again and again, which define in a nutshell the character's personality—and it certainly epitomizes Harpagon, who repeats it with mechanical Bergsonian regularity.

At the end of this seemingly endless reiteration, Valère cannot keep from commenting sarcastically:

VALÈRE: Yes, money is the most precious thing in the world, and you should thank the Lord for bestowing on you such a wonderful father. He knows what it's all about. When a man offers to accept a young woman "without dowry," that act epitomizes everything: it supersedes any consideration of beauty, youth, birth, honor, wisdom, or decency.[79]

Not surprisingly, Harpagon compliments his valet for agreeing to the *sans dot* style of matrimony.

Cléante, the desperate lover, now seeks advice from La Flèche about how to stop his father from marrying his beloved. The latter-day "clever slave" is astounded that Harpagon could actually feel love for another person, but has arranged with a shady money-lender to advance Cléante the necessary means to continue his suit for Mariane. The anonymous lender's rates are exorbitant *(Quel juif, quel Arabe!)* and the young man bemoans the fact that his father's stinginess has brought him to this pass:

> CLÉANTE: What else do you want me to do about it? Now you see the extremes that young men are driven to by the avarice of their fathers. Is it any wonder their children wish them dead?[80]

This very Plautine allusion to parricide is not a chance one. Montaigne has apposite observations about the miserliness of fathers, who characteristically hold tenaciously to their wealth until their sons entertain murderous thoughts.[81] We recall from Ovid that such sentiments began in the iron age with the introduction of money—the poet calls gold more corrupting than iron.[82] Charles Mauron goes as far as to remark that

> *The Miser* is without question the comedy which comes closest to the original Oedipus myth because the son, not satisfied with coveting the young lady that his father is going to marry, wishes almost openly for the death of the old man.[83]

The notion of a mortal battle between father and son is repeated in the next scene when the usurer tells Harpagon, who is actually the mysterious money-lender, that the borrower he has found is certain to be able to repay the loan very soon. For the young man's father will certainly be dead within eight months at most, and *then* he will have lots of cash.

Then in a bitter mini-*cognitio,* father and son suddenly realize that they are lender and desperate borrower respectively:

> HARPAGON: Ah, it's *you,* you wretched boy. Have you stooped to such despicable behavior?
>
> CLÉANTE: Ah, so it's *you,* father. Have you stooped to such unsavory business?[84]

Molière doubtless knew a similar scene in Plautus' *Mercator* (*The Merchant*), where father and son bargain for a girl, each on behalf of a "friend":

> DEMIPHO: Wait—*a certain older man's* commissioned *me*
> To buy a girl of just her type.
>
> CHARINUS: But father—*a certain younger man's* commissioned *me* to buy this very type of girl for him![85]

There is no need to say that in *The Miser,* after the unfortunate Oedipal confrontation between father and son, the deal is off. In fact, Cléante now has an additional reason for wishing his father dead—not only has Harpagon denied his son the money he needs, but he now intends to deny him the girl as well.

Act Two, Scene Five teems with financial references, with several puns on the pecuniary connotations of the verb *toucher.* Though he knows the girl is practically penniless, Harpagon nonetheless seeks reassurance from the sleazy matchmaker Frosine that, in addition to the girl, he will "get something tangible":

> HARPAGON: Frosine, have you had a business meeting with the mother concerning *(touchant)* what dowry she can give to her daughter for the wedding? Have you told her that it is very important that she gives us a helping hand, that she makes an effort, that she really squeezes herself for an occasion like this. After all, no one marries a woman unless she brings him a real asset.[86]

To this Frosine responds with sophistical arithmetic worthy of the Spanish bawd Celestina. The girl can guarantee him an annual income of twelve thousand *livres*. For she eats only simple foods like apples and cheese—a saving of three thousand right there. Nor does she like jewelry, fancy clothes, or antiques—another four thousand. And, unlike most women, she hates gambling—five thousand at least. And so on.

But Harpagon is not fooled by this Wrong Logic, astutely noting that "I am not going to write a receipt for something I don't receive." He encapsulates his whole philosophy of life with "It's an absolute condition that I get something tangible *(il faut bien que je touche quelque chose).*" And yet with a straight face Frosine asserts that the girl may someday come into money—a tantalizing and ironic hint of an ultimately happy outcome.

Passing to a more personal topic, Harpagon voices his anxiety that he might be too old for Mariane. Once again Frosine allays the miser's fears. Unlike ordinary girls, Mariane's walls are not decorated with posters of Adonis or Apollo. On the contrary, his bride-to-be has hung portraits of such worthy mythological senior citizens as Saturn, old King Priam, and the ancient Nestor. Nor need he fear any young rivals, since he himself will live to be one hundred and twenty:

> FROSINE: Why, you'll bury your children—and your childrens' children![87]

She is feeding Harpagon's ego by suggesting that he will triumph in the Oedipal battle, reversing the natural order to outlive both his son and his grandsons. This ultimately echoes Philocleon's promise in the *Wasps* to the pipe-girl ("Miss Piggy") that "when my son dies I'll purchase you and free you and make you my official mistress."[88]

Harpagon is not even in good health, yet Frosine continues to play to the miser's *alazoneia*, even complimenting him: "you have a charming cough" (this was not acting, it was Molière's own). At last he determines to pay a visit to the object of his affections, ornately dressed with huge spectacles ("the better to see your beauty, my dear"). The lovely Mariane, of course, is mortified at first sight. Is this her cruel destiny? *(Ah! Frosine, quelle figure!)* It will come as no surprise to learn that Harpagon avoids paying the matchmaker.

Thus, at the end of Act Three, all is in crisis. Poor Élise is about to marry the doddering (she imagines) Seigneur Anselme, Mariane is doomed to become the stepmother of her lover, and he is betrothed to an ancient widow. And still more trouble is brewing. Early in Act Four, Harpagon catches sight of his son being rather friendly with Mariane and murmurs with concern:

> HARPAGON: What's this? My son kissing the hand of his future step-
>   mother? And his future stepmother barely protesting! Is
>   there something fishy going on?[89]

The canny miser demands an explanation, and shows his shrewdness in searching out Cléante's true feelings. When the naive lad is tricked into revealing his affection for his father's fiancée, the miser erupts:

> HARPAGON: What's this, you criminal? You have the gall to go poach-
>   ing on my territory![90]

By the end of Act Four the Oedipal situation approaches the tragic: Harpagon abandons, disinherits, and curses Cléante. Rousseau was scandalized by this scene. But not by Harpagon's behavior, rather the *son's*![91] Matters cannot get any worse—which is the cue for the comic solution.

The servant La Flèche rushes in and tells Cléante that he has discovered—and stolen—his father's treasure. There follows one of the most famous scenes in French dramatic literature. Once again we find Molière elaborating a Plautine model, this time Plautus' *Aulularia (The Pot of Gold),* where the miser Euclio loses his mind when he discovers that someone has made off with his hoard. Molière has developed this into a bravura piece—for himself, of course. This celebrated aria contains almost every possible comic device, and is so brilliant that it bears examining at length. Harpagon enters, frantic, and calls for justice against the "robber—murderer—killer":

> HARPAGON: I'm killed, I'm finished, I'm assassinated!
>   My throat's been slit—someone's stolen my money![92]

His paranoia reaches a new height. Who could have been the villain? Where should he run? Where should he not run? Desperately looking everywhere, he gets hold of someone's arm and snarls: "Give me back my money, you rogue!" He then realizes that the limb he has attacked is his *own* arm. This is true comic self-ignorance: the inability to control one's own physical movements is one of the prime Bergsonian characteristics. It has a memorable modern analogue in the "Nazi" arm of Dr. Strangelove, which, although the rest of him is working for the U.S. Government, cannot keep from raising itself in the *Sieg Heil* salute of his former employers.

Harpagon finally realizes what he has done and lets go of his "prisoner," explaining to no one in particular that he had made his mistake because he is terribly distressed. The miser's affection seems to animate his buried treasure. Here he cries out like a parent who has lost a child:

> HARPAGON: Oh woe is me, woe is me! My money, my poor lovely
> money, my dearest friend. They've separated us forever . . .
> It's all over for me, I have nothing left in this world. I
> can't live without you.[93]

He now protests that he is already dead and, breaking the dramatic illusion, pleads with the audience (whom he also suspects): "Isn't there anyone here who wants to bring me back to life?" It is nothing less than a perversion of the traditional comic longing for rebirth.

His frenzy and irrationality increase still further. He demands that the police come and interrogate his whole household—"the maids, the valets, my son, my daughter and even *me!*" When still none of the spectators react with anything but laughter, the miser once again invokes all manner of law officers, voicing the ultimate threat:

> HARPAGON: I want everyone in the world to be hanged! and
> If I still don't find my money the I'll hang *myself!*[94]

His ravings again and again show Bergsonian ignorance of self. He has no idea how irrationally he is acting, and is not even aware that he is condemning himself to death. He remains at this lunatic level even in the next scene, where he demands that the chief of police put the entire force on the case:

> OFFICER: Whom do you suspect of this robbery?
> HARPAGON: Everybody! I want you to take the entire city prisoner—
> including the suburbs![95]

A man possessed, the miser also continues the investigation on his own. He turns on the ingenuous Valère—highly suspect as a new employee—and demands that the youth reveal his "crime." There follows a typical Molièresque *quiproquo*—a dialogue in which the speakers think they are discussing the same subject whereas they are actually alluding to two different things.[96] The scene was directly inspired by a parallel misunderstanding in the *Pot of Gold*,[97] but is especially propitious in the French where "pot" and "lady" can both be referred to by the feminine pronoun *elle:*

> VALÈRE: A treasure indeed, and beyond question the most precious thing you have, but not lost to you in becoming mine. I beg you on bended knees to grant me this most cherished of treasures. Surely you can't refuse your consent.[98]

When Harpagon demands that Valère return the treasure he has stolen, the naive young man replies:

> VALÈRE: Me! I didn't take [her] off anywhere. She's still at your house.
> HARPAGON: *(aside)* Oh, my beloved treasure! *(then to Valère)* Not left the house, you say?
> VALÈRE: No Sir.[99]

Harpagon remains monomaniacal even when Valère's declarations become more and more explicit. When the lover protests that his motive is "the passion inspired by her beautiful eyes," Harpagon is confused:

> HARPAGON: My money pot's "beautiful eyes?" The man speaks like a lover speaking of his mistress![100]

At last Valère makes it crystal-clear that the *elle* he is talking about is the miser's *daughter,* and officially announces their engagement. Harpagon's reaction is Vesuvian.

But just as things reach this desperate pass, Molière saves the day with a splendid *deus ex machina* in the person of Seigneur Anselme, his daughter's mature fiancé. Harpagon is delighted to see him: "you're just in time to see the arrest of this criminal who lied his way into my empiry to steal my money and seduce my daughter." Valère is astonished: "why are you making all this fuss—what could I possibly want with your money?" As Harpagon orders the constable to arrest and charge Valère, the young man insists:

> VALÈRE: I don't see how you can accuse me of any crime except the passion I feel for your daughter. The only punishment that you may think I deserve is for making her my fiancée. *(portentiously)* When everybody finds out who I really am—
> HARPAGON: I don't give a damn about any of your fairy tales. Nowadays the world is full of phony noblemen.[101]

But a splendid *cognitio* is in the offing when Valère reveals his true identity:

> VALÈRE: I have too much integrity to pretend to be something I'm not. All of Naples can attest to my birth.[102]

Anselme warns the young man to be careful, for he too is well acquainted with the crème de la crème of that city. "If you know Naples," Valère retorts, "then you must know the late Thomas d'Alburcy." To which Anselme replies, "no one knows him better than I." Harpagon, who is dying to retrieve his money, snaps: "I don't give a damn about any dom Thomas or dom Martin."

And then Anselme drops the bombshell of the traditional—but here politically updated—shipwreck scenario:

> ANSELME: This shameless impudence is unbelievable. Learn to your dismay that sixteen years ago the man you speak of perished at sea along with his wife and children. They were escaping the persecutions and disorders that so afflicted Naples at that time and forced so many noble families into exile.[103]

Valère now reveals that he too was in a shipwreck, but was saved by a Spanish vessel whose captain raised him. Having heard rumors lately that his father did not perish after all, he has come here in search of him. Naturally Anselme is dubious: does he have any evidence? Of course he does. Valère produces the traditional New Comedy trinkets (gnōrismata): an agate bracelet which his mother had placed on his arm, and a signet ring which belonged to his father.

And then a further surprise. (Or is it?) Moments later, Mariane, the miser's "fiancée," suddenly cries out, "Oh my god—you're my long-lost brother!" She quickly recounts that neither she nor her mother died in the shipwreck but were saved by a pirate vessel. After ten years of servitude the two women managed to escape and make their way to the place he now finds them.

Anselme is overcome with joy and offers the last surprise:

> ANSELME: Well, for your information, *I* am Dom Thomas d'Alburcy whom Heaven also protected against the waves, along with *all the money I was carrying.* I thought you were all dead and so after mourning for years, I decided to see if I could find happiness with someone sweet and clever in a second marriage.[104]

As in the *Comedy of Errors,* two young couples as well as their *parents* are "undrowned." For Mariane has already told us that her grieving mother is still at home. Thus she and Anselme—or is it dom Thomas?—will be reunited as well.

The conclusion is both typical and atypical. On the one hand it is firmly in the tradition of Menander's *Dyskolos,* which ends with a double wedding—when even the grouch of the title is forcibly carried into the festivities. But here in Molière there is no change in the character or status of the curmudgeon. As everybody goes off to a festive reunion dinner, Harpagon remains on stage—a loner—outside the circle of humanity. His monomania is undiminished, and he embraces the only thing he loves in life: *ma chère cassette.* An unregenerate agelast, he is incapable of enjoying the *kōmos.*

Significantly, none of the three plays that Molière produced in the year 1668 end like conventional comedies. *Amphitryon* concludes with the hero in an altogether unsatisfactory state. His absolute silence suggests that he can never be reconciled with his wife. There is none of the restored *antiqua gratia* that Plautus' Jupiter promises to bestow, and no kōmos of mutual forgiveness. Likewise, *George Dandin* ends with the humiliated cuckold, trapped forever in a painful marriage. The curtain falls with George on his knees, humbly begging forgiveness of his wife's pretentious family—a position he will doubtless stay in for the rest of his life. Of the trio of plays, *The Miser* seems closest to Northrop Frye's definition of the traditional comic ending, the "reintegration of society." But it too ends on a bitter note, for, like Malvolio, Harpagon is not persuaded to join the dance.

This is not to argue that the theme of cuckoldry and jealousy was exclusively the product of Molière's unhappy marriage. There was ample precedent in French literature, notably Rabelais' *Tiers Livre*, which abounds in "horning," and before that the medieval *fabliaux*, which "swarm with cuckolds."[105]

In fact, the subject is almost as old as comedy itself and was depicted in some of Molière's plays that antedate his marriage. In *La Jalousie du Barbouillé* we find many of the same elements that reappear in *George Dandin* (although more acerbic in the latter): the blatantly cheating wife who is discovered, and the old vaudeville trick of he-locks-her-out, she threatens suicide, he goes out to save her, and then she-locks-*him*-out—and then complains to her father, who rushes onto the scene, that her husband is an unreliable drunk.

Although still working in a conventional mode, Molière already betrays symptoms of what would become his obsession as early as 1660 in *Sganarelle (The Imaginary Cuckold)*. In what was to become the most successful play in the playwright's lifetime,[106] we find the hero lamenting:

> Oh it's much too lucky to have such a beautiful wife,
> But how unlucky to have this terrible disgrace!
> Their flagrant affair is now all-too-confirmed—
> She's cuckoldized me without shame—not even half a drop.[107]

But in the end Sganarelle's worst expectations turn out *not* to be true. He expresses the moral of the play in the admonitory epilogue:

> Has anyone ever thought himself more a cuckold than I?
> But now you see it is a fact that the most powerful appearance

Can throw a false belief into a soul.
Keep this example well in mind,
And even when you think you've seen *everything*, make yourself
   believe you've not seen *anything!*[108]

Sadly, Molière was not as lucky as the character he portrayed. Even on the eve of his marriage to Armande, we sense a change in his approach to this traditional theme. Is it mere coincidence that in *L'École des maris (School for Husbands)*, produced in 1661 six months before their marriage, we find a reversal of the May-December paradigm? For here spring does not triumph over winter, but vice versa. The old man gets the girl (shades of Aristophanes!) In his depiction of the heroine's preference for an older suitor—played by Molière, of course—do we not sense the playwright's own fantasy? As Léonor states in rejecting the offers of more "suitable" suitors:

> I prefer the enthusiasm of a mature man like this
>   to all the fancy and amorous effusions of a younger suitor.[109]

But as the playwright's marriage began to near the rocks—which was almost immediately—we see in his comedies an obsession with cuckoldry that grows more pathological with every play. He was evoking laughter on the topic which caused him the greatest pain.

Molière's final play was *The Imaginary Invalid*, praised by Gide as "the freshest, most enduring and most beautiful" of all Molière's great comedies.[110] It presents an old man who, like Harpagon, suffers from a monomania. In this case he is afflicted with a persistent hypochondria which so consumes him that he will not allow his daughter to marry anyone but a doctor. This is truly a comedy of humors in the Jonsonian sense, for until the eighteenth century "hypochondria" was regarded as a real condition—just as *melancholia*, according to the theory of the four humors, was regarded as an excess of black bile. Ever the professional, Molière incorporated his now-worsening cough, which he had used to such advantage in *The Miser*, as part of his characterization of Argan, the imaginary invalid.

The play, which is hilariously funny, ends with a symbolic death and rebirth. To test the fidelity of his second wife, Argan pretends to die and asks 'Toinette—perhaps the most versatile and charming of Molière's scheming servants—played by Armande, of course—to announce to everyone that he is dead at last. His would-be widow rushes in, sees 'Toinette weeping melodramatically over Argan's body, and chastises her:

> BÉLINE: O cut out those tears 'Toinette—he's not worth the trouble. What loss is he to anyone but himself? What good was he doing on earth? A man who annoyed the whole world—dirty, disgusting, always needing an enema or dose of something in his belly. Always blowing his nose or coughing or spitting. A bad-tempered, tiresome bore— scolding the servants day and night.[111]

At this eulogy, Argan "resurrects" himself, having now discovered his wife's true feelings. The test proved so revealing that 'Toinette suggests they try the same charade on his daughter. The hero once again plays dead and discovers to his delight that his daughter is truly heartbroken. She even tells her fiancé that at this moment her sadness prevents her from marrying him. Kneeling down to beg her father's forgiveness, she is surprised and delighted to see him "revive." The ending may be described by Oscar Wilde's famous definition: "the good end happily and the bad unhappily. That is what fiction means."[112]

In this play the hero suffers from a mania which—unlike Harpagon's—is indulged in the end, when he himself is persuaded to become a doctor. And unlike the miser, who absents himself from felicity and is left cold and alone, Argan joins everyone in a concluding dance of celebration. One wonders if any of the spectators of Molière's time could read in the playwright's face the painful feelings stirring in his heart.

Of course, the finale to *The Imaginary Invalid* was all wishful thinking on Molière's part. Armande—young enough to be his daughter—would more likely have reacted like Argan's heartless wife rather than his faithful daughter. In fact, the night Molière collapsed on stage, Armande had already left to go home (perhaps during the concluding "ballet of physicians"). Like a true man of the theater, Molière, though in terrible pain, had insisted upon going on with the performance to assure his actors' salary.

He ended his life by exiting from the stage and going straight to his deathbed. He was past any possible medical remedy, and near the end he began to hallucinate—about his wife's lovers. And yet it is said that as he died, Armande embraced him "with an affection that she had never shown before." Thus ended a painful life which still lives on in laughter.

19

The Fox, the Fops, and the Factotum

> Comic writers start by making certain devastating assump-
> tions about human nature, by questioning every man's hon-
> esty and every woman's virtue, even though they seldom
> push them to such drastic conclusions as *Mandragola, The
> Country Wife . . .* or *Volpone.*
>
> HARRY LEVIN, *Grounds for Comparison*

He was the Elizabethan equivalent of an angry young man. His comedy evoked the characteristically aggressive laughter of its age—what
Hobbes referred to as "sudden glory."[1] No one ever called Ben Jonson
"sweet" or "gentle"—his contemporaries' two favorite epithets for
Shakespeare, which even Jonson himself used (at least twice) to describe the Bard.[2] The best praise his contemporaries could muster for
Jonson seems to have been the epithet "learned," bestowed upon him
by the likes of Drayton and Milton.[3]

Yet he wore his learning heavily. Samuel Johnson referred to "His
studious patience and laborious art."[4] Dryden described Jonson as "a
learned plagiary of all classical authors."[5] And no less a cerebral play-

wright than George Bernard Shaw referred to Jonson as "a brutal pedant."

Edmund Wilson related the playwright's anal eroticism to that of his heroes—as well as his own excessive demonstration of learning.[6] The syndrome, characterized by compulsive orderliness, may in extreme cases take the form of pedantry, parsimony leading to avarice, and obstinacy leading to irascibility and vindictiveness. According to Wilson, this bifurcated Jonson's muse into vulgarity for the vulgar, and learning for the learned—hardly reconcilable opposites. And yet the evidence is there, as for example in Morose's dour statement: "I should always collect, and contain my mind, so suffering it to flow loosely." And the plays of Jonson are filled with innumerable references to matters scatological.[7]

As much by nature as design, his artistic temperament contrasted strongly with that of his more famous contemporary. This can be best seen in a comparison of their respective "transvestite" comedies. Shakespeare's *Two Gentlemen of Verona, As You Like It,* and of course *Twelfth Night* were light and airy, always concluding with a joyful *gamos* and a promise of happily ever after. Yet how different was Jonson's treatment of the same theme in 1609, when he produced *Epicoene*—whose very title ("sexless") bespeaks the playwright's harsh and unsentimental approach to the theme pioneered on the English stage by the genteel John Lyly. (The fact that Dryden regarded this as the playwright's best comedy says more about Dryden than it does about Jonson.)

It goes without saying that Jonson's brittle version of this theme is in complete contrast to Shakespeare's damsels in disguise. Whereas Viola ultimately "uncases" her masculine disguise to reveal that she is of the appropriate gender to marry her beloved Orsino, Morose, a bad-tempered old man obsessed with noise of all sorts, is finally persuaded to marry. He chooses a wife with a reputation for silence and yet, by comic irony, she turns out to be quite the opposite, an interminable babbler. Morose is so discomfited that he pleads with his "friends" to get him divorced. These cruel pranksters then dress up as judge and barrister and proceed to torture the old fellow even further with pedantic, incomprehensible Latin, searching for *duodecim impedimenta*—the classic twelve grounds for divorce. Morose is in torment and finally confesses to everyone:

> I am no man . . . utterly unabled in nature, by reason of frigidity to perform the duties, or in any way the least office of a husband.[8]

As if he were not already sufficiently shamed, his acquaintances throw off his "bride's" wig to reveal that Morose has "married" a boy. This is the polar opposite of the Shakespearean comedies, which in the end reveal the "other man" to be a *girl*. Indeed, we might go so far as to say that the play concludes with an anti-*gamos*. One editor has called *Epicoene* "Jonson's most daring departure from comedy's normal direction and purpose."[9]

This contrast may seem facile, but it is a valid appraisal of the character of the two playwrights' work. Nevertheless, we must beware the traditionally accepted view of Jonson versus Shakespeare as a literary grudge match—in which the forces of evil were knocked down by those of the good. For this bardolatry really began only after Jonson's death. Its prime mover was John Dryden, whose *Essay of Dramatic Poesy* (1668) deified Shakespeare and vilified all other poets as mere mortals. Nicholas Rowe,[10] Shakespeare's first biographer, took up the refrain, which ultimately reached its diapason in eighteenth-century critics like Dr. Johnson—not to mention such continental scholars as A. W. Schlegel (who referred to "*Unser* Shakespeare"!).[11] Only recently has this simplistic antithesis been called into question.[12]

All the same, the two playwrights' dramaturgical methods could not have been less similar. Jonson had strong artistic objections to the fantastical nature of Shakespeare's comedies, which ranged the map from the seacoast of Asia Minor to the "seacoast" of Bohemia, with many other exotic locales, real and imaginary, in between. *The Tempest* was an egregious example—set on an island "full of magic," and ending happily with men and fantastical creatures undergoing "a sea change." The metamorphosis of such unreal creatures as Ariel and Caliban, the transformation of the villains into men of good will, is crowned by the marriage of the innocents, noble Ferdinand and "admired" Miranda.

Without mentioning the Bard by name, Jonson launches a broadside against dramatists who

> ... make nature afraid in his plays, like those that beget *Tales, Tempests* and suchlike drolleries ...[13]

In fact, all through his career he pilloried the very notion of romantic (a euphemism for Shakespearean?) comedies in whose plots we find

> a duke to be in love with a countess, and that countess to be in love with the duke's son, and the son to love the lady's waiting maid; some such cross wooing, with a clown to their servingman.[14]

Any resemblance to *Twelfth Night* is purely intentional.

By contrast, Jonson's plays are realistic, ill-tempered, satirical broadsides—without the slightest element of fantasy. The writing of a comedy of twins was alien to his muse—which is why he could never finish his own version of the *Amphitryon* myth.[15] As he told Drummond, he could never find two actors "so like others that he could persuade the spectators they were one."[16]

At the same time that Shakespeare's gossamer creations were being acted at the Globe, Jonson was presenting his sharp, satirical comedies, nearly every one of which is set on the streets of urban London (*Volpone* is a conspicuous exception). Compare this with Molière, who set only half of his plays in Paris.[17] Jonson's theater teems with the crowds and smells of the city—even the noxious ones. It is hard to imagine a play of Shakespeare's mentioning aggressive flatulence as in the opening line of the *Alchemist,* where the title character shouts at Face, the housekeeper, "I fart at thee," followed with a rejoinder in the next line, "lick figs" (piles).[18] It goes without saying that none of the Bard's characters ever pronounce the "F-word" onstage,[19] whereas Jonson feels no such fastidiousness.[20] Instead of the fairies in a magic wood outside Athens, Jonson presents greasy housewives, pig women, cutpurses, and tapsters. The settings of his plays could have been painted by an early-seventeenth-century Hogarth. But these are Jonson's anglicizations of the traditional comedic *dramatis personae*. As the prologue to *The Alchemist* explains:

Our scene is London, cause we would make known,
   No country's mirth is better than our own,
  No clime breeds better matter, for your whore,
   Bawd, squire, impostor, many persons more . . .[21]

And yet, amazingly, the King's Men continued to produce them both. The remarkable coexistence of two such disparate playwrights in the same repertory is an indication of the wide panorama of the Elizabethan dramatic landscape. During one Christmas season in the early years of King James's reign, of the ten plays the company produced at court from their repertory, seven were by the Bard of Avon and two more "classical" offerings by the Pedant of Westminster. And Jonson was happy enough to have his artistic nemesis Will Shakespeare take the leading role in *Every Man in His Humour*—produced at the Globe in 1598, and the bad-tempered dramatist's first solo success as a writer, as well as being a leading player in *Sejanus*, Jonson's attempt at tragedy. The two men were that close—and that far apart.[22]

Since at one time or another Jonson attacked every one of his contemporary rivals, it was inevitable that some of his barbs would be cast at the revered Shakespeare. Witness his famous remark:

> I remember the Players have often mentioned it as an honour to Shakespeare, that in his writing, (whatsoever he penned) he never blotted out a line. My answer has been, would he had blotted a thousand.

And though but two sentences later Jonson concedes that "I lov'd the man and do honour his memory (on this side idolatry) as much as any,"[23] at times he could not suppress his jealousy. Witness his coupling of contemporary authors in *Epicoene,* where he cites "Daniel with Spencer, Jonson with tother youth."[24] Clearly at that moment he could not bear to refer to "tother youth" from Stratford by name.[25]

If nothing else, Jonson suffered an acute case of ambivalence toward his more successful contemporary. In his account of the winter he spent with Jonson, William Drummond reports his consistently contentious remarks about all other writers, even insisting that "Shakespeare wanted art."[26] The bard was also reviled by his contemporary

Robert Greene—a university wit with degrees from both Oxford and Cambridge—who referred to him (in the earliest extant mention of the playwright) as an "upstart crow, beautified with our feathers . . . in his own conceit the only Shake-scene in our country."[27]

But Jonson was not necessarily criticizing his Stratfordian rival for lack of talent or learning, rather perhaps for ignoring the Aristotelian unities of time, place, and character. As he wrote of his own technique in the prologue to *Volpone*:

> The laws of time, place, persons he observeth,
> from no needful rule he swerveth.[28]

Recall Malvolio's agelastic strictures in *Twelfth Night*—"Is there no respect of place, persons, nor time in you?"—perhaps Shakespeare's rejoinder to such pedantic criticism.[29]

In the prologue to *Every Man in His Humour*, Jonson further elaborates his artistic principles, this time paraphrasing Cicero:

> But deeds, and language, such as men do use:
> And persons, such as Comoedie would choose,
> When she would show an Image of the times
> And sport with human follies, not with crimes.[30]

"Sport" is an understatement. More characteristically, he both inculpates and prosecutes. As Levin observed, "Jonsonian comedy invariably tends in the direction of an arraignment."[31]

The man himself was a character of contradictions.[32] One cannot imagine Shakespeare fighting a duel—much less killing his opponent. But Jonson did so twice: once out of military duty, once out of civilian rage. His victim was Gabriel Spencer, an actor with the Admiral's Company—who likewise had a short temper. Imprisoned at Newgate, Jonson only escaped punishment by invoking "benefit of clergy"—that is, by proving that he could read Latin.

In the presence of witnesses—and, most important, a representative from the Bishop's office—he chose his own "neck verse" from the psalter and read it out.[33] When the judge inquired of the churchman *Legit ut clericus?* ("Does he read it like a clergyman?") the answer came back, *legit* ("he does"). Thus the second greatest playwright of the age literally got away with murder. All in all, the irascible Jonson was not a man you would drink a pint with at the Mermaid Tavern—although many younger aspiring men of letters, like Herrick, did come and listen to him venting his ire. Full of drink and of himself at his farewell dinner, Jonson embarrassed even his more fervent acolytes.

He had good reason to be bitter. His father was a minister—hence his son's biblical name—who died a month before he was born, and his mother subsequently married a bricklayer. Jonson went to Westminster School merely as a day boy, for he was not good enough to be one of the "Queen's Scholars" who had their tuition paid. His stepfather, lacking the funds to pay for university, apprenticed Ben to one of his fellow tradesmen. Thus while his schoolmates went on to Oxford and Cambridge, Jonson was forced into manual labor. Which is why perhaps he spent most of his life trying to prove his "intellectuality."

Ben loathed the work and soon threw in the trowel. We next find him working as an actor with Shakespeare's company—then known as the Chamberlain's Men. They would ultimately produce Jonson's first solo effort as a playwright. The state of the theater when Jonson began his career has been well described as being like

> Philip Henslow's [the legendary producer of the age] property room—a confused jumble of lion skins, crowns, dragons, rainbows, coffins, tombs, swords, steeples, snakes, arms and legs, and bedsteads—and Jonson saw himself replacing this clutter with the classic simplicity that Sidney had advocated.[34]

Jonson was so successful at the Globe that he was engaged to compose dramatic entertainment for the court of King James I (or more specifically his Queen).[35] Like the sometimes truculent Aristophanes, Jonson's muse also combined the satiric and the lyric. For the sensitivity of some of his poems is extraordinary. Such exquisite lines as the well-known "Drink to me only with thine eyes," from an adaptation of some epigrams by the imperial Greek writer Philostratus, are memorably preserved in song—a unique example of Jonson mixing both his pedantic and romantic sides. Other astonishingly tender lines are unsurpassed by any poet writing in English:

The voice so sweet, the words so fair,
As some soft chime had stroked the air,
And though the sound were parted thence
Still left an echo in the sense.[36]

Unfortunately, Jonson's rougher side quarreled with Inigo Jones, who was providing the set and stage machinery. Jones, the most respected architect and theatrical designer of the age—the inventor of movable scenery and other visual delights transcending words—remembered his collaborator as "the best of poets but the worst of men." He confronted his royal patrons and said, in so many words, "either he goes or I go." Jonson went.

Thus Jonson returned to the public theater and in 1606—the same season as Shakespeare's *Macbeth*—wrote what was unquestionably his masterpiece: *Volpone*. What is more astonishing is that he composed it in a mere five weeks, a feat explained to Drummond as occasioned by a Christmas gift of "some ten dozen of sack [sherry]." (We recall the moral of Cratinus' *Bottle:* "you can't compose anything clever by just drinking water.")[37] The play contains all of Jonson's thematic preoccupations—indeed too many, for it is rarely staged in its entirety.

The scene is Venice, Shylock's city—but in a very different kind of play. It is one of Jonson's rare ventures out of England, and the theme is as old as Petronius' first-century novel, the *Satyricon*. Here the inhabitants of Crotona live a dog-eat-dog existence—"they are either the victims or the victimizers" *(aut captantur aut captant)*—hungrily circling rich old men without families in the hope of gaining an inheritance. Jonson also drew from the Roman satirists Horace and Juvenal, both of whom describe the unscrupulous scheming of legacy-hunters.

Jonson's world is likewise populated by only rogues and fools. And the theme is always golden fleecing. As one character says in *Every Man in His Humour* (a close echo of Horace for the learned spectator):[38]

> KNOWELL: The rule, "Get money;" still, "Get money, boy.
> No matter by what means; money will do
> More, boy, than my lord's letter."[39]

For the ascension of James I marked a new age. London was infected by a pandemic hunger for riches, inspired by the discoveries in the New

World. Some have viewed this as the decline of civilization, others more positively as the birth pains of modern capitalism. One scholar forcefully emphasizes this point with a Jonsonian allusion, arguing that "in the early seventeenth century . . . Lady Pecunia became, in a special sense 'the Venus of time and state.'"[40]

Almost every Jonsonian play deals with avarice and the acquisition of wealth. This is aptly demonstrated by the fantastical fantasies of Sir Epicure Mammon, who dreams that the new technology—alchemy—will bring him untold riches:

> Come on, sir. Now, you set your foot on shore
> In *novo orbe;* here's the rich Peru:
> And there within, sir, are the golden mines,
> Great Solomon's Ophir! He was sailing to 't,
> Three years, but we have reached it in ten months.[41]

Jonson and Shakespeare, each at the height of his powers, reacted strongly to this plague of materialism, both with the same opprobrium but in characteristically different styles. One critic has compared *Volpone* and *King Lear* in this respect, which were both presented within the same year. Through the theme of disinheriting the good, each author treats "the corruption which greed works on the human soul."[42] There are a number of revealing verbal parallels. For example, when Corbaccio disinherits his son he declares, "he is a stranger to my loins." Lear disowns Cordelia in a similar way, calling her "a stranger to my heart and me."[43] The words of Shakespeare's Albany could also serve as an epigraph for *Volpone:*

> Humanity must perforce prey on itself
> Like monsters of the deep.[44]

But perhaps most important for the play under discussion is that with Jonson's Venetian comedy we return once again to the theme of Terence's *Eunuch.* Here, as we recall, the hero is a feigned castrato who uses the impersonation for erotic satisfaction. The climax of *Volpone* is almost a carbon copy of the *Mandragola,* where an impotent old husband also prostitutes his pure wife for selfish reasons. And yet there is a significant difference. In Machiavelli's play, the scheming hero Callimaco genuinely wants the sensual joy of sleeping with Lucrezia—if only once. Volpone (the Fox) would be satisfied with merely the conquest, not even the consummation. For although circumstances prevent him from completing the act, he gloats in the mischief he has already stirred up and trumpets to his lackey Mosca (the Fly) that the pleasure was greater "than if I had enjoyed the wench."[45]

Volpone's appetites tend more to the gold than the girl. He is first discovered in exactly the same inner stage occupied by Marlowe's anti-hero at the beginning of the *Jew of Malta* as he counts his "infinite riches in a little room." There Barabas describes his possessions with luxurious language:

> Bags of fiery opals, sapphires, amethysts,
> Jacinths, hard topaz, grass-green emeralds,
> Beauteous rubies, sparking diamonds . . .[46]

But to Marlovian preternatural greed, Jonson adds unabashed blasphemy. Volpone too in his theater-bed gleefully apostrophizes his treasures, with impieties in every line:

> O, thou sun of Sol,
> But brighter than thy father, let me kiss,
> With adoration, thee, and every relic
> Of sacred treasure, in this blessed room.
> Well did wise Poets, by thy glorious name
> Title that age, which they would have the best.[47]

These grandiloquent verses were said to have influenced Milton's famous apostrophe in *Paradise Lost*:

> Hail, holy Light, offspring of heaven first-born,
> Or of th' Eternal Coeternal beam
> May I express thee unblam'd? since God is light . . .[48]

Volpone's invocation has several more dimensions. For Sol is not only the Sun; in Jonson's day it was also the alchemists' term for gold—as well as a specific type of coinage. We will soon see Volpone's urge to "coin" his victims. Like a manic King Midas, he longs to gild everything—even human kindness.[49] To this Venetian sensualist, gold is "the best of things" (perhaps the pedant Jonson alluding to Pindar):[50]

> . . . and far transcending
> All style of joy in children, parents, friends,
> Or any other waking dream on earth.[51]

This is the nature of money-hungry misers. As we have seen, Molière's Harpagon also forsakes the human joys of children and friends in favor of his pot of gold. Riches eclipse all human feeling. We are reminded of Freud's observation that "happiness is the deferred fulfillment of a pre-historic wish. That is why wealth brings so little happiness; money is not an infantile wish."[52]

Volpone is devoid of human feelings. Avarice has so reified his desires that at no time in the play do we see him spend any of his riches:

> Yet, I glory
> More in the cunning purchase of my wealth,
> than in the glad possession . . .[53]

What kind of comic hero does not wish to enjoy his acquisitions? Volpone takes sadistic glee from those that have gathered around him like cormorants, waiting for him to die. The patient's bait is:

> I have no wife, no parent, child, ally,
> To give my substance to; but whom I make
> Must be my heir, and this makes men observe me.[54]

In Aesopian style, Jonson has peopled Volpone's world with birds of prey. Like Hamlet, they all "eat the air promise-cram'd." In a telling phrase, Volpone reveals how he will treat his victims' insatiable lust: he will "coin'em into profit."[55] This is the third repetition of this curious verb, which had an additional meaning in the seventeenth century, when the word also meant "fornicate." Human desire seems to animate every character.

At this point, we see a parade of Volpone's chosen dupes. They are a veritable aviary: Voltore (the vulture), an advocate; Corbaccio ("a filthie great raven"),[56] an old geezer with a handsome young son; and Corvino (the crow),[57] a wealthy merchant with a much younger wife. But Volpone intends "to fox" them all. This bestiary of characters reinforces Jonson's underlying theme—that men are animals, led by their baser instincts. The suitors have all given generously to their "dying" Volpone and here, assured by Mosca that each will be the sole heir, are encouraged to give still more.

Volpone is rich in one thing beyond his tangible treasures. He has been endowed by his creator with luxuriant language—hence T. S. Eliot, in a landmark essay, argued that Jonson was "the legitimate heir of Marlowe."[58] Indeed, one of Eliot's contemporaries went further, praising Jonson for "out-Marlowing Marlowe."[59]

The three "suitors" pay daily visits to Volpone. They are all absolutely heartless. When Mosca details to Corbaccio how very sick his master is, the miserly raven cannot keep from repeating reflexively "Oh good, good, good" at every symptom. This is true Bergsonian anesthesia of the heart, typified by Orgon in *Tartuffe* who is so besotted with his reverend guest that, when his maid is trying to tell him of his wife's severe illness during his absence, he ignores her and keeps asking the servant, "et Tartuffe?"

These legacy-hunters deserve to be gulled. Mosca now begins a further assault on Corbaccio's greed, convincing him to disinherit his own son in favor of Volpone. All of this evil brings true *Schadenfreude* to the dissemblers. At his heart Jonson is as much a moralist as a dramatist. For after this panorama of greed, the Fox remarks to the Fly: "What a rare punishment / Is avarice, to itself!"—ironic words that will come back to haunt him.[60]

But Volpone's money—as well as his appetite for mischief—grows apace. He asks Mosca to procure for him the most gorgeous woman in Venice. To which his minion replies that he cannot, for "she is untouchable." Is this not a precise reminiscence of *Mandragola*, where the hero sets a trap for the most exquisite woman in Florence—indeed in all of Europe—who, like Celia, Corvino's wife in this play, is kept under heavy lock and key?

> VOLPONE: Has she so rare a face?
> MOSCA: O, the wonder, the blazing star of Italy!
> O' the first year, a beauty, ripe, as harvest![61]
> Whose skin is whiter than a swan, all over!
> Than silver, snow, or lillies!, a soft lip,
> Would tempt you to eternity of kissing![62]

As in Menander, but to a more drastic degree, there are only two kinds of women in the world of Ben Jonson. His plays are replete with white-skinned virgins and hot-blooded sluts. Hence in contrast to the fabled courtesans of Venice, Celia is innocence itself, "whose skin is whiter than a swan, all over." Jonson's good women are constantly described with this color of purity, as for example in his lyric:

> Have you seen the white lily grow
> Before rude hands have touched it?[63]

The final stanza ends: "O so young, O so straight, O so chaste, so chaste is she!"

Volpone's lust is aroused; he must have this wonder. Nothing is more tempting to a sadist than the corruption of the innocent. Yet even now his obsession with riches is not dimmed. For what stirs him most is Mosca's description of Celia's beauty: "bright as gold, as lovely as your gold."[64]

For the moment at least, Volpone is so inflamed that he is willing to surrender to Mosca all of his possessions in exchange for access to Celia. Once again taking a page from Machiavelli's book, he combines sexual sensuality with the lust for inanimate gold as he commands his servant to "coin me":

> Gold, plate and jewels, all's at thy devotion;
> Employ them, how thou wilt; nay, coin me, too:
> So thou, in this, but crown my longings . . .[65]

At this rare moment, physical desire surpasses even Volpone's avarice. He instructs Mosca to tell the three voracious birds that his master is about to die and needs one final ministration to help him on his way:

> But some young woman must be straight sought out,
> Lusty, and full of juice, to sleep by him.[66]

Shades of King David—recall the Old Testament story of the lovely maiden Abishag who is put into David's deathbed in the hope of "warming him up."[67] The problem is presented to Corvino, who at first proposes a courtesan. But then Mosca informs him that "Signior Lupo the physician" has offered his own virgin daughter for the purpose.[68]

Hearing that the Wolf is willing to make so great a sacrifice, the Crow, driven to desperate measures, proposes his own wife. The Fly gratefully accepts on behalf of his moribund Fox.

As Corvino goes home to persuade her, there follows what at first appears to be a completely superfluous scene. In the street Mosca encounters Bonario, the handsome young son of Corbaccio, and mischievously reveals to him that his father is planning to disinherit him. He offers to hide the incredulous Bonario in Volpone's bedroom so he can hear the outrageous facts for himself.

No sooner is the young man stowed away than the sluttish Lady Politic Would-be arrives, breathing heavily. She too lusts after Volpone's gold, and, hearing he needs a bedmate, tries to foist herself upon the cringing patient. The other medicines she proposes sound like a parody of the Marlovian language used elsewhere in the play by Volpone:

> Seed pearl were good now, boiled with syrup of apples,
> Tincture of gold, and coral, citron-pills,
> Your elecampane root, myrobalanes . . .
> Burnt silk, and amber, you have muscerdel.[69]

At this Volpone groans, "Before I feigned diseases, now I have one." But this amusing interlude serves only as an overture to the great confrontation between the Fox and the innocent maiden he desires.

Corvino arrives with his innocent and anxious wife, commanding her to "respect my venture"—not by accident, a commercial term. Thunderstruck, she retorts:

> CELIA: Before your honour?
> CORVINO: Honour? tut, a breathe;
>   There is no such thing, in nature: a mere term invented
>   to awe fools. What is my gold the worse for touching?[70]

In a manner typical of the heartlessness of the fortune-hunters, Corvino compares his wife to an inanimate object that cannot feel anything—not even shame. His sophistical rejection of honor recalls (unconsciously?) Falstaff's famous catechism in *1 Henry 4*, "what is that word honour? . . . Who hath it? He that died a-Wednesday."[71]

Celia's protestations echo Lucrezia's own passionate determination to protect her *onore*. And if his wife refuses, Corvino threatens to denounce her as a whore and mutilate her face. (Is this really a comedy?) Like the original Roman heroine, Celia would rather die than suffer disgrace:

> CELIA: Sir, kill me, rather: I will take down poison,
> Eat burning coals, do anything—
> CORVINO: Be damned![72]

We have seen throughout this book that the quintessential theme of comedy is rebirth. But in *Volpone* it is perverse indeed. Left alone in the sensualist's bedroom, Celia looks around in panic as the "invalid," suddenly "resurrected," rises from his deathbed and begins to woo her:

> Why art thou mazed, to see me thus revived?
> Rather applaud thy beauty's miracle.[73]

Volpone is reborn: "fresh, / As hot, as high, and in as jovial plight."[74] Then he makes his first of several proposals to have sex in various shapes, like "blue Proteus, or the horned flood"—the latter adjective with its unmistakable connotations.

Then in a scene of utter cruelty, Jonson suddenly turns lyrical (and classical) with his translation of Catullus:

> Come, my Celia, let us prove,
> While we can, the sports of love . . .
> But if, at once, we lose this light,
> 'Tis with us perpetual night.[75]

Is such sentimentality appropriate at this moment? Far from being moved, Celia begs to be struck by lightning to avoid disgrace. Volpone persists with verse that shows Jonson at his most voluptuous:

> See, here, a rope of pearl; and each more orient
> Than that the brave Egyptian queen caroused:
> Dissolve, and drink'em. See, a carbuncle,
> May put out both the eyes of our St. Mark;

A diamant, would have bought Lollia Paulina,
When she came in, like starlight . . .[76]

He then proposes exotic delicacies like "tongues of nightingales, the milk of unicorns and panther's breath." But Celia remains adamant; she is even immune to Volpone's audacious proposal that the two of them

> in changed shapes, act Ovid's tales [sc. the *Metamorphoses*],
> Thou, like Europa now, and I like Jove,
> Then I like Mars, and thou like Erycine,
> So, of the rest, till we have quite run through
> And wearied all the fables of the gods.[77]

The inhuman Fox proposes further bestialities.[78] But to no effect. Exasperated, he resorts to rape ("Yield, or I'll force thee").

Just as it seems that Celia will lose her honor, Bonario leaps from his hiding place to her rescue: "Forbear, foul ravisher, libidinous swine." For an instant it looks like the end of Volpone's personal *kōmos*. Have the rogues finally met their nemesis? To think so is to underestimate the depth of the man's depravity.

When all the characters gather before the judges in the Scrutineo, the corrupt lawyer Voltore perjures himself to exonerate the villain, alluding to Celia as "this lewd woman" and Bonario as a "lascivious youth." Justice has been turned so topsy-turvy that Corbaccio now refers to his own son in bestial terms. And now the only two pure characters in the play who do not have animal names are here given them: her husband refers to Celia as a partridge (reputed in antiquity to have an insatiable sexual appetite), and his father describes Bonario as a "monster of men, swine, goat, wolf . . . viper."[79]

As proof positive of his client's innocence, Voltore has "the impotent Volpone" brought before the court. The alleged seducer is carried in on a stretcher as Voltore comments sarcastically:

> VOLTORE: See here, grave fathers, here's the ravisher,
> The rider on men's wives, the great impostor,
> The grand voluptuary! do you not think

> These limbs should affect venery? . . .
> Perhaps, he doth dissemble?
>
> BONARIO: (*outraged*)   So he does.[80]

Naturally, as one would expect from the cold-hearted Jonson, the villainous lawyer wins the case. The two innocents are sent off to prison "severed," that is, kept apart from one another. Volpone and Mosca indulge in an orgy of self-congratulation. Their utter depravity has brought a wholly undeserved triumph. Once again Volpone revels in *Schadenfreude,* declaring that he is happier "than if I had enjoyed the wench / The pleasure of all womankind's not like it."[81]

Mosca thinks that they have reached the limits of outrage. But Volpone is obsessed with pushing his luck—and perhaps the audience's patience—even further. He orders his underling: "straight away give out that I am dead."

The play reaches its devilish climax as the trio of scavengers scurry to Volpone's lair, where they come upon Mosca, who is serenely taking an inventory. To his eavesdropping master's delight, he declares that none of the three birds is Volpone's heir. In fact, *he* himself is. With typical Jonsonian severity the parasite upbraids the three, with special emphasis on their moral and physical defects. To Corbaccio he snarls:

> Go Home, and die, and stink;
> If you but croak a syllable, all comes out,
> Away and call your porters, go, go, stink.[82]

As Mosca revels in his new mastery, Volpone leaves in disguise to strut the streets of Venice and savor all the pain he has inflicted. At a far remove, is this not an echo of the role-switching of Dionysus and Xanthias in the *Frogs?* The evil servant now reveals to the audience his own cruel plan to trick his master: "Let his sport pay for't, this is called the Fox-trap."[83]

After all this boundless mischief, Jonson works a bitter justice on the principal villains. When Mosca appears before the hastily reassembled judges, resplendent in his master's garments, the servant cuts so grand a figure that one of the magistrates thinks out loud, "a fit match for my daughter." The Fly is so inebriated with *alazoneia* that he whispers an ultimatum to his master, demanding half his wealth in exchange for his returning to his servile role. When Volpone hesitates, Mosca informs him that the price has now doubled. At which the Fox loses his temper and control. (We recall Jonson's own famously short fuse.) Doffing his disguise, he declares:

> I am Volpone, and this is my knave;
> This, his own knave: this, avarice's fool . . .[84]

Both master and man have been hoist by their own petard. Ever moralizing, the playwright has one of the judges pronounce:

> These possess wealth, as sick men possess fevers
> Which, trulier, may be said to possess them.[85]

Jonson does not stop here. He insists upon meting out poetic justice to each malefactor. In its way this is a cruel *anagnōrisis,* as at long last the topsy-turvy values right themselves. The judges order Voltore the lawyer to be stripped of his profession and banished from Venice. All of Corbaccio's wealth is given immediately to his son, and the old man himself is to be sent to the monastery of San Spirito:

> Where, since thou knew'st not how to live well here,
> Thou shall be learn'd to die well.[86]

Corvino will be taken around Venice wearing asses' ears and pelted by "stinking fish / bruised fruit and rotten eggs." He will also have to return Celia *intacta* to her parents with her dowry tripled—an apt punishment for a pathological miser.

And as for the really stinking fish, Mosca is taken off to be whipped and thereafter become a perpetual galley slave. Volpone's treasure is confiscated, and he is to be confined at the Hospital for the Incurable— originally established in Venice for treating venereal disease—"Till thou be'st sick, and lame indeed."[87]

Thus all the rogues are suitably punished and will live unhappily ever after. And yet this is a comedy—should it not end with a joyous *gamos* between the two innocents, Celia and Bonario? This would certainly approximate at least the happy ending of the *Mandragola.* But we are denied this pleasure. Breaking with centuries of tradition, Jonson does not allow the valorous young man and beautiful young woman to unite in marriage. In fact, there is no indication that they will ever see each other again. As in *Epicoene*, Jonson undercuts the possibilities for a comic ending in *Volpone* in the final act: "the comedy concludes notoriously with no reconciliation, no sudden fortunes, no betrothals, no . . . lovers' meetings."[88] It is easy to see how this sort of ending has led to the view of Jonson as a miserly moralist, stingy with his feelings as well; his dour character would not allow him to give the audience what would satisfy them.

Jonsonian comedy has known a checkered history. He was much esteemed—even loved—in the Restoration, but has never really been in favor since. Perhaps John Dryden's observation (referring to Quintilian's description of Demosthenes) sums it up:

> A joke he gladly would present—
> If only jokes he could invent.[89]

⁕

In the end, Malvolio triumphed after all.

Since the remaining acting companies in England were encountering increasing financial difficulties, fewer and fewer plays were performed. When in 1642 the Puritans finally succeeded in having the theaters officially closed, they were already nearly defunct.[90] And legendary monuments like the Globe were not merely shut, they were razed. And so the keys to the playhouses were added to the chain of the agelastic steward.

After nearly a decade of civil war, King Charles I was formally tried and executed as the aristocracy fled into exile. The Commonwealth, with Cromwell as its first Protector, regarded theater as anathema. Yet Londoners produced proof in advance of Matthew Arnold's dictum that "the theater is irresistible." For, despite the official interdiction, there were occasional clandestine public performances in theaters like the Red Bull. Such productions were quickly shut down, however, and the participants harshly punished. A rare exception was Sir William Davenant (1606–1668), who even surpassed Ben Jonson by actually becoming "Poet Laureate." He also had the unique distinction of seeing his plays produced before, during, and after the Commonwealth.[91] And in 1660 he was given a patent to open a theater—the Lincoln's Inn Fields Theatre at the Duke's House.

The death of Cromwell and the subsequent collapse of his government was a victory for monarchy, dramaturgy, and lechery. Charles II took the throne, and his courtiers flocked back to enjoy their restored "nobility." Following the Puritans' 1650 law "suppressing detestable sins of incest, adultery, and fornication," what better revenge could the reinstated gentry enjoy than to make life one great debauch? Their behavior confirmed Newton's recently formulated third law of motion: "to every action there is always opposed an equal reaction." At first glance the golden days of Restoration seemed more like one continuous orgy. For whereas the Puritans had certainly exaggerated in referring to Jacobean and Caroline drama as "The Devil's work," this appellation would certainly have been an apt description for much of Restoration comedy—which was in a sense conceived under the presiding genius of Priapus.

The playhouses opened again to great enthusiasm. It was long widely accepted that, in contrast to the vast Elizabethan showplaces, Restoration drama was presented to a privileged few. But more recent views have called this into question.[92] Even in the Elizabethan age, whether at the Globe or in private performances, the aristocracy had already demonstrated their enthusiasm for the theater. As for the "privileged" nature of the Restoration audiences, this view has also been modified. For although theater was indeed a passion of the returned noblemen, the growing merchant class also made its presence felt— business had created a new nobility. Dryden summed this up in the prologue to *Marriage-à-la-Mode,* which promises to "oblige the town, the city, and the court"[93]—in other words, the plebs, the rising merchant class, and the aristocracy. (This is one of the earliest references to the "city" as a financial and commercial center.)[94]

But the newly opened theaters were no longer "open" architecturally, and for this reason had to be considerably smaller than the Globe. Indeed, the theater receipts for John Dryden's *All for Love* (1677) list a total audience of only 249.[95]

As far as the nobility were concerned, the plays were *by* themselves, *for* themselves, and *about* themselves. If one could have held a mirror alternately up to the actors and then the audience, the reflections would have shown exactly the same people, playing the same roles. Indeed, the drama of this age more than any other conformed to Cicero's definition of comedy as "a mirror of manners." The atmosphere in the theater recalled the Roman games as described by Ovid:

> All the girls come to look and be looked at,
> That place is a graveyard to chastity.[96]

A new breed (some might say swarm) called critics sat in a special circle. The dandies in "fops' corner" were self-styled wits who loudly criticized the play even while it was in progress. Wycherley mentions this anti-social practice in the Prologue to *The Plain Dealer*, referring to the fops as "The fine loud gentlemen o'th' pit / Who damn all plays."[97] The rest of the "beautiful people" occupied the pit or sat in the boxes. As the eighteenth-century literary critic John Dennis recalled, "that was an age of Pleasure."

Yet, despite their frivolous behavior, these returning aristocrats had a bitter outlook on life. The civil war had painfully uprooted them from their comfortable existence, and experience had taught them to assume a hedonistic outlook—life is uncertain, therefore *carpe diem*: seize the moment. Having been unseated once, they were haunted by the fear that it could happen again. This may at least partially explain the selfishness that pervaded society.

It was a cynical age. These "nobles" displayed a schizophrenic lifestyle. On the one hand, they lived a silk-and-silver existence—bowing, embracing, and wearing the latest fashions. Yet at the same time they used four-letter words liberally—even at the dinner table in front of their wives. They spat on the floor, and would even relieve themselves— not where "gentlemen" were meant to go—but in the fireplace. What these lads regarded as good entertainment were cock-fights, dog-fights, bear-baiting—or a trip to Charing Cross to watch the executions. When even these amusements palled, they would pay Thames boatmen to fight each other for a prize (whence the modern term for pugilists).[98] These were anything but genteel pursuits.[99]

And they got drunk at the pop of a cork. In a manner of speaking, the major milestones in sixteenth- and seventeenth-century English comedy can be distinguished by the alcohol in vogue. For Shakespeare and his early Elizabethan contemporaries it was "small beer," a cherished tipple as old as the pharaohs.[100] It was especially relished during Tudor times, as commemorated in the proverb:

> Hops, Reformation, bays, and beer
> Came into England all in one year.

The next drink in vogue was sack, a type of dry sherry which came into favor in the late sixteenth century. Ben Jonson claimed that his success and speed in writing *Volpone* were due to a Christmas gift of "some ten dozen of sack." We also recall Prince Hal's astonishment upon discovering Falstaff's bar bill, which included no less than two gallons of this aperitif: "O monstrous, / But one penny-worth of bread and this intolerable deal of sack."[101]

Finally, when King Charles II recovered the throne in 1660, the exiled aristocrats returned from France with a sparkling new potion they had discovered. Reputedly invented by the Benedictine monk Dom Pérignon, the drink was named champagne after the province in northern France. Like so many great discoveries, it was the result of hazard as much as planning. For the cleric simply opened a barrel of wine that had fermented too long—and fizzed into history.

But the liquid which best characterizes Restoration comedy is gall. On both sides of the stage, the preeminent value was wit—but not merely in the epigrammatic style that Oscar Wilde was to favor. It contained no small amount of undiluted hostility. Known as "hectors," these wits would break windows, mug pedestrians—even assault the officers of the watch. And when the hapless law officers were knocked to the ground, the bullies would shout, "Whip! Stitch! Kiss my arse!" In Wycherley's final play, *The Plain Dealer,* a character proclaims, "Where there is mischief there's wit." Another is chastised for denying that there is humour in "breaking of windows" and that "being mischievous is a sign of wit."[102] The most that can be said for this is that it vaguely conforms to what Freud defines as aggressive wit.

All this was the immediate heritage of Ben Jonson, who, many agree, represents the halfway point between Plautus and the Restoration.[103] One speech by True-Wit in *Epicoene* particularly illuminates the cynicism and immorality of the age:

TRUE-WIT: Alas, sir, do you ever think to find a chaste wife in these times? . . . If you had lived in king Etheldred's time, sir, or Edward the Confessor's, you might perhaps have found in some cold country-hamlet, then, a dull frosty wench, would have been contented with one man: now, they will as soon be pleased with one leg, or one eye.[104]

Fidelity was mocked, adultery the order of the day. The theater became the next thing to a bawdy house, and in addition "the plays presented a veritable textbook for seduction."[105] Gentlemen made their assignations with the "orange girls," damsels of dubious morality who went around hawking fruit which the spectators could either eat or—if the play displeased them—hurl at the actors.

Or the actresses. For the Restoration marks a milestone in the history of English theater. Female roles were no longer played by young boys with high voices but—*mirabile dictu*—by real women with real curves (many of them French imports), thus politically anticipating George Meredith's as-yet-unwritten rule that female "social freedom was the *sine qua non* for true comedy."[106]

Many of the first generation of actresses had begun their careers in fruit. Boswell wrote admiringly of "that delicious subject of gallantry, an actress."[107] The most famous of these voluptuous "green-grocery girls" was Nell Gwyn, who rose spectacularly from theater pit to stage, where she became a prima donna. After starring, for example, as the eponymous heroine in *Flora's Vagaries* (1663) by Richard Rhodes (which bears some traces of Molière's *George Dandin*), she graduated to her greatest role—that of mistress to Charles II, to whom she bore at least two sons, one of whom became the Duke of Buckingham.

Not only did the Restoration include women on stage, but there were even a fair number of female playwrights, the most famous and prolific of whom was Aphra Behn (1640-1689), the first woman to earn her living as a playwright in the English theater. She led a very romantic life. During the Dutch war she had worked as a spy, and was later imprisoned for debt. One of her famous comedies, *The Feign'd Curtizans* (1679), was dedicated to Nell Gwyn (she knew on which side her bread was buttered). She had as lesser colleagues Mary Pix (1666-1709),

Catherine Trotter (1679–1749), and the wildly promiscuous Delariviere
Manley (1672–1724), whose scandalous life-style did nothing to mitigate
the notoriety of the women of the theater.[108]

The new liberation, with its tacit acknowledgment that females
wanted sensual fulfillment as much as men, caused the male population some subliminal uneasiness. Sex was referred to by coy euphe-
misms like "the sport." Infidelity was euphemized as "honor." Ben
Jonson was a major influence on these early comic authors, his popularity for a time exceeding that of Shakespeare.[109] But while Jonson had
envisioned the world as divided into rogues and fools, the new Restoration playwrights saw it as peopled by rogues and cuckolds.

Molière was also a popular model, although the Restoration authors
added a kind of salacious twist to the Frenchman's dramatic situations—witness the frequency and brutality of the cuckolding theme
that London theatergoers obviously savored. Northrop Frye offers a
psychological explanation in his description of Congreve's *Love for Love*
(1695), in which we also hear distant echoes of Terence's *Eunuch:*

> There are two Oedipus themes in counterpoint: the hero
> cheats his father out of the heroine and his best friend vio-
> lates the wife of an impotent old man who is the heroine's
> guardian. A theme which would be recognized as a form of
> infantile regression, the hero pretending to be impotent in
> order to gain access to the woman's quarters . . .[110]

With a few alterations, this description could also fit Terence's
Eunuch. Typical of the new style comedy was Sir George Etherege's
She Would If She Could (1668). The principal characters are Sir Oliver,
an impotent skirt-chasing oldster, married to a nymphomaniac whose
proclivities are plagued by "adultery *interruptus*"—which is to say
that her assignations are always spoiled by someone or other. There
are, of course, other lewd women in the play. Here, with merely a
change of costume, we find the sexual incapacity of the typically
Plautine *senex.*

Arguably the first masterpiece of this era was William Wycherley's
Country Wife (1675). The author, an Oxford graduate, knew his classical
literature, which he adapted to suit the manners of the age. Yet even

among the jades of this society the play created an immediate scandal. And later on the eve of the twentieth century, the playwright and critic William Archer, echoing Goldoni's critique of the *Mandragola,* called it "the filthiest play in the English language." Its original performance created such a scandal that Wycherley himself alludes to it in his final play, *The Plain Dealer,* produced the following year.[111] In a scene similar to Molière's *Critique of the School for Wives* (where the characters all sit around criticizing the original play), Wycherley's prudish heroine Olivia remarks:

> Then you think a woman modest, that sees
> the hideous *Country Wife* without blushing, or publishing
> her detestation of it?[112]

Notwithstanding its cornucopia of obscenities, one may still ask why Wycherley's play was bowdlerized (by Garrick among others) for two centuries thereafter. In fact, New York only saw the unexpurgated *Country Wife* in 1931.[113] In its way it is like Nahum Tate's "happier" *King Lear* (1681), which held the stage for more than a century and a half.[114] We can only conclude that, in their extreme form, tragedy and comedy are for people with greater intestinal fortitude.

One may well ask what the original audiences found so shocking about Wycherley's play. To begin with, the insouciance of the characters in the face of outrageous behavior is itself startling. For it was neither fashionable nor comfortable for Restoration men to acknowledge that women could have an intelligence equal to theirs. The author here presents women more sophisticated than had yet been seen on the English stage, who consciously schemed to fulfill their suppressed desires. Paradoxically, Meredith did not like Restoration drama—otherwise he would have found there his own criteria for true comedy: for the *Country Wife* elevates women to an equal status with men.

With these observations as prologue, let us gird our intellectual loins to approach the play itself. It combines two motifs we have already encountered. From Terence, Wycherley has taken the theme of a young man's eunification, which gives him license to be left alone in the presence of women. Then there is a second model—the innumerable May-December comedies of Molière where an old man wants to marry a young girl, for example *School for Husbands, School for Wives,* and *The Miser.*

As is the fashion in Restoration comedy, the characters have "speaking names" that epitomize their personalities: Lady Wishfor't (a sex-starved matron), Mr. Trusty (of all things, a lawyer), Scrub and Snap (servants), Sir John Brute, Mrs. Love-it, Sir Fopling Flutter, and so on.

The "hero" of the *Country Wife* is Horner—the name bespeaks his favorite pastime—who conceives a novel way of seducing the fine ladies of London. Like Volpone, he has his physician, Dr. Quack (of course), breach professional confidentiality and let it be known throughout the town that on a recent trip to France (of course) his patient has caught the "pox," and subsequent treatment by Gallic healers has left him impotent.

Horner has a villainous streak. His motivation is to demonstrate the utter corruptibility of women—*all* women. First, as he explains to the physician, his medical problem will help him identify the veteran adulteresses at a glance: "now I can be sure she that shows an aversion to me loves the sport."[115] Thus the plan is set:

> Now may I have, by the reputation
> of an eunuch, the privileges of one . . .[116]

But Horner's appetite transcends obtaining the favors of the bored wives in his own milieu. His aim is to seduce an attractive newcomer to London: the innocent young Margery. In so doing he confirms John Donne's bleak misogyny in "Go and catch a falling star," which concludes:

> Though she were true when you met her,
> And last when you write your letter
> Yet she
> Will be
> False, ere I come, to two or three.

Her husband—himself an old whoremaster—is in the long tradition of characters like Dr. Nicia, Volpone, and Etherege's Sir Oliver. In English letters, this was already a familiar theme in Chaucer's "The Miller's Tale":

> This Carpenter hadde wedded newe a wyf,
> Which that he lovede moore than his lyf.
> Of eighteteene yeer she was of age.
> Jalous he was, and heeld hire narwe in cage,
> For she was yong and wylde, and he was old,
> And demed hymself been lik a cokewold . . .
> For youthe and elde is often at debaat.
> But sith that he was fallen in the snare,
> He moste endure, as other folk, his care.[117]

Wycherley's more immediate debt, however, is to Molière's *School for Wives*. There the mature (not to say overripe) Arnolphe intends to marry his lovely young ward and has tried everything to keep her from meeting a truly suitable—in other words, young and attractive—man. In the opening scene of the French play, the older man Arnolphe explains to his friend the reasoning behind his tactics:

> Since women's gift for trickery is great,
> I've taken measures to avoid this fate.
> I've picked a simple girl to be my wife,
> And keep my head away from horns for life.[118]

Likewise, Wycherley's Pinchwife is a stale, worn-out rake, insanely obsessed with protecting his wife's chastity—which strongly suggests his inability to perform like the young husband she deserves. He has wed a simple girl from the country who, he is certain, will not have known any other lover and therefore will not desire one. As he foolishly confides to Horner:

> Well, gentleman, you may laugh at me; but you
> shall never lie with my wife . . .[119]

He has taken all measures—or so he thinks—to keep Margery from straying or even finding temptation. Like Filippo in Boccaccio's tale, he foolishly believes that by keeping her ignorant of "the wicked city" he can prevent *la forza di natura* from giving her a private tutorial. For it is not Horner who seduces her, but her own instincts.[120] Pinchwife's efforts to discourage Margery only succeed in awakening her interest further: his admonitions are a *précaution inutile*. For at first Margery is scarcely aware of the rake's interest, and her husband's paranoia only serves to awaken her passion. And in trying to dissuade Horner, the would-be seducer, he merely whets the scoundrel's appetite.

Alithea, Pinchwife's sister, is the closest thing to a decent woman in the play, as indicated by her name, the Greek for "truth." We find her discussing with the naive Margery the various places for a woman to go in London. The young girl ingenuously asks why Pinchwife always keeps her locked up. Alithea responds, "He's afraid you should love another man."[121] Margery then confides that yesterday in the theater the play bored her, but "I liked hugeously the actors. They are the goodliest, properest men, sister."[122] Already we see her natural inclinations at work.

Pinchwife has had his ear to the door—there is a continual dimension of unsavory voyeurism to the play, especially with Dr. Quack. When he can bear this no longer he bursts in to scold Alithea:

> Do not teach my wife where the men are to be found . . .
> I beg you keep her in ignorance as I do.[123]

He once again warns his wife not to act "like naughty town women."[124] Indeed, the town looms so large in the play it is almost a character in itself—especially the familiar haunts for extramarital assignations in fashionable meeting places like Mulberry Gardens (where Buckingham Palace now stands) and St. James Park.

When he foolishly tells her that "one of the lewdest fellows in town" was in love with her, Pinchwife is crushed to find how captivated his young wife is and immediately regrets his mistake.[125] He is pushing her ever closer to Horner (he has not yet learned of the hero's alleged infirmity). And as his attempts to suppress his wife grow more cruel, he only increases her appetite. The irony increases as she grows ever more cunning.

Hearing company approach, Pinchwife frantically stuffs his wife into a closet ("in baggage, in"). A moment later the fop Sparkish enters to introduce his fiancée Alithea to his friend Harcourt—who immediately falls in love with her. This second plot is the closest thing to true love in the play. The young gentleman is so taken by her that he begins to woo Alithea right under the nose of the empty-headed dandy, who is too foolish to realize that his friend is making earnest advances to his fiancée. Alithea does, however, and protests that her foppish fiancé "loves me, or he would not marry me."[126] Harcourt offers an epigrammatic response:

> Marriage is rather a sign of interest than love; and he that marries a fortune covets a mistress, not loves her. But if you take marriage for a sign of love, take it from me immediately.[127]

Nevertheless, Alithea still feels honor-bound to marry her foppish fiancé and rejects Harcourt's advances, although she confesses in an aside (a typical feature of Restoration comedy):

> I am so far from hating him, I wish my gallant had his person and understanding. Nay, if my honour—[128]

Unlike the other women in the play, Alithea acts with honor in the accepted sense of the word. She declines her adolescent fiancé's invitation to the theater: "I will not go if you intend to leave me in the box and run into the pit."[129] She vainly hopes that Sparkish will retire from Fops' Alley and be a proper husband. Harcourt persists in his suit throughout the play, but Alithea remains admirably steadfast until the very end. She has given her word, and she will honor it. This is a rare—if misplaced—instance of fidelity.

Horner's stratagem begins to show results. A trio of little non-maids from the School for Scandal (to be slightly anachronistic) bustle in to take Margery to the play. As one critic baldly put it, their interests "do not rise above the belt."[130] Horner tells us in a sarcastic aside that Lady Fidget, Miss Dainty Fidget, and Mrs. Squeamish are "pretenders to honour, as critics to wit . . ."[131] Of course they are flagrant hypocrites. For when Sir Jaspar Fidget casually offers to tell Lady Fidget the "naked truth," she cringes: "Fy, Sir Jaspar! do not use that word 'naked.'"[132] ("Naked" is out but "honour" is in.) On hearing of Horner's "misfortune," the ladies are filled with revulsion:

MRS. SQUEAMISH: And I would as soon look upon a picture of Adam and
                Eve, without fig-leaves, as any of you . . .[133]

Yet because of his alleged impairment Horner is granted free access to these "women of honour." At the first possible moment he will reveal his secret to them. Lady Fidget is deeply moved and praises him perversely as "a man of honour" for his willingness to be reported "no man." Then she has a momentary qualm that epitomizes the hypocrisy of the age. To her lubricious mind, the only "sin" is being found out. "The crime is the less when 'tis not known"—this is reminiscent of Machiavelli's corrupt friar, Timoteo, to whom "a sin that's hidden is half forgiven." We find in Molière's Tartuffe another arch-hypocrite who assures his victim of seduction:

> Only sin in public causes scandal;
> A sin in silence is a sin that we can handle.[134]

By contrast, how fastidious the ladies are in discussing this new arrangement as their ring-leader expresses her misgivings: ". . . if you give me leave to speak obscenely, you might tell, dear sir."[135] Horner replies that the "reputation of impotency is as hardly recovered again in the world as that of cowardice, dear madam." Thus reassured, she invites him to "do your worst, dear, dear sir."

With the impression that his wife is in safe hands, Sir Jaspar leaves for Whitehall:

> Go, go, to your business, I say, pleasure,
> whilst I go to my pleasure, business.[136]

This antithesis, later expressed almost verbatim by Pinchwife,[137] is not new. We have already encountered the dichotomy as a theme in the *Menaechmi,* where the local twin returns from the enforced professional obligations in the forum, which have prevented him from enjoying the sensual delights at Erotium's house. Wycherley's sophisticated audience would grasp the double meaning in the word "business," which was also used to refer to sexual intercourse. Lady Fidget makes the theme even more emphatic in her closing epigram:

> Who for his business, from his wife will run
> Takes the best care, to have her business done.[138]

Pinchwife finally surrenders to Margery's pleas to take her into town on the condition that she be disguised as a boy. (What a far cry from

Lyly's transvestite heroines, much less Viola in *Twelfth Night* and the Bard's discreet reference to "the little thing!") They meet Horner, who immediately sees through the attempted gender change and begins to kiss the young "brother-in-law" affectionately, to the great irritation of Pinchwife, who is helpless to keep them from strolling off into the bushes.

When the two return several painful moments later, with Margery's hat full of fruit, Horner announces: "I have only given your little brother an orange, sir."[139] Margery then hands her husband the fruit Horner "gave her." To which Pinchwife mutters angrily to himself:

> PINCHWIFE: (*aside*) You have only squeezed my orange, I suppose, and
> given it me again.[140]

Pinchwife throws the proffered citrus away, saying, "I deserve it, since I furnished the best part of it." He concludes with the caustic couplet:

> The gallant treats presents, and gives the ball;
> But 'tis the absent cuckold pays for all.[141]

At the beginning of Act Four we see the saucy servant Lucy trying vainly to persuade her mistress Alithea to reject Sparkish and marry Harcourt, a truly worthy person. When her foppish suitor enters with "Ned Harcourt" (alleged to be a parson from Cambridge who bears a remarkable resemblance to her secret love), she immediately recognizes him beneath the clerical collar, but the dim-witted dandy does not. The scene contrasts Sparkish's *alazoneia* with Harcourt's irony.

The next morning an angry Pinchwife interrogates Margery as to what exactly Horner did with her. She reports ingenuously that the gentleman carried her into a house next to the Exchange and sent for "some dried fruit, and China oranges."[142] He also performed some "beastliness":

> MARGERY: Why he put—
> PINCHWIFE: (*in panic*) What?
> MARGERY: Why, he put the tip of his tongue between my lips . . .[143]

Her husband's temper boils over, and he forces Margery to compose a harsh letter to her would-be gallant:

> PINCHWIFE: Come begin, "Sir—"
> MARGERY: Shan't I say "Dear sir?" you know one says always something better than bare "Sir."
> PINCHWIFE: Write as I bid you, or I will write whore with this penknife in your face.[144]

What a way to address your wife! This is not Mack the Knife—this is a country gentlemen, threatening to mutilate his wife. That, one presumes, is also an act of "wit."

We have seen the same brutal treatment of an innocent wife when Corvino threatens Celia to comply with his command to sleep with Volpone:

> CORVINO: Yield . . . I will buy some slave, whom I will kill, and bind thee to him, alive; And at my window, hang you forth: devising some monstrous crime, which I, in capital letters, will eat into thy flesh, with aquafortis, and burning corsives, on this stubborn breast.[145]

At last Margery is cowed into transcribing what her husband dictates— or at least most of it. When he rereads what she has done, he snaps:

> PINCHWIFE: Thou impudent creature! where is 'nauseous' and 'loathed.'
> MARGERY: I can't abide to write such filthy words.[146]

Again, ordinary if unpleasant words become obscenities in the vocabulary of love. As further incentive, Pinchwife threatens to "stab out those eyes that cause my mischief." She is frightened and succumbs to this brutal threat.

But when Pinchwife briefly leaves the room, she quickly switches his stern missive with a love letter of her own which on his return he seals with wax. Having learned the use of words, Margery has now employed them for her own purposes that nature has instilled within her. And she will get to Horner because, as we have seen throughout, in comedy the force of nature will always triumph.

There then ensues the infamous China scene. It commences with Dr. Quack making another house call to see how his patient is faring. But the consultation is cut short by the early arrival of Lady Fidget for a romantic rendezvous (provided Horner will have a care for her "dear honour"). Horner responds, "in the mysteries of love it makes the charm impotent." At which the outraged lady castigates him: "Nay, fye, let us not be smutty."[147] He then promises her:

> HORNER: . . . to serve you, I'll lie with 'em all, make the secret their own, and then they'll keep it: I am a Machiavel in love, madam.[148]

His generosity knows no bounds. But just as they are about to commence "business," Sir Jaspar arrives inopportunely: "O my husband— prevented! . . ."[149] Lady Fidget protests that she was only tickling Mr. Horner, and her husband, who is aware of the gentleman's "infirmity," inquires why she was not out shopping for China as she had told him. The entrapped Horner quickly remarks, "that is my cue, I must take it."[150] He then explains to Sir Jaspar that he is merely showing his wife some of his own private China. Crockery now becomes a euphemism for lechery, which Wycherley exploits to the hilt.

As Sir Jaspar chuckles with relief, Horner takes the lady into another room to show her what else he has—entering by a second door, as Sir Jaspar calls out good-naturedly:

> SIR JASPAR: Wife! He is coming into you the back way.

To which his lady wife replies:

> LADY FIDGET: Let him come, and welcome, which way he will.[151]

Perhaps we now have an inkling why the play was bowdlerized.

Almost operatically, the rest of the women now arrive. Mrs. Squeamish appears ("Where is this women-hater, this toad, this ugly, greasy, slovenly villain . . . where is this odious beast?"), and at this very moment Lady Fidget returns from "toiling and moiling for the prettiest piece of china, my dear." This arouses Mrs. Squeamish's jealousy:

> MRS. SQUEAMISH: Oh, Lord, I'll have some china too. Good Mr. Horner, don't think to give other people china, and me none; come in with me too.

HORNER: Upon my honour, I have none left now. This lady had the
last there.[152]

After Wycherley milks the double-entendre for all it is worth,[153] they
all depart and we are reminded that there is an extra dimension to this
scene—the almost pathological voyeurism of Dr. Quack, who has been
observing all this time. This is totally gratuitous: it is nothing like the
eavesdropping in ordinary comedy, which is normally used to further
the plot. Once again serving as a dramatic chorus, the physician gasps:
"I will now believe anything he tells me."[154] So much for the filthiest of
all possible scenes.

This scene was so scandalous that Wycherley referred to it
metatheatrically in *The Plain Dealer*. The hero's mistress, Olivia, pretends to have been shocked by the author's earlier play, the *Country
Wife:*

> . . . the lewdest, filthiest thing, is his china—nay I will never
> forgive the beastly author for his china. He has quite taken
> away the reputation of poor china itself, and sullied the most
> innocent and pretty furniture of a lady's chamber—inso-
> much that I was fain to break all my defiled vessels. You see I
> have none left; nor you, I hope.[155]

With the subject of china finally exhausted, Pinchwife himself arrives to deliver his wife's "angry" letter and loudly protests:

PINCHWIFE: I'll not be a cuckold, I say. There will be danger in making
me a cuckold.

HORNER: Why, wert thou not well cured of thy last clap?

PINCHWIFE: (*angered*) I wear a sword.[156]

The phallic reference is unmistakable—a reinforcement of the more
blatant outbursts of her impotently raging husband. (Throughout the
play Pinchwife repeatedly threatens his wife with, among other things,
stabbing her eyes out or attacking her with a sword.)[157]

This is racier than ever Ben Jonson writ. Surely when one has em-
barked on a sea of innuendo, one can sail forever. At this the doctor offers yet another choral comment—that Horner would flourish in the

harem of the Sultan of Turkey. Quack finally serves a useful dramatic purpose: to remind the audience that Pinchwife is unique in his ignorance of Horner's pretended malady.

By now Margery's fever goes hand in hand with her growing cleverness. Like Dante, she is moved by love to speak. We find her moaning with delicious pain in the midst of writing her second love letter to Horner:

> I have got the London disease called love. I am sick of my husband and for my gallant. I have heard this distemper called a fever, but methinks 'tis liker an ague, for when I think of my husband I tremble and am in a cold sweat, and have inclinations to vomit, but when I think of my gallant ... my hot fit comes and I am all in a fever.[158]

Suddenly Pinchwife surprises her, and once again draws his sword. But she has learned the ways of the city so well that she quickly concocts an ingenious pretext to stave him off: she replies that the letter is not for herself but for Alithea, his sister, who is in love with Horner. Margery, who has come from the country ingenuous and innocent, is now a sophisticated urban schemer. Pinchwife is hoodwinked, murmuring to himself: "this changeling could not invent this lie ..." And then he adds in an aside:

PINCHWIFE: I'd rather be of kin to him by the name of brother-in-law than that of cuckold.[159]

Gulled into believing that it is Alithea who is the object of Horner's attentions, Pinchwife now leads his sister (actually Margery dressed as Alithea, and masked) straight to the lecher's bower. Here we find a direct echo of the finale of *Mandragola*, in which Dr. Nicia is the author of his own marital undoing as he himself escorts Callimaco into Lucrezia's bed. But Horner gives the scene an additional cruel twist, asking Pinchwife if the lady he has brought "is sound?"—that is to say, free of disease. To which the outraged cuckold-to-be retorts: "What, do you take her for a wench, and me for a pimp?" After another exchange of epigrams, Pinchwife leaves to fetch a parson, saying to the two lovers: "I'll leave you together, and hope when I am gone you will agree."[160]

Horner then tells the medical voyeur:

> Doctor, anon, you too shall be my guest,
> But now I am going to a private feast.[161]

Later, upon hearing from Pinchwife that "Alithea" is at Master Horner's, Sparkish is infuriated. When she enters, he hurls abuse at his unwitting fiancée, confessing:

> I never had any passion for you, till now, for now I hate you.
> 'Tis true I might have married your portion, as other men of
> the town do sometimes . . .[162]

He completes his valediction with an ambiguous farewell, punning on the word "servant," which in Wycherley's day could also mean lover: "there's for you and so your servant, servant."[163]

We now return to bedroom farce. Margery is still in Horner's bed when the "virtuous gang," as they call themselves, unexpectedly arrive for dinner ("a pox, they are come too soon—before I have sent back my new mistress!").[164] And so in an ironic replay of Pinchwife's incarceration of his wife Margery, now Horner locks the same woman—his mistress—in the bedroom as well. When the dinner party is over Horner frees the poor innocent-guilty woman, who is now so intoxicated with joy that she wants to marry him.

There ensues an operatic finale—all the characters are on stage, including the earnest Harcourt, the lovely Alithea, her clever maid Lucy—not to mention a parson ready to perform the traditional legal *gamos*. They all confront Horner with accusations. Pinchwife once again draws his sword on Margery—and then immediately menaces Horner, screaming that he has been cuckolded. Lucy tries to soothe matters, blaming herself with a flimsy pretext that Margery is innocent and the antics were all a concoction to help Alithea in "breaking off the match between Mr. Sparkish, and her, to make way for Mr. Harcourt."[165]

But Pinchwife is disabused of his suspicions when at last Sir Jaspar whispers to him the secret of Horner's recent "misfortune." The old man smiles:

> PINCHWIFE: An eunuch! Pray, no fooling with me.
> DR. QUACK: I'll bring half the surgeons in town to swear it.[166]

This now explains why Wycherley included the physician among Horner's dinner guests—he can offer professional testimony to his patient's "disability." An incredulous Pinchwife protests, "I'm sure when I left the town he was the lewdest fellow in't."[167] But the good doctor brings Pinchwife's knowledge up to date: "haven't you all heard the late sad report of poor Mr. Horner?"[168] The trio of "honourable" over-sexed harpies, oozing innocence, testify as one: "Ay, ay, ay."

And yet this is a difficult deception to make plausible—especially when Margery keeps insisting that she knows Horner's anatomy to be in fine working order. But since everyone else has a vested interest in the truth being covered up, Margery's ingenuous defenses of Horner's masculinity are totally ignored.

The play concludes with each set of characters pronouncing a homily on their particular views of marriage. For example:

> ALITHEA: Women and fortune are truest still to those that trust 'em.
> LUCY: And any wild thing grows but the more fierce and hungry for being kept up, and more dangerous to the keeper.
> ALITHEA: There's doctrine for all husbands, Mr. Harcourt.
> HARCOURT: I edify, madam, so much, that I am impatient till I am one.
> DORLIANT: And I edify so much by example, I will never be one.
> SPARKISH: And because I will not disparage my parts, I'll ne'er be one.
> HORNER: And I, alas! can't be one.
> PINCHWIFE: But I must be one—against my will to a country wife, with a country murrain to me![169]

Finally Margery is resigned to remaining a country wife, for "I find, for I can't, like a city one, be rid of my musty husband and do what I list."[170] Thus Horner has "enjoyed the outrage while being spared the consequences." By contrast, if Ben Jonson had written this play, Horner probably would have suffered the surgical punishment of Abelard. Instead, Pinchwife becomes a *mari philosophe,* sighing:

> For my own sake fain I would all believe;
> Cuckolds like mothers should themselves deceive.[171]

We recall the attitude toward infidelity of Sosie in Molière's *Amphitryon:*

> Would it not be better—to take no chances,
> And don't ask what's really going on?[172]

Is it too grand to liken Pinchwife to Plautus' heroic Amphitruo? Perhaps not, for after all horns are horns. And as John Dryden's 1690 adaptation of the same Latin play demonstrates, the Amphitryon myth was in its way the ideal paradigm for countless Restoration comedies. Nearly every ingredient is there: the innocent wife; the cuckolded husband; a greater power, whether monarchic or celestial, imposing his will and thus forcing the human husband to accept the unacceptable. Many of these features characterize the *Country Wife* as well, although Wycherley's tone is far more brittle and derisive.

All the above qualities were brought to perfection in Beaumarchais's matchless *Marriage of Figaro*—which has a daring political dimension as well. When the play was first completed in 1781, it radiated a thinly disguised subversive aura, which so troubled King Louis XVI that he declared categorically, "this play will never be produced." But the dramatist did not give up easily. He revised his text, employing a technique similar to Plautus' use of Greek characters to license un-Roman behavior. This time the camouflage was Hispanification. For what was the Château of "Fraiche Fontaine" in his original draft became "Aguas Frescas" in subsequent revisions. References to the Bastille were wisely reduced. And so on. The play was at last performed on 27 April 1784 by the Comédie Française, to wild acclaim from the all-star audience.

Figaro is a figure who is at once traditional and revolutionary—in both senses of the word. Audiences had already met him in Beaumarchais's earlier *Barber of Seville* (1774), in which he describes Figaro's long and colorful career as a factotum—a jack-of-all-trades.[173] He has finally ended up here in Seville as "a barber to anyone who needed me." And now at the count's urgent request, Figaro takes him on as a client to press his suit with Rosine. Like Figaro himself, Beaumarchais was a man with his finger in every pie. His many activities included setting up a trading company to send munitions and materials to the American revolutionaries. He had to go into exile in England three times for supplying arms to the rebels in America, but his talent for diplomacy proved indispensable.

On the one hand, the *Marriage* is rich with the familiar comic themes—like the *agōn* between servant and master, which is also a conflict between youth (Figaro) and age (the now-jaded Count). The outcome is completely conventional: the prize, as in Plautus' *Casina,* is the young girl—Figaro's fiancée—for whom both men are battling. The play also perfectly exemplifies Northrop Frye's formulation that "New Comedy unfolds from what may be described as a comic Oedipus situation."[174] In the subplot, Figaro makes a hairsbreadth escape from marrying his own mother, thanks to a traditional *cognitio* with the usual juvenile trinkets. The play also includes a traditional Saturnalian humiliation of the master by the slave's *ponēria,* just as we find in Plautus' *Epidicus,* where the title character, a bondsman—*after* he has already been liberated—demands further that his ex-master kneel and beg forgiveness.[175]

But Beaumarchais's comedy is also revolutionary in the literal sense. During the familiar mixup of identities—in the dark, as in *George Dandin*—Figaro appears and holds the stage for a long soliloquy. At this point thinking himself deceived by his beloved Suzanne, he rails against all women ("flighty and deceitful creatures"). This misogyny of course is not new. What is really audacious is Figaro's tirade against the unearned privileges of birth:

> No, my dear Count, you won't have my Suzanne. Just because you're an aristocrat, you think you're also a great genius. Nobility, fortune, rank, position—you're so proud of these trappings. But what the hell did you *do* to deserve them? You took the trouble of being born—that's it. Otherwise you're just a fairly run-of-the-mill chap.
>
> But I, a mere plebeian face in the crowd, have had to mobilize more skill and planning just to keep my head above water . . . Compare my life-story to yours . . . I'm the son of God-knows-who, kidnapped as a child by bandits . . . escaped to learn an honest trade—only to have every door slammed in my face. I studied Chemistry, Pharmacology, Surgery—and all the efforts of a great aristocrat could barely get me a job as a junior veterinarian . . .[176]

And yet the distinction is not the various employments that Figaro has tried—that would make him little better than Molière's Scapin. Figaro as good as says, "all men are created equal." Which is why this speech is regarded as the first call to arms for all Frenchmen to gain *liberté*, *égalité*, and *fraternité*.

But today Beaumarchais's comedy is better known for having inspired Mozart's most popular opera. (We recall that Rossini's *Barber of Seville* [1816], a musicalization of the first Beaumarchais play, was presented much later.) The young genius began composing the moment he read the newly published play—and indeed chose as his collaborator the multitalented and figaroesque Lorenzo Da Ponte.[177] *Figaro* was a marriage of mind and melody. It produced many memorable and enchanting moments, such as the servant's aria when he learns that his master has designs on his fiancée and resolves to thwart him (*Se vuol ballare signor Contino*):

> Count, if you're looking
> To dance with Susannah,
> Count, if you're seeking
> Romance with Susannah,
> I'll play the music on my guitar.
> But if you'd like some delayed education,
> You'll learn your lesson—you won't get far.

Whether or not Beaumarchais's *Figaro* was the first shot in the revolution that would explode five years later may be disputed. What is beyond doubt, however, is that the revolution that began with a simple quip by Susarion of Megara more than two millennia earlier had now reached in Beaumarchais its ultimate perfection.

20

Comedy Explodes

After reaching its apogee with Figaro, comedy had nowhere to go but down. Like the animated cartoons in which a character runs off a cliff and continues running in the air until he realizes there is no ground beneath him, the genre continued to flourish in the form we have been studying until the eve of the twentieth century.

One of the prime characteristics of post-classical comedy is the annihilation of logical discourse and coherent plot. The laughter comes not as a result of the audience "getting" the joke, but rather from the nonsense and illogic of the joke itself.

It is a matter of debate as to when the disintegration of classical forms began. The first theatrical offender is usually thought to be Alfred Jarry, the mad genius who burst upon the Paris intellectual scene like a Roman candle at the end of the nineteenth century, and whose life and luminescence were similarly brief. In his works all logic was destroyed. Yet one can find traces of the incipient disintegration of rational discourse as early as Molière, in the rambling hysteria of Harpagon's frantic outburst when his pot of gold is stolen. His hysterical cry to the authorities—to have everyone searched (including himself), and if the gold is still not found, to kill everybody (including himself)—teeters on the verge of lunacy.

But since *The Miser* has all the other elements of traditional comedy, we should perhaps seek the first frontal assault on the classic form in the plays of the mischievous George Bernard Shaw. We will see, as a general rule, that "assassins of comedy" are all intellectuals of one sort or another. Shaw, who in addition to being the leading English dramatist of the early twentieth century was also a music, book, and art critic, polemicist, essayist, linguistic reformer, and self-interpreter, certainly fits this description. Consider, for example, two of his most popular plays, *Man and Superman* (1905) and *Pygmalion* (1913).

In the first, after a long debate with the Devil, the legendary seducer Don Juan decides to forsake the fleshly delights of the netherworld and instead go to heaven. He opts for the *intellectual* stimulation of an ethereal—and asexual—existence:

> DON JUAN: I have done a thousand wonderful things unconsciously by merely willing to live and following the line of least resistance: now I want to know myself and my destination, and choose my path; so I have made a special *brain*—a philosopher's *brain* to grasp this knowledge for me . . . [emphasis mine][1]

This very long play is actually two dramas in one, which at first appear to be only marginally related but, as we ultimately come to see, form an integrated diptych which presents the pursuit of man after woman—or is it vice versa? The second drama presents the experience of Don Juan in Hell. All this verbiage could not disguise the fact that the hero of Shaw's play was nothing like the sensualist familiar to audiences for three centuries.

His desire to "know himself" aligns the hero directly with Plato's injunction to "know thyself," totally ignoring Bergson's dictum that a character is *comic* in proportion to his *ignorance* of himself. Shaw was all mind, preferring words to action. Thus his paragonal great lover embodies the antithesis of comedy, where the intellect triumphs over instinct. One wonders if Shaw was fully aware how much of his own personal eccentricity he was revealing in this atypical characterization. Indeed, here and elsewhere in his plays he displays an almost pathological fear of women. He complains that love is "not what I bargained for":

It was not music, painting, poetry, and joy incarnated in a beautiful woman. I ran away from it. I ran away from it very often: in fact I became famous for running away from it.[2]

In case it is not already clear, he becomes even more specific:

When I stood face to face with Woman, every fibre in my clear critical brain warned me to spare her and save myself.

Not to put too fine a point on it, the Shavian Don Juan suffers from a scarcely-hidden castration anxiety. Witness the following speech he places in his hero's mouth:

A woman seeking a husband is the most unscrupulous of all the beasts of prey . . . and marriage is a mantrap.[3]

One could even go so far as to call it sexual nausea, as evidenced by the following exchange:

DEVIL: Give me warmth of heart, true sincerity, the bond of sympathy with love and joy.
DON JUAN: You are making me ill.

In short, Don Juan is a prime example of *intellect* dominating *instinct*—a decidedly anti-comic stance.

Or perhaps he has not reached emotional maturity. This can be inferred from the hero's ingenuous—or disingenuous—remark:

When I was a child, and bruised my head against the stone, I ran to the nearest woman and cried away my pain against her apron. When I grew up, and bruised my soul against the brutalities and stupidities with which I had to strive, I did again just what I had done as a child.[4]

In Shaw's version, the great seducer still wants his mommy. Is this not a prime case of arrested development?

Yet Don Juan is far from being Shaw's only hero who is unduly attached to his mother. Another of his unwitting self-portraits is found in *Pygmalion,* his most famous play—thanks to *My Fair Lady*. In the original myth of Pygmalion, a misogynistic sculptor rejects all women on earth as not good enough and only finds perfection in one of his own statues. "Golden Venus" sees to it that his love is requited by turning his statue into a real woman.[5]

Shaw's version, however, is perverse. His hero, a professor of linguistics named Henry Higgins, after transforming a flower-girl into a lady, lets Liza Doolittle walk out of his life to marry the twittish Freddy, while he himself clings to the maternal apron strings. Apparently he has not grown "accustomed to her face." The musical adapters of course made the necessary comic corrections. All they had to do was replace the intellectual with the instinctual by bringing the lady back onstage, leaving us in no doubt as to what they would be doing after the curtain fell. ("I could have danced all night.")

In his Afterword, Shaw justifies this odd monasticism with considerable sophistry. He protests that Higgins' "indifference to young women" was because "they had an irresistible rival in his mother." By keeping Higgins in a state of prepubescent sexuality, Shaw denies the hero—and the audience—the traditional satisfaction of a *gamos*. This is why there is really no glory in his outrageous claim that

> there is no eminent writer . . . whom I despise so entirely as I
> despise Shakespeare when I measure my mind against his.[6]

But intellect is the enemy of comic instinct, and Shaw's superior mind—even if indeed it was greater than Shakespeare's—is not in the job description of a comic hero.

It is not difficult to see the author himself in this rationalization because, like his protagonist, Shaw was, among other things, involved in the creation of a new phonetic alphabet—which, to speak figuratively, was unable to spell "sex." This kind of apology gave much fuel to critics like H. G. Wells, who bluntly referred to Shaw as "an intellectual eunuch."[7]

At the same time as this cerebral Anglo-Irish playwright was denying his hungry audiences the conventional *gamos,* across the channel a more radical revolution was taking place. Arguably the first agent provocateur of the war was Alfred Jarry, whose *Ubu Roi* deliberately violated or methodically threw away all the traditional rules.[8]

Jarry was viewed by his contemporaries as a *potache*—half brat, half genius. By one of those coincidences that seem too good to be true, his teacher at the Lycée Henri IV was none other than Henri Bergson. Thereafter, in 1894, incredible though it seems, Jarry was drafted for military service. Not surprisingly, he did not find the discipline congenial, and in fact spent most of his time in the military on latrine duty—an experience which may have inspired his choice of a toilet brush as King Ubu's scepter. An overdose prematurely ended his army career and nearly his life. He then plunged into the Paris literary scene. Undaunted, he continued to enhance his geniality with lavish doses of alcohol and various mind-altering drugs.

But his greatest thrills still came from his wild imagination. To begin with, he furnished his bizarre low-ceilinged apartment with various miniatures, as well as a giant phallus—also a miniature, as he mischievously confided to his friends.[9] Similarly, in his plays, he aimed to shock as well as amuse. And he did so with a vengeance. His first play was nothing less than the first blow in the campaign that ultimately would destroy all cherished—that is, coherent and logical—dramatic form.

On the tenth of December 1896, when he was only twenty-three years old, the Théâtre de l'Oeuvre produced Jarry's magnum opus, *King Ubu*. It was shocking, scatological, unstructured, oneiric, and puerile. In fact, Jarry's works may be seen as the reverse of Wordsworth's famous description of Romanticism: not "the child is father of the man," but rather "the man is father of the child."

Ubu was a riot—literally. As with Stravinsky's *Rite of Spring*, there were no neutral opinions on the night of its premiere: members of the audience began attacking one another from the first word of the play. Why did the mayhem start after the very first word? Because the word was *merdre* ("shitto"). Nor did they watch the rest of the play quietly—they went berserk every time they heard that word.

This deranged travesty of *Macbeth*—spiced with other snippets from Shakespeare—begins with a scene between Mère and Père Ubu. Their style of acting demonstrates the persistence of Jarry's childhood fascination with Punch and Judy puppets. But the puppets lack all sexuality.[10] In his imagination, Jarry's characters were prepubescent. Yet in another sense, Jarry's characters have unbounded libido and no superego. Indeed, as one critic observes:

There is a striking similarly between the insights of Jarry and those of Freud. That Jarry could not, for purely chronological reasons, have known the works of Freud is beyond doubt.[11]

Jarry's introductory speech sets the tone of absurdity. "This play is set in Poland, which is to say nowhere."[12] And yet there is more than a grain of sense in even this seemingly preposterous statement. For after the Congress of Vienna in 1815 the sovereign state of Poland did not exist—at least cartographically—and would not reappear until the end of the First World War. Thus it temporarily joined such other fictive comic locations as Cloudcuckooville, Shangri-la, Illyria, and the sea-coast of Bohemia.

When the Ubus finish insulting each other, they scheme like Macbeth and his lady to kill King Venceslas and take over the country. And, in the delicate words of Mère Ubu, they must slaughter the whole of the royal family so that her husband can "put his ass on the throne."[13]

In the next scene, as they wait for their proposed victims to arrive for dinner, Père Ubu pays his wife a dubious compliment: "You are exceedingly ugly today, is it because we have visitors?" The only possible answer to this illogic is Mère Ubu's "Shitto."

After eating, Père Ubu tells his wife, "I've had a rotten dinner," to which Captain Bordure ("Captain von Rubbish"), their co-conspirator, comments:

CAPT. BORD.: It was very good sir, except for the Shitto.
PÈRE UBU: What? I thought the Shitto wasn't bad.

The hostility between husband and wife continues with the aid of their guest. When Ubu embraces him, Bordure cringes:

CAPT. BORD.: Ugh, you stink, Père Ubu. Don't you ever wash?
PÈRE UBU: Rarely.
MÈRE UBU: Never!
PÈRE UBU: I'll stamp on your toes. You're a mega shitto. (grosse merdre!)

The dialogue oscillates between puerilities and non-sequiturs, with occasional combinations of both. This unrestrained aggression characterizes the Theater of the Absurd, and colors the comedy of both Ionesco and Albee.

After he organizes his junta, they all move to attack the king, and Père Ubu's language grows noticeably babyish:

> PÈRE UBU: Now listen, I'll try to step on his toes, and when he kicks out at me I'll shout "Shitto" and that will be your signal to jump all over him.

The mad plot succeeds, and most—but not all—of the royal family are slaughtered. Ubu is now king! Yet despite their ascent to power, the new royal couple remain no less childish and markedly prepubescent in their behavior—not to mention sexually abstemious. In fact, there is no sexuality of any sort during the play.

Ubu's first priority as monarch is "I want to get rich." To accomplish this he puts the nobles, financiers, and other worthies to death (through a convenient trap door) by "disembraining" them so he can confiscate their possessions. Though his subjects rise up in protest, Ubu goes around collecting taxes. As he explains concisely:

> PÈRE UBU: With this system I'll soon have made my fortune, then we'll kill everybody and go away.

Before the apocalyptic assassinations, Ubu acts with a cruelty that surpasses even that of a depraved child, much like Strepsiades or Harpagon. When his starving subjects protest their hunger or his troops demand a salary, he bawls petulantly: "I won't give away any of my money." His sheer barbarity extends beyond staff to stable. As with Harpagon, Ubu's horses are starving to death—yet another prime example of Bergonsian anesthesia of the heart. Mère Ubu complains that they haven't been fed for five weeks and are too feeble for them to ride. Ubu simply asks for another horse—which he promptly falls off. He then rushes out to war prepared "to kill everybody." His wife's touching farewell is "Adieu, dear husband, be sure and kill the Czar." But in his absence the Poles turn on her, and Mère Ubu is put to flight.

Again as in *Macbeth*, one son of the murdered king—Bougrelas ("Dimwhittington")—survives. He reaches Moscow and obtains the support of the Russian monarch, who proceeds to attack "Poland." Ubu leads his Poles (in a manner of speaking) against the enemy, and a harsh battle ensues in which he is wounded. But despite his injuries he even confronts the Czar with his "saber of shitto." The Cossacks give chase.

The scene suddenly shifts to a cave in Lithuania where Ubu and his officers take refuge during a snowstorm. Out of nowhere a huge bear appears—perhaps a relative of the ursine creature who enters similarly unmotivated in Shakespeare's *Winter's Tale*. Père Ubu, petrified, scrambles to a high rock and begins to recite the Paternoster with supreme Wrong Logic. As he prays, the creature preys. After his less cowardly comrades dispatch the beast, Ubu praises himself for climbing out of reach—not out of cowardice, but to "get his prayers closer to heaven."

Too tired to go with his fellow soldiers, Ubu remains in the cave and takes a nap in which he sees a vision of two monsters—a bear and his wife. He shouts out nonsensically:

> PÈRE UBU: I've been dead for a long time, Bougrelas killed me and
> I'm buried in Warsaw, Cracow, and also in Thorn.

This is typical of the utterances of Absurdist characters, which always have a hypnotic, hallucinatory quality—especially appropriate here, since it is, of course, a dream.

The final act begins with Mère Ubu entering the tenebrous cavern. She speaks a reasonably heroic monologue, recounting how she has crossed all of Poland in four days with her beloved knight, Palotin Giron, to escape the revolution. She proudly tells how he went into raptures when he saw her, "and even when he didn't"—the greatest proof of love. He swore to have himself cut in two. Giron outdid himself and was cut in four by Bougrelas.

She suddenly notices her sleeping husband, and proceeds to enter his dream as a ghost of the Archangel Gabriel. In this divine disguise she praises herself and tries to dissuade Père Ubu of his low opinion of her:

PÈRE UBU: Certainly she is the vilest of old hags.

MÈRE UBU: You mean that she was a charming woman . . .

PÈRE UBU: A horror . . .

MÈRE UBU: Why she is at least the equal to Diana of the Ephesians.

Could this possibly be, in the midst of a *Macbeth* parody, an allusion to Shakespeare's *Comedy of Errors,* or *Pericles* for that matter? With Jarry you never know:

MÈRE UBU: At least she doesn't drink . . .

PÈRE UBU: Not since I took the key to the cellar, before that she was smashed before breakfast . . . My wife is a slut.

Through war and other cataclysms their relationship has remained unswervingly belligerent. As the specter, she instructs him to forgive his wife even though she might have taken some money. To which Ubu replies that he will forgive her "when she's had a good beating." A moment later the marital rivals recognize each other in a kind of *cognitio*. At this point he throws the carcass of the bear at her. She screams with fear and he comments snidely, "It's dead, you grotesque hag," and proceeds—like Falstaff at Shrewsbury Field—to claim credit for killing the bear himself. And then, in a manner typical of their tender relationship, Ubu begins, according to Jarry's stage direction, to "tear her to pieces."

In the penultimate scene the exiled pretender Bougrelas suddenly appears in the cave, and the two Ubus pour nonsensical insults on him—a time-honored comic routine:

PÈRE UBU: Take that, Pollack drunkard, bastard, hussar, tartar, dozener, cozener, liar, savoyard, communard!

His wife joins the drubbing:

MÈRE UBU: Take that! Swindler, porker, traitor, playactor, perjurer, dog-robber, bolster!

Yet another stage fight ensues, at the end of which the petrified Ubu suffers an Aristophanic dilemma:

PÈRE UBU: O my, I've done it in my pants.[14]

The Ubus win the mêlée and run off. If it has not yet been made clear, it is now beyond question that King Ubu is a big baby. In the tradition of Strepsiades in the *Clouds* and Dionysus in the *Frogs,* or the simple Sancho Panza, fear has inspired him to loosen his sphincter.

The final scene shows the hero and heroine on a ship at sea (Jarry had no sets, merely placards announcing each change of locale). According to Père Ubu's estimate, they are doing "at least a million knots per hour." He then puns: "these are special knots that never become undone." (The pun works in French as well: *un million de noeuds à l'heure.*) After passing such heroic sites as Prince Hamlet's Castle of Elsinore, Spain, the North Sea, and "Germania," Ubu pronounces the ultimate message of the play:

> PÈRE UBU: Ah my friends, as beautiful as it may be it is nothing compared to Poland. After all if there weren't any Poland there wouldn't be any Poles!

There can be no answer to that. And thus concludes the initial shot across the bow of dramatic coherence.

Such future immortals as Yeats and Mallarmé were among those present at this landmark event. The Irish poet described the occasion:

> The audience shakes their fists at one another . . . The players
> are supposed dolls, toys, marionettes, and they are all hopping like wooden frogs . . .

And yet, he concludes ominously, "that night . . . I am very sad for comedy, objectivity has displayed its growing power once more." And then the famous chilling words: "After us the Savage God."[15]

In a life scarcely longer than Jarry's, his friend and artistic heir Guillaume Apollinaire produced an enormous amount of literary and dramatic work including—like the master—art and music criticism. He could have run for mayor of Montmartre, so popular was he with the avant-garde of almost every artistic movement. But his primary purpose was always to shock—both in words and images. He gleefully deprecates bourgeois devotees of all "boulevard" genres. One of his earliest published works, the prose poem *Onirocritique,* contains the line "the sky was full of shit and onions."[16] This was hardly classical poetry.

Born out of wedlock, Apollinaire took mischievous delight in claiming that he had been sired by a cardinal in the Vatican.[17] Throughout his life he was known for his childlike laughter. In other words, like Jarry he preserved his infantile personality even in adulthood—a recurring quality of the avant-garde. His noble gesture of volunteering for service in the First World War cost him his life—he died at age thirty-eight from mortar wounds and the Spanish influenza.

Probably Apollinaire's most enduring legacy to literature was his coinage of the term "surrealism," invented for the preface to his 1918 Jarryesque play *Les Mamelles de Tirésias (The Breasts of Tiresias).* This work attempted

> a renovation of the theatre, at least an original effort . . . [a return to] nature itself without copying it photographically.[18]

In other words, he concludes quite candidly, his play is "a protest against that realistic theatre which is the predominating art today."

For history's sake it should be recorded that Apollinaire's coinage made its first public appearance the week before the opening of Cocteau's *Parade,* when the preface to *Les Mamelles* was published in the newspaper *Excelsior.* His own play, for which he had coined the term, was produced a month afterwards.[19]

Composed in the same year when Apollinaire met Jarry, *Les Mamelles* was not presented until a decade later. But the shock value of the play was not diminished by the delay. As Apollinaire wrote in the preface:

> I wrote my surrealist drama above all for the French as Aristophanes composed his comedies for the Athenians. I have warned them of the grave danger, recognized by everybody, that not making children holds for a nation that wishes to be prosperous and powerful and to remedy the evil I have shown them what must be done.

As with Jarry, the play is minimalist—the entire population of Zanzibar is represented by a single person who does not even speak. In fact, most of the dialogue is "shouted at the audience" through a megaphone. Cocteau also employs this device to emphasize the artificiality of the characters.

The heroine (at least for a few minutes) is Thérèse, who is dressed in blue—including her face. She is a modern woman:

> I am a feminist and I do not recognize the authority of men . . .
> I want to make war and I do not want to make children.

She then shouts into the megaphone the following nugget of nonsense:

> Because you made love to me in Connecticut
> doesn't mean I have to cook for you in Zanzibar.

Thérèse emphasizes her ambition to become a "mathematician philosopher chemist a page in a restaurant a little clerk in a telegraph office." Now, as an overture to the most crucial moment of the play, she sneezes, cackles, and choo-choos like a train. This is merely the first note in what will be a crescendo of depersonalization, indeed of reification. It concludes:

> THÉRÈSE: But I think I'm growing a beard and
> My bosom's falling off.

She now experiences a surreal reversal of the classical myth of Tiresias, the ancient seer who was blinded and turned into a woman by Juno for revealing that females enjoy the sexual act even more than males. By contrast, Thérèse becomes a man, opening her blouse and letting her breasts (one red, the other blue) fly off. She then announces through the megaphone:

> THÉRÈSE: I feel as virile as the Devil,
> I'm a stallion from my head down,
> I'm a bull.

Thérèse's husband (who has no name) now arrives and asks the creature wearing his wife's clothing what "he" has done with her. He hurls himself in anger at the epicene figure and, like farcical marionettes (again a Jarryesque feature), they brawl; then, according to Apollinaire's stage directions, "*she* overpowers *him.*"

This is a significant moment in comedy's dramatization of relations between the sexes. It rivals—and indeed surpasses—Aristophanes'

Lysistrata, not to mention his *Assemblywomen,* in which Euripides sends his kinsman disguised as a woman to plead on his behalf in the assembly of women gathered to condemn him.

He/she then announces to her stunned mate, "Thérèse is no longer a woman . . . from now on I will be called Tiresias." In a subsequent scene she subdues her husband again, takes off his trousers, puts them on, hands him her skirt, cuts off her hair, and dons a top hat. A wholly unmotivated pistol shot concludes this gambit. To make the transformation complete, the husband now imitates the locomotive sound she had previously made.

But this exchange of sexual identities is more than just a vaudeville routine. It signals an important moment in the development of avant-garde drama. After Thérèse/Tiresias's aggression, the husband sensibly proposes:

> HUSBAND: Since my wife is a man
> It is proper for me to be a woman.

Having triumphed in the war between the sexes, Thérèse/Tiresias emphatically states that women will no longer have babies at the whim/will of their husbands. Thus at the close of Act One the population of the world is in dire jeopardy.

And yet Act Two begins with a flagrant contradiction of what has just transpired. We see the husband tending to several cradles and holding an infant in each arm. He rhapsodizes:

> HUSBAND: O what a thrill it is to be a father
> 40,049 children in one day alone
> My happiness is complete.

This phenomenon even attracts a journalist from Paris ("a town in America"), who admiringly asks the husband how he intends to raise his thousands of offspring. Avoiding the question, he praises the talents of his little tykes. One has published a novel which sold 600,000 copies and won a literary prize consisting of twenty cases of dynamite—an amusing (and rather explosive) allusion to the Nobel family fortunes.

By the end of the interview the reporter is reduced not simply to monosyllables but to mere vowels, as he pronounces "a e i o u" into the megaphone. We shall see how this depreciation of language becomes a regular motif in subsequent comedy of the Theater of the Absurd.

The action grows more vertiginous as *Les Mamelles* cavorts toward its conclusion. At last, Thérèse and her husband are reunited—with a difference. When he presents her with a basket of balls so she will "no longer be as flat-chested as a bedbug," she refuses, saying, "We've both got along without them, why don't we keep it that way?"

They then throw the spheroids into the audience, an ancient Aristophanic routine here vested with new meaning. For, despite the recent population explosion, the play ends with a significant desexualization: neither husband nor wife is now of any distinguishable gender.

How then could a comedy end without a *gamos*?

The evolution of Absurd Comedy can be aptly compared to a relay race, with the baton passing in turn from Jarry to Apollinaire to Cocteau, who saw himself as their logical heir.

But perhaps the simile should be changed in the spirit of Jarry's penchant for cycling, which inspired his wildly sacrilegious piece, "The Passion Considered as an Uphill Bicycle Race."[20] Apollinaire later composed equally irreverent verses in the poem "Zone" about how "Christ ascended to the sky, higher than any pilot, breaking the world's altitude record."[21] Is there a possible athletic reference here to the high jump (*saut en hauteur*)?

It is remarkable that so many of the seminal pieces of the Theater of the Absurd deal with the same material as Menander—family matters—albeit from a radically different perspective. Typically it invokes a form only to destroy it, or in this case at least to emphasize how radically the phenomenon of *gamos* is regarded by the so-called avant-garde playwrights. A marked sexual regression can be seen in childish heroes like Mère and Père Ubu, or in the sexual ambiguity of Thérèse/Tiresias and her husband. And in the play we are about to examine, the wedding itself is annihilated.

Jean Cocteau, an eagle of the arts, was a direct descendant of Alfred Jarry via Apollinaire, although the young Cocteau had an ambivalent relationship with the latter. Indeed, in his program notes for Cocteau's ballet *Parade* (in which he rhapsodized about the music by Erik Satie and scenery by the young Picasso), Apollinaire minimized the scenario, using the term "surréaliste."[22] Perhaps this was a direct slap at Cocteau's earlier description of the work as *ballet réaliste*. (It was only after this production—in the last years of his life—that Apollinaire warmed to the young Cocteau.)[23] There had not been as many intellectual superstars gathered in one place since the début of Jarry's *Ubu*, and the play itself had the same effect—riots. Among the admirers, no less a luminary than Marcel Proust wrote the young author a fan letter.[24]

Cocteau played a major part—or at least dabbled—in most artistic movements of the avant-garde. Dramatist, poet, graphic artist, choreographer, and *cinéaste*, he was perhaps himself the embodiment of the artist he described as a "total athlete" *(athlète complet)*—a hypothetical ideal who could produce every aspect of a play for the theater:

> A work for the theater should ideally be written, designed, costumed, musically scored, played, and danced by one single person. This "total athlete" doesn't exist. It is therefore important that this (hypothetical) individual be replaced by someone who most resembles an individual—a convivial group.[25]

Cocteau was being disingenuous, for he himself came closest—more than anyone before or since—to being a compete athlete. He could best be described by paraphrasing his own *mot* about Victor Hugo: Jean Cocteau was a madman who thought he was Jean Cocteau. For at one time or another during his career, Cocteau would fill all of these roles. His appreciation for contemporary music was enormously perceptive, and he collaborated with most of the major French composers of the early twentieth century. In fact, Cocteau's play *The Wedding on the Eiffel Tower*, first performed on 19 June 1921 and published a year later, had music by no fewer than five of the famous "Les Six": Georges Auric, Arthur Honegger, Darius Milhaud, Francis Poulenc, and Germaine Tailleferre.[26]

The printed play is preceded by a Terentian—that is, polemic—preface, by now standard procedure in this new genre. Cocteau sets out his intentions, which aim to present "the ferocity of childhood and the miraculous poetry of daily life." To this end he proposes to "resurrect the cliché." Cocteau intended to paint life *plus vrai que le vrai*, that is, "more real than the real," although he does not use the term "surrealism" himself. He does speak of the *absurde organisé*, anticipating the adjective that would come to describe the genre to which he was contributing. He is not shy and sees his work in the tradition of Shakespeare, Molière, and *le profond Chaplin*.[27] This is by no means the only invocation of the Little Tramp by avant-garde artists, as we shall see.

To begin with, Cocteau's choice of setting is significant. The Eiffel Tower was not merely a tourist attraction. Built for the Centennial Exposition in 1889, it was a beacon of optimism, of the limitless future and progress of mankind in the twentieth century. (This idea will again be of significance in *Waiting for Godot*.)

With a drum roll, the curtain rises on the first platform of the Tower. As in the stylistic delivery of *Ubu* and the megaphone "shouting at the audience" in *Les Mamelles*, Cocteau has his dialogue spoken by two loudspeakers—clearly a technical advance. He describes these devices in great detail:

> Downstage, right and left, half-hidden behind the proscenium arch, are stationed two actors dressed as phonographs, their bodies the cabinets, horns corresponding to their mouths. These gramophones narrate the play and recite the parts of the characters. They speak very loudly, very quickly, and pronounce each syllable very distinctly.[28]

To this unnatural, reified speech—a continuing theme—the author has also added another modern invention: an enormous camera with a large bellows. This will prove to be an important player in the drama about to unfold. Lest the audience think for a moment that any logic would prevail, the phonographs describe an ostrich crossing the stage followed by a hunter who fires at him. The ostrich is unharmed, but a blue *pneumatique* (a distant ancestor of the fax) falls to the ground. "You killed a telegram," moans the First Phonograph. It turns out that the ostrich is a fugitive from the camera, where it was used to draw the subjects' attention when they were told to "watch the birdie."

The manager of the Eiffel Tower now appears and notices that the telegram is addressed to him. But this telegram is dead, complains the First Phonograph. To which the second machine replies with supreme illogic, "it is precisely because it is dead that everybody understands it." The message requests a reservation for a wedding party that day. As the guests enter to the strains of a wedding march by Darius Milhaud, the Phonographs announce the various clichéd members of the party. They include the bride "gentle as a lamb," the groom "a real heart-throb," the Father-in-Law "rich as Croesus," and the Mother-in-Law "devious as a car salesman."[29]

When the guests are gathered around the table, one of them, the General, makes a speech which consists of oratorical motions—but the only sound from the loudspeakers is that of percussive noises. Is this not yet another devaluation of the spoken word? Only at the end does one of the loudspeakers announce that "everyone is deeply moved." At this moment a cyclist enters and asks directions to Chatou. The General takes her for a mirage but answers her anyway. She pedals off. Where has she come from? Clearly this is Cocteau's homage to Jarry, his literary inspiration, who both rode and wrote about bicycles.

At this point, with an Ubuesque touch, a child "massacres the entire wedding party." The manager of the Eiffel Tower rushes in to urge them to be quiet and not "frighten the telegrams." By some miracle the guests revive and the party resumes. This time five telegrams flutter down from "New York, city of lovers and dim lights." There follows a "dance of the Telegrams," and then they exit. Somewhere a lion appears from the Camera and menaces the General, who reassures the party that this beast too is a mirage, before the lion eats him up. There follows, of course, the General's funeral, after which something very significant occurs. The little boy asks: "I want someone to buy me some bread to feed the Eiffel Tower." Once again there is the confusion of living and lifeless, and we note that no character remarks on the oddness of the lad wanting to give food to a steel structure. The Second Phonograph chastises him: "It's only fed at certain hours; that's why it has grilles around it."

Language and coherence are beginning to crumble.

The celebrants have their picture taken, and it is immediately declared to be a masterpiece. Understandably, then, an Art Dealer appears, followed by an Art Collector who asks:

COLLECTOR: Who painted it?
DEALER: It is one of the latest works of God.
COLLECTOR: Is it signed?
DEALER: God does not sign . . .

The businessman continues to praise the work: "Look at that style, that nobility, that *joie de vivre!*" And then contradicts himself, "It looks like a funeral to me." The collector dissents: "I see a wedding."

Life—death—it is all a question of how you view it. Is there not some wisdom in this? Are not comedy and tragedy, more than ever, contrasting views of the same event? We think of Charlie Chaplin's astute distinction between the two dramatic modes as merely different perspectives: "tragedy is the world in close up and comedy the world in long-shot."

The grand finale may seem light-hearted, but it marks another stage in the disintegration of "normal" comedy. First the bride and groom, then the mother and father-in-law, then the rest of the wedding party enter the Camera. They do not return. Is this merely a bit of stage business? Or is Cocteau, by setting this fluffy bit of comedy on a monument built to celebrate the limitless horizons of progress, anticipating what will be a major theme of the later avant-garde—the erosion of rationality in discourse, the gradual encroachment of machines on humanity, depersonalization, and "mechanization imposed on life"? (The latter phrase is Bergson's.)[30]

There is something menacing in the machine's engorgement of the vitality of the most passionate moment in life. Indeed, this play not only negates the happy effect of a *gamos,* it all but obliterates the possibility of any future *gamoi.*

Can comedy survive without a wedding? We shall see.

❧

The determining event in the history of the early avant-garde was the brutality and senseless carnage of the battlefields of the First World War. But far worse was the total inhumanity of the Second. Indeed, what was there left to portray but the utter depravity of man which was beyond words?

The final two stages in what I have chosen to call the Death of Comedy are marked in the plays of Eugene Ionesco and Samuel Beckett. Cocteau's adjective has now given its name to a genre. These are truly works of the Theater of the Absurd in the root sense, deriving their meaning from the Latin *surdus*—deaf. Human sensibilities were no longer able to express—or hear—the atrocities which had deprived them of life.

Like so many writers of the French avant-garde, Ionesco was an alien. Born in Romania, he was educated mostly in France, although he returned to Budapest for his university studies; a Ph.D. begun thereafter in Paris was never completed. French, however familiar it was to him, was not his mother tongue. We have seen of course, as in the case of Terence, that foreign birth need not preclude a mastery of style. Nevertheless, it gave Ionesco the crucial awareness and perspective which would enable him to sense more clearly the phenomenon of the death of language.

Other Absurdist authors had a similar distance from the French in which they composed. Arthur Adamov (1908–1970) left the Caucasus—and the Russian language—at the age of four, and was brought up thereafter in France and Germany. Like so many of the Absurdists, he must have experienced some feelings of alienation. He is perhaps more pessimistic—certainly more tormented—than any author we have encountered thus far. His masterpiece, *Ping Pong* (1955), presents life as an arcade game with man pushing away at various buttons to no real effect. This is life. You are born. You play. You die, having accomplished nothing. A grim view indeed.

The third and most famous of this alien trio was Samuel Beckett, an Irishman who chose to compose in French "parce que c'est plus facile d'écrire sans style" ("because it is easier to write without style").

Beyond this kinship with his fellow expatriates, Ionesco was influenced, like the master Jarry, by his earliest theatrical experience— puppet shows:

> My mother could not tear me away from the Punch and Judy
> show at the Luxembourg Gardens . . . I stayed there, enrapt,

for whole days. The spectacle of the Punch and Judy show held me there, as if stupefied, through the sight of these puppets that talked, moved, clubbed each other. It was the spectacle of the world itself, which, unusual, improbable, but truer than truth, presented itself to me in an infinitely simplified and caricatured form, as if to underline its grotesque and brutal truth.[31]

Ionesco's very first work for the theater, and perhaps his greatest, was *La Cantatrice chauve (The Bald Soprano)*—a title inspired by an actor's slip of the tongue during rehearsal.[32] Completed in 1949 and staged in 1950, it perpetuated the stylistic tradition initiated by Jarry. The characters—if they can be called that—speak in a staccato, machine-like manner. The playwright himself titled it an "anti-play," and later referred to it as "a comedy of a comedy." One may also view it as logic having a nervous breakdown. Though his friends found the play very funny, Ionesco himself regarded it as "the tragedy of language."[33] Or, as one critic has expressed it, "the demise of intellectual control . . . the subversion of reason."[34]

The Bald Soprano was inspired by Ionesco's study of the English language with the aid of the Assimil method on disks. This experience he later described facetiously as "the road to the discovery of new truths":

> I learned not English but some astonishing truths—that, for example, there are seven days in the week, something I already knew; that the floor is down, the ceiling up, things I already knew as well, perhaps, but that I had never seriously thought about or had forgotten, and that seemed to me, suddenly, as stupefying as they were indisputably true.[35]

But the *Bald Soprano* is no mere parody of language teaching methods—on the contrary, it argues for the death of language. Ionesco has woven his school book into the fabric of the play, but regardless of the triviality of the origin of this material, when the playwright uses it to describe the difficulty of communication in a modern world, it becomes his own intellectual property. (The same principle applies for the speech of Enobarbus in *Antony and Cleopatra* which describes the queen's splendid barge. Although it was drawn from North's English translation of Amyot's French translation of Plutarch's Greek original, once it entered the play it became Shakespeare's.)

Ionesco gives a hint of what is to come in his meta-banal description of the setting: "a middle-class English interior, English armchairs, and English evening etc. . . ."[36] In the initial dialogue, Mrs. Smith does all the talking as Mr. Smith continues to read the paper—his only response being a click of the tongue. She goes on to describe the trivialities of her mundane existence—the bland dinner they have had and various other forgettable minutiae.

The only hint of action is the fact that the meal made Mr. Smith "go to the w.c." (These people are obviously of an age when even the plumbing begins to deteriorate.) Perhaps the only important item in her observation that the children "have also eaten well and the daughter plays the piano and eats only porridge" is the fact that we will never see these children at all—a theme which is repeated in the Martins' description of their offspring. The hint of illogic in her observation that a local yoghurt "is good for the stomach, kidneys, the appendicitis, and apotheosis" goes unnoticed by her husband—and perhaps the audience.

It is only when she reports that their doctor never prescribes any medicine without having tried it on himself first that we have some inkling of the irrational conclusion to come:

MRS. SMITH: Before operating on Parker, he had his own liver operated on first, although he was not the least bit ill.

At last her husband speaks:

MR. SMITH: But how does it happen that the doctor pulled through and Parker died?

MRS. SMITH: Because the operation was a success in the doctor's case but not in Parker's.

Mr. Smith then submits that McKenzie is not a good doctor:

MR. SMITH: A conscientious doctor must die with his patient if they can't get well together. The captain of a ship goes down with his ship into the briny deep, he does not survive alone.

MRS. SMITH: Ah, I hadn't thought of that . . . perhaps it is true. And
then, what conclusion do you draw from this?

MR. SMITH: All doctors are quacks. And all patients too. Only the
Royal Navy is honest in England.

MRS. SMITH: But not sailors.

MR. SMITH: Naturally . . .

Cartesian logic has been thrown to the winds. Can this be real communication? This may well be the very point that Ionesco is making. He
presents a mad duet based on the history of a family, all of whom are
named Bobby Watson. Mr. Smith reads the notice that "Bobby Watson
has died." Mrs. Smith is shocked, but her husband chides her:

MR. SMITH: Why do you pretend to be astonished? You know very
well that he has been dead these past two years. Surely
you remember that we attended his funeral a year and a
half ago?

Is the audience yet tuned in to these bizarre details? Have they
given any logical attention to the fact that the man's funeral was a full
six months after he died? If not, they would certainly notice when Mr.
Smith observes: "it has been three years since his death was announced." And a moment later he says, "Poor Bobby, he had been dead
for four years and he was still warm." He is referring to the man's wife—
who is also called Bobby Watson (of course). She and another Bobby
Watson are planning to be married. The original couple had no children—except a boy and a girl named Bobby and Bobby.

There follows a virtual explosion of Bobbys—uncle, mother, cousin,
and so on. Spiced by Mr. Smith's informative observation that "all
Bobby Watsons are commercial travellers," these conclusions, made on
the basis of senseless evidence, represent the ultimate destruction of
the concept of "ergo." The Smiths continue to speak in a hostile fashion—a kind of tired, middle-aged Punch and Judy. At last Mrs. Smith
shows a glimmer of emotion:

MRS. SMITH: Men are all alike! You sit there all day long, a cigarette in
your mouth, you powder your nose, you rouge your lips
fifty times a day, or else you drink like a fish.

This attitude toward men as—at best—androgynous is characteristic of the Theater of the Absurd, where the line between genders is progressively blurred. We have already seen a hint of this in the prepubescent characters of their majesties the Ubus, as well as the sexual ambidexterity of Apollinaire's Thérèse/Tiresias.

When their guests the Martins arrive (chastized by the maid Mary for being late), a spectacular, incredible *cognitio* ensues—or at any rate a virtuoso parody of the familiar classical convention. Mr. Martin suddenly recognizes Mrs. Martin as someone "that I've met somewhere before. Was it in Manchester?" Mrs. Martin allows that it is possible, but:

> MRS. MARTIN: I do not have a good memory, Sir, I cannot say if it was there that I caught a glimpse of you.

They continue to disclose various coincidences that make it likely that they are man and wife. And despite the mounting evidence and the mutual exclamations of bizarre coincidences, Mrs. Martin continues to express terrifying (at least to the spectator) amnesia:

> MRS. MARTIN: It is certainly possible and not at all unlikely. But I do not recall it, Sir.

Mr. Martin admits that he does not recall it either. Even when they discover that they are living at the same address and in the same flat, neither of them recall each other. They do not even recall that *they sleep in the same bed*(!). Clearly, their sex life is anything but a *kōmos*.

Finally, with the discovery that they each have a daughter named Alice with blond hair and one white eye and one red eye, the gambit ends. It is heralded by the clock striking twenty-nine times. They rush into each other's arms.

Have we seen the longest, most labyrinthine of *cognitiones*? As they embrace and immediately fall asleep, the maid Mary steps forward and reveals the truth:

> MARY: Elizabeth is not Elizabeth. Donald is not Donald. And here is the proof . . . Whereas Donald's child has a white right eye, and a red left eye, Elizabeth's child has a red

right eye and a white left eye. Thus all of Donald's system
of deduction collapses . . .

This magisterial philosophical demonstration puts the gun to the head
of language and coherence. To what purpose? As Mary herself observes:

> MARY: But who is the true Donald? Who is the true Elizabeth?
> Who has any interest in prolonging this confusion? I
> don't know.

Appropriately, at this moment the clock strikes "as much as it likes,"
and Mr. and Mrs. Smith re-enter to greet the Martins. The two couples
seem to have a rudimentary exchange of short clichés punctuated by
long silences. Suddenly out of nowhere, Mr. Martin inquires of
Mr. Smith, "Don't you feel well?" After a pause, Mrs. Smith explains,
"No, he has wet his pants." This accident is totally ignored as they
volley more clichés. Mrs. Martin then excitedly reports having witnessed something extraordinary in the street that day—"a man tying
his shoelace." The others react with astonishment, and Mr. Martin
adds another marvel, "I saw a man, quietly sitting on a seat reading his
newspaper." Mr. Smith tries to employ logic: "perhaps it was the same
man."

After a pointless philosophical inquiry as to whether or not the ring-
ing of one's front door always indicates that someone is outside, the
Fire Chief enters. Mrs. Smith bids him "take off your helmet and sit
down." The officer responds by sitting down—and not removing his
helmet. Are these people speaking the same language? Perhaps, but it is
sorely debased. After an exchange of coughs and inchoate phrases, the
Fire Chief inquires diffidently, "is there a fire here?" Mrs. Smith is sorry
to disappoint, but promises to notify him if they do have one. The
official then laments that things are not going very well for the fire
fighters—the odd chimney or barn, but nothing important. The others
commiserate.

While it seems that the play is going nowhere, the Fire Chief offers a
story for entertainment which he tells with great emotion:

> FIRE CHIEF: "The dog and the cow," an experimental fable. Once
> upon a time another cow asks another dog "why have you

not swallowed your trunk?" "Pardon me," replied the
dog, "it is because I thought I was an elephant."

MRS. MARTIN: What is the moral?

FIRE CHIEF: That is for you to find out.

What is the sense of all this? That is for *us* to find out. The Fire Chief
continues as a raconteur of meaningless fairy tales, concluding with
"the head cold"—a wild proliferation of marriages and relatives that
makes the previous discussion of the Bobby Watsons seem like supreme logic. Just as the *cognitio* has previously been destroyed, here the
cognatio—the traditional discovery of familial relationships typical of
comedy from Menander onward—is made meaningless by the incoher-
ent inundation of the Fire Chief's countless relatives and relationships.
It is incomprehensible to anybody—even the teller of the tale. The two
couples press the official for more, but he can only reply that "it depends upon what time it is."

MRS. SMITH: We don't have the time here.

FIRE CHIEF: The clock?

MR. SMITH: It runs badly. It is contradictory and always indicates the
opposite of what the hour is.

Here we see another prime characteristic of the Theater of the Absurd: time is out of joint. As one critic has expressed it, "the avant-garde
is a drama of broken watches." In Adamov's *La Parodie* the characters
keep asking what the time is, but they cannot tell because the clocks in
the play have no hands.[37] When time vanishes, everything in the Universe is fast losing coherence.

But Ionesco still maintains the fragments of conventional comedy
when Mary enters and she and the Fire Chief enjoy an old-fashioned
cognitio. Astounded to see each other, they fall into a warm embrace.
Mrs. Smith rightly inquires, "what does all this mean?" She may well
ask. When they come up for air, the Fire Chief explains it was she who
extinguished his first fires.

Had it ended here, there might have been a chance of making sense
out of this play. But when the Fire Chief leaves, everything lapses into
monosyllabic incoherence. Mrs. Martin thanks him for helping them

pass a "truly Cartesian quarter of an hour," and the civil servant offers them a farewell non-sequitur:

FIRE CHIEF: Speaking of that—what about the bald soprano?

Only Mrs. Smith can offer an answer to this profound query:

MRS. SMITH: She always wears her hair in the same style.

The disintegration of meaning begins to accelerate. Initially the traces of Assimil records are distinguishable, as in observations like "a schoolmaster teaches his pupils to read, but the cat suckles her young when they are small." Nonsense gradually collapses into meaningless babble, and their mechanical Bergsonian dialogue continues with comments like:

MR. SMITH: Cockatoos, cockatoos, cockatoos, cockatoos, cockatoos, cockatoos, cockatoos, cockatoos, cockatoos, cockatoos.

There is a touch of scatology when Mrs. Smith daringly repeats the phrase "such caca" nine times. And Mr. Martin then repeats "such cascades of cacas" eight times. There follows an increasingly deteriorating effusion of nonsense, culminating in this exchange, which surely contains the least common denominators of speech:

MR. SMITH: A,e,i,o,u, a,e,i,o,u, a,e,i,o,u. u,i,!
MRS. MARTIN: B,c,d,f,g,l,m,n,p,r,s,t,w,x,z!

Perhaps this is a literary allusion to the monosyllables in Apollinaire. But in any case, discourse cannot be sabotaged by any further reduction—we think. And yet Mrs. Smith now begins to imitate a train:

MRS. SMITH: Choo, choo, choo choo, choo, choo, choo, choo, choo, choo, choo.

This is surely an intertextual echo of Thérèse's husband in *Les Mamelles,* whose speech also disintegrates into the sounds of a train.

Thus *The Bald Soprano* ends with an atomic nuclear meltdown of meaning. The only saving grace is Ionesco's *idée lumineuse*—to have the whole thing begin again, but this time with each couple speaking the exact same words that the other spoke in the first scene! Since this could go on forever, we can easily read Ionesco's message of the unchanging and unending banality of human existence. For *The Bald So-prano* is not so much a plot as a situation. Although there is some grim movement, this play is like the wheel of Ixion—much motion but no progress.

Ionesco presents a similar repetition of pain in *The Lesson* (1951), where the Professor tries to justify to the Maid why he has killed his fortieth Student of the day. She chastises him (the stage direction specifies that he holds his arm up, "to protect himself, like a child"). The maid scolds the infantilized professor:

> MAID: Now didn't I warn you just a little while ago: arithmetic leads to philology and philology leads to crime?

This play likewise ends with yet another turn of the wheel, as a new Student arrives to participate in another lesson of endless suffering and death.

Even from his first play, Ionesco was keenly aware of what he was doing—presenting not merely the extinction of meaning and the rigor mortis of human feelings, but the endless repetition of the act of absurdity. As he later explained.

> The Smiths and the Martins can no longer talk because they can no longer think; they can no longer think because they can no longer be moved, can no longer feel passions. They can no longer be; they can "become" anybody, anything, for, having lost their identity, they assume the identity of others . . . they are interchangeable.

Another way of viewing this endless repetition of senseless conversation is as a banalization of Camus's Sisyphus, condemned to roll his rock up the hill for the rest of eternity. Ionesco replaces the boulder with a meatball, but man's existential dilemma—and the pain—are the same.

This decay of language accompanies an increasing regression. The Absurdist authors, who were contemporaries of Shaw, echo his terror of females—especially domineering mothers. The figure appears in various forms—often offstage, but always a presence. She is a recurring character in Adamov, ever trying to prevent her son from growing up and having a relationship with another woman.[38] In *Les Retrouvailles*

(The Reunions), for example, after two of his fiancées have been murdered, the protagonist is wheeled offstage by his mother—in a baby carriage.

Ionesco's work is likewise infested with mothers—most of them castrating and tearful. Take for example *Jacques or the Submission*, in which the mother browbeats the eponymous hero in a melodramatic manner reminiscent of Mrs. Portnoy:

MOTHER JACK: *(weeping)* My son, my child, after all that we have done for you. After all our sacrifices! Never would I have believed you capable of this. You were my greatest hope.[39]

Again, in *Les Chaises* (*The Chairs*, 1952):

OLD MAN: Ah! Where are you Mamma, Mamma, where are you, Mamma? . . .

OLD WOMAN: But I'm here, my darling!

OLD MAN: It's not the same thing . . . I want my mamma, you, you're not my mamma.

They then jump out of the window, with the Orator himself speaking a bizarre epitaph in monosyllabic baby talk:

Mmm, Mmm, Guene, Gou, Gu, Mmm, Mmm, Mmm.

Perhaps this babbling infant is their lost child. (We find such a motif in Edward Albee's *American Dream*.) It is hardly a heroic conclusion.

In *King Ubu* the actors did not relate to one another, but spoke in stentorian tones to the audience—already an erosion of the spontaneous challenge of human speech. Apollinaire reduced the dialogue to its least common denominator—mere syllables. Cocteau's wedding party is swallowed by a huge camera, while the characters of Ionesco become like phonographs, spouting meaningless recorded phrases. *The Bald Soprano* also concludes with a total breakdown of communication. The characters exchange the same syllables that constituted "dialogue" in Apollinaire. In a word, as one scholar has described it, "Ionesco's message is that there is no message."[40]

We are but one step away from total silence.

21

Beckett: The Death of Comedy

In the end the head conquers and the heart dies. It is no accident that the artists of the Theater of the Absurd were all intellectuals. Jarry was a serious art and literary critic. Apollinaire was not only an art critic, but a painter in his own right. Cocteau was versed in mythology and every imaginable artistic discipline. Ionesco had a degree in French from the University of Bucharest, and published many serious articles on theater.

In every case these authors were acutely aware of the forms they were systematically destroying. And it was as much an act of intellect as mischief. We see a gradual decline in human faculties, from infantilism in Jarry, to infancy in Apollinaire, and finally to *infantia* (the total inability to communicate) in Ionesco. The root of all these words is the Latin *for, fari* ("to speak"). We can also express it with the Greek *aut-* ("self"), whereby the decline is from the autonomy of the classical hero, to automatons like Ubu, to the autism of Samuel Beckett, the subject of this final chapter.

In the progress of the anti-classical movement we witness the increasing dehumanization of the word in modern culture. The entire Theater of the Absurd is in a sense a long gloss on Theodor Adorno's famous remark that "it is barbarous to write a poem after Auschwitz." Kafka wrote ominously, "now the Sirens have a still more fatal weapon than their song, namely their silence."[1]

It is fitting then that one of the most popular artists of the early twentieth century was a silent film comedian—Cocteau's idol, *le profond Chaplin*. The avowed aim of a conventional hero is to win, as Balzac epitomized it, *une femme et une fortune*. But the little tramp's quest is usually far more modest: merely to keep on his feet. Take for example the ballroom scene in *The Gold Rush* (1925), where Chaplin keeps slipping on the dance floor as if it were an ice rink, unable to stand up. His costume was like the clown's traditional outfit, especially his baggy trousers—an acknowledged symbol of sexual incapacity.[2]

In the full maturity of his career, Chaplin began to widen his canvas and deal with more serious contemporary issues. But throughout his *oeuvre* (even in his later films), he continued to present the waning of sexuality—or, more specifically, masculinity. There are often moments when Charlie's gender seems dubious: for example, when he flirts effeminately with the bully in the *Gold Rush*. There is a similar scene in *City Lights* (1931), when Charlie bats his eyes coquettishly at the menacing boxer in the locker room and later, in the ring, jumps into his arms like a frightened little girl.

The hero longs for love in *City Lights* and uses all his ingenuity to restore the sight of the young heroine. But when she can actually see her benefactor for the first time, her face says all too clearly that Charlie is not the *man* of her dreams. The film ends with the epicene tramp waddling off into the sunset . . . alone. One critic has observed:

> A fool's thwarted love is the theme that recurs throughout
> the films of Chaplin, especially those that have a serio-comic
> element in addition to the farce that characterises his earlier
> film.[3]

It is no coincidence that other major silent comics were also virtually sexless: Buster Keaton, Harold Lloyd, and Bobby Clark with his limp, soft walking-stick.[4] Very often the fool does not win the girl in the "fullest" sense. This occurs in many of Buster Keaton's films, like *Go West*

(1925), where the stone-faced hero opts for the reward of a cow rather than the rancher's daughter.[5]

Chaplin continued to play the "little fellow" in subsequent masterpieces like *Modern Times* (1936), in which we find a repetition of the same twentieth-century comic themes we encountered in the work of Jarry, Apollinaire, Cocteau, and Ionesco: the reification of the world, machines encroaching on the humanity of human beings, with all of this underscored, so to speak, by silence. Though sound had already come to the cinema with *The Jazz Singer* nearly a decade earlier, Chaplin remained stubbornly silent.

Modern Times satirizes the destructive aspect of the Industrial Revolution. Man is no longer even a face in the crowd—he is a mere cog in the wheel.[6] This is the ultimate Bergsonian mechanization of life. The finale makes a half-hearted attempt at romance, as the film concludes with Chaplin and Paulette Goddard (who were actually married at the time) walking off together into the sunset. But there is no clinch.

Until this time, Chaplin had created but a single persona, "but that character is so rich that to describe it adequately you must compare it with such creations as Falstaff and Don Quixote . . . [He is] one of the great comic characters of world art."[7]

At last came *The Great Dictator* (1940), Chaplin's boldest film to date—and his first complete talkie. It was a passionate broadside against Fascism. We have seen again and again the fundamental comic conflict between *alazōn* and *eirōn,* the blusterer and the ironic man. This dichotomous duo appeared in various incarnations as early as Aristophanes' *Acharnians* (Lamachus and Dicaeopolis), followed by Plautus' *Miles Gloriosus* (with the slave and his military master), Terence's *Eunuch* (with the *alazōn* Thraso, whose boastfulness bequeathed to us the English term "thrasonic"). On rare occasions we find magnificent characterizations which embody both types. Falstaff, for example, is "not only witty in myself, but the cause that wit is in other men."[8]

In *The Great Dictator,* Chaplin embodies the extremes of humanity and inhumanity, playing two roles—the little Jewish barber (the tramp in a skull cap), and the bombastic villain Hynkel, a thinly disguised Adolf Hitler. Charlie's physical similarity to the Führer is uncanny. Of the two parts, Chaplin himself remarked enigmatically, "One of us is a tragedian, the other a comedian, I don't know which is which."[9] After discomfiting the German soldiers with his pranks, the barber is taken off to a concentration camp. He later escapes and is walking timidly down the streets of "Pretzelburg" when soldiers mistake him for the Great Dictator. He is haled to a massive rally, where he is hailed as "the future emperor of the world." There he surprises the huns with a speech which, though criticized by some as too mawkish, is undeniably a heartfelt plea for world peace and mutual understanding:

> I'm sorry, but I don't want to conquer anyone. I should like
> to help everyone—if possible—Jew, Gentile, black man, white.
> We don't want to hate and despise one another. In this
> world, there is room for everyone.

Many critics have commented on the passionate sympathy for the downtrodden that Chaplin expressed in this film. Understandably this awakened the anti-Semites, who always suspected that Chaplin was a member of the "inferior" race. To this snide racist criticism, he protested somewhat infelicitously, "I am not a Jew! I am a citizen of the world!"[10]

Chaplin is a very important figure in the history of comedy. But he also represents a significant stage toward its death in portraying the infantilized hero and the waning of the senses.

Samuel Beckett was a passionate devotee of silent film comedians, always first in line to see the latest film by Harold Lloyd, Buster Keaton, and later the Marx brothers. But he especially loved Chaplin.[11] Moreover, unlike the other Absurdists, Beckett was not a mere boulevard *philosophe,* but a serious academic. Upon receiving his first degree from Trinity College Dublin, he won a competition to teach English for two years at the *Ecole Normale Supérieur* as *lecteur d'Anglais.* Thereafter he returned to Trinity, where he received his M.A. by offering as his dissertation the book on Proust which he had completed in Paris. He was then appointed lecturer in French, at an annual salary of £200 with three years to tenure ("till death—or sin—do them part").[12]

But after two years Beckett was put off by the grinding routine of the Academy, and he returned to Paris. Having already made friends with

the Joyce family on his previous stay—occasionally even acting as aman-
uensis, taking dictation for *Finnegans Wake* from the nearly-blind emperor of words[13]—he made contact again.

Beckett often contrasted his own subject matter with that of his literary hero:

> The more Joyce knew the more he could. He's tending to-
> ward omniscience and omnipotence as an artist. I'm working
> with impotence, ignorance.[14]

Beckett intuitively linked the inability to communicate with loss of sexuality.[15] This itself is a new topic in dramatic literature—especially for a
comedy, which, as we have seen countless times, traditionally culminates in a potent, energetic *gamos*. But Beckett's heroes are all "inca-
pables," sexual cripples. The phallus is conspicuous in his dramatic
work—for its total *absence*.

Most of his plays end with a flourish of silence and a dance of immobility—not only *Godot* with its conflict of word and action, but also
smaller pieces such as *Act without Words I: A Mime for One Player,* which
emphasizes the fact that the single actor does not move. The French
concludes exactly as *Godot* does, with the repeated emphasis on the fact
that "he does not move."[16]

Indeed, *Endgame* begins in this fashion, with a symphony of pauses
and an echo of *Godot* in which the two main characters (Hamm and
Clov—another odd couple) try to separate themselves from each other:

> HAMM: Why do you stay with me?
>   CLOV: Why do you keep with me?
> HAMM: There's no one else.
>   CLOV: There's nowhere else.
>   *(pause)*
> HAMM: You're leaving me all the same.
>   CLOV: I'm trying.[17]

These qualities may be conveniently studied in Beckett's short play
Krapp's Last Tape (1958). The double-edged quality of his writing, and the
need to read his plays in both languages, is no better demonstrated
than in a comparison of the English and French titles.[18] *Krapp's Last*

Tape suggests the aging hero's fixation on his growing constipation, whereas *La dernière bande* refers as much to a final tape as to a "last erection." In both languages, Beckett is dealing with the end of life—but the French concentrates on the death of the libido.

The hero is old and feeble. He moves with difficulty. He is, the playwright informs us, "very short-sighted and hard of hearing. He has trouble walking." His table holds a recorder and many reels of tape. It has the only light in the room. Laboriously he unlocks a drawer and takes out a large banana, which he now brings to the edge of the stage. It would not be an exaggeration to see a phallic suggestion in Beckett's stage direction, "he caresses the banana"—perhaps even a reference to masturbation. When he has finished eating he throws the skin away, and on getting up nearly slips on it. He then tosses the peel over the edge of the stage.

Krapp has not as yet spoken. There is a sound of a cork being popped from a bottle and then another long pause. Beckett is perhaps most eloquent in his silences. He then puts his ledger on the table and starts to read from it an inventory of his many recorded reels. He squints at the book and reads:

> KRAPP: Mother at rest at last.

And then, a moment later, "slight improvement in bowel condition":

> KRAPP: Hmm, farewell to . . . (*he turns the page*) love.[19]

He then switches on his machine and listens to a much stronger voice than his present one reporting on a long-ago birthday:

> KRAPP: Thirty-nine today, sound as a bell, except for my old
> weakness, and intellectually I now have every reason to
> suspect at the . . . (*hesitates*) crest of the wave—or thereabouts.[20]

He is pleased with his new lamp ("with all this darkness round me I feel less alone"). But then he closes his eyes and meditates:

> KRAPP: Just been listening to an old year, passages at random. I
> did not check in the book but it must be at least ten or

twelve years ago. At the time I think I was still living off
and on with Bianca on Kedar Street.[21]

He then muses:

> KRAPP: Hard to believe I was ever that young whelp
> The voice! Jesus![22]

Beckett's dramatic heroes, like Aristophanes', are all well past their
prime. After an "engrossing sexual life," Krapp can only yearn for his
lost power and youth. He now only broods about his unattainable
laxation. Enigmatically, but with nostalgia, he speaks of "a girl in a
shabby green coat on a railway station."[23]

He then plays a tape and listens to his own lament for his mother's
"viduity"—an arch word—and then her death. And then again a flash of
light in his own dark life:

> KRAPP: One dark young beauty . . . all white and starch,
> incomparable bosom . . .[24]

But she was offended when he was "bold enough to speak to her." If
these are his most fervent memories, he must have had a very bleak life.
In nebulous retrospect, this is one of the rare appearances of a woman
in all of Beckett's dramas—and it is a long-ago fading memory at that.

There is not much heterosexual love in the plays themselves. The two
most notable female characters, Nell in *Endgame* and Winnie in *Happy
Days,* are both buried from the waist down, one in a garbage can and
the other in a sand-pile, thus removing their private parts from sight—
and use. The playwright demonstrates

> a profound hostility—all the more implacable for being at
> once restrained and informed with pity—towards woman. In
> Beckett's philosophy, love might seem to be a logical impos-
> sibility.[25]

Krapp continues to rehearse the past. He was obviously an author of
sorts, because he mentions:

> KRAPP: Seventeen copies sold, of which eleven at trade price to
> free circulating libraries beyond the seas.[26]

After which he sat shivering in the park drowned in dreams. He reminisces about another long-ago physical encounter with a woman. There is a pause. His lips move once again, but there is no sound. He sighs:

> KRAPP: Past midnight. Never knew such silence. The earth might be uninhabited.[27]

After yet another pause he speaks into the microphone:

> KRAPP: Perhaps my best years are gone. When there was a chance of happiness. But I would not want them back. Not with the fire in me. No, I wouldn't want them back.[28]

But now Krapp has exhausted his thoughts and his words, and the tape runs on into a wordless void. It goes without saying that this is no longer comedy as we know it—it is nostalgia for a life half-lived and a yearning for the minute transitory joys this character once experienced. This is the antithesis of the Aristophanic hero's desire to be young again, and his triumphant rejuvenation.

Endgame is another gloomy "comic" creation. Ionesco remarked that its true value consists in "its closer kinship to the Book of Job than to modern boulevard comedies."[29] This play expresses nostalgia for a once-living sexual relationship between Hamm and Clov ("if I could sleep I might make love"),[30] yet another Beckettian couple that is trying to separate without success, and each on his own incomplete. The world seems to have been destroyed by a nuclear holocaust; and it will be all the more desolate if Clov succeeds in leaving Hamm.[31] This is Beckett at his most pessimistic. In this final stage of comedy, he presents the ultimate progression—or rather regression—from Aristophanic *parrhēsia,* the license to say anything, to *aphasia,* the inability to say anything. Here is the shriveling of a once human being for whom there is no joy, no laughter, and no feeling. This is immeasurably sad, but archetypically Beckett. And yet, as Nell remarks at the beginning of the play, "nothing is funnier than unhappiness."[32]

Beckett was never a popular playwright, although his masterpiece, *Waiting for Godot,* actually was a *succès d'estime* on Broadway, with Bert Lahr giving an unforgettable performance as Didi. Written originally in French in 1948, it had its world premiere on 5 January 1953 in the tiny

Left Bank Théâtre de Babylone in Paris.[33] His English translation was staged in 1954 in London.[34]

There has been no end of speculation as to what these characters' names mean. One critic argues that Didi when read backwards reveals Id-Id, and Gogo is short for Ego-Ego.[35] Another has suggested that Didi was short for French *dis-dis* ("say, say"), while Gogo is simply the English "go-go," representing the division between thought and action which characterizes (if that is the right word) the two protagonists and explains their inability to part from each other.[36]

As for the name "Godot" itself, Charlie Chaplin's French nickname, Charlot, may be cleverly alluded to.[37] Whether or not Chaplin's name is hidden in the title, his influence is certainly visible throughout the play. The persona of the protagonists is but one step away from that of the "little tramp." Indeed, his first biographer comments on Beckett's own "curious lurching gait, legs stiff and feet turned out, very much like Charlie Chaplin's Little Tramp"—a quirk which provoked young playmates' jests.[38]

Another possible source for Godot is Balzac's play *Le faiseur* (also known as *Mercadet*), produced posthumously in 1851.[39] This presents a crooked financier who has embezzled all his clients' wealth, and has evasively promised his creditors that he will pay them as soon as his rich—and fictitious—partner "Godeau" returns to France. Just when the protagonist is on the brink of ruinous exposure, it is announced that a certain Godeau actually *has* arrived from the Far East, laden with wealth to save the day. Drunk with joy, the hero exclaims:

> I've invoked Godeau so many times that I much more than anyone have the right to see him. Come on, let's all go see Godeau!

Interestingly enough, Godeau is never actually seen.

It has been further speculated that "Godot" is a bilingual diminutive of God.[40] In a psychoanalytic approach, a provocative suggestion has been made that

> like Beckett's un-God Godot . . . Lacan's Symbolic Father does not possess the Phallus, as the power of meaning, the

ultimate signifier—so much as he possesses the Law of universal "castration" read as separation, renunciation, frustration of desire.[41]

But the exact identity of the title character is not important: "we are being teased by hints of a system, not to be much pursued."[42] In fact, the playwright himself has been quoted as saying (perhaps disingenuously) that, if he knew what the play was about, he would have said so.[43] As several critics have argued, Beckett's play is not about *Godot,* but about *waiting.*[44] Godot is a *deus ex machina* whose machine is broken.

The curtain rises on a scene of desolation. A leafless tree in the background is the only thing remotely resembling a landscape. The time is not specified; it might be yesterday or a hundred years from now. We see the first of the two tramps, Estragon (Gogo), trying to pull off his boot as his sidekick Vladimir (Didi) enters. Perhaps it is more accurate to call him Gogo's "better half" (in the common use of the phrase). His—and Beckett's—first words are "Nothing to be done." The play's title could have been the polar opposite of his mime *Acts without Words*— this one could be called *Words without Acts.* It is what Terence long ago called *fabula stataria*—a non-action play—but here reduced to total immobility.

The two greet each other as though they have been separated forever, although they have (allegedly) spent only the previous night apart. From the fragments of dialogue we learn that they have been waiting "for a long time." Their only emotion seems to be hope:

> VLADIMIR: What's the good of losing heart now, that's what I say. We should have thought of it a million years ago in the nineties . . . Hand in hand from the top of the Eiffel Tower, among the first. We were respectable in those days. Now it's too late. They wouldn't even let us up.[45]

Beckett's choice of imagery is not random. As we have already seen in reference to Cocteau, the Eiffel Tower, completed in 1889, was a symbolic testimony to the capabilities of twentieth-century man—and, at the time it was built, the tallest phallic symbol in the world. Clearly, if these tramps are emblematic, their failure to march in the vanguard of the new age could be seen as symbolizing the dissolution of twentieth-century optimism into terrible disappointment, leaving Vladimir (Didi) with his *mot de caractère:* "nothing to be done."

Throughout the play we will look for clues to exactly what they are waiting for, and find a suggestive hint in Didi's remark that "One of the thieves was saved. *(Pause.)* It's a reasonable percentage. *(Pause.)* Gogo."[46] This is a clear reference to the crucifixion, for which mankind still bears the guilt. Hence Vladimir's next proposal:

> VLADIMIR: Suppose we repented.
> ESTRAGON: Repented what?
> VLADIMIR: Oh . . . *(He reflects.)* We wouldn't have to go into the details.
> ESTRAGON: Our being born?[47]

In other words, they should try to purge themselves of the guilt of original sin, with which all of us come into the world. Gogo has spoken an awesome truth. Like everyone, these men—or at least fragments of men—are tainted with the sin of killing Christ—which cannot be expiated until He (Godot?) returns.[48] As Calderón expressed it in his famous line from *Life Is a Dream* (*La Vida es sueño,* 1635):

> The greatest sin of men is to have been born.

Gogo speaks nostalgically of the Holy Land, telling his friend:

> ESTRAGON: That's where we'll go for our honeymoon. We'll swim. We'll be happy.[49]

The allusion to a "honeymoon" is significant, perhaps strengthening the suggestion of a homosexual relationship. Vladimir responds with theology:

> VLADIMIR: Our Saviour. Two thieves. One is supposed to have been saved and the other . . . damned.[50]

The discussion is at the same time philosophical and a dramatic bit of business. The two banter back and forth like vaudeville clowns:

> VLADIMIR: Come on, Gogo, return the ball, can't you, once in a way?[51]

After running a gambit about the prospects of salvation, Gogo proposes, not for the last time:

> ESTRAGON: Let's go.
> VLADIMIR: We can't.
> ESTRAGON: Why not?
> VLADIMIR: We're waiting for Godot.
> ESTRAGON: Ah! You're sure it was here?[52]

This bit of business is repeated again and again, with Didi's knee-jerk reaction followed by Gogo's illuminated "Ah!" (I cherish the still-vivid memory of Bert Lahr's automatic raising of his finger in baffled comprehension of this reminder of their purpose.)[53] And yet they are still not certain:

> ESTRAGON: You're sure it was this evening?
> VLADIMIR: What?
> ESTRAGON: That we were to wait.
> VLADIMIR: He said Saturday. *(Pause.)* I think.[54]

Like any earthly being waiting for the Savior, Didi has remembered imperfectly. If it is Christ they are expecting, He will not rise until to-morrow—but it is well worth waiting for. On the other hand, Godot may be something more earthy. They could be seeking sexual redemption:

> ESTRAGON: Wait.
> VLADIMIR: Yes, but while waiting.
> ESTRAGON: What about hanging ourselves?
> VLADIMIR: Hmm. It'd give us an erection.
> ESTRAGON: *(highly excited.)* An erection!
> VLADIMIR: With all that follows. Where it falls mandrakes grow. That's why they shriek when you pull them up. Did you Not know that?
> ESTRAGON: Let's hang ourselves immediately!
> VLADIMIR: From a bough? *(they go towards the tree.)* I wouldn't trust it.[55]

The "plot" thickens with the arrival of the only two other genuine characters in the play—the flamboyant Pozzo and his slave, ironically named Lucky. The ever-hopeful tramps immediately think this is the man they are waiting for. One scholar expresses his certainty that Pozzo *is* Godot, and comments further: "on this interpretation the play becomes almost too tightly knit."[56] And yet Pozzo specifically denies this:

ESTRAGON: You are not Mr. Godot, Sir?
POZZO: (in a terrifying voice) I am Pozzo![57]

Pozzo then proceeds to picnic, tossing his bones to Lucky. All the while Lucky has held the baggage and Pozzo gives no thought to his slave, not unlike Xanthias in the *Frogs*. Pozzo declares that he wants to dispose of Lucky:

VLADIMIR: You want to get rid of him?
POZZO: Remark that I might just as well have been in his shoes
and he in mine. If chance had not willed otherwise. To
each one his due.[58]

Clearly, if he is correct in his thesis that only one of the two thieves was saved, Pozzo is trying to enslave Lucky to do his will—and so improve his odds of salvation. We recall that earlier in the play Gogo was unable to get into his shoes. The English idiom is here played upon in both senses.

At last it is time for the concluding aria of the act, which, appropriately, is sung by Lucky (many critics have discerned the influence of James Joyce in this torrent of words and many have denied it—the question remains open). When his master commands him to think, the words spill out of Lucky:

LUCKY: Given the existence . . . of a personal God quaquaquaqua
outside time without extension who from the heights
of divine apathia divine athambia divine aphasia
loves us dearly with some exceptions for reasons
unknown . . .[59]

At first it seems like incomprehensible nonsense. And yet *apathia, athambia,* and *aphasia* are anything but divine states. They represent respectively the inability to care, the inability to feel, and the inability to speak. Lucky is a twentieth-century version of the learned professor *gloriosus*, whose nonsensical pronouncements make a mockery of pompous philosophers.

But the speech is notable for more than its incoherence. It contains one of the few possible references to sexuality in the play: *"essy-in-possy,"* a corruption of Latin *esse* and *posse*, which might have any one of several connotations.[60] There is no doubt that Testu and Cunard, who are invoked again and again, are both allusions to the male and female genitals. In Cunard's case, this is an in-joke involving one of Beckett's Paris friends.

Aristophanic devices and themes are all inverted, subverted, and perverted, for this weak verbal *gamos* is the closest we come to sexuality. Gone are the traditional comic themes of rebirth, appetite, and phallic triumph. In their place we have senescence, frustration, and sexual inadequacy. Norman Mailer put it bluntly:

> Two men, two vagabonds, a male and female homosexual, old and exhausted, have come to rest temporarily on the timeless plain, presided over by a withered cross-like tree marooned in a purgatory of their failing powers . . . They are beyond sex, really neither old men or old women . . . They can only wait for Godot and they speculate about his nature, for Godot is a mystery to them, and after all they desire, not only sex and rebirth into life, but worldly power as well. They are looking for the potency of the phallus and the testes.[61]

Finally Pozzo and Lucky exit, leaving the tramps to their waiting. After a long silence they again discourse in a brief, meaningless dialogue, which concludes with the repetition of the leitmotif:

VLADIMIR: That passed the time.

ESTRAGON: It would have passed in any case.

VLADIMIR: Yes, but not so rapidly. (*Pause.*)

ESTRAGON: What do we do now?

VLADIMIR: I don't know.

ESTRAGON: Let's go.

VLADIMIR: We can't.

ESTRAGON: Why not?

VLADIMIR: We're waiting for Godot.

ESTRAGON: *(despairingly)* Ah![62]

The act ends with the arrival of a young boy who "minds the goats" for a Mr. Godot, who brings the message that his master will not be able to come that evening ("but surely tomorrow").

The boy exits, and for the tramps it is also time to depart. Gogo leaves his boots. They pause for an instant and look at the tree. This is very clever dramaturgy, as the tree is the single thing that will change in Act Two. Their final remarks hark back to their earlier purpose to commit suicide—if only to get an erection:

> ESTRAGON: Pity we haven't got a bit of rope.
> VLADIMIR: Come on. It's cold.
>   *(He draws Estragon after him as before.)*
> ESTRAGON: Remind me to bring a bit of rope to-morrow.
> VLADIMIR: Yes, come on . . .
> ESTRAGON: Well, shall we go?
> VLADIMIR: Yes, let's go.[63]

But, as Beckett indicates, they do not move. If nothing else, this proves that Beckett's tramps represent thought and action, each one half of mankind. (Note that they can still walk at the end of Act One.)

Act Two is reminiscent of Ionesco's *Bald Soprano,* in which a whole play is repeated again—and again. One wag has remarked that "*Godot* is a play in which nothing happens—*twice.*"[64] There is some wisdom in this wit, and yet, as we have seen with Ionesco, part of Beckett's "message," if we may be so bold as to call it that, is that there is *no* message.

The setting of Act Two is identical—almost. We find the same bleak landscape with the tree, but this time the playwright's stage directions specify that "*the tree has four or five leaves!*" In Beckett even the smallest things carry great meaning. The "heroes" enter and greet each other after a long night apart. Didi reports: "I didn't get up in the night"—a remark which the avant-garde director André Gregory has construed as a phallic reference. They are in a better mood:

> VLADIMIR: We are happy.
> ESTRAGON: We are happy. *(Silence.)* What do we do now, now that we
>   are happy?
> VLADIMIR: Wait for Godot.[65]

The tramps engage in a dialectic, questioning whether they were in this place yesterday or in a different place. Like Hamm and Clov, they live in a continuum ("it's the end of a day like any other day").[66] They are clouded by amnesia. Gogo reflects that they have been blathering about nothing in particular "now for half a century." Inasmuch as Beckett's play was first produced in 1953, this brings us back to the early days of the Eiffel Tower, when they were acceptable in society.

As they are going through the same routines, Didi suddenly calls attention to the new arboreal florescence:

> ESTRAGON: Was it not there yesterday?
> VLADIMIR: Yes of course it was there. Do you not remember? We nearly hanged ourselves from it. But you wouldn't. Do you not remember?
> ESTRAGON: You dreamt it.
> VLADIMIR: Is it possible you have forgotten already?[67]

Here at the end of the world, the senses are waning, memory is impaired (as Pozzo moans at one point). Or does Estragon *need* to forget that Godot did not come the day before in order to carry on? Here, faith is denying experience. As we have already seen in Ionesco, amnesia is a common motif of Absurdist theater.

The two tramps are neither able to part nor keep from talking. They want desperately to use their reason, but Didi remarks bitterly (as he does several times during the play):

> VLADIMIR: We are in no danger of ever thinking any more.
> *They look at the tree with astonishment.*
> VLADIMIR: Look at it.
> *They look at the tree.*
> ESTRAGON: I see nothing.
> VLADIMIR: But yesterday evening it was all black and bare. And now it's covered with leaves.
> ESTRAGON: Leaves?
> VLADIMIR: In a single night![68]

Has it really been only one night? The seasons have changed. Perhaps it was a hundred days ago, or even a thousand—their memory is not strong enough to calculate. It has been argued that the time span of the play is eternity. Beckett's notes, however, specify: *"Next day, same time, same place."* But how could the seasons have changed in so short a time?

In any case, Gogo's boots are still where they left them, but he denies ownership: his were black and these are brown. And now the shoe fits. Didi logically concludes that someone else has taken his and left theirs:

> VLADIMIR: His were too tight so he took yours.
> ESTRAGON: Mine were too tight.
> VLADIMIR: For you not for him.[69]

Didi's reasoning seems simple enough. And yet there is another, more radical explanation for why his friend can now fit into the shoes: it is not the same *Gogo!*

After this interlude of illogic we run the familiar gamut:

> ESTRAGON: Let's go.
> VLADIMIR: We can't.
> ESTRAGON: Why not?
> VLADIMIR: We're waiting for Godot.
> ESTRAGON: Ah![70]

This routine is repeated again a few minutes later, after which they conclude that perhaps they are a bit early for their appointment with Godot.

A moment later Pozzo arrives again—in drastically different condition. He is now blind, and the formerly babbling Lucky is now mute. It will come as no surprise to learn that Beckett's first choice for this role was Buster Keaton, the very epitome of silence, referred to by one critic as "the deadest man alive." (Keaton, baffled by what appeared to be a nonsensical script, roundly rejected the offer as a waste of his time. Beckett finally succeeded in getting the stone-faced actor for *Film.*)[71]

Pozzo's first word encapsulates his emotional state: "Help!" He repeats this several times and begs for pity. He who was once the cruel tyrant is now a helpless victim. These tramps are not uneducated, for when Pozzo reveals that he is blind, they remark, "Perhaps he can see into the future." Do they mistake him for Tiresias? Maybe these fragments of humanity were once intellectuals of some sort. Didi can even quote Latin (*memoria praeteritorum bonorum*, "the memory of past kindnesses"). In what century did he acquire this learning? As one critic observed:

> To cope with [Beckett] you will need some French and German, a resident exegete of Dante, a good encyclopedia, OED, the patience of Job and your wits about you.[72]

One scholar remarked to Beckett himself that in the English version of Godot he makes his heroes speak as if they had Ph.D.'s. "How do you know they hadn't?" the author replied.[73]

Still, we have no time to speculate as Didi is needed to help Gogo keep Pozzo erect. Indeed, in this posture the three of them look like an outsize penis. Ironically, they remember Pozzo, but he does not recall them:

> VLADIMIR: We met yesterday. *(silence)* Do you not remember?
> POZZO: I don't remember having met anyone yesterday. But tomorrow I won't remember having met anyone today.[74]

In this moribund and crumbling world, memory is the first faculty to deteriorate. And then eyesight, then hearing. Pozzo's slave Lucky is now dumb. Didi asks him how long he has been this way, a civil question which nonetheless infuriates Pozzo. He rails at them, approaching the nearest thing to eloquence in Beckett's dialogue:

> POZZO: Have you not done tormenting me with your accursed time! It's abominable! When! When! One day, is that not enough for you, one day he went dumb, one day I went blind, one day we'll go deaf, one day we were born, one day we shall die, the same day, the same second, is that not enough for you? *(Calmer.)* They give birth astride of a grave, the light gleams an instant, then it's night once more.[75]

Time has no meaning in this world. For what is human life compared with the eternity in which these people seem condemned to live? We are reminded of the other Absurdists' preoccupation with the passage—or stasis—of time, which they can never manage to capture. It is no coincidence that the topic of Beckett's M.A. thesis was *time* in Proust.

As Pozzo and Lucky exit, leaving the two hoboes alone to contemplate their predicament, Didi laments man's place in the universe. Beckett here attains a kind of eloquence in simplicity:

> VLADIMIR: Astride of a grave and a difficult birth. Down in the hole, lingeringly, the grave-digger puts on the forceps. We have time to grow old. The air is full of our cries. But habit is a great deadener.[76]

Once again we think of Calderón, *aun no acabas de nacer cuando impiezas a morir* ("you are scarcely born when you begin to die"). Human life is fleeting. Only Godot—whatever or whoever he may be—is eternal.

The play concludes with another arrival of the young boy. Vladimir is upset that the boy thinks they are meeting for the first time. But no matter. What is important is the tidings he brings:

> VLADIMIR: You have a message from Mr. Godot.
> BOY: Yes Sir.
> *(Silence.)*
> VLADIMIR: He won't be coming this evening.
> BOY: No Sir.
> VLADIMIR: But he'll come tomorrow.
> BOY: Yes Sir.
> VLADIMIR: Without fail.
> BOY: Yes Sir.
> *(Silence.)*[77]

The young messenger leaves, and once again they propose to hang themselves—on a willow tree. Surely this is the learned Beckett invoking the mournful yearning of the Israelites for the promised land in Psalm 137:

> By the rivers of Babylon, there we sat down, yea,
> we wept, when we remembered Zion.
> We hanged our harps upon the willows.

Didi and Gogo are likewise in exile from both paradise and the world. Their desire to meet Godot could lead them back forever. But they propose to hang themselves ... tomorrow. Surely this delay cannot be to wait once again for Godot. And yet their predicament is encapsulated in words and actions—or non-actions—which we have witnessed many times before:

> VLADIMIR: Well? Shall we go?
> ESTRAGON: Yes, let's go.
> *They do not move.*[78]

Once again their intent—if it be that—is thwarted by their inability to act. In a way they represent the dilemma of modern man, suffering and longing, but unable to marry word to action.

At first glance, it may be hard to view *Godot* as a comedy. And yet a minor adjustment could still bring it into the mainstream: for example, Godot—whoever he may be—could actually appear as some kind of angelic epilogue as in Euripides, or even perhaps as an Aristophanic messenger bringing the hero's beautiful woman for the *kōmos* finale. It could be as simple as an orgasm. Beckett is aware that we all yearn for a truly happy ending. Yet, like the other assassins of the genre, he deliberately denies it to us. It would perhaps be better then to refer to this play as an *anti*-comedy.

Godot marks the end of the life cycle of a genre—the death of comedy. For in it we can discern an echo of the play that has been deemed its apogee. Indeed, the similarity between *Godot* and Aristophanes' *Birds* is too remarkable to be mere coincidence. For Beckett is a chimerical post-modern classicist and a supreme ironist.[79]

Both plays begin with the identical *mise-en-scène:* a country road and a single tree. In each drama the first characters to enter are a pair of senescent tramps, dropouts from society. Moreover, these odd couples are on a similar quest. In the *Birds,* Euelpides says that he and his fellow hobo Peisetaerus have "flown away" from Athens—that city of fines, fees, and lawsuits—to search for a "do-nothing place" *(topon apragmona),* "a cozy, woolly city, soft as a rug, where a man can stretch out and relax in peace."[80] A similar sentiment is expressed by Beckett's tramps in a passage which appears in the French edition, but which Beckett omitted from the English version:

> VLADIMIR: Tonight perhaps we'll sleep at his place,
> warm, dry bellies full—on straw.
> That's worth waiting for isn't it?[81]

Both sets of tramps are sexually dysfunctional. The Athenian old-sters are inclined to pederasty,[82] and Beckett's anti-heroes are so worn out that they are beyond any sexual redemption. In their desperation they even propose to hang themselves—death is the only action which will produce an erection. But they cannot adhere to the wisdom of Feste in *Twelfth Night:* "He that is well hanged in this world needs to fear no colours."

The trajectory of Aristophanes' heroes is archetypal. They ascend from old age to rejuvenation; from sexual incapacity to priapic, Olympic athleticism; from social ostracism to universal dominion. As we recall, the play concludes with Prometheus, ever a friend to man, advising Peisetaerus to force the abdication of Zeus himself and to demand the divine king's surrender of Basileia, "potentateship" personified.

With the messenger hailing his triumphant final entrance and the chorus intoning a wedding hymn, Peisetaerus strides on stage, bathed and fresh in his regal wedding suit, leading a phallic procession to cries of *kallinikos.* The chorus' song compares the occasion to the wedding of Zeus and Hera where, significantly, Eros had served as the couple's charioteer.[83] They hail the marriage bed that the hero will visit with Basileia, who, before Peisetaerus arrived on the scene, had been the "constant companion" of Zeus. The joy is unbounded, as is the implicit immorality.[84]

Although the beginning of *Waiting for Godot* evokes the same starting point as the *Birds,* Beckett deliberately replaces Aristophanic *kōmos* with a tragicomic stasis. And yet he has cleverly set the scene for a similar victory—which, alas, never comes. For Godot can be equated with sexual potency. Or even the archetypal father ("little God"), setting the stage for another act of taboo-smashing. But unlike Aristophanes, there is no such happy ending.

Beckett celebrates the triumph of failure. His post-modern aesthetic is a belief that the aim of literature is to disappoint.[85] There is no need to say that this philosophy is quintessentially anti-comic. One thinks of Aristotle's remark that the ending of comedy comes from the spectators' own desires—more specifically, their "weakness" *(astheneia)*.[86] By contrast, Beckett asserts his strength as avant-garde author and consciously denies the audience their traditional expectations.

What Beckett's deficient duo really desire is not rejuvenation but re-gression. His hoboes are pale reflections of Charlot, the ultimate comic tramp. In Beckett, even the modest ennoblement of staying on one's feet is too difficult for the protagonists to manage. There are no fewer than forty-five stage directions in which the characters leave the up-right position—symbol of human dignity. Recall the Aristophanic tramps' original "desire" in their unrejuvenated state—to find a warm, safe place to lie down. Is this not the peacefulness of the womb? Do Beckett's characters, mere fragments of people, long—like the play-wright himself—to be unborn? (Beckett often claimed that he was haunted by vivid memories of his uterine existence.)[87] Is this not a comic variant of Nietzsche's "Terrible Wisdom of Silenus," or Heine's "the best would be never to have been born"? They were both antici-pated by Sophocles' bleak existential cry:[88]

> Not ever to be born is a blessing that surpasses speech.
> The next best is, once we are born,
> To go back where we came from.
> With greatest speed.

Such bleak views are temporarily refuted by the comic outlook. It revels not only in the joys of birth, but in the even greater pleasure of *re-birth*, momentarily conquering the reality of death and the agony of life, celebrating that "beautiful untrue thing"—the happy ending.

At the far extreme from Aristophanic triumph stands Beckett's the-ater of inadequacy. His hymn to impotence is a rejection of all language (not merely Joyce's grandiloquence). It is a statement of the futility of the word, but with abundant recognition of previous literature—espe-cially Aristophanes. It is this that makes Beckett's work a deliberate *coup de grâce* to the comic genre.

Didi and Gogo will wait forever for their appointment to be kept. The drama will have no happy ending. Indeed, it will have no ending at all. There will be no revel, renewal, or rejuvenation. For whatever Godot may represent, whether salvation or erotic rebirth, one thing is clear. The traditional happy ending is no longer possible—because comedy is dead.

Coda

This has been, as I confessed at the outset, only a metaphorical exercise. It was necessary to study the death of comedy the better to understand its complete life cycle. But as we have seen, comedy always thrives upon outrage and flouting the establishment—or common sense—whether it be an Aristophanic hero dethroning Zeus and marrying his queen, or Jarry's King Ubu defying all morality in pursuit of self-gratification.

But after the savage atrocities of two World Wars, comic authors had to seek ever more radical subjects to evoke in the audience the illicit pleasures of "enjoying the outrage and being spared the consequences." Even the Nazi concentration camps have been portrayed light-heartedly—first in Chaplin's *Great Dictator* and then more recently in Roberto Benini's prize-winning *La vit'è bella*, which dealt—albeit at a remove of half a century—with the unspeakable mass slaughters of the Second World War. Yet neither of these has what could be called a conventional comic ending, and it would seem that comedy could go no further. It no longer seemed possible to find any more Freudian objects of wit—moral or religious precepts that command so much respect that they can only be approached in comedy, and even then in disguise. What was left that evoked awe, respect, or fear?

Only nuclear holocaust.

That is why Stanley Kubrick's film *Dr. Strangelove: or How I Learned to Stop Worrying and Love the Bomb* (1963) took the subject of comedy into *terra incognita,* by evoking laughter from the prospect of the destruction of the entire world.

Ever since Hiroshima, the specter of nuclear annihilation has haunted mankind, and the fact that the bomb is now in the hands of many countries in the grip of unstable leaders is hardly cause for sleeping more easily. It was bad enough when Russia and the United States faced off as the only proud possessors of these weapons of mass destruction. Each country was amply populated by maniacs who would have pressed the button if they could have gotten their hands on it. This is so horrific a thought that it could only be approached artistically under the protective armor of comedy.

Peter Sellers played a triple role in the film. Group Captain Lionel Mandrake—a subtle phallic reference—is a diffident British officer who tries to dissuade the mad General Jack Ripper (note the charactonym) from inviting apocalypse by calling in an unauthorized attack on Russia. This would provoke an immediate retaliation—leaving the entire world in tatters.

Sellers also plays Merton Muffly—an unsubtle reference to the female pudenda—the bland, slightly dim President of the United States. Muffly tries to dissuade his Soviet counterpart from retaliation, on the grounds that Ripper is a freelance *miles gloriosus* who is worried about the enemy's contamination of his "precious bodily fluids" (which is why, as a matter of policy, he denies his "essence" to all women).

Sellers' third role is as the grotesque "rehabilitated" Nazi scientist Dr. Strangelove—a.k.a. *Doktor Fremdeliebe*—a masterly parody of Werner von Braun, who made the identical trip from Berlin to Washington, also with a slightly Anglicized name. Sellers displays a cornucopia of Bergsonian devices: ignorance of himself, anesthesia of the heart, and the inability to control his own bodily movements. Even while he is enthusiastically presenting his scheme for the salvation of humanity to the President, he cannot keep from raising his right hand in a Nazi salute. And like Molière's Harpagon, he also unwittingly tries to strangle himself with his own arm.

When troops are sent in by the President to capture General Ripper's base, rather than surrender the secret code that will call the planes back, the demented commanding officer—in the tradition of the perverted Aristophanic monomaniac—shoots himself.

Finally a desperate Captain Mandrake succeeds in cracking the code that will call back the bombers from their terrible mission. Not surprisingly, General Ripper's password turns out to be "precious bodily fluids." The English officer desperately tries to convince a wary Colonel Bat Guano to break into a soda machine to get the coins needed for an urgent call to alert the President. A furious Guano barks, "I can't destroy the property of Coca-Cola!" At long last Mandrake persuades him, and they are able to transmit to Washington the code that will call the planes back.

Except for one. Major T. J. "King" Kong cannot be contacted because his plane's radio has been damaged by enemy fire. As a good American, he is determined to drop his bombs on the Red Menace. Washington is at a loss, and President Muffly can only suggest that the Soviet Premier try to shoot down the rogue American plane. But because Major Kong has been forced to fly so low, their radar cannot locate him. Therefore, the trembling porcine Ambassador reveals, the Russian "Doomsday" machine will be automatically activated and emit enough nuclear power to annihilate the entire world. A furious General Buck Turgidson begins to grapple with the diplomat, and in the mêlée that ensues the President protests, "you can't fight in here—it's the War Room!"

The future of humanity is now in the hands of the bizarre Dr. Strangelove, who gleefully proposes that a select group of men and especially attractive women—in a ratio of ten females to every male—go deep underground to escape the fallout and work very hard to repopulate humankind. ("Naturally, they would have to breed prodigiously.") We are not wrong to sense in this finale a nuclear *kōmos/gamos* in the making.

With this festive solution for the happy few, the film concludes with Major Kong astride a nuclear bomb—an atomic phallic symbol of infinite potency—sailing blithely through the air toward an imminent Russian consummation. For most of humanity the "happy ending" is more like a catastrophe, a perversion of the sacred marriage. The bomb explodes, and as its mushroom cloud burgeons, we hear Vera Lynn singing, "We'll meet again, don't know where don't know when."

This is anesthesia of the heart on a global scale and sets the tone for further cinematic outrages to come.[1]

The mind boggles.

Notes
Index

Notes

1. Etymologies: Getting to the Root of It

1. The "Helen Ode" of Aeschylus' *Agamemnon* (681–698) best illustrates the ancients' belief in this principle. There the chorus puns on *helein* ("to destroy") in speculating how Helen came to be named "with such thorough etymology" *(etētumōs)*. She was such an evil force that she proved to be *helenas, helandros, heleptolis* (689), "Hell for ships, hell for men, hell for cities." This linguistic phenomenon is treated at length in Plato's *Cratylus*; see also W. B. Stanford, *Greek Metaphor* (Oxford, 1936), p. 115; William D. Woodhead, *Etymologizing in Greek Literature from Homer to Philo Judaeus* (Toronto, 1928).

2. See G. Kaibel, *Comicorum Graecorum Fragmenta* (hereafter *CGF*) (Berlin, 1899), who cites the author of *Peri tēs kōmōidias*, p. 14; scholion to Dionysius Thrax, p. 14; Tzetzes *Ad Lycophronem*, p. 34; *Peri diaphoras poiētōn*, pp. 35 and 38.

3. All comatose conjectures are definitively dispelled by H. Frisk, *Griechisches etymologisches Wörterbuch* (Heidelberg, 1970), vol. 2, pp. 61–62.

4. A more recent formulation is by Louis Breger: "Sleep is a unique state; it is probably the single most 'infantile' activity we engage in. That is, it persists from infancy with very little change . . . throughout life while other basic activities undergo tremendous modifications . . . [Sleep] manifests itself the same in the adult as in the infant. The comfortable warm bed, the relative lack of stimulus input, the lack of motor output, or, indeed, any

interchange with the external environment, all of these factors recreate a state present in earliest infancy and contribute to 'regression.'" "Function of Dreams," *Journal of Abnormal Psychology* 72, no. 5 (1967), 1–25, esp. 19.

5. S. Freud, "Jokes and Their Relation to the Unconscious," vol. 6, pp. 9–236, esp. 28–29, 236. Quotations from Freud are taken from *The Standard Edition of the Complete Pyschological Works of Sigmund Freud* (24 vols.), ed. James Strachey et al. (London, 1953–1974). Henri Bergson devotes many pages to the similarity between comic absurdity and dreams in *Le Rire: Essai sur la signification du comique* (Paris, 1940), pp. 142–147. Interestingly enough, as Michael Silk points out in his brilliant essay, "The Autonomy of Comedy," *Comparative Criticism* 10 (1988), 3–37, Freud was anticipated by Kierkegaard, who wrote: "Precisely because the pleasantry of humour consists in revocation . . . it naturally is often a regression to childhood." Søren Kierkegaard, "Concluding Unscientific Postscript," trans. D. F. Swenson and W. Lowrie (Princeton, 1941), p. 489.

6. Freud, "Jokes," p. 236. Norman O. Brown saw the comic as "a psychoanalytical reformulation of the truth contained in the Platonic doctrine of *anamnēsis*." *Life against Death: The Psychoanalytical Meaning of History* (New York, 1959), p. 60.

7. Plato *Republic* 9.571c.

8. Aristophanes *Clouds* 1078.

9. Aristophanes anticipates the atmosphere in Cloudcuckooville, which the Chorus leader describes as a situation in which all things disgraceful (*aischra*) will become lovely (*kala*). The first example he gives is father-beating (*Birds* 757–759). I have not misled the reader on the erotic nature of the common philosophical word *physis,* which is usually translated as simply "nature" or "essence." But as K. J. Dover points out in his edition of the *Clouds* (Oxford, 1968), here the word means "sexual desire" (p. 227 at 1075). Jeffrey Henderson, *The Maculate Muse: Obscene Language in Attic Comedy*[2] (New York, 1975), pp. 79, 218, demonstrates that *physis* is often used in Old Comedy as a euphemism for "phallus."

10. Homer *Iliad* 14.359. See Hippocrates' categorical distinction between *hypnos* and *kōma, Epidemiae* 3.3.6: "continuous *kōma,* not to be confused with sleep." See also the comment made by Hesychius, s.v.: "lethargic sleep, an attack of deep sleep." *Malakon kōma* is also the "soft sleep" of sexual longing at *Odyssey* 18.201. At Sappho 2.8 (Lobel/Page), the poetess bids Aphrodite enter her grove, promising a *kōma* (trance?), induced by what emanates from the foliage. For further discussion of this word's peculiarities, see Denys Page, *Sappho and Alcaeus* (Oxford, 1955), p. 37. The same is true of the word used for slumber at significant places in the Old Testa-

ment, as when Adam is put to sleep for his "Eve-ectomy"; the divine anesthetic is called *tardemar* (Genesis 2:21), a term also employed to describe "the sleep of God" in 1 Samuel 26:12 and elsewhere. See H. Gunkel, *Handkommentar um Alten Testament* (Göttingen, 1910).

11. See Kaibel, *CGF,* p. 14, *Peri tēs kōmōidias;* Schol. in Dionysus Thrax, Kaibel, *CGF,* p. 14; *Etymologicum Magnum,* Kaibel, *CGF,* p. 16; Tzetzes *Ad Lycophronem,* Kaibel, *CGF,* pp. 11–12, 34.

12. As A. Körte notes in his fundamental article "Komödie," in *Real-Encyclopädie der classischen Alterumswissenschaft* 11 (1921), col. 1216.

13. Plautus *Menaechmi* 1047.

14. *A Midsummer Night's Dream* 4.1.205–216.

15. Apuleius *Metamorphoses* 6.24.

16. Aristotle *Poetics* 1448a35–1448b2.

17. According to Dionysius Thrax, *Ars grammatica* 3.9.2, the Roman polymath Varro held this view. Other ancient supporters are cited by Kaibel, *CGF,* pp. 6, 11. The medieval and Renaissance opinions are discussed by A. Philip McMahol, "Seven Questions on Aristotelian Definitions of Tragedy and Comedy," *Harvard Studies in Classical Philology* 40 (1929), 97–198. Dante is among the many who, even without direct Aristotelian influence, trace comedy's relation to *kōmē.* Even as modern a scholar as Albin Lesky conceded that the notion of *kōmē* has "a grain of truth," in *Geschichte der griechischen Literatur²* (Bern, 1963), p. 219.

18. Aristotle *Poetics* 1448a38.

19. Compare the tradition that in Syracuse it was customary for the countryfolk *(agroikoi)* to compete in song, and that the victor remained in the city while the others went out to the villages collecting food for themselves and no doubt causing quite a comastic commotion. In this case the *kōmos*-singers were certainly from the *kōmai. Scholia in Theocritum Vetera,* ed. C. Wendel (Leipzig, 1914), pp. 2–3 *(prolegomena* B.a).

20. The Latin *rus,* "country," may be akin to Avestan *ravo,* "wideness," as in *ravas-čarāt,* "what moves in the open," as well as Greek *eurus,* "wide," "far reaching," and Gothic *rums* (cf. German *Raum* and English *room*). Thus we find the persistent connotation of "unbounded expanse" and "free range." See A. Walde and J. B. Hofmann, *Lateinisches etymologisches Wörterbuch⁴,* vol. 2 (Heidelberg, 1965), p. 454. For the opposition of country and city in New Comedy, see Dario del Corno, "Il problema del'urbanesimo in Menandro," *Dioniso* 43 (1969), 85–94.

21. See Plato *Republic* 9.571c. For Epicharmus' *Rustic (Agrostinos)* see Kaibel, *CGF,* p. 90; on Epicharmus himself see first A. W. Pickard-Cambridge, *Dithyramb, Tragedy and Comedy²,* rev. T. B. L. Webster (Oxford, 1968),

pp. 230–290. Other Aristophanic *agroikoi* are Trygaeus and Strepsiades. The type was discussed by Aristotle (*Nicomachean Ethics* 4.1128a7–10) and Theophrastus (*Characters* 4).

22. Plato *Laws* 626c; Thucydides 1.5.

23. *Hamlet* 3.2.112–116.

24. For the sexual overtones of "country matters," see Eric Partridge, *Shakespeare's Bawdy* (London, 1947), p. 95. See also the vivid description of Elizabethan festivals published by the Elizabethan moralist Phillip Stubbes in *The Anatomie of Abuses* (1583), a long tirade against the sinfulness of the theater: "Against May, Whitsunday, or other time, all the young men and maids, old men and wives, run gadding overnight to the woods, groves, hills, and mountains, where they spend all the night in pleasant pastimes, and in the morning they return, bringing with them birch and branches of trees to deck their assemblies withal."

25. J. G. Frazer, *The Golden Bough*[3] (London, 1926), vol. 2, pp. 97–119. Of this (sometimes maligned) work, John B. Vickery, *The Literary Impact of The Golden Bough* (Princeton, 1973), p. 81, writes: "Frazer stands with Marx and Freud, just behind Darwin as an influence on the thinking of the modern world. His greatest achievement was to have resolutely collected and classified a mass of apparently heterogeneous material, not in order to support the pretensions of some abstract explanation, some 'key to all mythologies,' but rather so as to transmit a concrete impression of an epoch of the human mind."

26. Both are typical of new year festivals in the ancient Near East. They have many features in common, including the fact that "excess" follows abstinence, that is, the period of jubilation is preceded by one of fasting, purgation, and atonement. Of significance for the present argument is the fact that the festival license took place *outside the city limits*. The rites of Akītu are epitomized and analyzed by Theodor H. Gaster, *Thespis: Ritual Myth and Drama in the Ancient Near East* (New York, 1961), pp. 62–64. It was traditional at the end of Yom Kippur for eligible girls to dance publicly outside the boundaries of the town, inspiring the arrangement of many a marriage. The Talmud acknowledges that these occasions sometimes lapsed into orgiastic events. See Mircea Eliade, *The Myth of the Eternal Return, or Cosmos and History*, trans. Willard R. Trask (Princeton, 1965), p. 61; Gaster, *Thespis*, p. 42.

27. See Frisk, *Griechisches etymologisches Wörterbuch*, p. 63: From the agent noun *kōmōidos* comes the action noun *kōmōidia*. Pickard-Cambridge, *Dithyramb, Tragedy and Comedy*[2], p. 132, vehemently (and rightly) asserts that *kōmos* is the only possible root. Walter Headlam, *Herodas: The Mimes and Fragments*

(Cambridge, 1922), pp. 82–84, assembles the ancient sources which describe the drunken, nocturnal ambles of Greek and Roman comasts.

28. Jane Ellen Harrison, *Themis* (Cambridge, 1912). On this pioneering scholar, see also Hugh Lloyd-Jones, "Jane Harrison, 1850–1928," in *Cambridge Women: Twelve Portraits,* ed. E. Shils and C. Blacker (Cambridge, 1996), pp. 29–72.

29. Gilbert Murray, "Excursus on the Ritual Forms Presented in Greek Tragedy," in Harrison, *Themis.* See also Murray's *The Classical Tradition in Poetry* (Oxford, 1927).

30. F. M. Cornford, *The Origins of Attic Comedy* (Cambridge, 1934).

31. Theodor Gaster in his introduction to F. M. Cornford, *The Origins of Attic Comedy*² (Gloucester, Mass., 1968), p. xxiii.

32. A. W. Pickard-Cambridge, *Dithyramb, Tragedy and Comedy* (Oxford, 1927). His attack was so ferociously personal that—even after Cornford's death— T. B. L. Webster, who edited the second edition (1968), felt it necessary to expunge some of the *ad hominem* derision. Curiously enough, Webster's redaction is somewhat at odds with Pickard-Cambridge's original arguments, showing more sympathy to Cornford's ideas. We have opted to refer to the second edition throughout since it is more generally available. Other antagonists to the ritualist approach included Andrew Lang, *Magic and Religion* (London, 1901); William Bascom, "The Myth-Ritual Theory," *Jahresbericht über die Fortschritte der klassischen Altertumswissenschaft* 70 (1957), 103–113; E. R. Leach presents a damning analysis of Frazer's methods in "Golden Bough or Gilded Twig?" *Daedalus* 90, no. 3 (Spring 1961), 371–387; Joseph Fontenrose, *The Ritual Theory of Myth* (Berkeley, 1966).

33. Walter Burkert, "Greek Tragedy and Sacrificial Ritual," *Greek, Roman and Byzantine Studies* 7, no. 2 (1966), 87–122; quotation from p. 114, n. 61.

34. Walter Burkert, *Structure and History in Greek Myth and Ritual* (Berkeley, 1979); *Homo Necans: The Anthropology of Ancient Greek Sacrificial Ritual and Myth* (Berkeley, 1983); *Creation of the Sacred: Tracks of Biology in Early Religions* (Cambridge, Mass., 1996). For a brief overview of ritualist scholarship and an examination of ritual as a motif in the extant tragedies, see Hugh Lloyd-Jones, "Ritual and Tragedy," in *Ansichten griechischer Rituale: Symposium for Walter Burkert,* ed. Fritz Graf (Stuttgart, 1998), pp. 271–295. He concludes: "Sacrificial ritual . . . play[s] an important part in tragedy . . . but I would prefer not to say that they pervaded tragedy . . . What does pervade tragedy is religion, and ritual is an important element in religion" (p. 295).

35. John J. Winkler and Froma Zeitlin in the introduction to *Nothing to Do with Dionysos?,* ed. Winkler and Zeitlin (Princeton, 1990), p. 3. The editors' approach may be epitomized by a passage from their preface. They argue

that their "analysis accords with the ancient views of Athenian comedy as well as with the consistent pattern of statements about itself inside comedy, and stands in opposition to the carnivalesque view that would see Attic comic discourse as a merely playful, 'anything goes' inversion of contemporary social reality" (p. 8).

36. John J. Winkler, "The Ephebes' Song: *Tragoidia* and *Polis*," in *Nothing to Do with Dionysos?*, pp. 20-62. As he sees it, both tragedy and comedy had an important pedagogical function: "those festivals [of Dionysus] were the occasion for elaborate symbolic play on themes of proper and improper civic behaviour . . . Such play at festivals . . . occurred in both serious and facetious formats" (p. 20).

37. Jeffrey Henderson, "The *Demos* and the Comic Competition," in *Nothing to Do with Dionysos?*, pp. 271-313, quotation from p. 286; reprinted in *Oxford Readings in Aristophanes*, ed. Erich Segal (Oxford, 1996), pp. 65-97, quotation from pp. 78-79.

38. As Gregory W. Dobrov recognizes in *The City as Comedy: Society and Representation in Athenian Drama*, ed. Dobrov (Chapel Hill, 1997), p. xi: "Our understanding of the complexities and nuances of the comic polis will always be a function of our grasp of the historical and cultural realia. Equally important, however, is an understanding of the comic forces by which these realia are shaped, distorted, and transformed."

39. C. L. Barber, *Shakespeare's Festive Comedy* (Cleveland, 1963), p. 78.

40. Ovid *Fasti* 3.525-526.

41. J. G. Frazer, *Ovid: Fasti* (Cambridge, Mass., 1931), p. 407 (at 3.523ff.). Cf. *Golden Bough*[3], vol. I, p. 363 on the Parilia. Martial mentions a fertile grove sacred to Anna Perenna which "rejoices in virgin blood" (*virgineo cruore gaudet*, 4.64.16). See Frazer, *The Fasti of Ovid*, pp. 111-112.

42. *Persuasit nox amor vinum adulescentia: / humanumst*, Terence *Adelphoe* 470-471.

43. Horace *Ars Poetica* 224.

44. *As You Like It* 4.1.68-69.

45. M. Bakhtin, *Rabelais and His World* (Cambridge, Mass., 1968), pp. 4-18.

46. Ernst Kris, *Psychoanalytic Exploration in Art* (New York, 1952), p. 185.

47. Freud, "Totem and Taboo" (1913), vol. 13 (1913-1914), pp. 1-161, quotation from p. 140.

48. Plato *Republic* 10.606c.

49. Johan Huizinga, *Homo Ludens: A Study of the Play Element in Culture* (Boston, 1955).

50. Tertullian *De spectaculis* 10.7.

51. Several scholars trace these two words to the root *koi* or *kei*, "to share, associate." They also relate them to other cognates including *koinos*, common.

See A. Bezzenberger, *Beiträge zur Kunde der indogermanische Sprache 27* (Göttingen, 1904), p. 168; Frisk, *Griechisches etymologisches Wörterbuch,* pp. 61-62; P. Chantraine, *Dictionnaire étymologique de la langue grecque* (Heidelberg, 1938), p. 544.

52. For the meaning "of a revel," see Pindar *Olympian* 2.47. "In the village" is found as a variant reading in Hesiod *Works and Days* 344. The MSS containing Hesiod's works read *enchōrion* ("in the place"). But *enkōmion* (the meaning "in the village" is given s.v. *kōmē* in a scholion to Proclus) is proposed by Stephanus of Byzantium, and the validity of this reading is indisputably proved by its appearance in a Hesiodic papyrus, P. Mich. inv. 6828. See M. L. West, "Three Papyri of Hesiod," *Bulletin of the American Society of Papyrologists* 3 (1966), 69-75, who, however, keeps *enchōrion;* Friedrich Solmsen adopts the *kōmē* etymology in his 1970 Oxford edition.

53. L. R. Palmer, "Mycenaean Greek Texts from Pylos," *Transactions of the Philological Society* (1954), 18-53, esp. 27-35; E. Boisacq, *Dictionnaire Etymologique de la langue grecque* (Heidelberg, 1950), p. 544.

54. Such a picture is also suggested by Pollux's catalogue of Laconian festival entertainments (*Onomasticon* 4.104-105). F. R. Adrados expounds the "festival matrix" in *Fiesta, Comedia y Tragedia: sobre los origines griegos del teatro* (Barcelona, 1972).

55. *Kōma* is generally derived from **kei,* "to lie down," found also in *keimai* and which most scholars have dissociated from the **kei/koi* root of *kōmos* and *kōmē.* Boisacq, *Dictionnaire Etymologique,* pp. 543-544 and 426; see also K. Brugmann, in *Griechische Grammatik* (Munich, 1913), p. 317.

2. The Song of the *Kōmos*

1. "The playwrights construct [happy endings] to satisfy the weakness *(astheneia)* of the spectators" (*Poetics* 1453a31-34). As Northrop Frye observed, "the happy ending comes from the audience side of the stage." *The Anatomy of Criticism* (Princeton, 1957), p. 171.

2. It is possible that Aristotle has in mind a comic treatment of the Orestes myth by Alexis: see W. Geoffrey Arnott, *Alexis: The Fragments* (Cambridge, 1996), pp. 501-502.

3. Homer *Iliad* 20.490.

4. Homer *Odyssey* 1.50.

5. Ibid., 5.218.

6. Ibid., 5.219-220.

7. As Dimock comments, "To pass from the darkness of the cave into the light, to pass from being 'nobody' to having a name, is to be born." G. E. Dimock, Jr., "The Name of Odysseus," *The Hudson Review* 9, no. 21 (Spring 1956), 56.

8. Homer *Odyssey* 13.79–80.

9. Ibid., 11.488–491.

10. *1 Henry 4* 5.4.78–79.

11. Ibid., 5.1.134–140.

12. Ibid., 5.3.58; 5.4.85–86.

13. Byron, *Don Juan,* canto 3, st. 9.

14. Of course, only the first play of the *Prometheia* is fully extant, but we have sufficient reason to believe that the third play *(Prometheus Purphoros)* concluded with a torchlight procession, as per Herbert Weir Smyth's third conjecture in the Loeb edition of the Aeschylean fragments (Cambridge, Mass., 1926, repr. 1995): "as the *Fire-bearer,* it followed the *Luomenos* [*Prometheus Unbound*], and described the inauguration of the *Prometheia,* the Athenian festival at which torch-races were held in honour of the Titan . . ." (p. 445).

15. Gilbert Murray, *The Classical Tradition in Poetry* (Oxford, 1927), p. 38.

16. Aeschylus *Agamemnon* 264–265.

17. Ibid., 1324; 1646.

18. C. J. Herington, "Aeschylus: The Last Phase," *Arion* 4.3 (Autumn 1963), 387–403, discusses "comic" endings in Aeschylus. Kenneth Cavander has offered the opinion in conversation that the ending of the *Oresteia* should be viewed as a triumph not of law, but of fertility. See for example the choral ode enumerating the blessings of fertility that will come to the Athenians at *Eumenides* 938–948.

19. As with the Greek Ouranos and Gaia (Hesiod *Theogony* 133–134). The same myth is prominent in Oceania from Indonesia to Micronesia, as well as in Asia, Africa, and the Americas. See Mircea Eliade, *The Sacred and the Profane: The Nature of Religion,* trans. Willard R. Trask (New York, 1959), pp. 147–151. Greater detail is provided in the same author's *Patterns in Comparative Religion,* trans. Rosemary Sheed (New York, 1958), pp. 239–262. On Near Eastern versions, see Theodor H. Gaster, *Thespis: Ritual Myth and Drama in the Ancient Near East*[2] (New York, 1961), pp. 62–64. Frazer, *Folklore in the Old Testament* (New York, 1925), p. 24, detected similarities in the cosmogonies of the Greeks, Hebrews, Egyptians, and Babylonians, though he remarked uneasily that the concept of a male and female deity posed problems for a Judeo-Christian: "How the distinction can be reconciled with the unity of the Godhead is a problem on which the writer vouchsafes us no information" (p. 25). Indeed, the conspicuous exception of the Old Testament, in which the Almighty is the procreator of the universe, may in fact be the result of a later redaction (Eliade, *Patterns,* pp. 354–357). According to some scholars, in fact, the editors of Genesis may have obfuscated an

earlier version of the Creation which involved a male divinity (Adam) and the earth goddess (Adama). On the suppression of the feminine Hebrew divinities, see Theodor Reik, *Pagan Rites in Judaism* (New York, 1964), pp. 68-71.

20. Feste's song at the end of *Twelfth Night* concludes with the lines, "A great while ago the world begun / with a hey ho the wind and the rain" (5.1.404-405). Leslie Hotson, *The First Night of Twelfth Night* (New York, 1954), p. 171 n. 2, first noted the conjugal allusion in these verses. In Shakespeare's day, moreover, the verb "begin" could also mean "beget." See Eric Partridge, *Shakespeare's Bawdy*[2] (London, 1968), p. 73.

21. Ovid *Fasti* 3.523-540 (the key lines are cited in chapter 1). Ovid's wording, *accumbit cum pare quisque sua* ("each fellow lies next to his girl"), is circumspect, as befits the tone of the *Fasti*. But the sexual connotations of *accumbere* are made clear by parallels at, for example, Plautus *Bacchides* 1189, *Menaechmi* 1142, and Catullus 61.164.

22. The fundamental study of "The Sacred Marriage" is Frazer, *The Golden Bough*[3] (London, 1926), vol. 2, pp. 120-170. See also Eliade, *Patterns*, pp. 255-262; for India with literature cited on sacred orgies in Muslim Persia, Russia, etc., see the same author's *Yoga: Immortality and Freedom*, trans. W. R. Trask (London, 1958), pp. 420-421; Marcel Granet, *La réligion des Chinois* (Paris, 1922), p. 14. Gaster discusses sex rites in the Ukraine (*Thespis*, pp. 41 and 56 n. 177), also mentioning the biblical version of the rape of the Sabine women (Judges 21:19-23) in which the men of Benjamin "wifenap" the women of Shiloh on the occasion of an annual festival in that town. Further research on the sacred marriage is collected in R. Goodland, *A Bibliography of Sex Rites and Customs* (London, 1931).

23. Frazer, *Golden Bough*[3], p. 97.

24. Eliade, *Patterns*, pp. 354-357.

25. Mircea Eliade, *Myths, Dreams and Mysteries*, trans. Philip Mairet (New York, 1957), p. 186.

26. Walter Burkert, *Homo Necans: The Anthropology of Ancient Greek Sacrificial Ritual and Myth*, trans. Peter Bing (Berkeley, 1983).

27. Athenaeus *Deipnosophistai* 6.267E-270A discusses the Golden Age comedies, listing in chronological order Cratinus' *Wealths*, Crates' *Beasts*, Teleclides' *Amphictyons*, Pherecrates' *Miners* and *Persians*, Aristophanes' *Tagenistai*, Nicophon's *Sirens*, and Metagenes' *Thuriopersians*. Important accounts of the Golden and Iron Ages are given in Vergil *Georgics* 1.118-159, 2.493-542, *Aeneid* 8.319-336; Ovid *Metamorphoses* 1.89-150; Hesiod *Works and Days* 106-201, 225-247 describes the successive races in similar terms.

28. Vergil *Georgics* 1.145.

29. The Saturnalia is first described by the playwright Accius in the mid-second century B.C., as quoted by Macrobius *Sat.* 1.7.37.

30. Saturnus may himself have been an agricultural deity in origin. See further E. Segal, *Roman Laughter*[1] (Cambridge, Mass., 1968), p. 177, n. 28.

31. Vergil *Eclogues* 10.69.

32. Ernst Kris, *Psychoanalytic Explorations in Art* (New York, 1952), p. 185.

33. On the so-called Anacreontic vases, see Françoise Frontisi-Ducroux and François Lissarrague, "From Ambiguity to Ambivalence: A Dionysiac Excursion through the 'Anakreontic' Vases," in *Before Sexuality: The Construction of Erotic Experience in the Ancient Greek World,* ed. David M. Halperin, John J. Winkler, and Froma I. Zeitlin (Princeton, 1990), pp. 211–256.

34. Philostratus *Imagines* 1.2.5.7–9.

35. See further W. T. MacCary, "The Comic Significance of Transvestism in Plautus, Shakespeare and Beaumarchais," in *Letterature comparate: Problemi e metodo. Studi in onore di E. Paratore* (Bologna, 1981), vol. 1, pp. 294–308.

36. As B. Seidensticker has argued in "Comic Elements in Euripides' *Bacchae,*" *American Journal of Philology* 99 (1978), 303–320.

37. "The quality of otherness that, in the form of transvestitism, is peculiarly prominent in the 'Anacreontic' *kōmos* is in fact a fundamental component of every form of *kōmos,* and in other representations we find other sorts of disguises" (Frontisi-Ducroux and Lissarrague, "From Ambiguity to Ambivalence," p. 229).

38. Plato *Philebus* 47–50.

39. Henri Bergson, *Le Rire: Essai sur la signification du comique* (Paris, 1940), p. 13.

40. Shakespeare's sylvan settings (in *Two Gentlemen of Verona, A Midsummer Night's Dream, As You Like It,* and *The Merry Wives of Windsor*) are but one species of what Frye called "the green world," symbolizing the victory of summer over winter (*Anatomy of Criticism,* pp. 58–73). Other comic utopias include Dicaeopolis' private peace in *Acharnians,* Cloudcuckooville in the *Birds,* the woman-controlled world of the *Ecclesiazusae* (perhaps a dystopia?), and the numerous Golden Age plays glimpsed in the Old Comedy fragments (such as *The Beasts* of Crates).

41. *1 Henry 4* 1.2.199–200.

42. *Love's Labour's Lost* 4.1.77.

43. Aristotle *Poetics* 1449a14.

44. Another tradition makes Arion the inventor of tragedy (*Suda,* s.v.). The testimonia for both these figures are collected and discussed by A. W. Pickard-Cambridge, *Dithyramb, Tragedy and Comedy*[2], rev. T. B. L. Webster (Oxford, 1968), pp. 9–20, 69–88. That Thespis dealt specifically with

Dionysiac myth is guaranteed by the *Suda* (s.v. Thespis), which records the names of four of his plays—one of which was *Pentheus*.

45. See A. W. Pickard-Cambridge, *The Dramatic Festivals of Athens²*, rev. John Gould and D. M. Lewis (Oxford, 1968), pp. 72–73, 112.

46. Ibid., p. 59.

47. This is memorably illustrated by Juvenal *Satires* 6.67–70. See further E. Segal, *Roman Laughter²* (Oxford, 1987), esp. pp. 42–70.

48. For a convenient overview of the comic festivals, see Margaret Bieber, *The History of the Greek and Roman Theatre²* (Princeton, 1961), p. 52 and n. 7.

49. The Aristotelian basis of the *Tractatus Coislinianus* has been argued most cogently by Richard Janko, *Aristotle on Comedy: Towards a Reconstruction of Poetics II* (London, 1984), p. 104 and passim. Its authenticity has been strenuously attacked by, among others, H. G. Nesselrath, *Die attische Mittlere Komödie* (Berlin, 1990), pp. 102–149.

50. Aristotle *Poetics* 1449a10. Some scholars believe that *hē men apo tōn exarchontōn ton dithurambon, hē de apo tōn ta phallika* should be taken chiastically in reference to the antecedents "tragedy" and "comedy," that is, with tragedy developing from *ta phallika* and comedy from the dithyramb. (See Lloyd-Jones, "Ritual and Tragedy," in *Ansichten griechischer Rituale* [Stuttgart, 1998], pp. 271–295, here pp. 274–275, citing Jürgen Leonhardt.) Since phallic worship was associated with the cult of Dionysus generally, this is conceivable. But it is much more economical to connect comedy with *ta phallika* given the omnipresence of the phallus in Old Comedy. This is especially evident from Dicaeopolis' private phallic procession in the *Acharnians* and the grand procession which concludes the *Birds*—each a sort of phallic play within a play.

51. See in general Eliade, *Patterns,* p. 357.

52. Consider the ancient description of two women's festivals, the Thesmophoria and Arretophoria: "[they are held] for the creation of fruits and human procreation . . . and they bring unmentionable sacraments prepared from bread dough: effigies of snakes and male organs" (scholion to Lucian *Dialogi Meretricii* 2.1 Rabe). In a fascinating discussion, N. J. Lowe raises the possibility that this account may ultimately derive from an actual participant in these festivals—perhaps even a priestess—who divulged the mysteries to one of the Hellenistic antiquarians who collected odd details of Attic history. "Thesmophoria and Haloa: Myth, Physics and Mysteries," in *The Sacred and the Feminine in Ancient Greece,* ed. S. Blundell and M. Williamson (London, 1998), pp. 149–173.

53. Cf. Eliade, *Patterns,* 259–262.

54. Frazer, *Golden Bough*³, vol. 7, p. 12.

55. Herodotus 2.49–51.

56. St. Augustine *De Civitate Dei* 6.21. For phallic boundary stones, see Burkert, *Homo Necans*, pp. 39 and 58, who explains this delimiting function of the phallus in biological and evolutionary terms. With some primates the males will sit on guard at the perimeter of their territory with erections as a show of force. This seems to derive from the deep-seated connection between aggression and the sex drive.

57. Aristotle *Poetics* 1449a11–12. See also the scholion to *Acharnians* 243.

58. Thucydides 6.27.

59. Aristophanes *Acharnians* 264.

60. The details of both anthems are recorded by Athenaeus *Deipnosophistai* 14.622b–d. Generally skeptical, Pickard-Cambridge (*Dithyramb, Tragedy and Comedy*², pp. 134–144) saw no grounds for connecting either these *phallophoroi* or *ithyphalloi* directly with the phallic ceremonies (*ta phallika*) mentioned by Aristotle. But this is to judge the issue too narrowly, for all three terms must simply designate local variations on a more or less pan-Hellenic cultural practice—whose broad features can surely help to explain this key element of comedy.

61. Malcolm Heath draws a further parallel between the abusive language of comedy and the frequent invective of political rhetoric, seeing the development of both in the Classical period as a reciprocal relationship. "Aristophanes and the Discourse of Politics," in *The City as Comedy: Society and Representation in Athenian Drama*, ed. Gregory W. Dobrov (Chapel Hill, 1997), pp. 230–249, esp. pp. 232–233.

62. See Martin P. Nilsson, *Geschichte der Griechischen Religion*³ (Munich, 1967), vol. 1, p. 119. We also recall the biblical account of Balaam, whose attempts at cursing the Children of Israel were turned into blessings by the Almighty (Numbers 22.6–34). This is especially interesting because the Hebrew verb for curse, *arar*, is almost identical with the double-edged Greek *ara*.

63. *Golden Bough*, vol. 7, p. 62. See also L. R. Farnell, *Cults of the Greek States* (Oxford, 1896–1909), vol. 3, p. 104. For Iambe's jokes in the *Hymn to Demeter* 202–204, see T. W. Allen, W. R. Halliday, and E. E. Sikes, *The Homeric Hymns* (Oxford, 1936), p. 150.

64. On the Haloa, see Nilsson, *Geschichte der Griechischen Religion*³, vol. 1, p. 467. The ancient references for these and other festivals that featured obscenity are conveniently collected by Maurice Olender, "Aspects of Baubo: Ancient Texts and Contexts," in *Before Sexuality*, pp. 83–113, esp. pp. 94–95.

65. Salomon Reinach, "Le rire rituel," in *Cultes, mythes et religions* IV (Paris, 1912), p. 112, n. 27.

66. Sándor Ferenczi, "On Obscene Words," in *Sex in Psychoanalysis* (New York, 1956), p. 122.

67. Fragments 110-111 (Lobel and Page). D. Page, *Sappho and Alcaeus* (Oxford, 1955), p. 120, doubted that these contained anything lewd. But G. S. Kirk, "A Fragment of Sappho Reinterpreted," *Classical Quarterly* N.S. 13 (1963), 51-52, and Hugh Lloyd-Jones, "Sappho fr. cxi," *Classical Quarterly* N.S. 17 (1967), 168, have both argued for a fescennine quality to these wedding songs.

68. Herodotus 5.82-83.

69. *Incompositum temere ac rudem,* Livy 7.2.7.

70. Horace *Epistles* 2.1.146-148.

71. The connection is not without dissenters. Alois Walde and J. B. Hoffman, *Lateinisches Etymologisches Worterbuch* (Heidelberg, 1938-1956), vol. 1, p. 488, connect the word with the city Fescennia in Etruria. Nonetheless, fescennine/*fascinum* has a basis in the *Glossariae Latinae* of Festus (85), cited in Robert Maltby's lexicon: "Fescennine verses, which are sung at weddings, are so-called in reference to the Fescennine city, or because they are thought to ward off enchantment [*fascinum*]." See also the convincing argument of G. L. Hendrickson, "The Dramatic Satyr and the Old Comedy at Rome," *American Journal of Philology* 15 (1894), 1-30, who posits a direct parallel between fescennine verses and Aristotle's *ta phallika*.

72. Burkert, *Homo Necans,* p. 5.

73. Peter Brown, "Bodies and Minds: Sexuality and Renunciation in Early Christianity," in *Before Sexuality*, pp. 479-493. See also the same author's *The Body and Society: Men, Women and Sexual Renunciation in Early Christianity* (New York, 1998).

74. St. Augustine *De Civitate Dei* 6.21. Phallic worship is also attested by Varro *De Lingua Latina* 7.97, who describes the phallic amulets worn around the neck by children.

75. See Paolo Toschi, *Le Origini del teatro italiano* (Turin, 1955), p. 112, who traces the continuous development of Saturnalia into Carnevale.

76. In medieval Western Europe dissipation at Carnival, and the abstinence from flesh on the eve of Lent, was largely characteristic of the southern countries. The north (including England) preferred Feasts of Fools and the like, closer to midwinter and the New Year. It was the suppression of these latter celebrations, which were typically blasphemous, by the Reformation and Counter-Reformation that made way for Carnival—which was

merely boisterous—to spread into those northern countries in which Roman Catholicism was retained or restored. Protestants of course felt they needed neither, having transcended the urgings of the psyche.

77. Cited by Toschi, *Le Origini,* p. 114.

78. Kris, *Psychoanalytic Explorations,* p. 226.

79. Aristotle *De partibus animalium* 673a8.

80. *Pour ce que rire est le propre de l'homme,* Rabelais, "Aux lecteurs."

81. *Aliquando praeterea rideo . . . homo sum,* Pliny *Epist.* 5.3.2.

82. See Gertrud Hauser et al., "The Biology of Laughter: Medical, Functional, and Anthropological—Human Ethnological Aspects," in *Laughter Down the Centuries,* vol. 3, ed. Siegfried Jäkel, Asko Timonen, and Veli-Matti Rissanen (Turku, 1997), pp. 9–23.

83. Quintilian *Inst.* 6.3.1.

84. As Kris puts it: "[in laughter] the ego is overwhelmed by instinctual claims or affects. The role of the instinct can be seen at once" (*Psychoanalytic Explorations,* p. 225). Konrad Lorenz views laughter as "one of the few absolutely uncontrolled discharges of an instinctive motor pattern in man." *On Aggression,* trans. Marjorie Kerr Wilson (New York, 1966), p. 295.

85. Kant, *Kritik der ästhetischen Urteilskraft,* 54.

86. Susanne Langer, *Feeling and Form: A Theory of Art* (New York, 1953), p. 340. Compare Herbert Spencer's (1820–1903) theory of laughter as an overflow: "a large amount of nervous energy . . . is suddenly checked in its flow . . . The excess must discharge itself in some other direction, and there results an efflux through the motor nerves to various classes of the muscles, producing the half-convulsive actions we term laughter." "The Physiology of Laughter," in *Essays,* Second Series (London, 1863), p. 114.

87. See Hauser et al., "The Biology of Laughter," pp. 17–19. The authors adduce the saying of Solomon, "A merry heart doeth good like a medicine."

88. Most familiar is Bergson's observation (*Le Rire,* p. 15) that "laughter is a social gesture." Lorenz strongly affirms this: "shared laughter not only diverts aggression, but also produces a feeling of social unity" (*On Aggression,* p. 179). James Sully earlier remarked on laughter's socially binding powers in *An Essay on Laughter* (London, 1902). Others who have expressed this view include Dupréel, Freud, Eastman, and Kris. See the convenient summaries of these thinkers by R. Piddington, *The Psychology of Laughter* (London, 1933).

89. Piddington, *The Psychology of Laughter,* p. 76.

90. Charles Darwin, *The Expression of the Emotions in Men and Animals* (1872; New York, 1929), chap. 5, pp. 115–145.

91. Cited and discussed by Reinach, "Le rire rituel," p. 112. See also the further discussion in Eduard Norden, *Die Geburt des Kindes: Geschichte einer religiösen Idee* (Berlin, 1924), p. 66.

92. Recounted by Morris Edward Opler, *Myths and Tales of Jicarilla Apache, Memoirs of the American Folklore Society,* vol. 31 (1938), pp. 1-18; summarized by Joseph Campbell in *The Masks of God: Primitive Mythology* (New York, 1959), p. 236.

93. Hesiod *Theogony* 194-195.

94. On the role of Iambe or Baubo in the myth of Demeter, see Olender, "Aspects of Baubo."

95. Homeric *Hymn to Demeter* 200; 305-469; 203; 14.

96. Isaac *(Yitzchak)* is a "child of laughter" not only because the Lord caused both Abraham and Sarah to laugh (Genesis 17.17; 18.12), but also because when he was born Sarah exclaimed: "God has made laughter for me; everyone that hears will laugh on account of me," *kol shomeya yitzchak-li* (21.6).

97. Reinach, "Le rire rituel," pp. 111, 121.

98. On the Easter Laugh, see, among others, Reinach, "Le rire rituel," pp. 127-129; H. Fluck, "Der Risus Paschalis: Ein Beitrag zur religiösen Volkskunde," *Archiv für Religionswissenschaft* 31 (1934), 188-212.

99. George Meredith, "An Essay on Comedy," in *Comedy,* ed. Wylie Sypher (New York, 1956), p. 4. Reprinted from *The Times,* 5 February 1877, 4/5. For *agelastes* in Rabelais, see L. Sainéan, *La langue de Rabelais* (Paris, 1923), vol. 2, pp. 269-270 ("qui ne rient pas . . . la plus grave injure selon la doctrine pantagruéline").

100. "The tendency of comedy is to include as many people as possible in its final society: the blocking characters are more often reconciled or converted than simply repudiated." Frye, *Anatomy of Criticism,* p. 165.

101. Aristophanes *Knights* 42.

102. See, for example, Darwin's remarks on primates in *The Expression of the Emotions,* p. 131, and J. Y. T. Grieg, *The Psychology of Laughter and Comedy* (London, 1923), p. 30. There seems to be consensus on the psychological analysis: see Martin Grotjahn, *Beyond Laughter* (New York, 1957), p. 198.

103. Aristotle *Poetics* 1453a34.

104. Freud, "Jokes," p. 235.

105. Catullus 31.7-10.

106. Martin A. Berezin demonstrates the psychic need for a well-structured "Happy End" not only in comedy but also in music as well: "Some Observations on Art (Music) in its Relationship to Ego Mastery," *Bulletin of the Philadelphia Association for Psychoanalysis* 7:2 (June 1958), 49-55 and passim.

3. The Lyre and the Phallus

1. Homer *Iliad* 2.270.

2. Ibid., 2.274. Certainly Sir Thomas Elyot appreciated "the witty Ulisses" at this moment. Compare *The Governour,* ed. A. T. Eliot (London, 1834), p. 13.

3. As forcibly argued by George E. Dimock, Jr., "The Name of Odysseus," *Hudson Review* 9 (Spring 1956), 52-77, reprinted in several anthologies including *Essays on the Odyssey,* ed. Charles H. Taylor, Jr. (Bloomington, 1963), pp. 54-72. More recently Walter Burkert has supported a non-Greek derivation of the name: *Homo Necans: The Anthropology of Ancient Greek Sacrificial Ritual and Myth,* trans. Peter Bing (Berkeley, 1983), pp. 131-132.

4. Dimock's translation of *Odyssey* 19.407-409, "The Name of Odysseus," p. 55.

5. Ibid.

6. S. Freud, "Jokes and Their Relation to the Unconscious," vol. 8, pp. 9-236, quotation from p. 102.

7. In *Leviathan* Thomas Hobbes wrote that laughter is "sudden glory arising from some sudden conception of some eminency in ourselves by comparison with the infirmity of others, or with our own formerly."

8. W. K. Wimsatt, "The Criticism of Comedy," in *Hateful Contraries* (Lexington, 1965), p. 91.

9. Ibid., pp. 94-95.

10. The fragment's authenticity is generally doubted (see Kassel-Austin [hereafter K.-A.], vol. 7, pp. 664-665). After all, if Susarion was from Megara, why is the fragment in Attic dialect? A. W. Pickard-Cambridge, *Dithyramb, Tragedy and Comedy*², rev. T. B. L. Webster (Oxford, 1968), pp. 162-187, went so far as to doubt whether Susarion was a historical figure at all. Though the Megarian claim to have invented comedy is probably an exaggeration, it seems certain at least that they had an early comic tradition. Their humor was proverbially tasteless—we shall see an Aristophanic parody in the *Acharnians.*

11. Scholion to Dionysius Thrax (= testimonium 9 K.-A.).

12. Susarion frag. 1. K.-A. (freely translated). Compare frag. 276.7-9, from Menander's *Misogynē* (*The Woman-Hater*): "A wife is expensive and troublesome and does not allow / her husband to live as he wants; but there is one good thing from them: children."

13. Aristotle describes marital dynamics at length, comparing them to the workings of government, in which some rule and others are ruled (*Nicomachean Ethics* 8.1160b32-1161a1).

14. Horace *Ars Poetica* 79: "rage armed Archilochus with its very own iamb" (*Archilochum proprio rabies armavit iambo*).

15. Hipponax frag. 68 West.

16. Semonides frag. 7.12–20 West.

17. Further memorable misogyny is found in Aristophanes *Clouds* 41–55; Pherecrates frag. 286 K.-A.; Alexis frag. 150 K.-A. ("We men forgive when we are wronged, but women do wrong and then on top of it make accusations!"); Xenarchus frag. 14 K.-A.; Antiphanes 220 K.-A.; Menander frags. 64, 65, 508, 804 K.-A. On anti-wife humor in Roman comedy, see further E. Segal, *Roman Laughter*[2] (Oxford, 1987), pp. 21–27.

18. Freud, "Jokes," pp. 108–109.

19. Caesar *Carm.* 1.3–4. "Comic violence" renders *vis comica,* but Caesar may have meant us to construe *comica* with *virtus* ("comic virtue").

20. We find a close approximation of the word in the Greek *epichairekakia* (Aristotle *Nicomachean Ethics* 2.1107a10); in Latin we have *laedere gaudes* in Horace *Sat.* 1.4.78.

21. Aristophanes *Frogs* 1–2.

22. Ibid., 12–18.

23. On the garrulity of women see Menander frags. 65, 186, 804, and 815 K.-A.

24. Eupolis frag. 232 K.-A. We have supplemented the context of the fragment.

25. See also Aristophanes *Lysistrata* 270. The name is also found in Menander frags. 188 and 815 K.-A.

26. Eupolis frag. 295 K.-A.

27. Plato Comicus frag. 105 K.-A.

28. Plato Comicus frag. 188 K.-A.

29. Aristophanes frag. 9 K.-A.

30. There is a learned dispute over whether this was spoken by Kaufman or Moss Hart, his collaborator on such zany comedies as *The Man Who Came to Dinner* (1939).

31. Scholion to Aristophanes *Birds* 283. Compare Plato *Protagoras* 314d–e.

32. Eupolis frag. 158 K.-A.

33. Ameipsias frag. 9 K.-A.

34. Eupolis frags. 386, 388 K.-A.

35. Cratinus frag. 2 K.-A.

36. My abbreviated translation offers merely the gist of a long passage (*Clouds* 1310–1443).

37. Plautus *Pseudolus* 120; 122.

38. See Herodotus 5.78: "It is clear in every way how freedom of speech (*isēgoria*) is a good thing, if the Athenians, when they were ruled by tyrants, were no better in war than any of their neighbors, but when they got rid of them they became foremost by far."

39. Scholion to Lucian *Dialogi Meretricii* 7.4.

40. Horace *Sat.* 1.4.1–5. K. J. Reckford, *Aristophanes' Old-and-New Comedy* (Chapel Hill, 1987), p. 470, reminds us that "the verb *notare* connects their work with that of the Roman censor, who struck immoral people from the Senate list."

41. Tzetzes *Peri kōmōidias* 3.16; see G. Kaibel, *Comicorum Graecorum Fragmenta* (Berlin, 1899), p. 18; Platonius *Peri diaphoras* (Kaibel, *CGF,* p. 6).

42. See first Pickard-Cambridge, *Dithyramb, Tragedy and Comedy*², pp. 194–212. It was in the choral structure of Old Comedy that F. M. Cornford, *The Origins of Attic Comedy* (Cambridge, 1934), attempted to find vestiges of an ancient seasonal ritual.

43. Of course, contests of all sorts are typical of festivals. We know of competitions for professional musicians and amateur choruses in the Archaic period: see M. L. West, *Ancient Greek Music* (Oxford, 1992), pp. 14–21. As a more immediate precedent for the comic *agōn,* compare also the tradition of rustic singers competing against each other in a comastic setting, later stylized by Theocritus and the other pastoral poets. See *Scholia in Theocritum Vetera,* ed. C. Wendel (Leipzig, 1914), pp. 2–3 (*prolegomena* B.a).

44. *Acharnians* 1227–1228, 1231; *Knights* 1254; *Birds* 1765.

45. See further G. M. Sifakis, *Parabasis and Animal Choruses* (London, 1971), who reviews the various theories on the ritual origins of the animal chorus, and considers their role in the development of Old Comedy.

46. See Pickard-Cambridge, *Dithyramb, Tragedy and Comedy*², p. 144 with n. 1.

47. As Oliver Taplin reminds us: "Comedy and the Tragic," in *Tragedy and the Tragic,* ed. M. S. Silk (Oxford, 1996), pp. 188–202, esp. p. 195 with n. 24. See also the same author's *Comic Angels* (Oxford, 1993), p. 60 with n. 11.

48. *Orsa Lakedaimōn paa,* Aristophanes *Lysistrata* 995–996. *Ors-* = *orth-,* "erect." Compare *Lys.* 834, *orthēn . . . tēn hodon,* "the long straight path," and the use of the epithet in *Ach.* 243 and 259—both noted by J. Henderson, *The Maculate Muse: Obscene Language in Attic Comedy*² (Oxford, 1991), p. 112—as well as *orthēn* [sc. *hodon*], the very first word of the *Birds* (echoed at *Thesm.* 1223).

49. Aristophanes *Birds* 1695–1696.

50. Aristophanes *Wasps,* 505. Translation from Alan H. Sommerstein's edition (London, 1983). The longest such word, found at *Assemblywomen* 1169–1175, is 76 syllables long. This tendency is already found in Epicharmus (frag. 46 Kaibel).

51. Cratinus frag. 271, 352 K.-A.; Aristophanes *Clouds* 907; Eupolis frag. 454 K.-A.; Plato Comicus frag. 201 K.-A.

52. Pherecrates frag. 138 K.-A.

53. See Henderson, *Maculate*², pp. 133–136.

54. Cratinus frag. 171 K.-A.

55. Cratinus frags. 342, 326 K.-A.

56. Cratinus frag. 73 K.-A.

57. Aristotle *Poetics* 1449a32-37.

58. Homer *Iliad* 2.216.

59. Aristophanes *Knights* 550; *Peace* 767-774.

60. Cratinus frag. 346 K.-A.

61. Heracles the glutton appears in comedy as early as Epicharmus (frag. 21 Kaibel), but his literary history is older still. See first the discussion in Athenaeus *Deipn.* 10.411a-412b, which includes many further citations. On this and other comic treatments of Heracles, see G. Karl Galinsky, *The Heracles Theme* (Oxford, 1972), pp. 81-100.

62. Aristophanes *Knights* 526-530. The passage contains a possible Homeric allusion, for the flood simile is used of Ajax (*Iliad* 11.492-5).

63. Aristophanes *Frogs* 357.

64. For Heracles the bull-eater, see Athenaeus *Deipnosophistae* 10.412a; Pausanias 5.5.4.

65. *Knights* 533-535. The joke lies in the substitution of "quaffing" for the expected "eating," since public heroes were awarded free *dinners* at the Prytaneum.

66. For Cratinus' bibulousness, see also *Peace* 695-703.

67. Testimonium 8 K.-A., inspiring confidence by relating Crates specifically to the date of Aeschylus' *Edonians*. Test. 9 K.-A., from Jerome's *Chronicle of Eusebius*, places Crates in the eighty-second Olympiad (450 B.C.)—after the death of Aeschylus. As usual with dates of flourishing, however, this is undoubtedly only a rough calculation.

68. Anonymous *Peri kōmōidias* (Kaibel, *CGF*, p. 7).

69. Crates frag. 16 K.-A.

70. Aristotle *Poetics* 1449b7-9.

71. In the *Fish* of Archippus (a contemporary of Aristophanes), the piscine chorus denounces the cruelty shown to fish by humans (frag. 23 K.-A.). So too in Aristophanes' *Birds* the chorus views man as its mortal enemy (369-374). As John Wilkins puts it, "food is closely associated with the products of the natural world, animals, fish, and plants. In the comic polis, access to that world may be gained by the animal chorus: in comedy the food talks back." "Comic Cuisine: Food and Eating in the Comic Polis," in *The City as Comedy: Society and Representation in Athenian Drama*, ed. Gregory W. Dobrov (Chapel Hill, 1997), pp. 250-268, quotation from p. 253.

72. Crates frag. 19 K.-A.

73. Anonymous *Peri kōmōidias* (Kaibel, *CGF*, p. 8).

74. Athenaeus *Deipnosophistae* 6.268e.

75. "It has often been claimed that Athenaeus' almost pathological penchant for everything about food and drink is very much to blame for a distorted picture we get about those comedies he cites from; the fact is, however, that no other period of Attic comedy provided him with more material on big eaters and drinkers in Athens than Middle Comedy; this can be no mere coincidence with Athenaeus' interests." Heinz-Günther Nesselrath, "The Polis of Athens in Middle Comedy," in *The City as Comedy,* ed. Dobrov, pp. 271-288, quoted from p. 277. Of course, this picture may be distorted by the aleatoric nature of the remains: there may have been as much emphasis on food in Old Comedy.

76. John Wilkins, "Comic Cuisine," p. 251. See also the same author's "The Significance of Food and Eating in Greek Comedy," *Liverpool Classical Monthly* 18 (1993), 66-74; and Emily Gowers's study of food in Plautus, *The Loaded Table* (Oxford, 1993), pp. 50-108.

77. On sexual double-entendres involving eating, see Henderson, *Maculate*[2], pp. 142-144.

78. Crates frag. 43 K.-A.

79. Pherecrates frag. 43 K.-A.

80. Pherecrates frag. 190 K.-A. The side-dish joke was popular throughout the entire history of Greek comedy. For a full discussion see Athenaeus *Deipnosophistae* 9.367B-368C, from which we get most of the comic fragments that use the word (although these do not all have a sexual overtone): Aristophanes frag. 191 K.-A. ("For all women it's the same: an affair is like a little side dish"); Alexis frag. 89 K.-A.; Antiphanes frags. 61, 225 K.-A.; Archedicus frag. 2 K.-A.; Eubulus frag. 6 K.-A.; Magnes frag. 2 K.-A.; Metagenes frag. 15 K.-A.; Nicophon frag. 22 K.-A.; Pherecrates 157 K.-A.; Plato Comicus frags. 32, 43 K.-A.; Sotades frag. 3 K.-A. ("Seems I'm a side dish to Krobylos: for he's gobbling down *that* guy, but he's only nibbling at me"). Perhaps the most famous usage of this term is by Aeschylus, when he has Clytemnestra exult in her lover Aegisthus as "a delicious bed-hors d'oeuvre" (*eunēs paropsōnēma tēs emēs chlidēs, Agamemnon* 1447).

81. Pherecrates frag. 185 K.-A.

82. Pherecrates frag. 164 K.-A.

83. Eupolis frags. 171 K.-A.; 247 K.-A.

84. For a fine introduction to this playwright and his relationship with Aristophanes, see Ian C. Storey, "Notus est Omnibus Eupolis," in *Tragedy, Comedy and the Polis,* ed. Alan H. Sommerstein et al. (Bari, 1993), pp. 373-396.

85. Eupolis frag. 106 K.-A.

86. See the scholia to *Clouds* 554 and *Knights* 1291; Aristophanes *Knights* 958, 1290–1299, 1372; *Peace* 446, 673, 675, 1295–1304; *Wasps* 19–20, 822; *Clouds* 353, 400, 673–675, 680; *Birds* 289, 290, 1473–1481; *Women at the Thesmophoria* 605.

87. Frag. 89 K.-A. Eupolis is said to have written from 1288 onwards (scholion at Aristophanes *Knights* 1291).

88. Aristophanes *Clouds* 553–555.

89. According to Athenaeus *Deipnosophistae* 14.621d-e, the foreign doctor (*xenikos iatros*) derived from Doric farce. A fragment of Alexis (146 K.-A.) describes how people are taken in by a foreign accent. See W. Geoffrey Arnott, *Alexis: The Fragments* (Cambridge, 1996), pp. 430–432, for a concise history of the comic physician in Greece (including a possible prototype in Epicharmus). Other early *medici gloriosi* are found in Crates frag. 46 K.-A., Alcaeus frags. 10–13 K.-A.?, Theopompus frag. 3 K.-A. We will soon encounter the *medicus* in Plautus' *The Brothers Menaechmus* and "Doctor" Callimaco in Machiavelli's *Mandragola*. In the commedia dell'arte the Doctor (*Il Dottore*) could be either a lawyer graduated from Bologna or a doctor graduated from Padua: see, among others, Albert Bermel, *Farce: A History from Aristophanes to Woody Allen* (Carbondale, 1990), pp. 88–89.

90. Eupolis frag. 99.90–97 K.-A. The text is badly damaged. We follow Edmonds' interpretation and supplements.

91. Eupolis frag. 173 K.-A.

92. Eupolis frag. 193 K.-A.

93. Eupolis frag. 261 K.-A.

94. Eupolis frag. 301 K.-A. See Henderson, *Maculate*, pp. 131–133, who distinguishes between "pig" and "piggie," the first alluding to a grown woman, the second a young one.

95. Compare *Frogs* 3–5 with frags. 339–340 K.-A. In both farcical instances, the slave character is struggling with too many packages and groaning "my neck/shoulder is getting crushed."

96. Vomiting: frags. 49, 365, 625 K.-A. Side-dish: frag. 191 K.-A. (compare old Magnes and Plato Comicus).

97. Aristophanes frag. 9 K.-A.

98. Aristophanes frag. 488 K.-A. In praise of himself: frag. 719 K.-A. Against Euripides: frag. 682 K.-A. In frag. 392 K.-A. he says that Socrates supplies Euripides with material for his "clever gossipy tragedies."

99. Aristophanes frag. 616 K.-A.

100. Aristophanes frag. 478 K.-A.

101. Aristophanes frag. 477 K.-A.

4. Aristophanes: The One and Only?

1. Plato *Republic* 2.373D-E; *Laws* 1.625E.
2. Werner Jaeger, *Paideia*², trans. Gilbert Highet (New York, 1945), vol. 1, p. 367. Karl Reinhardt, "Aristophanes und Athen," in *Von Werken und Formen* (Godesburg, 1948), p. 294. On the difficulty of assessing Aristophanes' views of Athenian politicians and policy, see most recently Malcolm Heath, "Aristophanes and the Discourse of Politics," in *The City as Comedy: Society and Representation in Athenian Drama,* ed. Gregory W. Dobrov (Chapel Hill, 1997), pp. 231-249. For a contrasting view, see Douglas M. MacDowell, *Aristophanes and Athens: An Introduction to the Plays* (Oxford, 1995), pp. 46-48.
3. Cicero *Rep.* 4.11-12.
4. See K. J. Dover's exhaustive discussion of the issue in his edition of *Clouds* (Oxford, 1968), pp. xxxli-lvii.
5. But as F. H. Sandbach, *The Comic Theatre of Greece and Rome* (New York, 1977), p. 15, wrote, "to say that we have eleven plays by Aristophanes is a half truth. We have the words of eleven plays. The text is not the play, the performance is."
6. *Acharnians* 647-651.
7. "It is certainly a curious feature which distinguishes Aristophanes' plays from all other forms of comedy, that they present a whole series of heroes who are old men and behave as such at the beginning, while at the end they are more or less transformed into youthful bridegrooms." F. M. Cornford, *The Origins of Attic Comedy*², ed. Theodor Gaster (Gloucester, Mass., 1968), p. 92. See also C. Whitman, *Aristophanes and the Comic Hero* (Cambridge, Mass., 1964), p. 52.
8. Pherecrates frag. 77 K.-A. See also frags. 78-79 K.-A.
9. S. Freud, "Totem and Taboo" (1913), vol. 13 (1913-1914), pp. 155-157; see also Bennett Simon, *Tragic Drama and the Family: Psychoanalytic Studies from Aeschylus to Beckett* (New Haven, 1988), chap. 1; and Ludwig Jekels, "Zur Psychologie der Komödie," *Imago* 12 (1925), 328-335.
10. Further fragments on old age are Pherecrates 156 K.-A., Cratinus 133 K.-A. We shall also see the complaints of the old men in *Wasps.* According to Pollux (*Onomasticon* 4.104-105) the imitation of old men, leaning on staffs, was part of the Dorian festival tradition (and was probably universal). Aristophanes claims to avoid this character (*Clouds* 541-542), which, if anything, suggests that his own old men are direct descendants.
11. Pherecrates frag. 283 K.-A.
12. Cratinus frag. 28 K.-A.
13. Aristophanes *Clouds* 1417, *dis paides hoi gerontes.*

14. For the phases of a child's sexual development, see S. Freud, "Three Essays on the Theory of Sexuality" (1905), vol. 7 (1901–1905), pp. 130–243, esp. 231–243.

15. Aristophanes' association with Callistratus was probably a sort of apprenticeship, but only in regard to the mechanics of production. See Douglas M. MacDowell, "Aristophanes and Callistratus," *Classical Quarterly* 32 (1982), 21–26.

16. Compare Eupolis frag. 388 K.-A.

17. Aristophanes frag. 206 K.-A.

18. *Acharnians* 27. Compare Eupolis frag. 219 K.-A.: "O polis, polis [polis]! / Up to now you've been so lucky, but not wise."

19. See J. Henderson, *The Maculate Muse*² (Oxford, 1991), p. 58.

20. *Acharnians* 30.

21. Ibid., 79.

22. Unlike the widespread modern perception which condemns the practice in totality, or the modern liberal sensibility which approves everything except pederasty, the ancient Athenian mentality distinguished between acceptable and unacceptable homosexual activities. Reprehensible acts were those which made the participant seem dominated or submissive, hence unmanly—notably pathic anal penetration and fellatio. These acts were strictly excluded from the conventions of honorable pederasty. See K. J. Dover, *Greek Homosexuality*² (Cambridge, Mass., 1989), pp. 91–109, 140–144.

23. *Acharnians* 100–165. For the fine distinctions between "unnatural and natural" sexual practices, see John Jay Winkler, "Laying Down the Law: The Oversight of Men's Sexual Behavior in Classical Athens," in *Before Sexuality: The Construction of Erotic Experience in the Ancient Greek World*, ed. David M. Halperin, John J. Winkler, and Froma I. Zeitlin (Princeton, 1990), pp. 171–210.

24. *Acharnians* 128. *Megas*, which beginning students are taught to translate simply as "big," was not uncommonly used by comic and lyric poets to refer to a mighty erection. Regius Professors *emeriti* of Greek at both Oxford and Cambridge have demonstrated this use, as well as the ithyphallic nature of the expression "big man," in Sappho and elsewhere. See G. S. Kirk, "A Fragment of Sappho Reinterpreted," *Classical Quarterly* 13 (1963), 51–52; H. Lloyd-Jones, "Sappho Fr. 111," *Classical Quarterly* 17 (1967), 168; also Henderson, *Maculate*², pp. 115–116. Of course, not every use of this very common word is phallic, but the connotation is common in the plays of Aristophanes.

25. *Acharnians* 198.

26. Paolo Toschi, *Le Origini del Teatro Italiano* (Turin, 1955), p. 112 and passim.

27. *Acharnians* 681.

28. See Hans-Joachim Newiger, *Metapher und Allegorie: Studien zu Aristophanes,* Zetemata 16 (Munich, 1957), p. 144.

29. *Acharnians* 214-218. For the record, Phaÿllus was not only a sprinter but an admirable pentathlete who set the record of 55 feet in the long jump. He refused to participate in the Olympiad of 480 in order to command a ship in July, August, and September in the supreme Athenian victory against the Persians at Salamis. See Herodotus 8.47, Pausanias 10.9.2; also H. A. Harris, *Greek Athletes and Athletics* (Bloomington, 1969), pp. 90-91.

30. *Acharnians* 243; compare 259.

31. We have another bit of incestuous eroticism in *Wasps* 606-609. When Philocleon comes home with his juror's pay, his daughter rewards him with sexy tongue-kisses: see K. J. Dover, *Aristophanic Comedy* (Berkeley, 1972), p. 127. This touchy subject will be considered further in relation to the comedies of Molière.

32. *Acharnians* 254-256.

33. Ibid., 263-275.

34. Ibid., 280-292.

35. Aristophanes *Frogs* 1010-1012.

36. *Acharnians* 396-400.

37. One famous early use of the *ekkyklēma* is in the *Oresteia.* In the first play, *Agamemnon,* Clytemnestra is revealed standing defiantly over the bodies of her husband and Cassandra. The scene is artfully mirrored in the second play of the trilogy, *The Libation Bearers,* where in a similar *mise en scène* Orestes stands over the bodies of Clytemnestra and her lover Aegisthus. Helene P. Foley correctly points out the comic use of this device in the *Acharnians:* "Aristophanes not only stresses in an untragic fashion the mechanics of tragic theatre, but suggests that comedy reveals the unglamorous but important truths that tragedy (drama that depends on dramatic illusion) hides behind the stage." Helene P. Foley, "Tragedy and Politics in Aristophanes' *Acharnians," Journal of Hellenic Studies* 108 (1988), 33-47, repr. in *Oxford Readings in Aristophanes,* ed. E. Segal (Oxford, 1996), pp. 117-142, quotation from p. 136.

38. See Aristotle *Poetics* 1460A32; Hyginus *Fabulae* 100, 244. A full list of references is given by Robert Graves in *The Greek Myths* (New York, 1955), pp. 285-286.

39. *Frogs* 1079-1080; Menander *Epitrepontes* 1123-1124.

40. *Acharnians* 497-500.

41. *Troilus and Cressida* 2.3.78.

42. *Acharnians* 557-571.

43. Is it mere coincidence that Lamachus is hailed as "stormer of city walls" (570) and Plautus' eponymous braggart warrior is saluted as *urbicape*, "sacker of cities" (*Miles Gloriosus*, 1055)?

44. *Acharnians* 574.

45. In Plato Comicus frag. 201 K.-A., nausea is also induced by a feather and an obnoxious person.

46. See Dover, *Homosexuality*, p. 204, and *Acharnians*, ed. Alan H. Sommerstein (Warminster, 1980), ad loc.

47. *Acharnians* 590–593.

48. Ibid., 664, *deilos kai lakatapygōn*.

49. *Acharnians* 977. See, for example, Crates frag. 16–18 K.-A.; Cratinus frags. 172, 176, 256–258 K.-A.; Pherecrates frag. 137 K.-A.

50. As Cornford explained this odd convention, "the expulsion of the intruder is the dark counterpart of the *kōmos*, which brings in the new god, victorious in the *agōn*." *The Origins of Attic Comedy* (Cambridge, 1934), p. 151.

51. For the sexual sense of "piglet," see Henderson, *Maculate²*, pp. 131–132; on this passage as a whole, see ibid., pp. 60–61, and Dover, *Aristophanic Comedy*, pp. 63–64. Piglets seem to have had more general sexual associations as well. At the Thesmophoria they were cast into the pits "as a symbol, because of their fecundity, of human and vegetable procreation." (Scholion to Lucian *Dialogi Meretricii* 2.1 Rabe.)

52. *Acharnians* 749.

53. Ibid., 789.

54. Ibid., 799–802.

55. Ibid., 967.

56. Ibid., 987.

57. Ibid., 988.

58. See Henderson, *Maculate²*, p. 142 for salt-fish; pp. 128–129 on feathers and wings; pp. 137–138 for doors, gates, and passageways. For an extended comic treatment of fish in a sexual context, see Antiphanes frag. 27 K.-A. from his play *The Fisherwoman* (*Halieuomene*) with Nesselrath's discussion, "The Polis of Athens in Middle Comedy," in *The City as Comedy*, pp. 271–288, esp. pp. 279–281. See also the discussion in James Davidson, *Courtesans and Fishcakes: The Consuming Passions of Classical Athens* (London, 1998), pp. 3–20.

59. *Acharnians* 991–994.

60. Ibid., 1058–1066.

61. According to the *Suda* (s.v.), the tragedian Phrynichus, an older contemporary of Aeschylus, was the first to portray women onstage. But the *mimēsis* of old women, like that of old men, seems to have been a regular part of

festival tradition. See A. W. Pickard-Cambridge, *Dithyramb, Tragedy and Comedy*², rev. T. B. L. Webster (Oxford, 1968), pp. 63–65 (for Phrynichus) and 162–166 (for old men and women).

62. *Acharnians* 1106–1108, 1140–1142.

63. Ibid., 1143–1149.

64. Ibid., 1214–1221.

65. Ibid., 1149, *deina*.

66. Ibid., 1231.

67. See F. M. Cornford, *Origins*², pp. 52, 57, 69.

68. *Knights* 42: *dyskolon gerontion*.

69. *Knights* 180; 166–167. Henderson, *Maculate*², p. 153, took the verb *laikazein* intransitively as "receive fellatio," just as other Athenian heroes were given dinners. But H. D. Jocelyn, "A Greek Indecency and its Students: *Laikazein*," *Proceedings of the Cambridge Philological Society* 206 (1980), 12–66, has argued exhaustively that *laikazein* is strictly equivalent to *fellare*. We must then take the verb actively, as does Alan H. Sommerstein, *Knights* (Warminster, 1981), ad loc., and this makes the joke even better. The city would thus maintain the Sausage-seller as he *performs* fellatio to his heart's content. Elsewhere he is proud of his pathic expertise: his well-worn anus is mocked at lines 423–426, 483–484, 963–964, 1242, 1262–1264: see Henderson, *Maculate*², p. 68.

70. Thucydides 2.43; Aristophanes *Acharnians* 144.

71. Dover, *Homosexuality*, p. 202.

72. *Knights* 732.

73. Ibid., 733.

74. Ibid., 1341–1344.

75. Ibid., 1121–1124.

76. Ibid., 1330; 1333.

77. Ibid., 1325.

78. Ibid., 1384–1386.

79. Ibid., 1387.

80. Ibid., 1388–1389.

81. Ibid., 1390–1391.

82. It is tempting to connect Trygaeus' theft of Opora with the "fruit-stealer" of the Dorian festival tradition (see Athenaeus *Deipnosophistae* 14.621d; Pollux *Onomasticon* 4.105), a character who appears as early as Epicharmus (frag. 239 Kaibel).

83. *Peace* 54–55.

84. See Whitman, *Comic Hero*, pp. 115–116.

85. Homer *Iliad* 6.200.

86. *Peace* 42. The audience would have been familiar with the cult of Zeus *katabatēs* ("he who descends in thunder"), and would appreciate the mere addition of a couple of letters to transform the epithet into a scatological sobriquet (*skataibatēs,* "shit-walker").

87. Whitman, *Comic Hero,* p. 106.

88. The classic work on "the play element in culture" is Johan Huizinga, *Homo Ludens,* trans. R. F. C. Hull (London, 1949). He sums up his theory as follows (p. 28): "Play is a voluntary activity or occupation executed within certain fixed limits of time and place, according to rules freely accepted as absolutely binding, having its aim in itself and accompanied by a feeling of tension, joy, and the consciousness that it is 'different' from 'ordinary life.'" See also Jacques Ehrmann, "*Homo Ludens* Revisited," *Yale French Studies* 21 (1968), 31-57.

89. *Peace* 236-237.

90. Ibid., 520.

91. Ibid., 551-552.

92. Ibid., 556-559.

93. Ibid., 706-708.

94. Ibid., 710 711.

95. Ibid., 726-728.

96. Ibid., 729-818.

97. See ibid., 335-336, 351-354.

98. Ibid., 860-867.

99. See Athenaeus *Deipnosophistae* 14.646f.

100. *Peace* 868-870.

101. See, for example, Asclepiades 35; Propertius 2.1.13, 2.15.5.

102. *Peace* 895-904.

103. Ibid., 1329-1331.

104. This is the conjecture of Alan H. Sommerstein, *Peace* (Warminster, 1985), ad loc.

105. *Peace* 1337-1340.

106. Ibid., 1351-1352.

107. As reported in the hypothesis to *Peace.*

5. Failure and Success

1. Oliver Taplin, *Comic Angels* (Oxford, 1993), pp. 89-92, correctly insists that the extensive archaeological remains in both Attica and Magna Graecia as a whole, as well as the great number of plays—he cites Alexis, for example, who by his reckoning composed 130 comedies, while the *Suda* (s.v.) claims that it was an astounding 245—require us to assume that plays were per-

formed outside Athens from an early time. Taplin further calls our attention to the contrast between the output of the Old Comic poets (for instance, Aristophanes' 40 plays) and the astounding fecundity of the later playwrights.

2. *Clouds* 520–524; *Wasps* 1047.

3. On this question, see C. F. Russo, "The Theatrical Seasons and the Dawn of Comedy," in *Aristophanes, An Author for the Stage,* trans. Kevin Wren (New York, 1992), pp. 1–12.

4. See *Clouds* 218.

5. Test. 3 K.-A. first gives Cratinus' age as 94, but then implies that he lived for 97 years.

6. See, for example, C. Whitman, *Aristophanes and the Comic Hero* (Cambridge, Mass., 1964), p. 137.

7. Aristophanes *Knights* 526–536. Compare Cratinus' *tou rheumatos* (frag. 198.1 K.-A.) of the drunken flood of his poetry which washes away all the land, with *Knights* 525–530 (cited in Chapter 3), esp. *rheusas* (526). Mary R. Lefkowitz, *The Lives of the Greek Poets* (London, 1981), pp. 112–113, quotes a bit of amusing "history" from the anonymous treatise on Comedy (quoting Aristophanes *Peace* 702–703), that "Cratinus died when the Spartans invaded Attica because he fainted; he could not bear to see a jar full of wine being broken." See G. Kaibel, *Comicorum Graecorum Fragmenta* (Berlin, 1899), p. 3. Lefkowitz even quotes the comically sentimental "fact" that when the playwright Eupolis died, his dog immediately died of grief (pp. 114–115).

8. Scholion to Aristophanes *Knights* 400 (= test. 2 K.-A.).

9. Cratinus frag. 193 K.-A. The text is corrupt, and its interpretation remains problematic. We follow the conjectures of Edmonds which, though by his own admission doubtful, at least adhere to what we know of the play from the summary found in the scholion to Aristophanes *Knights* 400.

10. Cratinus frag. 200 K.-A.

11. Cratinus frag. 203 K.-A.

12. Cratinus frag. 199 K.-A.

13. Victor Coulon, *Aristophane,* 5 vols. (Paris, 1952–1954), vol. 1, p. 153.

14. Ameipsias frag. 9 K.-A.

15. See the first Hypothesis to the play and K. J. Dover's definitive discussion of the two versions in his edition of *Clouds* (Oxford, 1968), pp. lxxx–xcviii.

16. Aristophanes repeated the titles of *Wealth, Women at the Thesmophoria,* and *Peace.* On the theatrical authorities and the appointing of "executive producers," see Aristotle *Athenian Politics* 56.3–6.

17. This is reported in the first Hypothesis to the play, and seems to be accurate.

18. See Athenaeus *Deipnosophistae* 171c.

19. On the other hand, it might be argued that the play was in fact staged but placed fourth or fifth and has thus eluded the records. Dover, *Aristophanic Comedy* (Berkeley, 1972), pp. 103–140, puts forth another possibility, that it was incompletely revised and put into circulation as a written text.

20. The original application of the saying is unknown, but it seems to have been used repeatedly as innovations took drama further and further from its Dionysian roots. See the discussion in A. W. Pickard-Cambridge, *Dithyramb, Tragedy and Comedy*², rev. T. B. L. Webster (Oxford, 1968), pp. 124–125.

21. *Clouds* 522.

22. Ibid., 317, *gnōmēn kai dialexin kai noun*.

23. Ibid., 129.

24. Ibid., 28–29.

25. A modern version of this is found in *Monty Python and the Holy Grail:* "I fart in thy general direction."

26. "I married the niece of Megacles—I a rustic, she from the city" (46–47). Strepsiades describes himself as an *agroikos*, a type described at length by Aristotle and Theophrastus.

27. Strepsiades constantly harps on his rusticity (see, for example, lines 43, 47, 51, 138 and elsewhere). For hints of his wife's gluttony as well as sexual insatiability, see for example line 52, which describes her extravagance and gourmandizing. The old man also alludes to *Cōlias*, which would be clear to a Greek audience as a place where women's festivals were held. And the *Genetyllis*, who are goddesses of procreation. As Sommerstein sums it up, "she was oversexed" (at 52).

28. Ibid., 75–76.

29. Ibid., 99, 101–102.

30. See *Clouds* 143–168.

31. In 1998 the McVities biscuit company funded research on the physics of "dunking" to see how well their best-selling Hobnobs could stand up to hot tea (at 80°C) in comparison with Ginger Nuts and Digestives. Digestives proved most durable—unless the Hobnob has a protective chocolate coating. *The Times* (London), 11 November 1998. In a similar vein, after an entire month's intensive research, Professor Jean-Marc Vanden-Broeck of the University of East Anglia proved that all teapot spouts, regardless of construction, will dribble.

32. *Clouds* 171–173.

33. Ibid., 734. See Dover, *Clouds,* ad loc., who thinks he is masturbating.

34. *Clouds* 295.

35. Ibid., 517, *sophian epaskei.*

36. For example, 178, *diabētēn* ("bestriding"): see the comments of Alan H. Sommerstein, *Clouds* (Warminster, 1982), ad loc.—the same pun is made by Metōn at *Birds* 1003; and the repeated appeal to the *euruprōktoi* in Wrong Logic's winning argument (1085–1104).

37. *Clouds* 1304, *erastheis.*

38. Freud, "Character and Anal Eroticism" (1908), vol. 7 (1906–1908), pp. 209–215. Freud further remarks: "The original erotic interest in defecation is, as we know, destined to be extinguished in later years. In those years the interest in money makes its appearance as a new interest which had been absent in childhood. This makes it easier for the earlier impulsion, which is in process of losing its aim, to be carried over to the newly emerging aim." See further Freud's observations in "Anal Eroticism and the Castration Complex" (1918), vol. 17 (1917–1919), pp. 72–88; "Two Lies Told by Children" (1913), vol. 12 (1911–1913), pp. 287–291; and the interesting suggestions in "Leonardo da Vinci and a Memory of his Childhood" (1910), vol. 14 (1910), pp. 151–231.

39. See *Clouds* 518–562.

40. Ibid., 367–381.

41. Ibid., 385–394.

42. See the first Hypothesis.

43. *Clouds* 522–525.

44. Ibid., 537–543.

45. Ibid., 544–548.

46. Ibid., 811–812.

47. Ibid., 973.

48. Ibid., 975–976.

49. Ibid., 991; 1005–1006.

50. Ibid., 1011–1014.

51. Ibid., 1015–1019.

52. Ibid., 1078–1080.

53. Ibid., 1384–1390.

54. Ibid., 1325, 1331.

55. Ibid., 1334.

56. Ibid., 1417; also found in Cratinus frag. 28 K.-A.

57. As Dover observes of this remark in his commentary: "the violence against one's mother is more abhorrent than the violence against one's father."

58. *Clouds* 1509.

59. Ibid., 423–426.

60. See especially Charles Segal, "Aristophanes' Cloud-Chorus," *Arethusa* 2 (1967), 143–161, repr. in *Oxford Readings in Aristophanes,* ed. E. Segal (Oxford, 1996), pp. 162–181.

61. E. Bentley, *Let's Get a Divorce and Other Plays* (New York, 1958), p. xiii.

62. J. Henderson, *The Maculate Muse*² (Oxford, 1991), p. 78.

63. W. Thomas MacCary, "Philocleon, *Ithyphallos:* Dance, Costume and Characters in the *Wasps,*" *Transactions of the American Philological Association* 109 (1979), 137–147, quotation from p. 138.

64. F. M. Cornford, *The Origin of Attic Comedy*², ed. Theodor Gaster (Gloucester, Mass., 1968), p. 147.

65. *Wasps* 54.

66. This criticism of the throwing of fruit as vulgar is repeated in *Plutus* 794–801.

67. See *Wasps* 54–62.

68. Ibid., 88–90.

69. Northrop Frye, *The Anatomy of Criticism* (Princeton, 1957), p. 168.

70. Henri Bergson, *Le Rire: Essai sur la signification du comique* (Paris, 1940), p. 29.

71. Sometimes the humors are explicitly mentioned. See, for example, Menander *Epitrepontes* 393, *Phasma* 57.

72. *Wasps* 89.

73. Ibid., 99.

74. Ibid., 523, 756–759.

75. Ibid., 126–128.

76. Ibid., 139–144.

77. Gregory Crane, "Oikos and Agora: Mapping the Polis in Aristophanes' *Wasps,*" in *The City as Comedy: Society and Representation in Athenian Drama,* ed. Gregory W. Dobrov (Chapel Hill, 1997), pp. 198–229, sees this scene as the crux of the play's concern with the conflict between *oikos* and *polis,* where the contemporary economic and historical forces which were changing the character of the *polis* were also threatening to subsume the individual *oikos.* By locking up his jury-crazed father, Bdelycleon attempts to secure the *oikos* against the intrusion of political forces, as represented by the patron-client relationship between Cleon and the old jurors.

78. "Does anyone still seriously believe that these were stingless wasps, or that their sting was a lance rather than an erection at the ready?" William Arrowsmith, "Aristophanes' Birds: The Fantasy Politics of Eros," *Arion* N.S. 1/1 (Spring 1973), 119–167, quotation from p. 136.

79. *Wasps* 357–359.

80. Ibid., 365.

81. Ibid., 441–444.

82. Ibid., 549.

83. Ibid., 572–573.
84. Ibid., 607–609. See Dover, *Aristophanic Comedy,* p. 127, and A. Sommerstein, *Wasps* (Warminster, 1983), ad loc.
85. K. Reckford, *Aristophanes' Old-and-New Comedy* (Chapel Hill, 1987), p. 236.
86. *Wasps* 578.
87. Ibid., 619–620; 625–627.
88. Ibid., 1015–1059.
89. *Frogs* 1491.
90. *Wasps* 727.
91. Ibid., 1060–1064.
92. Ibid., 1066, 1070.
93. Ibid., 1090.
94. Ibid., 1222.
95. Ibid., 1252–1261.
96. Ibid., 1296.
97. Ibid., 1303.
98. Ibid., 1299–1302.
99. Ibid., 1305–1323.
100. Ibid., 1341–1355.
101. Henderson, *Maculate*², p. 82, denies any sexual rejuvenation to Philocleon. He argues that the pipe-girl is not interested in "ministering to his lusts . . . despite our amusement and sympathy, we must agree with Bdelycleon, cast in the role of a stern father, who sees that this rejuvenation is . . . the drunken enactment of youthful exploits long past."
102. *Wasps* 1365–1366.
103. Ibid., 1386.
104. Ibid., 1450–1455.
105. "In his rejuvenated state Philocleon performs figures . . . to musical accompaniment whose rhythm is conventionally associated with proto-dramatic phallic performances in honor of Dionysos." MacCary, "Philocleon, *Ithyphallos,*" p. 147.
106. *Wasps* 1535–1537.
107. *Wasps* took the second prize, but it is not improbable that Aristophanes simultaneously won the first with *The Preview.* See MacDowell, *Wasps,* p. 124; and the introduction to Sommerstein, *Wasps,* p. xv.

6. The *Birds:* The Uncensored Fantasy

1. Thucydides 6.31.
2. Euripides *Iphigenia in Tauris* 398–420. Translation by R. Lattimore, *Iphigenia in Tauris* (London, 1974).

3. See Nan Dunbar's definitive edition, *Aristophanes, Birds* (Oxford, 1995), pp. 1–6, for the relationship between the play and contemporary political developments. Jeffrey Henderson, "Mass versus Elite and the Comic Heroism of Peisetaerus," in *The City as Comedy*, ed. Gregory W. Dobrov (Chapel Hill, 1997), pp. 135–148, has most recently argued that the play is a deliberate political satire: "The resemblance of the plot to the sensational events of the preceding year, though not explicit, is close enough that no spectator could fail to see it, and this resemblance clearly suggests that among the play's agenda was satire of the lofty imperial ambitions engendered in the Athenians by contemporary rhetors, just as the name of the hero suggests satire of their persuasive rhetoric" (p. 136).

4. "In no way could he have reached more subtly into the psychology of his contemporary audience." C. Whitman, *Aristophanes and the Comic Hero* (Cambridge, Mass., 1964), p. 176.

5. See Thucydides 1.70, 4.10, 6.24, 6.31.

6. Ibid., 6.27.

7. *Lysistrata* 1094.

8. Freud, *Introductory Lectures on Psychoanalysis* (1916–1917), Lecture 10, "Symbolism in Dreams," vol. 15, pp. 149–169, quotation from p. 155; compare J. Henderson, *The Maculate Muse: Obscene Language in Attic Comedy*[2] (Oxford, 1991), pp. 49–50.

9. John Boardman, "The Phallos-Bird in Archaic and Classical Greek Art," *Revue archéologique* 2 (1992), 227–242, favors a different etymology for English "cock," deriving it from the word's application to "water spout, tap or faucet, which may have been suggested by the crest-like presence of a handle above the spout-beak" (p. 235).

10. See the full discussion of Catullus' bird in J. N. Adams, *The Latin Sexual Vocabulary* (London, 1982), pp. 32–34.

11. On the phallus-bird, see William Arrowsmith, "Aristophanes' Birds: The Fantasy Politics of Eros," *Arion* N.S. 1/1 (Spring 1973), 119–167, who devotes an entire appendix of his article to demonstrating that *pterōs* is synonymous with phallus. Boardman, "Phallos-Bird," p. 236, n. 7, finds Arrowsmith's argument "laboured." He sees the winged phallus as representing "the satisfaction of female sexuality through heterosexual activity, physical or imagined, without the intervention of a live complete male" (pp. 239–240). The present reading of the *Birds*, however, should make it clear that the winged phallus was an image of greater range and potency than this. See also Walter Burkert's discourse on phallus-birds and other priapic creatures in *Homo Necans: The Anthropology of Ancient Greek Sacrificial Ritual and Myth* (Berkeley, 1983), p. 71.

12. Plato *Phaedrus* 252b4-c2.

13. Arrowsmith, "Fantasy Politics," p. 130.

14. Recall the messenger in *Lysistrata* who reports that "All Sparta is aroused" (*orsa Lakedaimōn paa*, 995), and compare line 834 in the same play.

15. *Birds* 1.

16. Ibid., 3-4. The translation attempts to convey a sense of the play's special imagery. Here, the Greek adverbs *anō* and *katō* ("upwards" and "downwards") indicate the phallus in its two polar positions, at rest or at attention. For *anō*, compare *Thesm.* 1223, *orthēn anō diōke*.

17. *Birds* 36-41.

18. Ibid., 44.

19. Thucydides 2.40.2-3.

20. *Birds* 46-48, 114-122.

21. Ibid., 64-66.

22. J. R. Green, "A Representation of the *Birds* of Aristophanes," *Greek Vases in the J. Paul Getty Museum* 2 (1985), 95-118. Oliver Taplin, *Comic Angels* (Oxford, 1993), pp. 101-104, counters that the most conspicuous features of this vase—the depiction of the birds as fighting cocks and their confrontational pose—are incompatible with any scene in the *Birds,* and suggests instead that they may represent Wrong and Right Logic in the first version of the *Clouds*—who, according to a scholiast's comment on line 839 of that play, were originally so costumed. As he concedes, however, the piper is strong evidence for the involvement of a chorus—and so the *Clouds* is really excluded. Yet the *agōn* between the birds and the two hoboes might easily have been staged as a cockfight, as suggested below. And the aggressive virility of cocks provides a context for understanding the aroused nature of the birds. Another bird chorus (not ithyphallic) is shown on an early fifth-century vase, possibly to be connected with the *Ornithes* of Magnes. See Richard Green and Eric Handley, *Images of the Greek Theatre* (London, 1995), pp. 49-50.

23. Sophocles' *Tereus* was staged c. 431 B.C. For a consideration of Aristophanes' use of this play, see Gregory W. Dobrov, "The Tragic and the Comic Tereus," *American Journal of Philology* 114.2 (1993), 189-234. See also H. Hofmann, "Mythos und Komödie: Untersuchungen zu den Vögeln des Aristophanes," *Spudasmata* 33 (1976).

24. When Tereus first appears and Euelpides likewise remarks on his wings and plumage, it may be another allusion to prominent sexual characteristics. Throughout the play the erectile quality of the bird's crest is played upon. See Green, "Representation," p. 116.

25. *Birds* 211-212, 217.

26. Ibid., 669.
27. Ibid., 114–118.
28. Ibid., 121–122.
29. Ibid., 137–142.
30. Ibid., 156–161.
31. Compare Theophilus fragment 11.2 K.-A., where two of the flowers mentioned here are found as names of courtesans.
32. *Birds* 162–163.
33. Ibid., 558–559.
34. Ibid., 559–560. To ensure that their athletes did not expend themselves sexually in any way, the ancient Greeks would infibulate or "disable" their penises with a kind of clip or seal.
35. Ibid., 422, *megan tin' olbon.*
36. Ibid., 321.
37. Ibid., 374, in the inspired translation of A. Sommerstein, *Birds* (Warminster, 1987).
38. Compare the representation of Right and Wrong Logic as fighting cocks in the *Clouds,* for which see Dover's edition (Oxford, 1968), pp. xc–xciii and xcvi. The skewer is one of the many pole-shaped objects documented as phallic by Henderson, *Maculate*[2], pp. 123, 144.
39. *Birds* 412–415. Compare 324.
40. Ibid., 433. Dunbar, *Birds,* ad loc., compares *Lysistrata* 669–670, where the same verb is used to describe the rejuvenation of old men.
41. *Birds* 468–470.
42. For instance, there are definite phallic allusions in the description of the activities of the cock (486–492). He was so strong and big (*megas* again) in the old days that even now when he sings his high-pitched rise-and-shine song, "men would immediately jump up to the job" (490). The word *orthrion,* literally "dawn song," would inevitably suggest morning erections to the audience with a pun on *orthos.*
43. *Birds* 478.
44. Ibid., 556.
45. Both the glyconics, which introduce their address, and the familiar anapests themselves are written with extreme delicacy. Michael Silk, "Aristophanes as a Lyric Poet," *Yale Classical Studies* 26 (1980), 99–152, argues that the playwright should not be ranked alongside the great lyric poets for passages like this. Rather, he had a gift for pastiche, and although his odes are competent they are not, and are not intended to be, great lyric poetry. Nevertheless, Aristophanes is a master of language in many different ways and is capable of some very beautiful effects. See for example

E. Fraenkel's discussion, "Die Parabasenlieder," in *Beobachtungen zu Aristophanes* (Rome, 1962), pp. 191–215. See also Dunbar, *Birds*, at 750 and 1748–1754.

46. *Birds* 703–704.

47. Ibid., 753–768; *Clouds* 1078.

48. *Birds* 790–792.

49. *Assemblywomen* 637–639. For more on this syndrome, see A. H. Maslow and Beta Mittelman, *Principles of Abnormal Psychology* (New York, 1955), s.v. Henry A. Murray, "American Icarus," in *Clinical Studies of Personality,* ed. Arthur Burton and Robert E. Harris (New York, 1955), vol. 2, pp. 615–641, cites a case history involving fantasies of airborne excretion (p. 635).

50. In lines 1003–1007, Metōn says he wants to put his "stiff rod" *(orthos kanōn)* in the hero's "parted legs" *(diabētēn,* with the same pun on "compass" used at *Clouds* 178) so that the city will have straight roads *(orthai hodoi,* recalling the opening words of the play) moving into its very middle *(pros auto to meson;* compare perhaps the song of the *ithyphalloi* in Athenaeus *Deipnosophistae* 14.622b-d, quoted in Chapter 2: "For [the phallus], erect and throbbing, wants to march through the middle of the place"). Finally, Peisetaerus expels him: "Why don't you go somewhere and 'measure' *yourself!*" (1020).

51. *Birds* 1054–1055. The suggestion of flatulence is from Sommerstein's edition (Warminster, 1987), ad loc., based on Peisetaerus' expression of disgust, *aiboi* ("phooey"). This would work well by punctuating the decree-seller's attempt at blackmail in line 1053 ("Remember how you used to shit on the decrees?").

52. Ibid., 1224–1237. Translation slightly condensed.

53. Ibid., 1253–1255.

54. Ibid., 1255–1256. J. Taillardat, *Les Images d'Aristophane: étude de langue et style* (Paris, 1965), p. 103, remarks of this passage that for Aristophanes' characters to "pierce with the sword three times" is a sign of virility and youth. See also Henderson, *Maculate*[2], p. 121.

55. *Acharnians* 994.

56. *Birds* 1279, 1284.

57. Ibid., 1534–1543. *Basíleia* ("Royal Lady") has been confused here with *Basileía,* "sovereignty." The two are identical except for the accent, yet metrical considerations prove that the former is intended. See Dunbar, *Birds,* at 1531–1536.

58. *Birds* 1633–1636.

59. Ibid., 1639.

60. Ibid., 1686–1687.

61. Ibid., 1731–1742.

62. See Dunbar, *Birds,* ad loc.

63. *Birds* 1747.

64. Ibid., 576, 1714; 1749–1750. There is perhaps a further tumescent pun here between *pyrphoron* ("firebearing") and *porphyrōn* ("swelling, growing crimson"), another poetic word, used both of flame (Apollonius of Rhodes 1.935) and of flushed skin (see *L.S.J.* s.v. II).

65. *Birds* 1753.

66. After giving a broad overview of the various theories, Hans-Joachim Newiger, *Metapher und Allegorie: Studien zur Aristophanes* (Munich, 1957), pp. 99–101, concluded that Basileia must be some real goddess (like Athena), and is not a random personification.

67. *Birds* 1731–1735, 1740–1742.

68. L. R. Farnell, *Cults of the Greek States* (Oxford, 1896), vol. 1, pp. 180–188 with testimonia at 241 n. 1, and 250 n. 42. Farnell argues that, though the cult itself is not explicitly attested at Athens, the Athenians would certainly have been familiar with its existence, as shown by Plato *Phaedrus* 253b. More recently, A. M. Bowie, *Aristophanes: Myth, Ritual and Comedy* (Cambridge, 1993), pp. 163–164, suggests that Peisetaerus' marriage may be compared to the *"hieros gamos* between the wife of the Archon Basileus (the 'Basilinna') and Dionysus at the Anthesteria, which marked acceptance of the god into the city in spring."

69. "Even in this unusually bold fantasy of a mortal taking over Zeus' power, it would have been impossibly sacrilegious to make Peisetaerus, an Athenian citizen, marry a real goddess such as Zeus' consort Hera or Athena, the virgin patron of the city." Dunbar, *Birds,* pp. 703–704. Carlo Fernando Russo, *Aristophanes: An Author for the Stage,* trans. Kevin Wren (London, 1994), p. 152, takes the opposite stance and comes closer to the mark by referring to Basileia as "a rejuvenated Hera."

70. S. Freud, "Totem and Taboo" (1913), vol. 13 (1912–1914), pp. 43–159; also "Dostoyevsky and Parricide" (1928), vol. 14 (1927–1931), pp. 437–461. For a post-Freudian revision of the Oedipus complex as regarding women, see Estela V. Welldon, *Mother, Madonna, Whore: The Idealization and Denigration of Motherhood* (New York, 1988).

71. Norman O. Brown, *Life Against Death: The Psychoanalytical Meaning of History* (New York, 1959), p. 270.

72. C. Lévi-Strauss, *Les Structures élémentaires de la parenté* (Paris, 1949), pp. 71–72. See also Jean Rudhart, "De l'inceste dans la mythologie grecque," *Revue française de psychanalyse* 4 (1982), 731–763, who traces the history of the concepts of incest. The Christian era saw new vocabulary which distinguished

between specific couplings, as against the more general Greek terms for "shameful gamos." The Greeks in turn regarded Egyptian practices as bizarre.

73. Otto Rank, *The Incest Theme in Literature and Legend: Fundamentals of a Psychology of Literary Creation,* trans. Gregory C. Richter (Baltimore, 1992), p. 341.

74. *Birds* 1765.

75. Plautus *Poenulus* 1219–1220.

76. *Birds* 1633–1635.

77. Northrop Frye, "The Argument of Comedy," in *English Institute Essays, 1948* (New York, 1949), pp. 58–73, quotation from p. 58.

78. "The total *mythos* of comedy, only a small part of which is ordinarily presented, has . . . a ternary form: the hero's society rebels against the society of the *senex* and triumphs, but the hero's society is a Saturnalia, a reversal of social standards which recalls a golden age in the past before the main action begins." Northrop Frye, "The Mythos of Spring," in *The Anatomy of Criticism* (Princeton, 1957), p. 171. Incidentally, *Birds* is one of the few Aristophanic comedies that conforms precisely to the paradigm of F. M. Cornford, *The Origin of Attic Comedy* (Cambridge, 1934).

79. *Birds* 1759–1761.

80. Ibid., 1764.

81. Gilbert Murray, *Aristophanes: A Study* (Oxford, 1933), p. 155. He could also have adduced Alcman frag. 1.16–39 ("let no man fly to heaven / nor seek to marry Aphrodite," etc.) or any of Pindar's frequent warnings not to attempt to rival Zeus (for example, *Isthmian* 5.14, *Olympian* 5.24).

82. See the first Hypothesis to the play.

83. As we are reminded by Whitman, *Comic Hero,* p. 120.

7. Requiem for a Genre?

1. Aristides 2.342D. Compare Valerius Maximus 7.2.7.

2. Charles Segal, "The Character and Cults of Dionysus and the Unity of the *Frogs,*" *Harvard Studies in Classical Philology* 65 (1961), 207–242, quotation from p. 230.

3. C. Whitman, *Aristophanes and the Comic Hero* (Cambridge, Mass., 1964), p. 231.

4. Dionysus was also travestied in Eupolis' *Taxiarchoi* (*The Commanders*), the *Dionysoi* and *Dionysalexander* of Cratinus, and Aristophanes' own *Dionysus Shipwrecked,* as well as comedies by Magnes, Plato Comicus, and others.

5. *Frogs* 18.

6. Ibid., 45–47, 108–109.

7. Notably in connection with the myth of Omphale. Nicole Loraux, "Herakles: The Super-Male and the Feminine," in *Before Sexuality: The Construction of Erotic Experience in the Ancient Greek World*, ed. David M. Halperin, John J. Winkler, and Froma I. Zeitlin (Princeton, 1990), pp. 21–52, observes of the present passage that "Dionysus-Herakles produces laughter of two sorts: first, there is the laughter internal to the comedy, the laughter of Herakles who, from the heights of his affirmed masculinity, is amused at the heroic get-up of Dionysus the Wimp; and then there is the secondary laughter of the spectator, who knows that Herakles has more to do with the wearing of the *krokotos* [a women's garment] than he admits" (p. 38). Perhaps Heracles the cross-dressed appeared in Ion's satyr-play *Omphale* or the *Omphale* of the Younger Cratinus.

8. *Frogs* 53.

9. See the brilliant ideas put forth by Eric Havelock in *The Literate Revolution in Greece and Its Cultural Consequences* (Princeton, 1982), especially where he describes the physiological and psychological pressures exerted in the process of a society's conversion from oral to written literature: "The clash of the senses . . . required prolonged alignment of hearing to vision. A psychological adjustment was required to bridge the gap between them . . . The skills, habits and institutions required to convert [the alphabet] into a complete cultural instrument have become perfected and familiar, obscuring the physiological problems created by its introduction, though by no means altogether removing them" (p. 262).

10. See J. R. Green, *Theatre in Ancient Greek Society* (London, 1994), p. 3.

11. *Frogs* 1409.

12. Ibid., 1113–1115. Jennifer Wise, *Dionysus Writes: The Invention of Theatre in Ancient Greece* (Ithaca, 1998), has recently argued that the development of the Classical dramatic forms was dependent upon the technology of writing to a hitherto unsuspected degree, and that the notion of a fixed text, as the Greek plays certainly were, is fundamentally at odds with oral composition.

13. *Frogs* 55–58; 66–67.

14. Ibid., 95.

15. See Dover's edition (Oxford, 1993), p. 202 at 95: "this might simply be a vulgar expression"; at 96: "*gonimon* suggests that the impotent is being contrasted with the fertile."

16. *Frogs* 345–347.

17. Ibid., 408–413.

18. See for example Hypothesis 1c.

19. *Frogs* 740.

20. Ibid., 1306–1308.

21. Ibid., 117–122.

22. Ibid., 129–133.

23. Ibid., 307–308. The reference is quite explicit. See Dover at *Frogs* 255, who translates *enchezein* as "to shit in one's clothes."

24. *Frogs* 479.

25. Ibid., 959.

26. Gregory Crane, "Oikos and Agora: Mapping the Polis in Aristophanes' *Wasps,*" in *The City as Comedy: Society and Representation in Athenian Drama,* ed. Gregory W. Dobrov (Chapel Hill, 1997), pp. 198–229, aptly comments: "The Athenian public found Aeschylus hard to understand, but, if *Frogs* presents a recognizable picture, Aeschylean complexity made the Athenians feel grand rather than small, enhancing their sense of worth more than emphasizing their intellectual inadequacy" (p. 201).

27. *Frogs* 1063.

28. Ibid., 1053.

29. Ibid., 1079–1081.

30. Ibid., 1206–1208.

31. C. Whitman's defense of this interpretation, *"Lēkythion apōlesen,"* *Harvard Studies in Classical Philology* 73 (1969), 109–112, is definitively supported by Dover, *Frogs,* pp. 337–339.

32. The success of the *Frogs* is recorded by one of the *Vitae* (*Prolegomena* 228.40–43 Koster), and by Dicaearchus (as adduced in Hypothesis 1). Alan H. Sommerstein, "Kleophon and the Restaging of *Frogs,*" in *Tragedy, Comedy and the Polis,* ed. Sommerstein et al. (Bari, 1993), pp. 461–476, has argued authoritatively that the encore of the *Frogs* was at the Lenaia of 404 B.C.

33. Eupolis frag. 219 K.-A.

34. Euripides' *Phrixus,* frag. 833 Nauck.

35. Gilbert Murray, *Aristophanes* (Oxford, 1933), p. 199; Whitman, *Comic Hero,* p. 2.

36. See Wilhelm Süss, *Aristophanes und die Nachwelt* (Leipzig, 1911).

37. Aristotle *Nicomachean Ethics* 1128a21. Note that Aristotle's distinction between Old and New Comedy could not yet have embraced Menander, and so his reference to the "new writers" *(hoi kainoi)* should correspond to what subsequent critics termed "Middle."

38. See for example the energetic attempts of F. M. Cornford, *The Origin of Attic Comedy* (London, 1934); O. Navarre, "Les Origines et la structure technique de la Comédie Ancienne," *Revue des études anciennes* 13 (1911), 245–295. Whitman, *Comic Hero,* pp. 9–11, offers a brief defense of Aristophanic structure. But K. Reinhardt, "Aristophanes und Athen," in *Von Werken und Formen*

(Bonn, 1948), p. 292, reviews the various generic explanations and cautions against attempts to fit Aristophanes into any "Gattungs- oder Ursprungsformel."

39. A. W. Schlegel, *Vorlesungen über dramatische Kunst und Literatur,* Lecture 13 (Stuttgart, 1966), p. 157. Ironically, Schlegel then asserts that New Comedy is not a real genre. Albin Lesky also opposed any attempt to link Old and New Comedy in an evolutionary scheme: see *Geschichte der griechischen Literatur*² (Bern, 1963), p. 425.

40. K. J. Dover, "Greek Comedy," in *Fifty Years (and Twelve) of Classical Scholarship* (Oxford, 1968), p. 147. H. Flashar, "Zur Eigenart des Aristophanischen Spätwerks," in *Poetica I* (1967), pp. 154–175, ed. Hans-Joachim Newiger (Darmstadt, 1975). See E. Segal, "The *physis* of Comedy," *Harvard Studies in Classical Philology* 77 (1973), 129–136.

41. Aristotle *Poetics* 1449b7–9.

42. Anonymous, *Peri kōmōidias.* See G. Kaibel, *Comicorum Graecorum Fragmenta* (hereafter *CGF*) (Berlin, 1899), p. 8.

43. F. M. Cornford, *The Origin of Attic Comedy*², ed. Theodor Gaster (Gloucester, Mass., 1968), p. 189.

44. Richard Janko has reconstructed a putative version of *Poetics II* in *Aristotle on Comedy* (London, 1984). In a lighter vein, Umberto Eco has mischievously made this mythical Second Book the motive for various murders by a mad monk in *The Name of the Rose.*

45. *Pollas metabolas metabalousa . . . epausato:* see Aristotle *Poetics* 1449a10–15. For the idea of *physis* as "the fullest natural form," see *Politics* 1.1252b33–36.

46. *Poetics* 1449b1–2.

47. E. R. Curtius, *Europäische Literatur und lateinisches Mittelalter* (Bern, 1948), pp. 275–276. G. Luck adapted the term as "normative" (opposed to "absolute") in "Scriptor Classicus," *Comparative Literature* 10/2 (1958), 150–158, esp. p. 151.

48. Aristotle *Poetics* 1447b6–16.

49. Heinz Günther Nesselrath, *Die attische mittlere Komödie: Ihre Stellung in der antiken Literaturkritik und Literaturgeschichte* (Berlin, 1990). See also "The Polis of Athens in Middle Comedy" in Dobrov, *The City as Comedy,* pp. 271–288. Earlier scholars who accepted Middle Comedy as a literary genre are A. Körte, *Real-Encyclopädie der classischen Altertumswissenschaft,* vol. 11.1 (Stuttgart, 1921), cols. 1256–1258; Philippe Legrand, *The Greek New Comedy,* trans. J. Loeb (London, 1917), passim; Karl Reinhardt, "Aristophanes und Athen," in *Von Werken und Formen* (Godesberg, 1948), p. 309; T. B. L. Webster, *Studies in Later Greek Comedy*² (Manchester, 1970), passim.

50. Eupolis frag. 99 K.-A.

51. Apuleius *Florida* 3.16. According to Athenaeus *Deipnosophistae* 11.482c, Antiochus of Alexandria wrote a work "On the Middle Comedy poets" (*Peri ton en tei mesei komoidiai komoidoumenon poieton*).

52. Alexis has now been restored to prominence by Arnott's new *Alexis, The Fragments: A Commentary* (Cambridge, 1996).

53. Tzetzes *Prol. com.* 3.16 (Kaibel, *CGF,* p. 18).

54. Platonius *Peri diaphoras* (Kaibel, *CGF,* p. 6); Tzetzes *Prol. com.* (Kaibel, *CGF,* p. 18).

55. See Pickard-Cambridge, *Dithyramb, Tragedy and Comedy²*, rev. T. B. L. Webster (Oxford, 1962), pp. 194–212.

56. Herodotus 5.78.

57. Geoffrey Arnott, *Menander, Plautus and Terence, Greece and Rome New Surveys in the Classics* 9 (Oxford, 1975), p. 18.

58. See J. R. Green and E. W. Handley, *Images of the Greek Theatre* (London, 1995), pp. 60–62. Niall Slater, "The Fabrication of Comic Illusion," in *Beyond Aristophanes: Transition and Diversity in Greek Comedy*, ed. Gregory W. Dobrov (Atlanta, 1995), pp. 29–45, here pp. 40–41 with n. 33, suggests that Menandrean plays as we have them might be the "touring" versions with the choral songs, which were performed in Athens, simply excised.

59. See *Poetae Comici Graeci*, ed. R. Kassel and C. Austin, vol. 4 (Berlin, 1983), p. 192; K. J. Dover, *Aristophanic Comedy* (Berkeley, 1972), pp. 216–217.

60. On the changing role of the chorus in Middle Comedy, see Kenneth S. Rothwell, "Continuity of the Chorus in Fourth-Century Attic Comedy," *Greek, Roman and Byzantine Studies* 33 (1992), 209–225, who notes that an interactive chorus is still found in some Middle Comedy fragments. On the chorus of New Comedy, see E. W. Handley, *The Dyscolos of Menander* (Cambridge, Mass., 1965), pp. 171–174; A. W. Gomme and F. H. Sandbach, *Menander: A Commentary* (Oxford, 1973), p. 12.

61. It is likely that this fund was only instituted in the mid-fourth century. See P. J. Rhodes, *The Athenian Boule²* (Oxford, 1985), p. 105.

62. Aristotle *Poetics* 1450a15, see also 1447a8, 1451a32–33. Horace *Ars Poetica* 23: "At any rate, be it what you wish, as long as it is simple and one."

63. As Horace enjoined, "Do not let a god intrude, unless a snarl has befallen which is worthy of such an untangler" (*Ars Poetica* 191–192).

64. Cratinus frag. 197 K.-A.

65. Aristotle *Poetics* 1449a32.

66. *Acharnians* 623–625; 720–728.

67. Ibid., 971–976.

68. Ibid., at 1018–1055.

69. Ibid., 1038–1039.

70. *Knights* 213–216.

71. *Lysistrata* 567–570.

72. *Wasps* 763–935.

73. Ibid., 799–803.

74. *Ecclesiazusae* 211, *en tais oikiais*.

75. S. Saïd argues that Aristophanes, in his two extant fourth-century plays, seems to advocate a *polis* organized on the model of the *oikos*. "L'Assemblée des femmes: les femmes, l'économie et la politique," in *Aristophane, les femmes et la cité*, Les Cahiers de Fontenay (Fontenay-aux-Roses École Normale Supérieure) 17 (1979), 33–69, reprinted in English translation, slightly abridged, as "The Assembly Women" in *Oxford Readings in Aristophanes*, ed. E. Segal (Oxford, 1996), pp. 282–313. H. P. Foley puts forth a similar argument in "The 'Female Intruder' Reconsidered: Women in Aristophanes' *Lysistrata* and *Ecclesiazusae*," *Classical Philology* 77 (1982), 1–21.

76. *Ecclesiazusae* 673–676.

77. References to money and materialism in the *Ecclesiazusae* include lines 184–188, 197–198, 204–210, 291–292, 304–309, 392–393, 412–413, 446–448, 659–661, 730–754, 778–783, 815–829, 872–876.

78. We know, for example, that in Plautus the cost of a party girl was 20 *minae*. See F. Ritschl, *Opuscula Philologica*, vol. 2 (Leipzig, 1868), pp. 308–309. In some plays the cost itself becomes a kind of leitmotif.

79. Quoted and discussed by Norman O. Brown, *Life against Death: The Psychoanalytical Meaning of History* (New York, 1959), p. 254. Brown describes sublimation as follows: "Whereas for archaic man the crucial defense mechanism is undoing (expiation), for civilized man the crucial defense mechanism is sublimation. The basic characteristic of sublimation is the desexualization of sexual energy by its redirection towards new objects. But as we have seen, desexualization means disembodiment. New objects must substitute for the human body, and there is no sublimation without the projection of the human body into things; the dehumanization of man is his alienation of his own body" (p. 281). See also Sándor Ferenczi, *Further Contributions to the Theory and Technique of Psychoanalysis* (New York, 1926).

80. Brown, *Life against Death*, p. 238.

81. See Lysias 19.11, 21.13, 27.2. Victor Ehrenberg, *The People of Aristophanes*[2] (Oxford, 1951), p. 253, concurs: "It lies beyond doubt that during the period of Old Comedy the economic factor became more important in the lives and minds of the Athenians."

82. *Acharnians* 33–36. There is an untranslatable pun on *prión*, meaning both "buy" and "saw."

83. Ovid *Metamorphoses* 1.89–90.

84. Ibid., 1.131; compare Vergil *Aeneid* 8.327.

85. Ovid *Metamorphoses* 138–140.

86. Ovid *Fasti* 1.209–226: 1.211, *opum furiosa cupido*.

87. See E. Segal, "The Business of Roman Comedy," in *Perspectives of Roman Poetry: A Classics Symposium*, ed. G. K. Galinsky (Austin, 1974), pp. 93–103.

88. Menander frag. 838 K.-A.

89. Menander frag. 218 K.-A.

90. For the record, the phallus did not totally disappear until the mid-fourth century. See A. W. Pickard-Cambridge, *The Dramatic Festivals of Athens²*, rev. John Gould and D. M. Lewis (Oxford, 1968), pp. 220–223.

91. W. Thomas MacCary, "Philokleon *Ithyphallos*: Dance, Costume and Characters in the *Wasps*," *Transactions of the American Philological Association* 109 (1979), 147.

92. Donatus *De comoedia* (Kaibel, *CGF*, p. 67) *(Comoedia est fabula diversa instituta continens affectuum civilium ac privatorum)*, rendering an earlier Greek definition which is also given.

93. Sander Goldberg, *The Making of Menandrian Comedy* (London, 1980), p. 3, observes that "unlike Dionysus and Xanthias, who are larger than life and whose relationship is exploited with comic brilliance and a touch of the grotesque, Chremylos and Karion are drawn on a human scale and are, at least by comparison, realistic."

94. See V. Ehrenberg, *The People of Aristophanes: A Sociology of Attic Comedy²* (Oxford, 1951), p. 186: "The master was always the absolute lord and owner, the *despotēs*. Therefore to kill one's own slave was not a legal crime." On the inhumane—or far too humane, according to the crusty Old Oligarch (1.10–12)—torture of slaves in Athens, see Eva Keuls, *The Reign of the Phallus: Sexual Politics in Ancient Athens* (Berkeley, 1985), p. 7. For the judicial torture of slave-witnesses, see Michael Gagarin, "The Torture of Slaves in Athenian Law," *Classical Philology* 91 (1996), 1–18.

95. *Plutus* 13–14.

96. Bernard Knox, *Word and Action* (Baltimore, 1979), p. 359.

97. *Plutus* 46; 48.

98. Euripides frag. 696.

99. *Plutus* 56–62.

100. Ibid., 72–79.

101. Ibid., 104–106.

102. Beaumarchais, *Barber of Seville* 1.2.

103. *Plutus* 99.

104. Ibid., 141–142.

105. See K. J. Dover, *Greek Popular Morality in the Time of Plato and Aristotle* (Oxford, 1974), pp. 114–115: "In comedy the crude sentiment that food and drink are the best that life can offer is apt to be uttered by slaves." Among the passages he cites is Menander, *The Girl Who Gets Her Hair Cut Short (Perikeiromenē)*, 288 (Sandbach): "To fill my belly is a pleasure, master, and I do deserve it after everything I've told you."

106. *Plutus* 188–192.

107. See Dover, *Aristophanic Comedy*, p. 210; Dover, *Greek Popular Morality*, p. 115.

108. *Plutus* 254, *tou ponein erastai.*

109. Ibid., 263, *psychrou biou kai dyskolou.*

110. See Aristotle *Poetics* 2.1448a15.

111. *Plutus* 298.

112. Ibid., 410–412.

113. See E. R. Dodds, *The Greeks and the Irrational* (Berkeley, 1951), p. 193.

114. *Plutus* 760–761.

115. Aristophanes *Clouds* 1078; *Wasps* 1305; Plato *Republic* 9.571c.

116. Aeschylus *Agamemnon* 810–813.

117. *Plutus* 795–799.

118. Ibid., 1184.

119. Ibid., 1189–1190.

120. *Vita Aristophanis* 28.65 (Dübn.) = test. 1.49–51 K.-A. Some of the younger comic playwrights, such as Anaxandrides (*Suda* s.v.), were toying with these innovations as well.

121. D. L. Page, *Actors' Interpolations in Greek Tragedy* (Oxford, 1934), p. 220.

8. The Comic Catastrophe

1. In addition to the earlier discussion of the *Telephus*, the extensive parody of the *Helen* in the *Thesmophoriazusae* is discussed in detail below. For specific parallels see Aristophanes *Thesm.* 519 and Euripides *Telephus* frag. 711 Nauck; *Thesm.* 855–857 and *Hel.* 1–3; *Thesm.* 859–860 and *Hel.* 16–17; *Thesm.* 864–865 and *Hel.* 52–53; (to a lesser extent) *Thesm.* 886 and *Hel.* 466; and, most notoriously (and significantly for *cognitio* in comedy), *Thesm.* 906–912 and *Hel.* 558, 561–566.

For a convenient catalogue of passages, see P. Rau, *Paratragödia* (Munich, 1967), pp. 185–212. See also more recently the important contribution of M. S. Silk, "Aristophanic Paratragedy," in *Tragedy, Comedy and the Polis*, ed. Alan H. Sommerstein et al. (Bari, 1993), pp. 477–504; C. Prato, *Euripide nella critica di Aristophane* (Galatina, 1955).

2. Aristophanes frag. 488 K.-A.

3. "At the same time as comedy plundered tragedy for parodic purposes, a tragic poet was not above borrowing from a comedian." K. J. Dover, *Aristophanic Comedy* (Berkeley, 1972), p. 149. For further verbal parallels, see M. S. Silk, "Aristophanes as a Lyric Poet," *Yale Classical Studies* 26 (1980), 99–151, esp. 101–103.

4. Euripides *Helen* 1107–1113; Aristophanes *Birds* 209–222. See R. Kannicht, *Euripides Helena* (Heidelberg, 1969), vol. 2, p. 281, n. 8. Further parallels in diction include *genuos xouthēs* (Ar.), *xouthan genuon* (Eur.); *synnome* (Ar.), *synergos* (Eur.). It seems unnecessary to consider Rau's view, *Paratragödia,* p. 195, that both passages are based on a single earlier original source. Apart from the general futility of discussing hypothetical texts—which is in this case still more irrelevant since the nightingale was a *topos* treated by many poets (for example Homer *Od.* 19.518–521, which Rau himself cites)— it would still be natural to see Euripides' song as a *reaction* to Aristophanes' very recent and memorable rendition of this motif, which is the point of interest. For the myth of the nightingale see J. Pollard, *Birds in Greek Life and Myth* (London, 1977), pp. 42–43, 164–165, 172–174; *Aristophanes: Birds,* ed. Nan Dunbar (Oxford, 1995), at 15; and also at 213, where she suggests as a parallel Pindar's use of *elelizein* to describe quivering lyre strings (*Ol.* 9.13, *Pyth.* 1.4). Though lyre strings cannot be said to "trill," it is a very convincing precedent given the consistent poetic association of the lyre with birdsong. See W. S. Anderson, *Music and Musicians in Ancient Greece* (Ithaca, 1994), pp. 1–26 passim.

5. Cratinus frag. 342 K.-A.

6. T. B. L. Webster, *The Tragedies of Euripides* (London, 1967), pp. 4–5, considered the *Danae* to be an early play (before 428 B.C.).

7. Pollux *Onomasticon* 4.III. According to Aristotle (*Poetics* 1456a29–30), Agathon introduced *embolima* (choral interludes) to tragedy, a device adopted by the comic poets from at least the *Plutus* onwards, and to which the chorus was restricted by the time of Menander.

8. As E. A. Havelock observed in a lecture at Yale—alas, never published.

9. Aristophanes *Frogs* 959.

10. *Alcestis* 944–949.

11. A. W. Schlegel, *Vorlesungen über dramatische Kunst und Literatur,* in *Kritische Schriften und Briefe,* ed. E. Lohner, 6 vols. (Stuttgart, 1962–1967), vol. 5, p. 103. Strictly speaking, domestic scenes were not totally absent from prior tragedy. There is Aeschylus' description of the baby Orestes soiling his diapers at *Choephoroi* 755–759. There is the baby scene in Aeschylus' *Dictyulci* frag. 47a (Radt), and full chamberpots are flung in Aeschylus frag.

180 (Radt) and Sophocles frag. 565 (Radt), but these were Satyr-plays. This sort of homey detail would be inconceivable in Roman tragedy.

12. Aristotle *Poetics* 1453a36.

13. Hypothesis 2: see *Euripides: Orestes*, ed. C. W. Willink (Oxford, 1986), pp. lvi–lvii. For a definition of *katastrophē* in a comic context, see the late Roman critic Donatus (*De comoedia*, Kaibel, *CGF*, p. 69; pp. 27–28 Wessner)—yet another scholar who clung to the derivation of comedy from *kōmē* (*De comoedia*, Kaibel, *CGF*, p. 67; p. 23 Wessner). In Shakespeare's day the word carried both its ancient and modern connotations. Hence, Don Armado can pun during the multi-matrimonial ending of *Love's Labour's Lost* (4.1.77), "The catastrophe is a nuptial."

14. Plato *Symposium* 223d. To cite only a few modern discussions, see R. P. Winnington-Ingram, "Euripides: *Poiētēs Sophos*," *Arethusa* 2.2 (1969), 127–142; and Oliver Taplin, *Comic Angels* (Oxford, 1993), pp. 63–66. For a fuller discussion, see B. Seidensticker, *Palintonos Harmonia. Studien zu kömischen Elementen in der griechischen Tragödie* (Göttingen, 1982), who examines the history of "tragicomedy" from Homer onwards. See also Oliver Taplin, "Fifth-century Tragedy and Comedy: A *synkrisis*," *Journal of Hellenic Studies* 106 (1986), 163–174, with literature cited there, who argues that tragedy and comedy helped to define each other "by their opposition and their reluctance to overlap." M. Silk, "The Autonomy of Comedy," *Comparative Criticism* 10 (1988), 3–37, believes that such a polarization of tragedy and comedy is an unhelpful and mostly pedantic distinction.

15. B. M. W. Knox, "Euripidean Comedy," in *Word and Action: Essays on the Ancient Theatre* (Baltimore, 1979), pp. 250–274.

16. Aristotle *Poetics* 1452a16.

17. *Ion* 54.

18. Ibid., 290.

19. Ibid., 74–75.

20. Ibid., 150.

21. G. M. A. Grube, *The Drama of Euripides* (London, 1941), p. 262.

22. *Ion* 237.

23. Ibid., 305–306.

24. Ibid., 321.

25. Ibid., 338–354.

26. Ibid., 398.

27. Ibid., 408–409.

28. Menander *Samia* 567.

29. *Ion* 515–516.

30. See Knox, "Euripidean Comedy," pp. 261–264.

31. *Ion* 517–519.

32. P. T. Stevens, *Colloquial Expressions in Euripides* (Wiesbaden, 1976), p. 66, comments: "This lively passage of dialogue in stichomythia has a flavour of comedy and eight, perhaps, nine colloquialisms contribute something to the liveliness and conversational tone of these exchanges."

33. *Ion* 517–523.

34. Ibid., 541.

35. Ibid., 545; 550–553.

36. *Persuasit nox amor vinum adulescentia: / humanumst,* Terence *Adelphoe* 470–471.

37. P. G. McC. Brown, "Love and Marriage in Greek New Comedy," *Classical Quarterly* 43 (1993), 189–205, quotation from p. 196. Political correctness should not blind us to the fact that in some cases the girls must have been willing or semi-willing partners. In the post-*kōmos* world, with its strict rules protecting young women of good birth from the stigma of illegitimate pregnancy, such festive frolic would necessarily be recast as rape. This is not to deny that in many cases the situation may indeed have been rape as we understand it. In fact, details of violence are not infrequent, as recently catalogued by Vincent J. Rosivach, *When a Young Man Falls in Love: The Sexual Exploitation of Women in New Comedy* (London, 1998), pp. 13–50. On this question see also Zola M. Packman, "Call It Rape: A Motif in Roman Comedy and Its Suppression in English-speaking Publications," *Helios* 20 (1993), 42–55; Elaine Fantham, "Sex, Status and Survival in Hellenic Athens," *Phoenix* 29 (1975), 44–74.

38. *Ion* 578–581.

39. Of course, strictly speaking, even early Greek values—as exemplified in Homer—do not exclude the acquisition of treasure (*olbos*). The Achaeans demanded repayment of stolen wealth as well as stolen wife in Herodotus' version of Paris' theft (2.118). What is important here is not the topic but the genre in which the topic is broached—tragedy, the noblest of them all.

40. Insightfully noted by Anne P. Burnet, "Human Resistance and Divine Persuasion in Euripides' *Ion,*" *Classical Philology* 58 (1967), 89–103.

41. Winnington-Ingram, "Euripides: *Poiētēs Sophos,*" 130–132, has demonstrated how "Euripides exploited and mocked the traditional choral conventions with metatheatrical gags that would be enjoyed by audience and actors alike."

42. *Ion* 796–797. Later, when the enraged populace clamors for Creusa's death, the chorus of her frightened followers echo her earlier desire to fly from this trouble (1238–1241): "What wingèd escape is there / Or what valleys under the dark earth shall I tread, / Fleeing the stony ruin of death" (lit. the stoning-ruin of death).

43. See *Ion* 1041.

44. Ibid., 1324.

45. Ibid., 1372.

46. Ibid., 1395.

47. Ibid., 1450.

48. Ibid., 1464-1467.

49. Ibid., 1488.

50. Ibid., 1512-1517.

51. Ibid., 1523-1526.

52. Ibid., 1556-1558.

53. Ibid., 1601-1603.

54. Ibid., 290, 293.

55. Otto Rank, *The Myth of the Birth of the Hero* (Leipzig, 1909), trans. F. Robbins and Smith Ely Jellife (New York, 1936), p. 71. S. Freud, *Die Familienroman* (1909), translated as "Family Romances," vol. 9 (1906-1908), pp. 237-241. See also Géza Róheim, "The Psychoanalytic Interpretation of Culture," in *Man and His Culture: Psychoanalytic Anthropology after "Totem and Taboo,"* ed. Warner Meunsterberger (New York, 1970), pp. 43-45.

56. Aristotle *Poetics* 1453a34. Compare the discussion of the audience's wish for a happy ending for Hamlet in Goethe's *Wilhelm Meisters Lehrjahre* 5.3 (1824).

57. See especially Webster, *Tragedies*, pp. 4-5; *Euripides: Helen*, ed. A. M. Dale (Oxford, 1967), p. xxviii; *Ion*, trans. A. P. Burnett (Englewood Cliffs, 1970), p. 1, who opts for "about 410 B.C."; K. Matthiessen, *Elektra, Taurische Iphigenie und Helena* (Göttingen, 1964), pp. 89-91, who argues for 413. See also the comments of Albin Lesky, *Greek Tragic Poetry*, trans. M. Dillon (New Haven, 1983), p. 316.

58. Thucydides 8.1.2.

59. The date is firmly established by the scholia to Aristophanes *Thesm.* 1012 and 1062, as well as to *Frogs* 53.

60. Cesare Questa, *Il ratto dal seraglio: Euripides, Plauto, Mozart, Rossini* (Bologna, 1979), p. 13, also mentions the minority view that regards the *Iphigenia* as a later play.

61. M. Platnauer, *Iphigenia in Tauris* (Oxford, 1938), outlines the extraordinary similarities between the two plays in his preface.

62. "Il *pathos* è sottolineato dal grande duetto in metrici lirici, squisitamenti 'melodramatico,' tra Oreste ed Ifigenia . . . un momento enfatico, particolare relievo da . . . il fatto metrico-musicale particolarmente esalto e concitato." Questa, *Il ratto*, pp. 11-32, quotation from p. 24.

63. See T. McEvilley, "Development in the Lyrics of Aristophanes," *American Journal of Philology* 91 (1970), 257-276.

64. See *Mostellaria* 1149–1151: *si amicus Diphilo aut Philemoni es, dicito eis, quo pacto tuos te servos ludicaverit: optumas frustrationes dederis in comoediis* ("If you're a friend of Diphilus or Philemon, go and tell him how your slave bamboozled you today: you'll be giving them the choicest tricking scenes [*frustrationes*] in comedy."

65. *Iphigenia in Tauris* (hereafter *I.T.*) 24–27.

66. Ibid., 50–51.

67. Ibid., 75.

68. Ibid., 964, 970–971. Though the decree of the Areopagus exonerated Orestes, some Furies would not accept this verdict but continued to pursue him.

69. *I.T.* 500–504.

70. Ibid., 568.

71. Ibid., 627.

72. Ibid., 630–631.

73. Ibid., 769–773.

74. Ibid., 788–792.

75. Ibid., 798–799.

76. Ibid., 803–807.

77. He also mentions the lock of her hair (line 820) that she sent back to their mother before she was "sacrificed"—perhaps a variation on the tonsorial *anagnōrisis* in Aeschylus' *Choephoroi (Libation Bearers),* where Electra recognizes a lock of Orestes' hair.

78. *I.T.* 829.

79. Ibid., 1002–1006.

80. Ibid., 1029–1051.

81. Ibid., 1032.

82. Winnington-Ingram, "Euripides: *Poiētēs Sophos,*" 133.

83. *I.T.* 1164–1167.

84. Ibid., 1189, 1193–1195.

85. Ibid., 1218–1221.

86. Ibid., 1223.

87. Ibid., 1319–1326.

88. Ibid., 1346.

89. Ibid., 1095, 1138–1139, 1141.

90. Ibid., 1475–1485.

91. In addition to the *Helen,* the *Thesmophoriazusae* includes parodies of Euripides' *Telephus, Palamedes,* and *Andromeda.* See Rau, *Paratragödia,* pp. 42–50, 51–89.

92. In addition to Agathon and the kinsman, compare Cleisthenes at 574; Euripides as Echo (1056–1095); the kinsman as Helen and Andromeda (850–

916, 1012–1135). For the more detailed significance of these impersonations, see C. Moulton, *Aristophanic Poetry* (Göttingen, 1981) = *Hypomnemata* Heft 68, pp. 120–121.

93. Aristophanes *Thesmophoriazusae* 850.

94. Aristophanes *Birds* 255–257.

95. On *kainos* in Aristophanes, see Thomas K. Hubbard, *The Mask of Comedy* (Ithaca, 1991), pp. 103 and 162; Moulton, *Aristophanic Poetry*, pp. 35 and 136 (on the "new" *Helen*). Armand D'Angour, "The Dynamics of Innovation: Newness and Novelty in the Athens of Aristophanes," Ph.D. diss., University College London (1998), pp. 21–26, has convincingly proposed to derive *kainos* from the root *kai-* ("burn") with the adjectival suffix *-nos* (also found in *dei-nos, ked-nos* and *klei-nos*), and adduces the English "brand-new" as a parallel metaphor. Hence *neos* refers to that which is naturally new through the passage of time, while *kainos* is a radical novelty which breaks with the past. The word's resonances give an extra twist to the parodic echo of the opening line of Sophocles' famous ode in the *Antigone* (332) at *Birds* 1470: "Many are the strange, wonderfully new, and awesome things have we seen from aloft." On the treatment of Helen in *Thesm.*, A. M. Bowie, *Aristophanes: Myth, Ritual and Comedy* (Cambridge, 1993), p. 223, observes with insight that "Aristophanes takes on an especially difficult task in choosing for parody a scene . . . which is itself highly comic: he must produce in effect a parody of a parody."

96. Antiphanes frag. 189 K.-A. See Eric Handley's insightful discussion of this celebrated fragment in *The Cambridge History of Classical Literature. Vol. 1: Greek Drama*, ed. P. E. Easterling and B. M. W. Knox (Cambridge, 1989), pp. 159–161.

97. See the discussion of G. Zuntz, *The Political Plays of Euripides* (Manchester, 1955), pp. 64–65, who, however, contests the traditional dating of the play.

98. *Electra* 1280–1283.

99. *Helen* 1, *kalliparthenoi rhoai.*

100. Euripides *Andromache* 218, *aplēstia lechous.*

101. Martial *Epigrams* 1.62.5–6.

102. *Helen* 59–60; 65.

103. Ibid., 66–67.

104. Ibid., 48.

105. Herodotus (2.116) claims that this innocent version of Helen's actions during the Trojan War was known even to Homer, who chose not to treat it. But the early sixth-century lyric poet Stesichorus, who seems to have specialized in odd versions of common myths, made a rendition of it, of which Plato preserves a fragment (*Phaedrus* 243a = frag. 15 Page).

106. *A Midsummer Night's Dream* 5.1.58–59.

107. For a full discussion see Kannicht, *Euripides Helena,* vol. 1, pp. 41-48.

108. *Helen* 765-769.

109. Herodotus 2.15.

110. *Helen* 63, *thērai gamein me.*

111. *Helen* 30, 32, 48, 65, 376, 427, 475, 584, 590, etc., for a total of 17 references against 15 in *Medea.*

112. *Helen* 69-70.

113. Ibid., 138-140.

114. Ibid., 160-161.

115. Ibid., 225.

116. *Ion* 881-922.

117. *Helen* 417-419.

118. Ibid., 386-392.

119. Ibid., 415-422.

120. Ibid., 449.

121. Ibid., 454.

122. Ibid., 471-478. Euripides' use of the verb *tarassō* ("to make topsy-turvy") in line 478 anticipates Bergson's famous description of the paradigmatic comic situation as *monde renversé.* Henri Bergson, *Le Rire: Essai sur la signification du comique* (Paris, 1940), p. 72.

123. See Dale, *Euripides Helen,* p. 99; and the remarks of Kannicht, *Euripides Helena* ad loc.

124. *Helen* 487-499.

125. Plautus *Amphitruo* 423.

126. *Helen* 540.

127. *I.T.* 229-235.

128. *Helen* 541-552.

129. Ibid., 544. In his long analysis of "characters," Aristotle (*Nicomachean Ethics* 2.1108a23-26) mentions the *agroikos* as a character type, as did Theophrastus (*Characters* 4), arguably the source-book for Menander, as we shall see. Plato also described the "uncivilized" behavior of the dream state as *agrion* (*Republic* 9.571c).

130. *Helen* 563-566.

131. Ibid., 567.

132. Ibid., 795.

133. *I.T.* 1029, *kainon exeurēma ti.*

134. *Helen* 1034; see also 813.

135. Ibid., 1186-1188.

136. Ibid., 1204.

137. Ibid., 1231-1233.

138. Ibid., 1253–1254.

139. Ibid., 1408–1420. These are the lines which F. Leo, *Plautinische Forschungen*[2] (Berlin, 1912), pp. 165–167, pointed out as being closely echoed in Plautus' *Miles Gloriosus* (1366).

140. *Helen* 1478–1479.

141. Ibid., 1513, *kaina pēmata*.

142. Ibid., 1621.

143. The victims were Phoebe and Hilaeira, the two daughters of Leucippus (Apollodorus 3.2.2; Hyginus *Fabula* 80).

144. *Helen* 1667.

145. Ibid., 1676–1677.

146. Ibid., 1686–1687.

147. See the comments of W. S. Barrett, *Euripides Hippolytos* (Oxford, 1964), pp. 417–418, who regards these and other Euripidean "tail-pieces" as actors' interpolations.

148. *Helen* 1688–1692.

149. Aristophanes *Frogs*, 52–54.

150. See Kyle M. Phillips, Jr., "Perseus and Andromeda," *American Journal of Archeology* 72 (1968), 1–23. In a similarly useful discussion, J. R. Green, *Theatre in Ancient Greek Society* (London, 1994), pp. 19–23, presents no fewer than four ceramic depictions.

151. Achilles Tatius III.7. Compare Apuleius *Metamorphosis* 4.32–35, where Psyche is melodramatically prepared for a *thalamus funereus* ("funeral chamber").

152. See also the heroine's face in the *Helen* and the image of Artemis in the *Iphigenia*, both originally thought to be works of art.

153. See A. D. Trendall and T. B. L. Webster, *Illustrations of Greek Drama* (London, 1971), p. III.5,4 ARV[2] 1336.

154. Euripides frag. 143.

155. See Gilbert Murray, *Aristophanes* (Oxford, 1933), p. 251.

156. Euripides frags. 141 and 142.

157. *Electra* 1342.

158. Christian Wolff, "On Euripides' *Helen*," *Harvard Studies in Classical Philology* 77 (1973), 82. Wolff also supports the argument of this chapter by emphasizing that "the movement of the play . . . is generally away from death and towards the prospect of marriage, Spring, new life, success and happiness."

159. *Helen* 1448–1449. Literally "to walk with a straight foot." Elizabeth Craik, "Tragic Love, Comic Sex," in *Tragedy, Comedy, and the Polis*, pp. 253–262, argues for this erotic innuendo in the recognition scene (261–262), maintain-

ing: "If we find such expressions in comedy—an auspicious foot, or an erection—their ambiguity is immediately obvious" (p. 261).

160. Ian C. Storey, however, argues that *Demoi* was staged in 416; see "Dating and Re-dating Eupolis," *Phoenix* 44 (1990), 1–30, esp. 24–27, following W. G. Forrest in *Yale Classical Studies* 24 (1975), 41. This version of the theme of rebirth seems to have been a favorite among Old Comic playwrights. In addition to Aristophanes' *Frogs* which brings Aeschylus back to life, Plato Comicus revives several great poets including Aesop, back from the underworld in his *Laconians* or *The Poets* (see scholion 6 on *Birds* 471).

161. Eupolis frag. 119 K.-A.

162. Compare *Frogs* 96.

163. E. R. Dodds, *The Greeks and the Irrational* (Berkeley and Los Angeles, 1966), p. 193.

164. Wolff, *"Helen,"* p. 83.

165. S. Freud, *Beyond the Pleasure Principle* (1920), section V, vol. 18 (1920–1922), pp. 34–43.

166. Exceptions are Cnemon *(Dyskolos)* and Smicrines *(Aspis, Epitrepontes)*. They are nonetheless blocking characters.

167. This plural title is supported by W. G. Arnott, "First Notes on Menander's *Sikyonioi,"* *Zeitschrift für Papyrologie und Epigraphik* 116 (1997), 1–10, esp. 1–3.

168. A. R. W. Harrison, *The Law of Athens: Family and Property* (Oxford, 1968), pp. 25–29.

169. See Albin Lesky, *A History of Greek Literature²*, trans. J. Willis and C. de Heer (London, 1966), p. 386; see also Matthiessen, *Elektra, Taurische Iphigenie und Helena*, pp. 93, 127–143.

170. T. B. L. Webster, *An Introduction to Menander* (Manchester, 1974), p. 130.

171. *Helen* 560.

9. O Menander! O Life!

1. Eight, according to Apollodorus (Aulus Gellius *Noctes Atticae* 17.4.6 = K.-A. test. 46). Martial recalled, in complaining of his own lack of contemporary success, that "few theaters applauded for a laurelled Menander" (*rara coronato plausere theatra Menandro*, 5.10.9 = K.-A. test. 98).

2. Aulus Gellius (*N.A.* 17.4.1 = K.-A. test. 71) preserves an anecdote about Menander's reaction to the fact that his own superiority was not recognized by his contemporaries. One day when he came across Philemon, his more successful rival, he asked him, "don't you blush every time you beat me?" As subsequent history shows, Menander went on to fulfill Quintilian's prediction (Inst. Orat. 3.7.18 = K.-A. test. 99) that posterity would vindicate the playwright's true worth: *quidam sicut Menander, iustiora*

posterorum quam suae aetatis iudicia sunt consecuti ("Just like Menander, about whom critical judgment was better in subsequent ages than his own time").

3. See Plutarch *Moralia* 853e (= K.-A. test. 103).

4. *Inscriptiones Graecae* 14.1183c (= K.-A. test. 170).

5. Syrian. in Hermog. (= K.-A. test. 83).

6. Plutarch *Moralia* 853–854.

7. Menander fell foul of the stylistic fashion that swept over the Greek world for recreating classical Attic; he was too late and his language—as Phrynicus Arabius vehemently asserts (*Epit.* 418, 433)—"was incorrect." (Byzantine schoolmasters, unlike the Victorian ones, were less afraid that Aristophanes would corrupt their students' morals than that Menander would corrupt their Greek.)

8. The phrase occurs five times in the fragments.

9. Probably sometime between 1950 and 1959. See E. G. Turner, *Greek Papyri: An Introduction* (Oxford, 1968), p. 52.

10. "The world of scholarship was swept by an epidemic of an illness which Eduard Fraenkel called Dyscolitis." Hugh Lloyd-Jones, "Ritual and Tragedy," in *Birthday Symposium for Walter Burkert*, ed. Fritz Graf (Stuttgart, 1998), pp. 271–295, quotation from p. 271. For the history of the Menandrian finds, see A. W. Gomme and F. H. Sandbach, *Menander: A Commentary* (Oxford, 1973), pp. 2–4.

11. Horace *Ars Poetica* 139.

12. This was when the Regius Professor of Greek at Cambridge was visiting at Yale.

13. But see Timothy P. Hofmeister's subtle evocation of the political scene in Menandrian comedy, "*Hai Pasai Poleis: Polis* and *Oikoumene* in Menander," in *The City as Comedy*, ed. Dobrov, pp. 289–342, and David Wiles in the same volume.

14. Gilbert Murray, *Aristophanes* (Oxford, 1933), p. 251.

15. There is no evidence of a marital ending to the *Epitrepontes*. The *Hecyra* (*The Mother-in-Law*) of Apollodorus, later adapted by Terence, ends not in marriage but with the estranged couple's reconciliation.

16. Ovid *Tristia* 2.369.

17. Plutarch *Moralia* 854a-b (= K.-A. test. 103). Elaine Fantham, "Roman Experience of Menander," *Transactions of the American Philological Association* 114 (1984), 299–309, has argued that theatrical performances of Menander, even in the time of Cicero, were not as common as generally supposed. Moreover, since these writers' allusions to Menander are strangely evasive, she concludes that many Roman writers may not have known Menander

at first hand. But since Cicero (*Fin.* 1.4), Propertius (3.21.25–28), Horace (*Sat.* 2.3.11–12), and Ovid (*Trist.* 2.369–70) all clearly imply or state explicitly that they have read Menander—and we know that they could all read Greek—it is better to accept Ovid's statement at face value.

18. Horace *Ars Poetica* 189–190. Richard Hunter, *The New Comedy of Greece and Rome* (Cambridge, 1985), pp. 40–41, discusses how in Menander the climax often comes in the fourth act. Perhaps this is a heritage of the *kōmos*—business is settled in the fourth act so everyone can party in the fifth. Terence returns to the nuptial *catastrophe,* the wedding in the final act.

19. Quintilian *Inst.* 10.1.71–72 (= K.-A. test. 101). A depraved taste caused his contemporaries to prefer Philemon over Menander (Apul. *Flor.* 16 = K.-A. test. 114; Aul. Gel. *N.A.* 17.4.1 = K.-A. test. 71). As Gellius reports, Menander was often defeated by Philemon—whose dramatic skill it is difficult to assess from his fragments—because of intrigue, favoritism, and partisanship.

20. Sander Goldberg, *The Making of Menandrian Comedy* (London, 1980), pp. 22–26. On Menander's adaptation of tragic diction, see further F. H. Sandbach, "Menander's Manipulation of Language for Dramatic Purposes," in *Ménandre,* ed. E. G. Turner, Entretiens Fondation Hardt 16 (Geneva, 1970), pp. 124–136; T. B. L. Webster, *An Introduction to Menander* (Manchester, 1974), pp. 56–57; C. Moulton, "Menander," in *Ancient Writers: Greece and Rome,* ed. T. J. Luce (New York, 1982), pp. 435–447, esp. pp. 443–445. See also A. Blanchard, *Essai sur la composition des comédies de Ménandre* (Paris, 1983), esp. p. 19, who argues that the essential problem is to discover why Menander insists upon continuity between his dramaturgy and that of Euripides.

21. Webster, *Introduction,* p. 22, compare p. viii. Similarly, Vladimir Propp, *The Morphology of the Folktale,* trans. Laurence Scott (Austin, 1968), argued that the Russian fairy tales of the Arne Thompson collection could be reduced to a single modular plot-structure.

22. Plutarch *Moralia* 347e (= K.-A. test. 70). See Eric Handley's discussion in *The Dyskolos of Menander* (London, 1965), p. 10. There is a similar anecdote about Ravel, who is said once to have quipped that he had already composed his new symphony—and only needed to write the notes.

23. Aristotle *Poetics* 1450a38.

24. Philemon frag. 118 K.-A.

25. *P. Oxyr.* 1176, frag. 39, col. 7.8–22.

26. Quintilian *Inst.* 10.1.69.

27. Ibid., 10.1.69–70.

28. See Aristotle *Poetics* 1452a16.

29. Northrop Frye, *The Anatomy of Criticism* (Princeton, 1957), p. 163.

30. We have reference to and a mere four lines of an *Oedipus* by the Middle Comic poet Eubulus (Athenaeus *Deipnosophistae* 6.239a). And in Aristophanes' *Assemblywomen*, a young girl says to the revolting (in both senses) old women that if their insurrection succeeds, "the entire land will teem with Oedipuses" (1042).

31. On the other hand, piratical kidnapping was quite common in the ancient Greek world—and still is in modern Italy.

32. Frye, *Anatomy of Criticism*, p. 170.

33. *Tychē* or *tyche* appears over three hundred times. See also the remarks of Gomme and Sandbach, *Menander*, at frag. 417 (= 372 K.-A.).

34. See for example *Dyskolos (The Grouch)* 545; *Epitrepontes* 1108; *Misoumenus (The Hated Man)* 449; *Perikeiromenē (The Girl Who Gets Her Hair Cut Short)* 151; *Samia* 55, 163.

35. Theophrastus frag. 493 (FHS&G, = Cicero *Tusc.* 5.25); see also Menander *Aspis* 411; Nicostratus frag. 18.4 K.-A.; Demosth. 2.22; Alciphr. 3.8.3; Plato *Leg.* 4.709b; Plut. *De fortuna* 97.c.1; Iambl. *Theol. ar.* 71.12; Libanius *Or.* 25.11.3.

36. Menander frag. 372.7–8 K.-A.

37. Aristotle *N.E.* 3.1112a2–13.

38. Aristotle *N.E.* 2.1108a20–31. See also Frye's brilliant discussion of these four types and the endless ways they may be combined and counterposed (*Anatomy of Criticism*, pp. 171–185).

39. The relationship between Theophrastus and Menander is established by Diogenes Laertius 5.36–37 (= K.-A. test. 8).

40. Theophrastus *Charact.* 23.4.

41. For *dyskolos*, compare also Aristotle *N.E.* 2.1108a-b.

42. Handley, *Dyskolos*, p. 9.

43. Menander frag. 707 K.-A.

44. *Nomina personarum in comoediis dumtaxat habere debent et rationem et etymologium*, Donatus at Ter. *Ad.* 1 (p. 12 Wessner).

45. A miserly *micrologos* appears in Menander frag. 106 K.-A.

46. The action of the *Perikeiromenē*, however, takes place in Corinth.

47. The *Dyskolos* is exceptional for its setting on a path in Phyle, a country district of Attica.

48. Rare exceptions include the *Perikeiromenē*, where there is a crude scatological insult in line 394 and an accusation of "cock-sucking" (*laikastria*) at 483–485. *Skatophagos* ("shit-eater") also occurs at *Samia* 427. Frag. 351.11 K.-A., *hypobinētiōnta brōmata* ("aphrodisiac foods"), is hardly obscene.

49. See for example *Dyskolos* 892, and the two cooks' banter in lines 280–288 of Plautus' *Aulularia*. The type has persisted to our own day and may be seen

in the "Gourmet Night" episode of *Fawlty Towers,* written by John Cleese and Connie Booth. This series also featured Manuel, a running servant *(servus currens),* and The Major, a windy veteran who owes as much to Southern English folklore as to the classical *miles gloriosus.*

50. Aristotle *Poetics* 1449a23–26.

51. Rare exceptions are a passage of lyric dactyls at *Theophoroumene (The Girl Possessed),* 36–41 (Arnott); and an anapestic chant at *Leukadia* 11–16 (Arnott).

52. Plutarch *Moralia* 854c.

53. See the excellent discussion by W. Geoffrey Arnott, "Humour in Menander," in *Laughter Down the Centuries,* vol. 3, ed. Siegfried Jäkel, Asko Timonen, and Veli-Matti Rissanen (Turku, 1997), pp. 65–80.

54. This wedding formula is found (with variations) many times in Menander: for example, *Dyskolos* 842–844; *Misoumenus* 444–445; *Perikeiromenē* 1013–1014; *Samia* 727.

55. *Sonnets* 1.1–2.

56. *Much Ado About Nothing* 2.3.242.

57. See H. Lloyd-Jones, *Sophocles: Fragments* (Cambridge, Mass., 1996), pp. 106–109, who also notes that Euripides and at least six other tragedians wrote on the theme of Thyestes.

58. W. T. MacCary and M. M. Wilcock, in the introduction to their edition, *Plautus Casina* (Cambridge, 1976), p. 5.

59. *Perikeiromenē* 153–157.

60. Ibid., 162–163; 167–169.

61. Ibid., 301–303.

62. Ibid., 305.

63. Ibid., 308–309.

64. Ibid., 370, 390; 404.

65. Ibid., 541. Gomme and Sandbach, *Menander,* ad loc., interpreted *synestēkōs* as "absorbed in thought," but admitted that "there is no real parallel." But M. Gronewald, "Bemerkungen zu Menander," *Zeitschrift für Papyrologie und Epigraphik* 107 (1995), 57–59, has demonstrated by analogy that the word, which I have rendered as "aroused," must mean "tensed-up" or "on edge."

66. *Perikeiromenē* 548–550.

67. Netta Zagagi, *The Comedy of Menander: Convention, Variation, and Originality* (London, 1994), p. 84.

68. *Perikeiromenē* 777–778.

69. Ibid., 985–986.

70. Ibid., 1013–1014.

71. Ibid., 1025–1026. W. Geoffrey Arnott, "Two Notes on Menander," *Zeitschrift für Papyrologie und Epigraphik* 115 (1997), 73–74, argues that Moschion makes a counterproposal of some bridal candidate more suited to his own tastes, drawing a parallel with the ending of Terence's *Self-Tormentor*.

72. S. Caritonidis, L. Kahil, and R. Ginouvès, *Les mosaïques de la Maison du Ménandre à Mytilène = Antike Kunst,* Beiheft 6 (Berne, 1970), p. 57 and color plate 8. The interpretation of the scene is uncertain. See the discussion in *Menander,* ed. W. G. Arnott (Cambridge, Mass., 1979–1996), vol. 2, pp. 250–251.

73. At line 685, for example, Getas is recounting a conversation between both Demeas and Kratea in which the old man demands that Thrasonides release her because she is a free woman. Thrasonides threatens suicide. Getas later reports to the father and daughter that his master has indeed committed suicide.

74. *Misoumenus* 216–221.

75. The subject of incest averted is discussed by the characters themselves at *Epitrepontes* 341–343, and is also treated in Plautus' *Epidicus*.

76. *Samia* 21.

77. The verb *aischunomai* is repeated twice (23, 27, and again at 47–48).

78. *Samia* 82–83.

79. *Ibid.,* 130. See H. Lloyd-Jones, "Menander's *Samia* in Light of the New Evidence," *Yale Classical Studies* 22 (1972), 119–144, esp. p. 131, n. 18, who explains the joke by saying that it would be understood by the Athenian audience as a playful allusion to the familiar jest that *hetairai* are for pleasure, wives for procreation, and whores for relief of the general needs of the body.

80. *Samia* 137–138.

81. Ibid., 246–248.

82. Ibid., 267–274.

83. Ibid., 311.

84. Ibid., 336–342.

85. Ibid., 352–354.

86. Ibid., 381–383.

87. Ibid., 407–409. The translation is somewhat condensed here.

88. Ibid., 429–430.

89. Ibid., 433–439.

90. Ibid., 452–454; 477–479.

91. Ibid., 485–487.

92. Ibid., 488–491.

93. Ibid., 495–497.

94. There are instances of fathers marrying daughters to stepsons, although it was officially frowned upon.

95. *Samia* 516–517.

96. Ibid., 535–536.

97. Ibid., 589–591.

98. Ibid., 592–593.

99. Ibid., 595–597.

100. Ibid., 600–602. This is reminiscent of Roberto Rossellini's 1948 film *The Miracle* (screenplay by Fellini et al.) in which a simple peasant girl is seduced, believing that she is the next Virgin Mary.

101. Euripides *Ion* 341.

102. This was legal in Athens. The only instance in which a brother could marry a sister would be if they were half-siblings and only a *homopatrios* at that, that is, if the father was the common parent. By contrast, at Sparta it was children of the same mother by different fathers who could marry; at Rome neither.

103. *Georgos* 58–59.

104. The play is very fragmentary, with lacunae that would allow other interpretations for the play. The story as analyzed here has the enthusiastic support of at least four major scholars: Webster, *Introduction,* pp. 141–144; Arnott, *Menander,* vol. 1, pp. 106–107 and 117 n. 2; Gomme and Sandbach, *Menander,* pp. 105–107.

105. *Dyskolos* 189–191.

106. Ibid., 205–206. Compare *Romeo and Juliet* 2.2.70–72:

> JULIET: If they do see thee, they will murder thee.
> ROMEO: Alack there lies more peril in thine eye than twenty of their swords.

107. See Zagagi, *Menander,* p. 101. In Menander's Athens this kind of behavior would have been regarded as outrageous. Freeborn women were normally kept at home—and segregated from the men at that.

108. Frye, *Anatomy of Criticism,* p. 167.

109. Two notable examples: Barabas, the eponymous Jew of Malta, hates Christians but has an angelic daughter who rejects him and converts. Likewise, Shylock has an equally angelic daughter who also rejects him and his values. The archetype concludes with either assimilation to ordinary society, e.g., Shylock being "punished" by having to turn Christian, or total rejection—like Barabas being hurled into a boiling cauldron.

110. Aristophanes *Knights* 42, *dyskolon gerontion.*

111. See Goldberg, *Menandrian Comedy,* p. 86.

112. *Dyskolos* 6, *apanthrōpos tis anthrōpos.*
113. *Dyskolos* 40.
114. Ibid., 641–642.
115. Ibid., 713–719.
116. One thinks of the *Persae* of Aeschylus, where water from a "virgin spring" is among the sacred ingredients needed to summon the ghost of Darius from the dead (607–620). Recall the "beautiful-virginal waters" next to the tomb of "deathless" Proteus in Euripides' *Helen* (*kalliparthenoi rhoai*, 1). And in Vergil's underworld the shades awaiting rebirth must first be cleansed of memory in the river Lethe (*Aeneid* 6.710–751).
117. E. K. Chambers, *The Medieval Stage* (Oxford, 1925), vol. 1, p. 122.
118. *Dyskolos* 685–686.
119. Some critics, for example Goldberg, *Menandrian Comedy*, p. 86, maintain that Knemon cannot change his character. Nevertheless, the old grouch will join the dance.
120. *Dyskolos* 739.
121. Ibid., 754–755.
122. Ibid., 795–796.
123. In lines 327–328 we learn that Knemon's property is worth two talents, a sum equal to the large dowry which is being provided by his son's future father-in-law.
124. *Dyskolos* 797–812.
125. Ibid., 842–844.
126. Ibid., 846–847.
127. Ibid., 855–859.
128. For *pannychizein* ("to keep a vigil, and be up all night"), see Aristophanes *Clouds* 1069 and J. Henderson, *The Maculate Muse: Obscene Language in Attic Comedy*[2] (Oxford, 1991), pp. 157–158. We recall Pannychis, the frisky sub-nymphet in Petronius' *Satyricon*, 65.
129. *Dyskolos* 959.
130. *Aspis* 356–359.
131. Ibid., 33.
132. Ibid., 89–90.
133. Ibid., 94–96.
134. Ibid., 117–121.
135. *Ponēros* and *ponēria*: 48, 116, 140, 309, 316, and 369. *Chrēstos*: 125, 130.
136. *Aspis* 135–136.
137. Ibid., 146–148.
138. Ibid., 149–152.
139. Ibid., 260–267.

140. See Arnott, *Menander,* ad loc.

141. *Aspis* 256–260.

142. Ibid., 297–298.

143. Ibid., 309–310.

144. Ibid., 329–330.

145. Ibid., 339–344.

146. Ibid., 348–353.

147. Ibid., 374–375.

148. Ibid., 388–390. This is reminiscent of Palaestrio's words in Plautus' *Miles Gloriosus* as he prepares *his* scheme to bamboozle the soldier (1143–1144).

149. See Goldberg, *Menandrian Comedy,* p. 38; Margarete Bieber, *The History of Greek and Roman Theatre*² (Princeton, 1961), p. 102.

150. In the *Epitrepontes* (387–390) there is the literate rhetoric-spouting slave Syriscus, whom the editors describe as "subtle and ingratiating, capable of more complicated periods, and proudly employing many of the devices of the practised orator." Gomme and Sandbach, *Menander,* pp. 302–303.

151. Menander frag. 462 K.-A.; see also Philemon frag. 38 K.-A; frag. Adespot. 1093 K.-A.

152. Ovid *Amores* 1.15.17–18.

153. Ben Jonson, *Poetaster* 1.59–60.

154. Frag. 722 K (= Adespot. 1027 K.-A.).

155. As Gomme and Sandbach, *Menander,* remind us ad loc., "There were schools of medicine in Sicily and Kos and in Knidos, in all of which places a man might acquire his professional knowledge. All these places were Doric-speaking, and Doric-speaking doctors appear in Crates frag. [41 K.-A.], Alexis Fr. [142 K.-A.], Epicrates Fr. [10 K.-A.]."

156. *Aspis* 447–449.

157. H. Lloyd-Jones, "Menander's *Aspis,*" *Greek, Roman and Byzantine Studies* 12 (1971), 189, has suggested that the play concluded with a ragging of the miser much the way Knemon is taunted in the *Dyskolos.* See also Webster, *Introduction,* pp. 126–127.

158. Beaumarchais, *Barber of Seville* 5.8.

10. Plautus Makes an Entrance

1. At least two biographical sources describe this merry death: pseudo-Lucian, *Macrobioi* 25 s.v. Philemon (test. 5 K.-A.); *Suda* s.v. Philemon (test. 1 K.-A.). For similar jolly demises of comic poets, see Mary R. Lefkowitz, *The Lives of the Greek Poets* (London, 1981), pp. 105–116, esp. pp. 112–113.

2. Schol. on Ovid *Ibis* 591–592 (test. 17 K.-A.). There is some scholarly disagreement over the exact dates of both poets' deaths. Those interested in

pursuing this should begin with W. G. Arnott s.v. Philemon in *The Oxford Classical Dictionary*³ (Oxford, 1996); see also *Menander,* ed. Arnott (Cambridge, Mass., 1979–1996), vol. I, p. xiv; S. Schröder, "Die Lebensdaten Menanders," *Zeitschrift für Papyrologie und Epigraphik* 113 (1996), 35–42.

3. Figures vary. See Aulus Gellius *Noctes Atticae* 17.4.4–5 (test. 46 K.-A.); *Suda* s.v. (test. 1 K.-A.); Anon. *De com.* 53 (test. 3 K.-A.).

4. Oliver Taplin, *Comic Angels* (Oxford, 1993), pp. 12–20, describes the evolution of the audience for plays beyond Athens. On the touring companies see also Niall Slater, "The Fabrication of Comic Illusion," in *Beyond Aristophanes: Transition and Diversity in Greek Comedy,* ed. Gregory W. Dobrov (Atlanta, 1995), p. 41.

5. For more details about comic activities in Tarentum specifically, see Taplin, *Comic Angels,* p. 14 with n. 10, and J. R. Green, "Notes on Phylax Vases," *Quaderni ticinesi di numismatica e antichità classiche* 20 (1991), 49–56, esp. p. 55.

6. *Livy* 7.2. The circumstances of Livius Andronicus' "transfer" to Rome are the subject of much debate among historians. Those wishing to investigate the matter should begin with the earnest discussion of Cicero (*Brutus* 8.71–74), who did not rate the trailblazing poet's dramatic gifts too highly. See also G. Duckworth, *Nature of Roman Comedy* (Princeton, 1952), pp. 39–40.

7. Livy 7.2.8: *ab saturis ausus est primus argumento fabulam serere* ("From mere improvisations he was the first who dared to write a play with a plot"). Friedrich Leo, "Varro und die Satire," *Hermes* 24 (1889), 67–84, astutely noted that the similarities between Livy's account and Aristotle's description of the development of comedy in the *Poetics* were too great to be merely coincidental. See also G. L. Hendrickson, "The Dramatic Satura and the Old Comedy at Rome," *American Journal of Philology* 15.1 (1894), 1–30.

8. These were the *ludi Plebeii* (November), *ludi Apollinares* (July), and *ludi Megalenses* (April). See Lily Ross Taylor, "The Opportunities for Dramatic Performances in the Time of Plautus and Terence," *Transactions of the American Philological Association* 68 (1937), 284–304; Duckworth, *Roman Comedy*², pp. 76–79.

9. See for example Tacitus *Ann.* 14.20. Early performances also took place at the Circus Maximus (Livy 41.27; Polybius 30.22). See further Dwora Gilula, "Where Did the Audience Go?" *Scripta Classica Israelica* 4 (1978), 45–49, esp. pp. 47–48 with n. 9.

10. Tertullian *De Spect.* 10.4–6. For the *theatrum Pompei* see further Cic. *Off.* 2.60; Hor. *Carm.* 1.20.3–8; Pliny *N.H.* 7.34, 158, 8.20–21, 36.115 (number of

seats); Tacitus *Ann.* 3.23, 3.72, 13.54, 14.20; Suet. *Cal.* 21, *Cl.* 21.1, *Nero* 46.1; Vell. 2.130.1; Aulus Gellius *N.A.* 10.1.7–9; *CIL* 6.1191. The theater has left its impression in the curving outline of the piazza di Grottapinta. There were other attempts to build a permanent theater from as early as 179 B.C., but these were all aborted by patrician disapproval. See, among others, Duckworth, *Roman Comedy*², pp. 79–80.

11. See the discussion of W. Beare, *The Roman Stage*³ (London, 1964), pp. 137–148.

12. Horace *Epist.* 2.1.170–174.

13. "Titus" is Roman slang for phallus, "Maccius" an allusion to the fool in Atellane farce, and "Plautus" may be a contraction of Planipes, meaning "Flatfoot," a mime player. See J. N. Adams, *The Latin Sexual Vocabulary* (London, 1982), p. 32; A. S. Gratwick in the *Cambridge History of Latin Literature* (Cambridge, 1982), vol. 2, p. 809; and the same author's "Titus Maccius Plautus," *Classical Quarterly* n.s. 23 (1973), 78–84. See also *Plautus' Menaechmi*, ed. Gratwick (Cambridge, 1993), p. 3.

14. Aulus Gellius *N.A.* 19.8.6, *linguae latinae decus.*

15. Ibid., *N.A.* 3.3.14, *in operis artificium scaenicorum.*

16. See further E. Segal, *Roman Laughter* (Cambridge, Mass., 1968), pp. 1–7.

17. The point was made by Eduard Fraenkel, *Elementi Plautini in Plauto* (Florence, 1960), revised edition of *Plautinisches im Plautus* (Berlin, 1922), p. 324. John Wright, *Dancing in Chains: The Stylistic Unity of the Comoedia Palliata* (Rome, 1974), has contributed much to our understanding of Roman comedy by demonstrating how all Plautus' contemporaries, except of course the later Terence, wrote in "Plautine" style.

18. Vergil *Aeneid* 2.65–66.

19. Terence *Eunuchus* 7; *Ars Poetica* 268–269.

20. *Trinummus* 19, *Philemo scripsit: Plautus vortit barbare.*

21. In lyricizing his models, rather than simply translating them, he was anticipated by both Ennius and Accius. See Thomas Cole, "Opera in Ancient Rome," *Ventures* (Magazine of the Yale Graduate School)(Spring 1967), 35–36.

22. Horace *Ars Poetica* 47–55.

23. Aulus Gellius *N.A.* 3.3.4.

24. *Casina* 694.

25. *Epidicus* 350, *nil moror vetera et volgata verba.*

26. On Shakespeare's use of North's Plutarch, see E. Segal, *Roman Laughter*² (Oxford, 1987), p. 6. On the process of Roman "translation," see further Bruno Gentili, *Theatrical Performances in the Ancient World* (Amsterdam, 1979), pp. 96–105.

27. Aulus Gellius *N.A.* 2.23.

28. In the first century B.C., the grammarian Volcacius Sedigitus in his lost *De poetis* (cited by Aulus Gellius *N.A.* 15.24) placed Caecilius first, Plautus second, and Terence a mere sixth, while Ennius was given an honorable mention (tenth place) "for old time's sake" *(causa antiquitatis)*. Unfortunately, the author of the *Plokion* now exists only in this and a few other fragments—not enough to gauge his quality. The ancient appraisals of Caecilius are conveniently collected by Leofranc Holford-Strevens, *Aulus Gellius* (London, 1988), p. 158, n. 80. A full edition of Caecilius is now being prepared by K. Kleve. See also the same author's "How to Read an Illegible Papyrus: Towards an Edition of *Pherc.* 78, Caecilius Statius, *Obolostates sive Faenerator,*" *Cronache ercolanesi* 26 (1996), 5-14.

29. Aulus Gellius *N.A.* 2.23.12, *nescio quae mimica inculcavit.*

30. Published as *Menander and Plautus: A Study in Comparison* (London, 1968).

31. Fraenkel, *Elementi Plautini,* p. 2340.

32. Handley, *Menander and Plautus,* p. 18. Handley has now fully edited the *Dis Exapaton* papyrus in *Oxyrhynchus Papyri,* vol. 64 (1997), pp. 14-42.

33. *Stichus* 446-448.

34. Pliny (*N.H.* 8.209-210) specifically refers to the "sumptuary laws" of Plautus' age which restricted the consumption of items that outraged the stern Cato—*abdomina, glandia, testiculi, vulvae, sincipita verrina.* These are some of the very dishes featured in Menaechmus' menu. See further Emily Gowers's discussion in *The Loaded Table: Representations of Food in Roman Literature* (Oxford, 1993), pp. 66-76, who argues incisively that "not only did the ban help to redefine the structure of weekday and festival in the Roman year: the limited proportions of the everyday human or animal body, the meagre fowl on the table, also supplied a model for the proper limits of the Roman state's consumption" (p. 75).

35. *Menaechmi* 208-212; compare *Captivi* 902-905. A closer translation of the foods he is ordering would be "pork sweetbreadettes, hamletty fat bacon, pork half-heads."

36. *Miles Gloriosus* 901-903, 919, 1139.

37. *Pseudolus* 117-120, 122.

38. Occasionally, as in the *Perikeiromenē*, Menander has the young man "punished" by being forced to marry.

39. *Casina* 1015-1016.

40. *Trinummus* 1183-1185.

41. Cf. Segal, *Roman Laughter²,* pp. 7-14 and passim.

42. *Casina* 319-320.

43. Ibid., 353-354.

44. See Aristophanes *Clouds* 40–55.

45. See Aulus Gellius *N.A.* 2.23.12.

46. Aristotle *N.E.* 8.1161a1. Aristotle describes these marital dynamics at length, comparing them to the dynamics of government, in which some rule and others are ruled.

47. For unmotivated outbursts against *uxores dotatae,* see for example the speech of Periplectomenos in *Miles Gloriosus* (679–699), Simo's lament in *Mostellaria* (690–710), and Megadorus' outburst in *Aulularia* (478–535).

48. *Menaechmi* 12.

49. E. Stärk, *Die Menaechmi des Plautus und kein griechisches Original, ScriptOralia* 11A1 (Tübingen, 1989). This was subsequently refuted by Gratwick, *Menaechmi,* pp. 23–30 and n. 27.

50. H. Levin, "Two Comedies of Errors," in *Refractions* (Oxford, 1966), pp. 128–150.

51. If Plautus uses divinities at all, they are figures like Luxuria and Inopia ("Want") in the *Trinummus,* and Auxilium ("Help") who speaks the prologue to *Cistellaria*—that is, minor abstractions relevant to the plot of the play. Is Arcturus, the blazing star in the *Rudens,* really a god?

52. As cited by Henri Bergson, *Le Rire: Essai sur la signification du comique* (Paris, 1940, repr. 1969), p. 26.

53. *Menaechmi* 152.

54. Ibid., 569.

55. Ibid., 114–118.

56. Ibid., 121–124.

57. Ibid., 189.

58. Ibid., 202.

59. Ibid., 259, *voluptarii atque potatores maxumi.*

60. Ibid., 262. See Ovid *Amores* 3.7.55–58 for the sexual magnetism inherent in *blanda* and *blanditia.*

61. *Menaechmi* 258–264.

62. Gratwick, *Menaechmi,* pp. 164–165, comments: "'Trieste, Ibiza and thereabouts, Marseilles, Albania/Yugoslavia, *(Hilurios),* the whole Adriatic *(mare superum* as opposed to *inferum,* the Tyrrhenian sea), and all round the foot of Italy and Sicily' *(Graecia exotica).* The order is random: 'Epidamnus' is *somewhere,* but somewhere garbled. Indeed, by including the real Illyria in the middle of the list of places already visited, Pl[autus] was implying that 'Epidamnus' was *not* where it really was at all."

63. *Menaechmi* 473–476.

64. Ibid., 588–589.

65. Ibid., 114, *retines, revocas, rogitas.*

66. To emphasize the "tenacity" of these restrictions, Plautus employs three variations of the verb *tenere* ("to hold"): first *retinere*, in reference to the henpecking matron, and here *attinere* and *detinere* to describe the clinging client (114; 589).

67. See Fraenkel, *Elementi Plautini*, p. 152; D. C. Earl, "Political terminology in Plautus," *Historia* 9 (1960), 237; R. Perna, *L'originalità di Plauto* (Bari, 1955), p. 291.

68. *Menaechmi* 588–589.

69. Ibid., 698.

70. Ibid., 713–717.

71. Ibid., 1062.

72. Ibid., 1143–1144.

73. Ibid., 1047.

74. Ibid., 1160.

75. *Casina* 34–35.

76. Ibid., 65.

77. Ibid., 68–72.

78. In one of my earliest exposures to Plautus, an Italian translation of the *Casina* staged in the Stadio di Domiziano in 1962, I admired how subtly the character of Lysidamus could be played: Camillo Pilotto evoked not only laughter but wonderful sympathy for his vain attempts to be the young lover.

79. *Casina* 225.

80. Ibid., 682.

81. Ibid., 227.

82. Ibid., 233–246.

83. Ibid., 262–264.

84. Ibid., 419.

85. Ibid., 491–492.

86. Ibid., 517–519.

87. Ibid., 549–550.

88. Ibid., 526.

89. Ibid., 559; 535.

90. Ibid., 563–573.

91. Ibid., 652.

92. Ibid., 670–671.

93. Ibid., 694.

94. Ibid., 758.

95. Ibid., 759–762.

96. Ibid., 797.

97. Ibid., 815.
98. Ibid., 856.
99. Ibid., 860–861.
100. Gordon Williams, "Some Aspects of Roman Marriage Ceremonies and Ideals," *Journal of Roman Studies* 48 (1958), 23.
101. *Cistellaria* 175.
102. *Casina* 907–914.
103. Ibid., 937–942.
104. Ibid., 1001–1003.
105. Ibid., 1005–1006.
106. Ibid., 1015–1018.
107. *Epidicus* 180.
108. Plutarch *Cato Maior* 16.4, 24.
109. Val. Max. 6.7.1.
110. Aulus Gellius *N.A.* 10.23.5. On Romulus' law, see Susan Treggiari, *Roman Marriage: Iusti Coniuges from the Time of Cicero to the Time of Ulpian* (Oxford, 1991), p. 265.
111. *Love's Labour's Lost* 4.3.213.

11. A Plautine Problem Play

1. See for example Aulus Gellius *Noctes Atticae* 2.23.13.
2. See E. Segal, "Perché *Amphitruo*," in *Dioniso* 46 (1975), 247–267, reprinted in the author's own translation as "Why Plautus chose *Amphitryo*," in the same author's *Roman Laughter*[2] (New York, 1987), pp. 171–191.
3. See E. Lefèvre, *Maccus vortit barbare: vom tragischen Amphitryon zum tragikomischen Amphitruo* (Wiesbaden, 1982).
4. *Amphitruo* 785–786.
5. See for example E. Frenzel, *Stoffe der Weltliteratur*[5] (Stuttgart, 1981), pp. 43–46; Udo Reinhardt, "Amphitryon and Amphitruo," in *Musa Iocasa; Festschrift Andreas Thierfelder* (Hildesheim, 1984), pp. 95–130.
6. *Amphitruo* 51.
7. Ibid., 52–55.
8. Ibid., 59–61.
9. Ibid., 100.
10. Ibid., 104–106.
11. Ibid., 107–109.
12. For *usura* in the mercantile sense, see for example Cicero *Verr.* 2.3.72.168; *Att.* 9.12.3 and 12.22.3.
13. *Amphitruo* 1135–1136.
14. Ibid., 498; 980–981.

15. Ibid., 112, 132.

16. Ibid., 113–114.

17. Ibid., 132, *cubat complexus cuius cupiens maxume est;* 134–135, *cum moecho est.*

18. Ibid., 287–288.

19. Ibid., 289–290.

20. Gordon Williams, "Some Aspects of Roman Marriage Ceremonies and Ideals," *Journal of Roman Studies* 48 (1958), pp. 24–25, argues that "*obsequi* and its derivatives are so frequent in this use that the word seems almost to be a technical term and arouses the suspicion that it may have been pleonastically linked with *morigera* . . . At any rate obedience in wives is praised as a virtue on their epitaphs from early times to late." See also E. Segal, *Roman Laughter*[1] (Cambridge, Mass., 1968), pp. 21–26.

21. *Amphitruo* 465, 472, *satietatem capiet.*

22. Ibid., 488.

23. Ibid., 492–493.

24. Ibid., 498, *uxor usuraria;* 504, *summus imperator.*

25. Ibid., 506.

26. Ibid., 497, *Amphitruo subditivos.*

27. Horace *Odes* 3.5.13–56.

28. *Amphitruo* 523. Elsewhere in Plautus we find *surripio* with an overtone of amorous clandestinity. See for example *Asinaria,* 929–930; *Menaechmi,* 200, 394, 510.

29. Erich S. Gruen, "Plautus and the Public Stage," in *Studies in Greek Culture and Roman Policy* (Leiden, 1990), pp. 148–157, recounts that "the amounts of cash and booty at the disposal of victorious commanders reached unprecedented levels. And the display of captured loot dazzled contemporaries" (p. 133). Compare ibid., pp. 137–138, for his discussion of Amphitryon's portrayal as a Roman general.

30. *Amphitruo* 546.

31. Ovid *Amores* 1.13.40.

32. *Amphitruo* 594.

33. See for example the comatose allusions at *Amphitruo* 298, 314, 351, 407, 623–624, 697–698, 726.

34. *Amphitruo* 621.

35. Ibid., 623–624.

36. Ibid., 635, 637, 641.

37. Ibid., 638, *parumper datast.* Contrast Lucretius 4.1116, *parva fit ardoris violenti pausa parumper* ("the relief from the searing passion is but fleeting"). Then there is Petronius' cynical formulation *foeda est in coitu et brevis voluptas* ("The pleasure of sexual intercourse is brief and base," *PLM* 101.1), or, in

Ben Jonson's terse translation (*The Underwood* 88.1–2): "Doing, a filthy pleasure is, and short; / and done, we straight repent us of the sport."

38. *Amphitruo* 648–653.

39. J. A. Hanson, "Plautus as a Source-Book for Roman Religion," *Transactions of the American Philological Association* 90 (1959), 48–60.

40. *Amphitruo* 677.

41. Ibid., 688–689.

42. Ibid., 696, 697.

43. Ibid., 726, *vigilans vigilantem.*

44. Ibid., 735.

45. Ibid., 840, *sedatus cupido.*

46. Ibid., 760–761.

47. Ibid., 762.

48. *Menaechmus* 655–656.

49. *Amphitruo* 797, *dedisti . . . clanculum.*

50. Most scholars would take *dedi* here only as an innocent outcry. But for a confirmation of *dare* in a sexual sense, see Ovid *Amores* 1.4.69–70, where the poet beseeches his girlfriend, who is going to bed with her husband, not to give in to his advances—or at least not admit it to Ovid on the morrow: "But whatever happens between you two tonight / tomorrow be loyal, and deny that you 'gave' him anything" *(cras mihi constanti voce dedisse nega!).*

51. *Amphitruo* 802–804.

52. *Menaechmi* 475, 1142.

53. *Amphitruo* 805.

54. Ibid., 808.

55. Ibid., 810–811. On the possible connotation of rape in the word *vitium,* see J. N. Adams, *Latin Sexual Vocabulary* (London, 1982), p. 199.

56. *Amphitruo* 819.

57. Ibid., 831–832; 23; 833–834.

58. Ibid., 838.

59. Ibid., 839–842.

60. Ibid., 1086.

61. Horace *Odes* 3.24.21–24.

62. *Amphitruo* 852 (see below).

63. Ibid., 861, 864.

64. Ibid., 868.

65. Ibid., 874–875. We encounter the term *frustratio,* in the sense of a theater trick, elsewhere in Plautus, most memorably at the farcical conclusion of the *Mostellaria.* The slave Tranio harshly abuses the bamboozled *senex*

Theoproprides, boasting that his own clever stratagems could provide the playwrights Philemon and Diphilus with "ideal trickery plays" (*optumae frustrationes*, 1151) for their own comedies.

66. *Amphitruo* 869, 872, 895.

67. Ibid., 879.

68. Ibid., 898.

69. Ibid., 928, *valeas, tibi habeas res tuas, reddas meas.* See *XII Tabulae* 4.3 = E. H. Warmington, *Remains of Old Latin* (London, 1938), vol. 2, pp. 442–443; see also Cicero *Phil.* 2.28.

70. *Amphitruo* 933–934.

71. Ibid., 935.

72. Ibid., 980–981, *cum hac usuaria / uxore nunc mihi morigero.*

73. Ibid., 995, *amat: sapit; recte facit, animo quando obsequitur suo.*

74. Ibid., 1004, *meo me aequomst morigerum patri, eius studio servire addecet.*

75. Hesiod *Scutum* 1–56; Pindar *Isthmian Odes* 7.5; Apollodorus 2.4.7–8; Hyginus *Fabulae* 29; Tzetzes *On Lycophron* 33 and 932.

76. Beginning after line 1034.

77. Frag. 16.

78. We discount the battle scenes in the *Iliad*—where in every case the gods appear in human guise.

79. *Amphitruo* 1039.

80. Ibid., 1051.

81. Ibid., 1062, *trepitus, crepitus, sonitus, tonitrus.*

82. Ibid., 1100, *sine dolore.*

83. Ibid., 1072.

84. Ibid., 1032.

85. Ibid., 1074.

86. Ibid., 1076–1078.

87. Ibid., 1087–1088.

88. Ibid., 1089.

89. Ibid., 1121.

90. *Amphitruo* 1121–1122. Note that *consuetum*, as the past participle of *consuescere* ("to do something habitually"), clearly intimates that he has been with her more than once.

91. Ibid., 1125–1126.

92. Ibid., 1141.

93. The image of the "horned" cuckold first appears in the Middle Ages.

94. Aristophanes *Lysistrata* 107, 212–213; *Thesmophoriazusae* 395–397; *Ecclesiazusae* 225, 522.

95. Aristophanes frag. 191 K.-A.

96. *Amphitruo* 1143, *mea vi subactast facere.*

97. Ibid., 996. Timothy J. Moore, *The Theater of Plautus: Playing to the Audience* (Austin, 1998), p. 122, observes that Mercury's vocabulary is emphatically similar to that of other bondsmen.

98. "That concept, so fertile for Mediterranean thought, gesture, insult, and comedy, seems not to have been invented until later. It is difficult even to find sober texts which attest the concept of 'wronged husband.'" Susan Treggiari, *Roman Marriage: Iusti Coniuges from the Time of Cicero to the Time of Ulpian* (Oxford, 1991), p. 312. Yet the *stupidus* of the mimes was a cuckold, while under Augustus' legislation a Roman whose wife betrayed him was guilty of pimping if he did not take action; Claudius' ignorance of Messallina's antics made him look a fool.

99. *Amphitruo* 290.

100. Ibid., 1122. Compare also 132, *cubat complexus cuius cupiens maxime est*; 290, *qui complexus cum Alcumena cubat amans animo obsequens*; 735, *Immo mecum cenavisti et mecum cubuisti*; 808, Amph.: *ubi tu cubuisti?* Alc.: *in eodem lecto teum una in cubiculo.*

101. *Oxford English Dictionary*[2] (Oxford, 1989), s.v.; and Eric Partridge, *Origins: A Short Etymological Dictionary of Modern English*[4] (London, 1966), p. 133.

102. See the brief but stimulating article by J. N. Hough, "Jupiter, Amphitryon, and the Cuckoo," *Classical Philology* 65 (1970), 95–96, quotation from p. 96. The scene Hough refers to involves the inebriated playboy Callidimates, whom his buxom sweetheart, as he lies ogling on her bosom, accuses of being drunk. He replies with the semiconscious pun: *Tun me ais mammamadere* (*Mostellaria* 331), "You really think I'm tit-tit-tipsy?" See also Seyffert's attractive emendation *ex aqu-aqu-aqua ar-arerem* at *Rudens* 534 ("Would that I were as dry as a qua-qua-qua-quacking duck out of water"), adopted by, among others, H. T. Fay in his edition of the play (London, 1969).

103. *Love's Labour's Lost*, 5.2.897–901.

104. See Richmond Lattimore, *Themes in Greek and Latin Epitaphs* (Urbana, 1962), pp. 295–299, and Williams, "Some Aspects of Roman Marriage," p. 23.

105. *Amphitruo* 1135–1136.

106. Ibid., 1143.

107. Ibid., 1144–1145.

108. Val. Max. 7.1.

109. The first divorce in Rome was traditionally held to be that of Sp. Carvilius Ruga, c. 230 B.C., which caused great excitement and was regarded as a sign of imminent moral decay. See for example Dionysus of Halicarnassus 2.25.7. Tertullian (*Apol.* 6.6, *Monog.* 9.8) allows the City's pagans 600 years before the first divorce. Plutarch *Comparison of Theseus and Romulus* 6.4, and

Comparison of Lycurgus and Numa 3.7, mistakenly fixes the date as 230 years from the founding of Rome, that is, under the decadent Tarquins. See the comments of C. Ampolo and M. Manfredini, *Le Vite di Teseo e di Romulo* (Milan, 1988), p. 343. In fact, divorces are attested still earlier than this, as listed by Treggiari, *Roman Marriage*, p. 516.

110. Cato ap. Aulus Gellius *N.A.* 10.23.5.

12. Terence: The African Connection

1. The interruptions in the *Hecyra* came in the first act (*primo actu placeo, quom interea rumor venit; Hecyra* 39).

2. See Horace *Ars Poetica* 58–59.

3. Alessandro Ronconi, "Sulla fortuna di Plauto e di Terenzio nel mondo romano," *Maia* 22 (1970), 19–37.

4. *Carm.* 1.3–4 (= Suetonius *Vit. Ter.* 7, p. 9 Wessner): *lenibus atque utinam scriptis adiuncta foret vis / comica ut aequato virtus polleret honore.* It is not certain which word the poet intended to modify with *comica.*

5. Ibid., 1.1.

6. Quintilian *Inst.* 10.1.99.

7. Aulus Gellius *Noctes Atticae* 3.3.4.

8. Sander Goldberg, *Understanding Terence* (Princeton, 1986), pp. 40–60, has demonstrated the playwright's debt to contemporary oratory.

9. There is, for example, the splendid Terence manuscript in the Lessing J. Rosenwald Collection, Washington, D.C. See the article by E. Segal in *Vision of a Collector: The Lessing J. Rosenwald Collection in the Library of Congress* (Washington, 1991), pp. 172 173.

10. See G. E. Duckworth, *The Nature of Roman Comedy* (Princeton, 1952), pp. 396–397, 404.

11. Gilbert Norwood, *The Art of Terence* (Oxford, 1923). For the record, Shakespeare based his dramatizations of Plutarch not on the original but rather on the celebrated English translations of Thomas North (c. 1535–1601)— who was himself at a remove from the Greek, having based his own version on the French translation of Jacques Amyot (1559).

12. Erich Reitzenstein, *Terenz als Dichter* (Leipzig, 1940), p. 10.

13. Heinz Haffter, *Terenz und seine künstleriche Eigenart* (Darmstadt, 1967), in Italian translation as *Terenzio e la sua personalita artistica* (Rome, 1969), quotation from p. 67. Although there has been critical dissension from some of Haffter's views, his monograph remains perhaps the best general introduction to the playwright.

14. See especially Walther Ludwig, "Von Terenz zu Menander," *Philologus* 103 (1959), 1–38, reprinted in E. Lefèvre, *Die römische Komödie: Plautus und Terenz* (Darmstadt, 1973), pp. 354–408; Ludwig, "The Originality of Terence and

his Greek Models," *Greek, Roman and Byzantine Studies* 9 (1968), 169–182, esp. p. 180, reprinted in *Oxford Readings in Menander, Plautus, and Terence,* ed. E. Segal (Oxford, 2002). The original language of this essay was English, later translated into German.

15. Donatus at *Andria* 10–14.

16. Ludwig concluded that the changes wrought by Terence would in our own age be the province of a director or producer. Then again, modern playwrights are often present at the first reading of their new work to hear the actors read their play, judging whether their dialogue is light or limp. This could possibly have been the case with Terence.

17. Ludwig, "The Originality of Terence," p. 180.

18. Suetonius *Vit. Ter.* 1 (p. 3 Wessner).

19. As noted by F. H. Sandbach, *The Comic Theatre of Greece and Rome* (New York, 1977), p. 135.

20. See Frank Snowden, *Blacks in Antiquity* (Cambridge, Mass., 1970), p. 270, who also points out that in the Vergilian *Moretum* 32–33 the Negroid Scybale is described as *afra genus* and *fusca colore.*

21. See R. M Brown, *A Study of the Scipionic Circle* (Jacksonville, Fla., 1934); H. Strasburger, "Der Scipionenkreis," *Hermes* 94 (1966), 60–72; A. E. Astin, *Scipio Aemelianus* (Oxford, 1967), pp. 294–296; Goldberg, *Understanding Terence,* pp. 13–15.

22. This tale is found in Suetonius *Vit. Ter.* 5 (pp. 7–8 Wessner). Aulus Gellius 17.4.4 (= K.-A. test. 46) cites a tradition which attributed 108 dramas to Menander, as against the more reliable testimony of Apollodorus' *Chronica* (244 F 43 Jacoby) which puts the number at 105. This colossal figure seems to have been due to a scribal error in copying the text of Suetonius, who was quoting or paraphrasing the critic Quintus Cosconius (first century B.C.): *Q. Cosconius redeuntem a Graecia perisse in mari dicit cum fabulis conversis a Menandro* ("Cosconius says that [Terence] perished in the sea returning from Greece with plays adapted from Menander"). A later—but not much later—copyist seems to have mistaken *cum* ("with") for the Roman numeral CVIII and read *fabulis conversis* as an ablative absolute: that is, "108 comedies having been adapted" versus "with adapted comedies." This explanation doubtless accounts for the alternate figure attributed by late sources to Menander, and assuages the pain of scholars who might otherwise mourn the loss.

23. On Roman jokes see Gordon Williams, *Tradition and Originality in Roman Poetry* (Oxford, 1968), pp. 285–296.

24. *Conversum expressumque Latina voce Menandrum.* From his commonplace book *Limon,* as recorded by Suetonius *Vit. Ter.* 7.

25. Horace *Ars Poetica* 224.

26. *Heauton Timoroumenos* (hereafter *H.T.*) 36.

27. Euanthius *Exc. de Com.* 4.4 (p. 22 Wessner).

28. *H.T.* 37-40.

29. *Eunuch* 23.

30. Ibid., 35-40.

31. Ibid., 41.

32. *Mostellaria* 233-234.

33. *Adelphoe* 519-520.

34. Donatus ad Ter. *Adelphoe* 521 (vol. 2, p. 108 Wessner).

35. See further E. Segal, *Roman Laughter*² (Oxford, 1987), pp. 16-19.

36. Terence uses *fabula* more than twice as often as *comoedia,* and more than five times as often if we take its many other utterances in a metatheatrical sense.

37. *Hecyra* 4.

38. See for example *And.* 113, 236, 278; *H.T.* 77, 99, 552, 1046; *Eun.* 880; *Phorm.* 509; *Hec.* 499, 553; *Adelph.* 145, 471, 687.

39. Cicero *De off.* 1.9.30.

40. *H.T.* 77, *homo sum humani nil a me alienum puto.*

41. Prologue to *Andria* 15-19.

42. Suetonius *Vit. Ter.* 4 (pp. 5-7 Wessner) records an occasion on which Gaius Laelius, a nobleman involved in the new philosophical movements (and called Sapiens, "the wise"), came home late for the Matronalia, an important dinner in honor of married women. Explaining to his irate wife that he was delayed trying to finish an important verse, he then quoted the verse which is now line 723 of the *Self-Tormentor.* Cicero hurls a similar accusation of aristocratic assistance (*Att.* 7.3.10). Quintilian (*Inst.* 10.1.99) repeats the anecdote, making the ghost-writer Scipio himself. Suetonius himself records the doubts of his source Santra, on the grounds that Scipio and Laelius were too young at the time.

43. Montaigne, *Essays,* I.xxxx (trans. M. A. Screech): "And if a perfect mastery of language could contribute anything worthy of a great public figure, Scipio and Laelius would certainly not have allowed the credit for their comedies, with all their grace and delightful language, to be attributed to an African slave—for the beauty and excellence of these works are adequate proof that they are really theirs, and Terence himself admits it. I would be deeply displeased to have that belief of mine shaken."

44. Though he left Czechoslovakia at an early age, Stoppard spoke only Czech from the ages of three to five—enough to implant Czech as the primary language.

45. Although Cicero regarded Caecilius as "a poor model of Latinity" (*malus auctor Latinitatis, Att.* 7.3.10), this did not stop the playwright from achieving great success: he was rated the best Roman dramatist by Volcacius Sedigitus (see Aulus Gellius *N.A.* 15.24) and Cicero (*Opt. Gen.* 2), while Quintillian reports his primacy among the ancients (*Inst.* 10.1.99).

46. *Aspis, Heros,* and *Perikeiromenē.*

47. The old Chambers' dictionary refers to such a reader as an end-dipper, one who turns to the last page "to see if she got him." G. K. Chesterton inveighs splendidly against this bean-spilling ("The back of the cover will tell you the plot").

48. *A Midsummer Night's Dream* 3.1.8–20.

49. *Adelphoe* 22–24. There is a briefer version of these same remarks, using some of the same language, in the prologue to Plautus' *Trinummus* (16–17): "Don't count on hearing all the plot from me right now. / The oldsters coming on will then come out with everything." A still earlier statement is found in Menander *Dyscolus* 45–46.

50. "Creating suspense of this kind was a very daring thing to do. Greco-Roman comedy generally provided the audience with fuller knowledge of the dramatic situation than the characters possess . . . By refusing to grant any superior knowledge, Terence seeks to put us on the same level as his characters. He wants them to seem no better or worse than ourselves." Goldberg, *Understanding Terence,* pp. 160–161.

51. Compare Horace *Ars Poetica* 179: *Aut agitur res in scaenis aut acta refertur* ("a matter is either acted out on stage or it is reported as having been done").

52. *Curculio, Epidicus, Mostellaria, Persa* and *Stichus.* In the *Menaechmi* the prologue, in setting the scene, gives no indication how the play will turn out. Caecilius may have withheld prologues as well (see Duckworth, *Roman Comedy,* pp. 48–49).

53. Haffter, *Terenzio,* p. 50.

54. Holt Parker, who has recently argued vigorously for a reassessment of Terence's popularity in relation to Plautus, somewhat perversely uses the Plautine examples to downplay Terence's achievement in the invention of suspense on the grounds that the elimination of the expository prologue was as old a practice as Menander's *Misoumenos.* This damaged play may in fact contain traces of a lost, postponed prologue, as discerned by T. B. L. Webster, *An Introduction to Menander* (Manchester, 1974), pp. 163–164. Furthermore, of the Plautine examples cited as anticipating Terentian suspense, the *Cistellaria* actually *has* a very long expository prologue—by Auxilium ("First Aid"). Although it is postponed until well into the play, it runs a full fifty-three lines (149–202). "Plautus vs. Terence: Audience and

Popularity Re-examined," *American Journal of Philology* 117 (1996), 585–617, esp. pp. 601–604.

55. G. E. Lessing, *Hamburgische Dramaturgie*, 48.

56. See Erich S. Gruen, *Culture and National Identity in Republican Rome* (London, 1993), pp. 212–218.

57. *H.T.* 22, *malevolus vetus poeta.*

58. Ibid., 16–20.

59. *Andria* 18.

60. Ibid., 18–21.

61. See for example Moschus frag. 2, "Pan loved his neighbor Echo, but Echo was infatuated with a horny satyr, the satyr was madly in love with Lyde" (and so forth).

62. *H.T.* 77, *humani nil a me alienum puto.*

63. Ibid., 1046, *nimisque inhumane.*

64. *Andria* 10–12.

65. As defined by Euanthius *Exc. de Com.* 3.2 (p. 19 Wessner), protatic characters are "extra parts brought in beyond those required for the plot . . . often used by Terence, so that through their exposition the plot may be more readily laid out." Shakespeare's Valentine is another such device in *Twelfth Night,* not to mention the *confident* of classical French drama, whose function is to be told things that persons in the principal's confidence know already but the audience does not.

66. See Gomme and Sandbach, *Menander,* p. 15.

67. *Andria* 31–34, *ars . . . fide et taciturnitate.*

68. Ibid., 61; 68.

69. Ibid., 88–89, *symbolam / dedit, cenavit.*

70. See W. Geoffrey Arnott, *Alexis: The Fragments* (Cambridge, 1996), p. 87.

71. *Andria* 89.

72. Ibid., 103.

73. Ibid., 109, *conlacrumabat.*

74. Ibid., 110–112.

75. Ibid., 119–120.

76. Ibid., 126. Compare Cicero *Pro Caelio* 25/61; Horace *Ep.* 1.19.41; Juvenal *Sat.* 1.168.

77. *Phormio* 99–100.

78. In another of Terence's plays, *The Brothers,* an angry father takes consolation in his wayward son's reaction to his scolding: "he's blushed—then all is good" (643).

79. *Andria* 129, *fletur.*

80. Ibid., 135–136.

81. Ibid., 144–146.

82. Ibid., 184–185.

83. Ibid., 187, *iniquus pater;* 190, *redeat iam viam.*

84. Ibid., 194.

85. Ibid., 197.

86. Ibid., 215–216; 218.

87. Ibid., 224; 220.

88. Ibid., 294.

89. In *A Midsummer Night's Dream,* for example, many would agree that the second story line of Helena and Demetrius is, if anything, more interesting than that of Hermia and Lysander.

90. *Andria* 315–316.

91. Ibid., 326–327.

92. Ibid., 375–411.

93. Ibid., 412–458.

94. Ibid., 498–516.

95. Ibid., 535.

96. Ibid., 553; 538–573.

97. Ibid., 599–606.

98. Ibid., 620.

99. Ibid., 625–668.

100. Ibid., 669–672.

101. Ibid., 673–674.

102. Ibid., 691–693.

103. Ibid., 806.

104. See A. R. W. Harrison, *The Law of Athens: The Family and Property* (Oxford, 1968), p. 132.

105. *Andria* 844, *ego commodiorem hominem adventum tempus non vidi.*

106. Ibid., 855.

107. Ibid., 906.

108. Ibid., 933.

109. According to data from the U.S. Department of Statistics, obtained at the beginning of the third millennium, this figure would be approximately U.S. $250,000.00. Anthony Rosenfelder called these data to my attention. But seeking modern equivalents is a minefield best avoided. In Menander the dowries are still large (between one and four talents), and the heiress of the *Plokion* brought more into the marriage than the dowry of the *Andria,* though it is clearly a fantasy figure. Gomme and Sandbach, *Menander,* pp. 296–298, note that the size of Greek dowries may have increased in the later part of the fourth century, and in the ever-richer Rome

of the second century B.C. it would not be surprising if they had grown apace. In Plautus' *Cistellaria* there is a dowry of twenty talents, in *Mercator* ten.

110. *Andria* 971–972.
111. Ibid., 980–981.

13. The Mother-in-Law of Modern Comedy

1. In fact, John Barsby's was the first—and may well be the last—edition of the play in English: *Eunuchus*, ed. John Barsby (Cambridge, 1999).
2. Gilbert Norwood, *The Art of Terence* (Oxford, 1923), p. 57.
3. *Eunuchus* 912–916. And thus we have a typical garden-variety *cognitio:*

> PYTHIAS: Have you shown the baubles to the nurse yet?
>
> CHREMES: Every single one of them.
>
> PYTHIAS: Please tell me quick, did she recognize them?
>
> CHREMES: Absolutely.

4. Ibid., 1038, *unast domus.*
5. Barsby, *Eunuchus*, p. 178.
6. Suetonius *Vit. Ter.* 3 (p. 5 Wessner).
7. J. G. Frazer, *The Golden Bough*[3] (London, 1926), vol. 3, pp. 83–85, 338–346.
8. Douglas Gilbert, *American Vaudeville: Its Life and Times* (New York, 1968), p. 202.
9. See Dwora Gilula, "Terence's *Hecyra:* A Delicate Balance of Suspense and Dramatic Irony," *Scripta Classica Israelica* 5 (1979/1980), 137–157, esp. pp. 140–141.
10. *Hecyra* 4.
11. Sander M. Goldberg, *Understanding Terence* (Princeton, 1986), pp. 42–60, makes this point in his incisive discussion of the prologues, demonstrating their debt to contemporary Roman rhetoric, as is made quite clear in the opening speech to the *H.T.*: "The author wanted me to be defense attorney, not a prologue. Therefore he's made you be the jury, and me the lawyer" (*oratorum esse voluit me, non prologum: / vostrum iudicium fecit: me actorem dedit,* 11–12).
12. *Hecyra* 28–30.
13. Ibid., 30, *ita eam oppressit calamitas.*
14. Ibid., 33.
15. F. H. Sandbach, "How Terence's *Hecyra* Failed," *Classical Quarterly* 32 (1982), 135, suggests that "the first prologue may say nothing of the boxers because the speaker's object there is to depreciate the audience's taste, and funambulism was an art less widely acclaimed than pugilism. Boxing was

understood and watched by the educated as well as the general run . . . In the second prologue Turpio more tactfully implies that the renown of the boxers was an adequate cause for the failure of the comedy."

16. *Hecyra* 42, *meum non potui tutari locum.*

17. Ibid., 46–47.

18. Holt Parker, "Plautus vs. Terence: Audience and Popularity Re-examined," *American Journal of Philology* 117 (1996), 585–617, quotation from pp. 591–592. Parker gives much weight to the huge financial reward. Yet it is not clear whether this *pretium* was a fee or a bonus for his success: we know nothing of such financial arrangements, except that drama was the one form of writing for which one could expect to be paid (Juvenal *Sat.* 7.87). Parker first admits that a reward is more likely, but then consistently clouds the issue by referring to it as the largest payment in theatrical history. Parker tends to imply that, by virtue of his popularity, Terence could *command* such a price. Moreover, as Rome became richer prices would become correspondingly inflated: nothing can be deduced from the high *pretium* about Terence's ability or popularity compared to members of an earlier generation.

19. *Hecyra* 40.

20. Ovid *Rem. Amor.* 580.

21. As demonstrated by Sandbach, "How Terence's *Hecyra* Failed," p. 135. See also E. Lefèvre, *Terenz' und Apollodors Hecyra = Zetemata* 101 (Munich, 1999), pp. 175–179.

22. See Sandbach, "How Terence's *Hecyra* Failed," p. 135; Parker, "Plautus vs. Terence," pp. 595–596.

23. Vergil *Georgics* 2.527–531.

24. Horace *Ep.* 2.1.185–186. This statement is not, as Parker claims ("Plautus vs. Terence," p. 597), merely Horace's inference from or allusion to the *Hecyra* prologues. Are we to believe that these were the later poet's only exposure to crowd psychology? He had surely seen more animal hunts *(venationes)* than Terence—who at any rate does not mention bears—since, by Augustus' own calculations (*Anc.* 22), 3,500 African beasts had been killed in the course of the eighty hunts he sponsored.

25. Polybius 30.22. The tale is repeated by Athenaeus *Deipnosophistae* 14.615b-d.

26. Parker, "Plautus vs. Terence," p. 596, n. 46.

27. See *Amphitruo* 64–95; *Asinaria* 4–5; *Captivi* 10–14; *Poenulus* 1–43.

28. Horace *Ep.* 2.1.170–176. When Horace compares Plautus to Epicharmus, he presumably refers to the vulgarity of the language and the fast and loose dramaturgy (*Ep.* 2.1.58, compare 2.1.168–176). Consider also Horace's *quantum sit Dossennus edacibus in parasitis* (*Ep.* 2.1.173) in relation to the early ap-

pearance of parasites in Epicharmus. On the prominence of vaudevillian improvisatory devices in Plautus, see G. Voigt-Spira, "Traditionen improvisierten Theaters bei Plautus," in *Griechisch-römische Komödie und Tragödie,*" ed. B. Zimmerman (Stuttgart, 1995), pp. 70-93.

29. *Stichus* 220.

30. *Casina* 879-880.

31. Timothy J. Moore, *The Theatre of Plautus: Playing to the Audience* (Austin, 1998), p. 29 and passim.

32. Horace *Ep.* 2.1.168-176.

33. Velleius Paterculus 1.17.1. Horace does in fact mention Plautus, but not with much enthusiasm (*Ep.* 2.1.59-60): *Plautus ad exemplar Siculi properare Epicharmi, / vincere Caecilius gravitate, Terentius arte* ("Plautus races helterskelter across the stage like the Sicilian Epicharmus. Caecilius is more serious; Terence more skillful").

34. Suetonius *Vit. Ter.* 10 (p. 10 Wessner), *Hecyra saepe exclusa uix acta est.*

35. Aulus Gellius *N.A.* 15.24.

36. Suetonius *Vit. Ter.* 2.

37. Ibid., 2.

38. Dwora Gilula, "Who's Afraid of Rope-Walkers and Gladiators (Ter. *Hec.* 1-57)," *Athenaeum* 59 (1981), 29-37, esp. pp. 30-31 (followed by Parker, "Plautus vs. Terence," p. 591), gives undue weight to Suetonius' "correction" of Volcacius, supporting his authority only with the observation that the earlier critic's "evaluation of poets (Aul. Gell. *N.A.* 15.24.1) seems idiosyncratic, and is probably quoted by Gellius precisely because of its striking incongruity with views commonly held by others . . . so also the ranking of Terence's comedies is quoted by Suetonius as a strictly personal opinion of a peculiar individual." But this is mere conjecture. Volcacius' value is that his opinions were formed before the onset of Augustan literary tastes which held Plautus and other comic poets in contempt, and before the archaic revival made its own new judgments. Thus, though we do not know the criteria used by Volcacius in ranking Terence, he is much more likely to reflect the playwright's contemporary popularity than Cicero, Horace, or Suetonius. At any rate he has no extant peers who can demonstrate that he is "idiosyncratic."

39. See Quint. *Inst.* 10.1.99.

40. Aulus Gellius *N.A.* 15.24.

41. See Charles Homer Haskins, *The Renaissance of the Twelfth Century* (Cambridge, Mass., 1927), pp. 110-111.

42. Many critics have remarked on the fact that *Hecyra* represents Terence's most sophisticated use of suspense. See among others Lefèvre, *Terenz,*

pp. 126–128. As Ireland remarks: "For audiences accustomed to the often blatant transparency of Plautine comedy the depth of misapprehension which Terence imposed on those who viewed the *Mother-in-Law* must have come as no small dramatic shock and we cannot but wonder if the two abortive productions, first in 165, then in 160, were caused as much by the complex uncertainties of the action as by the extraneous interference." *Hecyra,* ed. Stanley Ireland (Warminster, 1989), p. 9. This position was first stated by T. Frank, "Terence's Contribution to Plot Construction," *American Journal of Philology* 49 (1928), 320: "There is not one ancient play before the day of Terence . . . where an audience was left in such complete suspense before an accumulating mass of perplexities." Gilula, "Who's Afraid," p. 34, objects that, since the climactic disclosure of the rapist occurs in line 829 while the first two performances were interrupted in the first act, "it is highly unlikely that the spectators could have become dissatisfied with a technique of whose existence they were unaware . . . or a tension that had not yet built up." But that is just the point of suspense: in the absence of exposition, the effect is *immediate*. If the audience was not absolutely patient and attentive—and there are always distractions at such festivals—they would soon have become bewildered.

43. Using the word "zany" in its original Italian sense. *Lo Zanni* [singular *sic*] was one of the stock servants in the commedia dell'arte. In English comedy he was most likely to be a fumbling imitator of his master, certainly the sense in which Jonson employed him. His name has been derived variously—perhaps a descendant of the Sannio who appeared in the *fabulae Atellanae,* or a corruption of the Lombardic form of the name Giovanni. See Pierre Duchartre, *The Italian Comedy,* trans. Randolph T. Weaver (New York, 1966), p. 29.

44. *Hecyra* 448–449, *nam me parenti potius quam amori obsequi / oportet.*

45. Ibid., 145, *virgo integra.*

46. Ibid., 157, *cotidie.*

47. Ibid., 164–166.

48. Ibid., 169–170; 393.

49. Ibid., 201–204.

50. Ibid., 241–242.

51. Ibid., 277–279.

52. Ibid., 281.

53. Ibid., 480–481.

54. Ibid., 312, *mulieres sunt ferme ut pueri levi sententia.*

55. Ibid., 355.

56. Ibid., 376–379.

57. Ibid., 405–406.

58. Ibid., 476.

59. Ibid. 480–481.

60. Ibid., 488, *amoque et laudo et vehementer desidero.*

61. Ibid., 524.

62. Ibid., 527.

63. Ibid., 527–528.

64. Ibid., 531.

65. S. Ireland, *Hecyra,* pp. 163–165, discusses at length the time-frame of the pregnancy. The only way to reconcile the various clues given by the characters is to assume a premature birth at seven months (recognized as feasible by Donatus at 531). This explains Phidippus' initial suspicion (*ex qui,* 527), and we must assume that he drops the issue in the face of his wife's vehement denial of illegitimacy.

66. *Hecyra* 572–574.

67. Ibid., 600.

68. Ibid., 602, *hanc matrem habens talem, illam autem uxorem.*

69. Eric Bentley, "The Making of a Dramatist 1892–1908," in *G. B. Shaw: A Collection of Critical Essays,* ed. R. J. Kaufmann (Englewood Cliffs, 1965), p. 57. Elsewhere Bentley quotes the protest of Mrs. Patrick Campbell, who played the first Eliza: "The last act of the play did not travel across the footlights with as clear a dramatic sequence as the preceding acts—owing entirely to the fault of the author." See the same author's *Bernard Shaw*[2] (New York, 1957), p. 122.

70. *Hecyra* 638–639.

71. Ibid., 662–663.

72. Ibid., 719.

73. Ibid., 735, *nam mores facile tutor.*

74. Ibid., 157.

75. Ibid., 774–776.

76. Euanthius *Exc. de Com.* 3.4 (p. 19 Wessner).

77. Dwora Gilula, "The Concept of the *bona meretrix:* A Study of Terence's Courtesans," *Rivista di filologia* N.S. 108 (1980), 156–157, argues that the "respectful prostitute" is a figment of scholarly imagination. But this is well-countered by the more persuasive comments of Ireland, *Hecyra,* at 752: "Only now is the negative picture of Bacchis established by Parmeno at 158f. shown to be little more than a subjective and inaccurate interpretation of events."

78. *Hecyra* 866–868.

79. Ibid., 852–853.

80. Ibid., 875.
81. See M. Bakhtin, *Rabelais and His World,* trans. Hélène Iswolsky (Bloom-ington, 1984), pp. 1-58.

14. Machiavelli: The Comedy of Evil

1. On the *Nachleben* of Plautus and Terence in antiquity, see A. Ronconi, "Sulla fortuna di Plauto e di Terenzio nel mondo romano," *Maia* 22 (1970), 19-37.
2. Cicero *Pro Roscio comoedo* 20.13; Cicero also mentions a Plautine play at *De senect.* 14.50.3.
3. As evident from the letters of Fronto, tutor to Marcus Aurelius (c. 95-c. 166 A.D.). See also Aulus Gellius *N.A.* 1.7.17, who praises Plautine diction.
4. Aulus Gellius *N.A.* 3.3.1-11.
5. Macrobius 2.1.10.
6. Scholion to Gregory of Nazianzus. See A. Nicoll, *Masks, Mimes, and Miracles* (New York, 1963), p. 141.
7. Though the Emperor Constantine's "enlightenment" came before the bat-tle at the Milvian Bridge in 312 A.D., he was only baptized on his deathbed in 337 A.D. "Thus Constantine's attitude to the church is unambiguous but the true nature of his 'conversion' remains as enigmatic as his charac-ter." M. Cary and H. H. Scullard, *Rome Down to the Reign of Constantine*[3] (London, 1979), p. 547.
8. Tertullian *De spectaculis* 30.2-5.
9. M. Bakhtin, "Comedy and Carnival Tradition" (1968), reprinted in *Comedy: Developments in Criticism,* ed. D. J. Palmer (London, 1984), pp. 95-102, quota-tion from p. 96.
10. "If we are to approach the drama of the Middle Ages intelligently we must dismiss all our own contemporary notions of what a theatre should be and how a play should be written, and then go on to substitute the idea of community games in which the actors are the contestants (mi-metic or athletic or both) and the theatre is any place appropriate or convenient both to them as performers and to the rest of the com-munity as spectators." Glynne Wickham, *The Medieval Theatre* (London, 1974), p. 4.
11. E. K. Chambers, *The Medieval Stage,* vol. 1 (Oxford, 1903), pp. 10-11, presents the same story, albeit with a different saint as martyr, and argues that all these histrionic saints can be traced to an original Greek story about an anonymous *mimus* (= *Acta SS Aug.* v. 122).
12. Homer *Odyssey* 11.488-491.
13. See Wickham, *Medieval Theatre,* with the diagrams on pp. 16 and 17, and his further comments on open space in early churches, pp. 18-19.

14. L. D. Reynolds and N. G. Wilson, *Scribes and Scholars*³ (Oxford, 1991), pp. 95–96.

15. Charles Homer Haskins, *The Renaissance of the Twelfth Century* (Cambridge, Mass, 1927), pp. 4–10 and passim.

16. Jacob Burckhardt, *The Civilization of the Renaissance in Italy,* trans. S. G. C. Middlemor (London, 1990), p. 104.

17. There was of course no "Italy" when Boccaccio wrote. It was rather a scattering of city-states—both petty despotisms and republican communes—of which the author's was by far the most glorious.

18. F. Ritschl, *Opuscula philologica* (Leipzig, 1868), vol. 2, pp. 5–8. The new plays were *Bacchides, Mostellaria, Menaechmi, Miles Gloriosus, Mercator, Pseudolus, Poenulus, Persa, Rudens, Stichus, Trinummus, Truculentus.*

19. There were at least 440 editions of Terence completed in France between 1400 and 1600.

20. For the record, the plays were *Epidicus, Bacchides, Miles Gloriosus, Asinaria, Casina.*

21. Baldassar Castiglione, *Tutte le opere,* vol. 1, *Le lettere,* ed. Guido La Rocca (Rome, 1978), p. 345.

22. See Douglas Radcliff-Umstead, *The Birth of Modern Comedy in Renaissance Italy* (Chicago, 1969), p. 63.

23. The Italian text used for the arguments in this chapter is based on Niccolò Machiavelli, *Mandragola* [and] *Clizia,* with commentary by Gian Mario Anselmi (Milan, 1938), preface by Ezio Raimondi.

24. Carlo Goldoni, *Mémoires* 1.10.

25. See the discussion of W. Geoffrey Arnott, *Alexis: The Fragments* (Cambridge, 1996), pp. 419–421.

26. Alexis frag. 146 K.-A.

27. The commedia dell'arte, which reached its flowering in the mid-eighteenth century, owes part of its existence to the revival of ancient Roman comedy. Undoubtedly, however, it grew from an unbroken improvisatory tradition which stretched back to antiquity.

28. Francesco di Sanctis, *History of Italian Literature,* trans. J. Redfern (New York, 1931), p. 563. He goes on to say: "He has no need to be an Iago, because Nicia is not an Othello. He is a common cheat, and if he were only a little more witty we should laugh at him. But he is only hateful and contemptible, the worst type of man that Machiavelli conceived in *The Prince.*"

29. A play on a medical theme was particularly apt for one whose family saints were Cosmas and Damian. Indeed, it may have been performed for Leo on their day in 1520. See Bonnie J. Blackburn, "Music and Festivities at the Court of Leo X," *Early Music History* 11 (1992), 1–37, esp. pp. 26–28.

30. Ovid *Fasti* 2.832–834.

31. Enobarbus puns on the dual sense of "dying," that is, performing the sexual act, when he remarks of Cleopatra: "I have seen her die twenty times upon far poorer moment. I do think there is mettle [sexual prowess] in death which commits some loving act upon her she hath such a celerity in dying" (*Antony and Cleopatra* 1.2.141–144).

32. See especially Livy 1.57.6–1.58.12 and Ovid *Fasti* 2.685–852.

33. A modern popular example of this is in the television comedy "Fawlty Towers" where the Spaniard Manuel, a latter-day *servus currens,* is recast as Mario the *Italian* when the program is playing in Spain.

34. *Mandragola* 1.3.

35. Ibid., 2.2.

36. Ibid., 2.6.

37. Ibid., 2.6.

38. Ibid., 3.11.

39. There is a similar motif in the Apocryphal book of Tobit, where the devil Asmodeus kills seven of Sarah's bridegrooms. Tobit's son Tobias, with the aid of the angel Raphael, chases away the evil demon, marries Sarah, cures Tobit's blindness, and restores his wealth.

40. *Mandragola* 4.9.

41. Ibid., 5.2.

42. Ibid.

43. Ibid., 4.10.

44. Ibid., 5.2.

45. Ibid., 5.4.

46. Ibid.

47. Ibid.

48. Ibid., 5.5.

49. Ibid., 3.11.

50. Ibid., 5.5.

51. Ibid., 5.6.

52. Ibid.

15. Marlowe: *Schade* and *Freude*

1. Plato *Republic* 3.388e–389b. To the modern mind, the Homeric term *asbestos gelōs* suggests inanimate, unfeeling laughter, reminiscent of Bergson's definition of the comic as "something mechanical stuck upon the living."

2. Plato *Philebus* 49d; Aristotle *Nichomachean Ethics* 4.1128a4–8.

3. Aristotle *Poetics* 1449a33–35.

4. Homer *Iliad* 2.216.

5. Plato *Philebus* 49d.

6. Although at one point Aristotle specifically decries *epichairekakia* (*Nicomachean Ethics* 2.1107a10, 1108b). Horace objects to *laedere gaudere* ("to enjoy giving pain") in *Sat.* 1.4.78-85 and passim.

7. See especially Walter Burkert, *Homo Necans, The Anthropology of Ancient Greek Sacrificial Ritual and Myth* (Berkeley, 1983).

8. Adler is retrospectively discussing his first statement on aggression. Cited in *The Individual Psychology of Alfred Adler*, ed. Heinz L. Ansbacher and Rowena R. Ansbacher (New York, 1956), p. 38.

9. S. Freud, *Civilization and Its Discontents* (1930), vol. 21 (1927-1931), pp. 64-145, quotation from p. 111.

10. Ibid., p. 122. Otto Rank accepts the essence of Freud's view on "this primary evil in man." See *Life Fear and Death Fear*, trans. Mabel E. Moxon, in *The Myth of the Birth of the Hero*, ed. Philip Freund (New York, 1951), p. 275. The theory of aggression was also put forth by Konrad Lorenz, *Das sogenannte Böse. Zur Naturgeschichte der Aggression* (Vienna, 1963), and Burkert, *Homo Necans.*

11. And yet Socrates was not unaware of "the aggression principle." Throughout the *Philebus* passage already cited, he speaks of man's innate *phthonos* toward his fellow man. The Greek term is usually rendered as "envy," but there is legitimate basis for translating *phthonos* as "hostility." Compare its usage (though in all cases in its verbal form) in *Iliad* 4.55-56; Pindar *Pythian* 3.71; Euripides *Ion* 1025.

12. *Defense of Poesie*, in *The Complete Works of Sir Philip Sidney*, ed. A. Feuillerat (Cambridge, 1923), vol. 2, p. 41.

13. *Timber: Or Discoveries Made Upon Men and Matter*, in vol. 8 of *The Complete Works of Ben Jonson*, ed. C. H. Herford, Percy Simpson, and Evelyn Simpson (Oxford, 1947), p. 643.

14. Lord Chesterfield's letter from Bath, 9 March 1748, is quoted in *The Idea of Comedy*, ed. W. K. Wimsatt (Englewood Cliffs, 1969), p. 150.

15. M. Esslin, "Violence in Modern Drama," in *Reflections: Essays on the Modern Theatre* (Garden City, 1969), p. 167.

16. My translation, from Lazarillo de Tormes in *La novela picaresca en España*, ed. Angel Valbuena y Prat (Madrid, 1962), p. 91.

17. Moreover, the first extant French farce in the vernacular is the late thirteenth-century *Le garçon et l'aveugle.*

18. Giovanni Boccaccio, *Il Decameron*, ed. Charles S. Singleton (Bari, 1955), vol. 2, p. 111, *uomini sollazzevoli molto, ma per altro avveduti e sagaci.*

19. Boccacio, *Decameron*, p. 173.

20. Henri Bergson, *Le Rire: Essai sur la signification du comique* (Paris, 1940), p. 4.

21. Nietzsche, *Menschliches, Allzumenschliches* 2.1, 202.

22. "The Reeve's Prologue," 4275-4276. All quotations from Chaucer are from the second edition of F. N. Robinson (Boston, 1957).

23. Ibid., 4307-4308.

24. "The Miller's Tale," 3812-3813.

25. Ibid., 3855-3858.

26. Ibid., 3867-3868, 3874.

27. T. S. Eliot's essays, "Notes on the Blank Verse of Christopher Marlowe" and "Ben Jonson," are published in *The Sacred Wood* (London, 1920), pp. 86-94, 104-122. The words quoted here are from the essay on Marlowe, p. 92. For further comparisons between Marlowe and Jonson, see Harry Levin, *The Overreacher: A Study of Christopher Marlowe* (Cambridge, Mass., 1952), p. 148.

28. *Doctor Faustus* 446. All quotations from Marlowe are from the edition of C. F. Tucker Brooke (Oxford, 1910).

29. Bernard Spivack, *Shakespeare and the Allegory of Evil* (New York, 1958), pp. 134-140; 346-353; quotation from p. 141.

30. George E. Dimock, Jr., "The Name of Odysseus," *Hudson Review* 9 (Spring 1956), 52-77, reprinted in several anthologies including *Essays on the Odyssey*, ed. Charles H. Taylor, Jr. (Bloomington, 1963), pp. 54-72, quotation from p. 55.

31. Levin, *Overreacher*, p. 61.

32. As noted by Mario Praz, "Machiavelli and the Elizabethans," in *The Flaming Heart* (New York, 1958), p. 104.

33. David M. Bevington, *From Mankind to Marlowe* (Cambridge, Mass., 1962), pp. 222, 224.

34. Levin, *Overreacher*, p. 157.

35. *Turcismus enim Judaismo cognatus admodum et affinis est.* From an anonymous tract quoted by Leon Kellner in "Die Quelle von Marlowes 'Jew of Malta,'" *Englische Studien* 10 (1887), 110.

36. Barabas is "bottel-nosed" like the morality devil (Spivack, *Allegory of Evil*, pp. 134-135). An equation between Turks and devils is made by Urbanus Regius in *An Homely or Sermon of Good and Euill Angels* (1583).

37. *Jew of Malta* 1-3. That the Marlovian caricature has not a single real characteristic of the Florentine philosopher is methodically demonstrated by Irving Ribner, "Marlowe and Machiavelli," *Comparative Literature* 6 (Fall 1954), 348-356.

38. *Jew of Malta* 30.

39. Ibid., 35.

40. Ibid., 165.

41. Nathaniel Woodes, *The Conflict of Conscience* 1.1.83–84, ed. Edgar T. Schell and J. D. Shuchter, in *English Morality Plays and Moral Interludes* (New York, 1969).

42. *Jew of Malta* 42.

43. Ibid., 67.

44. Ibid., 72.

45. Ibid., 73.

46. Ibid., 115–117.

47. Ibid., 118.

48. Ibid., 191–192.

49. Ibid., 176. And Barabas must once again have Agamemnon in mind when he comments on Lodowick's desire for his daughter's hand: ". . . e're he shall haue her / I'le sacrifice her on a pile of wood" (812–813).

50. *Jew of Malta* 414.

51. Jonson, *Volpone* 1.1.16–17.

52. *Jew of Malta* 212.

53. Ibid., 218.

54. Ibid., 225–229.

55. Ibid., 2292.

56. "I am Enuy . . . O that there would come a famine through all the worlde, that all might die, and I liue alone." *Doctor Faustus* 744.

57. *Jew of Malta* 14.

58. Ibid., 531–532.

59. Ibid., 501–504.

60. Ibid., 539.

61. Ibid., 705.

62. Ibid., 712.

63. Ibid., 751.

64. Ibid., 772.

65. Ibid., 805–807.

66. Ibid., 851.

67. Aristophanes *Knights* 45, *panourgotaton kai diabolōtaton.*

68. Ibid., 328–332.

69. Ibid., 1206, *Oimoi kakodiamōn hyperanaideuthēsomai.*

70. *Decameron* 1.29.

71. Molière, *Dom Juan* 1.1. Sganarelle continues, describing his master as "un enragé, un chien, un diable, un Turc, un hérétique, qui ne croit ni Ciel ni Enfer, ni loup-garou" (a madman, a dog, a devil, a Turk, a heretic who doesn't believe in Heaven or Hell or the Big Bad Wolf!).

72. *Jew of Malta* 939–941, 946–961.

73. For example, Barabas' hyperbolic allusions when discussing the poison for the nuns (1399). The characters in the subplot are also given to exaggeration; see Bellamira's boast that clients once came to her from as far as Padua and Venice (1155). Barabas' "aria of evil" can also be compared with the boasts of Lightbone in *Edward the Second* ("I learned in Naples how to poison flowers," 5.4.30–37, and others).

74. In significant contrast to his daughter's first words in the play, "Not for my selfe . . ." (462).

75. See Kellner, "Die Quelle," pp. 89–90.

76. *Jew of Malta* 1317.

77. Ibid., 1345.

78. Ibid., 1354–1355.

79. Ibid., 1418.

80. Ibid., 1626–1627.

81. Jonson, *Volpone* 5.1.30–31, 128.

82. *Jew of Malta* 2213.

83. Ibid., 2329–2330.

84. Ibid., 2370. See Eugene Waith, "Marlowe and the Jades of Asia," *Studies in English Literature* 6 (Spring 1965), 239.

85. See W. K. Wimsatt, "The Criticism of Comedy," in *Hateful Contraries* (Lexington, 1965), pp. 94–95.

86. "De l'essence du rire," in *Curiosités ésthétiques* (Paris, 1962), p. 256.

87. *Asinaria* 495.

16. Shakespeare: Errors and *Erōs*

1. Leo Salingar, *Shakespeare and the Traditions of Comedy* (Cambridge, 1974), p. 75.

2. Harold Bloom, *Shakespeare: The Invention of the Human* (London, 1999), p. 21; he continues: "[*Errors*] shows such skill, indeed mastery—in action, incipient character, and stagecraft—that it far outshines the three *Henry VI* plays and the rather lame *Two Gentlemen of Verona*." For the conventional evidence of the early dating, see, among others, R. A. Foakes's excellent Arden edition of *The Comedy of Errors* (Walton on Thames, 1962), p. xxiii. Kenneth Muir, *Shakespeare's Comic Sequence* (Liverpool, 1979), pp. 15–16, at first straddles the fence, saying: "The chronology of Shakespeare's early comedies is uncertain, but *The Comedy of Errors, The Two Gentlemen of Verona,* and *The Taming of the Shrew* (in whichever order) were the first three." He subsequently retreats to join the general consensus, conceding that "it seems probable, therefore, that the *Comedy of Errors* was the first to be written."

3. Northrop Frye, *A Natural Perspective: The Development of Shakespearean Comedy and Romance* (New York, 1965), p. 87.

4. Plautus *Menaechmi* 247.

5. The relevant New Testament passages are all printed in Appendix I of Foakes's edition.

6. *Comedy of Errors* 1.1.18–19.

7. Ibid., 1.1.51–52.

8. Ibid., 1.1.103–106.

9. Ibid., 1.1.97.

10. Ibid., 1.2.30.

11. Ibid., 1.2.35–38.

12. *Menaechmi* 1088–1090.

13. *Comedy of Errors* 1.2.39–40.

14. Ibid., 1.2.77–81.

15. Ibid., 1.2.45–46.

16. Ibid., 1.2.97–102.

17. *Menaechmi* 264, *nemo ferme huc sine damno devortitur*.

18. Acts 19.13–19.

19. Sonnet 1.1–2.

20. *Comedy of Errors* 2.1.7.

21. Ibid., 2.1.10.

22. Ibid., 2.1.18–24: "The beasts, the fishes, and the winged fouls / Are their males' subjects, and at their controls; / Man, more divine, the master of all these, / Lord of the wide world and wild wat'ry seas, / Indued with intellectual sense and souls, / Of more pre-eminence than fish and fowls, / Are masters to their females, and their lords . . ."

23. Ibid., 2.1.29. Compare Ephesians 5.22.

24. *Comedy of Errors* 2.1.96–99.

25. Ibid., 2.1.114–115.

26. Ibid., 2.2.110; 119–123.

27. *1 Henry 4* 5.1.126.

28. *Love's Labour's Lost* 5.1.17–22.

29. *Comedy of Errors* 1.1.51.

30. Ibid., 2.2.149.

31. Ibid., 3.1.97.

32. Ibid., 5.1.281.

33. Ibid., 5.1.296. The adjective "strange" and its verb "estrange" occur frequently in Shakespeare's first play, reinforcing the sense of enchantment and magic that pervades his Ephesus. *Strange* swells to a veritable tidal wave in *The Tempest*, his final play, where it occurs no fewer than 21 times. He is not using it in the familiar modern sense, but rather to denote something that contains a certain magic and wonder—most famously expressed: "Full fathom five thy father lies / Of his bones are coral made; /

Those are pearls that were his eyes: / Nothing of him that doth fade, / But doth suffer a sea-change / Into something *rich and strange*." (*The Tempest* 1.2.399–404.)

34. Ibid., 2.2.125–129.

35. *Romeo and Juliet* 2.2.133–135.

36. *Comedy of Errors* 2.2.148.

37. Ibid., 2.2.152.

38. These false but apt etymologies include *lucus ex non lucendo* ("glade from shade") or asparagus from "sparrow grass."

39. *Comedy of Errors* 2.2.182–184.

40. *Midsummer Night's Dream* 5.1.423–426.

41. *Comedy of Errors* 2.2.212–214.

42. See Leviticus 18.16.

43. Harry Levin, *Refractions: Essays in Comparative Literature* (Oxford, 1966), p. 130.

44. *Amphitruo* 456.

45. *Comedy of Errors* 3.1.44.

46. *Amphitruo* 423, *aliud nomen quarendum est mihi.*

47. *Comedy of Errors* 3.2.35.

48. Ibid., 3.2.39–40.

49. *Romeo and Juliet* 2.2.50.

50. *Comedy of Errors* 3.2.72–77.

51. Ibid., 3.2.131–138.

52. Ibid., 3.2.143.

53. Ibid., 3.2.179–180.

54. Ibid., 4.2.19–22.

55. *Menaechmi* 1039–1043; 1047.

56. *Comedy of Errors* 4.3.1–4; 10–11.

57. Ibid., 4.3.78–90.

58. Ibid., 4.4.90.

59. Ibid., 4.4.92.

60. Ibid., 5.1.45–46.

61. Ibid., 5.1.85–86.

62. Ibid., 5.1.270–271.

63. Ibid., 3.2.45–46.

64. Ibid., 5.1.287–288.

65. Ibid., 5.1.307–310.

66. Ibid., 5.1.331.

67. Ibid., 5.1.332–334.

68. Ibid., 5.1.400–402.

69. Foakes, *Comedy,* p. 106, calls attention to the arithmetic but omits mention of christological evidence.

70. Frye, *Perspective,* p. 107.

71. Another more remote possibility is that, as in a production of *Comedy of Errors* in Stratford, Connecticut, in the early 1960s, both Antipholi were played by the same actor. This worked without masks. If the same tactic was adopted in Shakespeare's version, one of the twins would have been doubled in the finale by an extra who, though dressed the same, was unable to speak lines.

72. On the reunion of twins see Frye, *Perspective,* p. 78: "When they meet they are delivered, in comic fashion, from the fear of the loss of identity, the primitive horror of the Doppelganger which is an element in nearly all forms of insanity, something of which they feel as long as they are being mistaken for each other."

73. *Pericles* 5.3.43–44.

17. *Twelfth Night:* Dark Clouds over Illyria

1. The title of the entire collection was *Riche His Farewell to Military Profession.* See also Kenneth Muir, *The Sources of Shakespeare's Plays* (London, 1977), pp. 136–138.

2. *Gallathea* 3.2.13–25. See also the plaint of Phillida at 3.2.1–5.

3. Compare the sexual pun on "will" in Sonnets 135.11–12: "Thou being rich in *Will,* add to thy *Will* / And one will of mine to make thee large *Will* more."

4. Occasionally "clever" modern directors have reversed the initial scenes of *Twelfth Night,* putting the appearance of Viola first and that of the lovesick Duke second. This is a monstrous distortion. If Shakespeare had wanted it this way he would have done so himself.

5. *Twelfth Night* 1.1.1–4.

6. See Eric Partridge, *Shakespeare's Bawdy²* (London, 1968): "Appetite," p. 58; "die," p. 93; "fall," p. 103; "play," p. 162; "surfeit," p. 195. For "appetite," see *Venus and Adonis* 34: "with leaden appetite, unapt to toy" (in other words, not keen to have sex); and Malvolio's "distempered appetite" below. There are those who balk at ascribing so many sexual innuendos to a melancholy nobleman and remind us that Orsino is not the clown whose stock in trade is bawdy language. These dissenters might cite Quintilian's castigation of Celsus' statement that there is a phallic innuendo at Vergil *Georgics* 1.356–357 (*freta ponti / incipiunt agitata tumescere,* "the stirred up sea begins to swell"). The schoolmaster scolds the encyclopedist: "If one accepts this far-fetched interpretation, then nothing is sacred" (*quod si recipias, nihil tutum est; Inst.* 7.3.47). On the other hand, there are those who believe that

even the Duke could speak in double-entendres—especially at the beginning of a play.

7. Critics are divided between those who regard the entire play and not merely the beginning as sad and elegiac, and those who generally view Illyria as a joyous, carefree place. Middleton Murray found in it Chekhovian melancholy. W. H. Auden viewed the playwright as "in no mood for comedy." Most optimistically, Northrop Frye finds in the play "the triumph of life over the wasteland." For the full spectrum of interpretations, see the excellent Arden edition of the play by J. M. Lothian and T. W. Craik (1976, repr. Walton-on-Thames, 1997), pp. l–lxi.

8. *Twelfth Night* 1.1.20–23.

9. St. Augustine *Confessions* 3.1.

10. The patron saint of lovers had already been established in England for at least a century.

11. *Twelfth Night* 1.1.27–30.

12. Recall how in *The Girl from Andros* the father is pleased by his son's tears at the death of a relative stranger: "how much more will his father's death affect him?" (110–112).

13. *Twelfth Night* 1.2.4–7.

14. Ibid., 1.2.15–16.

15. Herodotus 1.23–24, the first attestation of this story (which was adapted by Aulus Gellius and appended to editions of Aesop), mentions a single dolphin; Plutarch has a school (*Moralia* 160e–162b).

16. *Twelfth Night* 1.2.42.

17. Ibid., 1.2.53–56.

18. Although there are extant musical settings for Shakespeare's lyrics as far back as the seventeenth century (including those by Henry Purcell), none of the original songs has survived. For a complete listing of musical compositions related to this and other plays, see *A Shakespeare Music Catalogue,* ed. Bryan N. S. Gooch and David Thatcher, 5 vols. (Oxford, 1991). For a splendid discussion of music and its imagery in Shakespeare, see John Hollander, *The Untuning of the Sky* (New York, 1970).

19. See M. C. Bradbrook, *Shakespeare the Craftsman* (1969), p. 233, as quoted in *Shakespeare: Twelfth Night,* ed. D. J. Palmer (Basingstoke, 1972).

20. *Twelfth Night* 1.3.126–128. The joke is bilingual, and refers to the *cinque pace,* a five-step dance like the Galliard.

21. Ibid., 1.3.2.

22. Ibid., 1.3.26–27.

23. Ibid., 1.3.90–92.

24. Ibid., 1.4.13–14.

25. Ibid., 1.4.31–34.

26. Sonnet 20.1–2. It closes suggestively: "But since Nature prick'd thee out for women's pleasure / Mine be thy love, and thy love's use their treasure."

27. For this liking of ambiguity, compare Anacreon frag. 360.1–2 (Page): "O lad, your virgin eyes" (ō pai parthenion blepōn); and Horace *Odes* 2.5.21–4 with the notes of R. G. M. Nisbet and M. E. Hubbard, *Odes Book 2* (Oxford, 1970).

28. *Twelfth Night* 1.4.40–42.

29. Ibid., 1.5.4–6.

30. Ibid., 1.5.19.

31. Leslie Hotson, *The First Night of Twelfth Night* (London, 1954), p. 168.

32. Elena Glazov-Corrigan, "The Clown as a Form-Creating Principle in the Shakespearean Corpus," in *Laughter Down the Centuries*, vol. 3, ed. Siegfried Jäkel, Asko Timonen, and Veli-Matti Rissanen (Turku, 1997), pp. 131–139, quotation from p. 134. As she explains, "the position of the clown vis-à-vis the rest of the play shows the raw mixture of the two separate public forms of entertainment, namely, one form involving a theatrical troupe narrating a story with a beginning, middle and end, and the other involving the clown, the most popular market entertainer resistant by his very calling to any imposed structure" (p. 134).

33. Muir, *Sources,* p. 138, notes that Malvolio's name was probably suggested by the phrase *mala voglia,* which recurs frequently in Bandello's version of the story.

34. *Twelfth Night* 1.5.158–160.

35. Ibid., 1.5.89–90.

36. Ibid., 1.5.237–241.

37. Sonnet 1.1–4.

38. *Twelfth Night* 2.4.38–39.

39. Aristophanes *Lysistrata* 596–597.

40. Garcilaso de la Vega, Sonnet 23.

41. *Twelfth Night* 2.1.24–31.

42. Ibid., 2.2.16; 25.

43. Ibid., 3.4.55.

44. Ibid., 2.2.32–38.

45. Ibid., 2.3.48–53.

46. *1 Henry 4* 1.2.1, 6–12.

47. *Twelfth Night* 2.3.86–93.

48. Ibid., 2.3.114–115.

49. Ibid., 2.3.163.

50. Ibid., 2.4.26.

51. Ibid., 2.4.27; 30.

52. Ibid., 2.4.50–53.

53. *Much Ado About Nothing* 5.2.99–101.

54. *Twelfth Night* 2.4.107–109.

55. Ibid., 2.4.111–116.

56. Ibid., 2.4.120–121.

57. *As You Like It* 4.1.106–108.

58. See Michael Mangan, *A Preface to Shakespeare's Comedies 1594–1603* (London, 1996), p. 235.

59. H. Levin, *Shakespeare and the Revolution of the Times: Perspectives and Commentaries* (New York, 1976), p. 141.

60. *Twelfth Night* 2.5.32.

61. Ibid., 2.5.42.

62. Ibid., 2.5.73.

63. Ibid., 2.5.87–90.

64. As the editors of the Arden Shakespeare note, there is no "C" or "P" in Olivia's name. The joke may be based either on the Latin *cunnus* or the word "cut" in the sense of a geological declivity. (*O.E.D.,* "cut" 2.21b). But another reading supplies the "N" out of "and." In Dutch, the part in question is known as *kut, kont* meaning the "backside" (like "fanny" in American versus British English).

65. Nevertheless, a great deal of effort has been spent in deciphering the puzzle. See for example Peter J. Smith, "M.O.A.I.: 'What should that alphabetical position portend?' An Answer to the Metamorphic Malvolio," *Renaissance Quarterly* 51 (1998), 1199–1224, which reviews earlier treatments.

66. *Twelfth Night* 2.5.132–134.

67. Ibid., 3.1.135–138.

68. Ibid., 3.1.149.

69. Ibid., 3.1.160–162.

70. Ibid., 3.2.34.

71. Ibid., 3.3.19.

72. Ibid., 3.4.46–54.

73. Ibid., 3.4.55.

74. Ibid., 3.4.144.

75. C. L. Barber, *Shakespeare's Festive Comedy: A Study of Dramatic Form and its Relation to Social Custom* (Princeton, 1959), p. 120.

76. *Twelfth Night* 3.4.119–120.

77. Ibid., 3.4.226–227; 254–255.

78. Ibid., 3.4.307–308.

79. While Lothian and Craik concede a sexual innuendo in *The Merchant of Venice* 3.4.60–63, they do not acknowledge one here.

80. *Your Own Thing* made theatrical history for being the first off-Broadway production to be favored over current Broadway productions for the Drama Critics Circle award, as reported in "Broadway Calendar: June 1, 1967 through May 31, 1968" (New York, 1968).

81. Barber, *Shakespeare's Festive Comedy*, p. 245.

82. *Twelfth Night* 3.4.375–378.

83. Ibid., 3.4.384–385; 389–390.

84. Ibid., 3.4.392–394.

85. Ibid., 4.1.26.

86. Ibid., 4.1.48–51.

87. Ibid., 4.1.56–59.

88. Ibid., 4.3.234.

89. *As You Like It* 3.5.82.

90. *Twelfth Night* 5.1.74–77.

91. Ibid., 5.1.207.

92. Ibid., 5.1.214–215.

93. Ibid., 5.1.263.

94. Ibid., 5.1.230–231.

95. Ibid., 5.1.257–258.

96. Shakespeare actually uses this bit of doggerel twice, in *Love's Labour's Lost* (5.2.875) and *Midsummer Night's Dream* (3.2.461).

97. *Twelfth Night* 5.1.265–266; 270–271.

98. Northrop Frye, "The Mythos of Spring," in *The Anatomy of Criticism* (Princeton, 1957), p. 165.

99. *Twelfth Night* 5.1.377.

100. *Much Ado About Nothing* 2.3.242.

101. *Twelfth Night* 5.1.388–391.

102. *Romeo and Juliet* 2.4.93.

103. *Twelfth Night* 5.1.404–407.

104. See Partridge, *Shakespeare's Bawdy*[2], p. 171, citing for example *Midsummer's Night Dream* (1.1.128–130):

> LYSANDER: How now, my love! Why is your cheek so pale?
> How chance the roses that do fade so fast?
> HERMIA: Belike for want of rain.

105. Hotson, *The First Night*, p. 171.

106. 1 Corinthians 13.11.

107. S. Freud, "Jokes and Their Relation to the Unconscious" (1905), vol. 8 (1905), p. 236.

18. Molière: The Class of '68

1. Raymond Fernandez, *Molière: The Man Seen Through the Plays*, trans. Wilson Follet (New York, 1958), p. 172.

2. Victor Hugo, *Préface de Cromwell*.

3. P. Pichout, J. D. Guelfi, and C. Hakim, *La Personalité*, vol. 3: *Pathologie* (Paris, 1973). Excerpted in Molière, *Le Malade imaginaire*, ed. Cécile Pellissier-Intartaglia and Marc Vuillermoz (Paris, 1997), p. 192.

4. Patrick Danchey devotes hundreds of pages to Molière's sad condition in *La Médecine et la mélancolie dans le théâtre de Molière*. Vol. 1: *Sganarelle et la médecine ou De la mélancolie érotique*. Vol. 2: *Molière de la maladie imaginaire ou De la mélancolie hypocondriaque* (Paris, 1998).

5. Aulus Gellius *N.A.* 2.23.12.

6. Nicolas Boileau Despréaux, *Art poétique* (1674), 3.

7. Paul Bénichou, *Morales du Grand Siècle* (Paris, 1948, repr. 1967), p. 263. He adds further that "his silly or hateful characters are always all associated with a certain bourgeois vulgarity. That is not surprising considering Molière's milieu."

8. "My conclusion is this: I am certain that Armande was Madeleine's daughter, that her birth was secret, in an unknown place, and from an unknown father. There is no convincing proof that the rumors of incest were justified and that Molière married his daughter. But neither is there any evidence to disprove this terrible rumor." Mikhail Bulgakov, *Life of Monsieur de Molière*, trans. Mirra Ginsburg (New York, 1970), pp. 145–149, quotation from p. 148.

9. See for example the discussion in W. G. Moore, *Molière: A New Criticism* (Oxford, 1949; repr. Garden City, New York, 1962), esp. p. 4, n. 9, who deals with the whole controversy.

10. Aulus Gellius *N.A.* 20.4.1. Gellius also cites pseudo-Aristotle *Problems* 30.10 (96b12–16), where we find a similar outlook on the morals of players.

11. Athenaeus *Deipnosophistae* 12.535a.

12. Some biographers report that Molière himself was romantically involved with one of his male actors, but *pudeur* causes most to ignore this. Even if true, this would hardly alleviate Molière's agony over his wife's antics.

13. See, for example, the introduction to the play in the Pléiade edition, *Oeuvres complètes*, ed. Georges Couton (Paris, 1971), vol. 2, pp. 249–357.

14. This penchant for special effects dates back to 1645, when Giacomo Terelli, the famous Italian designer and painter, was invited to contribute

his talents and knowledge of stage machinery to further delight the French audiences.

15. Prologue to *Amphitryon* 91–92.

16. Ibid., 66–69.

17. *Amphitryon* 1.2.349–351.

18. Plautus *Amphitruo* 423, *aliud nomen quaerundum est mihi.*

19. *Amphitryon* 1.2.424–427; 430–431.

20. Ibid., 1.4.648–651.

21. Ibid., 2.1.746–748.

22. Ibid., 2.1.796–798.

23. Henri Bergson, *Le Rire: Essai sur la signification du comique* (Paris, 1940; repr. 1969), p. 56.

24. *Amphitryon* 2.2.899–900.

25. Ibid., 2.2.941.

26. Ibid., 2.2.1016–1022.

27. This was also Jocasta's advice to Oedipus in Sophocles (*Oedipus Rex* 1056–1072); women, like servants, are permitted unheroic common sense.

28. *Amphitryon* 2.6.1304–1307.

29. Ibid., 2.6.1408–1409.

30. Ibid., 3.1.1470–1475.

31. Ibid., 3.2.1550–1555.

32. Ibid., 3.3.1559–1560.

33. Ibid., 3.5.1617–1618.

34. Ibid., 3.5.1644–1645.

35. Ibid., 3.5.1703–1704.

36. Ibid., 3.7.1860–1861.

37. Ibid., 3.10.1898–1899.

38. Rotrou, *Les sosies* 5.5.1761–1766. Text of Jean de Rotrou from *Les sosies,* ed. Damien Charron (Geneva, 1980).

39. *Amphitryon* 3.5.1942–1943.

40. During the Third Republic, presidents "gilded the bitter pill" for "philosophical" husbands with the Légion d'Honneur.

41. In Rotrou, "this blameless princess has given birth to two sons" (5.5.1704).

42. Boccaccio, *Decameron* 4.7.

43. "Dandin" means "nincompoop."

44. *George Dandin* 1.1.

45. Ibid., 1.2.

46. Ibid., 1.3.

47. Ibid., 1.4.

48. Ibid.

49. Ibid.
50. Ibid., 1.6.
51. Ibid.
52. Ibid.
53. Ibid.
54. Ibid., 1.7.
55. Ibid., 2.2.
56. Ibid.
57. Ibid., 2.6.
58. Ibid., 3.6.
59. Ibid., 3.8.
60. Not divorce in the modern sense, but a judicial separation or an annulment on theological grounds.
61. Fernandez, *Molière*, p. 203, believes that "*The Miser* is the least original of Molière's great plays. There is scarcely a scene that is not borrowed from Plautus or the skits of the *Commedia dell'arte*, from Ariosto, Larivey or Bois-Robert."
62. *L'Avare* 1.2.
63. Northrop Frye, *The Anatomy of Criticism* (Princeton, 1957), pp. 164–165.
64. *L'Avare* 2.4.
65. Another instance of Bergson's theory that laughter is born of repetition of "an anesthesia of the heart" can be found in a dialogue between the protagonist of *Tartuffe* and Dorine. When the maid tries to tell him of his wife's recent illness, he is so obsessed with his spiritual adviser's welfare that he cannot pay attention to what she is saying:

> DORINE: Your wife had awful fever, sad to say,
>   It was so bad she stayed in bed all day.
> ORGON: What about Tartuffe?
> DORINE: Tartuffe? Why Sir, *he's* fat and fine,
>   he gorged himself on lots of food and wine.
> ORGON: *(sighing)* poor chap!

66. *L'Avare* 3.1.
67. Menander *Dyskolos* 6, *apanthrōpos tis anthrōpos.*
68. *L'Avare* 2.4.
69. Bergson, *Le Rire*, p. 53.
70. *L'Avare* 1.3.
71. Ibid., 1.4.
72. Ibid.

73. Immanuel Kant, "Critique of Pure Reason," in *Gesammelte Schriften* (Berlin, 1908), Part One: Vol. 5, pp. 334–335.
74. *L'Avare* 1.4.
75. Ibid., 1.4.
76. Ibid., 2.1, *mon père est mon rival.*
77. Ibid., 1.4.
78. Ibid., *Voilà qui est fait.*
79. Ibid., 1.5.
80. Ibid., 2.1.
81. Michel de Montaigne, *Essais,* 2.8, "De l'affection de pères aux enfants" (Paris, 1834), pp. 214–216 and passim.
82. Ovid *Metamorphoses* 1.128–143.
83. Charles Mauron, *Psychocritique du genre comique* (Paris, 1964), p. 61. He further notes that the nuance of incest is still omnipresent, but the guilt is displaced onto the old man who is vaguely suspected of wanting to marry a young girl who could perhaps be his own daughter.
84. *L'Avare* 2.2.
85. Plautus *Mercator* 425–427.
86. *L'Avare* 2.5.
87. Ibid.
88. Aristophanes *Wasps* 1352–1353.
89. *L'Avare* 4.2.
90. Ibid., 4.3.
91. Jean-Jacques Rousseau, "Lettre à d'Alembert sur les spectacles" (1758).
92. *L'Avare* 4.7.
93. Ibid.
94. Ibid.
95. Ibid., 5.1.
96. There are numerous *quiproquos* in Molière. Perhaps the most notorious is in *School for Wives.* The elderly hero is so desperate to know what occurred between his ward (whom he was grooming as a bride) and Horace, her new young suitor, that he cannot let the girl finish her sentence: "He took my—". This evokes all sorts of erotic possibilities, and yet it turns out that the young man had taken nothing more than her little ribbon.
97. Plautus *Aulularia* 731–761.
98. *L'Avare* 5.3.
99. Ibid.
100. Ibid.
101. Ibid., 5.5.

102. Ibid.

103. Ibid. The reference is to the Neapolitan revolt led by the fisherman Masaniello in 1647. He was already a subject of dramatic representation by 1682.

104. Ibid., 5.6.

105. Mauron, *Psychocritique*, p. 51. Mauron contrasts the taboos of Aristophanes and Molière. The Greek playwright had complete liberty to deal with subjects which were totally off-limits for the Frenchman, namely modesty, political power, and religion. By contrast, Aristophanes was unable to mock a deceived husband, a theme with which medieval farce teems.

106. The (anonymous) editor of the play notes in the Seuil edition, *Oeuvres Complètes* (Paris, 1962), p. 112, that contemporary critics regarded it as Molière's best play—it especially pleased the king. See also Andrew Calder, *Molière: The Theory and Practice of Comedy* (London, 1993), p. 28.

107. *Sganarelle* 349–353.

108. Ibid., 14.653–657.

109. *L'École des maris* 1051–1052.

110. André Gide, *Journal*, ed. Martine Sagaert, 2 vols. (Paris, 1997), vol. 2, p. 766 (entry for 2 July 1941).

111. *Le Malade imaginaire* 3.12.

112. Compare Tom Stoppard's parody of this sentiment in *Rosenkrantz and Guildenstern Are Dead:* "The bad end unhappily, the good unluckily. That is what tragedy means."

19. The Fox, the Fops, and the Factotum

1. Hobbes, *Leviathan*, quoted by W. K. Wimsatt, "The Criticism of Comedy," in *Hateful Contraries* (Lexington, 1965), pp. 91, 94–95.

2. See "Ungathered Verse," 25, the introduction to Shakespeare's First Folio, at the very beginning "to the reader": "This Figure, that thou here seest put, / It was for *gentle* Shakespeare cut." And then at 26 in his famous dedicatory Epistle: "Yet I must give not give Nature all: Thy Art, / My gentle Shakespeare, must enjoy a part." Nevertheless we should not ignore Ian Donaldson's astute reminder that in the age of Jonson and Shakespeare the word "gentle" was also used to convey fluidity, as of a river. See *Jonson's Magic Houses: Essays in Interpretation* (Oxford, 1997), p. 20.

3. Drayton, "To Henry Reynolds, Of Poet and Poesy": "Learn'd Jonson in this list I bring / who had drunk deep of the Pierian spring." Compare Milton's phraseology in "L'Allegro," 131–134: "Then to the well-trod stage anon, / If Jonson's learnèd Sock be on, / Or sweetest Shakespeare fancy's child, / Warble his native Wood-notes wild."

4. Samuel Johnson, "Prologue Spoken by Mr. Garrick at the Opening of the Theatre in Drury Lane" (1747), reprinted in *Samuel Johnson on Shakespeare,* ed. W. K. Wimsatt (New York, 1960), p. 1.

5. See John Dryden's "Essay of Dramatick Poesie" (1668), as reprinted, for example, in Barrett H. Clark, *European Theories of the Drama,* rev. Henry Popkin (New York, 1965), p. 133. The critique continues, "If Horace, Lucan, Petronius Arbiter, Seneca, and Juvenal, had their own from him, there are few serious thoughts which are new in him . . . I loved their fashion, when he wore their cloths."

6. Edmund Wilson, "Morose Ben Jonson," in *The Triple Thinkers* (London, 1952), p. 207.

7. See for example *Epicoene* 4.4.139.

8. Ibid., 5.4.41-44.

9. *Epicoene or The Silent Woman,* ed. R. V. Holdsworth (London, 1979), p. xxviii. He continues: "Comedy conventionally leads its characters from sorrow to joy, reuniting couples and families, achieving the triumph of young lovers over the opposition of crabbed age, reaffirming the harmony of the social group through the defeat of splintering, antisocial forces. Its ending is usually a celebration of this new sense of human order and wholeness, symbolized by a dance, a feast, and, almost always, a marriage. *Epicoene* negates this pattern; lack, loss, and disharmony are the qualities it affirms."

10. Rowe picked up Dryden's laudatory poem to the bard: "*Shakespear,* who, taught by none, did first impart / To *Fletcher* Wit, to Lab'ring *Johnson* [*sic*] Art . . . / But *Shakespear's* Magick could not copied be, / Within that Circle none durst walk but he." Reprinted in Frank Kermode, *Four Centuries of Shakespearian Criticism* (New York, 1965), p. 55.

11. See Kermode, *Four Centuries,* pp. 74-100 (Johnson); pp. 108-111 (Schlegel).

12. See for example Donaldson, *Jonson's Magic Houses,* p. 44, who points out that "the notion of Jonson's warfare with Shakespeare, and of his moroseness, malignity and envy, was . . . an eighteenth century invention, an intrinsic part of the simultaneous construction of the modern idea of Shakespeare."

13. Induction to *Bartholomew Fair* (1614), ed. E. A. Horsman (London, 1960), lines 130-132.

14. M. Chute, *Ben Jonson of Westminster* (New York, 1953), p. 88.

15. See Anne Barton, *Ben Jonson: Dramatist* (Cambridge, 1984), pp. 29-32.

16. Jonson, *Conversations with William Drummond of Hawthornden* (1618), in *Ben Jonson,* ed. C. H. Herford and Percy and Evelyn Simpson (Oxford, 1941-1947), vol. 8, pp. 420-430.

17. H. C. Knutson, *The Triumph of Wit: Molière and Restoration Comedy* (Columbus, 1988), p. 10, notes that all of the Restoration comedies (with the exception of two by Farquhar) are set in contemporary London.

18. *The Alchemist* 1.1.1–3. This is far from the only example of "bathroom" humor in Jonson. Take for example the quite revealing instance when Sir Epicure Mammon fantasizes that when he is enriched by the philosopher's stone, there will be in his retinue great poets like "the same that writ so subtly of the fart . . ." And there is the childishly gross exchange in *Epicoene* (4.5.133–135):

    TRUE-WIT: Whether were you going?
    LA-FOOLE: Down into the court, to make water.
    TRUE-WIT: By no means, sir, you shall rather tempt your breeches.

    We should recall that anal erotic types are preoccupied with such unsavory topics.

19. And yet one might adduce the suggestive allusions in the Latin lesson given by the parson Sir Hugh Evans to young William in *Merry Wives of Windsor* (4.1), although surely his reference to the "focative case," among other mistranslations, would be lost on most of the spectators, as would Evans' further explanation that "the focative is *caret*," punning on "carrot," then a synonym for penis. But somehow none of these allusions—compiled so exhaustively by Eric Partridge in *Shakespeare's Bawdy*[2] (London, 1968)—seem nearly as crude in the mouths of Shakespeare's characters, whereas Jonson's vulgarities seem truly vulgar.

20. *Epicoene or The Silent Woman* 1.4.71:

    CLERIMONT: Did you ever hear such a wind-fucker, as this?

21. Prologue to *The Alchemist* 5–8.

22. This continued throughout their careers. Jonson produced his scathing satire *Epicoene* in the same year (1609) that Shakespeare presented his gentle *Cymbeline*.

23. Jonson, "Timber or Discoveries Made Upon Men and Matter," in Herford and Simpson, *Ben Jonson*, vol. 8, p. 583.

24. *Epicoene* 2.2.114.

25. Although some literal-minded litterateurs have proposed other candidates for "tother youth," Donaldson, *Magic Houses,* 8–25, argues convincingly that the reference is to Shakespeare.

26. Drummond was not a friendly interlocutor, noting that Jonson was "a great lover and praiser of himself, a contemner and Scorner of others, given rather to lose a friend, than a Jest" (Jonson, *Conversations,* 680–689).

27. Robert Greene in *A Groatsworth of Wit Bought with A Million of Repentance* (1592). The full quotation is: "For there is an upstart crow, beautified with our feathers, that with his tiger's heart wrapped in a player's hide, supposes he is as well able to bombast out a blank verse as the best of you; and being an absolute Johannes fac totum, is in his own conceit the only Shake-scene in our country."

28. Prologue to *Volpone* 31–32.

29. *Twelfth Night* 2.3.93.

30. Prologue to *Every Man in His Humour* 21–24. Cicero's definition is preserved by Euanthius *De Comoedia* I (p. 22 Wessner): "[Comedy is]: an imitation of life, a mirror of customs and the image of truth."

31. Levin, *Grounds,* p. 48.

32. One scholar describes him as: "Boisterous, energetic, witty, fond of drink, competitive to the point of hating all rivals and violent enough to kill, he was at the same time a meticulous scholar, a classicist and a literary and moral authoritarian." *The Revels: History of Drama in English. Volume 3, 1576–1613,* ed. Clifford Leech and T. W. Craik (London, 1975), p. 327.

33. The term commonly refers to Psalm 50.3 in the Vulgate, 51.1 in Protestant versions.

34. Chute, *Ben Jonson,* p. 60.

35. Some scholars have mistakenly asserted that Jonson was actually *the* Master of the Revels. But although he never quite achieved the post—nor the knighthood rumored to be in store for him—he was undisputedly held in great royal favor during the last decades of his life. It would have been a brilliant career if the man who began his career as a jailbird had concluded it as an important courtier. See Richard Dutton, *Mastering the Revels: The Regulation and Censorship of English Renaissance Drama* (Basingstoke, 1991), pp. 220–222 and passim.

36. Jonson, *Eupheme* 4, "The Mind" (1640).

37. Cratinus frag. 203 K.-A.

38. Horace *Epistles* 1.1.65–66: *rem facias, rem, / si possis recte, si non, quocumque modo rem.*

39. *Every Man in His Humour* 2.5.48–49.

40. L. C. Knights, *Drama and Society in the Age of Jonson* (London, 1937), pp. 121–122.

41. *The Alchemist* 2.1.1–5.

42. S. Musgrove, "Tragical Mirth: *King Lear* and *Volpone,*" in *Jonson Volpone: A Casebook,* ed. Jonas A. Barish (London, 1972), pp. 118–132, quotation from p. 118.

43. *King Lear* 1.1.114. Musgrove, "Tragical Mirth," pp. 120–121, even finds verbal echoes of *Lear* in *Hymenaei,* a masque Jonson wrote about the same time.

He further notes that "nature" and "monster" sound through both plays "like the tolling of a bell" (p. 124).

44. *King Lear* 4.2.49–50.

45. *Volpone* 5.2.10.

46. *Jew of Malta* 1.1.25–27.

47. *Volpone* 1.1.10–15.

48. *Paradise Lost* 3.1–3.

49. *Volpone* 1.1.85–87.

50. See Pindar *Olympian* 1.1–2: "As precious as water, gold, like a shooting star at night—shines more brightly than all other noble wealth."

51. *Volpone* 1.1.16–18.

52. Norman O. Brown, *Life Against Death: The Psychoanalytical Meaning of History* (New York, 1959), p. 67.

53. *Volpone* 1.1.30–31.

54. Ibid., 1.1.73–75.

55. Ibid., 1.1.86.

56. According to the contemporary Italian-English dictionary of John Florio, *A Worlde of Wordes* (1598).

57. Florio adds "of a ravens nature or colour."

58. T. S. Eliot, "Ben Jonson," in *Selected Essays 1917–1932* (London, 1932), p. 154.

59. G. Gregory Smith, *Ben Jonson* (London, 1919), p. 110.

60. *Volpone* 1.4.142–143.

61. As one commentator has suggested, the learned Jonson may be making an obscure reference to describe Celia's innocence, that "O' the first year" may be an allusion to Leviticus 9 and the sacrificial lamb who must be "without blemish." Is not Celia such a victim?

62. *Volpone* 1.5.107–112.

63. "A Celebration of Charis: The Underwood" (spelling modernized).

64. *Volpone* 1.5.114.

65. Ibid., 2.4.22–24.

66. Ibid., 2.4.34–35.

67. But of course, "the monarch knew her not" (Kings 1.1.1–4).

68. Lupo (the wolf) is possibly a contemporary allusion to Doctor Rodrigo Lopez, the crypto-Jewish physician who was hanged in 1594 for allegedly plotting to kill Queen Elizabeth I.

69. *Volpone* 3.4.51–54; 56.

70. Ibid., 3.7.38–40.

71. *1 Henry 4* 5.1.134–140.

72. *Volpone* 3.7.93–95.

73. Ibid., 3.7.145–146.

74. Ibid., 3.7.158.
75. Ibid., 3.7.166–167; 172–173, translating Catullus 5.
76. Ibid., 3.7.191–196. "Lollia Paulina" is a learned reference to the Emperor Caligula's wife, who was famous for her bejeweled, dazzling outfits (see for example Pliny *N.H.* 9.117).
77. *Volpone* 3.7.221–225.
78. Holdsworth, *Epicoene,* p. xxix, has also observed that no character in that play engages in conventional sex. And yet, as he notes, "a pervading concern is sexual decorum."
79. *Volpone* 4.5.110–111.
80. Ibid., 4.4.23–29.
81. Ibid., 5.1.10–11.
82. Ibid., 5.3.74–76.
83. Ibid., 5.5.17.
84. Ibid., 5.12.89–90.
85. Ibid., 5.12.101–102.
86. Ibid., 5.12.132–133.
87. Ibid., 5.12.124.
88. Donaldson, *Magic Houses,* p. 123.
89. In Dryden's "Introduction" to *An Evening of Love,* he cites Quintilian in Latin (of course), "non displicuisse illi jocos, sed non contigisse": the quotation is from Quintilian's *Institutio Oratoria* 6.3.2.
90. Information for this section was drawn from *The Revels: History of Drama in English. Volume 4, 1613–1660,* ed. Philip Edwards et al. (London, 1981).
91. Before: *The Wits* (1634); during: operas like the *Siege of Rhodes* (1656); after: adaptations of Shakespeare's plays, for example, the *Tempest* with Dryden (1667) and *Macbeth* (1673).
92. See for example Harry William Pedicord, "The Changing Audience," in *The London Theatre World, 1660–1800,* ed. Robert D. Hume (Carbondale, 1980), p. 239. And even more recently Anne Jennalie Cook, *The Privileged Playgoers of Shakespeare's London, 1576–1642* (Princeton, 1987), has argued that *all* classes of society attended the Elizabethan theater as well. In fact, "the privileged probably dominated the huge public theaters as well" (p. 9).
93. Prologue to *Marriage-à-la-Mode* 37.
94. See *Oxford English Dictionary*² (Oxford, 1987), s.v. "city," 5b.
95. Knutson, *Triumph of Wit,* p. 29. Also in his prologue to *Marriage-à-la-Mode,* Dryden alludes to the three significant social groups who composed his audience: "the Town, the City, and the Court."
96. Ovid *Ars amatoria* 1.99–100.

97. Prologue to *The Plain Dealer,* 11–12.
98. The first recorded use of this sporting term is in 1703. See *O.E.D.*[2], s.v. "prize fighter."
99. The information in this paragraph owes much to John Harold Wilson, *A Preface to Restoration Drama* (Boston, 1965), pp. 36–38.
100. See also *2 Henry 6* 4.2.68, and the exchange between Hal and Poins in *2 Henry 4* 2.2.6–12:

> PRINCE: Doth it not show vildly to desire small beer?
> POINS: Why, a prince should not be so loosely studied as to remember
>   so weak a composition.
> PRINCE: Belike then my appetite was not princely got, for, by my troth. I
>   do now remember the poor creature, small beer.

101. *1 Henry 4* 2.4.540–541.
102. *The Plain Dealer* 5.2.
103. Levin, *Grounds,* p. 190, viewed the playwright as the central figure in the transition from Elizabethan sonnet to Jacobean satire—and more significantly the midpoint of comedy's evolution from the festivity of Plautus to the cold cynicism of the Restoration.
104. *Epicoene* 2.2.28–36.
105. Cook, *The Privileged Playgoers,* p. 157.
106. "Where they have no social freedom, Comedy is absent: where they are household drudges, the form of comedy is primitive: where they are tolerably independent, but uncultivated, exciting melodrama takes its place and a sentimental version of them . . . But where women are on the road to an equal footing with men . . . pure Comedy flourishes, and is, as it would help them to be, the sweetest of diversions, the wisest of delightful companions." George Meredith, "An Essay on Comedy and the Uses of the Comic Spirit" (1877, repr. New York, 1897), pp. 54–55.
107. Boswell, *London Journal,* entry for Saturday, 18 December 1762.
108. See Elizabeth Howe, *The First English Actresses: Women and Drama 1660–1700* (Cambridge, 1992), pp. 16–17 and passim.
109. See Gerald Eades Bentley, *Shakespeare and Jonson: Their Reputations in the Seventeenth Century Compared* (Chicago, 1945), p. 138.
110. Northrop Frye, *The Anatomy of Criticism* (Princeton, 1957), p. 181.
111. Wycherley wrote four plays and retired from the stage to spend the rest of his life in penury and debauchery.
112. *The Plain Dealer* 2.1.384–386.
113. *The Country Wife,* ed. James Ogden (London, 1991), p. xxxiii.
114. Hazelton Spencer, *Shakespeare Improved* (Cambridge, Mass., 1927), p. 75.

115. *Country Wife* 1.1.164.
116. Ibid., 1.1.169–170.
117. "The Miller's Tale," 3221–3226; 3230–3232.
118. *School for Wives* 1.1.76–80.
119. *Country Wife* 1.1.457–458.
120. In its way the portrait of contemporary arranged marriages is also in the mainstream of comic literature, recalling that all-important rule of the triumph of nature as later epitomized by Figaro's concluding remarks to Doctor Bartholo in Beaumarchais' *Barber of Seville* (1775):

> FIGARO: Let's be frank, doctor: when youth and love combine to trick an oldster, whatever he may do to try and avoid it may rightfully be called *A Useless Precaution*.

121. *Country Wife* 2.1.10.
122. Ibid., 2.1.20–21.
123. Ibid., 2.1.56–58.
124. Ibid., 2.1.80.
125. Ibid., 2.1.113.
126. Ibid., 2.1.234.
127. Ibid., 2.1.237–240.
128. Ibid., 2.1.287–288.
129. Ibid., 2.1.315.
130. Norman N. Holland, *The First Modern Comedies: The Significance of Etherege, Wycherley and Congreve* (Bloomington, 1959), p. 75.
131. *Country Wife* 2.1.438.
132. Ibid., 2.1.420.
133. Ibid., 2.1.434–435.
134. *Tartuffe* 4.5.
135. *Country Wife* 2.1.579–581.
136. Ibid., 2.1.602–603.
137. Ibid., 3.2.399–400.
138. Ibid., 2.1.609–610.
139. Ibid., 3.2.559.
140. Ibid., 3.2.560–561.
141. Ibid., 3.2.604–605.
142. As Ogden, *Country Wife*, comments ad loc., "the phrase links the bawdy association of oranges and china." Ironically, china shops were a favorite meeting place for lovers' assignations.
143. *Country Wife* 4.2.36–37.
144. Ibid., 4.2.92–96.

145. *Volpone* 3.100–105.
146. *Country Wife* 4.2.109–110.
147. Ibid., 4.3.50.
148. Ibid., 4.3.67–69.
149. Ibid., 4.3.77.
150. Ibid., 4.3.86.
151. Ibid., 4.3.131–132.
152. Ibid., 4.3.190–193; 196.
153. For example (4.3.194–204):

MRS. SQUEAMISH: Nay, nay I have known you deny your china before now, but you shan't put me off so. Come.

HORNER: This lady had the last there.

LADY FIDGET: Yes indeed, madam, to my certain knowledge he has no more left.

MRS. SQUEAMISH: Oh, but it may be he may have some you could not find.

LADY FIDGET: What, d'ye think if he had any left I would not have had it too? For we women of quality never think we have enough china.

HORNER: Do not take it ill, I cannot make china for you all, but I will have a roll-wagon for you too, another time.

154. *Country Wife* 4.3.233.
155. *The Plain Dealer* 2.1.422–434.
156. *Country Wife* 4.3.309–312.
157. See for example *Country Wife* 4.4.44, 5.1.4, on which Holland, *The First Modern Comedies,* p. 75, comments: "Wycherley, of course, had not read Freud: we cannot expect that he was aware of the overtones of swords and knives. Nevertheless, his insight here is brilliant."
158. *Country Wife* 4.4.1–7.
159. Ibid., 5.1.82–83.
160. Ibid., 5.2.73.
161. Ibid., 5.2.110–111.
162. Ibid., 5.3.69–71.
163. Ibid., 5.3.76. See *O.E.D².*, s.v. "servant," 3b, which cites, among others, Ben Jonson, *Every Man and His Humour* (4.2): "servant in troth you are too prodigal Of your wits treasure, thus to powre it forth Upon . . . my worth."
164. *Country Wife* 5.4.1–2.
165. Ibid., 5.4.329–332.
166. Ibid., 5.4.364–365.
167. Ibid., 5.4.372.
168. Ibid., 5.4.376–377.
169. Ibid., 5.4.394–407.

170. Ibid., 5.4.409–410.
171. Ibid., 5.4.425–426.
172. *Amphitryon* 2.3.1079–1080.
173. Figaro speaks (1.2) of his experience in Madrid in the "republic of letters," which he describes as "a pack of wolves, constantly at each other's throats . . . a bunch of insects, flies, gnats, mosquitoes, critics [as we shall see, "critic" is also a term of abuse in Beckett], jealous journalists . . . [who] suck the blood out of all writers—if they have any left." This long description of his picaresque adventures in the *Barber* anticipates his tirade in favor of the equality of man in 5.1, cited below, where he also reviews his checkered career.
174. Northrop Frye, "The Argument of Comedy," in *English Institute Essays, 1948* (New York, 1949), p. 74.
175. *Epidicus* 728–730.
176. *Marriage of Figaro* 5.3.2685–2701. Figaro then plunged into the theater with an exciting play about a sultan's harem. But an Arab sheik used his influence to have the play closed. Indeed, everything he did ran into censorship. Thus he ended up as a *croupier*—the last resort of a desperate man. "In short, I've seen everything, done everything, worn everything, borne everything." And then finally, just when he was on the verge of getting his life on an even keel, "my mother shows up just in time for me to marry her!"
177. Da Ponte also provided the text for *Don Giovanni* and *Così Fan Tutte,* as well as words for dozens of other composers. His love songs were lyrical, and for the funnier bits his nimble use of words can sometimes be as joyously clever as W. S. Gilbert's patter songs. His extraordinary life makes him seem like one of Plautus' ever-resourceful slaves. He ultimately found his way to New York, bringing opera to America, and was appointed to the first chair of Italian at Columbia University—but not before he had provided the words for some thirty-five operas. The subject of *Don Giovanni* seems to have been in part inspired by Da Ponte's own hyperactive womanizing—an interest which he shared with his good friend Casanova. The character of Don Juan seems to have entered European literature with a play by the Spanish cleric(!) Tirso de Molina entitled *El burlador de Sevilla y convidado de piedra* (1630). See Jean Rousset, *Le Mythe de Don Juan* (Paris, 1978), pp. 107–129, who treats the origins of the figure.

20. Comedy Explodes

1. *Man and Superman,* Act 3, p. 685.
2. Ibid., p. 634.
3. Ibid., p. 670.

4. Ibid., p. 680.

5. See for example Ovid *Metamorphoses* 10.243–297.

6. Shaw, *Dramatic Opinions and Essays* (London, 1907), vol. 2, p. 52.

7. Shaw's marriage to Charlotte Payne-Townsend was never consummated— at her insistence. He was only sexually initiated at age twenty-nine, and it was a brief flowering.

8. In a way, Jarry was anticipated by Lope de Vega in his "The New Technique of Making Comedies in Our Time" (1609), a light-hearted practical manual which advises the modern playwright to ignore the antiquated strictures of Aristotle.

9. In true comic tradition, Jarry devoted an entire play to the celebration of the male member: *Le Surmâle (The Super Male)*.

10. As noted by Roger Shattuck, *The Banquet Years: The Origins of the Avant Garde in France: 1885 to World War I* (New York, 1968), p. 209.

11. Keith Beaumont, *Alfred Jarry: A Critical and Biographical Study* (Leicester, 1984), p. 171.

12. Ibid., p. 113. Beaumont calls our attention to the program notes of December 1896: "Nowhere is everywhere, beginning with the country in which one finds oneself," adding "a theory cherished by Jarry, just as geographical contradictions cancel each other out to produce an abstract 'Nowhere-Everywhere,' so too historical chronological contradictions cancel each other out to produce an abstract 'Eternity.'"

13. Quotations from Jarry's *Ubu Roi* are taken from *Ubu Roi,* trans. Barbara Wright (New York: New Directions, 1961).

14. *Ah! J'en fais dans ma culotte!*

15. W. B. Yeats, *Autobiographies* (London, 1955), pp. 348–349.

16. *Le ciel était plein de fèces et d'oignons.*

17. Shattuck, *The Banquet Years,* p. 257.

18. *Une rénovation de théâtre, du moins un effort personnel . . . [un retour] à la nature même, mais sans l'imiter à la manière des photographes.* Translations from *Les Mamelles de Tirésias* are the author's.

19. See Francis Steegmuller, *Cocteau: A Biography* (Boston, 1970), pp. 182–183.

20. Shattuck, *Banquet Years,* pp. 236–237.

21. *Le record du monde pour la hauteur.*

22. Steegmuller, *Cocteau,* pp. 182–183.

23. Ibid., p. 148.

24. A long excerpt from the letter is reprinted in Steegmuller, *Cocteau,* pp. 188.

25. Cocteau, *Les Mariés de la Tour Eiffel,* Preface, in *Théâtre,* vol. 1, p. 48.

26. See "Les Six" in *New Grove Dictionary of Music and Musicians* (London, 1980), vol. 17, pp. 358–359.

27. He makes this comparison in the prologue to the play under discussion.

28. Cocteau, *Les Mariés,* p. 52.

29. The French says "deceitful as a *faux jeton"*—a counterfeit token for the Métro.

30. Henri Bergson, *Le Rire: Essai sur la signification du comique* (Paris, 1940, repr. 1969), p. 25.

31. Eugène Ionesco, "Lorsque j'écris . . .," *Cahiers des Saisons* 15 (Winter 1959), 209-211. See Martin Esslin, *Theatre of the Absurd* (New York, 1969), p. 105.

32. Instead of saying the blond schoolmistress *(institutrice blonde),* the fellow playing the fire-chief erred and said *cantatrice chauve.*

33. David I. Grossvogel, *The Blasphemers: The Theater of Brecht, Ionesco, Beckett, Genet* (Ithaca, 1962), p. 67, has observed that "in nearly every play of Ionesco's someone laments the failure of language."

34. Ibid., p. 55.

35. Esslin, *Theatre of the Absurd,* p. 109. Ironically, he uses language to present the radical devaluation of language.

36. Quotations from Ionesco's *Bald Soprano* are taken from Eugene Ionesco, *The Bald Soprano and Other Plays,* trans. Donald M Allen (New York: Grove Press, 1958).

37. As Esslin observes in *Theatre of the Absurd*[3] (New York, 1985), p. 110.

38. Ibid., p. 113.

39. We see a similar—if not more drastic—maternal caricature in Arthur Kopit, *Oh Dad, Poor Dad, Mama's Hung You in the Closet and I'm Feelin' So Sad* (1960). Madame Rosepetal is a wildly flamboyant creature who travels around the world with her dead husband in a coffin as a means of stifling the development of her witless son's sexuality. There is plenty of castration anxiety expressed—consider, for example, the carnivorous Venus Fly Traps.

40. Jacques Guicharnaud with June Beckelman, *Modern French Theatre: From Giraudoux to Beckett* (New Haven, 1961), p. 189.

21. Beckett: The Death of Comedy

1. George Steiner discusses this phenomenon at length in *Language and Silence: Essays on Language, Literature and the Inhuman* (New York, 1972), pp. 36-54.

2. Martin Grotjahn, *Beyond Laughter: Humor and the Subconscious* (New York, 1957), pp. 91-92. "The symbol of the ridiculed penis returns to the contemporary scene in the walking-stick as used by Charlie Chaplin, W. C. Fields and Bobby Clark . . . Fields . . . was a master, a true artist at expressing the

impotence of the father in a symbolic way without making his children—
the audience—feel guilty or sorry."

3. William Willeford, *The Fool and His Scepter: A Study in Clowns and Jesters and
Their Audience* (Evanston, Illinois, 1969), p. 188.

4. Grotjahn, *Beyond Laughter*, p. 94.

5. Willeford, *Scepter*, p. 253.

6. This is a theme emphasized by Günther Anders, *Die Antiquiertheit des
Menschen: Über die Seele im Zeitalter der zweiten industriellen Revolution* (Munich, 1956), which begins with a broadside launched against the "tyranny
of technology which is substituting machines for feelings" (p. 120).

7. Edward Wagenknecht, *The Movies in the Age of Innocence* (Norman,
Oklahoma, 1962), p. 180.

8. *2 Henry 4* 1.2.10.

9. Theodore Huff, *Charlie Chaplin* (New York, 1951), p. 264.

10. Ibid., p. 284.

11. Deirdre Bair, *Samuel Beckett* (New York, 1978), p. 50. Anders, *Die
Antiquiertheit*, p. 231, also stresses the influence of Chaplin.

12. Bair, *Beckett*, p. 103.

13. Martin Esslin, *The Theatre of the Absurd³* (New York, 1980), p. 34, emphasizes
that Beckett was not at any time Joyce's regular stenographer. This chapter owes an immense debt—especially for biographical details—to all three
editions of Esslin's magnificent work.

14. As quoted by Israel Shenker, "Moody man of letters," *New York Times* (section 2, 6 May 1956), cited by Norman Mailer, "A Public Notice on *Waiting
for Godot*," reprinted in Ruby Cohn, *Casebook on Waiting for Godot* (New
York, 1967), pp. 69-74, quotation from p. 70.

15. To this Richard N. Coe adds, "the main theme of his work is impotence of
mind just as much as it is of body." *Samuel Beckett* (New York, 1964, rev.
1968), p. 11.

16. "Il ne bouge pas"—it is almost like a mantra, or the paralysis of a deeply
psychotic mental patient. See pp. 122-124 of the Frence edition (entitled
Acte sans Paroles); pp. 90-91 of the English. The text is published with that
of *Endgame* in both languages; see note 17.

17. P. 20 of the French edition, *Fin de Partie* (Paris, 1957); p. 6 of the English,
Endgame (New York, 1958).

18. In an enlightening essay, Ann Beer demonstrates that Beckett's plays must
be read not as original and translation (in whichever direction) but as two
parts of a single whole: "Slipping from world to world, the author maintains a voice that inhabits margins, thresholds and anonymous quiet
spaces, often in transit or in solitude." "Beckett's Bilingualism," in *The*

Cambridge Companion to Beckett, ed. J. Pilling (Cambridge, 1994), pp. 209–221, quotation from p. 216.

19. Pp. 12-13 of the French edition, *La dernière bande de Krapp* (Paris, 1958); p. 13 of the English, *Krapp's Last Tape and Other Dramatic Pieces* (New York, 1959).
20. P. 14 French; p. 14 English.
21. P. 16 French; pp. 15–16 English.
22. P. 17 French; p. 16 English.
23. P. 18 French; p. 17 English.
24. P. 21 French; p. 19 English.
25. Coe, *Beckett,* p. 109.
26. P. 28 French; p. 25 English.
27. P. 32 French; p. 28 English.
28. P. 33 French; p. 28 English.
29. Eugène Ionesco, "Lorsque j'écris . . .," *Cahiers des Saisons* 15 (Winter 1959), 211.
30. P. 33 French; p. 18 English.
31. Lionel Abel, "Joyce the father, Beckett the son," *The New York Leader* (New York, 14 December 1959), has suggested that Hamm and Clov may represent Beckett and Joyce themselves.
32. P. 33 French; p. 18 English.
33. *En attendant Godot* (Paris, 1952).
34. *Waiting for Godot* (New York, 1954).
35. Bernard F. Dukore, "Gogo, Didi, and the absent Godot," *Drama Survey* (Winter 1962), 302–303. He goes on to explore at great length these manifestations of Freudian divisions of the unconscious.
36. Professor Henri Peyre's remark was made in a memorable off-the-cuff lecture at Yale—which unfortunately he never published.
37. See Jacques Guicharnaud, *Modern French Theatre* (New Haven, 1961), p. 211. Coe, *Beckett,* p. 93, offers a veritable alphabet soup of possible meanings for the title character's name:

Godot. Godeau, the veteran French racing-cyclist, the "man-on-a-bicycle," Fr.: *godillot,* "a hob-nailed boot." Russ.: *god,* "a year"—old Father Time himself. Or Charl-ot, Pierr-ot, God-et. Just clowns. Comic grotesques, incarnations of impotence . . . like God? One may speculate till the cows come home, the only certain answer is that there is no answer.

38. Bair, *Beckett,* p. 387.
39. As per the ingenious suggestion of Eric Bentley, *What Is Theatre?* (Boston, 1956), p. 158.

40. *Per contra*, Dukore, "Gogo, Didi," p. 302, argues that Beckett is somehow making a pun on *godenot* ("runt"). But this seems less likely.

41. J. A. Flieger, *The Purloined Punch Line: Freud's Comic Theory and the Postmodern Text* (Baltimore, 1991), p. 217.

42. Hugh Kenner, *A Reader's Guide to Samuel Beckett* (New York, 1973), p. 121.

43. Alan Schneider, "Waiting for Beckett," *Chelsea Review* (New York, Autumn 1958).

44. First broached by Anders, *Die Antiquiertheit*, p. 220. The same thought is expressed—in practically the same words and the same year—by both Esslin, *The Theatre of the Absurd*³, p. 50, and Jacques Guicharnaud, *Modern French Theatre: From Giradoux to Beckett* (New Haven, 1961), p. 212.

45. *Waiting for Godot* (1954), p. 7.

46. Ibid., p. 9.

47. Ibid.

48. For a discussion of Godot as "a modern morality play, on permanent Christian themes," see G. S. Fraser, *"Waiting for Godot,"* in *Casebook on Waiting for Godot*, ed. Ruby Cohn (New York, 1967), pp. 133–137, quotation from p. 134. This volume contains a sampling of the wide spectrum of interpretations: Christian, Marxist—even Norman Mailer. Guicharnaud, *Modern French Theatre*, p. 212, n. 9, also supports a Christian interpretation. He sees the empty tree "as an empty Cross and Godot as the absence of God."

49. *Godot*, p. 8a.

50. Ibid., p. 9.

51. Ibid.

52. Ibid., p. 10.

53. Hugh Kenner, *Samuel Beckett: A Critical Study* (Berkeley, 1961), p. 136, calls our attention to the fact that the French is more vague and manages an inclusiveness denied to English idiom: "Pourquoi?" "On attend Godot." Not "nous" but "on": Didi, Gogo, and the audience alike.

54. *Godot*, p. 10a.

55. Ibid., p. 12.

56. Vivian Mercier, *Beckett/Beckett* (New York, 1962), p. 76.

57. *Godot*, p. 15a.

58. Ibid., p. 21a.

59. Ibid., p. 28a.

60. *Esse* may be taken as the infinitive of *edo* ("to eat"), and *possum, posse* ("to be able") can refer to the sexual act. For example, Martial 11.97.1–2: "I can make it *(possum)* four times a night, but with you, Telesilla, I couldn't

make it *(possum)* even once in four years." See also Horace *Epodes* 12.15, Martial 3.32.1. Another possible sexual allusion is "Feckham, Peckham, Fulham, Clapham."

61. Mailer, "Public Notice," p. 72.

62. *Godot,* p. 31a.

63. Ibid., p. 35.

64. Mercier, *Beckett/Beckett,* p. 74.

65. *Godot,* p. 39.

66. *Endgame,* p. 13 English.

67. *Godot,* p. 39.

68. Ibid., p. 42a.

69. Ibid., p. 43a.

70. Ibid., p. 44.

71. See Bair, *Samuel Beckett,* pp. 481–485.

72. Gerry Dukes, "How it is with bouncing Bel," *Irish Times,* 31 October 1992, as quoted by James Knowlson, *Damned to Fame: The Life of Samuel Beckett* (London, 1996), p. 147.

73. Mercier, *Beckett/Beckett,* p. 46.

74. *Godot,* p. 56a.

75. Ibid., p. 57a.

76. Ibid., pp. 58–58a.

77. Ibid., p. 58a.

78. Ibid., p. 60a.

79. Beckett's prodigious learning is emphasized by nearly every commentator. See for example Ruby Cohn, *Samuel Beckett: The Comic Gamut* (New Brunswick, 1962), p. 284. By coincidence, my comparison of *Birds* and *Waiting for Godot* resembles Bennett Simon's approach to *Endgame* in the light of themes from classical tragedy: see *Tragic Drama and the Family* (New Haven, 1988), pp. 212–249. See also Simon, *The Fragmented Self: The Reproduction of the Self in Beckett and in the Theater of the Absurd,* in *The World of Samuel Beckett: Psychiatry and the Humanities,* ed. Joseph H. Smith, vol. 12 (Baltimore, 1991), pp. 157–180.

80. Aristophanes *Birds* 44; 121–122.

81. *En attendant Godot* (Paris, 1952), p. 5. The passage has been omitted from the English translation.

82. *Birds* 139–142.

83. Ibid., 1731–1739.

84. In Aristophanes, it is scarcely an exaggeration to say that the comic hero becomes the phallus: see Peisetaerus' boasts that he will "wave my prow

three full times" between the legs of the goddess Iris (*Birds* 1256). By contrast, the death of the phallus is prominent everywhere in Beckett. Two ready examples: the metaphor of spectacle at the beginning of *Endgame* hinting at the last orgasm of the world, and the bilingual pun in the title *La dernière bande,* which can be construed as either the last tape of Krapp, or his last erection.

85. See the valuable discussion of Flieger, *The Purloined Punch Line,* pp. 197–202.
86. Aristotle *Poetics* 1453a34.
87. As recalled by Peggy Guggenheim, *Confessions of an Art Addict* (London, 1960), p. 50.
88. Sophocles *Oedipus at Colonus* 1224–1227.

Coda

1. Not every delicate issue in the modern psyche can be treated with comic impunity. Two years after *Dr. Strangelove,* Tony Richardson's *Loved One* was released. It too had a screenplay by Terry Southern. The film, which mocks the foibles and antics of the funeral business, failed miserably despite an all-star cast. For it was not so much the topic but the treatment that did not succeed in generating real anesthesia of the heart.

Index

❦